BIKE
LONDON

BIKE LONDON

A GUIDE TO CYCLING IN THE CITY

Charlie Allenby

ACC ART BOOKS

London is home to all sorts of cyclists – from road bike racers to fans of Penny Farthings.

INTRODUCTION

Cycling has been a part of my life for as long as I can remember. It all started when my grandad took the stabilisers off my Raleigh Wolf Cub and I made my first unassisted ride up and down his driveway. I was hooked. As the years progressed, so did the bikes – mountain bike to BMX to road – but that simple joy I got from the freedom of exploring on two wheels never diminished. Wherever I went, there was a bike in tow. Chelmsford, Essex, was my oyster, and each new addition to my collection allowed me to explore a new side to it.

From my home in the commuter belt, cycling in London seemed like a different world. Busy streets, constant gridlock and news reports of accidents painted it as a place with an ingrained hostility to cyclists – far from the nirvanas of Amsterdam or Copenhagen. On moving to London in 2014, I was nervous about taking the plunge and commuting the four miles to my job by bike. I had cycled all my life, but would I end up being another statistic? The reality was completely different. Cycling gave me an alternative to having my face stuck in someone's armpit on the Tube. It had the added benefits of fresh air and keeping me fit – not to mention that door-to-door, it was generally faster.

Ask most people and they'll tell you that London is a car-friendly space. However, the capital has a rich history of cycling, dating back to the 1800s. London hosted many of the earliest organised races in the UK (some of which, in Crystal Palace's case, still continue), while the first clubs for everyday people sprouted up around the city at a similar time. The

biggest boosts for bicycle lovers can be traced back to London's hosting of the Olympics in 1948 (for the status it gave to Herne Hill Velodrome) as well as the 2012 games, the legacy of which I, and every other cyclist in London, feel to this day.

Even before London 2012, the attitude to cycling had started to shift. After decades spent feeding off scraps of success (Tom Simpson at the 1962 Tour de France, Chris Boardman at the 1992 Barcelona Olympics), Britain rose to become a dominant cycling force, both on the track and the road. As this trickled down to the grassroots level, cycling grew in popularity, a boom never before seen.

In 2008, construction started on infrastructure improvements announced by the then Mayor of London, Ken Livingstone. While these efforts had their faults, space in the city was being made for cyclists.

Although positive cycling stories may not make both front and back pages again (as they did during that golden summer of sport in 2012), people no longer need superhuman athletes to inspire them to hop on a bike. Green travel awareness has helped get more bums on saddles, while better, segregated lanes make cycling a more attractive option to those scared of mixing with traffic. And that's before you factor in the impact of Covid-19.

The coronavirus pandemic once again shifted our perceptions of cycling. With people stuck at home and advised away from public transport, getting around London by bike became a default option for some. Those who had never cycled before discovered the freedom that comes with being behind a set of handlebars. Combine that with traffic-free roads, and it's easy to see why cycling experienced another boom – if a different kind to the one a decade earlier. The demographic of these new cyclists wasn't restricted to MAMILs (Middle-Aged Men in Lycra). People took to two wheels regardless of age, gender or ethnicity. Even once traffic returned, the habit had been formed; a whole new group of people considered themselves cyclists, and London was theirs to explore.

Thankfully, this explosion of interest shielded the majority of London's cycling-based businesses from the economic downturn of the coronavirus pandemic. Local bike shops were included on a list of essential shops that could stay open, and experienced a swell of customers – new and old – looking for that first bike or wanting the old one in the shed made roadworthy. Others (frame builders, kit makers) also benefitted, while the more socially focused aspects of cycling in London (clubs, cafés and events) pulled through, finding novel ways of operating in the new normal.

This book is a celebration of all of the above, highlighting the best bits of London's ever-expanding two-wheeled community. Whether you're new to riding or a hardened commuter with decades of pedalling under your belt, there will be something useful for you in this guide to cycling in the city.

While London might have a way to go before it's mentioned in the same breath as its continental cousins, there has never been a better time to be a cyclist in the UK capital. I hope that *Bike London* proves the city isn't so far behind your Copenhagens and Amsterdams; and showcases the rich and varied community, founded on independent businesses run by passionate cyclists, who call the capital home. In years to come, I also hope that this book acts as a snapshot in time, introducing the people who laid the foundations for cycling in London.

Charlie Allenby, London

NOTE TO READER

Each chapter focuses on a different element of the capital's cycling scene, providing information, history and recommendations for all your saddle-based needs. Entries are organised in geographical (or in the case of events, chronological) order, helping you find your nearest spot – whether that's for a caffeine fix, or to get your bike fixed. There is also a selection of routes, suitable for a range of abilities and bikes. Each includes an illustrative map and an overview of the route. For turn-by-turn directions, it's possible to download a GPX file for a cycling computer by visiting bikelondon.co.uk.

www.pedalbackcycling.com
@pedalbackcycling
We're Open!
FOR
BIKE SALES
ICED +
COFFEE

CYCLING CAFÉS

Coffee and cycling have always, and will always, go hand in hand. Whether it's the pre-ride prepper, mid-ride pit stop or post-ride debrief, coffee is always on the menu. Something of a continental influence (where the humble cup of tea isn't as popular) that hit of caffeine can offer up a timely boost. But its popularity isn't solely to do with the performance benefits of an espresso – or six, if you're a professional (rider, not coffee drinker). There's also a social side to it.

Enter the cycling café. What constitutes a cycling café can vary. You have your standard coffee shop that has been adopted by cyclists because of its proximity to popular routes (such as Regent's Park Bar & Kitchen (see page 10)) or as the meeting point of a local cycling club's weekly run. Others go all-out to attract the community, setting themselves apart from your run-of-the-mill coffee shops with events, exhibitions and walls lined with memorabilia and merchandise. Some even have on-site workshops, meaning you can grab a flat white and get your flat tyre fixed in one transaction. But one thing remains common throughout: their dedication to serving up quality coffee, and lots of it.

A sandwich board promises bikes and beverages.
© Ben Fisher, Pedal Back Cycling

· CENTRAL

REGENT'S PARK
BAR & KITCHEN
The Regent's Park, Inner Cir, NW1 4NU
Opening hours: 8am-5pm (Mon-Sun)
royalparks.org.uk

Head to the Regent's Park Bar & Kitchen first thing on any day of the week and you'll find a pack of cyclists sipping freshly brewed coffee. Situated in Regent's Park's Inner Circle, the Regent's Park Bar & Kitchen is the perfect post-ride stop for those who have been doing training laps of the park's Outer Circle (see page 120).

It's more of a cycling-friendly café than an out-and-out bike-bedecked coffee spot, but there are plenty of places to park your pride and joy safely out the front and the café serves a mean line of cakes to go with your coffee (you'll have earned it, after all).

RAPHA SOHO
85 Brewer St, Soho, W1F 9ZN
Opening hours: 8am-7pm (Mon-Sat);
11am-6pm (Sun)
rapha.cc

This London-based manufacturer has an active presence in the city as a result of its two 'Clubhouses' – essentially shops that double up as cafés, meeting points and event spaces. Although the brand also has a store in the Old Spitalfields Market, the Brewer Street location was the first physical embodiment of all things Rapha when it opened its doors to the London cycling community in 2012.

While the store is, first and foremost, one of the only places in London where you can try on and buy new Rapha kit, there are many more reasons to swing by, even if you're not in the market for some premium Lycra. The café is a great meeting point to start or finish a ride, with regular Rapha Cycling Club morning laps of Regent's Park finishing with a coffee and some breakfast at the Soho spot. And if you prefer watching to riding, the café has a handful of televisions that broadcast the action live from some of the biggest cycling events of the professional calendar.

The Rapha Soho Clubhouse on Brewer Street is home to the Rapha Cycling Club. © *Tim Robinson, Rapha Soho*

NORTH

THE SPOKE

710 Holloway Rd, Archway, N19 3NH
Opening hours: 7:30am-10pm (Mon-Fri);
8am-10pm (Sat); 8am-9pm (Sun)
thespokelondon.com

With a name like 'The Spoke', you know you and your bike will be welcomed with open arms at this Islington joint. Just over the road from Whittington Park – Islington CC's pre-ride meeting point – the all-day café is perfect for that caffeine boost before a long loop or for a post-session pit stop before heading home.

As well as serving up great coffee, a tempting array of baked goods line the counter, and it's completely acceptable to stuff one (or more) in the back pockets of your jersey for some extra sustenance. But the full English (served until 3pm) is worth a pilgrimage all on its own. It's probably best to reserve it for after your ride though – otherwise it could soon be repeating on you as you stomp your pedals up Archway Road hill.

London's cycling cafés serve as start/finish points for rides out to Kent, the Surrey Hills and beyond.
© Tim Robinson, Rapha Soho

EAST

LOOK MUM NO HANDS!

49 Old St, EC1V 9HX
Opening hours: 7:30am-10pm (Mon-Fri);
8:30am-6pm (Sat); 9am-6pm (Sun)
lookmumnohands.com

This Old Street spot is probably the capital's most iconic cycling café – and for good reason. Opened in 2010, the space and what it stands for truly reflect London's growing cycling scene. From the outside, this might just look like a regular café – albeit a bike-mad one that generally has displays of drool-worthy machines in the window – but step inside and it's clear that it does much more than serve up cups of coffee and pints of beer.

The space is home to a workshop, where you can get your bike repaired, buy some spares or even learn the ropes yourself on a maintenance course. There's the

Look Mum No Hands! runs several summer pop ups, but their central location is at 49 Old Street.
© *Look Mum No Hands!*

exhibition space, which, as you'll have probably guessed, puts on cycle-themed displays of art from around the world. And then you have the regular series of events held at Look Mum No Hands! From screenings and book launches, to a monthly pub quiz (where you can flex your cycling knowledge) and live showings of key races during professional tours, this café's calendar is jam packed year-round with pedal-powered fun. And what's more, you don't even need to own a bike to get immersed in the action.

"I really love Look Mum No Hands! I think it's big enough that you can hide yourself away; it's a really lovely, warm space and everyone that works there is really nice. It's my second home – I just go there, do work and I know that the food I'm going to eat is going to be really good."

Jenni Gwiazdowski, London Bike Kitchen

SOUTH EAST

LONDON VELO
18 Deptford High St, New Cross, SE8 4AF
Opening hours: 8am-6pm (Mon-Sat);
9am-6pm (Sun)
ldnvelo.co.uk

Beneath a tattered red awning bearing the names of proprietors long past (New Vision Hair Salon, if you're interested), the only thing that marks out this little spot of Deptford High Street as a cycling café is the workshop-standard bike pump chained out front. That and its name, of course.

Inside though, it's hard to miss the riding paraphernalia. Frames of different shapes and sizes line the walls, while the sound of mechanics tinkering away in the on-site workshop blends seamlessly with the hissing of the coffee machine. The café's bagels are the perfect post-ride pick me up, and its garden is a great little sunspot come summer to catch some rays after putting in the hard miles on the bike.

SOUTH

MACHINE
97 Tower Bridge Rd, Bermondsey, SE1 4TW
Opening hours: 8am-6pm (Mon-Thur);
8am-5:30pm (Fri); 9am-5pm (Sat);
10am-4pm (Sun)
machinelondon.cc

At what point does a café stop become a local bike shop? This SE1 spot blends the two seamlessly, serving up locally roasted coffee from neighbours Monmouth while also having an on-site workshop that can fix any of your bike's squeaks, rattles or creaks. It also stocks bikes from the likes of Genesis and Cinelli, so don't be surprised if you leave with more than you bargained for.

Established in 2011 as the area's first ever cycle café, Machine has become a firm favourite for those who live south of the river, and its outdoor seating is a popular spot for chewing the fat and comparing stats over a coffee and slice of cake. Machine also hires out high-quality bike boxes – crucial if you're looking to take your pride and joy further afield.

SOUTH WEST

COLICCI
ROEHAMPTON GATE
138 Priory Ln, SW15 5JP
Opening hours: 8am-6pm (Mon-Fri);
8am-6:30pm (Sat-Sun)
royalparks.org.uk

While there are a number of places to get your caffeine fix when riding laps of Richmond Park – from car park-based coffee stalls to the Petersham Nurseries on the park's outskirts – most pale in comparison to Colicci. Located directly on the iconic loop (see page 142), the café is the perfect place for a post-ride pit stop before heading home.

For those colder days, the café does an extensive line in hot food (bacon bap, anyone?) while its Devonshire ice creams are hard to beat when the sun is shining. And, once you're finished, you can ogle all the expensive bikes that line the cycle racks out front.

G!RO CYCLES
2 High St, Esher KT10 9RT
Opening hours: 7am-5pm (Mon-Sun)
girocycles.com

Another spot that falls into the 'is it a café stop or is it a bike shop?' bracket is Esher's G!ro Cycles. Situated on the southwestern outskirts of the city, the café-cum-bike shop is easily a destination in itself, but most use it as a meeting place before heading deep into Surrey proper.

The café is great, whether you're after a simple slice of toast or a full-blown breakfast burrito, and you'll be able to wash it down with a caffeine fix courtesy of Bethnal Green's Workshop Coffee. In terms of the shop, G!ro stocks bikes and components from a handful of high-end independent manufacturers (Curve and Argonaut). It has an impressive line of apparel and accessories – including its own branded cycling kit.

If you're new to the area and not sure where to ride, the shop organises a number of runs throughout the week (including a gravel-focused Belgie loop) that are perfect for exploring the lesser-known roads and routes of Surrey.

THE DYNAMO
200-204 Putney Bridge Rd, Putney, SW15 2NA
Opening hours: 7:30am-10pm (Mon-Wed; Sun); 7:30am-11pm (Thur-Sat)
the-dynamo.co.uk

Porridge, pedalling, pizza and pints. A quartet that, when combined in that order, will leave a smile on most cyclists' faces. At Putney's The Dynamo, you can get three of the four (and you won't be judged if you don't actually do the second one, either).

It's hard to miss the spot thanks to the painted bikes that line its awning, but step inside and it's a shrine to all things cogs and chains. Casquettes (those iconic peaked cycling hats), jerseys and cycling-inspired prints adorn the walls, while there are hooks on hand for you to hang your ride while you sample the food and drink. If it's sustenance you're after, you can't go wrong with a bowl of 100-mile porridge, while a hand-crafted sourdough creation straight out of the woodfired pizza oven is a welcome reward after a day in the saddle.

G!RO café is well worth the pilgrimage down to Surrey. © *Jordan Addison*

PEDAL BACK CYCLING

24 Lillie Rd, Hammersmith, SW6 1TS
Opening hours: 7am-4pm (Mon-Fri);
9am-3pm (Sat); closed (Sun)
pedalbackcycling.com

If the bike in the window doesn't make it clear that this is a cycling café, then the dishes on the menu surely will. The Beryl (named in honour of one of Britain's most successful female cyclists, Beryl Burton) and The Cav (who probably doesn't need any introduction) are the highlights of the breakfast and brunch menu, while Britain's three Tour de France winners have been turned into toasties.

Outside of scrumptious food, this West Brompton hangout stocks essential accessories (casquettes, ass savers and bells), and its on-site workshop can fix your fixie while you wait. It also hosts a few Saturday morning rides each month aimed at those who are new to group runs. Starting and finishing at the café, they're a great introduction to riding on the road without the pressure of having all the right gear.

Offering three levels of service, Pedal Back Cycling is a workshop as well as a café. © Ben Fisher, Pedal Back Cycling

INTRODUCTION TO BIKEPACKING

Riding your bike and exploring new routes is one of the most enjoyable ways to spend a sunny Saturday. But why restrict it to just one day? Enter bikepacking. Essentially a crossover between camping and cycle touring, the pursuit sees you carry all your kit, hunker down for the night (anything from a hotel to a spot of wild camping is accepted, although the latter is the preferred option of purists), and wake up ready for another day in the saddle.

The traditional panniers and luggage rack set-up is eschewed for bags that are Velcroed and strapped to your bike. This leaves you with a lighter overall package, meaning you can ride faster, for longer, or explore off-road trails.

Although popularised by ultra-endurance events that see participants traverse countries and continents, your first bikepacking trip can be a much more enjoyable and relaxing experience – and just a stone's throw from your front door. Simply find somewhere to stay for the evening, plot a route to and from your destination and you're all set. From there, the possibilities are endless.

A typical bikepacking kit loads minimalist camping supplies onto an adventure bike. © *Charlie Allenby*

CYCLE HIRE

If you're out and about in London without a bike in tow, or want to go on a memorable sightseeing tour, or maybe just like the idea of starting your journey on two wheels, you're in luck. There are a number of ways to see the city from the comfort of a saddle you don't own, and the possibilities are increasing all the time. Whether it's an iconic 'Boris bike' or the electrically assisted Lime range, a variety of cycle-hire schemes cover everything from short trips to longer days spent exploring the city centre. And, if you want something more race-y, or for an extended period of time, there are a number of dedicated cycle-hire operators too.

But what if you're in London for the first time and haven't got a clue where you're going? A cycling tour might be your best bet. As can be expected, there is a rich selection of tourist-focused sightseeing spins – but some of these guided rides would even see a born-and-bred Londoner covering new ground.

Brompton's iconic fold-out bikes, made in London since 1976, are available to hire. © *Brompton*

CYCLE-HIRE SCHEMES

Although not as established as in other European cities, the concept of cycle-hire schemes has exploded in the capital since Santander Cycles (formerly Barclays Bike Hire) was launched by Transport for London (TfL) in 2010. In fact, there are now a variety of options available – from docked to dockless, pedal-powered to electrically assisted – depending on what you fancy doing and where you are in the city. This last point is important, as it's fair to say that the available cycle-hire schemes are still somewhat patchy. Some schemes are restricted to a handful of boroughs centred around the, well, centre, and there are still numerous blackspots where none operate (south east London, in particular, doesn't have many).

BERYL

Where you can find them: City of London, Hackney
Costs: Pay as you ride: £1 unlocking fee, £0.05 per minute; Day pass: £12
beryl.cc

One of the newest bike share schemes on the scene, Beryl is a cross between the docked and dockless competitors that have gone before it. Rather than users being able to leave the bikes wherever they want once they've finished their ride, the bikes have to be left in designated bays – similar to the established Santander Cycles. While this might not sound as convenient as the more liberated competition, there are currently 100 bays dotted across its operating location where a bike can be left, so there should be one not too far from your final destination.

The bikes, of which there are currently 350 available, are pedal operated (unlike others, there will be no electric boost to get you up any hills), and include handy features such as lights, a front basket and a seat that can be adjusted to suit most heights – anywhere between 4'11" (150cm) and 6'5" (196cm). The bikes are unlocked using an app, so you will need a smartphone to access your ride.

Beryl's range of micromobility hire-out options include adjustable bikes and electric scooters. © *Beryl*

Brompton bikes are a favourite choice for London commuters. © *Brompton*

BROMPTON BIKE HIRE

Where you can find them: Acton Town, Ealing, Hammersmith, King's Cross, Leyton Station, Leytonstone Road, Peckham Rye, Shepherd's Bush, Stratford 3 Mills, Surbiton Station, Twickenham Station, Walthamstow Central, Whittington Hospital
Costs: Leisure membership: £5 annual fee, £6.50 per day; Frequent membership: £25 annual fee, £3.50 per day
bromptonbikehire.com

No, your eyes aren't deceiving you. It is possible to hire one of these handy, London-made folding bikes from various locations in the capital. A sister company of the famous manufacturer, Brompton Bike Hire has quietly gone about helping its members get from A to B across the city (and further afield) since 2011. But as its hire bikes look exactly the same as the producer's other machines, it's not surprising you were none the wiser. Aimed at those after more than a quick spin to the office, Brompton Bike Hire is perfect if you're in the city for a number of days and want a quick, convenient and easy way to get around.

Thanks to the bikes' fold-up nature, the docks resemble lockers rather than the road-based alternative commonly seen with Santander Cycles. To book a bike, you simply have to become a member and reserve one at your nearest dock. You have to book a slot in a dock to return it, too. Sure, it takes a bit more effort, but the pleasure you'll get out of taking one of these iconic cycles for a spin makes everything worthwhile. What's more, as the scheme runs in cities outside of London (including Manchester and Birmingham) it's possible to hire a Brompton in London, take it with you on the train and drop it off in another city once you've finished with it.

FREEBIKE

Where you can find them: London-wide
Costs: E-bike: £1 per 10 minutes; Pedal bike: Free for first 20 minutes, £0.50 per 10 minutes after. Ending rental: Virtual stations: Free; Elsewhere: £1 (£3.50 in City of London).
london.freebike.com

While it wasn't the first to offer up electrically assisted cycling in the city, Freebike does have one unique selling point (and yes, its name is a bit of a giveaway). That's right: it's the only venture (dock or dockless) that offers up cycling for absolutely nothing. To do so, you need to opt for the pedal bike (rather than e-bike) when unlocking, and hey presto, you've got 20 minutes of free cycling – although you will need to park it in one of the 'virtual stations' detailed on the app to avoid any parking charges.

The bikes themselves are robust rides and come with a battery that, when full, can provide almost 80km of assisted riding. It's also possible to change the amount of support on offer, but if you're opting for an e-bike, you might as well always have it on the max setting to save having to slog away on a weighty machine.

LIME

Where you can find them: Bromley, Croydon, Islington, Brent, Ealing and Bexley
Costs: £1 to unlock, £0.15 per minute.
li.me

London's first ever e-bike cycle scheme has brought electrically-assisted pedalling to the masses since December 2018, turning the city's hills (not that there are many of note) into child's play. A growing trend in the world of cycling, this battery-powered option was a welcome addition to London's cycle-hire spectrum. It has sparked a movement that has seen others enter the fray and compete to get Londoners' bums on their speedy saddles.

Lime was the first player on the e-bike scene in London. © *Lime*

TIPS FOR RIDING SAFELY IN LONDON

KNOW YOUR ROUTE

Figuring out your route before setting off makes for a much more enjoyable experience. You don't need to memorise turn-by-turn navigation like a human Google Maps – just be aware of quiet roads, cycle paths or canal paths that will help keep you away from traffic.

STAY SEEN

Lights on the front and back of your bike are a legal requirement when riding at night or in poor visibility. Add some reflective clothing to help you stand out from the crowd.

POSITION YOURSELF WHERE CARS CAN SEE YOU

When on the road, don't feel obliged to ride in the gutter. You have as much right to be there as all other traffic, so aim to ride as centrally in the road as you can – not only will you be more visible but it'll stop dangerous passes. When at traffic lights or junctions, get yourself to the front of the queue and avoid being on the left of traffic as it might turn across your path.

STAY 1 METRE FROM CARS WHEN PASSING

Stationary cars can soon become moving ones, either through pulling out or opening doors. Ride a metre away from parked cars to give yourself time and space to avoid potential collisions.

OVERTAKE ON THE RIGHT

As intimidating as it might seem, it's better to overtake slower-moving traffic on the right, rather than squeezing along the inside between a car and the pavement. There's generally more room to ride in, drivers are more likely to see you in their mirrors and there's a smaller risk of a car turning left and cutting you off.

STAY AWARE OF SURROUNDINGS

Oncoming obstacles sorted: time to focus on what's to the side of and behind you. Get into the habit of frequently glancing over your shoulder when riding. This lets you see how close other road users are to you, and that split second of eye contact will make you more visible to them too.

SIGNAL CLEARLY

Indicate clearly, using your arms. This helps other road users know where you're going (even if you're not too sure yourself). Try to extend your arm out straight, but be mindful of the tip from above – don't clothesline a fellow cyclist. If you aren't comfortable riding one handed, it's worth brushing up on your balancing skills.

FOLLOW THE RULES OF THE ROAD

Jumping traffic lights isn't big or clever. Not only are you putting yourself and any pedestrians crossing the road at risk but you give people even more ammunition to think 'bloody cyclists'. Just wait like everyone else, safe in the knowledge that, once you get going, you can cut through traffic in no time at all.

Tackling London's busy streets can be dangerous. Always be aware of your surroundings and ensure you are seen.
© George Marshall / Rapha

One of the better represented cycle-hire options in terms of geographical spread, you can find a Lime from Southall in the west to Rotherhithe in the east, Balham in the south to Crouch End in the north. As with all schemes, you're limited to where you can park them (there's no dumping in a park, for example) and your top speed is restricted if you go outside of the bike's operational boundaries (marked with a thick red line on the app). But, unlike others, so long as you're within Lime's zone, you're free to park the bike wherever you wish.

Since summer 2020, Lime has also added the previously Uber-operated Jump bikes to its platform, providing customers with even more choice.

SANTANDER CYCLES

Where you can find them: Hammersmith and Fulham, Kensington and Chelsea, Westminster, Camden, Islington, the City, Hackney, Tower Hamlets, Southwark, Lambeth and Wandsworth
Costs: £2 per day, free for first 30 minutes, £2 per 30 minutes after
santandercycles.co.uk

The original TfL-backed cycle-hire scheme landed on London's streets back in 2010, and although it's changed its looks over the years (turning from blue to red after a 2015 sponsor shift from Barclays to Santander), there's no denying the project has been a massive success. After plans were unveiled by Mayor of London Ken Livingstone back in 2008 (making their 'Boris bike' nickname a slight exaggeration), the bikes have gone on to become synonymous with cycling in the city, and more than 10 million journeys are made on them each year.

Their success has a lot to do with their availability and spread. There are more than 13,600 individual bikes dotted around almost 1,000 docking stations, covering an area of 100 square km – making it the largest cycle-hire scheme in Europe. But Santander Cycles' popularity isn't solely down to sheer numbers. Designed by the iconic Warwickshire-based bicycle manufacturer Pashley, the bikes themselves are comfortable to use, robust without being impossible to ride and can offer a full day of cycling for just £2 (if you're sneaky and keep docking them before your free 30 minutes runs out).

The Santander Cycle, or 'Boris bike', is a staple of the London streets. © *Transport for London*

The red Jump e-bikes have been relaunched by Lime. © *Jump*

CYCLE-HIRE SHOPS

GO FURTHER CYCLING
4 Bury Road, E4 7QJ
Types of bikes available to hire: road,
mountain, e-bike, children's, trailers,
tag-a-longs
gofurthercycling.co.uk

LIVELO
Types of bikes available to hire: road
livelo.bike

LONDON BICYCLE TOUR COMPANY
74 Kennington Road, SE11 6NL
Types of bikes available to hire: hybrid,
road, mountain, tandem, folding, children's
londonbicycle.com/hire

LONDON RECUMBENTS
Dulwich Park and Battersea Park
Types of bike available to hire: hybrid,
recumbents, trikes, children's, cargo
londonrecumbents.com

ON YER BIKE
3-4 London Bridge Walk, SE1 2SX
Types of bike available to hire: road, hybrid,
touring, e-bike
onyourbike.com

While cycle-hire schemes are good for short trips and
pottering around town, what if you want a bike to explore
the road and off-road routes the outskirts of London has to
offer? Or a set of wheels you can keep for a whole weekend
(or longer)? A solid (and cost-effective) bet is to look into
a dedicated cycle-hire operator. From Epping Forest's
mountain bike-toting Go Further Cycling to the laidback
team at London Recumbents, you're sure to find a bike that
suits you and your needs. Plus, it saves you spending an
uncomfortable afternoon riding a Boris bike around gravelly
canal paths or up punchy hills.

7 LONDON CYCLE TOURS

London is world famous for its iconic landmarks. Historically, if visiting for the first time and looking to tick off some sights, you had to settle for traipsing around after a tour guide or sitting in traffic on an open-top bus, chugging past Big Ben, the Houses of Parliament, 10 Downing Street and Buckingham Palace. Not anymore. The city is home to loads of great bike-based tour companies, and each offers a number of different experiences – from the classic big hitters to 'secret' spots with drinking stops.

Even if you live in London and regularly ride in the capital, there's likely to be a tour for you. Biker's Delight's River Wandle jaunt (complete with wine tasting) and The Merry Pedaller's ride out to Windsor, in particular, are worth investigating if you're looking to explore new ground and learn something along the way.

BAJA BIKES
Tours on offer: Highlights of London, West End, Secrets of London, London by night
bajabikes.eu/en/bike-tours-london

BIKER'S DELIGHT
Tours on offer: Saturday Markets, Sunday Markets, Thames Path, River Wandle and wine tasting
bikers-delight.com/cycle-tours

BRAKEAWAY BIKE TOURS
Tours on offer: Grand London, Secret London
biketouroflondon.com

FAT TIRE TOURS
Tours on offer: Royal London, River Thames evening tour with beer tasting, Royal Scandals
fattiretours.com/london

LONDON BICYCLE TOUR COMPANY
Tours on offer: Classic, Love London, Original, Sunset, Gold Classic
londonbicycle.com/tours/half-day

THE MERRY PEDALLER
Tours on offer: Hampton Court Palace, Royal Deer Park, Ale tasting, Windsor Castle
merrypedallerbiketours.co.uk

TALLY HO!
Tours on offer: Landmarks and Gems, City and Secrets, London gin safari, Penny Farthing ride
tallyho.cc/#tours

CYCLING APPAREL AND ACCESSORIES

While London might not be as renowned as the likes of Paris and Milan for its fashion credentials, when it comes to cyclewear, this city is arguably the birthplace of some of the biggest disruptors the two-wheeled world has ever seen. At the heart of each of the capital's clothing and accessories brands is an urge to tear up the status quo. Whether they were already immersed in the industry (Le Col) or simply passionate cyclists (Milltag), the founders of these labels were tired of what was on offer and decided they could do better. Their continued successes prove them right.

The most well-known of the bunch is Rapha, which, since its inception in the mid-noughties, has become a globally recognised brand. Rapha wasn't a one off though: it paved the way for other like-minded dreamers.

Not all have plans of worldwide domination. There is a subsection of producers whose *raison d'être* is to create a crossover with cycling and the arts – from Romance's collaborations with artists to Hackney GT's musical origins. Don't panic if you're not a Lycra lover, either. Both Ride with Wolves and Vulpine produce functional cycling attire that wouldn't look out of place down the pub.

Rapha offers a wide range of understated, high-quality cycle wear.
© George Marshall / Rapha

CENTRAL

PAUL SMITH
No. 9 Albemarle Street, Mayfair, W1S 4BL
paulsmith.com

Paul Smith needs no introduction. A mainstay of the British fashion industry, his eponymous menswear brand oozes sophistication with a large helping of contemporary London. Aside from fashion, Smith has one other love – cycling.

As a teenager, one of his early ambitions was to become a professional cyclist. Although a bad bike accident ultimately saw him embark on a different path, his love of all things two wheeled remains. Cycling is a recurring theme in a number of Paul Smith designs, from prints on T-shirts to a line of fashion-focused bib shorts and jerseys.

In recent years, he has lent his stylish skills to a number of collaborations with cycling brands. Smith has a rich history of working alongside fellow London company Rapha to craft limited edition lines, while a one-off £20,000 tandem created with the Derbyshire-based framebuilders Mercian is the pinnacle of crossovers between cycling and this renowned fashion house.

NORTH

APIDURA
Condor Cycles, 49-53 Gray's Inn Road,
Holborn, WC1X 8PP
apidura.com

Although based in London, the idea for Apidura was sown on the far side of the Atlantic. Founder Tori Fahey was undertaking a 4,200km self-supported solo bikepacking ride from Canada to Mexico when she decided she no longer wanted to use a pannier and rack system to transport her kit cross-continent. Her solution: bikepacking bags, attached to various parts of the bike using Velcro and straps, which remove the need (and subsequent weight) of a rack.

Since 2013, Apidura has been supplying ultra-distance racers, globe-trotting explorers and everyday commuters with premium kit that helps them stay light and go further. The brand's range has grown over the years to include a city-focused messenger bag alongside its expedition and racing lines. At its core are durable designs that will last you for years to come.

RAPHA
Rapha London, Old Spitalfields Market, 61-63 Brushfield St, Shadwell, E1 6AA
rapha.cc

If one brand can claim to have done more to change the image of road cycling in the 21st century than any other, it's Rapha. Before this brand came along, cycling clothing was generally ill-fitting and the designs were on the lurid side. Founders Simon Mottram and Luke Scheybeler decided they could do better. They launched Rapha in 2004 – a

Apidura specialises in sleek, convenient bike bags. © *Apidura*

high-quality clothing company where the focus was on looking good as much as performance.

Taking its name from a 1960s team, the brand's early understated designs contrasted with the brash colours and sponsor-heavy kit of the time. They also featured the now signature asymmetric armstripe – a further nod to the retro kits sported by the likes of Jacques Anquetil and Eddy Merckx.

Sponsorship deals with professional teams big and small (including a certain Team Sky, when it was putting British riders on the top step at Le Tour de France) catapulted Rapha to international renown. It now has shops (or 'Clubhouses') on four continents, but its headquarters and creative heart remain firmly in London.

Rapha has been making cycle clothing since 2004. © *George Marshall / Rapha*

EAST

HACKNEY GT
16 Leaside Road, Clapton, E5 9LU
hackneygt.com

Cycling and music have a history of crossovers, although they've met mixed success – for every Kraftwerk's *Tour de France* album, there's a Queen's 'Bicycle Race'. Hackney GT is one of the better hybrids.

In 2011, its founder decided to make a one-off jersey design for his music production company, Hackney Globe Trotter. A self-confessed cycling nut and weekend racer, Russ Jones's appetite wasn't going to be sated with a single piece – and so the apparel brand Hackney GT was born. The range spans all disciplines of cycling, from aero-inspired road cycling jerseys to easy-breezy long-sleeve mountain bike tops, with the designs taking their cues from 1970s Americana.

MILLTAG
25 Flanchford Road, W12 9ND
milltag.cc

If Rapha was responsible for ushering in an era of understated kit, defined by block colours and monochrome detailing, Milltag is the brand's antithesis. It injects loud, brash designs back into road cycling, albeit with the help of graphic designers who make those in-your-face patterns look sharp rather than shameful.

Milltag was started by Ed Cowburn and Pete Kelsey in 2010 with the production of limited edition jerseys and collaborations. Since then, it has snowballed into *the* company for custom kit. Milltag's entire range – from jerseys to gilets – can be crafted with any design or print, while a bespoke service is on hand if you want an experienced kit creator to guide you through the process. The company has London club credentials too; it's the kit supplier of choice for the likes of Islington CC, Velociposse and Black Cyclists Network.

ROMANCE
rmnc.cc

East London is the creative heart of the UK capital, and resident Romance is one of the most exciting and boundary-pushing independent apparel creators around. Taking cues from international art- and fashion-focused brands such as Copenhagen's Pas Normal Studios and Vienna's Brilliant Brilliant Unicorn, Romance is rewriting the rulebook on cycling clothing, bringing streetwear-inspired style to two wheels.

To date, its collaborations with creatives such as Kate Moross and Camille Walala have brought splashes and blocks of colour to the world of cycling, while partnerships with established players such as GORE® Wear are surely just the starting point. Like all of the hottest designers, Romance's kit is only available in limited runs. Selling out as soon as it 'drops', you have to be quick off the mark to get your hands on it.

SOUTH

MONO.CC
monocycling.cc

Traditionally, a cycling club or team will work alongside a kit maker to alter an already established jersey and bib short combination to meet their needs – whether that's getting it printed in the club's colours or tweaking a piece to fit a particular rider's measurements. Not Mono, though. Its race team was the starting place for this small, independent brand, and it has only recently started sharing its designs with the rest of the world.

Subtle in style and with a premium price tag, the focus is on creating timeless pieces that will last beyond a season and won't look out of place in years to come – even as fashions change. Throw in a racing pedigree that means each garment has been tested during the heat of the moment, and you know your investment should withstand the demands of most pursuits.

RIDE WITH WOLVES
facebook.com/ridewithwolves

Despite what you might think from the London-based brands featured in this chapter, not all cycling apparel is skin-tight and made from Lycra. In fact, it's possible to ride a bike in normal clothes, and (whisper it) sometimes it can be more practical to arrive at your destination without looking like you're ready for a stage of Le Tour de France. The only issue is, most normal clothes haven't been created with the practicalities of city cycling in mind.

Enter Ride With Wolves. Founded by Ester van Kempen in 2016, this Etsy-based business specialises in clothing that makes a statement. The designs turn heads for all the right reasons. They come to life after nightfall as the reflective ink transforms you into a shining beacon of light. Gender neutral, body positive and made from environmentally sound organic cotton, Ride With Wolves' creations are a great way to add some non-Lycra cycling clothing to your wardrobe.

VULPINE
vulpine.cc

The ethos of Vulpine is to create functional cycling clothes that look good both on and off the bike – the litmus test being whether you can walk into a pub wearing some kit without standing out as a cyclist.

While it does have a line of full-zip jerseys that are unmistakably 'cyclist' in style, the rest of its range fits the bill. Instead of bib shorts and tights, you'll find stylish-looking shorts, jeans and trousers that are packed with cycling-friendly features, including breathable materials, water-resistant treatments and discreet reflective tabs.

This focus on practical pieces that wouldn't look out of place in an office environment makes Vulpine a must for commuters. City-based cycling is at the heart of everything it does.

Ride With Wolves specialise in unisex, ethical clothing featuring designs in reflective ink. © *Martin Gingerdope*

WEST

LE COL
lecol.cc

Professional road cyclists practically live in their kit, spending hours in the saddle year-round, putting technical garments to the test in all conditions. When former Team GB cyclist Yanto Barker retired from the peloton, he decided he could improve on everything he'd previously ridden in. Le Col was his answer, and since its founding in 2011 the company has risen to the heady heights of the WorldTour.

Designed in west London and produced in the shadows of Monte Grappa, Italy, Le Col's focus is on unparalleled quality and performance. Its signature style matches block colours with gold detailing – reinforcing its premium nature – while collaborations with the likes of Sir Bradley Wiggins have elevated the brand's status in a competitive high-end market.

ESSENTIAL COMMUTING KIT

BIKE

You won't get far without one. See the guide to Types of Bike (page 76) for a full breakdown of the different variations available. If in doubt, a hybrid is your best bet.

HELMET

While not a legal requirement, a helmet is recommended by the Highway Code. All have to pass a specific safety standard to be sold in the UK, but, generally, the more you spend, the more protective features you get.

LIGHTS

Unlike helmets, a white front light and red rear one are legally required to ride a bike on public roads at night. Look for rechargeable lights to save you spending a fortune on batteries.

LOCK

If you want to keep your bike safe and secure, it's worth investing in a decent lock. As a rule of thumb, you should look to spend 10% of the value of your bike on a lock.

BACKPACK

Commuting by bike means carrying everything you need for a day at the office, plus other essentials you wouldn't be lugging about on public transport (be it a lock, multitool or pump). A cycling-specific backpack is a good investment. Not only will it have better ventilation than a bog-standard bag, but most are waterproof and have reflective details to keep you seen.

WATERPROOF JACKET

Even if you're a fair-weather commuter, it's worth packing a waterproof, just in case. The conditions can change in an instant, and no one wants to turn up to work looking like a drowned rat.

PUNCTURE REPAIR TOOLS

Stashing inner tubes, a multitool, tyre levers and a hand pump in your commuting kit might seem excessive, but at least you'll have everything you need to repair a puncture. Not sure how to do that? Take a look at the How to Repair a Puncture guide (page 106). You'll be fixing flat tyres at the roadside in no time.

CYCLING CLUBS

Got a bike to commute on but not sure where to ride it, outside of the office-bound A to B? Or maybe you want to meet like-minded individuals who enjoy the thrill of exploring the world by pedal power? Then it might be an idea to join a cycling club.

Although intimidating to the uninitiated, most clubs are like any other social group – just on wheels. While they might appear like professional racers, with their matching kit and group formation when riding, the majority of clubs aren't competitive at all, and each is likely to organise rides that suit your ability and speed – even if you're a beginner. That's not to say it's all fun and games – a selection of London-based clubs do focus on racing, and count professional cyclists both past and present among their alumni.

Whether it's an established group with over 100 years of history, or a new collective born out of an aim to get more people from different backgrounds in the saddle, you'll finish your first club run with a smile on your face.

Whether you're a racer or a casual rider, membership with a club like the Black Cyclists Network will take you to the next level.
© *Black Cyclists Network*

CENTRAL

BLACK CYCLISTS NETWORK
Membership: 1,000+
Types of riding: Road, Track
blackcyclistsnetwork.cc

After joining a cycling club in 2013, Mani Arthur found there weren't many cyclists who looked like him. Rather than accepting the lack of diversity in the sport, he decided to establish the Black Cyclists Network. Launched to provide a space for cyclists of colour to connect, work together and share knowledge, its goal is to raise the profile of cycling within minority ethnic groups and inspire more people to saddle up for the first time.

In its relatively short history, the club has gone from strength to strength. It now boasts a diverse membership with hundreds of people from all backgrounds and hosts club sessions ranging from laps of Regent's Park to epic rides from London to Brighton and back. It also successfully crowdfunded to create the first British amateur cycling race team made up of riders from BAME backgrounds. Boasting a race team and a development squad, there are ample opportunities for members to get stuck in with some road and track action.

LONDON PHOENIX
Membership: 220
Types of riding: Time trials, CX, MTB XC, Road, Track, Women-only
londonphoenix.co.uk

Rather than committing itself to one set location, London Phoenix has a number of different club runs across the week that cater to most areas in the capital. Although the majority of its riding takes place north of the river, there is something on offer for those who live in the south-west and south-east corners of the city too, in the form of weekend rides that depart from Richmond Park or Cadence Performance (Upper Norwood).

The Black Cyclists Network is the predominant BAME-centric cycle club in London. © *Black Cyclists Network*

The London Phoenix club takes tours up into the hills. © *Neal Mackintosh, London Phoenix*

As well as the standard cycling club morning session (which takes place on a Friday and consists of laps of Regent's Park Outer Circle (see page 120) and weekend rides, London Phoenix supports a number of different types of riding throughout the year – from cyclo-cross in the off-season and track sessions at the Lee Valley Velopark, through to off-road cross-country mountain biking for the adventurous among us, who enjoy exploring bridle paths, fire roads and singletrack (often getting covered in the brown stuff along the way).

RAPHA CYCLING CLUB

Membership: 2,400
Types of riding: Time trials, CX, Road, Track, Women-only
rapha.cc/gb/en/rcc

The services provided by this premium London-based clothing and accessories maker don't end at snazzy kit. In 2015, the manufacturer and lifestyle brand extended into cycling clubs, creating what has become one of the biggest international riding fraternities around. Members are spread far and wide, from Amsterdam to Tokyo, Portland to Perth.

Its London 'chapter' was its first, and with a membership numbering more than 2,000, is one of its most popular too. Centred around two city Clubhouse locations (Soho and Spitalfields), the club runs regular weekday morning rides (including a gruelling Wednesday hill session), while weekends are for exploring the Home Counties. Members aren't limited to a strict set of ride outs though, and unofficial sub-groups form to ride where and when they want.

Being a RCC member also gets you exclusive access to Rapha kit, half-price coffee and bike hire opportunities at all Rapha Clubhouses worldwide – handy if you're in a new city and want a nice road bike to explore on.

VELOCIPOSSE

Membership: 45
Types of riding: Road, Track, Women-only
velociposse.cc

There is a gender imbalance when it comes to cycling in London, and this is something Velociposse strives to fix. Founded in 2015 as an all-women's track cycling team, the club has since transformed into a space for women of all abilities and interests to come and participate in riding and racing.

Unlike the others in this list, you won't find a set schedule of led club rides into the capital's suburbs at Velociposse. While longer rides do happen, it's on more of an ad-hoc basis and organised between members. Instead, the focus is on improving bike-handling skills and technique at training sessions in a relaxed and supportive environment. There are coaches on hand to help you get more confident with riding fast, cornering and coordination. And, if you discover a new-found love, you'll receive advice and support for all sorts of racing – from road and time trials, to fixed-gear criteriums and ultra-distance audaxes.

NORTH

ISLINGTON CC

Membership: 680
Types of riding: Time trials, CX, Road, Track, Women-only
islington.cc

Although only set up in 2013, this north London club has gone on to become one of the city's most popular – and it's easy to see why. The ethos is accessibility for all, and it delivers in spades with a total of nine different rides per week. On weekdays, these come in the form of shorter evening spins (much more approachable than having to get up at the crack of dawn!) up into Hertfordshire or tackling the hills of Alexandra Palace and Muswell Hill, while at weekends you'll find two speeds of Regent's Park laps (hard at 7am, more relaxed at 8am) and a whopping four different options for the Sunday ride – from a 35kph-plus smash fest down to a sedate 20kph jaunt. All rides (apart from Saturday mornings) depart from Whittington Park.

FAMOUS LONDON CYCLISTS

MAURICE BURTON

A product of Herne Hill Velodrome and VC Londres, Maurice became the first Black British champion in cycling when he won the Junior Sprint title on the track in 1973. He later moved to Belgium after growing tired of the racist abuse he received when riding in the UK. On retiring from racing, he returned to London and took over Streatham's De Ver Cycles shop, which he runs to this day.

BRADLEY WIGGINS

Although born in Ghent, Belgium, 'Wiggo' is an out-and-out Londoner. He moved to the city as a toddler and grew up in Maida Vale, joining Westbourne Grove's Archer Road Club aged 12, after being inspired by Chris Boardman's pursuits at the 1992 Barcelona Olympics. He cut his teeth racing at Herne Hill Velodrome and Crystal Palace before embarking on a hugely successful track and road career. His most iconic season was 2012, when he won Le Tour de France and the men's time trial at the 2012 London Olympics, becoming Britain's most decorated Olympian in the process.

TAO GEOGHEGAN HART

The Hackney-born Geoghegen Hart took on one of his first organised rides – the legendary Dunwich Dynamo – aged just 13 and joined CC Hackney shortly after. A Saturday job at Condor Cycles followed, which soon turned into sponsorship for bikes and equipment as a junior, with fellow London brand Rapha getting in on the act and supporting his precocious talent. Success led him to a three-year stint racing in America before signing to INEOS (formerly Team Sky) in 2017. In 2020, he became the second Londoner – after Wiggins – to win one of road cycling's 'Grand Tours'; the Giro d'Italia.

JOANNA ROWSELL SHAND

Another VC Londres alumni, Joanna came to prominence on the track with wins in the Individual Pursuit at the National Junior Track Championships in 2005 and 2006. She went pro a year later, competing on the track and road, and chalked up her first Team Pursuit Track World Championship win in 2008. Further success followed (including a further four Track World Championships), but the most defining victories of her career came in the 2012 London Olympics and 2016 Rio Olympics – both times as part of the gold medal-winning women's Team Pursuit trio.

Wiggins leading the 2012 Tour de France in the coveted yellow jersey. By Josh Hallett, Wikimedia Commons

The club also organises a number of different events every year. The most iconic is its 'Great Escape' – a 200km ride into the heartlands of Essex and back – while its 'Italian Job' heads into the Chiltern Hills.

CC LONDON
Membership: 150
Types of riding: Time trials, CX, MTB XC, Road, Track, Women-only
cc-london.com

Ideal for those who live slightly closer to the North Circular than the aforementioned Islington CC, CC London offers up six days per week of cycling from three different spots throughout the year. From Tuesday to Friday, members gather at our old friend, Regent's Park, where the club puts on pre-work race skills training (Tuesdays), social laps (Wednesdays and Fridays) and a faster chaingang session (Thursday). Come the weekend, CC London breaks free from the magnetic pull of the park and ventures further afield, setting off from Winchmore Hill on Saturdays and East Finchley on Sundays. Both of these rides are on the intermediate end of the spectrum when it comes to distance (roughly 72km and 95km respectively), but the various pacing groups and the pledge that 'no one is left behind' will make them more achievable than you think.

Outside of rides and runs, the club organises races and time trials if you fancy getting competitive, while many members also dip their toes in cyclo-cross, track and mountain biking.

NORTH EAST

HORNBEAM JOYRIDERS
Membership: NA
Types of riding: Women-only
hornbeam.org.uk/joyriders

Joining a cycling club doesn't have to mean endless laps of a Royal Park or clocking up the kilometers at the weekend, as this Walthamstow-based group proves. Founded in 2017 by the Hornbeam Centre, the initiative aims to introduce cycling to women from the area's diverse community, giving them the ability to empower themselves through riding a bike.

The JoyRiders has a strong track record of turning unsure novices into confident cyclists through its weekly social guided rides, advice on where to find free women-focused cycle skills lessons and ride leader training. Plus, it removes one of the key barriers to riding by offering up a number of bikes that can be borrowed for free.

As with any good cycling club, all rides include an obligatory café pit stop – after all, riding your way around Lea Valley, Hackney Marshes, Epping Forest or the Olympic Park can be thirsty work!

EAST

EAST LONDON VELO
Membership: 60
Types of riding: Time trials, CX, MTB XC, Road, Track
eastlondonvelo.com

While East London Velo's membership numbers might look on the smaller side compared to other groups listed, size doesn't always matter when it comes to cycling clubs – in fact, the smaller the outfit, the more involved you tend to feel.

East London Velo is more racing-focused than most, but that doesn't mean a need for speed is a must. The club organises a grassroots criterium series and is represented by members at all sorts of events – from hill climbs around the UK to local time trials. So, it's the perfect option for those who like their cycling with a slice of competition. East London Velo is still a great choice if you just like turning the pedals at a fair lick, though. Its Sunday club run averages 30kph (and can be 'livelier'). It tends to take in an 80km loop of Essex countryside from its start at The Castle, Woodford Green.

CC HACKNEY
Membership: 240
Types of riding: Time trials, CX, MTB XC, Road, Track, Women-only
cyclingclubhackney.co.uk

With an alumni including the professional road cyclists Tao Geoghegan Hart and Alex Peters, this small Homerton-based club must be doing something right. Its extremely active youth section can be thanked for refining raw talent into some of the most promising British riders to come out of London since a certain Bradley Wiggins, but its involvement with young people goes beyond being a production line for the professional teams. The club's Interlinkx CiC coaching programme works with eight to 18-year-olds from disadvantaged backgrounds in the borough, creating opportunities for physical activity through cycling that, otherwise, would be beyond their reach.

Outside of its youth team's amazing work, the club holds a regular senior Sunday club ride that departs from Lower Clapton and is split into three different speed categories (35kph, 30kph and 25kph). It also offers women-only rides, roller and turbo training evenings, and even a weekly session for those who want to learn the basics of bike maintenance (yes, including how to change an inner tube).

SOUTH EAST

VC LONDRES
Membership: 430
Types of riding: CX, MTB XC, Road, Track, Women-only
vcl.org.uk

Despite its French feel, VC Londres (or Velo Club Londres, to give it its full Francophile name) is based out of south-east London's Herne Hill Velodrome, and is merely named in homage to the cycle fanatics across the Channel.

Similar to CC Hackney, VCL goes big on its work with young people, and under 18s make up around half of the membership. In fact, development-focused sessions on the track start from as young as the under-12s group.

Thanks to its access to a track, a lot of the club's regular training takes place on the legendary velodrome. It is expected that you master riding in a group here before progressing to the Sunday club run – rides of two-to-three hours in duration that depart from Bromley and take in the country lanes of south London.

If you fancy putting all that training into practice, many VC Londres members compete across all levels and disciplines of cycle-sport, so there will be advice on hand, whether you're just starting out as a Category 4 rider (a new junior or senior license holder) or want to take the next step up.

SOUTH

BRIXTON BMX
Membership: 190
Types of riding: BMX
brixtonbmx.co.uk

London's first BMX (which stands for bicycle motocross, FYI) club was founded back in 1981, and has been offering up coaching and racing ever since. Based out of Brockwell Park's BMX track, this is *the* place to head to if you like going fast on some of the smallest bikes around.

The volunteer-led organisation puts a strong emphasis on providing young people with the skills and expertise needed to complete the course as quickly as they can. There's no upper age limit, though – all are welcome to head down to Brixton BMX's Saturday and Sunday morning sessions. They offer a great opportunity to become au fait with an adrenaline-fuelled sport that has managed to establish itself as an Olympic discipline, after debuting at the 2008 Beijing Olympics.

Haven't owned a BMX since you were in your teens? Don't worry – the club has a limited number of bikes available, as well as the all-important protective gear. All you have to do is turn up and be ready to race.

Young cyclists from the Brixton BMX club take on the Brockwell Park track. © *courtesy of Mike Woof*

BRIXTON CYCLES CLUB

Membership: 200
Types of riding: BMX, Time trials, CX, MTB XC, MTB Downhill, Road, Track, Women-only
brixtoncycles.cc

If you've ever been on a bike ride south of the river, there's a good chance that you will have come across a member of Brixton Cycles Club. Linked to the Brixton Road bike shop of the same name, the club's distinctive red, yellow and green striped jersey is hard to miss.

The group's main focus is on the social side of cycling – think Sunday runs down to the lanes of Kent and Surrey, potted with stops at cafés and pubs, rather than a reenactment of a Tour de France stage. Its members aren't so laid back they should be riding a recumbent, though. There is a small yet dedicated subsection who enjoy nothing more than diving into the 'pain cave' of track, road and cyclo-cross racing. So, if you live in south London and are looking for the best of both worlds, Brixton Cycles Club is as good it gets.

SOUTH WEST

LONDON DYNAMO

Membership: 550
Types of riding: Time trials, CX, MTB XC, Road, Track
londondynamo.co.uk

Richmond Park is a favourite amongst London-based cycling clubs, and it's easy to see why. Bigger and (in this writer's opinion) better than its north London counterpart (Regent's Park), the 11.6km triangular course offers up a variety of gradients – from pan-flat parcours to the thigh-burning 'peaks' (for London, anyway) of Broomfield and Dark Hills – that add a bit of spice to proceedings. It also makes it the perfect training spot for London Dynamo.

The club has been running its Saturday morning 'parkride' for more than 20 years. The meet sees groups of eight head off in chaingangs and complete four laps of the park (41.8km) before finishing up with the all-important coffee stop.

Dynamo also uses Richmond Park for its Wednesday night rides and Thursday evening coaching sessions, while

Surrey Hills and Windsor are the destinations of choice for Sunday club runs and its 'slacker's ride' – Tuesday and Thursday mornings for 'those lucky few who don't need to be at work… or prefer not to'.

TWICKENHAM CC

Membership: 175
Types of riding: Time trials, CX, MTB XC, Road, Track, Women-only
twickenhamcc.co.uk

While the bikes and races of the 19th century may be worlds apart from their modern-day evolutions, not many of London's clubs can say they've been promoting competitive cycling since its very start. Founded in 1893, Twickenham CC still has racing at its heart, and its members compete in a number of disciplines both locally and nationally – in fact, the former Team Pursuit World Champion Dani Rowe (née King) was part of the club's youth set-up.

Run from All Hallows Church in Twickenham, the club is a hive of activity year-round – whether that's putting on roller sessions in the darkest depths of winter, or coaching marginal gains to time trialists come summer.

Although it helps to love a good race, a competitive edge isn't a must to join Twickenham CC. The club's coaches are on hand whatever your goal – be it getting used to riding in a group or improving your time on an upcoming sportive – and all are welcome to join on its longer weekend rides.

WEST

SADDLEDRUNK CC

Membership: 70
Types of riding: Road
saddledrunk.cc

Cyclists based in west London have a rich variety of destinations on their doorsteps. Directly west lies Windsor; while if you venture further north you'll find yourself coming into Chiltern Hills territory; and in the opposite direction lie the ascents of Surrey. The Ealing-based SaddleDrunk

CC group takes advantage of all these options during its Sunday morning ride. Setting off from Munson's Coffee + Eats, the rides are members-only, but don't let this put you off – no-one is left behind, the group goes at the speed of the slowest rider and there's even a pre-planned coffee and cake stop midway.

Outside of the weekly club run, this adult-only club runs ad-hoc rides (generally an earlier Sunday spin and a Wednesday morning session) that are either led or self-guided. In these meets, the emphasis is on the riders to sort themselves into evenly matched groups. While the no-drop rule remains in place, if you're struggling and there's no slower group, you should be prepared to finish the route on your own.

NORTH WEST

WILLESDEN CC
Membership: 190
Types of riding: BMX, Time trials, CX, MTB 4X, MTB XC, MTB Downhill, Road, Track
willesdencyclingclub.co.uk

If you like spending your Sundays exploring the quiet country lanes of the London suburbs, then this Denham-based cycling club is probably the group for you. Founded as the Willesdon Socialist Cycling Club by a group of Labour supporters who wanted to spread the message of the working-class political party after the 1926 General Strike, the group soon discovered that it enjoyed being out on bikes as much as it did championing left wing causes. The club held its first race a year after it was formed and, by 1931, cycling won out when it was decided that 'socialist' would be dropped from its name.

Almost a century on from its founding, the club has had its ups and downs, but currently holds a position of strength with almost 200 members. Its weekly club runs meet throughout the year at Shane's Nursery, Denham, and you can expect to cover 80-130km depending on daylight.

It's the audaxes which are the stuff of legend, though. One of the UK's earliest pioneers of the discipline, the club organises a number of rides throughout the year, with some reaching 600km in distance.

WESTERLEY CC
Membership: 130
Types of riding: Time trials, CX, Road, Track, Women-only
westerley.cc

Cyclists come in all forms – be they TT-focused speed merchants or rambling randonneurs who love nothing more than exploring the world by bike. Westerley CC manages to cater for them all.

The British Cycling-affiliated club has a very active presence across west London throughout the year, whether it's organising crit races at Hillingdon Cycle Circuit or introducing first-time cyclists to group rides. And although club runs depart from the Polish War Memorial roundabout on the A40 in South Ruislip, its membership travel from as far afield as Kensington and Buckinghamshire to join in with the pedal-powered fun.

Westerley CC goes big on riding throughout the 12 months of the year. It offers up a full schedule of Rapha Festive 500 rides (a Strava challenge that sees people attempt to ride 500km in the eight days between Christmas Eve and New Year's Eve), ranging from 30km routes when the weather isn't playing ball, to 201km jaunts for those looking to take big chunks out of the total in one hit.

One thing is for sure: if you join Westerley CC, don't expect to solely be doing the club run for long.

CYCLING MANUFACTURERS

For as long as there have been bicycles in London, there have been bike builders. In the early 20th century, each of the capital's 'villages' had its own artisan who specialised in welding, brazing and filing steel tubing into a frame and a fork. The bikes of today tell a rather different story. Most are made thousands of miles away, where labour is cheap and prices are low. The legendary names of framebuilding (think Holdsworth, F.H. Grubb, Hetchins, Roberts) exist in name only, have relocated away from London or closed their doors for good.

But that doesn't mean the art of creating a frame from scratch is dead. If anything, the craft is going through something of a renaissance. A growing number of frame builders are still doing it the old-fashioned way – with a brazing torch in one hand and tubing in the other.

Their creations aren't all custom (and therefore expensive), either. London is home to a number of notable companies pushing the boundaries of what's possible with a frame and two wheels: be it the UK's biggest bike manufacturer (Brompton), or a workshop-based initiative looking to make cycling even more sustainable (Bamboo Bicycle Club).

The Isen workshop welds frames by hand. © *Bobby Whittaker*

CENTRAL

CONDOR CYCLES
49-53 Gray's Inn Rd, Holborn, WC1X 8PP
condorcycles.com

Established in 1948 by Monty Young, Condor Cycles has had a presence on Gray's Inn Road for more than 70 years. The frames are no longer made in London, but are still designed in the capital, while production takes place in Italy. The brand has focused on road-ready race bikes since its inception, and enjoys a long and storied connection to the professional peloton, supplying bikes to riders at Le Tour de France, world champions and (until 2018) its own racing outfit, JLT Condor.

While it's possible to buy a bike off the peg from Condor Cycles, it's worth heading in store to get something unique, tailored to your requirements and budget. After settling on a style (the brand crafts everything from velodrome-ready track bikes to pannier-laden tourers), a free bike fitting will ensure you're getting the perfect, personalised bike for you. Want to go fully custom? Whether it's tweaks to the geometry or a wild paint scheme, everything is up for grabs at Condor Cycles. Look no further if you're after a one-of-a-kind ride that you can help design.

"I was a customer of Condor Cycles for 10 years before starting Rapha, and Grant Young and the team there became valuable and helpful partners after we launched. They championed Rapha when we were a tiny upstart, and we had 10 years of racing together with the Rapha Condor sponsored teams."

Simon Mottram, Co-founder and CEO, Rapha

NORTH

FREDDIE GRUBB
47A Barnsbury St, Islington, N1 1TP
freddiegrubb.com

Although you might not know the name, Freddie Grubb arguably kicked off the British invasion into the world of professional road cycling. A born and bred Londoner, Grubb won two silver medals (individual road race and team road race) at the 1912 Stockholm Olympics, and was the first Brit to ever start the Giro d'Italia (although he wasn't one of the eight riders to finish the 1914 edition's eight stage, 3,150-plus km slog). Grubb is also the legend of cycling past who inspired the name of this modern London bike builder.

Established in 2015, the brand focuses on small-batch, handmade, steel city bikes. The frames, produced in London, are classic in design. They match a traditional road frame (including a women-specific step-through crossbar option) with Porteur handlebars to offer an upright ride perfect for commuting. The use of internal hub gears (from two- to eight-speed) keeps everything clean in terms of maintenance and design, while the potential additions of front racks and bottle cages make each bike fit for an adventure the original Freddie Grubb would be proud of.

EAST

BAMBOO BICYCLE CLUB
Unit 8, Caxton works, Jude St, E16 1FF
bamboobicycleclub.org

While most bike frames are created using steel or aluminium (or carbon or titanium, if you're feeling fancy), one London-based frame builder is taking this already 'green' mode of transport up a notch, towards true sustainability. Founded in the capital in 2012 (and with outposts in Munich, Germany, and Amersfoort, The Netherlands), the Bamboo Bicycle Club uses – you guessed it – bamboo as the main raw material for the frame. What's more, as there's no welding involved, you're able to assemble the frame yourself, either at a two-day workshop or as part of a build-at-home kit.

There are three different build kits to choose from (road, MTB or gravel) and each comes in a variety of options, meaning a wide spectrum of styles – track, tourer or trail-cruising fatbike – are catered for. While not a common frame material, there are a number of benefits to using bamboo, aside from its sustainable credentials. Bamboo has strong vibration dampening qualities, meaning it promises a smooth ride over even the roughest terrain. Plus, it's generally lighter than steel or aluminium, and a fraction of the price of carbon.

DONHOU BICYCLES
86b Main Yard, Wallis Rd, E9 5LN
donhoubicycles.com

Hidden away on an industrial estate in Hackney Wick lies one of the UK's most sought-after bike producers. Tom Donhou founded his eponymous brand in 2010 and has since established himself as the king of premium, handmade, steel creations. Bespoke builds were the foundations his company was built on. The most famous is arguably the Land Speed bike – a project that saw Tom design and build a machine capable of reaching speeds upwards of 100mph.

Tom now creates a number of off-the-peg signature models alongside his bespoke builds. The Signature Steel range has a road-influenced design, but models vary from a gravel-focused tourer through to an out-and-out racer developed inline with the Kibosh Racing team.

Even if you opt for a signature design, there's the chance to upgrade the standard builds with features such as rack and mudguard mounts. You can also get measured up for a custom size, and go as garish (or subtle) as you want at the in-house paint workshop.

QUIRK CYCLES
86b Wallis Rd, Hackney Wick, E9 5LN
quirkcycles.com

A stone's throw from Donhou Bicycles lies Quirk Cycles – a similarly brilliant steel-specialising frame builder (it must be something in the water of the neighbouring River Lee). Set up by Rob Quirk in 2015, the brand's focus has been on the endurance side of cycling, thanks in part to Rob's penchant for pushing himself and his bike to the limits. Each of its completely customisable models has been crafted and honed with long-distance events in mind – be it the Transcontinental Race or the Silk Road Mountain Race – and can therefore withstand anything that's thrown at them.

Like Donhou Bicycles, putting down your deposit only gets you a place in the build queue, but the end product is more than worth the wait. Whether you want to work

The Mamtor: Quirk Cycles' all-terrain, versatile road bike. © *Nikoo Hamzavi*

with Rob to craft the bike of your dreams, or just tinker with the paint job, the possibilities are endless. The only thing standing between you and your ultimate creation is your bank balance.

STAYER
Acacia Business Centre, 5, Howard Rd,
E11 3PJ
stayercycles.com

Frames and wheels go hand-in-hand. Get both right and you're on the path to creating a bike that will be a joy to ride for years to come. At Stayer, you can have both frame and wheels hand-built from scratch and customised for you.

Founded in 2015 by Sam Taylor and Judith Rooze, Stayer has become something of a go-to independent builder for those in the know. The steel frames are hand crafted by Sam, and the stock designs focus on the gravel-grinding all-road bikepacking cyclo-cross trend that has been growing in popularity over the last few years. Meanwhile, Judith takes care of the wheels, lacing the brand's own carbon fibre rims to Halo, DT Swiss or even dynamo hubs.

Once you've selected your frame and wheels, Stayer works with a handful of local bike shops to complete your bike to your specifications – whether you want something to cross continents on, or just something you can reliably use for commuting in all conditions.

"One of the things that's always come across is how genuine and free with their knowledge both Sam and Judith are. It's never been a case of trying to protect their skills and secrets as arcane knowledge that can't be shared, but about wanting to help other shops and other people who are interested in the same things they are."

David Donker Curtius, Founder, Clever Mike

SOUTH

ISEN
Unit 14, Menin Works, Mitcham CR4 3HG
isenworkshop.com

Set up by Caren Hartley (Hartley Cycles) and Matt McDonough (Talbot Frameworks) as a way of creating beautifully handmade steel production bikes in 2017, Isen (the Old English word for iron) has quickly turned from a short-run collaboration between two of the capital's most sought after bespoke builders into the pair's main business. All aspects of the company's frame builds take place within the four walls of its Mitcham workshop – from the cutting of the steel tubing all the way through to the brand's eye-catching fade paint jobs. Each frame is tested throughout the build process to make sure it matches up to Isen's extremely high standards.

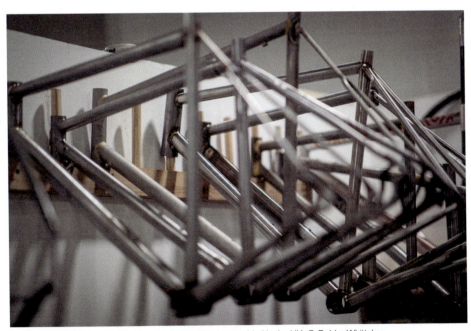

Isen's range of bikes are designed, manufactured and assembled in the UK. © *Bobby Whittaker*

A race-ready road-bike from Isen workshop. © *Bobby Whittaker*

The brand has a variety of builds on offer – from the All Season gravel grinder that started it all, through to the Mountain G.O.A.T. hardtail (perfect for downhill, singletrack and even punchy off-road climbs). Although basic in design, Hartley and McDonough offer up some customisation for those who want to really push the boat out, whether with extra luggage mounts, colour-matched components, or fully stainless steel builds.

SAFFRON FRAMEWORKS
TB-10, Unit 8, Thames-Side Studios,
Harrington Way, SE18 5NR
saffronframeworks.com

Good things come to those who wait. That's certainly the case with Saffron Frameworks, where you can expect a lead time of roughly eight months between paying the deposit and picking up your bike. The reward for your patience? A completely custom bike, from tyres to handlebar tape, that you have been involved in every step of the way.

Set up in 2011 by Matthew Sowter, who learnt the ropes at East Sussex's Enigma Bikes, the brand has gone from strength to strength, winning countless industry awards. Each design starts as a blank slate, and Matthew collaborates with the rider to find out what they want from their investment. Whether it's a globetrotting tourer or a Sunday-best bike, you'll end up with something that fits you perfectly and will leave you grinning ear to ear every time you saddle up.

VARONHA FRAMEWORKS
25 Mallet Road, Hither Green, SE13 6SP
varonha.co.uk

Located on an unassuming residential street in the deepest depths of south London lies one of the most experienced steel-frame builders in the city, if not the country. Winston Vaz has been welding, brazing and filing steel tubing into amazing pedal-powered machines since he was 16, starting at Holdsworth before it was sold to a rival company, and Roberts Cycles, where he was the master framebuilder for 27 years, until it closed in 2014.

Two years before Roberts shut its doors, Vaz decided to set up Varonha with his brother, Mario, a well-respected frame sprayer. The result is a relatively new name in the world of cycling, but one with the skills and experience common to the heritage brands of decades past. All frames are completely custom, designed to the individual after a consultation on sizing and requirements, and the pricing is competitive. Vaz will also work on any repairs or renovations – from filling dents in tubes, through to replacing entire frame parts – while his brother is on hand upstairs if your pride and joy needs a new lick of paint.

"Winston is probably the most underrated frame builder in the UK. He's also one of the most prolific, if not the most prolific. They're from where I grew up in Lewisham and they're still there knocking stuff out."

Matt McDonough, Co-Owner, Isen

WEST

BROMPTON
1 Ockham Dr, Greenford, Middlesex, UB6 0FD
brompton.com

Brompton bikes need no introduction – but here's one anyway. Founded by Andrew Ritchie in 1976, the brand has gone on to become one of the most renowned in the world; its unique folding design is often imitated but never bettered. The bikes themselves haven't changed much over the years – each one is still constructed by hand from roughly 1,200 parts – but that's why they're so cherished. They're practical, dependable and can be folded away in 10 seconds flat.

They're also – surprisingly – still made solely in London. While other manufacturers of its size have moved production overseas to keep costs down, Brompton has remained true to its roots, only upping sticks from its railway arch-based factory in Brentford for a state-of-the-art Greenford plant in 2015. The impetus was increasing output, and Brompton's move has been more than successful. Despite each model's small stature, the company is now the biggest bike manufacturer in the UK, in terms of the number of bikes created.

Varieties now include an electric version and a line of special editions – the titanium-framed collaboration with ex-professional David Millar's CHPT3 is a particular highlight. It's also possible to take a tour of the factory, where you'll get an insight into how each Brompton bike is made.

Fun fact: Brompton's name is inspired by the Brompton Oratory. The church was visible from founder Andrew Ritchie's bedroom workshop, where the first prototypes of this iconic folding bicycle were created.

One of Brompton's world-renowned bikes, containing upwards of 1000 parts. © *Brompton*

TYPES OF BIKE

ROAD

Skinny tyres, dropped handlebars and a Lycra-toting rider are all the hallmarks of a road bike. Designed for going fast on asphalt, many are used for inner-city commuting in the week, then let loose on the country lanes of London's outskirts at the weekend.

MOUNTAIN

Cross-country, enduro, downhill, trail… mountain bikes come in a range of styles that can be confusing to the uninitiated. All have flat handlebars and fat tyres, and are made for going off-road. Most will have some form of suspension to smooth out the rough riding.

HYBRID

The best of both worlds, a hybrid bike straddles the middle ground between a road bike and a mountain bike. Their comfortable upright position and ability to tackle tarmac and the odd bit of off-road makes them perfect for commuting. It's easy to see why they're the most-sold style of bike.

GRAVEL

A fairly new design, gravel bikes take the general geometry of a road bike and whack on some wider, mountain bike-style tyres. This means that, while great on the road, they can also handle bridleways and woodland trails.

CARGO

A favourite amongst cycle couriers, cargo bikes add a load-carrying aspect to the humble bicycle. The majority are used for transporting parcels and packages, but some have been adopted by parents as an alternative, greener way to ferry the kids around.

FOLD-UP

The fold-up is the bike-of-choice for workers who commute by train into the UK capital. Public transport-approved, they swarm around London's transport hubs at rush hour. A perfect choice if you like the idea of a hybrid but lack the storage space.

ELECTRIC

While all of the above rely on pedal-powered propulsion, there is a new and exciting world of electrically-assisted bikes to choose from. Available in all of the styles listed above, there's an e-bike for all pursuits.

FIXIE

A 'fixie' or fixed-gear bike is one of the simplest designs around. It has one gear, the pedals are directly coupled to the rear wheel (meaning you can't move forward without pedalling), and most have just a front brake (or in extreme cases, none at all!). Not to be confused with a single-speed bike (which often look identical but allow you to coast), fixies are generally reserved for the adrenaline-fuelled setting of a velodrome, though a growing minority of cyclists ride them on the streets.

The 'fixie' has become a familiar sight on London's streets in recent years. Image © *DrimaFilm / Shutterstock.com*

CYCLING EVENTS

If you're a cyclist in London, you're spoilt for choice when filling your calendar. From trade shows to ultra-endurance sportives, there's something for every rider, regardless of ability. As can be expected, the majority of participant-focused events take place in the summer months when the days are long and the weather is more likely to play ball (although, being the UK, this is no guarantee). But that doesn't mean it's slim pickings for the rest of the year.

Between the two events (Route Beer Ramble and Rouleur Classic) that bookend the riding season, there's a wealth of riding on offer – from the serious (Crystal Palace Crits, May-August) to the silly (The Tweed Run, May). Explore everywhere from the city streets (Nightrider, June) to the country lanes around the metropolis's far-flung outskirts (Route Beer Ramble, March; London Revolution, May).

So, what are you waiting for? Grab your diary and get on your bike!

Cyclists take part in the London edition of the World Naked Bike Ride. © *Steve Ritter, steveritterlife.com*

MARCH

ROUTE BEER RAMBLE
pannier.cc

Bikepacking (think the cooler, hip alternative to cycle touring (see page 21)) is a firm favourite amongst cyclists who want their weekend ride to be just that: a full weekend of cycling. Although there are no limits or set rules for a self-supported bikepacking expedition – the concept just combines a minimum of two days in the saddle with evenings spent under the stars – it is possible to join an organised tour or event. Following a predetermined route allows you to focus solely on keeping your pedals turning and having a little fun.

The Route Beer Ramble is one such tour, organised by bikepacking experts Pannier. It guides participants between the cities of London and Bristol. Run over two days, the ride sets off from Richmond Park and wends its way across a 230km route that offers a mixture of tarmac, bridleway and gravel terrain. Highlights include riding through the North Wessex Downs Area of Outstanding Natural Beauty, and a welcome (and well-earned) beer on arriving at Tapestry Brewery taproom in Bristol, which marks the end of the ride.

Don't have any gear (or any idea of what's required) for a bikepacking jaunt? Don't worry. It's possible to hire everything you need – including the bike – when securing your spot.

MAY

CRYSTAL PALACE CRITS
dulwichparagon.com/index.php/cpcrits

Crystal Palace Park is one of the oldest cycling venues in the world. From the first reported race that took place in the shadows of The Palace at Sydenham Hall in 1869 to its numerous dedicated Victorian-era cycle tracks, this south-

The Route Beer Ramble takes riders out on an organised bikepacking event. © *pannier.cc @panniercc*

east London spot has been a home of cycle-sport events for more than 150 years. Today, the racing on offer at Crystal Palace is as strong as ever, and various disciplines – from cyclo-cross to triathlons – have a home on its grounds. But nothing can compare to its summer criterium series.

Essentially a closed-course road event where competitors complete a set number of laps on the park's northern paths, the racing is fast and furious from the off, and some of London's best cyclists turn out for elite-level competition. You don't need to be the next Bradley Wiggins to take part, though. Racing is open to youth, junior and category 3-plus senior riders. Even if you don't fancy donning the Lycra, spectators can enjoy some free adrenaline-fuelled action in a friendly, welcoming atmosphere.

"Crystal Palace is renowned for being one of the best crit circuits in the UK, if not the world – the calibre of riders that have ridden there over the years is phenomenal. From the top end to the low end, people love it and it builds proper racing cyclists.

"You're in Crystal Palace, you're racing on parts of the old motor racing circuit – part of the straight you're racing on was part of the course that James Hunt and Niki Lauda fought on – and everyone says it's such a hard race but it's so fun. It's like no other bicycle race I've been to and I think that's what I love about it so much."

Alec Briggs, Tekkerz CC

THE TWEED RUN
tweedrun.com

Got a need for tweed? Do you know the difference between Harris and Highland varieties? Then this is the ride for you. Established in 2009, the Tweed Run sees hundreds of people with a passion for old fashion don their best woollen gear and saddle up on vintage steeds for a 19.3km spin around the city.

As you may have expected, this is no race, but rather an afternoon of appreciation for the creations of yesteryear. But that doesn't mean it's a competition-free zone, with a whole host of prizes up for grabs – including best vintage bicycle, best head gear and (obviously) best moustache.

The ride itself is ticketed, meaning no Tom, Dick or Harry can turn up on the day to take part – it's best to check the website in early Spring to find out how to enter. But if you miss out on a spot, or just like watching the clocks turn back on London's streets for an afternoon, the route is posted online on the day of the event, enabling you to head along, wave some flags and see the action for yourself.

LONDON REVOLUTION
london-revolution.com

If you've ever thought "I wish I could circumnavigate London by bike", then you're in luck (and no, this doesn't involve hugging the M25's hard shoulder). The London Revolution is a road bike-focused event where competitors get to take in the sounds and sights of central London before exploring the amazing countryside and quaint villages around the capital's edge.

The ride starts and ends at Lee Valley Athletics Centre. You have a mere 250.5km to tackle before reaching the chequered flag, including a thigh-trembling 2,246m of elevation gain thanks to sections through the North Downs and the Chiltern Hills. But before you think this is only for the climbing specialists, it's worth remembering that you won't have to clear both on the same day, with a well-earned rest (and complimentary massage) waiting for you at the Windsor Great Park base camp. Unless you opt for the Ultra distance, that is, where – you guessed it – you'll do the whole thing in one go.

PRUDENTIAL RIDELONDON
prudentialridelondon.co.uk

Cyclists in London have a lot to thank the 2012 Olympic games for, and RideLondon is just one of them. Started the year after the city hosted the Summer Olympiad, the weekend-long festival is a celebration of all things two-wheeled in the capital. While the marquee attraction used to be the RideLondon-Surrey 100 – a 100-mile (160km) sportive based on the route of the road race from the 2012 Olympics – attendees now have to settle for a 50km route instead. But there is a lot more to the proceedings than the iconic closed-road sportive.

On the first day of the festivities, the FreeCycle sees an 11km circuit of roads in central London closed to traffic, giving cyclists of all abilities the chance to spin their way around the capital and pass landmarks such as Buckingham Palace and St Paul's Cathedral as they go. The Saturday also sees the hosting of the Brompton World Championship with its Le Mans-style start, and the RideLondon Classique – a WorldTour-level women's criterium race where the best in the world battle it out during laps of the 5.5km circuit.

JUNE

THE CYCLE SHOW
cycleshow.co.uk

This annual fair of all things two-wheeled takes over Alexandra Palace for three days of pedal-powered fun in the summer. As you can expect from such an event – it's essentially a public-friendly trade show – visitors have the opportunity to get up close and personal with products from more than 100 brands, and ask the experts questions you simply can't find the answers to online. The Cycle Show hosts companies from across the cycling spectrum – road, mountain biking, commuting or kid-focused. All offer the chance for potential clients to discover the latest releases and technology available on the market. That's not all. An on-site test track allows you to hop on the saddle and try out new bikes for size (or just ride something really expensive that you'd never afford in your wildest dreams). The Cycle Show stage hosts conversations and Q&A opportunities with some of the biggest names in cycling, while mechanics are on hand to answer any query (big or small) you might have about bike maintenance. The weekend will also be hosting its own Balance Bike Championships – ideal if you're the proud parent of a future Olympian.

WORLD NAKED BIKE RIDE LONDON
wnbr.london

If you happen to be in central London on one of the first weekends in June, don't be surprised if you see a bit more than you bargained for as a peloton of cyclists whizzes past you in nothing but their shoes. You'll have just witnessed

The World Naked Bike Ride raises awareness for cyclists and protests against car culture.
© WNBR London, WNBRLondon.UK

the London edition of the World Naked Bike Ride – one of more than 100 rides like it that happen around the world in protest against car culture and promote the rights of cyclists.

The event sees more than 1,000 cyclists saddle up in as much or little clothing as they please. They ride from a number of starting points in the capital (from as far out as Kew Bridge to the central location of Marble Arch) before converging on Westminster Bridge and continuing the route around to Hyde Park Corner. And, quite surprisingly, it's all completely above-board – nakedness isn't illegal in England, unless it's done with the intention to alarm or distress someone.

If you fancy taking part yourself, all you've got to do is make your way to a start point and join in with the fun – although it's best to wait until you've arrived before getting your kit off...

LONDON TO BRIGHTON
bhf.org.uk

One of the most iconic bike rides in the cycling calendar, this pilgrimage from capital to coast has taken place annually since 1976. While there are other events like it, it's hard to beat the original – as agreed by the 30,000-plus cyclists who complete it each year.

Setting off from Clapham Common, the 87km route meanders south through the closed-off streets of the capital before hitting the punchy ascents of the Surrey Hills. From here, it's undulating countryside all the way as you pass through the idyllic villages of Smallfield, Turners Hill and Ardingly. On reaching Haywards Heath, you'd be forgiven for thinking it's plain sailing to the finish line, but there's the small matter of Ditchling Beacon to tackle. A hill so hard it was even included in the 1994 edition of Le Tour de France, the climb's

The London-to-Brighton nighttime trek sees cyclists tackling off-road trails after dark. © *Rough Ride Guide*

A London-to-Brighton off-road ride can also be taken during daylight hours. © *Rough Ride Guide*

figures speak for themselves – 1.4km long with an average gradient of 9% and a maximum of 16%. No surprise then, that many attempting the London to Brighton are left pushing their bike to the top. On reaching its summit, the hard work for the day is done. All that's left is a descent to the finish line and an obligatory portion of chips on the beach to celebrate.

LONDON TO BRIGHTON OFF-ROAD AT NIGHT
roughrideguide.co.uk

While road-riders might prefer the basic long-running London-to-Brighton trek, which takes place solely on tarmac, there are a couple of alternatives for those who like a bit of the rough stuff. There is, of course, the slightly more 'official' London to Brighton Off-Road (L2BOR) – again organised by the British Heart Foundation – that takes place in September. But if a 110km off-road route with 1,200-plus meters of elevation sounds too straightforward, an even harder mid-summer alternative adds a slice of darkness to proceedings.

Setting off from the capital in the twilight hours, you'll be deep into the countryside in no time at all with just the moon and your bike lights to guide the way. Although 10km shorter than its day-time cousin (setting off from Kempton Race Course instead of Richmond Park), the course still packs in the same amount of climbing, and features a lot of technical, twisting singletrack that would test the best riders. But all will be worth it on reaching the ride's *pièce de résistance* – watching the sun rise from the sea atop the South Downs, as dawn breaks over Brighton.

NIGHTRIDER
nightrider.org.uk

Sorry Hoff fans – the only kit at this event will be of the cycling variety. What started out in 2010 as a group of 300 is now an annual nighttime ride that comes to the streets of London (with other editions in Bristol and Liverpool) every summer to raise money for a number of charities. Not touted as a sportive or race, the event is instead a chance for its 1,000-plus participants to experience a different side to the city on two wheels, while doing their bit for a handful of worthy causes.

There are two routes available (100km and 50km) that start and finish at the iconic Lee Valley Velopark, with the first wave of riders setting off at 10:30pm. Although the course changes each year to keep things fresh, you're always guaranteed to see London's best sights as you spin around the city after dark.

It is worth noting that, while fully signposted, this is an open-road event, so it's best if you're comfortable cycling in and around traffic. You will receive a hi-viz vest on the night, but you're responsible for providing your own lights.

TIMELINE OF CYCLING IN LONDON

1869

First velocipede (the precursor to the modern bicycle) race held in London, in the grounds of The Palace at Sydenham Hall (known today as Crystal Palace Park).

1870

Pickwick Bicycle Club founded at the Downs Hotel, Hackney. The club was named after Charles Dickens' first novel, *The Pickwick Papers*, in honour of the author after his death. The invitation-only club still survives, but is mainly social nowadays.

1878

The Islington Agricultural Hall (today known as the Business Design Centre) hosted the world's first velodrome-based race. David Stanton waged £100 that he could ride 1,000 miles in six days, and completed the distance in just 73 hours.

1880

First dedicated cycling track opened in the city at Crystal Palace, followed by an updated version in 1896.

1891

Herne Hill Velodrome founded by amateur racer George Hillier. The venue hosted the cycling events of the 1948 London Olympics and has a passionate community of supporters to this day.

1934

London's first segregated cycle path opened between Hanger Lane and Greenford. There are now hundreds of miles of cycle lanes that connect the city, with more added and planned all the time.

1975

Lee Valley Eastway Cycle Racing Circuit opened. The popular east London venue hosted road, cyclo-cross and mountain bike racing until 2006, when it was bulldozed to make way for the site of the 2012 London Olympics (now known as Queen Elizabeth Olympic Park).

1978

London Cycling Campaign founded to lobby for better conditions for cycling. It now has more than 11,000 members.

2007

Le Tour de France came to London for the first time. The race started in the capital with a five-mile prologue time trial beginning on Whitehall and passing the likes of Parliament Square, Buckingham Palace and Hyde Park before finishing on The Mall. The following day's stage set off from Greenwich, heading south east from the city in the direction of the Canterbury finish line. Le Tour visited again in 2014 when stage three of the race finished on The Mall.

2008

TfL's cycle-hire scheme is unveiled. Launched in 2010 as Barclays Cycle-Hire (now Santander Cycles (see page 30)), 5,000 bikes and 315 docking stations were distributed around central London. The 'Boris bike' has become as iconic as a red routemaster bus, and there are now 11,000-plus bikes and 800 stations.

2012

London hosted its third Olympic Games, and the Lee Valley VeloPark took centre stage. Great Britain won seven out of the 10 gold medals available on the velodrome track, while Bradley Wiggins won the men's time trial on the road just 10 days after becoming Britain's first Tour de France winner. The Olympic legacy has had a lasting impact on the city, inspiring the annual RideLondon event series.

Cycling at the Summer Olympics in 1908, London; final lap of the 100km race. United States public domain.

A competitor in the London Prologue of Le Tour de France, 2007. © Ant Clausen / Shutterstock.com

JULY

DUNWICH DYNAMO
southwarkcyclists.org.uk

What starts in a Hackney pub on the Saturday night closest to a full moon in July, and finishes with a dip in the Suffolk sea? No, this isn't the start of a joke. First ridden in 1992 by a handful of dedicated riders, the Dunwich Dynamo has morphed into a 'must ride' cult event that each London-based road cyclist should attempt once.

The meeting point of this free, unsupported nighttime jaunt is Pub On The Park in London Fields. Riders tend to set off between 8pm and 9pm, giving themselves the last slithers of light to navigate their way out of Hackney in the direction of Epping Forest and the Essex and Suffolk country lanes that lie ahead. In terms of distance, the Dunwich Dynamo is a vague entity – some claim 200km, others around 193km. But one thing's for sure – you should be prepared to ride through the night and arrive at the Suffolk coastline anywhere between 3am and 9am the following day (depending on ability). Here, a quick dip in the bracing waves (it may be July, but the North Sea is never warm) or a celebratory tipple at Dunwich village local, The Ship, is your reward. To get back, Southwark Cyclists organises a ticketed coach and wagon service for you and your bike – it's best to book well in advance to secure your spot. Or, if you're feeling particularly hardy, some hop back in the saddle and retrace their steps all the way to London.

SEPTEMBER

URBAN HILL CLIMB
urbanhillclimb.com

Get ready to enter the pain cave as the capital's very own closed-road hill climb race comes to north London's Swain's Lane. Something of an odd British pastime (like cheese rolling and welly wanging), a hill climb event sees cyclists set off from a standing start at the bottom of a steep hill and pedal their way to its summit as quickly as they can. The races follow a time-trial format, meaning it's just individuals against the clock. This makes for a great spectator sport, with a full spectrum of facial expressions on display from competitors as the lactic acid in their legs starts to burn.

The Highgate-based event takes place on one of the capital's most notorious hills – Swain's Lane. While relatively short, at 0.7km in distance, the road has an average gradient of 8.5%, including a nasty 13.7% sting in its tail. While you'll see weight weenies of all ages flying to the top in times as fast as 80 seconds, the real fun comes in the more obscure categories, such as the Flying Dutchman Cargo – where a 30kg weight (usually a couple of beer kegs) is strapped to the front of a cargo bike for the competitor to carry up.

OCTOBER

SIX DAY LONDON
sixday.com

London has a rich history of six-day racing. The city was, in fact, the location of this velodrome-based pursuit's first ever iteration. That was back in 1878 at the Islington Agricultural Hall. The race was born out of the success of the previous year's six-day walking event, which had attracted crowds of 20,000 a day (those Victorians certainly knew how to have fun!). The first bike-based version saw a lone professional cyclist, English champion David Stanton, attempt to complete 1,000 miles over six days, all for a £100 bet. Stanton won his dues in just 73 hours, and a cult cycling competition was born. A larger scale version of the event was held at the same venue later that year, after which such races spread as far and wide as Madison Square Gardens in New York, as well as various European cities.

Despite its illustrious history, this might be the first you've heard of the sport. That's because its popularity waned towards the latter stages of the 20th century, with the last of the capital's six-day races taking place at Wembley Arena in 1980. Until 2015, that is, when a new Six Day Series was born.

Held in six velodromes across the world, the series kicks off at the Lee Valley Velodrome and sees some of the biggest names in track and road cycling turn out for six evenings of fast and furious action. The racing itself has changed – competitors now take part in various track cycling events (including the Madison, Derny and Keirin) rather than attempting to clock up 1,000 miles. But one thing that hasn't altered is the atmosphere, which can only be described as electric.

NOVEMBER

ROULEUR CLASSIC
rouleurclassic.cc

Warning – this show might just burn a hole in your pocket. Essentially a physical incarnation of the premium London-based road cycling magazine, Rouleur Classic assembles the biggest names in the sport and enthusiast-pleasing displays of memorabilia, all under one roof. Held over three consecutive days, Rouleur Classic is the chance for you to get up close and personal with road cycling at its finest. Whether that's listening to legends of the peloton (Eddy Merckx, Mark Cavendish and Lizzie Deignan have all previously graced the stage), or ogling historic mementos and the latest top-of-the-line products in the exhibition hall, it's very easy to while away an hour (or six).

A panel from Rouleur Classic, 2019. © *Rouleur*

BIKE SHOPS

Bike shops are the beating heart of any cycling community. From selling you a bike and caring for it throughout its lifespan (even if you aren't the most loving owner), to mechanics answering any bike-related question you might have (big or small), a local bike shop is an institution that you can rely on for anything two wheeled.

While London is home to hundreds of bike shops, from one-man bands that operate out of an industrial estate to the glittering flagship stores of national brands, not all are made equal. The best tend to be fiercely independent (so you'll find no Evans Cycles or Halfords in the following pages). They're supportive of each other and the wider cycling community and will treat every customer the same, whether they arrive on a carbon fibre creation fit for the professional peloton or an old banger dredged from a canal.

Sure, you might have to pay slightly more for a service or the actual RRP for some kit, but you'll do so safe in the knowledge that you're helping to keep a crucial component of your local cycling scene going for future generations of cyclists to come.

The Sigma Sports store stocks bikes, components and clothing.
© Sigma Sports, London, Hampton Wick

CENTRAL

BIKEFIX
44 Emerald St, Holborn WC1N 3QH
bikefix.co.uk

While a local bike shop is all well and good if mechanical issues arise at home (including those embarrassing times when a DIY attempt goes awry), what do you do if your trusty steed has a problem when you're in the middle of town, far from your favourite spot? If you happen to come a cropper in Holborn, you're in luck. Tucked away down a side alley off Lamb's Conduit St lies Bikefix, a workshop with more than 30 years' experience.

There's no booking system, so it's potluck where your bike will be in the queue. But, if it's a small job that doesn't require any special parts, it can be done on the same day – or even, if you time it right, while you wait (ideal for those annoying punctures you get just after leaving the office on your way home). The workshop can handle bigger projects as well. From electric bike servicing to repairs on steel or aluminium frames (perfect for when you've crashed, or just want something customised), Bikefix does what it says on the tin.

CLOUD 9 CYCLES
38 Store St, Bloomsbury WC1E 7DB
cloud9cycles.com

Since opening the doors of its Camden workshop in 2009, Cloud 9 Cycles has become one of the go-to places in London if you're looking for a custom bike – be it upgrading components on your current ride or starting from scratch. Now in a plush spot off Tottenham Court Road, Cloud 9 is a welcoming shop open to all levels of cyclist. Come along and learn about which bike best suits your needs, whether you've just started commuting or are on the hunt for a continent-crossing rig. The shop stocks fully built-up bikes and framesets from smaller, lesser-known brands (Orro, Brother, Litespeed, and Yeti) across a spectrum of road, mountain biking and city commuters, while its workshop can handbuild a wheel ready for any terrain.

Happy with your current bike? It's possible to pop it in for a service or repair (best to pre-book your spot online if you need it sorted as soon as possible). The shop hosts a number of events throughout the year, including launch parties for new bike models and talks by legends from the cycling community.

FULLY CHARGED
37 Bermondsey St, Bermondsey SE1 3JW
fullycharged.com

If you like your riding with an extra boost, then Fully Charged's flagship London Bridge shop is worth a visit. The chain specialises in all things e-bike, stocking battery-assisted machines of all shapes and sizes – from humble hybrids to Harley Davidson-inspired pedelecs.

Cloud 9 hosts several events year-round, including talks and bike model launches. © *Cloud 9 Cycles, Taylor Doyle*

Fully Charged focuses on the new e-bike sector of the cycling market. © *Fully Charged.*

The growing world of electric bicycles can seem like a confusing and, at times, intimidating space – especially for newcomers who see e-bikes as an accessible gateway into cycling, rather than dyed-in-the-wool riders after a bit of a turbo-boost on the hills. Fortunately, Fully Charged's team is on hand to offer expert advice. They'll find the right bike for you and your needs. It's even possible to book an appointment with one of the shop's specialists, where you can try out a handful of e-bikes to find the one that suits you best.

The shop's services don't end once you've bagged yourself a battery-assisted bike. A fleet of specially trained mechanics are on hand to keep your new investment in tip-top shape, from run-of-the-mill services through to full-blown repairs.

NORTH

CLEVER MIKE
465B Hornsey Rd, N19 4DR
clevermike.co.uk

Deriving its name from the cockney rhyming slang for 'bike', David Donker Curtius' Hornsey-based shop has gained an ever-expanding loyal tribe of customers since opening its doors on an unsuspecting industrial estate in 2013. Clever Mike is loved for its honest and welcoming approach to bike repairs. Whether you turn up with a cheap commuter or a top-of-the-line carbon fibre creation, you'll get the same reception from its small team of knowledgeable mechanics. You can trust that your pride and joy is in good hands – and that it'll be returned with no nasty surprises, either on the bike or the bill.

As well as offering everything from check-up services to full strip downs, Clever Mike has become something of a go-to destination if you go gaga for steel-framed bikes from

American brands such as Surly and All-City. Whether you're after an off-the-peg ride; or a fully custom creation featuring hand-built wheels from fellow Londoners, Stayer Cycles; David and his team will only be happy to help.

MICYCLE
47 Barnsbury Street, N1 1TP
micycle.org.uk

Give a man a fish and you feed him for a day; teach a man to fish and you feed him for a lifetime. That's the ethos at Micycle, a local bike shop with a difference. The small Barnsbury Street space does everything you could possibly want from a repairs-focused shop – bookable check-ups, full-blown services and first-come-first-served, while-you-wait puncture repairs and brake adjustments. But it also offers a variety of courses that will stop you pushing your broken bike round to the shop every time something goes wrong.

Micycle splits its bike maintenance course down into four sessions: an overview, wheels, brakes and gears. Once complete, this will give you all the knowledge you need to keep your bike well-maintained year-round. In addition to these repair-focused classes, Micycle runs a 'complete beginner' lesson that aims to get anyone (regardless of age) riding on two wheels, while a 'journey accompaniment' session sees a member of the Micycle team join you for a ride. They'll show you cycle-friendly routes to and from your place of work, as well as great tips for taking the commuting-by-bike plunge.

PEDAL PEDLAR
106 Balls Pond Rd, Mildmay Ward, N1 4AG
pedalpedlar.co.uk

While most modern bike designs focus on being lightweight, practical and fast, you can't beat the look of a classic steel bicycle. Pedal Pedlar knows this more than most. The shop has been specialising in vintage bikes since it opened its doors in Newington Green in 2011 (and even before then, online).

The store keeps a large selection of second-hand and new-old stock from the 1950s through to 1990s. It's *the* place to go if you dream of an Eroica-era bike that wouldn't look out of place beneath cycling legends Eddy Merckx or Fausto Coppi. From complete builds to a customisation service, the possibilities – stock permitting – are endless.

Pedal Pedlar's passion for the past doesn't end at bikes. You can get yourself fully kitted out, from vintage team kits down to casquettes and musettes (cotton bags stuffed with food, which are handed to professional cyclists mid-race).

Despite Pedal Pedler's vaunting of vintage, you don't need a bike built in the last millennium just to set foot in the shop. The on-site workshop is happy to tinker away at anything with two wheels. They have four levels of service available, from a light spruce-up through to a full strip, rebuild and polish.

NORTH EAST

TWO WHEELS GOOD
165 Stoke Newington Church St, Stoke Newington, N16 0UL
twowheelsgood.co.uk

Opened in 1998, Stoke Newington's Two Wheels Good has been around for long enough to see various cycling fashions, fads and trends peddle past. The shop has built up decades' worth of problem-solving experience in the process. If an issue has stumped the mechanic at your recently opened local bike shop, there's a good chance the guys at Two Wheels Good will have seen (and repaired) the same problem countless times. They'll get you out of any squeeze in a jiffy.

Proudly honest with their assessments and pricing, you'll know you can trust their unbiased opinion about any bike woes. The staff are a friendly bunch, and you'll receive the same level of service even if your bike's value doesn't stretch into four (or five) figures.

In addition to servicing, repairing and replacing in the workshop, Two Wheels Good stocks a small range of bikes from Trek, Surly, Pashley, and Gazelle, while its line of Frog bikes are perfect for little ones just getting started on their cycling journey.

EAST

LONDON BIKE KITCHEN
16 Whitmore Rd, N1 5QA
lbk.org.uk

While most shops see you drop off your bike for a mechanic to fix, at London Bike Kitchen, you drop yourself off to become the mechanic. Although getting stuck in may not be everyone's cup of tea, if you've got the time and desire, it's a great way to learn about your bike's inner workings in a safe and friendly environment.

Customers pay a flat hourly rate for access to tools, cleaning and greasing materials, as well as the knowledge of on-hand experts. If parts need replacing – or if you want to fit some plush new accessories – London Bike Kitchen stocks most bits and bobs you'd find in any regular bike shop.

As well as these drop-in sessions (which are first-come first-served), it hosts regular classes and lessons on everything from an introduction to bike maintenance through to wheel building. London Bike Kitchen also runs a free fortnightly workshop for women and non-binary people. It co-runs a Women of Colour cycling group, with the aim to get more underrepresented people comfortable with both riding and maintaining their bikes.

HOW TO REPAIR A PUNCTURE

YOU WILL NEED

- Inner tube and/or puncture repair kit
- Tyre levers
- Pump
- Adjustable spanner (if your bike doesn't have quick-release axles on its wheels)
- Gloves (optional, but things can get mucky)

STEP 1

Undo the quick-release skewer (or unscrew the axle's bolts) and remove the punctured wheel from the bike.

STEP 2

Use the tyre levers to prise one side of the tyre off the wheel's rim.

STEP 3

Slide the punctured inner tube out from the rim and remove it completely by pushing the valve up and through the hole in the rim (you might have to unscrew a nut that is holding it in place).

STEP 4

Run your hand carefully around the inside of the tyre to check for any sharp objects that might have caused the puncture. Remove anything sharp that you find.

(If replacing the punctured inner tube with a new one, skip to step 6).

STEP 5

Find the hole in the punctured inner tube (the easiest way: inflate it slightly, pop it in a bucket of water and watch for bubbles). Follow the instructions on the puncture repair kit to patch the hole.

STEP 6

Slightly inflate the new or repaired tube, insert its valve into the hole in the rim and slide the inner tube into the rim bed.

STEP 7

This is the tricky bit. With the valve at its furthest point from you, lever the tyre's bead back onto the inside of the rim. Work your way around the tyre until it's refitted. If you're left with a stubborn part that just won't cooperate, try pushing the valve up into the tyre. This will hopefully give you more room to work with and make it easier to ease the tyre back on.

STEP 8

Check that there aren't any parts of the inner tube trapped between the bead and the rim and inflate slightly. If there are any bulges, your inner tube is trapped. It might require a bit of massaging to get it sitting correctly.

STEP 9

Once clear, you're all set to inflate the tyre using your pump. Don't know your PSIs from your Bars? There will be a recommended pressure on the side of the tyre.

The Basic Maintenance Course from Look Mum No Hands! includes puncture repair. © *Look Mum No Hands!*

If you don't want to repair your bike yourself, the shop is more than happy to fix any problems you may have – but where's the fun in that?

SBC CYCLES
41 Cropley St, Hoxton, N1 7HT
sbccycles.com

Got a crazy idea for a custom bike unique to you and your requirements? Or maybe you want a set of hand-built wheels that can handle whatever you throw at them? Mark Boswell and Jamie Kirkham at this Shoreditch spot will be all too happy to help.

A pair of mechanics with almost three decades of combined experience, the SBC (Skull Bike Club) Cycles guys have a cult following that transcends their shop's east London location. This is mostly thanks to their build gallery, which is teeming with drool-worthy creations. Whether you're after a fixed-gear track bike, a trail-slaying mountain bike or a gravel-grinding all-road machine, the endless array of inspirational previous builds proves nothing is out of the question in SBC's workshop. The space also has an extensive menu of options when it comes to repairs and servicing. Got a problem? SBC will get you back in the saddle in no time at all.

BRICK LANE BIKES
118 Bethnal Green Road E2 6DG
bricklanebikes.co.uk

Born out of the street racing, cycle courier-inspired fixie boom of the late '00s and early '10s, Brick Lane Bikes is renowned for its role in bringing road-ready track bikes to the hip crowds of east London. It soon became *the* place to go if you were in need of the latest pedal-powered fashion accessory or some obscure vintage component, attracting enthusiasts from all over Europe with its collection of track bike treasures.

Although its roots are in the single-speed scene – and it still stocks a wide range of fixies – Brick Lane Bikes has expanded into a bit of an all-rounder. New hybrids rub shoulders with vintage Colnago racers, and the store's own BLB-branded builds include all-out track bikes, step-through town bikes and gravel-focused adventure bikes.

The Shoreditch-based space is home to its own workshop where a team of experienced mechanics are on hand, and will generally turn around small jobs on the same day. No booking is required, so all you have to do is drop your bike off – though the shop can take bookings if you require something specific, or if you want a guarantee that your bike will get seen to as a priority.

HUB VELO
215, 217A Lower Clapton Rd, Lower Clapton E5 8EG
hub-velo.co.uk

This Clapton store is the beating heart of the local cycling scene. Whether you're after a new bike, your current steed is in need of some love or you just fancy a coffee and slice of cake, you'll be welcomed at this friendly space with its attached café, which draws in cyclists from far and wide.

The shop stocks bikes from across the cycling spectrum from brands such as Trek, Cinelli and Brompton. It'll have something for you, be it a new road-racing machine or just something to pootle on down to the shops. Its on-site workshop is happy to work on anything from tandems to track bikes, but recommends booking your bike in if you're after a service. Small jobs such as a puncture repair can be done on the spot, and you can always enjoy something from the Hub Velo café while you wait.

Hub Velo is also home to a 150-strong cycling club (Hub Velo CC) and regular rides leave from the shop on Wednesday and Saturday mornings in the direction of the Essex lanes. As well as access to some snazzy Santini kit, club runs and even entry to races, membership gets you a handy 15% discount on the majority of items in the shop, so will start paying for itself in no time.

"Hub Velo in Lower Clapton is my go-to local bike shop. The staff are really friendly, they offer a great service and there's even a café too. They're a really important part of the local community."

Russ Jones, Hackney GT

THE HACKNEY PEDDLER
89 Stoke Newington Rd, Stoke Newington
N16 8AA
thehackneypeddler.co.uk

Steel bikes are enjoying something of a renaissance, and it's easy to see why. More durable than aluminium and carbon fibre, they make the perfect companion for inner city commuters, where the focus is robustness and reliability rather than the bike's performance in a wind tunnel.

This Stoke Newington-based shop specialises in all things steel, and stocks a broad selection of bikes, from dependable runarounds to classic vintage restorations. Its staff are on hand to talk you through *that* custom bike you've always dreamed of, with a selection of frames from iconic builders such as Hetchins, Colnago and Roberts for you to construct your period-correct or neo-retro build around.

The Hackney Peddler is also home to an in-store workshop that provides three different levels of service as well as more ad-hoc repairs. Punctures can be patched while you wait, and mechanics aim to complete all other jobs in 24 hours. The staff are an approachable bunch – so do ask them if you want a quick demo on how to make minor adjustments yourself.

The Hackney Peddler, an independent shop based in Stoke Newington. © *Andy Donohoe*

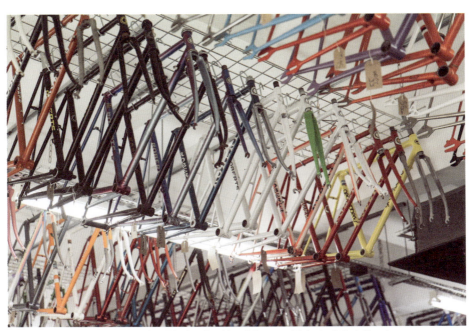

The Hackney Peddler stock frames from Mercian, Hetchins, Colnago and Roberts. © *Andy Donohoe*

SOUTH EAST

THE BIKE PROJECT
12 Crossthwaite Avenue, Herne Hill SE5 8ET
thebikeproject.co.uk

Cycling is such a beneficial form of transport. More than just an environmentally friendly way to get from A-to-B, it's good for your physical and mental health – not to mention a lot of fun. But it can also be a way of giving back to those less fortunate in society, as The Bike Project proves. A local bike shop with a difference, this charity takes donated second-hand bikes, repairs them, and then gives them to refugees and asylum seekers in the city. This provides the beneficiaries with mobility, opening up greater opportunities in the process.

The Bike Project also sells a proportion of these restored wonders in its online shop. Any profits are used to fund

The Bike Project workshop. © *The Bike Project*

the charity's work, doing up even more donated bikes. The same applies to any accessories it sells. It is possible to add a 'gift' for refugees to any order – be it a cycling safety kit or a full-blown bike.

Not in need of a new pre-loved bike? The Bike Project has its own workshop in Deptford that can carry out a service on your cycle and replace any old parts that have seen better days. Unlike some other local shops, you do need to book in your bike for a service, but it's possible to borrow a courtesy bike to keep you on the road while your pride and joy enjoys some much-needed attention.

CADENCE PERFORMANCE
2A Anerley Hill, Upper Norwood SE19 2AA
cadenceperformance.com

Since opening its doors in Crystal Palace in 2013, Cadence Performance has gone from strength to strength, and now has outposts as far and wide as Radlett, Hertfordshire, and Shoreham-on-Sea, West Sussex. Set up by co-founders Frank Beechinor-Collins and Ray Vella as a true hub for cycling, Cadence is a one-stop-shop for all your cycling needs – whether it's a new bike, a bike fit, coaching or even a sports massage. A stone's throw from Crystal Palace, its True Heart Cafe acts as a de facto clubhouse for the park's summer crit racing series, while its affiliated cycling club puts on the occasional event as well as its regular Saturday rides.

The shop itself is a stockist of Giant and Liv bikes, from humble hybrids to trail-taming e-MTBs. It sells everything you need to get started on your cycling journey (including clothing, footwear, locks and lights). Cadence is also home to a fully fitted workshop that provides a free estimate for any repair. The mechanics won't start work until you give the go-ahead – meaning you won't wind up with any nasty surprises on the bill.

SOUTH

BRIXTON CYCLES
296-298 Brixton Rd SW9 6AG
brixtoncycles.co.uk

One of the oldest bike shops in London, Brixton Cycles has been keeping wheels turning in south London and beyond since 1983. A workers' co-operative from the off, the shop prioritises people before profit, and the business model and ethos has seen some staff rack up multiple decades of service.

Dreamed up by a group of friends during a ride from Land's End to John O'Groats, it has grown from a humble local bike shop to a cornerstone of the Brixton community in its near 40-year history. Although it has moved around over the years (the co-op left its original Coldharbour Lane spot in 2001, while the second Brixton Beach shop was demolished in 2016), its latest Brixton Road iteration is an impressive space that sports a café as well as a workshop and shopfront.

Brixton Cycles can carry out servicing and repairs of any description. It also stocks new bikes from Surly, Specialized, Genesis and Trek, if you're in need of a fresh set of wheels. And, as with all good local bike shops, Brixton Cycles provides a free-to-use pump and tool board out front in case you get stuck mid-ride and need to carry out some roadside repairs.

DE VER CYCLES
632-636 Streatham High Rd SW16 3QL
devercycles.co.uk

Just over four miles down the road from Brixton Cycles you'll find this iconic, eye-catching establishment. Founded in 1977, De Ver was bought by Maurice Burton – the three-time British Track Champion and first Black British cycling champion – just ten years later. It's been under Maurice's management ever since, becoming a mainstay of Streatham High Street.

The shop sells all you need to push off the ground and start peddling, from bikes to bottle cages, stocking big-name brands like Cinelli, Genesis and Giant. The space also houses a comprehensive workshop, where mechanics are happy to diagnose and prescribe for any bike-related problems, while a state-of-the-art bike-fitting room ensures your ride is adjusted in the optimum way.

It wouldn't be a bike shop owned by a former professional if it didn't have an accompanying team. Team De Ver CC has a 60-strong membership and club rides start from the shop every Saturday morning. All ages and abilities are welcome, and there's even the chance to join Maurice for a pre-season training camp in Lanzarote. Not many local bike shops can offer that!

SEABASS CYCLES
261 Rye Ln SE15 4UR
seabasscycles.co.uk

Founded in 2013 by Sam Lewin and Charlie Roberts, Seabass Cycles has gone from strength to strength during its relatively short lifespan, and now has two spaces in south-east London to call home. The original Camberwell Church Street shop sticks to its roots, offering three levels of services and general repairs. Meanwhile, the Rye Lane location has its own workshop, where they stock a range of complete bikes from the likes of Specialized and Soma, as well as frames and hand-built wheels.

It is these custom creations that Seabass Cycles has become renowned for. The gallery of builds on its social media channels are a smorgasbord of cycling's latest and hottest trends. From rack-laden utility bikes to mile-munching all-road machines built around frames from Brother Cycles, Ritchey or All City, you can customise to your heart's content. Seabass Cycles will work with you to make your one-of-a-kind bike dreams a reality.

SOUTH WEST

FLAG BIKES
324 Battersea Park Rd, Battersea SW11 3BX
flagbikes.com

Handily located on London's Cycling Superhighway CS8, Flag Bikes has been serving stuck commuters since it opened its doors in 2014. But this is much more than a go-to shop for when you find yourself with a puncture en route to work. Flag Bikes' on-site workshop is Cytech-accredited and can carry out everything from a standard service through to a custom bike build – plus, of course, that all-important inner tube replacement.

Flag Bikes also carries a wide range of bikes from brands such as Cinelli, Genesis, Saracen and Tifosi. If the staff don't have your size or model in stock, they can soon order one in for you. This store understands that customers need to try out a bike before buying, as simply sitting on one won't simulate all the miles ahead. You're allowed to take bikes out on proper test rides around the nearby Battersea Park – all you need to do is bring some photo ID. As well as providing all the accessories and clothing new cyclists might need, other services on offer at Flag Bikes include bike-fitting appointments and a very reasonably priced bike box hire, if you fancy taking your bike on holiday.

SIGMA SPORTS
37-43 High Street, Hampton Wick KT1 4DA
sigmasports.com

It might be hard to believe now, but this online behemoth started life in 1991 as a small, mail-order business, run out of a spare bedroom. A brick and mortar premise in Hinchley Wood followed just one year later, before Sigma Sports made the move to Hampton Wick in 1996. Fast forward to today, and Sigma Sports is one of cycling's biggest online retailers – though the flagship store is arguably the jewel in its crown.

A three-storey space dedicated to all things cycling, running and triathlon, this shop is a mecca for road cyclists. Well worth the pilgrimage, a visit can be combined with a loop of Richmond Park (see page 142). Sigma Sports stocks bikes, components and clothing from the biggest brands around – and reserves space for independent British makers, too. Its state-of-the-art workshop is able to work on bikes of all shapes and sizes: no job is too big or too small. Sigma Sports also runs day-long mechanics courses for those hoping to gain a better understanding of how their bikes work. Want to learn how to carry out small jobs yourself at home (or by the roadside)? Sigma Sports is the shop for you.

Sigma Sports supplies cyclists, runners and triathlon athletes. © *Sigma Sports, London, Hampton Wick*

CYCLING ROUTES

London is one of the most interesting places to ride a bike in the world. Whether you're ambling along the Thames, ticking off landmarks as you go, or weaving your way towards the rolling fields on the outskirts, few other locations allow you to pass such a variety of sights from the comfort of your saddle. Stay in the centre and, thanks to some serious recent infrastructure investment, you'll find a wealth of segregated cycle lanes. Venture outside the city limits, and the suburbs boast a welcoming network of country lanes, quaint villages and the odd challenging hill. It's between these areas that difficulties arise. This no man's land, where cyclists and motorists share busy, narrow roads, puts off many prospective peddlers. But (in this cyclist's experience, anyway) the city's bark is worse than its bite.

Whether you're a first-time cyclist or an old hand, there's a route here for you. Those that focus on escaping the city include a train station en route – ideal if you'd rather skip the 'no man's land', or if you fancy cutting a ride short.

(Detailed directions for each route can be found at bikelondon.co.uk.)

See the sights of London from your saddle, from Buckingham Palace to Westminster Abbey and far beyond. © *Charlie Allenby*

CENTRAL

REGENT'S PARK LOOP

Start point: ZSL London Zoo entrance
End point: ZSL London Zoo entrance
Distance: 4.5km
Duration: 10-15 minutes
Train station: NA

Henry VIII's former hunting ground has become something of a mecca for cyclists who live north of the river (and even some who don't). The Outer Circle loop that lines the park's border is now a de facto training area for those who want to ride hard on some surprisingly quiet streets (for central London, anyway). The route attracts individuals, cycling clubs and full-blown pelotons most weekday mornings.

The circuit itself isn't visually anything to write home about – other than the dome-shaped roof of London Central Mosque and the BT Tower in the distance, there's not a lot to look at. But that's not really the point of doing the Regent's Park loop. Cyclists go there to train, and thanks to the lack of traffic, can focus on doing just that.

The start and end points are movable, although most ride outs meet at the London Zoo entrance with the aim to simply complete a lap (or as many as you can in a set time). Although not challenging (at 4.5km it should be achievable, regardless of ability), it's a great route to hone your skills as a cyclist – be that building endurance, riding in a group or just getting used to cycling on central London roads. Plus, thanks to its location, you could even squeeze a lap or two in before continuing your commute to work.

SIGHTSEEING SPIN

Start point: London Bridge station
End point: Marble Arch station
Distance: 12.1km
Duration: 45-60 minutes
Train station: NA

London has an embarrassment of riches when it comes to landmarks, and this route is something of a Greatest Hits tour: Tower Bridge, the Tower of London, the London Eye, the Houses of Parliament, Buckingham Palace, Hyde Park… Admire all of these and more as you travel from east to west. The best bit is that the route follows segregated cycle lanes from the Tower of London onwards. Plus, thanks to the numerous cycle-hire schemes on offer in central London, you don't even need your own bike to take part.

Setting off from Tooley Street, the road takes you past the shops of Hay's Galleria and More London before bringing you neatly to Tower Bridge. Riding over this landmark offers an amazing view out across the Thames, but if you'd rather stay away from motor traffic, it's worth starting your journey at the Tower of London instead. Here, the route picks up the East-West Cycle Superhighway 3 – a segregated cycle lane that runs all the way to Lancaster Gate.

You'll soon find yourself spinning through the City, rejoining the Thames once you reach Blackfriars, then onto Westminster. After crossing Parliament Square, next up is St James's Park and Buckingham Palace. And, after stopping for the obligatory picture, you'll soon find yourself at the tip of Hyde Park Corner. The 350-acre Grade I-listed park is perfect for exploring by bike, but if you're a stickler for routes, following Cycle Superhighway 3 takes you along South and West Carriage Drive, over the Serpentine and past its gallery. A right turn onto North Carriage Drive brings you to Marble Arch, where you can drop off your hire bike and take in a talk at the world's oldest free-speech platform, Speaker's Corner.

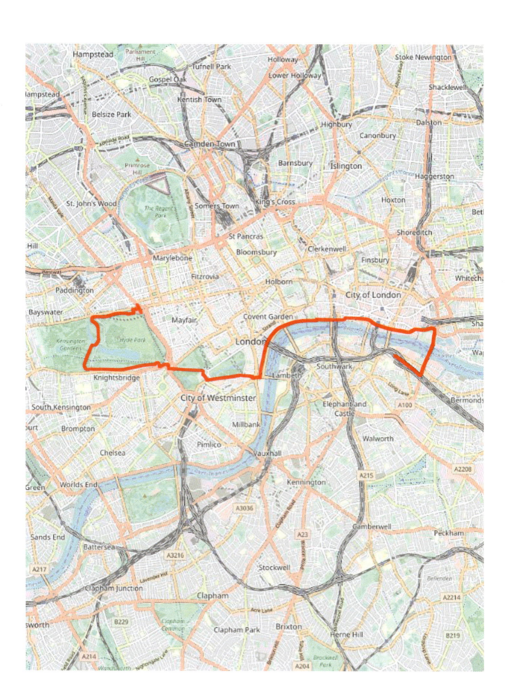

NORTH

AN INTRODUCTION TO THE CHILTERN HILLS

Start point: Finsbury Park
End point: Finsbury Park
Distance: 105.7km
Duration: 4-7 hours
Train station: Bushey

The Chiltern Hills are something of a road cyclist's playground. North London's equivalent to the South Downs, the area has a plethora of quaint villages and quiet country lanes, as well as the odd thigh-burning climb (it does have 'hills' in the name, after all). Although the region has quite a geographical spread – spanning the counties of Oxfordshire, Buckinghamshire, Bedfordshire and Hertfordshire – it's possible to start and finish a ride in London while getting a taste of what the Chilterns have to offer.

Finsbury Park is the starting point of the route, which, after tackling the first ascent of the day up Muswell Hill, heads in a northerly direction until turning west at Whetstone. Cycling out of London is never the nicest experience – more a means to an end – and can be skipped by getting the train directly to Bushey. From this point, there's still a solid 50km of good riding to be had, the majority of which takes in roads with little traffic.

Regardless of where you start though, you'll have a handful of hills to tackle along the way. Highlights include the climb through woodland up to the red brick houses of Flaunden village, the testing trip up Tom's Lane (which will leave you cursing whoever this 'Tom' is) and the rise up into Shenley with its steep sting in the tail.

From there, it's a simple spin back towards Finsbury Park along the High Road from High Barnet; breathe a sigh of relief – it's mainly downhill, with the appetite suitably whetted for future exploration of the Chilterns and its many hills.

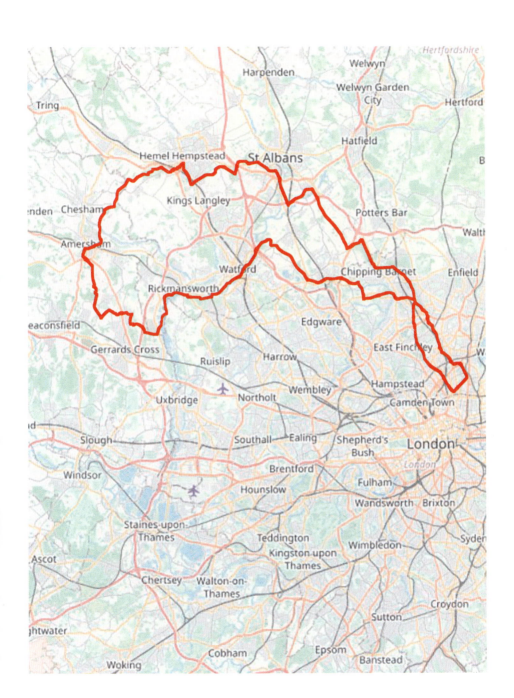

The River Colne is just one of the many beautiful spots en route to the Chilterns. © *Charlie Allenby*

HERTFORDSHIRE LANES

Start point: Kentish Town Tube station
End point: Kentish Town Tube station
Distance: 81.2km
Duration: 3.5-5 hours
Train station: Potters Bar

Hills in London are quite hard to come by. But that's not to say they don't exist. Take Swain's Lane, for example. The Highgate road is notorious amongst the city's road cyclists as being one of (if not *the*) hardest climbs the capital has to offer, and is even host to the Urban Hill Climb every September (see page 93). It's also, rather cruelly, about five minutes into the start of this route – but you'll feel suitably warmed up on reaching the top.

After tackling Swain's Lane, it's time to join the traffic as you meander your way through Finchley and up (literally) to High Barnet. A right at the church points you in the direction of Potters Bar, which is where you can join this route if opting to take the train.

From here starts a loop that offers up some of the best riding the outskirts of London has to offer (although, as it is my local loop, I might be somewhat biased). The settlements of Newgate Street, Epping Green and Hoddesdon are punctuated by a few short, sharp hills, before it's time to turn onto Lord Street and enjoy one of the nicest winding country lanes around. Once the roundabouts of Hertford have been carefully navigated, it's time to turn back towards Potters Bar – but not before completing the leg-sapping climb of Robins Nest Hill and freewheeling down to Cucumber Lane.

After a quick pit stop at De Beker café on reaching Potters Bar, it's time to return to London. Instead of retracing your steps, sample the thrilling descent of Stagg Hill on the way into Cockfosters and finish your ride with one final climb up Alexandra Palace's South Terrace.

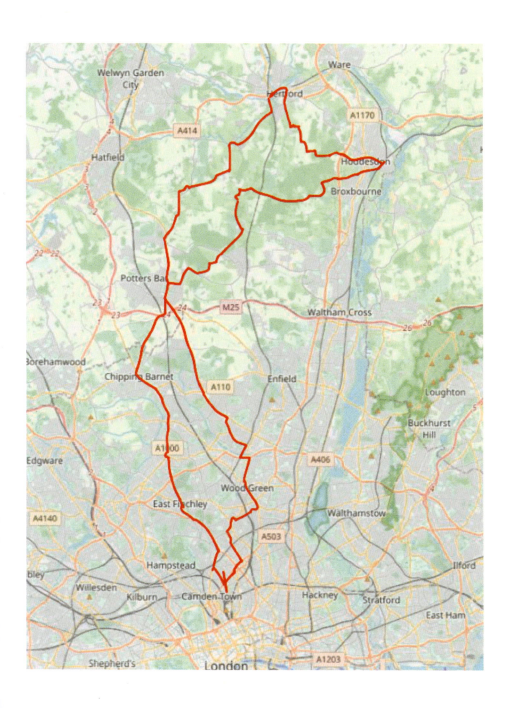

Swain's Lane is one of the steepest hills in London. © *Charlie Allenby*

Roundabout at the Coach and Horses, Newgate Street, in the Hertfordshire Lanes. © *Charlie Allenby*

Epping Forest offers many opportunities for off-road, traffic-free cycling. © *Charlie Allenby*

EAST

OFF-ROADING IN EPPING FOREST

Start point: Chingford Plain Car Park
End point: Chingford Plain Car Park
Distance: 20.8km
Duration: 1-2 hours
Train station: Chingford

Riding off-road and city living might seem to be polar opposites, but there are some absolute all-terrain gems in London (if you know where to look). Epping Forest is easily the most iconic of the bunch. Stretching from the depths of the East End out to the Essex hinterlands, the park is a traffic-free dream, offering countless woodland trails and open paths to explore on two wheels. It's also a favourite spot for the city's mountain bikers.

Starting from Chingford Plain Car Park (although you can join the loop from any point along the way), this route follows a predominately gravel path around the forest's circumference – leaning heavily on the park's 'main' and 'green' paths. The terrain makes it perfect for most bikes come summer when the trails are dry, but it's best sticking to a mountain bike or gravel bike when things are a bit damp. The route doesn't use a single road (although you have to cross a few), making it perfect for children and those not confident riding alongside motorised traffic.

There are a few speedy descents and short, sharp climbs to keep things interesting (pedestrians share these paths though, so bear that in mind before bombing downhill at full pelt). Those who like their riding with some airtime thrown in should note the odd dirt jump, dotted just off the paths. On reaching the tip of the loop (9.5km), there is a short section of the route that is best described as 'all-out off-road'. If you or your bike aren't up to the task, simply turn right instead of left, cutting off 2km of muddy ruts and loamy paths.

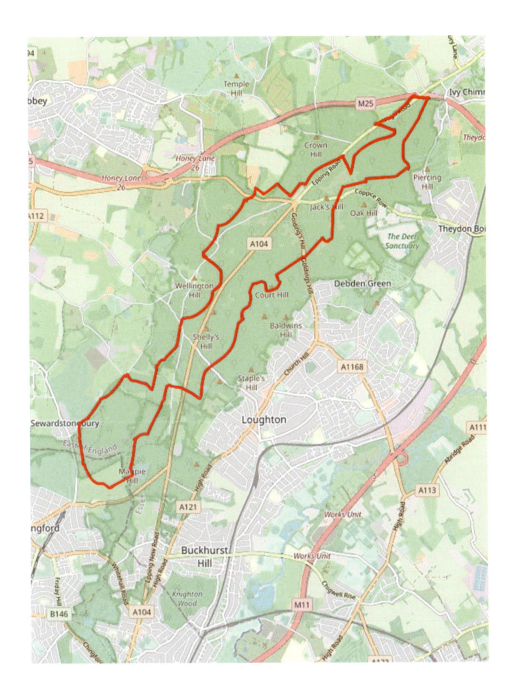

EXPLORING THE THAMES ESTUARY

Start point: The Tower of London
End point: Dartford
Distance: 40.2km
Duration: 2.5-3.5 hours
Train station: Maze Hill

The Thames Path is renowned for the riches it offers when travelled in a westerly direction from central London. After the landmarks and sights of the city, it turns into a trail flanked by picturesque countryside all the way to the river's source in Gloucestershire. But head in the opposite direction, and you're left with an edgier, gritter route along the inlet-packed bends of its estuary.

Setting off from the Tower of London, this path roughly follows the National Cycle Route 1 – a 2,769km trail that hugs the east coast of the UK from Dover to the Shetland Islands. After crossing Tower Bridge, you'll find yourself winding your way around the back streets and old industrial areas of Bermondsey until emerging on the Thames' southern bank and its quiet, traffic-free path. Greenwich's Old Royal Naval College, the *Cutty Sark*, the O2 and views out across to Canary Wharf are all ticked off before reaching the Thames Barrier – at which point you truly feel like you've left London, the city a mere speck on the horizon behind you.

From here, the paved path hugs the river and its occasional sandy beaches until entering the town of Erith. After a whistle stop tour of its high street, it's not long before you're back in the estuary, following a gravel track that meanders its way through the marshland flanking the river Darent (if travelling by road bike, it's best to skip this off-road section and navigate your way to Barnes Cray). A short spin along segregated cycle paths brings you to Dartford and a regular train service back to the city.

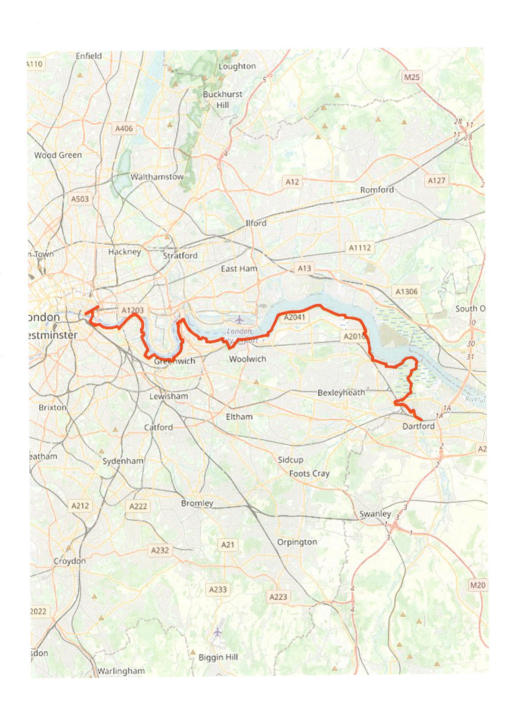

The Thames Estuary route follows part of National Cycle Route 1. © *Charlie Allenby*

SOUTH

ICONIC CLIMBS OF THE SURREY HILLS

Start point: Houses of Parliament
End point: Houses of Parliament
Distance: 137.5km
Duration: 5-7 hours
Train station: Dorking

Mention the words 'Box Hill' to any half-serious cyclist in London and watch their eyes light up in joy and pain. Put on the map by the 2012 London Olympics road race, the zig-zagging road (literally named 'Zig Zag Road') is a pilgrimage destination for road bike riders across the country. Although its reputation is crueller than its slope – the gradient is a manageable 4% over 4.2km from start to finish – the experience is definitely worth the trip. No wonder Box Hill welcomes thousands of cyclists every weekend.

This route loosely follows the old 100-mile RideLondon-Surrey sportive course. A-roads that were closed during the event have been switched out for cycle-friendly alternatives. You can also head straight for the hills by catching the train to Dorking (and skipping the busier sections of the route by doing so). If you complete the whole ride, your route is bookended by a split lap of Richmond Park (more information on page 142) and you'll get to sample the rolling greenery of London's southwestern suburbs. The hills start in earnest on the approach to West Horsley, and from there it's 50km of undulating lanes with the occasional punchy peak. Climbs of note other than Box Hill include the rise out of Sutton Abinger en route to Holmbury St Mary and Leith Hill, which, in my opinion, is actually harder than Box Hill. After a well-earned pitstop at the Box Hill café, it's a speedy descent down to Leatherhead and, from here, either a long ride back to central London or a diversion in the direction of Dorking and a comfortable train ride.

Fun fact: During the 2012 London Olympics road race, female competitors had to complete two laps of a 15.5km circuit that included Box Hill, while male riders had to head up the Zig Zag Road a thigh-burning nine times.

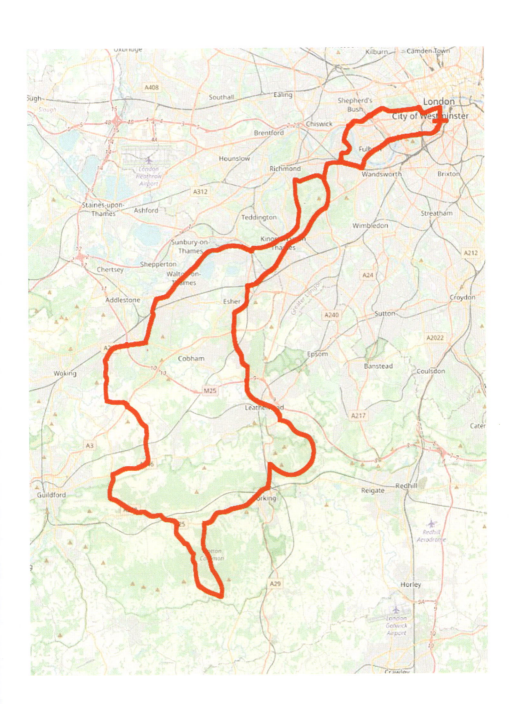

ESCAPE TO THE SEASIDE

Start point: Clapham Common
End point: Brighton Pier
Distance: 85.8km
Duration: 4-6 hours
Train station: Carshalton

The ride from London to Brighton is an absolute classic for the city's cyclists, up there with Regent's Park and Richmond Park in terms of pilgrimages to make on two wheels. The route has been enshrined by the British Heart Foundation-organised event that takes place every June, but you don't have to sign up to take on this 85.8km challenge.

Starting at Clapham Common, the first 10km or so of the route sees you navigate the busy streets of south London before rising up into Carshalton for the start of the Surrey Hills.

It's fairly lumpy going from here on out; the short, sharp climb to Nutfield and the longer affair to Selsfield Common the picks of the bunch. The scenery and settings make up for any thigh-burn, though; the country lanes are a welcome change from the city streets. The villages and settlements of High Weald national park fly by on a gradual descent down into Haywards Heath. Then you're onto the final quarter of the route – crossing Ditchling Beacon on the way.

This South Downs climb is the stuff of legend. Located within the final 15km of the London to Brighton route, it has claimed many victims over the years, who are left with no alternative but to push their bikes up by foot. An average gradient of 9.1% is certainly no walk in the park – add in some tired legs and it feels twice as steep. The view from its peak is motivation to push through the pain, as it's possible to see Brighton and the sea for the first time. A long descent into the city is your reward – along with a hearty helping of chips on the seafront.

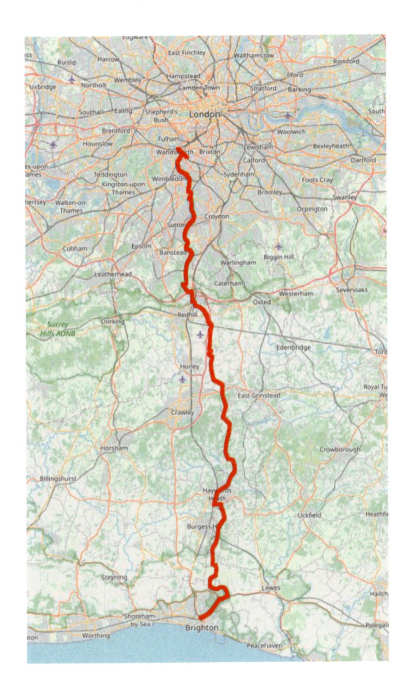

WEST

RICHMOND PARK LOOP

Start point: Colicci café
End point: Colicci café
Distance: 10.8km
Duration: 20-40 minutes
Train station: NA

Like Regent's Park in the north, we can thank the royals for this south-city cycle spot. Created by Charles I as a deer-hunting destination, London's largest park is still defined by its four-legged residents, though the only thing being chased down nowadays are personal bests around the 10.8km cycling circuit. Groups of cyclists take to the park's roads every day of the year, with the early morning weekend laps being the most popular. There are two ways of completing the Richmond Park loop – clockwise and anticlockwise. Both contain at least one hill that will see you out of the saddle. This anticlockwise loop tackles the longer, shallower climb of Dark Hill. It also means you get to whizz down Broomfield Hill, letting gravity do the work, while those on the other side of the road struggle up its 12%-gradient peaks.

The route sets off from Colicci café, though it can be joined from any of the entrances that line the park. After turning left at Roehampton Gate roundabout (another benefit of the anticlockwise loop: you just take the first exit on the park's three main roundabouts) the first stretch is a straight line up the false flat of Sawyer's Hill. While not steep, it'll get you nicely warm for what's to follow. The second, undulating segment takes in Queen's Road, passing Pembroke Lodge on your right and Thatched House Lodge on your left. After the final main roundabout at Kingston Gate, you meet Dark Hill. Its tree-lined 6.4%-average gradient makes it one of the city's steeper climbs, although at 500m in distance, you're soon back on the flat. From here, it's plain sailing – descending the snaky bends of Broomfield Hill, before you return to your start point. A single lap is enough for most, but if you want to push yourself, see how quickly you can do three. You'll have definitely earned a coffee and a cake after that.

A ROYAL RIDE
OUT TO WINDSOR

Start point: Hampton Court Palace
End point: Hampton Court Palace
Distance: 77.6km
Duration: 2.5-4 hours
Train station: Windsor

Windsor and its Great Park are a favourite of west London-based cycling clubs, as the Berkshire town is a manageable distance for an out-and-back ride from the capital. It's also a good destination for those easing themselves into longer rides thanks to quiet country lanes, with an easy gradient and a regular train service to whizz you back to various London terminals.

Starting from Hampton Court Palace, the route loosely follows the path of the Thames until reaching the town of Chertsey. A short, sharp climb up Ruxbury Road takes you up and over the M25 and the sleepy settlements of Stonehill and Burrowhill. A gradual descent on Chobham Common leaves you at Sunningdale and the edges of Windsor Great Park.

Say goodbye to traffic for a bit while exploring the historical hunting ground's car-free tracks, passing lakes, ponds and polo courses as you make your way into the park. Be sure to stop at the Copper Horse Statue of King George III (40.1km) for amazing views down the iconic Long Walk towards your mid-ride stop – Windsor Castle.

After an obligatory selfie at the world's oldest occupied castle, it's either off to the train station for an easy journey back to London or on to Eton and a 30km spin back to Hampton Court. The ride is pan-flat from here on, meaning you could be back within the hour if you're quick. You're soon back in familiar territory as you retrace your steps along the Thames from Chertsey onwards. A diversion south of the river, just past Shepperton, helps keep things interesting before you hit Hampton Court Bridge.

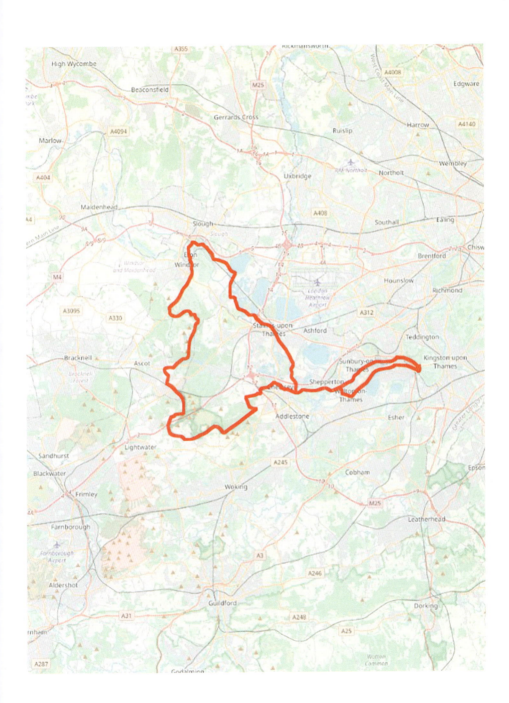

TYPES OF CYCLIST

NERVOUS NEWBIES

After taking up cycling during the heady days of lockdown, these first-timers are finding it difficult now that traffic has returned to normal. Give them extra space and an encouraging smile – you were in their position once upon a time.

MAMILS

Middle-Aged Men in (tight-fitting) Lycra can be found flying around Regent's and Richmond Park at weekends, but come the week, the city's streets are their race course. Although the Lycra might seem a bit much for a ride into the office, it does mean you aren't sitting in sweaty clothes all day.

CARGO-BIKE COURIER

Cycle couriers are renowned for whizzing around the capital on fixies, messenger bags bulging with packages and parcels. But a new breed of bike-based deliverers are helping save the environment as they go – the cargo-bike courier. Expect an explosion in their numbers as the capital leans green.

BIKELIFE LADS

Menacing or mesmerising? Whatever your opinion of these wheelie-ing youths, you can't deny that they are seriously skilled in balancing on their mountain bike's back wheel. Until it all goes wrong, that is...

CYCLE-HIRE TOURIST

While visitors should be applauded for exploring a new city on two wheels, they have a tendency to not know where they're going, let alone the rules of the road, and often stop without any prior warning. Most will be aboard a cycle-hire bike and can be spotted by their slightly confused expression. If you come across a group, it's worth giving them a wide berth.

RETRO RIDERS

Why have a new bike when you can buy vintage off eBay? Sure, your pride and joy might not run as smoothly as a modern machine, but it'll certainly turn heads (both for the aesthetic, and because it sounds like a bag of nails).

Keep a watchful eye out for the Cycle Hire enthusiast. © *Transport for London*

CYCLING VENUES

Cycling routes often rely on roads shared with motorised vehicles. However, there are a handful of spots in the city designed specifically with riding a bike in mind – whether you want to race as fast as you can or just enjoy a car-free spin. A lot of these have the 2012 Olympics to thank for their existence: they were either created to host events, or were given serious investment as part of the games' legacy.

That's not to ignore the good smattering of cycle spaces jammed with history. From the world's longest continuously used skate spot to a velodrome that dates back to the Victorian era, London has catered for its cyclists for as long as there have been bicycles.

Riders change during a mixed Madison (relay) at Herne Hill Velodrome's annual Velofete fundraiser.
© Tom Dunn (www.tommydunnit.com)

CENTRAL

SOUTHBANK SKATE SPACE
337-338 Belvedere Rd, Bishop's, SE1 8XT
southbankcentre.co.uk

Although officially regarded as the world's oldest skate spot (in terms of continuous use), the protected status of the area beneath the Southbank Centre is a relatively recent development. Opened in 1967 and first used by skateboarders as far back as 1973, the location is one of the UK's most well-known areas for Street BMX, with its graffitied concrete walls the backdrop for numerous iconic photographs and video segments.

The space was subjected to anti-skate measures from 1990, which came to a head in 2013 with plans to redevelop the entire Undercroft space into shops and restaurants. The group Long Live Southbank was born out of this threat to the local skate and BMX community, and, a year later, the long-term future of the space was secured after a successful campaign that garnered a lot of public support.

Today, the space is a hive of activity. Skaters, BMXers and graffiti artists all use it as an area to express their creativity – whether it's on the numerous benches or rails, or the brutalist structures.

HOUSE OF VANS
Arches, 228, 232 Station Approach Rd,
Lambeth SE1 8SW
houseofvanslondon.com

Afraid of taking your first tentative spin into the world of freestyle BMX? There's a central London spot where you can learn the ropes before throwing yourself into the Southbank Skate Space or one of London's other numerous purpose-built skateparks.

Opened in 2014, House of Vans has become an alternative lifestyle hub in the capital, hosting everything from gigs to art shows in its Waterloo Vaults location. On top of that, it's also home to a concrete bowl, halfpipe and street-inspired obstacles. The space opens its doors most Sunday afternoons for a free all-ages two-hour BMX session, where you get to ride its park and street courses without the crowds found at some of the city's more popular spots. Once you've got the knack, be sure to head along to House of Vans' monthly BMX Support Group night. Cash prizes are up for grabs for the best tricks, and there are free burgers and beers.

NORTH

REDBRIDGE CYCLING CENTRE
Forest Rd, Ilford, Romford IG6 3HP
visionrcl.org.uk

Although only opened in 2008, Redbridge Cycling Centre (or Hog Hill as it is otherwise known) has become a staple of the cycling scene north of the river. Built with compensation money after the compulsory purchase of the old Eastway track (located in Hackney, demolished to make way for the Olympic Park), Hog Hill has taken up the mantle where its predecessor left off.

The site is home to a 2km road track that has seven different possible arrangements, a 3.25km mountain bike course featuring descents, berms and jumps, and a BMX pump track suitable for racing. This ability to cater for different disciplines really makes Hog Hill stand out. The quality of the facilities means you're guaranteed to find a race meet here most weekends, and even weekday summer evenings – whether for road, mountain biking, cyclo-cross or BMX.

It's not all about racing, either. The centre is open year-round as a place to come and ride a bike in a car-free environment, and there's a range of bikes available to hire if you don't own your own.

EAST

LEE VALLEY VELOPARK
Abercrombie Rd, E20 3AB
visitleevalley.org.uk

This east London spot probably doesn't need any introduction. The site of Team GB's triumphs at the 2012 Olympics, the Lee Valley Velopark is home to the iconic Pringle-shaped velodrome – London's only indoor cycle track. Touted as the 'fastest track in the world', the space hosts numerous professional races throughout the year, including the Six Day series (see page 93). It's not just for the pros, though. Take to the boards for an experience like no other, as you spin your way around the scene of some of Britain's most memorable recent sporting moments.

Beyond the walls of the track, the Velopark is home to a number of other cycling-focused courses. To the side of the velodrome lies the 1.6km floodlit road circuit, where races and training events are held throughout the year on its smooth tarmac course. When not booked out, you can take on the course during the Velopark's pay and ride session – just beware: the climbs are punchier than you think.

For those who prefer things off-road, the Velopark also houses the berms and jumps of the Olympic BMX track, as well as 8km of cross-country mountain bike trails, with introductory and training sessions available for both.

HADLEIGH PARK
Hadleigh Country Park, Chapel Lane, Benfleet, Essex SS7 2PP
explore-essex.com

The eagle-eyed amongst you will have noticed that Hadleigh Park isn't actually in London. But while this Essex-based spot falls outside of the M25, it deserves a mention because of its ties to the capital. Yes, it may be closer to Southend-on-Sea, but the cross-country mountain biking on offer makes it worth the excursion.

The trails at Hadleigh Park, specially built to host the cross-country mountain bike competition during the 2012 London Olympics, have been adapted and maintained as part of the games' legacy. The site is now home to four different routes – from the 9km family-friendly green trail to the 5km red trail and its optional black-graded sections – making it a fun day out for first timers and pro-level athletes alike.

Thanks to their well-built construction, the trails are rideable in all weather, and are generally fairly quiet even on the sunniest days of the year. If you've yet to take the plunge on an off-road ride, the on-site shop offers up various mountain bikes, child-sized bikes and even e-bikes for hire.

SOUTH

HERNE HILL VELODROME
104 Burbage Rd, Dulwich, SE24 9HE
hernehillvelodrome.com

On an unassuming street in south London lies one of the oldest velodromes in the world. Formerly named the London County Grounds, Herne Hill Velodrome has been the beating heart of cycling in the city since first opening in 1891.

The open-air 450m-long concrete bowl has survived two world wars, countless threats of closure and competition from other London-based velodromes over the years. Hosting the stars of cycling past and present, from the likes of Fausto Coppi and Tom Simpson in the 1950s and 1960s to a 12-year-old Bradley Wiggins as he took his first tentative pedal strokes, Herne Hill was even the site of the track events at the 1948 Olympics. While it's hard to imagine this tucked-away venue attracting such massive audiences (crowds of more than 10,000 attended certain meets during the velodrome's '20s and '30s heyday), there is a strong and committed support of the velodrome from both the local and wider cycling community. Herne Hill still has a role to play today, more than 125 years since it first opened its track to cyclists.

One of Herne Hill's biggest assets is its comprehensive training sessions for those who want to get into, and improve, their cycling. Ages from two and above are catered for across a wide range of classes – from the basics of learning to ride, to introductions to track cycling, to all-out race training. Head along to a session and do your bit to support this key part of London's cycling history.

"I never would have thought to do any form of competitive cycling had it not been for Herne Hill. I started going to the women-only sessions on Sunday evenings – if you've never done track before, they give you a bike; you can do an induction during the session and then you join the rest of the women. I just fell in love with it and started going to that session religiously every week and I've not really stopped since then."
Jess Morgan, North London ThunderCats

WEST

HILLINGDON CYCLE CIRCUIT
11-12 Springfield Rd, Hayes UB4 0JS
hillingdoncyclecircuit.org.uk

Like Redbridge Cycling Centre in the north and the Velopark's closed-road track in the east, this purpose-built circuit is the perfect place to come and ride without having to worry about traffic. Located in Minet Country Park, the 1.5km asphalt loop was born out of races that were organised on the unopened Hayes Bypass in the 1990s. Once the road opened, the park – which had previously been an area where waste earth was dumped during the road's construction – was touted as a potential location for a closed-road track, and the circuit successfully opened in 1997.

The circuit is still an active and popular spot for riding and racing, with events and training held year-round by local clubs. The Hillingdon Slipstreamers youth club are based at the venue, too. When not booked out, the circuit is open to the general public for free, providing access to a well-maintained and safe space for everyone in the community to ride their bikes.

Riders get ready to roll away at Herne Hill Velodrome Women's League, the UK's largest women-only track league. Image © Sam Holden (*www.samholdenagency.com*)

BMX PUMP TRACKS

London is home to a strong collection of BMX pump tracks. While a large proportion of the city's spots germinated as a result of the 2012 London Olympics legacy funding, there are some, such as Brockwell Park, which have rich histories and strong club-based communities attached. The geographical spread means that there's one not too far from most Londoners' doorsteps. And, given the city's lack of trail centres or bike parks, the pump tracks are often the closest you can get to in-city off-road riding.

NORTH

LORDSHIP LOOP TRACK
Broadwater Farm Community centre, Adams Road, Tottenham, London
N17 6HE

EAST

CHENEY ROW PARK BMX TRACK
Cheney Row, Walthamstow, London E17 5ED
cogcycling.co.uk

HAGGERSTON PARK BMX
Haggerston Park E2 8QE
hackneybmx.com

LAKE FARM BMX TRACK
Lake Farm Country Park, Dawley Road, Hayes, Middlesex UB3 1JD
hawksbmx.co.uk

MILE END BMX TRACK
Mile End Park, Burdett Road E3 4TN
towerhamlets.gov.uk

SOUTH

BROCKWELL PARK BMX
Brockwell Park, Brixton, London SE24 0PB
brixtonbmx.co.uk

BURGESS PARK BMX
Wells Way, London SE5 0PX
peckhambmx.co.uk

CROYDON BMX TRACK
Norbury Park SW16 3LY

HORNFAIR PARK BMX TRACK
Hornfair Park, off Shooters Hill Road, SE18 4PE
facebook.com/GreenwichBMX

LEWISHAM BMX TRACK
Beckenham Place Park, Old Bromley Road, Bromley, BR1 4JZ

MERTON BMX TRACK
Acacia Rd, Mitcham CR4 1ST
mertonsaintsbmxclub.com

WEST

CHALKHILL BMX TRACK
Barnhill Road, London, HA9 9BU
brent.gov.uk

GURNELL LEISURE CENTRE BMX TRACK
19 Ruislip Rd E, West Ealing, London W13 0HT
ealingbmx.com

WORMWOOD SCRUBS BMX TRACK
Wormwood Scrubs, London, W12 0HU

BMX riders at Brockwell Park. Image © *courtesy of Mike Woof*

British Library Cataloguing-in-Publication Data
A catalogue record for this book is available from the British
Library

The author and publisher gratefully acknowledge the permission
granted to reproduce the copyright material in this book. Every
effort has been made to trace copyright holders and to obtain
their permission for the use of copyright material. The publisher
apologises for any errors or omissions in the text and would be
grateful if notified of any corrections that should be incorporated
in future reprints or editions of this book.

Front cover: Cycle routes allow travellers to pass some of
London's most famous landmarks.
© *Alena Veasey / Shutterstock.com*
Back cover: A number of London's bike shops and cycling cafés
also offer repairs and maintenance. © *Look Mum No Hands!*
Frontispiece: A sign guiding riders around the London Cycle
Network.
© *Hadrian / Shutterstock.com*
Maps on pages 121, 123, 125, 129, 133, 135, 139, 141, 143
and 145: © openstreetmap.org contributors
Inside cover: Charlie Allenby on his bike. © Andy Parsons

Printed in China
for ACC Art Books Ltd., Woodbridge, Suffolk, England

www.accartbooks.com

**ACC
ART
BOOKS**

14ᵗᵈ June 1988

RESEARCH PROGRESS IN PARKINSON'S DISEASE

Research Progress in Parkinson's Disease

Edited by
F CLIFFORD ROSE FRCP
*Consultant Neurologist, Charing Cross
Hospital, London
Consultant Neurologist, Medical
Ophthalmology Unit, St Thomas' Hospital
London.*

RUDY CAPILDEO MB, MRCP
*Senior Registrar
Department of Neurology
Charing Cross Hospital
London*

PITMAN MEDICAL

First published 1981
Reprinted 1981

Catalogue Number 21 0404 81

Pitman Books Limited
39 Parker Street, London, WC2B 5PB

Associated Companies:

Pitman Publishing Pty Ltd, Melbourne
Pitman Publishing New Zealand Ltd, Wellington

British Library Cataloguing in Publication Data

Research progress in Parkinson's disease. —
(Progress in neurology series).
    1. Parkinsonism
    I. Rose, Frank Clifford
    II. Capildeo, Rudy   III. Series
    616.8'33   RC382

ISBN 0-272-79601 8

ISSN: 0260-0013

Set in 10/11 pt IBM Press Roman by
Gatehouse Wood Limited, Sevenoaks, Kent
Printed and bound in Great Britain
at The Pitman Press, Bath

CONTENTS

PART V L-DOPA AND ITS PROBLEMS

PART VI OTHER DRUGS

CONTRIBUTORS

Sir Roger BANNISTER, CBE, MD, FRCP, Consultant Neurologist, National Hospital for Nervous Diseases, Queen Square, London

A BARBEAU, MD, FRCP (C), Professor, Department of Neurology, Clinical Research Institute of Montreal, Montreal, Quebec, Canada

N BATHIEN, Service de Neurologie, Centre Hospitalier Sainte Anne, Paris

R BAUER, MD, Wayne State University Medical Centre, Detroit, Michigan

P BEDARD, University Department of Neurology, Institute of Psychiatry and King's College Hospital Medical School, London

P O BEHAN, MD, FRCP (G), FACP, FRCP (Lond), Reader, Department of Neurology, Institute of Neurological Sciences, Glasgow

Wilhelmina M H BEHAN, MB, ChB, MRCPath, Institute of Neurological Sciences, Glasgow

R BERMAN, MS, Merck, Sharpe and Dohme Research Laboratories, West Point, Pa. 19486

W BIRKMAYER, University Professor of Neurology, Evangelica Hospital, Vienna, Austria

W BLACKWOOD, FRCSE, FRCPE, FRCPath, Honorary Visiting Consultant, Department of Neurology, Charing Cross Hospital, Emeritus Professor, Department of Neuropathology, Institute of Neurology, University of London

Ivan BODIS-WOLLNER, MD, Department of Neurology, Mount Sinai School of Medicine of the City University of New York, New York, USA

A H BONE, PhD, BSc, MRIC, Department of Biochemistry, Charing Cross Hospital Medical School, London

Michael Graham BRAMBLE, MB, ChB, MRCP, Senior Registrar, Royal Victoria Infirmary, Newcastle upon Tyne

Donald B CALNE, DM, FRCP, Experimental Therapeutics Branch, National Institute of Neurological and Communicative Disorders and Stroke, National Institutes of Health, Bethesda, Maryland, USA

Rudy CAPILDEO, MB, MRCP, Senior Registrar, Department of Neurology, Charing Cross Hospital, London

M CRITCHLEY, CBE, MD, FRCP, Emeritus President, World Federation of Neurology, Honorary Consulting Neurologist, National Hospital, Queen Square, and King's College Hospital, London

P DAS, MD, PhD, Research Fellow (Parkinson's Disease Society) Department of Neurology, Charing Cross Hospital, London

B I DIAMOND, PhD, Department of Neurological Sciences, Rush-Presbyterian, St Lukes Medical Centre, Chicago, USA

J DICK, University Department of Neurology, King's College Hospital and Institute of Psychiatry, London

R DOROW, Schering AG, Berlin

M DUNNING, MCSP, Physiotherapist, University College Hospital, London

P N C ELLIOTT, School of Pharmacy, Liverpool Polytechnic, Liverpool

L FINDLEY, MB, MRCP, DCH, Senior Registrar, Department of Neurology, St. Mary's Hospital, Lately Registrar, Department of Neurology, Charing Cross Hospital, London

G FIRNAU, PhD, Department of Nuclear Medicine, McMaster University Medical Centre, Hamilton, Ontario, Canada

Karen FISHER, MSc, Lately Psychologist, Charing Cross Hospital, London

Beryl FLEWITT, FCST, Research Physiotherapist (Parkinson's Disease Society of the UK) Department of Neurology, Charing Cross Hospital, London

K FLOWERS, MA, PhD, Lecturer, Department of Psychology, University of Kingston upon Hull

S FRANKLYN, MCSP, Physiotherapist, University College Hospital, London

E S GARNETT, FRCP, Department of Nuclear Medicine, McMaster University Medical Centre, Hamilton, Ontario, Canada

M J GAWEL, MB, MRCP, Lecturer, Department of Neurology, Charing Cross Hospital, London

F B GIBBERD, MD, FRCP, Consultant Neurologist, Westminster and Queen Mary's Hospitals, London

R B GODWIN-AUSTEN, MD, FRCP, Consultant Neurologist, Nottingham Medical School, Nottingham

Vivette GLOVER, MA, PhD, Research Biochemist, Institute of Obstetrics and Gynaecology (University of London), Queen Charlotte's Maternity Hospital, London

G GOPINATHAN, MD, FRCP (D), Experimental Therapeutics Branch, National Institute of Neurological and Communicative Disorders and Stroke, National Institutes of Health, Bethesda, Maryland, USA

M GRESTY, PhD, MRC Hearing and Balance Unit, Institute of Neurology, National Hospital, Queen Square, London WC1N 3BG

S HABERMAN, FIA, Research Fellow, Neuroepidemiology Unit, Charing Cross Hospital, Senior Lecturer, Department of Actuarial Sciences, City University, London

G W HANKS, MB, BSc, MRCP, Research Fellow, Sir Michael Sobell House, Churchill Hospital, Oxford

L HARRIS, MB, MRCP, FCP, Medical Director, Sanofi-Reckitt, Regent House, Stockport, Greater Manchester

H HOEHN, MD, University of Colorado Medical Center, Denver, Colorado

R HOROWSKI, Schering AG, Berlin

F J IMMS, MB, BS, PhD, Scientific Officer, MRC Environmental Physiology Unit, London School of Hygiene and Tropical Medicine

P JENNER, Senior Lecturer, University Department of Neurology, Institute of Psychiatry and King's College Hospital Medical School, London

F B JOLICOEUR, PhD, Department of Neurobiology, Clinical Research Institute of Montreal, Montreal, Quebec, Canada

R KERWIN, BA (Hons), PhD, Department of Pharmacology, Medical School, University of Bristol, Bristol

E KINNEAR, MCSP, Physiotherapist, Queen Mary's Hospital, Roehampton

Harold L KLAWANS, MD, Department of Neurological Sciences, Rush-Presbyterian, St Luke's Medical Center, Chicago, USA

L. J. KOHOUT, PhD, Department of Neurology, University College Hospital, London

William C KOLLER, MD, PhD, Department of Neurological Sciences, Rush-Presbyterian, St. Luke's Medical Center, Chicago, USA

Cecilie M LANDER, MB, FRACP, Department of Neurology, University College Hospital, London

A J LEES, MD, MRCP, Senior Registrar, Department of Neurology, University College Hospital, London

M G MARMOT, MB, BS, MPH, PhD, Department of Medical Statistics and Epidemiology, The London School of Hygiene and Tropical Medicine

J McFIE, MD, Consultant Neuropsychologist, Charing Cross Hospital, London

John McFIE, MD, Consultant Neuropsychologist, Charing Cross Hospital, London

D L McLELLAN, PhD, MA, MB, MRCP, Senior Lecturer in Neurology, University of Southampton, Honorary Consultant Neurologist, Wessex Neurological Centre, Southampton

C D MARSDEN, MD, FRCP, Professor and Head, University Department of Neurology, Institute of Psychiatry and King's College Hospital Medical School, London

M MUENTER, MD, Maho Clinic, Rochester, Minnesota

C NAHMIAS, BSc, Department of Nuclear Medicine, McMaster University Medical Centre, Hamilton, Ontario, Canada

H NARABAYASHI, MD, Professor of Neurology, Juntendo University Hospital, Hongo, Tokyo, Japan

P A NAUSIEDA, MD, Department of Neurological Sciences, Rush-Presbyterian, St Luke's Medical Center, Chicago, USA

D W NIBBELINK, MD, PhD, Merck Sharp and Dohme Laboratories, West Point, Pa. 19486

N C R PAGE, MB, MRCP, Neurological Registrar, Westminster Hospital, London

D M PARK, MA, BM, MRCP, Consultant Neurologist, Southend Hospital, Essex

J D PARKES, MA, MD, FRCP, University Department of Neurology, Institute of Psychiatry and King's College Hospital Medical School, London
Iris PEARCE, MB, BS, Research Fellow, Department of Neurology, Hull Royal Infirmary, Hull
G D PERKIN, MB, MRCP, Consultant Neurologist, Charing Cross Hospital, London
S PERLIK, MD, Rush-Presbyterian, St. Lukes Medical Center, Chicago, USA
Alison R PERRY, LCST, Senior Speech Therapist, Department of Speech Therapy, Charing Cross Hospital, London
A E PRATT, MB, FRCP, Consultant Neurologist, Hull Royal Infirmary, Hull
P PRICE, University Department of Neurology, Institute of Psychiatry and King's College Hospital Medical School, London
C PYCOCK, Department of Pharmacology, Medical School, University of Bristol, Bristol
P RIEDERER, University-Doz. Dipl-Ing, Chief, Neurochemistry Group, Ludwig Boltzmann Institute of Clinical Neurobiology, Lainz Hospital, Vienna, Austria
G REIN, MSc, Research Fellow, Department of Chemical Pathology, Institute of Obstetrics and Gynaecology (University of London), Queen Charlotte's Maternity Hospital, London
G P REYNOLDS, Visiting Research Fellow, Neurochemistry Group, Ludwig Boltzmann Institute of Clinical Neurobiology, Lainz Hospital, Vienna, Austria
D B RONDEAU, PhD, Department of Psychology, University of Moncton
P RONDOT, Professeur, Service de Neurologie, Centre Hospitalier Sainte-Anne, Paris
F Clifford ROSE, FRCP, Physician in Charge, Department of Neurology, Charing Cross Hospital, London
Madeleine ROY, MD, MSc, Department of Neurobiology, Clinical Research Institute of Montreal, Montreal, Quebec, Canada
M SANDLER, MD, FRCP, FRCPath, Professor of Chemical Pathology, Institute of Obstetrics and Gynaecology (University of London), Queen Charlotte's Maternity Hospital, London
M SCHACHTER, MB, BSc, MRCP, University Department of Neurology, King's College Hospital and The Institute of Psychiatry, London
M SHEEHY, MB, FRACP, University Department of Neurology, King's College Hospital and The Institute of Psychiatry, London
B SMITH, MSc, Clinical Laboratories, The Bethlem Royal and Maudsley Hospitals, London
K M SPENCER, MB, MRCP, Neurological Registrar, Westminster Hospital, London
E G S SPOKES, BSc, MD, MRCP, Senior Registrar, Department of Neurology, St James (University) Hospital, Leeds
S STELLAR, MD, St Barnabas Hospital, Livingston, New Jersey
G M STERN, MD, FRCP, Consultant Neurologist, Department of Neurology, University College Hospital, London
H TERAVAINEN, MD, Experimental Therapeutics Branch, Intramural Research Programme, National Institute of Neurological and Communicative Disorders and Stroke, National Institutes of Health, Bethesda, Maryland, USA

A M THOMAS, MB, BS, MRCP, Institute of Neurological Sciences, Glasgow

J THORNTON, PhD, Department of Neurology, Mount Sinai School of Medicine of the City of New York, New York, USA

S VINCENT, Department of Medical Physics, Charing Cross Hospital, London

C WARD, MB, MRCP, Department of Neurology, University College Hospital, London

W J WEINER, MD, Department of Neurological Sciences, Rush-Presbyterian, St Lukes Medical Center, Chicago, USA

M P I WELLER, MA, MB, MRCPsych., Senior Lecturer, Department of Psychiatry, Charing Cross Hospital, London

A WILLIAMS, MD, MRCP, National Hospital for Nervous Diseases, Queen Square, London

J B WILLIAMS, MBAOT, Occupational Therapist, Queen Mary's Hospital, Roehampton

A WILSON, MSc, Clinical Laboratories, The Bethlem Royal and Maudsley Hospitals, London

M D YAHR, MD, Chairman and Professor, Department of Neurology, Mount Sinai School of Medicine of the City University of New York, New York, USA

M YOKOCHI, MD, Department of Neurology, Juntendo University Hospitals Hongo, Tokyo, Japan

PART I

GENERAL ASPECTS

Chapter 1

INTRODUCTION

Melvin D Yahr

It is is indeed a pleasure for me to have the opportunity of writing this introductory chapter devoted to a volume on progress in Parkinson's disease research. The World Federation of Neurology through its Research Committee on Extrapyramidal Disease was most delighted to join with the Parkinson's Disease Society of Great Britain in its sponsorship of the symposium on which this book is based.

It is, of course, particularly fitting that this symposium was held here in London where James Parkinson lived, worked and wrote his now famous monograph. One cannot help but be impressed by the keen clinical perceptions of this remarkable physician—for James Parkinson's description of the "shaking palsy" was not only accurate and vivid, but has withstood the test of time. As impressive, if not more so, is his motivation in undertaking the task of writing his monograph. In the final section, he wrote:

> Before concluding these pages, it may be proper to observe once more, that an important object proposed to be obtained by them is, the leading of the attention of those who humanely employ anatomical examination in detecting the cause and nature of diseases, particularly to this malady. By their benevolent labours its real nature may be ascertained, and appropriate modes of relief, or even of cure, pointed out. [1]

I am not certain that this had any immediate impact on the morbid anatomist for it took some 75 years or more before attention was drawn to the seat of the pathological changes in the substantia nigra (SN) by Blocq and Marinesco (1893) [2], and 100 years before Tretiakoff (1919) [3] put them on firm footing. Though parkinsonism continued to interest the neurological community from a phenomenological, morphological and to some extent physiological viewpoint, I believe it is safe to say that no groundswell of research effort was evident in the succeeding years. Indeed, except for the spurt of interest occasioned by the epidemic of von Economo's disease in 1918 [4], it was rather a fallow field until some 15 years ago, when dramatic and impressive advances in our knowledge of the basal ganglia in regard to their unique chemical topography and pharmacological properties became available. Central to these developments was the demon-

3

stration of the role of neurotransmitters, particularly those related to the mono-amines in the control of motor activity and behaviour. The work in this country of Martha Vogt [5] on noradrenalin showing its preferential regional distributions; that of Carlsson in Sweden in regard to dopamine (DA) and the actions of reserpine, [6] and the development of techniques to demonstrate the localisation of the monoamines *in situ* by Flack and Hillarp [7] as well as means for their biochemical assay, led to a virtual explosion of research interest in this field. Fortuitously, what was going on in the laboratory about monoaminergic pathways found ready and rapid application to human disease—particularly parkinsonism. The demonstration of striatal DA loss in the parkinsonian brain by Ehringer and Hornykiewicz [8] in Austria led to the discovery of the strio-nigral pathway and a meaningful inter-pretation of the morphological changes in the SN.

Hard on the heels of these discoveries came a new and certainly more rational approach to the therapy of parkinsonism—the use of agents capable of replenish-ing brain DA. The contributions of Birkmayer [9], Barbeau [10], Cotzias [11], and our own [12] in this area will be covered and expanded in some depth in the chapters that follow, but there is no doubt that the effect of the systemic administration of L-dopa in modifying the symptoms of parkinsonism has been a milestone in the therapeutics of neurological disorders. It was the first instance of what has been termed replacement therapy for essential biochemical components of neural tissue lost as a result of disease. Its success has led to exploring new approaches for treatment of other neurological disorders with some reward to date such as the use of 5-hydroxytryptamine (5HTP) in action myoclonus. Whether the concept of replacement therapy is truly applicable is still debateable—what is not, is the ability of L-dopa to activate dopaminergic activity in the brain. Unfortu-nately, such action is not limited to the striatum, the target site where it is re-quired, nor does it occur with the precision necessary for the intricate function of this structure. At best, our present pharmacological approaches to parkinsonism must be considered as rather primitive and crude in both concept and practice. I am afraid it will remain so until more information regarding the underlying physio-logical and morphological substrate of this disorder as well as its aetiology are forth-coming; that such may well be on the horizon is evident by the content of this volume. One cannot help but be impressed by the number of scientific disciplines now involved in research bearing on parkinsonism, an effort, I am certain, that will lead to significant inroads into those areas of this devastating disorder where our information is sorely lacking, which I shall now emphasise.

The underlying anatomical substrate whose dysfunction leads to the symptoms of parkinsonism is still poorly understood. In this regard the striatum, a nodal struc-ture in this disorder with extensive connections to cerebral cortex and substantia nigra and a virtual storehouse of neurotransmitter substances, must be more fully explored. It is already apparent that its components, the caudate nucleus and putamen are less than homogeneous, containing a variety of cell populations with numerous types of dendritic arrangements and multiple classes of receptors for each of the neurotransmitters. Understanding the nature of these various elements and the mechanisms by which intrastriatal events occur, as well as their effects on other

4

neuronal systems, will lay the foundation necessary for a better understanding of parkinsonism and improved means for its treatment.

Though the operational concept of parkinsonism as solely a striatal dopamine deficiency syndrome has proven most useful over the past decade, it presently is in need of revision. Evidence for a role for other neurotransmitters is rapidly accumulating. Too little attention I believe has been given to altered levels of noradrenaline, acetylcholine and serotonin, nor have we yet applied information regarding the peptide containing pathways. All of these may be amenable to manipulation by using various therapeutic strategies.

Perhaps the area where little if any progress is being made concerns aetiological factors in parkinsonism. Although a variety of agents have induced parkinsonism as a result of their involvement of the nervous system, the cause of Parkinson's disease itself remains unknown. It has been suggested by some that genetic factors play a role; others have suggested that viral agents are the cause; still others claim that an enzymatic defect is acquired as part of the ageing process which specifically affects the monoaminergic cells of the nervous system or acts in a more generalised fashion.

Support for a genetic basis is primarily derived from family studies, for which historical documentation can be produced to indicate that 5-15 per cent of family members may suffer from the disease [13]. An on-going study in our Clinic of the incidence of Parkinson's disease in identical twins has to date failed to show concordance. Leaving aside the controversy still present in this regard, there is general agreement that if inheritance does play a role it is neither dominant nor fits a monogenic model. Whether it fits some polygenic model is open to question.

Considerable effort during recent years has been made to relate Parkinson's disease to the epidemic of encephalitis lethargica (von Economo) which occurred from 1918 to 1926. In a retrospective analysis of the age of onset of parkinsonian symptoms, supporters of this concept point to a cohort who have been ageing together and in whom the date of onset of their parkinsonism has been rising by one year for each calendar year [15]. Based on these data, they have proposed that Parkinson's disease is post-encephalitic and a late consequence of subclinical infection with the virus of encephalitis lethargica. The inferences drawn from these data are that there is a single aetiology for all parkinsonism and that a sharp decline in its incidence can be expected in the coming decades when those at risk have died off [16]. Indeed, a virtual disappearance of Parkinson's disease is predicted by the end of this century. Apart from methodological objections concerning the collection and analysis of these data and alternate explanations for their occurrence [17], pathological, clinical and immunological findings indicate that post-encephalitic parkinsonism and Parkinson's disease are very separate entities [18, 19]. The former, though affecting the substantia nigra, produces other widespread changes in the nervous system and is characterised by neurofibrillary changes and the absence of Lewy body formation. Recent studies of the immunological properties of post-encephalitic brains reveal antigenic sites which bind with Influenza A virus. No such sites are found in the brains of patients with Parkinson's disease [20]. Clinically,

5

post-encephalitic parkinsonism has certain distinctive features such as oculogyric crises which do not occur in Parkinson's disease. Lastly, the response to therapeutic agents varies considerably. Although post-encephalitics are most tolerant to anti-cholinergic agents, they can tolerate only limited amounts of levodopa [21]. It appears to the author that it is an error to formulate a unitary aetiological hypothesis for these two types of parkinsonism, nor has it been possible to uncover a relationship with any of the known viruses that invade the nervous system. None-theless, one would be equally in error to exclude the possibility that some types of viral infection, presumably of the "slow virus" variety, may well underlie Parkinson's disease. If it does, however, it is highly unlikely that it is the same agent which caused encephalitis lethargica and its sequelae.

Since the demonstration that striatal monoamines, particularly dopamine, are decreased in all forms of parkinsonism, attention has centred on its role in the aetiogenesis of Parkinson's disease. Conceivably, this loss, rather than being secondary to the degeneration of cells for its production, could result from a primary defect in its metabolism. In regard to the latter, it is of some import that the therapeutic response in Parkinson's disease which results from levodopa cannot be obtained with L-tyrosine, its immediate precursor. Since this reaction is de-pendent on tyrosine hydroxylase, the question arises as to whether there is a deficiency of this enzyme or its co-factors. In the limited number of postmortem studies performed to date, it is suggested that tyrosine hydroxylase activity is diminished in the brains of parkinsonians. It is not clear, however, whether such a decrease is a primary factor of the disorder or occurs secondary to cell loss, par-ticularly of the substantia nigra, and to the resultant degeneration of the nigro-striatal pathway. In view of the age specific onset of Parkinson's disease, in that it makes its appearance in the latter years of life, it might result from mechanisms related to ageing of neuronal cells, indeed, an accelerated ageing process of nigral cells in those so predisposed. Such increased vulnerability of nigral cells may be related to their monoamine metabolic activity. Several mechanisms exist which pro-tect such monoaminergic cells against damage by oxidative products which result from metabolic activity. In aged cells these tend to fail resulting in their de-struction. In particular, the formation of quinones, hydrogen peroxide and organic peroxides are lethal agents which depend on enzymatic processes for their removal. That they may be unavailable to do so allows such amine oxidative products to accumulate and eventually destroy the cell. There is a need to fully explore this hypothesis not only in Parkinson's disease but in central nervous system ageing as well.

In conclusion, I believe there is little doubt that of the many disabling neuro-logical disorders Parkinson's disease has profited the most from the research de-velopments of the past two decades. Not only is this evident in the availability of new pharmacological agents for its treatment, but the heightened level of interest it commands from clinical and basic scientists. In the1940s when I first became in-volved in the care of parkinsonian patients, a volume such as this would hardly be possible since the number of investigators actively engaged in research in this field were exceedingly few. Parkinsonism was, so to speak, on the "back burner".

Today, it is the forefront of research in central nervous system disease which bodes well for those afflicted with this disorder. Hopefully, these efforts will be fruitful in the not too distant future.

Acknowledgement

Supported in part by the Clinical Center for Research in Parkinson's and Allied Disease NIH Grant #NS11631-06 and NIH Grant #RR-71 Division of Research Resources, General Research Center Branch.

References

1   Parkinson, J. *An essay on the shaking palsy, 1817.* London: Sherwood, Neely and Jones
2   Blocq, P, Marinesco, G (1893) *CR Soc. Biol.* (Paris) *5,* 105–111
3   Tretiakoff, C (1919) Paris, These.
4   Association for Research in Nervous and Mental Disease: *Acute epidemic encephalitis (lethargic encephalitis)* Paul B Hoeber, New York, 1920
5   Vogt, M (1954) *J. Physiol.* (London) *123,* 451–481
6   Carlsson, A (1964) *Acta Neuroveg, 26,* 454–493
7   Flack, B, Hillarp, N A, Thieme, G, and Torp, A (1962) Fluorescence of cetchol amines and related compounds condensed with formaldehyde. *J Histochem. Cytochem, 10,* 348–354
8   Ehringer, H and Hornykiewicz, O (1960) Verteilung von Noradrenalin und Dopamin (3-hydroxytramin) im Gehirn des Menschen und ihr Verhalten bei Erkankungen des Extrapyramidalen System *Klin, Wschr. 38,* 1236
9   Birkmayer, W and Hornykiewicz, O (1961) Der L-3-4-dioxyphenylalanin (DOPA) Effekt bei der Parkinson–Akinese *Wien, Klin. Wschr. 45,* 787
10 Barbeau, A "Biochemistry of Parkinson's Disease" In Proceedings of the Seventh International Neurological Congress, Rome *Societa Grafica Romana,* 1961, vol. 2 pp 925–927
11 Cotzias, G C, van Woert, M H and Schiffer, L M (1967) Aromatic amino acids and modification of parkinsonism *New Eng. J. Med. 276,* 374–379
12 Yahr, M D, Duvoisin, R C, Schear, M J, Barrett, R E and Hoehn, M M (1969) Treatment of parkinsonism with levodopa. *Arch. Neuro. v. 21*
13 Martin, W E, Young, W I and Anderson, V E (1973) Parkinson's disease: A genetic study, *Brain, 96,* 495
14 Poskanzer, D C and Schwab, R S (1963) Cohort analysis of Parkinson's syndrome: Evidence for a single aetiology related to subclinical infection about 1920 *J. Chron. Dis. 16,* 961–973
15 Brown, E L and Knox, E G (1972) Letter to the Editor, *Lancet, i,* 974
16 Poskanzer, D C, Schwab, R S and Fraser, D W (1969), In *Third Symposium on Parkinson's Disease,* p. 8 (Eds) F J Gillingham and J M L Donaldson, Livingstone, Edinburgh
17 Duvoisin, R C, Yahr, M D, Schweitzer, M and Merritt, H H (1963) Parkinsonism before and since the epidemic of encephalitis lethargica, *Arch. Neurol. 9,* 323–236
18 Duvoisin, R C and Yahr, M D (1965) Encephalitis and parkinsonism, *Arch. Neurol. 12,* 227–239
19 Stadlan, E M, Duvoisin, R and Yahr, M D (1965) In *Proceedings of the Fifth International Congress of Neuropathy,* p. 568 Excerpta Medica. International Congress Series

20 Gamba, E T, Wolfe, A, Yahr, M D, Harter, D H, Duffy, P E, Barden, H and Hsu, S C (1974) Influenza virus antigen in postencephalitic parkinsonism brain. *Arch. Neurol.* *31,* 228
21 Duvoisin, R C, Antunes, J L and Yahr, M D (1972) Response of patients with post-encephalitic parkinsonism to levodopa, *J. Neurol. Neurosurg. Psychiat. 1972; 35:* 487

Chapter 2

MORTALITY AND PARKINSON'S DISEASE

M G Marmot

In the excitement and activity surrounding the therapeutic advances in Parkinson's disease, the epidemiological patterns have often been neglected. In analysing the epidemiology of Parkinson's disease I should like to illustrate two uses of epidemiology: 1) examination of mortality trends leading to aetiological inferences and 2) filling in the natural history of Parkinson's disease by examining the mode of death.

Mortality Trends and the Viral Hypothesis

The distinction between post-encephalitic and idiopathic Parkinson's disease has been questioned on epidemiological grounds by Poskanzer and Schwab [1]. They noted that, at the Massachusetts General Hospital, the average age of onset of parkinsonism had been increasing over time. The increase was approximately 1 year of age each calendar year and was seen in those patients diagnosed as "idiopathic" as well as those diagnosed as "post-encephalitic". This was consistent with the concept of a "cohort" of people all exposed to a single agent at a particular time period—the development of Parkinson's disease having a variable latent period. Poskanzer and Schwab suggested that the vast majority of new cases of so-called "idiopathic" Parkinson's disease was developing in this cohort as a result of exposure to von Economo's encephalitits. The implication is that "idiopathic" and post-encephalitic parkinsonism are not two diseases but are ends of the one clinical spectrum. Poskanzer and Schwab [1] predicted that as this cohort of people died off, so the incidence of Parkinson's disease would fall in the 1970s and 80s.

Similar increases in average age of onset of Parkinson's disease have been found in other series [2-4]; but the "cohort" explanation has been questioned [5, 6]. It has been pointed out that an increasing age of onset is compatible with a "two-disease" explanation: (a) an idiopathic form affecting old people with no change in incidence rate over time and (b) post-encephalitic parkinsonism affecting younger people that was common in the 1920s and has been gradually decreasing thereafter.

Duvoisin and Schweitzer [8] further doubt the cohort hypothesis because they felt that in England and Wales "mortality rates (from paralysis agitans) have been stationary for the past 40 years or more (1921-1962) at most ages." On this basis they conclude that there can have been no long term residual effect of the epidemic of encephalitis lethargica. In recent years there have been interesting divergent trends in age-specific mortality rates from paralysis agitans. We have examined these trends in mortality in England and Wales for the period 1931-1975. This provided the opportunity for a re-examination of the cohort (viral) and two-disease hypotheses of the aetiology of Parkinson's disease.

Time-trends

Figure 1 (a and b) shows for males and females the trends in age-specific mortality rates from paralysis agitans in England and Wales. The data are the average of successive quinquennia: 1931-1935, 1936-1940 etc. Plotted on a log scale, it can be seen that the secular trends are different at different ages. Among men aged 75-84 there has been an increase in mortality. Among younger men, there has been a decrease—the younger the age group the greater the relative decline. The picture in women is somewhat similar.

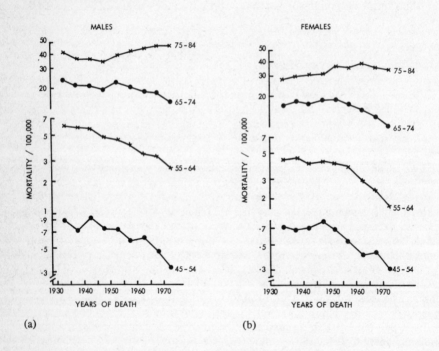

(a)   (b)

Figure 1a Paralysis Agitans Mortality, England and Wales, 1930–1973 (males)

Figure 1b Paralysis Agitans Mortality, England and Wales, 1930–1973 (females)

Encephalitis lethargica

To appreciate more closely whether this pattern is consistent with a cohort pattern, the mortality experience of each cohort or generation should be followed through its life time. In particular, if we wish to know if the mortality experience of each cohort is related to its exposure to encephalitis lethargica in 1918-1926, we should have information on the age and distribution of encephalitis lethargica. The age distribution of one published series from 1920 is shown in Figure 2 [9]. These figures are for numbers of cases, not incidence rates, but they give a rough guide to the age-distribution of encephalitis lethargica. The peak age of occurrence is in the age range 20-40. A similar age distribution was reported from other outbreaks [10].

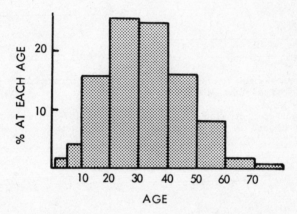

Figure 2 Age Distribution of 864 Cases of Encephalitis Lethargica 1918-1920*
  * Strauss and Wechsler (9)

Cohort analysis

Cohorts were then classified according to their age in 1920, and their subsequent mortality experience over the period 1931-1975 is shown in Figure 3, for England and Wales. The age-adjusted mortality is presented as a standardised mortality ratio for each cohort—100 being the average for all cohorts. Those shown as minus were born in 1930, which was close to the last reported year of any outbreak of encephalitis lethargica.

The picture for men and women is similar. Those who were aged 30-50 in 1920 had a higher mortality from paralysis agitans over the period 1931-1975 than those who were younger or older in 1920.

It could be argued that this excess mortality from paralysis agitans among cohorts apparently most heavily exposed to encephalitis lethargica might all have occurred in the early years after the epidemics when post-encephalitic parkinsonism was well recognised. That this is not the case can be shown by repeating the

11

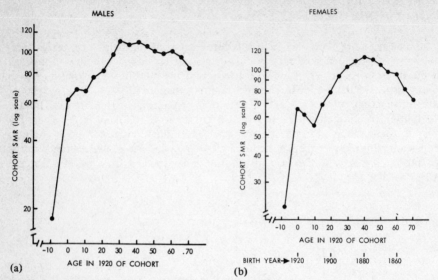

Figure 3a Lifetime Mortality from Paralysis Agitans (1931–1975) of Successive Cohorts by Age in 1920–England and Wales–Men

Figure 3b Lifetime Mortality from Paralysis Agitans (1931–1975) of Successive Cohorts by Age in 1920–England and Wales–Women

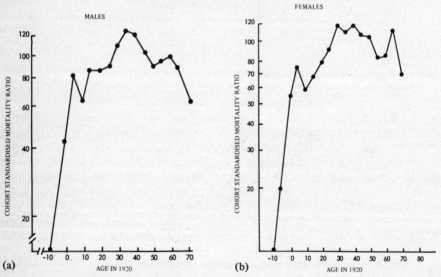

Figure 4a Lifetime Mortality from Paralysis Agitans (1931–1975) of Successive Cohorts by Age in 1920–Scotland–Men

Figure 4b Lifetime Mortality from Paralysis Agitans (1931–1975) of Successive Cohorts by Age in 1920–Scotland–Women

12

cohort analysis, examining only the later period of follow-up. When this was done for the last 20 years (1956-1975) the results were substantially unchanged: the highest standardised cohort mortality ratio occurred in those aged 30-50 in 1920.

The analysis of paralysis agitans mortality by cohorts in Scotland showed very similar results (Figure 4). Among both men and women, cohorts aged 30-40 in 1920 showed a higher standardised mortality ratio over the period 1931-1975 than cohorts that were younger or older in 1920.

Implications

In view of the decrease of one half to two thirds in the mortality from paralysis agitans at younger ages and the increase at older ages, the statement that "the risk of dying with paralysis agitans is about the same today as it was in the 1920s" [8] does not give a complete description of the changes.

An analysis based solely on death certificate data is fraught with difficulties, especially with a chronic disease such as Parkinson's disease. The disease may not be diagnosed or, if diagnosed, may not be listed as the underlying cause of death. These "Errors" of classification may act differently at different ages and in different time periods. It seems more likely, however, that such differences would mask a cohort effect than be responsible for a spurious cohort pattern. For this latter to happen the errors would have to be cohort specific. It seems unlikely, for example, that doctors certifying deaths in 1950, should be biased towards favouring a diagnosis of Parkinson's disease for a 50 year old and against this diagnosis for a 40 year old or a 70 year old; whereas in 1970 he should be biased towards this diagnosis for a 70 year old and against it for a 50 year old.

A simpler explanation of this apparent cohort pattern of mortality is that there has been a real change over time in the age of occurrence of Parkinson's disease. The clinical data, showing an increase in the average age of onset of Parkinson's disease, were held to be compatible not only with a single disease occurring in an ageing cohort, but with the dying out of a younger population of post-encephalitic parkinsonians. This two-disease explanation is not compatible with the present findings. The increased mortality of the cohorts most heavily exposed to von Economo's encephalitis in the 1920s continued right through to the 1950s, 60s and 70s, a period when the majority of parkinsonians were thought on clinical grounds to be idiopathic [7]. It seems possible then that the majority of so-called idiopathic Parkinson's disease occurring in these exposed cohorts is in fact post-encephalitic in origin.

Poskanzer and Schwab [1], pursuing the logic of their cohort hypothesis, predicted that as the exposed cohort died off, the mortality from Parkinson's disease would decline. The present data, showing a decline in mortality at younger ages, support that prediction. Of course, well-controlled studies of the effect of this treatment on survival are lacking, but most clinical opinion holds that the new treatment improves the quality of survival for Parkinsonians without an appreciable effect on mortality.

The fact that the "newer" cases of Parkinson's disease may be different epidemiologically from the older ones does not preclude a viral aetiology for them. If

13

it is true that clinically-defined idiopathic Parkinson's disease may be a very late result of a viral infection that has been unrecognised clinically, it is possible that new epidemics of viral infection could be responsible for an upsurge in the occurrence of Parkinson's disease.

Parkinson's Disease and Death from Cancer

An examination of the mode of death of patients with Parkinson's disease may give us useful information on the natural history of Parkinson's disease. It may also provide a way of exploring existing aetiological hypotheses and developing new ones. For example, if patients with Parkinson's disease were found to have an increased risk of dying from a particular disease, it might suggest an aetiology common to both the disease and Parkinson's. Alternatively, if a factor associated with disease x is thought to decrease the risk of developing Parkinson's, one might expect patients with Parkinson's disease to have a decreased risk of dying from disease x.

It was this latter alternative that prompted an attempt to assess the frequency with which sufferers from Parkinson's die of cancer, lung cancer in particular. It has been reported, from longitudinal studies, that Parkinson's disease occurs with low frequency among cigarette smokers [11]. If this association is real, one would expect a low frequency of lung cancer among Parkinsonians.

We have taken advantage of the fact that Parkinson's disease is not always listed as the underlying cause of death but may be listed as an associated cause on the death certificates of people who die with Parkinson's disease. The Office of Population Censuses and Surveys in London has been coding samples of death certificates according to all the causes listed on them, ie. not limiting the coding to the underlying cause. Table I shows data from the Birmingham Hospital Region in 1970 made available to us by Dr A Adelstein. Of 409 death certificates that mention paralysis agitans (Parkinson's disease), only 148 or 36 per cent had it listed as the underlying cause. Table IIA shows that, amongst the remaining 261, only 9 or 3.4 per cent had cancer as the underlying cause of death, and only 1 had lung cancer as the underlying cause. If the men and women who had Parkinson's disease listed on the death certificate had had the same frequency of cancer as all

TABLE I Death Certificates that Mention Paralysis Agitans—Birmingham Region 1970

Paralysis Agitans (PA)	Death Certificates No.	%
ANY MENTION	409	100
of which:		
UNDERLYING CAUSE	148	36.2
P A NOT UNDERLYING CAUSE	261	63.8

14

TABLE II Observed and Expected* Cancer Death Certificates that Mention Paralysis Agitans
(n = 261)—Birmingham 1970

A. Expecteds Based on all Deaths

Underlying Cause	Observed n	%	Expected n	%
All Cancer	9	3.4	54	20.6
Lung Cancer	1	0.4	14	5.5

B. Expecteds Based on Death Certificates that List more than One Cause

Underlying Cause	Observed n	%	Expected n	%
All Cancer	9	3.4	47	18.0
Lung Cancer	1	0.4	11	4.2

* Expected numbers are age-sex corrected.

persons who died at similar ages one would have expected 54 cancers and 14 lung cancers.

It is possible that this deficit in cancer might result from the doctor, certifying the cause of death, neglecting to record paralysis agitans, in a patient who died of cancer. Table IIB shows the "expecteds" recalculated on the basis of only those death certificates where the doctor had recorded at least two diagnoses. There is still a striking deficit in cancer deaths among those with paralysis agitans. As a further test of the assumption that a doctor, faced with a person dying of cancer, might neglect a long-standing chronic disease, the expected number of cancer deaths among those with Parkinson's disease was recalculated on the basis of death certificates that recorded rheumatism and arthritis. The difference between the observed and the expected was diminished but still showed fewer cancer deaths among the parkinsonians.

The decreased frequency of lung cancer deaths is consistent with smoking protecting against Parkinson's disease. The decreased frequency of "all cancer" deaths suggests the possibility of some more general biological process that protects Parkinsonians from cancer. We are currently exploring this further in a follow-up study of patients with Parkinson's disease.

Further Research

With Dr Gerald Stern and Dr Richard Godwin-Austen, we are conducting a case-control study of Parkinson's disease. This study will allow us to examine the relationship between smoking and Parkinson's disease in greater detail. It also

15

provides the opportunity to explore other aetiological leads; exposure to heavy metals, psychiatric illness, viral illnesses, previous operations and injuries, family history and consumption of certain foods.

Unfortunately a direct test of the viral hypothesis is difficult if not impossible using epidemiological methods. If a slow virus were the aetiological agent this would not be detected using standard virological techniques. If the mortality decline represents a true decline in incidence and continues into the 1980s, perhaps that will be considered proof enough for the Poskanzer-Schwab hypothesis.

References

1   Poskanzer DC, Schwab RS. *J Chron Dis 1963; 16:* 961
2   Brown EL, Knox EG. *Lancet 1972; i:* 974
3   Leibowitz U, Feldman S. *Isr J Med Sci 1973; 9:* 599
4   Kaplan SD. *Neurology (Minneap.) 1974; 24:* 972
5   Kessler II. *Prev Med 1973; 2:* 88
6   Kurland LT, Kurtzke JF, Goldberg ID, Cho NW, Williams G. In *Epidemiology of Neurologic and Sense Organ Disorders 1973;* 41. Harvard Univ Press
7   Duvoisin RC, Yahr MD, Schweitzer MD, Merritt HH. *Archives of Neurol 1963; 9:* 232
8   Duvoisin RC, Schweitzer MD. *Brit J Prev Soc Med 1966; 20:* 27
9   Strauss I, Wechsler IS. *Int J Publ Hlth 1921; 11:* 449
10   Matheson. *Report Vol 1 Epidemic Encephalitis 1979;* New York, Columbia Univ Press
11   Doll R, Peto R. *Brit med J 1976; 2:* 1525

Chapter 3

THE CLASSIFICATION OF PARKINSONISM

Rudy Capildeo, S Haberman and F Clifford Rose

Introduction

The Manual of the International Statistical Classification of Diseases, Injuries and Causes of Death (ICD) has its origins in the "Classification of Causes of Death" introduced by Jaques Bertillon (1893). The sixth revision was published under the auspices of the World Health Organisation (WHO) following an International Health Conference held in New York City (1949), when International Lists of Causes of Morbidity were added. Since then, subsequent revisions have continued to be decennial (7th revision in 1957, 8th in 1967 and 9th in 1977). One immediate drawback created by each revision is that, with the introduction of new rubrics and rearrangement of disease categories, it is not possible to make direct comparisons with statistics coded by previous revisions. Dissatisfaction with some of the changes incorporated into the 8th and 9th revisions has meant that they have also been "Adapted for use in the United States" (ICDA) and for "categorisation of diseases in hospital" (H-ICDA-2).

From the International Conference held to discuss the 9th revision (1975), it was reported that the WHO "had drafted a classification of therapeutic, diagnostic and prophylactic procedures in medicine, covering surgery, radiology, laboratory and other procedures" which would be published as a supplement. This was in response to a number of requests from Member States that alternative types of classification were required, such as the classification of impairments and handicaps. It was also noted that in three areas, classifications introduced by specialists for their own use had been incorporated into the 9th revision (oncologists, dentists and ophthalmologists). In a recent review of the 9th revision, Kurtzke [1] has demonstrated that "it is a regression towards a less specific and more symptom-orientated code than its predecessors . . . particularly poor in the category of neurologic disorders."

There was a need to devise a new classification for the neurological diseases because the existing problems had not been resolved.

17

Methodology

The methodology was originally developed for stroke by the present authors [2, 3], subsequently developed to provide a computerised data bank of stroke cases [4], and the clinician can obtain a discharge summary from the computer print-out for any individual case. Multiple sclerosis has been similarly classified [5].

There are three broad principles on which this new classification is based:

(i)   to define the diagnostic basis for each disease
(ii)   to provide data for epidemiological purposes
(iii)   to define the medico-social aspects of each disease

In order to accomplish this task, each neurological disease has to be considered separately since each offers its own particular problems for classification. A concise series of tables are developed for each disease which will provide the *essential* information to meet the three requirements listed above. (Table A).

TABLE A Classification of Diseases

1	Define disease
2	Determine diagnostic base:

Anatomy	Aetiology
Pathology	Clinical Findings
Histology	Investigations

3	Determine disability/social network:

Premorbid ability	Other causes of disability
Acute illness	Social network
Present status	Outcome

4	Determine other factors

Family history
Associated conditions
Habits, eg. smoking

The '*cumulative numbering system*' is used for the coding of each table. Although fully described previously [3] a brief description is pertinent. Basically, more than one item can be selected in each table, the cumulative number being derived from the total. If in Table I, Rigidity (2) and Bradykinesia (4) are selected, the cumulative number is '6' (ie. 2 + 4). This cumulative number is unique since it is dependent on the items selected, and no other combination in Table I

TABLE I Clinical Features—Major

0	Unknown
1	Tremor
2	Rigidity
4	Bradykinesia
8	Dementia
99	None

can add up to '6'. Any cumulative number can be decoded to indicate the individual items constituting that number, eg. a cumulative number of '23' in Table II is decoded by subtracting the immediate highest number below it and so on until the cumulative number of '23' in Table II is decoded by subtracting the immediate highest number below it and so on until the cumulative number is reduced to zero, ie. 23 = 16 + 4 + 2 + 1, indicating (16) 'Parkinsonian facies', (4) 'dysphonia', (2) 'excessive salivation (1) 'glabellar reflex—positive'.

TABLE II Clinical Features—Minor

0	Unknown
1	Glabellar reflex—positive
2	Excessive salivation
4	Dysphonia
8	Micrographia
16	Parkinsonian facies
32	Parkinsonian posture
64	Festinant gait
128	Other
999	None

Definition of Parkinsonism

In the 9th revision of the ICD [6], Parkinson's disease can be coded using 3 or 4 digits (Table B). Syphilis can be coded using alternative numbers, ie. syphilis as main category not Parkinson's disease. An additional code, the 'E code', can be used to "identify the drug, if drug-induced". Examination of the rubrics used (see Table C) indicates the problems of coding for drugs, since they were in use when the study group was convened to discuss the revision (1969) or even perhaps when the Conference of the Member States was held (1975) but were 'out-of-date' by the time of publication (1977). The 'E code' is a 3 or 4 digit code.

Since Parkinson's disease is an important, common neurological disease, it should be classified separately from "other extrapyramidal disease and abnormal movement disorders". The separation is to be found in ICD:9 viz. 332 and 333. It is possible that 'Parkinson's disease' is not a single disease entity but that a number of different disease processes may give rise to the symptoms and signs of 'Parkinsonism' and for this reason, the latter term is suggested to describe this type

19

TABLE B ICD: 9th Revision

332	Parkinson's Disease
332.0	Paralysis agitans

	Parkinsonism or Parkinson's disease:
	  NOS
	  idiopathic
	  primary

332.1	Secondary Parkinsonism

	Parkinsonism:
	  due to drugs
	  syphilitic (094.8)

NOTE: NOS = "Not otherwise specified"
  E code can be used to identify drug, if drug-induced
  094.8 = Alternative code for syphilis

TABLE C ICD: 9th Revision—E Code

E936	Anticonvulsants and anti-Parkinsonism drugs
E936.4	Anti-Parkinsonism drugs: Amantadine Profenamine (ethopropazine) Levodopa
E941.1	Parasympatholytics (anticholinergics and antimuscarinics) and spasmolytics: Atropine Hyoscine Homatropine Quaternary ammonium derivatives

of neurological disorder. The diagnosis is clinical since there is, as yet, no single, pathognomonic laboratory test to confirm the diagnosis; even though it has been defined as the clinical manifestations of central (brain) dopamine depletion, other disorders may arise from this.

Diagnostic Base

In stroke patients, it is possible to make an anatomical or pathological diagnosis from the results of all the investigations carried out, but this is not possible in parkinsonism where the diagnosis is purely clinical (Tables I and II).

The *major clinical features* have been separated from the *minor clinical features*.

Although not strictly 'minor', Table II qualifies Table I in terms of diagnostic certainty from the clinical standpoint. If a patient presented with 'tremor' only in Table I and had no 'minor features' coded in Table II, then the diagnosis of Parkinsonism would be highly suspect. The question would then arise, for example, are we dealing with essential, familial, or senile or other type of tremor? Again, a patient presenting with dementia and rigidity without any other 'minor features' could not be labelled from the outset as 'Parkinsonism—definite'.

The typical Parkinsonian patient will present with a combination of tremor, rigidity and bradykinesia, coded in Table I, and some or all of the features in Table II. Since Table II is not meant to be 'all-embracing', the category 'other' is included which can be excluded in a subsequent revision if used infrequently. If, for example, 'swallowing difficulties' consistently appeared under 'other' then this would have to be added.

TABLE III Aetiology

1	Idiopathic
2	Drug-induced
4	Viral
8	Arteriosclerotic
16	Central nervous system degeneration
32	Other

An *aetiological diagnosis* would be the ideal but this is rarely possible (Table III). Post-encephalitic Parkinsonism could be coded under 'viral' as could those cases considered to be of slow-viral aetiology. Of the listed causes of Parkinsonism few are ever substantiated, eg. syphilitic, viral, post-traumatic or toxic, the vast majority being labelled 'idiopathic'. In the new classification, 'unknown' is coded as 'O' but 'idiopathic Parkinsonism' is so frequently used as a 'definitive' diagnosis that it has been assigned to '1' in this table. The two aetiological diagnoses that are important are '(2) Drug-induced' and '(16) Central nervous system degeneration'. 'Arteriosclerotic' should only be coded if the Parkinsonism is clearly related to a cerebrovascular episode, such as cerebral infarction.

TABLE IV Response to Drug Therapy

a	Anticholinergics	Code:	0	=	Unknown/Untried
b	b L-dopa		1	=	Initial response—good
c	Bromocriptine		2	=	Side effects
d	Amantadine		4	=	Withdrawn—side effects
e	Other		9	=	No response

Response to drug therapy is shown in Table IV, which is used to measure the patient's response to a new drug regime. In the future, it may be possible to show that the patient's reaction to L-dopa, for example, whether favourable or unfavourable, correlates with a specific neuropharmacological or neuropathological disturbance. Such a finding would form a new diagnostic basis for defining the different types of Parkinsonism. For the present, Parkinsonian patients can be subdivided according to their response to different drug therapies, and newer drugs (eg. lisuride) may be useful in this respect. Initial response to treatment may eventually prove to be of prognostic significance. Table VI indicates *current drug therapy.*

Disability

Table V indicates which limbs are affected and whether the symptoms and signs are predominantly right sided or left sided (ie. hemiparkinsonism). Parkinsonism can occur as part of other neurological syndromes (eg. Parkinsonism-dementia; Parkinsonism-amyotrophic lateral sclerosis) and for this reason, the presence of low motor neurone (LMN) signs and upper motor neurone (UMN) signs can be recorded. LMN signs in the arm would include wasting of the small muscles of the hand whilst UMN signs might include hyper-reflexia or an extensor plantar response. Disability can be linked to 'bradykinesia' (Table I) and also to 'social network/outcome' (Table VIII) and 'other causes of disability' (Table IX).

TABLE V Disability: Limbs Affected

	a	Right side		b	Left side
		Rt. Arm			Lt. Arm
	1	Tremor		1	Tremor
	2	Rigidity		2	Rigidity
	4	LMN signs present		4	LMN signs present
		Rt. Leg			Lt. Leg
	8	Tremor		8	Tremor
	16	Rigidity		16	Rigidity
	32	LMN signs present		32	LMN signs present
	64	UMN signs present		64	UMN signs present

TABLE VI Current Drug Therapy

0	Unknown
1	Anticholinergics
2	L-Dopa
4	Sinemet
8	Madopar
16	Bromocriptine
32	Amantadine
64	Other
99	None

Surgical Treatment (Table VII) is now rarely used but the indications for treatment would be suggested in Table V, eg. tremor affecting the left arm only. Disability (Table V) could be measured pre- and post-operatively.

The *social network/outcome* table (Table VIII) contains information concerning the medico-social effects of the disease in terms of loss of earnings, dependence on family, friends or social services and outcome (living at home, chair or bed-bound, institutionalised or dead).

TABLE VII Surgical Treatment

0	Unknown
1	Left hemisphere
2	Right hemisphere
9	None

TABLE VIII Social Network/Outcome

0	Unknown
1	At work—full time
2	At work—part time
4	At home
8	Family at home
16	Outside support—family/friends
32	Social services support
64	Chair or bed-bound
128	Institutionalised
256	Dead

TABLE IX Other Causes of Disability

0	Unknown
1	Visual problems
2	Arthritis
4	Orthopaedic
8	Depression
16	Stroke
32	Dementia
99	None

Other causes of disability (Table IX) may co-exist with Parkinsonism and are important because they may increase the overall level of disability.

Other factors

The only other table included in the classification of Parkinsonism relates to the presence or absence of a *family history* of tremor, rigidity, bradykinesia or dementia (Table X). This table can be linked with the major clinical features noted in Table I).

Development of the New Classification

For any Parkinsonian patient, the major category coded would be for *'Parkinson-*

23

ism', eg. Code 332. The places after the decimal point would be used to define:

(i)	the diagnostic base	:	Tables I–IV
(ii)	disability	:	Table V
(iii)	treatment	:	Tables VI and VII
(iv)	social network/outcome	:	Table VIII
(v)	other causes for disability	:	Table IX
(vi)	family history	:	Table X

Table VIII ('Social network/outcome') can be used in the same format to measure 'premorbid ability/disability', ie, what the patient was like before his illness.

Table V ('Disability') can be used in the same format to measure the effects of medical (Table IV or Table V) or surgical (Table VII) treatment.

TABLE X Family History

0	Unknown
1	Tremor
2	Rigidity
4	Bradykinesia
8	Dementia
99	None

With the exception of Table X ('Family history') all tables can be used for the purpose of medical follow-up.

Conclusion

A new classification has been developed for Parkinsonism using the methodology developed for the classification of stroke and other cerebrovascular diseases and multiple sclerosis. The new system has many advantages over the existing ICD:9, particularly since it indicates the basis for each and every diagnosis. The epidemiologist can use all the information from the tables in addition to basic demographic data. The new classification measures the medico-social impact of the disease. For the clinician, coding is quick and simple as he is only required to circle the appropriate items listed in each table. The information can be stored on a computer and individual print-outs for every patient obtained in the form of a discharge summary.

References

1   Kurtzke JF. *Amer J Epidemiology 1979;109:*383
2   Capildeo R, Haberman S, Clifford Rose F. *Brit med J 1977;2:*1578
3   Capildeo R, Haberman S, Clifford Rose F. *Quart J Med 1978;47:*177
4   Capildeo R, Haberman S, Clifford Rose F. In Greenhalgh RM, Clifford Rose F, eds. *Progress in Stroke Research 1 1979;*153. Tunbridge Wells: Pitman Medical Ltd
5   Capildeo R, Haberman S, Clifford Rose F. In Clifford Rose F, ed. *Clinical Neuroepidemiology 1980;*28. Tunbridge Wells: Pitman Medical Ltd
6   *Manual of the International Statistical Classification of Diseases, Injuries and Causes of Death, 1977.* 9th revision. Geneva, World Health Organisation

Chapter 4

MORBID ANATOMY

W Blackwood

A person of over 65 years of age, who is unaware of tremor or of rigidity, but perhaps a little slower than previously with minimal intellectual impairment, can expect to have some cell loss from the substantia nigra or locus coeruleus [1] [2], and some, but not many, neurofibrillary tangles in the frontal cortex and hippocampus [3] [4]. At this stage, Nature's reserves will not have been overstepped but when they have been, Parkinsonism in some form can be expected, when there will be pallor of substantia nigra and locus coeruleus (a nucleus which, though small in cross section, is 12mm long). Microscopically, the substantia nigra, instead of being richly innervated by melanin containing nerve cells, will show a loss of neurones with melanin in phagocytes and an increase of astrocytic nuclei and fibres. In the nerve cells that remain, and often elsewhere in the nervous system, there will be cytoplasmic inclusions, either Lewy bodies which are rounded with central cores, or neuro-fibrillary tangles, similar under light microscopy to those seen in the cortex in Alzheimer's disease or senile dementia.

If we knew the origin of the tangles and the Lewy bodies, we might well know the aetiology of Parkinsonism, and whether they were genetically or environmentally determined. Alzheimer type tangles are composed of protein and are related to microtubules or neurofilaments, though there is argument as to whether they come from one or the other, or both. Electron microscopy, chemical analysis and immunological methods still leave the answer obscure, as shown below.

With regard to Lewy bodies (LBs), we know rather less. Electron microscopically, Duffy and Tennyson [13] showed that in the outer zone there were filaments which were radially arranged and loosely packed, the core was dense and seemed to result from alteration of the filamentous material so that it formed a homogeneously granular mass. They were not prepared to state that the filamentous structure came from neurofilaments, though they might. Roy and Woolman [14] thought that they did come from neurofilaments, whilst Lipkin [15] stated that LBs were likely to be of protein nature. Bethlem [16] found that LBs did not contain lipid, mucopolysaccharide, glycogen, mucin, fibrin, calcium, iron, other heavy metals, mucoproteins, glycoproteins or nucleoproteins and that the core contained aromatic alpha-aminoacids.

25

TABLE I Neurofibrillary Tangles of Alzheimer Type

Microtubular Origin		Neurofilamentous Origin
Terry (1963) [5]: twisted tubules		Kidd (1964) [6]: paired filaments in double helix
Wisniewski et al (1970) [7]: ditto		
	Oyanagi (1974) [8]: both in continuity	
to B monomer tubulin ←	Iqbal et al (1978) [10]: protein similar in peptide maps	Wisniewski et al (1976) [9]: to major neurofilament protein
Grunde-Iqbal et al (1979) [11]: immunological cross reactivity between normal microtubules and tangles		Ishii et al (1979) [12]: suggest that tangles contain neurofilament protein

TABLE II Tangles in Progressive Supranuclear Palsy

Straight tubules	Straight and twisted tubules	Filaments
Powell et al (1974) [26]:		Tellez-Nagel and Wisniewski (1973) [27]
Interlacing bundles of straight tubules in parallel array 13–15 nm.		Straight filaments 15 nm
Roy et al (1974) [28]: 15 nm.	Tomonaga (1977) [29] Yagishita et al (1979) [30]	

Figures 1–5 show the schematic distribution of lesions in the different entities which are characterised clinically by Parkinsonism and microscopically by definite histological change, the substantia nigra and locus coeruleus always being involved. It is not my purpose to consider Parkinsonism due to drugs, trauma or vascular disease.

The distribution is shown in two diagrams, that on the left being a coronal section of the brain at the level of the red nucleus, that on the right at the level of the hypothalamus. The density of shading indicates the degree of involvement, all lesions being bilaterally symmetrical.

The inclusions are most often Lewy bodies but, as Alvord *et al* [2] found, although LBs alone are the most frequent (34.5%), sometimes there are only neurofibrillary tangles (26%), sometimes both (21.8%) and occasionally neither (17.7%). When LBs are present, they may also be found in other regions, including the spinal cord and autonomic ganglia [19–22].

My clinical colleagues tell me that, with modern drugs, these patients live longer, and are more liable to dementia, which occurs in up to 50 per cent of patients.

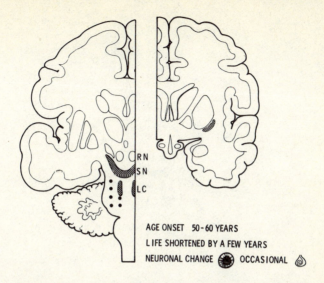

Figure 1 Paralysis Agitans. Involved are substantia nigra (SN) especially the central part of zona compacta, locus coeruleus (LC), dorsal nucleus of the vagus, nucleus basilis (or substantia innominata [17, 18] bilaterally.

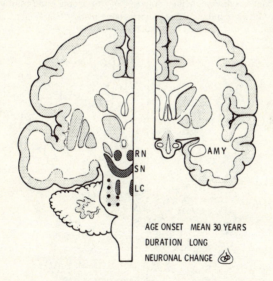

Figure 2 Post encephalitic Parkinsonism. Involved here are SN and LC, reticular nuclei of brainstem, red nucleus, dentate, around the aqueduct, subthalamic nucleus, extensively in the basal ganglia, hypothalamus and in the cortex [17, 24] bilaterally. Inclusions are neurofibrillary tangles.

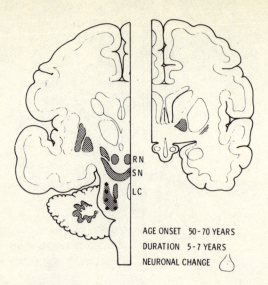

AGE ONSET 50-70 YEARS

DURATION 5-7 YEARS

NEURONAL CHANGE

Figure 3 Progressive Supranuclear Palsy. Involved are SN and LC, pontine tegmentum, red
nucleus, superior colliculi, periaqueductal grey matter, dentate and subthalamic nuclei,
globus pallidus and nucleus basalis [25a and b] bilaterally. In progressive supranuclear palsy
the nerve cells contain neurofibrillary tangles. These are slightly different from those
observed in Alzheimer's disease, being composed of interlacing bundles of straight structures,
in parallel array and of slender calibre. There seems to be disagreement as to whether they
are tubular or filamentous, straight or both straight and twisted.

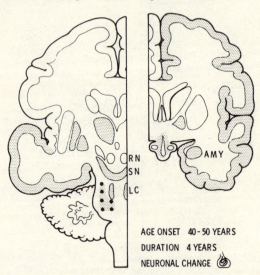

AGE ONSET 40-50 YEARS

DURATION 4 YEARS

NEURONAL CHANGE

Figure 4 Parkinsonism-dementia complex of Guam. Involved here are SN, LC, brainstem tegmentum, globus pallidus, thalamus, hippocampus, hypothalamus, amygdaloid nucleus,
frontal and temporal cortex [31–34] bilaterally. The inclusions are neurofibrillary tangles.

28

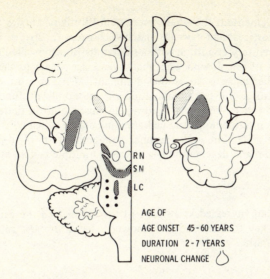

Figure 5 Striato-nigral Degeneration. Involved here are SN, LC, putamen, caudate (but less than putamen), sometimes subthalamic nucleus, bilaterally. There are few or no tangles [35, 36].

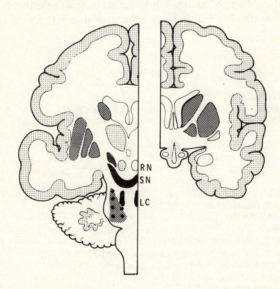

Figure 6 Putting all these conditions together, with density of shading indicating the number of times involved, we have the substantia nigra and locus coeruleus most often involved, with either LBs or more often tangles.

When they are demented, they have more neurofibrillary tangles and argyrophile plaques in their cortices than have age matched controls [2, 23].

There is a hereditary condition with a similar distribution called Joseph's disease [37], the legacy of one Joseph who, many years ago, came to the United States. The mode of inheritance is autosomal dominant. Mention must be made of the Shy-Drager syndrome [38] a combination of autonomic dysfunction with cerebellar, pyramidal and Parkinsonian features. In this condition there is a severe loss of cells from the intermedio-lateral cell columns of the spinal cord. This is perhaps not a distinct disease, but an occasional concomitant of olivo-ponto-cerebellar atrophy or striato-nigral degeneration—a so called multiple system atrophy.

Conclusion

It is suggested that increased knowledge of the nature and the causation of these inclusions is the key to increased knowledge of the nature and aetiology of many types of Parkinsonism.

Acknowledgement

I should like to thank Jill Mather and R Barnett of the Department of Histopathology, Helen Machilhenny and Marion Hudson of the Department of Medical Illustration and Rita Campolini and Jan Hutchins of the Department of Neurology, Charing Cross Hospital for technical and secretarial assistance with this chapter.

References

1   Forno LS. *J Neurosurg 1966;24:*266
2   Alvord EC, Forno LS, Kusske JA, Kauffman RJ, Rhodes JS, Goetowski CR. In McDowell FH, Barbeau A, eds. *Advances in Neurology No 5 1974;*175. New York, Raven Press
3   Tomlinson BE, Blessed G, Roth M. *J Neurol Sci 1968;7:*331
4   Dayan AD. *Acta Neuropath 1970;16:*85
5   Terry RD. *J Neuropath exp neurol 1963;22:*629
6   Kidd M. *Brain 1964;87:*307
7   Wisniewski HM, Terry RD, Hirano A. *J Neuropath exp neurol 1970;29:*163
8   Oyanagi S. *Adv Neurol (Jpn) 1974;18:*77
9   Wisniewski HM, Narang HK and Terry RD. *J Neurol Sci 1976;27:*173
10   Iqbal K, Grunde-Iqbal I, Wisniewski HM, Terry RD. *Brain Res 1978;142:*321
11   Grunde-Iqbal I, Johnson A, Wisniewski HM, Terry RD, Iqbal K. *Lancet 1979;i:*578
12   Ishii T, Haga S, Tokutake S. *Acta neuropath (Berl) 1979;48:*105
13   Duffy PE, Tennyson VM. *J Neuropath exp neurol 1965;24:*398
14   Roy S, Wolman L. *J Path 1969;99:*39
15   Lipkin LE. *Amer J Path 1959;35:*1117
16   Bethlem J. *J neurol neurosurg psychiat 1960;23:*74
17   Greenfield JG, Bosanquet FD. *J neurol neurosurg psychiat 1953;16:*213
18   Bottcher J. *Acta neurol scand 1975;suppl 52:*62

19   Hartog-Jager den WA, Bethlem J. *J neurol neurosurg psychiat 1960;23:*283
20   Forno LS. *J neuropath exp neurol 1973;32:*159
21   Forno LS, Norville RL. *Acta neuropath (Berl) 1976;34:*183
22   Ohama E, Ikuta F. *Acta neuropath (Berl) 1976;34:*311
23   Alvord EC. In McDowell FH, Markham CH, eds. *Recent advances in Parkinson's disease 1971.* Oxford: Blackwells
24   Yahr, DD. In Vinken, Bruyn, eds. *Handbook of Clinical Neurology 1978;34(2):* 451
25a   Steele JC, Richardson JC, Olszewski J *Arch. neurol (Chicago) 1964;10:*333
  b   Idem. *J Neurosurg 1966;24:*253
26   Powell HC, London GW, Lampert PW. *J neuropath exp neurol 1974;33:*98
27   Tellez-Nagel I, Wisniewski HM. *Arch neurol (Chicago) 1973;29:*234
28   Roy S, Datta CK, Hirano A, Chatak NR, Zimmerman HM. *Acta Neuropath (Berl) 1974;29:*175
29   Tomonaga M. *Acta neuropath (Berl) 1977;37:*177
30   Yagishita S, Itoh Y, Amano N, Nakana T, Saitoh A. *Acta neuropath (Berl) 1979;48:*27
31   Hirano A, Malamud N, Kurland LT. *Brain 1961;84:*662
32   Hirano A, Zimmerman HM. *Arch neurol (Chicago) 1962;7:*227
33   Hirano A, Malamud N, Elizan TS, Kurland LT. *Arch neurol (Chicago) 1966;15:* 35
34   Anderson FH, Richardson Jnr EP, Okazaki H, Brody JA. *Brain 1979;102:*65
35   Adams RD, van Bogaert L, van de Eecken H. *J neuropath exp neurol 1964;23:*584
36   Borit A, Rubinstein LJ, Ulrich H. *Brain 1975;98:*101
37   Rosenberg RN, Bay C, Shore P. *Neurology 1976;26:*703
38   Spokes EGS, Bannister R, Oppenheimer DR. *J neurol sci 1979;43:*59

PART II

CLINICAL ASPECTS

Chapter 5

CLINICAL CHARACTERISTICS OF JUVENILE PARKINSONISM

M Yokochi and H Narabayashi

The authors are interested in that specific group of parkinsonian patients in which onset of the disease is relatively earlier than in classical idiopathic parkinsonism (IP). They are also idiopathic in aetiology, but often show a familial predisposition and respond to L-dopa therapy in a very characteristic way. These cases, where symptoms start before the age of thirty-nine, are tentatively classified by the authors as juvenile parkinsonism (JP), and their frequency in Japan has been reported as 18.4 per cent by Izumi *et al* (1971) [1], 10.6 per cent by Yokochi (1976) [2] and about 11.5 per cent in a joint study on patients in seven general hospitals [2]. (Figure 1).

In this chapter, clinical observations on forty cases of JP observed in our department in the years from 1973 to 1976 will be described.

1 Familial incidence was noted in 17 (42.5%) of 40 cases, ie. it was much higher than that found in the classical form. Familial incidence was mostly confined to siblings, but in a few cases two successive generations were affected.

2 The forty cases were subdivided into three groups depending on the slight difference in the clinical picture and response to L-dopa.

The first group were ten cases with onset of the disease from 19 to 39 years of age. The clinical course and neurological symptoms of these cases did not differ much from the classical cases. The relative difference was that tremor was less than in IP and in most of the cases the dominating feature was rigidity. When tremor exists, it is slight and of minimum amplitude. However, the most characteristic observations were the dramatic response to L-dopa in all of these cases without exception and this was followed by a severe dyskinesia of choreo-ballistic type in the limbs in all cases except one. One of the cases is illustrated in Figure 2. This was a male of 44 years old, whose onset of rigidity with cogwheeling was at the age of 38. After four years of L-dopa administration which was quite dramatically effective in normalising the patient's activities of daily living (ADL), severe dyskinesia tended to appear within twenty minutes of L-dopa intake.

Four of ten cases tended to become L-dopa addicted, which was difficult to manage and it became almost impossible to continue L-dopa therapy with calm sustained effects in these cases.

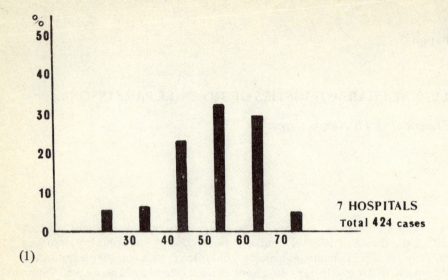

(1)

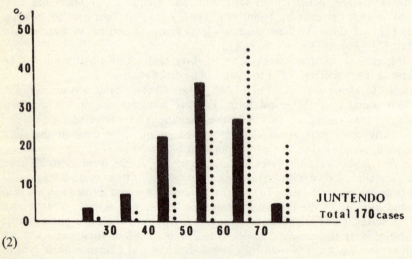

(2)

Figure 1 Age of onset of Parkinson's disease. 1. Joint study of seven general hospitals. 2. At Neurology Department of Juntendo Medical School.

The second group were 22 cases, with symptoms starting between the ages of 16 and 38, with clinical features similar to the former group, but differing in that the response to L-dopa was moderate and less conspicuous, but still belonging to the grade of marked improvement, as seen in cases of classical parkinsonism. Pro-

36

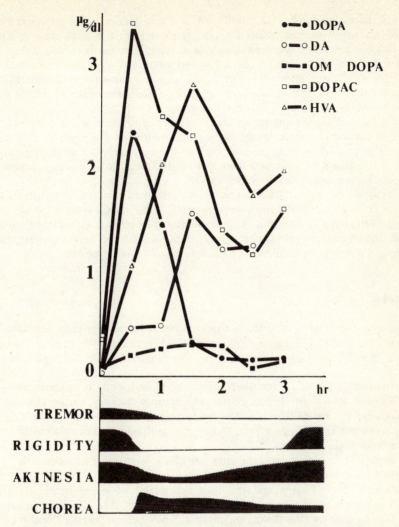

Figure 2 Marked fluctuations of the clinical picture of parkinsonism and of Dopa-induced dyskinesia in Case 9, with serum concentrations of Dopa, DA, DM-Dopa, Dopac and HVA.

duction of dyskinesia of the extremities in the later stage was also less, ie. there was marked dyskinesia in only one case and slight dyskinesia in four cases. Orofacial or neck dyskinesia, the usual type of dopa-induced dyskinesia observed in elderly patients, was not seen.

The third group consisted of eight cases of much younger onset than in the former two groups, ie. from 6 to 16 years of age. Symptoms usually started in the feet and often bilaterally. Deformity of feet and tendency to inversion were noticed in two cases, resembling the clinical pictures of the early stage of idiopathic dystonia. Tremor was seen in only two cases. Response to L-dopa therapy in this group was also very marked as in the first group and often dramatic. In three cases this effect was later accompanied by severe dyskinesia of choreo-ballistic type of extremities with a tendency to L-dopa addiction, both of which were difficult problems to control, as in the first group.

3 In all forty cases, the autonomic signs such as hypotension, severe constipation, or hypersecretion (drooling or oily-face) were not obvious. The psychological traits attributable to parkinsonian patients such as hypochondriasis, mutism, depressed mood, nervousness or insomnia were also much less in this JP series. Delirium, hallucinations or delusions were not observed.

4 In general, the course of progression in JP seemed much slower than in the classical IP, since survival with a well-preserved psychological state for more than twenty years was not rare, but it must be remembered that in ordinary parkinsonism the disease process almost always overlaps with the ageing process, thus resulting in a shorter survival period and more psychological problems.

Discussion

1 The higher familial occurrence in this group of JP has already been described by Okuma *et al* (1958) [3], and by Yokochi (1976 [2]. In the series of cases reported in this chapter, the higher incidence was also remarkable, viz. 42.5 per cent of forty cases.

2 In the forty cases of JP described above, the second group of patients seems to be somewhat similar in clinical course and symptomatology to the classical IP starting after the age of fifty. But the fewer cases of tremor, with slighter degree, and a more marked L-dopa effect, though not as dramatic as in classical IP, may still be important differences.

3 The other two groups, viz. the first and third, were more characteristic. The remarkable and specific observations in these groups were the dramatic change and improvement with L-dopa and the later appearance of severe dyskinesia after several months to years treatment. Compared with this marked effect, the influence of L-dopa in classical IP is slower and modest. Single peroral 500 mg Dopa or intravenously given 50 mg Dopa produced quick and almost complete disappearance of parkinsonian rigidity and akinesia in these two groups of patients; sooner or later, a period of severe choreo-ballistic dyskinesia follows when such trial is made in chronically treated patients. These quick and remarkable improvements with severe reverse side-effects are not usual in the classical IP.

The pharmacological studies, especially on the serum concentration of dopamine and its metabolites in these juvenile cases, will be published in detail elsewhere and will explain such quick changes in the clinical picture.

4 The third group of younger age patients, in which the average age of onset of the disease was twelve years, pose the question whether these cases have any similarity

to idiopathic dystonia, because of their much younger age of onset, presence of foot deformity in some cases etc. Idiopathic dystonia in childhood does not respond well to L-dopa and there is little known about its neuropathology and neurochemistry. However, the specific group of dystonia with diurnal fluctuation in child cases reported by Segawa *et al* [4] responded well to L-dopa therapy, and it remains to be seen whether some of the cases of our third group of JP may be related to the specific group of dystonia cases of Segawa *et al*.

Since all these cases are still alive, no postmortem study is yet available, and perhaps the final understanding and classification of these cases will need to await neuropathological examination.

Summary

Forty cases of juvenile parkinsonism with onset of the disease below the age of thirty-nine years are reported. Their characteristic features were mainly rigidity dominating, with less tremor, slow progression, dramatic response to L-dopa medication and very high occurrence of Dopa-induced dyskinesia in the later stages of treatment.

References

1   Izumi K, Kuroiwa Y. Naika *Intern Med 1971; 27:* 311
2   Yokochi M. Rinsho Shinkeigaku *Clin Neurol 1976; 16:* 871
3   Okuma T, Shikiba S, Endo S, Nago T, Narabayashi H. Seishin Shinkeigaku Zasshi *Psychiat Neurol Jap 1958; 60:* 882
4   Segawa M, Hosaka A, Miyagawa F, Nomura Y, Imai H. In Eldrige R, Fahn L, eds. *Advances in Neurology 1976 vol 14;* 215. New York, Raven Press

Chapter 6

ARTERIOSCLEROTIC PSEUDO-PARKINSONISM

Macdonald Critchley

It would be wrong to date our ideas as to the secret of Parkinson's disease from the discovery of dopamine deficiency 20 years ago. Nothing of the sort.

In this chapter, I feel rather like a defendant at an inquisition, called upon to defend a notion that some might regard as untenable: 'Arteriosclerotic Parkinsonism'. Is this just another example of that small but interesting group of mythical maladies of the nervous system? Let me take you back 50 years, when my paper on this subject appeared in *Brain*.

Few can possibly realise that in the second decade of this century, neurologists were actually seeing far more cases of post-encephalitic Parkinsonism than of conventional paralysis agitans. The appearance of this striking extrapyramidal disorder in young adults had something dramatic about it, for almost never before, since James Parkinson in 1817 published his monograph on 'the shaking palsy' had this syndrome been observed except in the middle-aged. The excitement aroused was considerable, every bit as widespread and profound as the resurgence of interest triggered off by the L-dopa story.

Neurologists of the last generation also became alive to the fact that a chronic inflammatory process was not the only aetiological factor which might provoke the onset of a syndrome which emulated the shaking palsy. My chief, Kinnier Wilson, who devoted most of his professional life to uncovering the mysteries of what he called "the old motor system", isolated a clinical variant associated with neurosyphilis—then quite a common disorder. He spoke of "mesencephalitis syphilitica", preferring it to the alternative terms "syphilitic Parkinsonism" or "paralysis agitans combined with tabes".

About the same time it was also realised and never disputed that Parkinsonism could appear as an industrial disease in those who worked with crude manganese.

Occasional references also appeared in the literature suggesting that a Parkinsonian-like state could develop in patients with deep-seated infiltrating brain tumours. Admittedly this was a rarity. Then arose the suggestion that sometimes a Parkinsonian-like picture would develop after head injury. The important medicolegal conception became, as you can imagine, a source of heated argument, with

40

flushed and angry clinicians maintaining an attitude either strongly for, or violently against. Sometimes their viewpoint actually varied as chance took them from one High Court to another. However shaky the scientific basis for such a hypothesis, no neurologist who has had a considerable experience of punch-drunk boxers—as I have—can deny that extrapyramidal signs are often so prominent in some patients with dementia pugilistica, as to raise difficulties in differential diagnosis.

Thus arose the conception that Parkinsonism was a syndrome, with multiple aetiologies, and that paralysis agitans was merely the clinical model whose causation was obscure, possibly abiotrophic.

Then came the Second World War and interest waned. However, the idea of symptomatic Parkinsonism became resuscitated in the 40s, when our psychiatric colleagues found themselves furnished with pharmacological weapons whose nature they only dimly understood. We now began to witness iatrogenic Parkinsonian states consequent upon the prodigal employment of such drugs as phenothiazine, reserpine, and many others.

It was against the background of this realisation that there was something vulnerable about the extrapyramidal system, that arteriosclerotic Parkinsonism saw the light. There was nothing novel about it, and it was no rarity: anything but. Those conversant with the rich Continental literature of that time were aware that the Germans were very familiar with a syndrome they called *"arteriosklerotische Muskelstarre"* that was liable to develop in hypertensive middle-aged arteriopaths. A comparable picture was also familiar to the pioneer neuro-geriatricians, and Jakob had described a syndrome of dementia, advanced age and Parkinsonism. Those who were acquainted with this picture in nonagenarians called it Jakob's disease—not to be confused with the Jakob-Creutzfeldt syndrome.

That scintillating galaxy of French neurologists likewise were aware that a disability reminiscent of Parkinson's disease could arise in patients known to be arteriosclerotic. Pierre Marie in particular was eloquent on this subject. He demonstrated a pathological situation where the basal ganglia and adjacent white matter were riddled with minute perforations like a sieve, an appearance which he called the *état criblé*. This worm-eaten state was partly due to multiple small infarctions, but partly also to a shrinkage of the white matter in the posterior perforated zone, away from the tiny blood vessels coming up from below. Pierre Marie described this entity as a "progressive lacunar degeneration", and it became customary to refer to an individual patient as a *"lacunaire"*.

There is no real difference between my arteriosclerotic Parkinsonism, the arteriosclerotic muscle-rigidity of the Germans, and the French conception of progressive lacunar degeneration.

Far from being a rarity, it is quite a commonplace, and, as I have repeatedly emphasised, one is perhaps more likely to meet with such cases socially rather than professionally. Indeed, on one occasion when I spoke of this condition before a distinguished if sceptical audience of my colleagues, there was seated in the front row a most striking and unmistakable sample of the syndrome, a friend whom I viewed with mixed feelings of sadness, embarrassment, but clinical understanding.

I have stressed the similarities between the arteriosclerotic and the idiopathic types of Parkinsonism: are there any differences? The answer is "yes".

1 Tremor does not occur.

2 Additional focal manifestations may complicate the arteriosclerotic cases, depending upon the presence and site of other ischaemic foci. Hence pyramidal, cerebellar, pseudobulbar pictures may co-exist.

3 The psychical state may differ. Emotivity is common, and mild dementia not rare, especially in the later stages.

4 The course of the disability is not the same. Rarely is there a steady downhill progression. The descent may be step-like, rather like a shopper who prefers to walk downstairs rather than use an escalator. The prognosis really turns upon cardiovascular and cerebrovascular considerations.

5 Arteriosclerotic Parkinsonians are not helped by L-dopa, and presumably no cellular deficiency in dopamine exists. Consequently, studies which are epidemiological, genetic and pharmacological in nature should be strictly confined to the idiopathic cases of paralysis agitans and exclude all symptomatic types, whatever their aetiology. Otherwise the statistics become hopelessly disarrayed and meaningless.

It can, therefore, be argued that all the symptomatic cases of Parkinsonism—syphilitic, post-encephalitic, arteriosclerotic, etc.—are states which are merely mirrors of the picture painted by Parkinson 160 years ago. In self-defence, I will concede that it would have been more appropriate to have spoken of arteriosclerotic *pseudo*-Parkinsonism, but no other disclaimer will I make.

Chapter 7

CLINICAL, PSYCHOMETRIC AND CAT SCAN CORRELATIONS IN PARKINSON'S DISEASE

J M S Pearce,
K Flowers,
I Pearce and
A E Pratt

Introduction

It is common experience that, when they present initially, patients with Parkinson's disease of idiopathic type generally have little mental abnormality. After some years, when admission to hospital becomes necessary for refined adjustment of drug therapy, many of the patients show aberrations which range from vague dottiness to eccentric behaviour, or more commonly a resistant apathetic state. We are all familiar with the ease with which such patients are precipitated into transient hallucinatory and confusional states by anticholinergic drugs, dopamine replacement therapy and dopamine agonists. In time this combination of apathy and transient psychosis is replaced by an insidiously progressive dementia.

Earlier studies [1, 2, 3] have suggested that these mental symptoms are an intrinsic part of Parkinson's disease, and many claims [4, 5] have been made which suggest that a diffuse cerebral atrophy becomes an essential part of the pathology which complicates the primary lesion in the substantia nigra. The purpose of this chapter is to examine more critically the relationships between the clinical features and natural history of the disease with selected psychometric tests, which have been chosen because of their suitability for Parkinsonian patients and for the existence of normal values in similar age groups. In addition we have studied a series of unselected patients by means of CT (CAT) scanning, using a series of radiological measurements of cerebral and cortical atrophy. We have preferred these methods to the somewhat subjective impressions of "mild", "moderate", or "severe" atrophy which characterise many studies of this type.

Material and Methods

A CT Scan in Parkinson's Disease and Controls

A consecutive series of 45 ambulant patients suffering from idiopathic Parkinson's disease who were attending a special clinic were examined by serial clinical tests and

43

Table I Measurement of Cerebral Atrophy

1	Ant'r horns—max diam	
2	Int diam skull	½ = Evan's ratio
3	Min diam Ant'r horns	1 + 3 = Huckman index
4	3rd ventricle	
5	Number sulci	

by CT scanning. Patients with incidental known cerebral pathology, eg. strokes, were excluded. Measurements (Table I) on the CT scans (AEP) were made utilising:-

1   The Evans ratio which expresses the maximum width of the anterior horns of the lateral ventricles with the maximal internal diameter of the skull at the same level.
2   The Huckman index [10] which summates the maximal anterior diameter of the lateral ventricles with the minimal diameter of the lateral ventricles.
3   The third ventricle was measured in the horizontal plane and
4   A count was made of the cortical sulci in the top horizontal slice.

These scans were performed on an EMI CT 1010 Head Scanner. Some were recorded on Polaroid film and some on X-ray film, using a Multiformat Imager. The necessary magnification factor for these was obtained by scanning a standard EMI phantom and recording this on Polaroid and X-ray film. The measurements were made using a Numonics Clinical Analyser and the images of the phantom were then measured. The Analyser computed the magnification factor for Polaroid and X-ray film and utilised this figure to give true measurements directly from the scans. In addition, each measurement was taken several times and the Analyser gave a mean for these measurements. Variation between these measurements and the error between two different observers (AEP and JMSP) were checked and were less than 5 percent. The use of this technique greatly facilitated the difficulties in accurate definition and measurement which are encountered when measuring Polaroid films or other projections with a ruler, and much greater precision of measurement was possible.

Clinical data in these patients included serial recording of the ten constituent measurements included in the Webster rating scale (IP). The total rating at the time of the CT scan was recorded along with the duration of illness, age of the patient and the predominant pattern of the disease.

The control group for the CT scans were selected from 44 patients submitted for this test who had no clinical symptoms or signs to indicate any gross cerebral pathology. Controls were selected from each decade to match as closely as possible in respect of age and sex of those suffering from Parkinson's disease. Controls included patients with functional symptoms, nonspecific headaches, and those with cancer of the buccal cavity, nasopharynx and sinuses in whom the test had been requested for evidence of intracranial spread. If any focal cerebral lesion was detected, the patient was excluded from the control group.

Table II Psychometric Tests in PD

WAIS—verbal, performances and total IQ
Raven matrices—non verbal IQ
Gottschaldt's hidden fig's—perceptual
Word recall—memory
Digit span + 1—learning

B Psychometric Measurements in Selected Parkinsonian Patients

Thirteen patients were examined (KF) by psychometric tests (Table II). These included WAIS scores (verbal, performance and total IQ); Raven's matrices; the hidden figures tests (Gottschaldt); digit span; digit span plus one and a free recall word list. These tests were selected for their value in assessing overall intelligence at both verbal and performance levels, the perceptual and spatial factors of Raven's test, the perceptual and cognitive features of Gottschaldt's test and the memory and learning aspects of the digit span tests and word list recall. These patients were unselected provided they were sufficiently intellectually preserved to be able to do the tests. The repeated measurements however deter the patient with impaired intellectual faculties, and there is probably some element of selection favouring those of higher intelligence and ability evident in this group. These 13 patients were derived from the original 45 (Study A) and clinical and CT scan measurements were available as above.

Results

Study A

The individual CT scan measurements all correlated with each other in the Parkinsonian patients and in the control series (Spearman Rank correlation coefficients significant at $p < .01$ or better). Absolute criteria for normality or abnormality were *not* assumed, since we relied on any statistical deviation from patients and controls to indicate significant differences. Patients with Parkinson's disease all showed a clear trend for increasing measurement of ventricular size and cortical atrophy with increasing age, and in each decade showed measurements indicating a greater degree of atrophy than in the control group. However in only the 70–79 year age group was this difference statistically significant (Mann-Whitney U-test for independent groups) (Figures 1,2,3). This figure in controls is probably spuriously low, the numbers being small.

Radiological evidence of atrophy did not correlate with the clinical severity of Parkinsonism judged by the Webster rating scales. The duration of the disease and the age of the patient similarly showed no statistically significant correlation with the degree of cerebral atrophy (Spearman Rank correlation coefficients all non-significant).

45

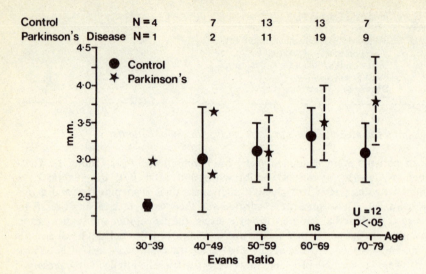

Figure 1 C.T. Measurements in Parkinson's Disease and Control–Evans Ratio

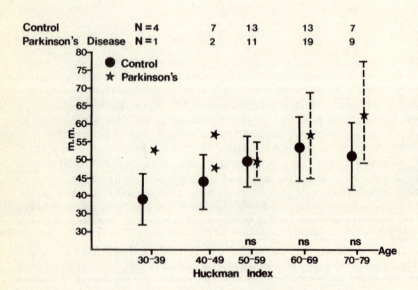

Figure 2 C.T. Measurements in Parkinson's Disease and Control–Huckman Index

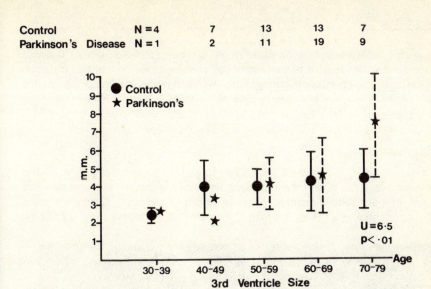

| Control | N = 4 | 7 | 13 | 13 | 7 |
| Parkinson's Disease | N = 1 | 2 | 11 | 19 | 9 |

Figure 3 C.T. Measurements in Parkinson's Disease and Control—3rd Ventricle Size

TABLE III Spearman Rank Correlations in Parkinson's Disease—Clinical, Radiological and Psychometric indices

	n	WEBSTER	r_s req'd	EVANS, HUCKMAN, 3 rd. V on C.T. Scan
WAIS verbal	13	-0.214	0.506	NS
perf	13	-0.115	0.506	NS
total	13	-0.272	0.506	NS
RAVEN's MATRICES	11	-0.61* p<.05 (2-tailed)	0.564	NS
HIDDEN FIG's Gottschaldt	12	-0.252	0.506	NS
DIGIT SPAN	13	-0.111	0.506	NS
DIGIT SPAN + 1	13	+0.327	0.506	NS
WORD LIST free recall	12	-0.60* p<.05 (2-tailed)	0.506	NS

Study B

Psychometric measurements showed no significant correlations in any of the tests performed with the CT scan measurements of atrophy (Table II). In two instances there was a strong correlation between the Webster rating and the psychometric measurements. These reached significance in respect of Raven's matrices and the word list free recall tests (Spearman Rank correlation coefficients: r_S = -0.610, p <.05 and r_S = -0.600, p <.05 respectively, both two-tailed).

C Additional Findings

In this series of 45 patients there were three instances of unexpected gross hydrocephalus *ex vacuo*. In two of these subjects in their early sixties there was evidence clinically of only mild dementia, but one had had increasing headaches intermittently for three years (Figure 4). In this patient, in retrospect a carotid arterio-

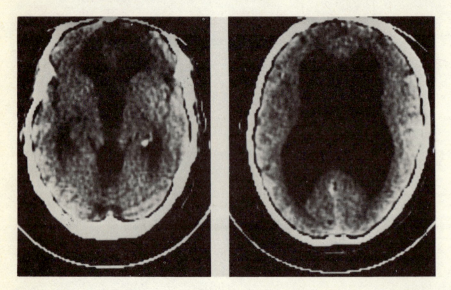

Figure 4 (See text)

gram performed seven years earlier showed evidence of hydrocephalus which had been overlooked. This patient responded well to ventriculo-atrial shunting, both headaches and mental impairment improving but the Parkinsonian signs remained mild and unchanged. In the second patient the hydrocephalus was an accidental discovery, though the patient had mild dementia which very rapidly increased following metrizimid ventriculography and was not relieved by ventriculo-atrial shunting. The third patient (Figure 5) aged 68 showed only minimal mental impairment (IQ = 115) and mild Parkinsonism and has not been subjected to surgical intervention.

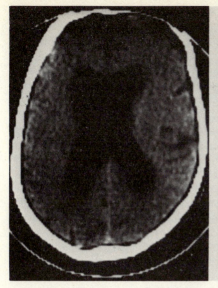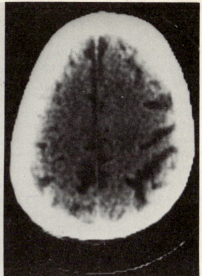

Figure 5 (See text)

Discussion

Before the advent of CT scanning, evidence of cerebral atrophy was obtained only in highly selected and unrepresentative patients (Table IV). These were seen at ventriculography when patients were treated with stereotactic surgery [5]. Pneumoencephalographic findings [4, 6] had similarly demonstrated a degree of cerebral atrophy which was regarded as being abnormal. In Gath's series [6], pneumoencephalograms of 19 patients with unilateral Parkinsonism and 26 patients with generalised Parkinsonism disclosed cortical atrophy in 46.7 per cent and ventricular atrophy in 77.8 per cent. As in the present studies, there appeared to be no relationship between the enlargement of the frontal horns and the duration of the illness and the severity of the clinical symptoms.

Table IV Evidence of Cerebral Atrophy in PD

1	ventriculography at stereotaxic op'n
2	selected cases at air encephalography
3	pathological data
4	CAT

In a more recent study of CT examination in Parkinson patients, Becker *et al* [7] reported scans in 172 patients and described abnormalities in 63.9 per cent of them. They found cerebral atrophy depended on age, and noted a high incidence of isolated cortical atrophy in 33 per cent of women. The criteria for normality were based on other arbitrary indices, and no control group was included. In a further paper [8], Fischer *et al* reported 58 patients where clinical examination and CT scan were performed before treatment. Twenty-three cases (40%) showed moderately, and nine per cent showed severely, abnormal findings. Again no control data are included. This group noted a significant age effect, those with cerebral atrophy being 11 years older than those with normal or slight findings. They also observed the frequency of cerebral atrophy in elderly patients which they felt could not be explained by the duration of Parkinson's disease. As in the present study there was no correlation between cerebral atrophy and the pattern of Parkinsonism—rigid/akinetic or tremor types. These workers did however claim a significant connection between cerebral atrophy and the state of well being and mood of the patient.

At the outset of this work our own impression [1, 3] was that cerebral atrophy occurred at an earlier stage in Parkinsonian than in normal subjects. We had also formed the impression there was some correlation between ventricular dilatation and sulcal enlargement with the presence of organic psychosis and dementia. We had believed that those patients precipitated into transient psychoses by the introduction of small doses of anticholinergic drugs and dopamine replacing drugs were in general those in the older age group who had cerebral atrophy (Table IV). The evidence from this work however contradicts some of these impressions. We have found no close correlation between the clinical scores for Parkinsonism and the degree of cerebral atrophy. The only positive results have been the high correlation between the Parkinsonian Webster score and a difficulty with the problems of Raven's matrices, indicating that clinical deterioration may be associated with a deficit in non-verbal reasoning. Similarly there was a positive correlation between the Webster score and the ability to recall words from a standard list, suggesting a similar association of clinical symptoms with memory dysfunction in these patients. These psychological deficits are instructive in that they are said to indicate incipient dementia in the elderly [11].

TABLE V Significance of Cerebral Atrophy in Parkinsonism

1	? associated with age or duration
2	? rigid/akinetic OR tremor at onset
3	? effect ofL-dopa OR anticholinergics
4	? relationship to dementia
5	? evidence for involvement of cortex primary / secondary

It is possible that within this mass of data there lie significant and positive correlations which we have not so far analysed. And we should not ignore the occurrence of three instances of unsuspected gross hydrocephalus *ex vacuo* with extremely severe cortical and white matter atrophy. These are unusual findings, but there is no reason to suppose that they are co-incidental to the basic cerebral pathology in these individual patients.

This study differs from similar previous papers in that a strictly selected control group has been used. We have been impressed by the striking degree of brain

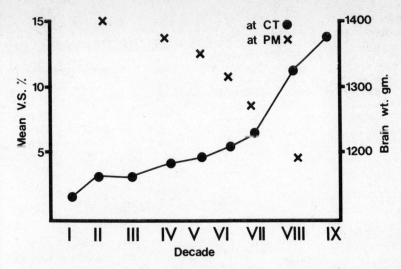

Figure 6 Normal brain ageing—perimetry and weight. (After Barron, Jacobs and Kinkel (1976)
[9] 135 CTs and von Braunmuhl (1957))

atrophy which occurs as a result of normal ageing. This was emphasised by Barron,
Jacobs and Kinkel [9] whose data correlate closely with our own showing a progressive increase in ventricular size from the first through sixth decades, and then a
dramatic increase after the age of 70 (Figure 6). It has thus become clear to us that
to demonstrate any precocious or excessive degree of cerebral atrophy in any degenerative lesion in this age group would require a very gross destructive process
indeed for it to become manifest in any systematic evaluation. It would therefore
require very much larger numbers to disclose any such acceleration of the atrophic
process in Parkinson's disease, and it is possible that the three isolated cases of in-
disputably gross atrophy may represent a very significant extreme end of the spectrum, the remainder of which has been submerged by the ageing process itself.

Acknowledgement

This work was supported by the Parkinson's Disease Society of Great Britain (IP)
and by a grant (JMSP and KF) from the Yorks Regional Health Authority.

References

1   Pearce J. *Brit med J 1974;2:*445
2   Pearce J, Pearce I. *Lancet 1975;i:*1245
3   Pearce J. *Europ Neurol 1974;12:*94
4   Svennilson E, Torvik A, Lowe R et al. *Acta Psychiat Scand 1960;35:*358

5   Selby G. *J Neurol Sci 1968;6:*517
6   Gath I, Jorgensen A, Sjaastad O, Berstad J. *Arch Neurol 1975;32:*773
7   Becker H, Grau H, Schneider E, Fischer PA, Hacker H. In Lanksch W, ed. *Cranial Computerised Tomography 1976;*250. Springer
8   Fischer PA, Jacobi P, Schneider E, Becker H. In Lanksch W, ed. *Cranial Computerised Tomography 1976;*244. Springer
9   Barron SA, Jacobs L, Kinkel WR. *Neurology 1976;26:*1011
10 Huckman MS, Fox J, Topel J. *Radiology 1975;116:*85
11 Miller E. *Abnormal Ageing 1978.* John Wiley

Chapter 8

INTELLECTUAL CHANGES IN OPTIMALLY TREATED PATIENTS WITH PARKINSON'S DISEASE

Karen Fisher and L Findley

Summary

Ten patients previously treated with Levodopa and ten previously untreated patients were assessed intellectually and then started on Levodopa combined with peripheral decarboxylase inhibitor, Carbidopa (Sinemet). Assessments were repeated after six months and two years of this treatment. Intellectual impairment was demonstrated initially which was reversed most effectively in the previously untreated group in whom improvement was maintained.
Parkinson in his monograph described an entirely motor disorder—"the senses and intellect being unimpaired" [1]. However, this original statement has been challenged many times since. A survey of the recent literature on intellectual functioning of patients with Parkinson's disease suggests that, while there is still an element of controversy, the disease is associated with some degree of dementia. Horne has looked at seven studies of Wechsler Adult Intelligence Scale (WAIS) results and discovers that in no instance was the overall IQ range significantly different from average. [2] This is undoubtedly the case with a small sample of patients, all of whom contribute to a normal distribution of results, but it cannot therefore be concluded that the disease process is not associated with loss of intellectual skill. It is important to examine each individual's results and, for this purpose, calculation of the deterioration quotient, while only roughly indicative, is none the less a useful standardised guide. [3]

Since the advent of L-dopa therapy for Parkinson's disease, studies have concentrated on improvement of intellectual functioning following treatment. This, of course, presupposes that deterioration has taken place, and on the whole the results suggest that such an improvement is a real feature of this form of therapy. [4] However, one must take into consideration first that this may be due to practice effects and secondly that it is not merely motor dexterity that is improved [5]. Certainly, those researchers who espouse the intellectual improvement theory show greater gains in IQ on the performance scale, but Briggs has studied the effects of asking normal and psychiatric subjects to perform the Block

53

Design and Object Assembly subtests with one hand, either dominant or non-dominant, and found that they did as well on these tests with either hand alone as they did with both hands together [6]. Meier also suggests that change is found in the perceptual organisation of material and this bears no relationship to dexterity. [7] Horne has investigated this with a non-motor perceptual matching task and concludes that the disturbance of basal ganglia function is implicated in an "information processing deficit". [2, 8] Botez *et al,* however, suspect that the disease process occurs in cortical as well as sub-cortical areas. [9] This is upheld by experimental work by Demassio, [10] and Selby has shown that 57.2 per cent of patients with Parkinsonism had significant cortical atrophy as assessed by air encephalography. [11] In addition, Botez pointed out that the slope of intellectual deterioration continued unabated after the first 2 months of the treatment with L-dopa, whether this was continued or discontinued. [8]

It seemed appropriate therefore to study the effects of L-dopa on the intellectual functioning of patients with Parkinson's disease and to see whether any improvement occurred when treatment clinically appeared optimal and, if it did, whether this was maintained.

Patients

These were 23 consecutive referrals to the Department of Neurology, Charing Cross Hospital, of patients suffering from Parkinson's disease. They were 13 males and 10 females, mean age 62 years (range 45–80 years). The mean duration of their symptoms was 9.08 years (range 1–33 years). The patients were divided into two groups, in that group 1 had previously received Levodopa but on clinical grounds were felt to be undertreated and would benefit from an increase in L-dopa. Group 2 patients were those who had not received L-dopa before. Between groups 1 and 2 the differences in sex distribution were not important and the age differences were not significant (t = 0.76 p > 0.52 two tailed test). However, the groups differed significantly at the age of onset of symptoms (t = 2.38 p < 0.05) and also in the duration of illness (t = 2.19 p < 0.05). This had implications in the analysis of scores (see results).

After six months of treatment, when all patients were recalled for testing, 21 were available for follow-up. After a further 18 months one patient had died from a myocardial infarction, reducing the final number on whom all data were available to 20 (10 in each group).

Methods

All subjects were given the Wechsler Adult Intelligence Scale, although not all the subtests. [12] The following subjects were used:- Comprehension, Arithmetic, Similarities, Digit Span, Vocabulary, Picture Completion, Block Design, Picture Arrangement and Object Assembly. It was decided that the Information subtest was redundant for our purpose since it is highly "g" loaded. [13] Digit Symbol subtest was also omitted because of its dependence on motor control.

Patients were either changed to or commenced on Levodopa in the combined preparation with the peripheral decarboxylase inhibitor Carbidopa (Sinemet), the ratio of Levodopa to Carbidopa being 10:1. This was slowly increased over two months until maximum therapeutic response had occurred or until unacceptable side effects had appeared necessitating a dose reduction. During the period of dose increase the patients were assessed weekly by a physician and an occupational therapist. The final mean total daily dose of Sinemet was 750 mg (range 125 mg–1500 mg), as equal divided doses three or four times daily. Throughout the period of follow up, patients were seen at approximately monthly intervals. None of the patients exhibited wide fluctuations in the control of the disease, marked end of dose deterioration or "on–off" effects. Once the patients had been individually stabilised their dose of Sinemet remained unaltered for the period of the trial. None of the patients, at the time of the trial, were receiving anticholinergic drugs.

Results

Means of the subtest, IQ scores and Deterioration Quotients for all subjects at the three occasions of testing (pre-treatment, after six months and after two years of treatment) are summarised in Table I. A t-test performed on these Deterioration Quotient data at this early stage of the analysis revealed a statistically significant improvement (both groups combined) at the time of the second assessment which had attenuated by the time of the third (Figure 1).

TABLE I Summary of Results of Intellectual Assessment

Test	Mean Score 1st Administration I	Mean Score 2nd Administration II	Mean Score 3rd Administration III
Comprehension	10.00	10.90	12.00
Arithmetic	9.30	9.40	10.43
Similarities	9.48	10.35	10.00
Digit Span	10.35	11.45	10.86
Picture Completion	9.34	10.15	10.81
Block Design	7.91	9.25	8.85
Picture Arrangement	7.74	9.30	8.80
Object Assembly	7.95	9.47	9.31
Verbal Scale IQ	99.83	103.05	106.58
Performance Scale IQ	91.91	98.98	100.43
Full Scale IQ	98.21	102.97	104.14
Deterioration Quotients	17.10	11.00	13.21

The subjects were then divided into two groups according to whether they had previously received L-dopa or not, and Table II summarises the important variables in matching the groups. Group 1 (previously treated) had 5 men and 5 women and group 2 (previously untreated) 7 men and 3 women.

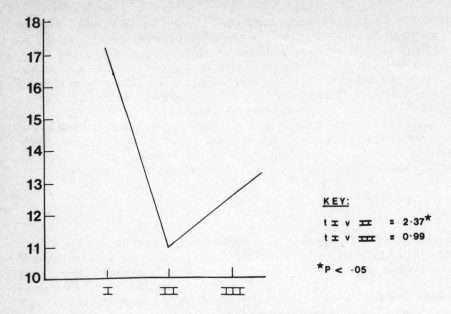

Figure 1 Mean deterioration quotients, Groups 1 and 2 combined, at pre-treatment (I), after 6 months (II) and after 2 years (III) of Sinemet treatment.

TABLE II Age, duration of illness, and Deterioration Quotient, differences between patients who had previously received L-dopa and those who had not.

	Mean L-dopa Group	Mean Non L-dopa Group	t
AGE	61.36 years	64.15 years	0.77
DURATION OF SYMPTOMS	8.00 years	2.30 years	2.22*
DETERIORATION QUOTIENT	19.80 years	15.17 years	0.92

* p < .04

Table III summarises the results of analysis of variance using the appropriate computer program from the Statistical Package for the Social Sciences (SPSS). Previously treated and untreated groups are compared on the scores obtained on each occasion of testing. Since both the Verbal and Performance IQ (and Block Design) results are significantly different before Sinemet treatment was instituted, and as we have seen there is no difference in the amount of deterioration found in

TABLE III Analysis of Variance between previously L-dopa and non L-dopa treated patients. F values of WAIS scores obtained before (I) after 6 months (II) and after 2 years (III) of Sinemet treatment.

	I	II	III
Comprehension	0.60	6.24*	9.33**
Arithmetic	1.67	8.87**	4.34
Similarities	2.14	0.96	1.61
Digit Span	2.94	2.74	4.22
Picture Completion	1.12	10.55	4.53
Block Design	4.23*	4.55*	6.42
Object Assembly	0.01	2.49	1.19
Verbal IQ	4.30	11.67**	5.46
Performance IQ	5.09*	6.65*	3.23
Full Scale IQ	2.73	7.96	5.03

* $p < .05$
** $p < .01$

each group, we must assume the two groups are drawn from different populations in respect of certain intellectual abilities. Table III also indicates that the groups are becoming discrepant in their scores following response to Sinemet, particularly on Comprehension, Arithmetic and Picture Completion subtests. However since the previously untreated group were generally brighter and since the duration of symptoms was likely to affect the potential for improvement, the data were further treated by an Analysis of Covariance (duration of illness covarying with the previous L-dopa/non L-dopa factor), and changes in scores rather than absolute scores were used as the independent variables, to compensate for the initial discrepancy.

TABLE IV Analysis of covariance. Changes in WAIS scores over time. L-dopa and non L-dopa groups compared, duration of illness controlled. F values after 6 months (II) and 2 years (III) of Sinemet treatment.

	II	III
Comprehension	1.50	2.93*
Arithmetic	3.20	3.38*
Similarities	1.25	0.98
Digit Span	3.25	2.63
Picture Completion	1.53	2.42
Block Design	3.37*	3.97*
Picture Arrangement	2.26	2.24
Object Assembly	1.39	1.29
Verbal IQ	4.76*	5.77**
Performance IQ	5.39**	5.75**
Full Scale IQ	3.01	3.51*

* $p < .05$
** $p < .01$

Table IV summarises the results of this analysis. After 6 months of Sinemet treatment, Block Design and Verbal Performance IQs have differentially improved, and after two years significant effects are also seen on Comprehension, Arithmetic and Full Scale IQs.

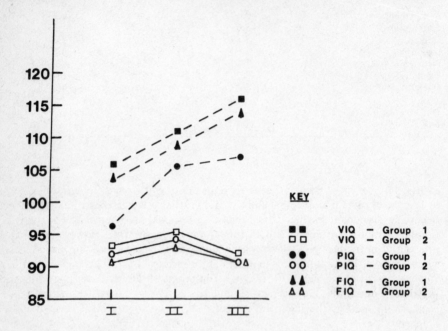

Figure 2 Means of IQ scores, Groups 1 and 2 compared, at pretreatment (I), after 6 months (II) and after 2 years (III) of Sinemet treatment.

Figure 2 shows the mean IQ differences for each group on the 3 occasions of testing. The analysis has corrected for the effect of the differences in duration of illness and compared the differences in slopes of change.

On no occasion was the interaction between L-dopa, duration of illness and subtest factors significant.

Discussion

Our findings have shown that the deterioration quotient was significantly smaller after 6 months treatment, indicating that there had been a degree of intellectual impairment associated with the disease. With the duration of illness and previous treatment with L-dopa controlled for, L-dopa in the form of Sinemet was able to produce significant gains in performance on intellectual tasks which were lasting at the two year assessment. These are more optimistic findings than those of Botez [9].

It is unlikely that the significant results we have shown can be attributed to the familiarity of the test material since the intervals between testing were great and Berkowitz and Green [14] suggested that over an extended period of time, the tendency is for scores to decline. Although these authors have calculated correction factors for practice effects, these are only appropriate up to a four month interval and only for raw scores rather than the age corrected ones we have used here, and are not significant for Comprehension, Arithmetic and Picture Completion.

It is known that Parkinson's disease can be associated with a wide variety of psychiatric disorders including depression [15, 16]. Any improvement in the assessment of intellect by WAIS may relate to the effects of L-dopa preparations on this aspect of the disease. However, although there is some controversy, in Loranger's series an analysis of the IQ scores of the patients whose depression improved with L-dopa, as contrasted with those whose depression did not improve, revealed no statistically significant differences [4]. Furthermore, Mindham *et al* [17] in a series of 50 treated Parkinsonian patients found that L-dopa was not an effective antidepressant. If then, it can be argued that improvement in intellectual functioning in L-dopa treated patients with Parkinson's disease is not due to improvement in motor performance, familiarity with test material, or change in affective state, it is probable that such improvement reflects the effects of the drug on the disease substrate itself rather than some epiphenomenon. The original work of Ehringer *et al* [18] showed depletion of striatal dopamine in brains of patients with Parkinson's disease and this is considered to be of major significance in the evolution of the neurological and mental symptoms [19]. However, both biochemical [20] and structural changes [11] are found outside the nigro-striatal system. More recently Lenzi *et al* [21] showed specific impairment of oxidative metabolism in the parietal cortex of hemi-Parkinsonian patients on the affected side. This cortical abnormality may be a primary deficit of the disease or relate secondarily to loss of dopaminergic or other neurotransmitter pathways, and thus possibly be responsive to neurotransmitter replacement therapy. Additional evidence for changes outside the extra-pyramidal system is supported by interesting work on the visual evoked potentials in patients with Parkinson's disease [22].

The more marked and sustained improvement in intellectual function in the previously untreated group (Group II) may reflect that Group I subjects had received some L-dopa before the trial period. This may have affected the capacity for further improvement and contributed to the observed fact that, in spite of the difference in duration of symptoms in the two groups, there was no statistically significant difference in the mean deterioration quotients at the initial assessment. However the ages of onset of symptoms in the two groups were significantly different and it could be that they represent two different disease sub-groups in their ability to respond to L-dopa preparations [19].

Acknowledgements

We would like to thank Dr F Clifford Rose for his support and for allowing us to carry out this work on patients under his care.

References

1   Parkinson J. In *An essay on the shaking palsy 1817*. Sherwood, Nealy and Jones, London
2   Horne D. *Brit med J 1973;2:*865,547
3   McFie J. In *Assessment of organic intellectual impairment 1975*. London, Academic Press
4   Loranger A, Goodell H, McDowell F, Lee J, Sweet R. *Arch Gen Psychiat 1972;26:*2,163
5   Asso D. *Brit J Psychiat 1969;115:*555
6   Briggs PF. *J Clinic Psychol 1960;16:*318
7   Meier M, Martin W. *JAMA 1970;213:*465
8   Horne D. *JNNP 1971;34:*192
9   Botez M, Barbeau A. *Lancet 1973;ii:*836,1028
10 Demassio J. *Personal Communication 1977*
11 Selby G. *J Neurol Sci 1968;6:*517
12 Wechsler D. In *Manual for the Wechsler Adult Intelligence Scale 1955*. New York, The Psychological Corporation
13 Vernon PE. In *Structure of Human Abilities 1960;*9. University of London Press
14 Berkowitz B, Green R. *J Genetic Psychol 1965;107:*179
15 Celesia GC, Wanamaker WM. *Dis Nerv Syst 1972;33:*577
16 Mindham RHS. *Brit J Hosp Med 1974;11:*411
17 Mindham RHS, Marsden CD, Parkes JD. *Psychol Med 1976;6:*23
18 Ehringer H, Hornykiewicz O. *Klinische Wschrift 1960;38:*1236
19 Rinne KR. *Acta Neurol Scand 1978;57:*Supplement 67,77
20 Farley IJ, Price KS, Hornykiewicz O. *Advances in Biochem Psychopharmacol 1977;16:*57
21 Lenzi GL, Jones T, Reid JL, Moss S. *JNNP 1979;42:*1,59
22 Bodis-Wollner I, Yahr MD. *Brain 1978;101:*661

Chapter 9

DYSPHAGIA IN PARKINSON'S DISEASE
Another Manifestation of Dopamine Acetyl Choline Imbalance?

M G Bramble

Introduction

The explanation that dysphagia in Parkinson's disease is due to delayed relaxation of the cricopharyngeal muscle [1] is almost certainly an oversimplification of the mechanisms involved. Although several radiological abnormalities have been described as occurring more frequently in Parkinson's disease [2-4], these studies were performed whilst patients were on anti-Parkinsonian therapy, and a similar problem is encountered in those few patients studied using manometric techniques [5].

In a group of 20 patients with Parkinson's disease, all therapy was stopped 48 hours prior to the manometric studies, in the hope of elucidating the true incidence of abnormalities. The methods are discussed elsewhere [6]. Results were compared to those obtained from age and sex matched controls. The study also included the administration of bethanechol and atropine to both groups, although not all the patients received these drugs.

Results

a Peripheral Dopaminergic Mechanisms

Detailed examination of peristaltic pressure waves failed to detect any increase in amplitude which might be associated with peripheral dopamine depletion. The results, as shown in Table I, are remarkably similar for both groups of patients. The response to bethanechol and atropine was also similar in the two groups.

The lower oesophageal sphincter pressure (LOSP) also showed no convincing evidence of dopamine depletion (again assuming that this might result in an increase in LOSP, which it may not). In severe, and very severe, Parkinsonian patients the LOSP (mean ± SEM) was 19.0 ± 3.6 mm Hg compared to 13.8 ± 2.4 mm Hg in mild to moderate cases and 13.4 ± 1.6 mm Hg in controls. The mean increase in LOSP after bethanechol was less marked in patients with severe Parkinson's disease

TABLE I Amplitude and duration of wet swallows (10 mls water) in Parkinson's disease and controls.

	Parkinson n = 20	Control n = 20
AMPLITUDE (mm Hg)		
Resting	22.9 ± 1.6	22.8 ± 0.9
Bethanechol	25.3 ± 1.9	24.9 ± 1.4
Atropine	14.7 ± 1.3	14.6 ± 0.9
DURATION (secs)		
Resting	8.4 ± 0.3	8.8 ± 0.3
Bethanechol	8.8 ± 0.4	9.6 ± 0.4
Atropine	7.8 ± 0.5	8.6 ± 0.4

(12.0 ± 3.5 mm Hg) compared to those with mild to moderate disease (22.0 ± 5.3 mm Hg), although these differences were not significant. No firm conclusions can be drawn at the present time as to whether or not peripheral dopamine depletion exists.

b Central Dopaminergic Mechanisms (Co-ordination)

Co-ordination in the Parkinsonian group was abnormal in only one patient and, overall, no consistent pattern emerged in the resting traces. Responses to both wet and dry swallows were no different from those observed in controls. The response to bethanechol (2.5 mg SC) is shown in Table II. Patients with Parkinson's disease showed an increase in non-peristaltic activity when compared to the resting motility ($p < 0.02$), but not when compared to controls. Parkinsonian patients also exhibited a correlation between the number of nonperistaltic swallows in the resting trace and the number after bethanechol ($r = 0.70$; $p < 0.01$) (Figure 1). No such correlation existed in the control group ($r = 0.49$).

TABLE II Increase in non-peristaltic swallows after bethanechol.

GROUP	Mean difference ± SED	Significance within group	Mean difference ± SED between groups	Significance between groups
Controls	3.7 ± 6.4	n.s.	11.3 ± 8.5	n.s.
Parkinsons	15.0 ± 5.3	$p < 0.02$		

Atropine (0.6 mg IV) resulted in a 30 per cent increase in nonperistaltic swallows in controls ($p < 0.001$) and a 50 per cent increase in Parkinsonian patients ($p < 0.001$). In neither group did a correlation exist between the number of non-peristaltic swallows in controls ($p < 0.001$) and a 50 per cent increase in Parkin-

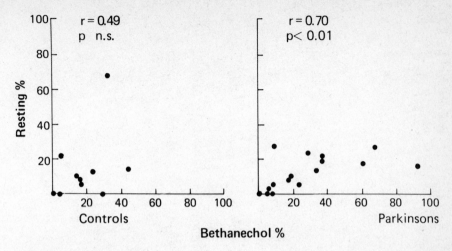

Figure 1 Correlation between non-peristaltic swallows before and after bethanechol.

sonian patients (p < 0.001). This response was significantly greater in patients with Parkinson's disease when compared to controls (p < 0.05, Table III). In neither group did a correlation exist between the number of non-peristaltic swallows in the resting trace and the number after atropine, but both groups did show a positive correlation between the number of non-peristaltic swallows after atropine and after bethanechol (p < 0.05, Figure 2).

TABLE III Increase in non-peristaltic swallows after atropine.

GROUP	Mean difference ± SED	p	Mean difference between groups	p
Controls	30.7 ± 6.9	< 0.001		
			21.7 ± 9.3	< 0.05
Parkinsons	52.4 ± 6.2	< 0.001		
D→	65.7 ± 6.7	< 0.001		< 0.1
Parkinsons			18.2 ± 10.3	
N→	47.5 ± 7.8	< 0.001		> 0.5

c Dysphagia

Eight of the 20 patients studied had this symptom to a greater or lesser degree but none showed any gross motility disorder. Dysphagia tended to be more frequent in more severely disabled Parkinsonian patients, and those patients with this symptom were more sensitive to atropine with an increase in non-peristaltic swallows of 65.7 ± 6.7 per cent compared to 47.5 ± 7.8 per cent for those without (0.1 < p > 0.05).

63

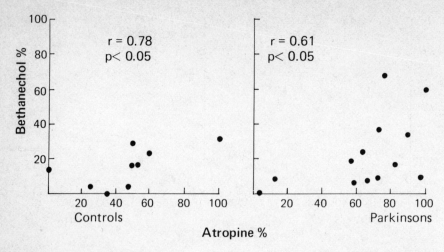

Figure 2 Correlation between non-peristaltic swallows after bethanechol and after atropine.

Discussion

With reference to the gastrointestinal tract, dopamine is the commonest catechol-amine present in several species [7] and undoubtedly has an important role in the regulatory mechanisms controlling alimentary function. In the oesophagus the picture is complicated by the presence of both excitatory and inhibitory dopamine receptors [8]. Dopamine reduces the amplitude of peristaltic pressure waves and lowers the LOSP [9], but whether or not dopamine depletion produces the opp-osite effect is unknown. No firm conclusions can be drawn from these data regard-ing the status of peripheral dopamine in Parkinson's disease.

Co-ordination of peristalsis, that complex sequence of motor activity which follows voluntary deglutition, is controlled by the brain stem nuclei and reticular formation [10–12]. Dopamine appears to be one of the most important neuro-transmitters in the initiation and facilitation of spontaneous and reflex swallowing [13] which may be affected in Parkinson's disease. Morphologically the Xth n. nucleus is abnormal [14] and it seems likely that there is a loss of dopaminergic neurones normally functioning in the initiation and co-ordination of deglutition.

Despite previous reports [2–5], this study failed to detect any gross differences in the resting traces of patients with Parkinson's disease, when compared to age and sex matched controls. In view of the normal resting oesophageal motility, initial interpretation of the increased incidence of non-peristaltic swallows following atropine was that cholinergic neurotransmission in the dorsal vagal nucleus was more important in patients with Parkinson's disease than in controls [6]. Un-fortunately this effect may be more complex than realised and several factors have to be taken into account.

64

Firstly, atropine would not only block central muscarinic receptors but also reduce dopamine turnover in the striatum [15,16]. As dopamine appears to be an important neurotransmitter in the initiation of swallowing [13], this effect alone may explain the findings. Increased disruption of peristalsis in Parkinson's disease could be explained by this effect on the fewer surviving dopaminergic neurones. Against this explanation is the fact that bethanechol, which should increase dopamine turnover [17], also disrupts peristalsis in patients with Parkinson's disease, when one might expect it to improve co-ordination.

Another explanation for the effects observed is that cholinergic inter-neurones replace the functions of degenerating dopaminergic neurones [18]. Whilst this is also possible, it has to be postulated that these neurones can alter their mode of action. In addition, receptor sites would have to be non-specific or new receptor sites become available. If this theory is correct, then cholinergic mechanisms would 'take over' the control of co-ordinating motor activity in the oesophagus, whilst maintaining normal function. However, if one considers that normal function is maintained by a delicate balance between dopamine and acetyl choline, it is difficult to explain how the same neurotransmitter can effect the same balance. Also, if the total of cholinergic neurones increases above normal then atropine would probably have less effect than in controls, not more. The effect of bethanechol also remains unexplained as a cholinomimetic agent should not alter the 'status quo' in this situation.

A more feasible explanation for these results is that cholinergic neurones also degenerate or are 'switched off' in some way to compensate for reduced dopaminergic activity. In this way the balance between dopamine and acetyl choline would remain, as would normal function. Atropine would thus produce greater blockade because fewer functioning cholinergic neurones are present. If cholinergic neurones did degenerate or were 'switched off' to maintain the balance, this would also result in an increase in the number of 'vacant' receptor sites available to bethanechol, and allow bethanechol to upset the balance by reducing this compensatory effect. This also explains the positive correlation between the number of non-peristaltic swallows after bethanechol and atropine as both are due to decreased cholinergic activity. This correlation is also seen in controls implying that not only is the dopamine acetyl choline ratio important, but so also is the neurotransmitter—receptor ratio.

Recent studies would confirm less cholinergic activity in Parkinsonian brains as levels of acetyl-cholinesterase are significantly reduced in the substantia nigra and several nuclei, compared to controls [19, 20].

Conclusions

Under normal circumstances patients with Parkinson's disease have normal oesophageal motility. The response to atropine and bethanechol would suggest a 15-20 per cent functional decrease in cholinergic activity, compared to controls. These changes probably compensate for loss of dopaminergic neurones thereby maintaining the acetyl choline dopamine ratio. If dysphagia is due to a dopamine acetyl choline imbalance, then excessive dopaminergic neuronal degeneration, or failure of cholinergic mechanisms to compensate may contribute to this symptom. Allowing for small numbers this study may indicate that dysphagia is associated with excessive loss of cholinergic neurones. This in itself is probably associated with, or secondary to, excessive dopaminergic neuronal loss. There is no circumstantial evidence of peripheral dopamine depletion.

Acknowledgements

I should like to thank Mrs P Groom for typing this manuscript.

References

1   Palmer ED. *JAMA 1974;229:*1349
2   Penner A, Druckermann LJ. *Am J Dig Dis 1942;9:*282
3   Eadie MJ, Tyrer JH. *Aus Ann Med 1965;14:*23
4   Gibberd FB, Gleeson JA, Gossage AAR, Wilson RSE. *J Neurol Neurosurg Psych 1974; 37:*938
5   Fischer RA, Ellison GW, Thayer WR, Spiro HM, Glaser GH. *Ann Int Med 1965;63:*230
6   Bramble MG, Cunliffe, J, Dellipiani AW. *J Neurol Neurosurg Psych 1978;41:*709
7   Heilman RD, Lum BK. *J Pharmacol Exptl Therap 1971;178:*63
8   Rattan S, Goyal RK. *Gastroenterology 1977;70:*377
9   Mukhopadhyay AK, Weisbrodt N. *Am J Physiol 1977;232:*E19
10 Sumi T. *Jap J Physiol 1972;22:*295
11 Roman C, Tieffenbach L. *J Physiol (Fr) 1972;64:*479
12 Jean A. *J Physiol (Fr) 1972;64:*227
13 Bieger D, Giles SA, Hockman CH. *Neuropharmacol 1977;16:*245
14 Eadie MJ. *Brain 1963;86:*781
15 Andén NE, Bédard P. *J Pharm Pharmacol 1971;23:*460
16 Bartholini G, Pletscher A. *Experientia 1971;27:*1302
17 Nose T, Takemoto H. *Eur J Pharmacol 1974;25:*51
18 Spehlman R, Stahl SM. *Lancet 1976;i:*724
19 Reisine TD, Fields JZ, Yamamura HI. *Life Sci 1977;21:*335
20 Rinne UK. *Acta Neurol Scand 1978;67:*77

Chapter 10

SCHIZOPHRENIA, NEUROLEPTICS AND PARKINSON'S DISEASE

Malcolm P I Weller

There are many points of contact between schizophrenia and Parkinson's disease. The two may co-exist in postencephalitic Parkinsonism [1] deaths from lung cancer are thought to be lowered in both disorders [2, 3], a viral aetiology has been proposed for both [3, 4] and there may be an inverse biochemical relationship between the two disorders.

The various categories of drugs used to treat schizophrenia share a common property of blocking dopamine (DA) effects [5, 6]. The early treatment with rauwolfia alkaloids is now believed to have succeeded by reducing the availability of DA. The DA blocking property of modern neuroleptics has been demonstrated as crucial. Only one of the two stereoisomers of flupenthixol, cis-flupenthixol, has anti-psychotic properties [7], and it is over 1,000 times more potent than the trans-form in blocking DA receptors [8]. The anti-psychotic potency is related to the neuroleptics avidity for DA receptor sites [9, 10].

Schizophrenia-like states can be induced by drugs which indirectly increase DA such as amphetamines [11-13] and psychotic side effects have been observed with L-dopa [14], bromocriptine [15] and indeed all the other DA agonists which have been successfully used in the treatment of Parkinson's disease [16]. The metabolic products of phenylethylamine, an endogenous amphetamine-like compound, is elevated in the urine of paranoid schizophrenic patients [17] and in the CSF of schizophrenic patients not receiving neuroleptic medication [18].

An increase in mesolimbic DA receptor sites has been demonstrated in postmortem schizophrenic brains, including five patients who had not had neuroleptic medication for over a year [19].

Parkinson's disease and schizophrenia rarely co-exist and, when they do, the Parkinson's disease tends to succeed the schizophrenia [20]. The few cases which have been reported are suspect and do not seriously challenge the contradiction between a proposed DA overactivity in schizophrenia and an underactivity in Parkinson's disease. In the eight cases reported by Hollister and Glazener [20], four were post-encephalitic and one arteriosclerotic; the remaining three cases were not described individually but the symptoms of the group as a whole included "confusion". Clear consciousness is considered a diagnostic *sine qua non* for schizophrenia. Of the four cases collected by Crow, Johnstone and McClelland [21], two had post encephalitic Parkinson's disease and the other two developed their illnesses in their sixties. They had good premorbid personalities which seemed preserved despite their illness. These features, together with marked deafness, merit re-classification of the disorders as paraphrenia, a condition with familial and epidemiological characterstics which Kay and his colleagues argue distinguish it from schizophrenia [22, 23], and which is often associated with a sensory impairment such as cataract or deafness [24]. The evidence for psychosis of whatever type is further weakened by the equivocation of one of the two cases who described her auditory hallucinations as "probably real". These often cited reports do not contain a satisfactory case of a concurrence of idiopathic Parkinson's disease and schizophrenia.

As would be expected, the common property of blocking DA receptors [25] causes neuroleptic drugs to induce extrapyramidal side effects, manifested most commonly by akathisia, classical symptoms and signs of Parkinson's disease and acute dystonias.

Different drugs, at equivalent neuroleptic dosage, vary in their propensities to produce these side effects. Various explanations have been advanced. Neuroleptics vary in their antagonism to GABA [26], which affects the extrapyramidal system [27, 28]. Two populations of DA receptors have recently been distinguished [29], but the proportions of the two populations are not sufficiently different in the two systems for this explanation to be convincing [30].

The intrinsic antimuscarinic activity of various neuroleptic compounds differs markedly [31] and may be sufficient to cause blurred vision, dry mouth, constipation and difficulty in initiating urination in some patients. Chlorpromazine, and particularly thioridazine, have strong anticholinergic actions. Trifluoperazine on the other hand is weak in this side effect and is particularly prone to cause acute dystonic reactions; the same is true for the butyrophenone, haloperidol.

The first few exhibitions of a neuroleptic are most likely to cause acute extrapyramidal side effects which is thought to be a result of a reactive overproduction of presynaptic DA, perhaps due to the blockade of presynaptic receptors. This does not persist, tolerance quickly develops and "plateaus" over a period of some twenty-five to seventy-five days [32], a period consistent with the increase in DA observed in the rat striatum with chronic neuroleptic medication after three months [33].

Anticholinergic drugs remedy these side effects and are desirable when neuroleptics are first introduced. There is no depletion of DA *per se* and L-dopa is additionally inappropriate because the primary action of the neuroleptic is to block DA transmission. L-dopa carries the hazard of exacerbating psychotic symptoms.

Although anticholinergic agents are initially helpful they may be maintained unnecessarily [34, 35]. On the other hand, akinesia, characterised by lessening of spontaneity, paucity of gestures, diminished conversation and apathy, is responsive to anticholinergic medication [36, 37] and may be mistaken for depression, or residual schizophrenic deficit. Since tricyclic antidepressants are strongly anti-

68

cholinergic [38], a beneficial response may be falsely attributed and compound the diagnostic mistake.

Coffee, and particularly tea, form an insoluble precipitate with many neuroleptic agents [39], which is likely to reduce absorption from the gastro-intestinal tract partly explaining the 100 fold difference in plasma concentration between individuals taking equivalent doses of chlorpromazine [40]. In a ward comparison, 32 out of 34 psychotic patients were noted as high coffee users against 13 out of 101 patients with other diagnoses [41]. The patients may have learned a way of overcoming their side effects by unwittingly cutting back their effective dosage. Anticholinergic agents also reduce plasma levels [42] which may account for their popularity with patients when there seems little justification for their maintenance.

An apparently paradoxical improvement in acute extrapyramidal reactions has been claimed with particular high doses of some neuroleptic agents. Extraordinarily high doses of fluphenazine, up to 1,200 mg per day for up to nine months, have been used with few extrapyramidal problems [43]. The explanation may reside in an exploitation of the relatively weak anticholinergic side effects after a plateau has been reached in the dose responding relationship *vis-à-vis* the DA receptors [44].

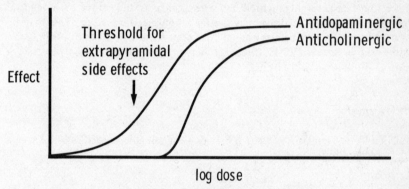

Figure 1 Extrapyramidal side effects occur beyond a threshold level. At higher dosage, the weaker anticholinergic properties of the drug become increasingly important. The separation between the curves at any particular dosage is a measure of the residual extrapyramidal side effects. This diminishes near the plateau in the dose/response relationship.

Two further apparently paradoxical responses will be considered. After prolonged usage, a *reduction* in the dose of neuroleptics may lead to a characteristic pattern of repetitive involuntary movements of a choreoathetoid type particularly of the mouth, lips and tongue. At a further stage in treatment these movements become apparent *without* any reduction in dose and may be suppressed by an *increase* in dose. Anticholinergic agents often exacerbate the symptoms. This so called *tardive dyskinesia* is a hazard of prolonged neuroleptic usage and demonstrates the development of supersensitivity of the nigro-striatal DA receptors to prolonged pharmacological blockade [45] anticholinergic agents are likely to highlight this supersensitivity [46], whereas beneficial claims have been made

69

for the acetylcholine precursors, deanol and choline [47]. However, treatment response is disappointing and many agents have been suggested without conspicuous success. The remedy lies either in increasing the dose of neuroleptic medication, and risking the later development of a more intense problem, or in stopping neuroleptic medication altogether and awaiting reversion of the supersensitivity. The potentials for further sensitisation is illustrated by the observations of Burt and his colleagues [48] that lesions of the nigro-striatal pathway produce double the augmentation of dopamine receptor binding in the corpus striatum to that with chronic neuroleptic blockade.

Reversion of supersensitivity may take from one to three years. An acceleration of the restorative process can be achieved at the expense of an immediate deterioration in the tardive dyskinesia, and also in the psychosis, by the administration of dopamine agonists [49], and very low doses of apomorphine produced an immediate improvement [50, 51] perhaps by stimulating presynaptic inhibitory DA receptors [52]. Low doses of L-dopa [53] and apomorphine [54] conferred beneficial effects on schizophrenic symptoms, probably by the same mechanism.

Tardive dyskinesia is highlighted by stress, such as the stress of a medical examination, and anxiolytic drugs may confer a non-specific benefit. This may be

Tardive dyskinesia is highlighted by stress, such as the stress of a medical examination and anxiolytic drugs may confer a non-specific benefit. This may be the reason why an apparent improvement was seen with high doses of propranolol (Yorkston *et al* in preparation), although other mechanisms may be involved since low doses of propranolol did not help.

Acknowledgement

Grateful thanks is given to Professor S R Hirsch for valuable suggestions and access to work in preparation.

References

1   Davison K, Bagley CR. In Herrington RN, ed. *Current Problems in Neuropsychiatry 1969. Brit J Psychiat.* Special Publication No 4, Ashford, Headley Bros
2   Rice D. *Brit J Psychiat 1979;134:*128
3   Marmot. Chapter 2 this volume
4   Tyrrell DAJ, Crow TJ, Parry RP, Johnstone E, Ferrier IN. *Lancet 1979;i:*839
5   Anden NE, Butcher SG, Corrodi H, Fuxe K, Ungerstedt U. *European J Pharmacol 1970; 11:*303
6   Nybäck H, Sedvall G. *European J Pharmacol 1970;10:*193
7   Crow TJ, Jonstone EC, Longden A, Owen F, Riley G. *Proc Roy Soc Med 1977;70 Suppl 10:*15
8   Miller RJ, Horn AS, Iversen LL. *Molecular Pharmacology 1974;10:*759
9   Iversen LL. *Science 1975;188:*1084
10 Seeman P, Lee T, Chau-Wong K. *Nature 1976;261:*717
11 Connell PH. *Maudsley Monograph No 5 1958.* London, Chapman and Hall
12 Angrist B, Sathananthan G, Wilks S, Gershon S. *J Psychiat Research 1974;11:*13

13   Snyder SH. *Arch Gen Psychiat 1972;27:*169
14   Jenkins RB, Groh RH. *Lancet 1970;ii:*177
15   Fahn S, Cote LJ, Snider SR, Barrett RE, Isgreen WP. *Neurology 1979;29:*1077
16   Price. This volume
17   Potkin SG, Karoum F, Chuang L-W, Cannon-Spoor HE, Phillips I, Wyatt RJ. *Science 1979; 206:*470
18   Sandler M, Ruthven CRJ, Goodwin BL, King GS, Pettit BR, Reynolds GP, Tyrer SP, Weller MPI, Hirsch SR. *Communications in Psychopharm 1978;2:*199
19   Owen F, Crow, TJ, Poulter M, Cross AJ, Longden A, Riley GJ. *Lancet 1978;ii:*223
20   Hollister LE, Glazener FS. *Dis Nerv Syst 1961;22:*187
21   Crow JJ, Johnstone EL, McClelland HA. *Psychol Med 1976;6:*227
22   Kay DWK, Roth M. *J Ment Sci 1961;107:*649
23   Kay DWK, Cooper AF, Garside RF, Roth M. *Brit J Psychiat 1976;129:*207
24   Cooper AF, Curry AR. *J Psychosom Res 1976;20:*97
25   Carlsson A. *Biol Psychiatry 1978;13(1):*3
26   Marco E, Mao CC, Cheney DL, Revuelta A, Costa E. *Nature 1976;264:*363
27   Cools AR. *2nd World Congress of Biological Psychiatry, Barcelona 1978;*104 Abstracts
28   Gale K. *Nature 1980;283:*569
29   Kebabian JW, Calne DB. *Nature 1979;277:*93
30   Creese I, Usdin T, Snyder SH. *Nature 1979;278:*577
31   Miller RJ, Hiley CR. *Nature 1974;248:*596
32   Post RM, Goodwin FK. *Science 1975;190:*488
33   Clow A, Jenner P, Theodorou A, Marsden CD. *Nature 1979;278:*59
34   Orlov P, Dasparian G, Dimascio A, Cole JO. *Arch Gen Psychiat 1971;25:*410
35   Klett CJ, Point P, Caffey E. *Arch Gen Psychiat 1972;26:*374
36   Rifkin A, Quitkin F, Kane J, Strove F, Klein DF. *Arch Gen Psychiat 1978;35:*483
37   Chien C-P, Castaldov, Thornton A, Maltbie A. *Psychopharmacology Bulletin 1979; 15(2):*75
38   Janowsky DS, David JM, El-Yousef MK, Sekerke HJ. *Lancet 1972;ii:*632
39   Kulhanek F, Linde OK, Meisenberg G. *Lancet 1979;ii:*1130
40   Hirsch SR. *Lancet 1979;ii:*1130
41   Winstead DK. *Am J Psychiat 1976;133(12):*1447
42   Gautier J, Jus A, Villeneuve A, Jus K, Pires P, Villeneuve R. *Biol Psychiat 1977;12(3):* 389
43   Rifkin A, Quitkin F, Carrillo C, Klein OF, Oaks G. *Arch Gen Psychiat 1971;25:*398
44   Hollister LE. *Clinical pharmacology of psychotherapeutic drugs.* New York, Edinburgh and London, Churchill Livingstone
45   Burt DR, Creese I, Snyder SH. *Science 1977;196:*326
46   Gerlach J. *Am J Psychiat 1977;134(7):*781
47   Davis KL, Hollister LE, Barchas JD, Berger PA. *Life Sciences 1976;19:*1507
48   Burt DR, Creese I, Snyder SH. *Mol Pharmacol 1976;12(5):*800
49   Friedhoff AJ, Alpert M. In Lipton MA, Dimascio A, Killam KF, ed. *Psychopharmacology: a Generation of Progress 1978:*797. New York, Raven Press
50   Carroll, BJ, Curtis, GL, Kokmen E. *Am J Psychiat 1977;134:*785
51   Smith RC, Tamminga C, Haaszti J, Pandey GN, Davis JM. *Am J Psychiat 1977;134(7):* 763
52   Raiteri M, Cervoni AM, Del Carmine R, Levi G. *Nature 1978;274:*706
53   Inanaga K, Inque K, Tachibana H, Oshima M, Kotorii T. *Folia Psychiatrica et Neurologica Japonica 1972;26:*145
54   Smith RC, Tamminga CA, Davis JM. *J Neural Transm 1977;40:*171

PART III

NEUROPHYSIOLOGY

Chapter 11

TREMORS IN PARKINSON'S DISEASE

M A Gresty and L J Findley

Introduction

We have used the technique of spectral analysis to examine the frequency content of involuntary movements in Parkinson's disease. For the present, little emphasis has been placed on movement wave forms which vary considerably, nor were we concerned with the amplitude of movements which may fluctuate for many reasons and are difficult to control experimentally. Specifically, we have examined resting tremor, exaggerated (or "symptomatic") postural tremor, cogwheel phenomena, intention tremor and clonus. During the course of our investigations it became apparent that postural and intention tremor, cogging and clonus, which have hitherto been thought of as unrelated phenomena, have similar frequency spectra and, although they occur in different circumstances, once initiated they have similar characteristics. Therefore, with respect to Parsimony, we suggest that the rhythmicity of these tremors is subserved by the same mechanism.

Subjects

The subjects consisted of 25 randomly selected patients, 13 men and 12 women, with idiopathic Parkinson's disease. Their average age was 65.5 years (range 52-71) and the average duration of their symptoms was 7.2 years (range 3-12). All the patients were taking L-dopa in a combined tablet with a peripheral decarboxylase inhibitor, Carbidopa (Senemet). The average daily amount of the drug taken was 370 mg (range 110-825 mg) in equidivided doses three times a day. Four patients were also taking anticholinergic drugs. The recordings were all taken in the morning and patients were asked to discontinue medication from the night before, that is, at least 12 hours before assessment. Despite the variations in individual drug regimes the frequency structures of the tremors we investigated were similar in all patients examined. For the present we are not concerned with any effect of the drugs on the amplitude or the actual occurrence of symptomatic tremor.

Experimental Method:

Movement transducers

Acceleration of the upper limb was transduced using a linear accelerometer, with a frequency band of DC to 7 kHz, a sensitivity of 40 picoCoulombs/g and a dynamic range of 0.001 g to 2000 g. The accelerometer was strapped with surgical tape to the first phalanges of the first and second fingers with its sensitive axis placed to transduce movement in flexion–extension.

Position of the finger of the upper limb during finger/nose testing was transduced using a Schottky barrier photodetector (United Detector Technology SC 50). The detector gives direct-coupled, differential voltage signals proportional to the displacement in the X and Y directions of the centroid of light falling onto the detector surface. The detector is mounted in the focal place of a 35mm camera which is placed to view the limb from a suitable angle. A small source of DC light is strapped to the tip of the index finger of the subject who undergoes conventional finger–nose testing. Movements of the light source are projected onto the sensitive surface of the detector via the camera lens and are hence transduced into electrical signals (after the method of Findley *et al* 1979).

The two methods of recording limb movement are complementary for the accelerometer, which is sensitive to tremor, is not suitable for recording motion during finger–nose testing as its sensitive axis is likely to deviate from the trajectory of the motion resulting in false readings. In contrast, the Schottky detector provides an independent frame of reference for the transduction of translational movement.

Spectral Analysis

The raw data records derived from accelerometric and displacement detectors were subjected to on-line spectral analysis using a Computer Automation Alpha LSI-2. The fast Fourier transform programme was supplied by Cambridge Electronic Design and consisted of 1024 point transforms with a maximum dynamic range of 96 dB. The sampling interval was 10 m/sec resulting in a Fourier series from 0.1 Hz to 50 Hz in 512 steps and a power spectrum from 0.1 Hz to 25 Hz. The data were hammed and filtered using a Butterworth filter with corner frequency of 1/10th the spacing in the buffer. Accelerometer data were filtered with an analog high pass filter having a time constant of 0.1 second.

Conditions of Recording

Tremor in the upper limbs was measured systematically in the positions listed below.

First: hand and arm at rest with the patient sitting comfortably and the arm resting on the arm of a chair. The hand was held dangling from the wrist over the edge of the arm of the chair in as relaxed a position as possible.

Second: hand posture. The arm rested on the arm of a chair whilst the hand was held over the edge of the chair in a horizontal position.

Third: forearm posture. The patient sitting upright with the elbow resting on the arm of the chair held out his forearm and hand in a straight line at an angle of about 30° to the horizontal.

Numerous power spectra were computed for each position until we were satisfied that the pattern of tremor had been established. On-line computation with the aid of a fast Fourier transform enabled many measurements to be made in each position.

Intention tremor was tested in the conventional finger—nose test.

Results

The collective findings relating to tremor and other involuntary movements for all our patients are represented in Appendix 1. In brief, the statistical analysis shows that resting tremors had an average frequency of 4.5 Hz whereas the mean frequencies of symptomatic postural tremor, cogging and intention tremor were all between 6.3 and 6.5 Hz. It is to be emphasized that these were consistent findings within and between patients and the data exhibited so little variance that the collective data could well represent any individual patient. Accordingly our findings can be adequately illustrated with the recordings taken from selected patients who are paradigmatic in the sense that they exhibit all the varieties found in Parkinson's disease.

Resting tremor in Parkinsonian patients

The fundamental frequency of resting tremor in our patients had a modal value of 4.3 Hz and was finely tuned (Figure 1). In each case 2nd, 3rd, 4th and even 5th harmonics could be detected and close examination of surface EMG taken during the tremor showed that some of these harmonics were generated by muscle activity and were not entirely due to passive resonances in the limb.

In terms of frequency content we found that the resting tremor in Parkinson's disease was indistinguishable from rubral tremor and tremor generated deliberately to simulate resting tremor. It is also similar in frequency and wave form to postural and intention tremors attributable to lesions of the cerebello-rubral pathways.

Postural tremor in Parkinsonian patients

The universally encountered postural tremor of the affected limb in Parkinsonian patients was finely tuned with a peak frequency between 6 and 7 Hz with a second harmonic at 12 to 13 Hz as illustrated from our patient in Figure 2. In some of our patients this was the finding irrespective of the presence or absence of tremor on clinical examination.

Such postural tremor can be shown to be distinct from resting tremor since, in some patients, whose resting tremor was evident on posture, both a 4 Hz and a 6 Hz tremor was seen to coexist producing double peaks on the power spectrum which were not harmonically related and, therefore, unlikely to be subserved by the same rhythm generating mechanism. Nor is 6 Hz tremor exaggerated physio-

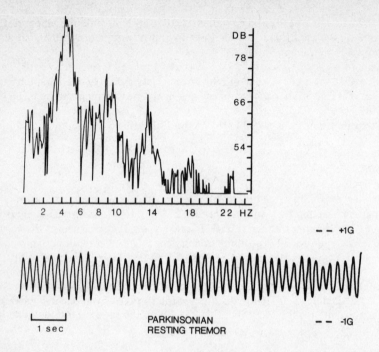

Figure 1 Power spectrum and raw accelerometer recording of resting tremor of the forearm in flexion/extension in a patient with Parkinson's disease. The axis horizontal is in units of frequency and the vertical axis in logarithmic units on an arbitrary scale adjusted by the computer to maximise the peak frequency. The important characteristics to note about the power spectrum are the overall shape of the spectrum and the occurrences of distinct peak values. In the power spectrum of resting tremor there are five distinguishable separate peaks at 4.5, 9, 13.5, 18 and 22.5 Hz which decreases in amplitude with increasing frequency. The peak at 4.5 Hz is the fundamental frequency of the tremor which also has the highest amplitude, this would correspond to the symptomatic tremor frequency. The higher frequency peaks are 2nd to 5th harmonics of the fundamental. The harmonic relationship suggests that they could be generated by the same timing mechanism as the fundamental frequency of oscillation. Each peak has a certain width which is a measure of the harmonic distortion of the signal, which represents variations in the timing of the oscillation. Other signals present in the power spectrum which are not either harmonic distortions nor harmonics represent signals which are probably derived from a separate timing mechanism. Thus between 6 and 8 Hz there are significant frequency components present which probably represent the higher frequency tremors of Parkinsonism such as symptomatic postural tremor. The calibration of the recording is with respect to gravity (G).

logical tremor as postulated by Lance et al [1]. This can be demonstrated in several ways. First, in hemi-parkinsonian patients the asymptomatic limb has a postural tremor which resembles physiological tremor in a normal person whilst the symptomatic limb has exaggerated 6 Hz tremor which is quite different in frequency content. This point is illustrated in Figure 3. Second, in some patients an affected limb may have 6 Hz tremor together with a tremor at higher frequency

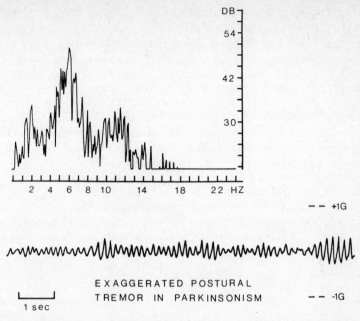

EXAGGERATED POSTURAL
TREMOR IN PARKINSONISM

1 sec

Figure 2 Power spectrum and accelerometer recordings of symptomatic postural tremor of the forearm in a patient with Parkinson's disease. The peak frequency of the tremor is 6 Hz with a broadly tuned harmonic at around 12 Hz. Low frequency signals at 1.5 to 2 Hz represent postural sway. Further explanation as for Figure 1.

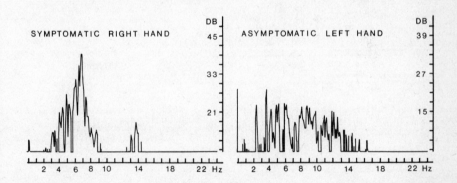

Figure 3 Power spectra of postural tremor of the hands from a patient with hemi-parkinsonism. The symptomatic hand has a finely tuned tremor at 7 Hz (with a second harmonic at 14 Hz) whereas the unaffected hand has a broadly tuned tremor with significant components throughout the frequency spectrum which is indistinguishable from the spectrum which could be obtained from a normal person. The conclusion is that the tremor of the affected hand is not an exaggeration of that of the more normal limb. The vertical scales provide direct comparison of amplitudes. Further explanation as for Figure 1.

79

of 8 to 10 Hz which is the normal range of physiological tremor in the healthy adult. The mixture of 6 and 8–10 Hz tremor produces two peaks in the power spectrum which are not harmonically related. Finally, if one examines postural tremor in unaffected parts of the body other than the limb in question, there is frequently a normal looking physiological tremor with a peak about 8–10 Hz which is quite different in structure from the 6 Hz tremor.

Cogging and intention tremor in Parkinsonian patients

Cogging and intention tremor in a Parkinsonian patient are illustrated in Figures 4 and 5 respectively. The recordings are taken from the same patient whose postural tremor and resting tremor have been presented earlier.

The cogging was evoked by the patient whilst resting his elbow on the arm of a chair and flexing and extending his outstretched forearm as smoothly and as rhythmically as possible. The overall movement, which is shown by the slow fluctuation in the raw record, has a powerful spectrum with high values at low frequencies (about 0.3 Hz) and little content in the higher frequency range in which

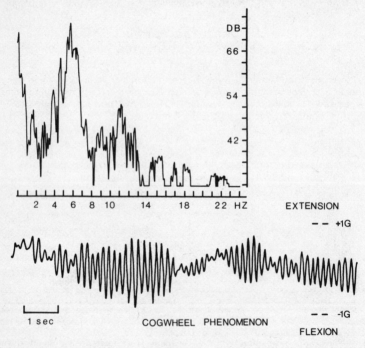

Figure 4 Power spectrum and raw accelerometer recording of cogwheel phenomena in a patient with Parkinson's disease actively flexing his wrist. The peak tremor frequency is finely tuned at 6 Hz. The very high values at below 1 Hz represent the overall flexion/extension movement and are not concerned with the cogging. In the raw data record the "spindling" occurring during the trace is the acceleration due to the cogs whereas the overall fluctuations represent the total movement.

80

tremor occurs. The large spindles on the raw data record in Figure 4 represent the cogging which, on hand measurement, was about 6 Hz. Thus the frequency content in the region of 6 Hz and above is largely representative of the cogging and not of the overall flexion and extension movements of the arm, which reflect in the low frequency content of the spectrum and can be ignored. The remainder of the spectrum, which is the frequency content of the cogging, consists of a finely tuned peak at 6 Hz with irregular subsidiary peaks at higher frequencies which are harmonics of the fundamental. Cogging in all patients, whether at the forearm or wrist, consisted of a transient rhythm with a peak frequency between 6 and 7 Hz which, on spectral analysis, was finely tuned with one or two harmonics. At this point one may compare the frequency spectrum of cogging as shown in Figure 4 with that of symptomatic postural tremor illustrated in Figure 2 to establish their similarities.

Intention tremor was measured in the conventional finger—nose test and was transduced by means of the Schottky photo detector. The frequency of the sinusoidal transient tremor which occurs in some patients during the termination of movement can be established by measurement on the raw records. In the case of the example shown in Figure 5 the periodic spindling represents the intention

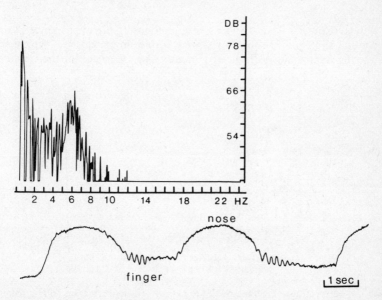

Figure 5 Power spectrum and Schottky barrier photodetector recordings of flexion/extension of the forearm of a patient with Parkinson's disease during finger/nose testing. A peak value is seen at 6.5 Hz although the spectrum is severely harmonically distorted due to artefacts from the overall movement. The high values at less than 1 Hz represent the large amplitude movements to and from the nose. The intention tremor occurs only at the termination of extension and may be measured with respect to the time base at 6 to 7 Hz. Further explanation as for Figure 1.

tremor found by hand measurement to be 6 Hz. The raw data record may be compared with that of postural tremor and also cogging in Figures 2 and 4 to show that these three are similar in frequency and structure. The mean frequency of cogging in our patients was 6.5 Hz.

A clinical observation which supports the identification of cogging with clonus is that, in some patients who exhibit brisk cogging, sustained pressure on the hand produces a constant deflection of the wrist which may initiate a strong tremor at 6 Hz and which is indistinguishable in "feel" from clonus.

Consistency of findings within and between patients

The most significant finding, which cannot be illustrated without reference to the records and spectra of every patient examined, is that whichever tremor was dominant, ie. postural tremor, intention tremor or cogging, the power spectrum remained similar in form, within 0.2 Hz and had similar peak frequencies. These findings were consistent even in the frequency analysis of cogging and intention tremor when other grosser movements contaminated the spectrum and tended to obliterate the pattern of frequency content attributed to the tremor alone (Also vide Appendix 1).

Clonus

The characteristics of flexion and extension clonus of the upper limbs in patients with cerebral and cervical cord lesions were further investigated. A typical result is shown in the frequency spectrum of Figure 6. The frequency of the tremor had a

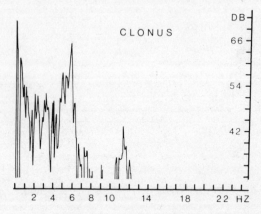

Figure 6 Power spectrum of clonus of the forearm in flexion/extension from a patient with high cervical cord lesion. The tremor is finely tuned at 6 Hz. The high values at low frequencies less than 1 Hz represent flapping movements of the arm and instinctive attempts on the part of the patient to arrest the movement. Further explanation as for Figure 1.

peak value at 6 Hz, was finely tuned and had a harmonic resonance of 12 Hz. Comparison of this pattern of spectrum with those of 6 Hz rhythmical movements in Parkinson's disease shows that they are similar.

Discussion

The identity of cogging, clonus, intentional and postural tremor in Parkinson's disease

We have demonstrated that in the Parkinsonian patient the frequency spectra of cog-wheel phenomena, exaggerated postural tremor and intention tremor in the upper limb are similar to the frequency spectra of clonus.

On the basis of these findings we suggest that cogging, intention tremor and postural tremor are subserved by the same mechanism. Furthermore, this mechanism is likely to be that which produces clonus in the spastic patient.

Evidence from clinical observation supports these identities. Clonus in the spastic patient is evoked by stretching the limb or by asking the patient to adopt a posture which are precisely the manoeuvres which evoke postural tremor and cogging in the Parkinsonian patient. In our interpretation the intention tremor in the Parkinsonian patient which occurs, particularly when the arm is reaching outwards, is a self-induced cogging phenomenon.

These views contrast with those of Lance *et al* [1] in the following respects. Lance *et al* considered that postural tremor in the Parkinsonian patient was exaggerated physiological tremor. This we reject because concomitantly a postural tremor, akin to physiological or normal tremor, can be demonstrated in the same subject. Lance *et al* hold that cogging has a variable frequency caused by the "superimposition of the stretch reflex on either resting tremor or action tremor, whichever was engaging the anterior horn cell at the moment of testing". In contrast we have found that once steady cogging has been established, its frequency remains constant and that whenever evoked it abolished resting tremor and took precedence (an example of this occurring is illustrated in Findley *et al* [2]). However, if single cycles of cogging are initiated at different times during the stretch then the cogging will appear to be of variable frequency whereas if several cycles of continuous cogging are triggered then an accurate estimate of frequency can be made. The measurement of frequency based on occasional single cycles which are assumed to be continuous is invalid.

Diagnostic value of tremor recording

Some observers tend to group together all tremors into the two frequency bands 3–6 Hz and 7–10 Hz with the comment that both frequencies in some sense represent physiological tremor [3, 4]. An implicit assumption of this classification is that the underlying mechanisms of the tremor are the same, thus Jung [5] and Dietz [6] note the similarity between Parkinsonian (presumably resting) tremor, and clonus. Rondot *et al* [7] assume that the 4 Hz resting tremor of Parkinson's disease increases in frequency to 7 Hz as if on a continuum when the limb moves into posture.

Our experience, with few exceptions, has been different. We have found that resting tremor in Parkinson's disease has always had a fixed frequency between 4 and 5 Hz with harmonic resonances and fine tuning. Furthermore, this frequency is never seen in clonus, cogging or postural or intentional tremor in Parkinson's disease which all have a dominant frequency at about 6 Hz. When a 4 Hz tremor occurs during posture in a Parkinsonian patient it does so in co-existence with a 6 Hz tremor. The 6 Hz tremor may also co-exist with a 9 Hz tremor which could be considered to be within the "normal" physiological range. Thus there is a distinct separation between tremors around 6 Hz and those around 4 Hz or 9 Hz which may imply different origins. In cerebello-rubral lesions which may produce tremor of postural or intentional variety, the tremor may vary between 3.5 Hz and 5 Hz thus overlapping with Parkinsonian resting tremor but tending to be more variable in frequency and not finely tuned. Stewart and Holmes [8] and Holmes [9] suggested that the origins of both Parkinsonian resting tremor and cerebello-rubral tremor were mesencephalic on the grounds that each was of a similar frequency and, in the case of rubral tremor at rest, indistinguishable. In terms of spectral analysis they could certainly be related, both being regulated, as it were, by the same "clock".

The ability to find definite patterns of frequency spectra of tremor in association with various disease states of the nervous system suggests that, with experience and given a "library" of identified patterns of tremor, spectral analysis of involuntary movement could have diagnostic value and help in the clarification of problems which are difficult to evaluate in the routine clinical situation.

These points can be illustrated by considering the results from recordings taken from a patient referred from out-patients because of some clinical doubts as to the origin and nature of his tremor. The patient was a 55 year old Indian business man who had always been in good health. He had noticed a postural and intentional tremor in his right hand for more than 30 years. Over the two years before coming to the clinic this has progressed in severity and was similarly involving the left hand. In addition more recently he had noted an intermittent tremor of the right hand at rest. His younger brother is similarly affected, symptoms beginning at the age of 25 years.

On examination the salient features were that with reinforcement there was cogging detectable on flexion and extension movements of the right wrist. He had an intermittent resting tremor of the right hand and a bilateral postural and intention tremor. Dorsiflexion of the right wrist exhibited clonus.

The spectral analysis showed a finely tuned intermittent resting tremor in the right hand at 4 Hz with harmonics at 8 Hz and 12 Hz. In addition on posture there was a 6 Hz tremor bilaterally also seen towards the termination of movement on the standard finger—nose test. These 6 Hz tremors were indistinguishable on analysis from that of cogging recorded in flexion–extension from the right wrist. On repeated analysis at the same sitting occasionally a 4 Hz postural tremor was present co-existing with the 6 Hz tremor.

From the history one would have been inclined to place this patient in the "essential" or "heredo-familial tremor" group. However, the spectral analysis of tremor revealed an additional 4 Hz resting tremor which was sometimes present on posture. This is the hallmark for extra-pyramidal disease and it could be argued that this patient had developed early super-added Parkinson's disease or be one of the small groups of patients who show extra-pyramidal or cerebellar features in the natural history of these tremors [10]. The importance of this patient for the present discussion is that he showed cogging and clonus in the same muscle groups of the same limb at identical frequencies when the wrist was dorsiflexed and at times it was difficult to be sure whether one was feeling clonus or cogging, ie. one seeming to be a continuum of the other without fundamental changes in frequency or wave form. This raises the question as to the origin of the important physical signs.

The clinical assessment supplemented by spectral analysis of the involuntary movements would lead one to conclude that both cogging and clonus are dependent on the same underlying 'timing' mechanism. In addition occasionally rigid Parkinsonian patients will show a marked 'intention' tremor at the termination of the finger—nose test, which persists into posture as an exaggerated 'clonic' tremor, indistinguishable from clonus as seen in cervical cord lesions. From our on-going studies we have found consistently that patients with low frequency type of essential or heredo-familial tremor do not respond to Propranolol or other beta blocking drugs.

The spinal origin of the 6 Hz tremor

The clock-like mechanism which regulates the periodicity of clonus is located in the spinal cord. This is demonstrated by the fact that clonus may be evoked in the isolated spinal state and that peripheral input during clonus does not alter the periodicity [11, 12]. For sustained clonus to occur, suprasegmental mechanisms must be present and activated, and the stretch reflex mechanism must be intact. Given the identity between 6 Hz rhythmical involuntary movements in Parkinson's disease and clonus we are provided with the explanation that these phenomena are the consequences of heightening of the conditions at a spinal level which give rise to rigidity.

In overview, the 6 Hz tremors of Parkinson's disease are attributable to the primary pathology in the basal ganglia giving rise to an increased level of activity in descending pathways which control spinal excitability, producing rigidity and the tendency to develop clonic-like rhythmical movements when stretch reflexes are activated.

Appendix I

Statistical data describing the distribution of peak or dominant frequencies of symptomatic tremor under various conditions of movement and posture in 25 patients with Parkinson's disease. Individual limbs are considered separately. The statistical estimates are based on single values for peak frequency for each limb/ condition/patient which were derived from numerous power spectra as described below. Hand and forearm posture are grouped together because no differences were found in the peak tremor frequencies recorded under these two conditions.

85

Type of Movement	Resting Tremor	Postural Tremor	Cogging	Intention Tremor
Incidence of individual tremors (out of 50 limbs)	28	24	13	9
Mean frequency	4.5	6.3	6.4	6.5
Standard deviation	0.5	0.5	0.4	0.4
Range total	4–5.5	6–8	6–7	6–7.5
Shape of distribution	Skewed to lower values	Normal with outlying high values	Normal	Normal with outlying high values

Statistical conclusions: There are no statistical differences between the frequency distributions of postural tremor, cogging and intention tremor by two standard deviations from the mean.

Estimation of peak tremor frequencies

For each condition of tremor recording numerous power spectra were calculated until we were confident that the typical pattern of tremor, free from other movement artefacts and abrupt changes in characteristics had been established. To a large extent this process was an attempt to identify intuitively "statistically stationary" samples of tremor recording. However, we found that the peak frequency of the tremor would be invariant to within 0.1 Hz for all samples which were free from artefact. Peak frequency was independent of amplitude of tremor although changes in amplitude did produce variations in the phase relationships between harmonics. Fluctuations in amplitude within a sample of tremor produced increased harmonic distortion.

Criteria for acceptance or rejection of data

Where a clinically evident resting tremor continued uninterruptedly and at the same frequency through movement and posture this was *not* considered to be a postural or intention tremor but a continuation of the resting tremor. In a resting limb in which there was no resting tremor evident we sometimes found 6 Hz "subliminal" tremor which became exaggerated into a symptomatic 6 Hz tremor on posture, such tremor at rest was *not* considered to be a 'Parkinsonian resting tremor' but evidence of increased tone producing an approximation to posture.

References

1 Lance JW, Schwab RS, Peterson EA. *Brain 1963;86:*95
2 Findley LJ, Gresty MA, Halmagyi GM. Abnormal arm movements. Submitted to *Archives of Neurology*
3 Freund HJ, Dietz V. In Desmedt JE, ed. *'Physiological tremor, pathological tremor and clonus'. Prog in clin Neurophysiol 1978;vol 5:*66. Basle, Karger

4   Stein RB, Oguztorelli MN. In Desmedt JE, ed. *'Physiological tremor, pathological tremor and clonus'. Prog in clin Neurophysiol 1978;vol 5:*   Basle, Karger

5   Jung R. *Z ges Neurol Psychiat 1941;173:*263

6   Dietz V. Reported by Freund and Dietz In Desmedt JE, ed. *Physiological tremor, pathological tremor and clonus'. Prog in clin Neurophysiol 1978;vol 5:*66. Basle, Karger

7   Rondot P, Jedynak CP, Ferrey G. In Desmedt JE, ed. *'Physiological tremor, pathological tremor and clonus'. Prog in clin Neurophysiol 1978;vol 5:*95. Basle, Karger

8   Stewart TG, Holmes G. *Brain 1904;27:*522

9   Holmes G. *Brain 1904;27:*360

10 Critchley Macdonald. *Brain 1949; 72:* 9

11 Walshe EG. *J Neurol Neurosurg Psychiat 1978;39:*266

12 Dimitrijevic MR, Sherwood AM, Nathan P. In Desmedt JE, ed. *Prog in clin Neurophysiol 1978;vol 5:*173. Basle, Karger

Chapter 12

RIGIDITY

D L McLellan

Rigidity was not mentioned in Parkinson's *Essay on the Shaking Palsy* (1817) [1] but is now accepted as a characteristic component of the syndrome. It is elicited by passive movement of the patient's limb, which induces involuntary contraction in the muscle that is being stretched. This gives rise to a resistance to stretch. The resistance may be smooth or intermittent ('cogwheel') but its mean amplitude feels relatively constant throughout the range of stretching, and does not obviously reflect the speed at which stretching occurs. This helps clinically to distinguish it from the velocity-sensitive stretch responses of spasticity.

Physiological basis of rigidity

It is barely possible to isolate single physiological mechanisms in man. Firstly, there are many ways in which an input from a limb can be directed on to moto-neurones, using pathways controlled from the brain. The sign of these pathways differs so that the net effects of the input can be facilitatory, inhibitory, or nil. Secondly, rigidity is only one of the features of Parkinsonism and physiological measurements may be misleading when other features are present. For example, the electromyographic 'silent period' induced by electrical stimulation of a per-ipheral nerve serving a tonically contracting muscle is abnormally prolonged in some patients. It was initially assumed that this threw light on the mechanism of rigidity but analysis of the patients' signs showed that the silent period was pro-longed only in patients with tremor [2]. The silent period produced in this way reflects the activity of an inhibitory reflex elicited by the stimulus [3]. There is other evidence of concurrent motoneurone inhibition with facilitation in Parkin-sonism [4] so that the result of a particular investigation depends not only on which particular reflex systems are tested, but upon the precise balance of abnor-mality in the patient.

An attempt to correlate clinical features of post-encephalitic Parkinsonism with histopathological examination at autopsy has shown an association between rigidity and the combination of severe damage to the putamen with relative sparing of the globus pallidus [5].

The slow (tonic) stretch response

Muscle activation in rigidity results from progressive recruitment of new motor units as the muscle is stretched, with progressive fall out of previously recruited units [6]. The muscle is usually silent at rest but electromyographic activity resumes if the muscle is stretched by passive joint movement of more than 5 or 10 degrees [7]. Injection of the muscle belly with procaine [8] or deafferentation of the limb [9] abolishes this response, confirming that it is induced by the activation of sensory receptors in the limb.

By subjecting rigid limbs to repeated sinusoidal flexion and extension movements, and averaging the electromyographic responses, Andrews and his colleagues [10, 11] identified the characteristic patterns of slow stretch response that occur in rigid muscles. Despite the clinical impression of 'plastic' or 'lead-pipe' responses, velocity-sensitive components were identified, particularly in extensor muscles, and especially in mild rigidity. A length-dependent component was greater in flexor than in extensor muscles and was relatively more prominent in severe rigidity. Except in the hamstring muscles, both components were facilitated when the length of the muscle increased. Responses in the triceps muscle were similar to those in the quadriceps but the biceps responses differed from those of the hamstrings. In the hamstrings, both length-dependent and velocity-dependent responses were maximal with the knee partly flexed and both responses diminished when the knee was fully extended. The responses were re-examined after the limb had been rendered ischaemic, preferentially inactivating wide-diameter peripheral nerve fibres, including the IA input from the equatorial regions of the intrafusal ('spindle') muscle fibres. Ischaemia abolished the velocity-sensitive component of the biceps stretch response and unmasked a length-dependent inhibition. The authors concluded that in rigidity, the input from group II spindle afferents inhibits the biceps and facilitates the triceps muscles. They argued that this would be expected because the biceps is an antigravity muscle in man. This inhibitory influence is normally submerged by the facilitatory responses in rigid muscles.

These findings could have been explained by a pathological increase in the tonic activity of dynamic and static fusimotor nerve fibres. However, single fibre recordings from IA afferents from rigid muscles have shown that the increased muscle tone is accompanied by a sustained spindle discharge, similar to that accompanying weak or moderately sustained voluntary contractions in normal subjects—in other words, the level of fusimotor activity is appropriate to the level of muscular contraction that is taking place [12].

The shortening reactions (Westphal Phenomenon)

Although it cannot be detected clinically, an electromyographic response can be seen in muscles that are passively *shortened*. A brief contraction often occurs during shortening (the dynamic shortening reaction) and may be maintained for as long as the muscle remains in the shortened position (the static shortening reaction). It is not clear whether the prominence of this phenomenon correlates with the severity of rigidity or with some other feature of the disease. Prominent dynamic shortening reactions occur in athetotic limbs [13] and sometimes in spinal cord transection [14]. The dynamic shortening response is abolished only transiently by infiltrating the muscle with procaine and the response in the antagonist is unaffected [10]. Procaine does, however, abolish the static shortening response in the antagonist of the injected muscle. Both responses are diminished by ischaemia. The static response is probably induced by an input from the stretched muscle and the dynamic response from a non-specific activation of both muscles by the process of the movement. The distribution of shortening reactions in flexors and extensors cannot be explained on the basis of the known differential effects of IA and II afferents on the motoneurones of flexor and extensor muscles [10].

Muscle contraction 'at rest'

Patients with mild Parkinsonism can relax their muscles completely at rest, especially when they make a conscious effort to do so. Exteroceptive reflexes may be enhanced though this does not necessarily reflect the degree of rigidity [15]. Later, the ability to relax is lost, and the muscles develop a state of continuous contraction that produces the characteristic flexed posture of Parkinsonism. Should such contraction be called a 'stretch response'? It is dependent upon an input from the muscle and forms the background upon which the response to added stretch is superimposed. The background activity and the stretch responses are increased by reinforcement (for example by Jendrassik's manoeuvre) but the profile of the slow stretch response differs from the contraction induced by a Jendrassik's manoeuvre or voluntary effort in a normal subject [11].

The Cogwheel effect

The cogwheel effect is characterised by bursts of activity in the stretched muscle at a frequency of about 8 Hz [16]. This differs from the rate of resting tremor which is usually slower at 4-5 Hz, and can often be detected in muscles in which no resting tremor is apparent. Where resting tremor is severe it may, of course, be of such amplitude that it interrupts the assessment of tone and imparts a spurious 'cogwheeling' to all attempts at movement. Many patients with Parkinsonism have an 'action' or 'postural' tremor at 6–8 Hz which appears to be independent of the resting tremor. It is accentuated by vibration of the muscle and in an individual patient passive stretch, voluntary effort and vibration all induce bursts of contraction at a similar frequency which is higher than the frequency of the patient's resting tremor (McLellan, 1972b, [17] Figure 1). Cogwheel bursts appear to result when tonic activation of the muscle is accompanied by an increased input from the muscle, whether generated by passive stretch, applied vibration, or spindle co-activation.

Where rigidity co-exists with resting tremor, dorsal root section abolishes the rigidity but not the tremor [9]. However, cogwheel bursts are not the inevitable expression of motoneurone activation for they are replaced by tonic contraction once the process of stretching ceases and the muscle is held at its new length.

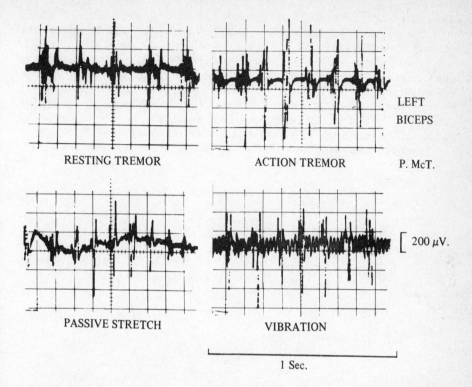

RESTING TREMOR

ACTION TREMOR

LEFT
BICEPS

P. McT.

PASSIVE STRETCH

VIBRATION

200 μV.

1 Sec.

Figure 1 Surface electromyogram of the left biceps muscle of a patient with the rigidity of Parkinsonism, showing synchronisation at about 5 Hz at rest (resting tremor) compared with a rate of 7-8 Hz during voluntary contraction (action tremor), passive stretch and vibration of the muscle.

Tendon jerks in rigidity

The amplitude of the tendon jerk is usually normal but in a personal series they were moderately increased in 80 of 191 rigid limbs and were more likely to be increased when the rigidity was severe. They were reduced in only 6 limbs, none of which had severe rigidity. The tendon reflex is a monosynaptic reflex, unlike rigidity which is determined by polysynaptic reflexes. A great deal of work has been done on the H response, a monosynaptic response induced electrically so that the muscle is not tapped and the muscle spindle is not activated. The amplitude of the H response, often expressed as a percentage of the maximal twitch response (the M response of the muscle) has been considered to reflect the level of the excitability of the motoneurone pool, but there are some objections to this view [18]. The input along the Ia afferent is susceptible to presynaptic inhibition. Voluntary muscular contraction is achieved by co-activation of alpha and gamma neurones [19] and in rigidity there is a tonic Ia input from a muscle with resting tone which

91

could alter the excitability of the motoneurone pool [12]. Finally, the amplitude of monosynaptic responses does not necessarily increase or decrease when muscle tone increases or decreases [20, 21].

Analyses of the recovery of H response amplitude after a single conditioning shock have suggested an increased state of motoneurone facilitation (or reduced inhibition) in rigidity [22, 23]. In a group of 15 patients, the amplitude of single H responses was significantly higher than normal [20] but when plotted against the duration of the H refractory period, the usual relationship between amplitude and the refractory period was lost and the amplitude values lay above the regression line of normal controls (Figure 2). This implies that the monosynaptic reflex arc

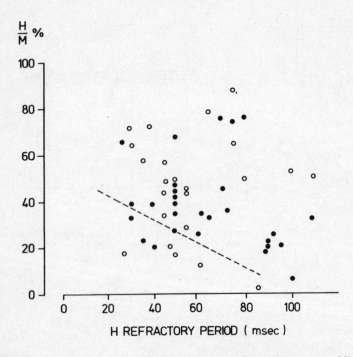

Figure 2 Relationship between the H refractory period and H/M ratio (a measure of H response amplitude) in 15 patients with Parkinsonism before (dots) and during (circles) treatment with levodopa. No consistent relationship was found. The dotted line is the regression line (X = −0.66) obtained from data from healthy subjects.

can be biassed so as to potentiate single volleys but not double volleys. Other authors have reported no increase in the amplitude of single H responses in their patients [24, 25]. In a group of patients in whom the soleus H response amplitude to single volleys was normal, the inhibitory effect of a conditioning stimulus to the posterior tibial nerve at the ankle was nevertheless reduced [26].

The tonic vibration response and rigidity

Vibration of the tendon or belly of the muscle induces a contraction in it that is principally due to activation of primary spindle endings, though secondary endings and other sense receptors in the limb are activated at the same time. The secondary endings that respond to vibration are probably less sensitive than primary endings and are likely to have either a dynamic or static type of response to stretch [27]. The response induced in the relaxed muscle (TVR) increases if the length of the muscle is increased and it builds up and falls away more quickly under isometric than under isotonic conditions; it is augmented by the presence of underlying voluntary contraction [28]. During vibration, the amplitude of the H response is considerably reduced [29]. The TVR in conscious man is thus a polysynaptic phenomenon, unlike the response studied in isolated animal preparations.

Marsden *et al* (1969) [30] studied the ways in which this TVR can be potentiated in man and concluded that it did not depend upon direct potentiation of fusimotor or of motor neurones but must be generated in 'higher centres'. It further differed from the monosynaptic reflex in being capable of suppression by voluntary effort and this suppression appears to take place also 'somewhere along the central pathways responsible for the development of tonic contraction'. In the intact cat, the TVR can be inhibited either by stimulation of the medial medulla or by stimulating areas of the cerebral cortex not all of which projected to the medial medulla [31]. The effects of cortical stimulation differed from the effects of medullary stimulation in being contralateral instead of bilateral, 'supporting the concept of a primitive activating mechanism being given specific direction from higher centres'. Stimulation of the lateral reticular formation and of the contralateral red nucleus potentiated this TVR.

In Parkinsonism, the TVR is difficult to measure in some patients because of accentuation of tremor [32] but, when patients with tremor are excluded and the TVR is elicited under isometric conditions, the strength of the induced contraction correlates positively with the severity of rigidity [20]. The TVR is absent in cord transection, confirming that when measured in this way it is a polysynaptic response requiring normal connections between the brain and the spinal cord.

In summary, the TVR and rigidity show many similarities. Both involve polysynaptic mechanisms requiring an intact spinal cord. Both show bursts of contraction of 'cogwheel' frequency in Parkinsonism (Figure 1) and both can be augmented or suppressed by voluntary effort. The strength of the isometric TVR correlates positively with the severity of rigidity but this could simply result from the super-imposition of vibration upon a muscle that is already contracting. It is not known whether the degree of enhancement of the TVR is similar in rigid (involuntarily contracting) muscle to that which occurs during comparable levels of voluntary contraction. Both rigidity and the enhanced TVR are reduced by L-dopa therapy as described below.

Rigidity and voluntary contraction

Although severe rigidity tends to be associated with severe bradykinesia, the correlation is poor (Figure 3) and there is no doubt that bradykinesia is a separate dis-

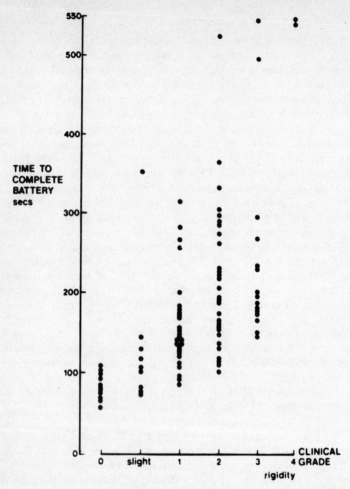

Figure 3 Relationship between time taken to perform a battery of manual tasks and the severity of rigidity in 82 patients with untreated Parkinsonism. Each point represents one upper limb.

order. The mechanism of reciprocal inhibition is intact in rigid muscles even at rest [33] and rigid antagonist muscles are usually silent during a simply voluntary effort except for bursts of action tremor [34]. The failure of the arms to swing normally when walking is associated with inappropriate contraction, usually rhythmical, in shoulder girdle muscles. These contractions do not appear to result from muscle stretch and the arm swings normally in some patients whose rigidity is severe [35]. Such observations invalidate simplistic explanations for bradykinesia but it is possible that a disorder of central motor programming could disrupt movement and release stretch responses at the same time.

94

Effects of therapy

Rigidity is relieved by anticholinergic drugs, stereotactic thalamotomy and dop-aminergic drugs. The concomitant improvement of bradykinesia is far greater with dopaminergic drugs than with other treatments, providing further evidence that rigidity and bradykinesia are separate disorders. Therapy not only reduces muscle tone but also abolishes 'cogwheeling'.

When L-dopa reduces rigidity, the isometric TVR is also reduced despite an *increase* in the amplitude of the soleus H responses [20]. This paradoxical in-crease in H response amplitude (Figure 4) could be due to a combination of the

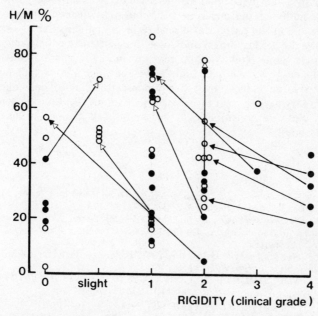

Figure 4 Relationship between clinical grade of rigidity and H/M ratio (a measure of H response amplitude) in 15 patients with Parkinsonism before (dots) and during (circles) treatment with levodopa. Solid-headed arrows indicate changes in limbs in which rigidity improved by 2 grades or more. Hollow-headed arrows show limbs in which H/M ratio in-creased by more than 28 per cent. The H response becomes larger as rigidity improves.

removal of the reciprocal inhibition from the tibialis anterior muscle and the facilitatory effects of L-dopa upon a descending noradrenergic facilitatory path-way to motoneurones, the effects of which can be blocked by phenoxybenzamine [34].

The anti-spastic drug baclofen reduces the amplitude of the H response in rigidity but it has no effect upon muscle tone or the TVR in this condition [21]. It is interesting that in spasticity, baclofen reduces both the amplitude of the H responses and muscle tone, without affecting the TVR. These are further illustrations of the frequent discrepancies that exist between the excitability of mono-synaptic and polysynaptic stretch responses.

Conclusion

Rigidity is a characteristic but not an essential feature of Parkinsonism. In mild cases it can be detected only by passive movement, augmented by reinforcement. In severe cases there is resting tone in the muscles, causing the abnormal flexed posture and this tone is augmented by stretching the muscle. Neurophysiological testing has provided evidence that is superficially contradictory in showing normal, facilitated or inhibited motoneurone behaviour. The different results sometimes reflect differences in the pattern of disability in the patients (which can be greatly altered if they are taking drugs) and sometimes differences between the experimental methods used. Monosynaptic reflexes and polysynaptic reflexes can be modulated separately by the brain and the way in which a single incoming volley is handled may give no indication of the response to a train of incoming impulses. Rigidity and cogwheeling cannot be explained simply by tonic enhancement or inhibition of alpha motoneurones, or by an isolated change in the activity of fusimotor neurones.

References

1   Parkinson J. *Essay on the shaking palsy 1817.* London, Sherwood, Neeley and Jones
2   McLellan DL. *J Neurol Neurosurg Psychiat 1972a;35:*373
3   McLellan DL. *J Neurol Neurosurg Psychiat 1973a;36:*334
4   Simpson JA. In Andrew BL, ed. *Control and Innervation of Skeletal Muscle 1966;*171. Edinburgh, Livingstone
5   Martin JP. *The basal ganglia and Posture 1967.* London, Pitman Medical Ltd
6   Denny-Brown D. *Lancet 1960;ii:*1155
7   Denny-Brown D, Seyffarth H, Chambers R. *Arch Neurol Psychiat (Chic) 1953;69:*252
8   Rushworth G. *J Neurol Neurosurg Psychiat 1960;23:*99
9   Pollock LJ, Davies L. *Arch Neurol Psychiat (Chic) 1930;17:*303
10   Andrews CJ, Burke D, Lance JW. *Brain, 1972;95:*795
11   Andrews CJ, Neilson PD, Lance JW. *J Neurol Neurosurg Psychiat 1973;36:*329
12   Wallin BG, Hongell A, Hagbarth K-E. In Desmedt JE, ed. *New Developments in Electromyography and Clinical Neurophysiology 1973;Vol 3:*105, Basle, Karger
13   Andrews CJ, Neilson P, Knowles L. *J Neurol Neurosurg Psychiat 1973;36:*94
14   Burke D, Andrews CJ, Gillies JD. *Brain 1971;94:*455
15   Delwaide PJ, Schwab RS, Young RR. *Neurology (Minneap) 1974;24;*820
16   Lance JW, Schwab RS, Peterson EA. *Brain 1963;86:*95
17   McLellan DL. *J Physiol (Lond) 1972b;227:*13
18   Granit R, Burke RE. *Brain Res 1973;53:*1
19   Vallbo AB. *Acta Physiol Scand 1970;80:*552
20   McLellan DL. *J Neurol Neurosurg Psychiat 1973b;36:*342
21   McLellan DL. In *Baclofen: Spasticity and Cerebral Pathology 1978:*52. Northampton, Cambridge, Medical Publications Ltd
22   Ioku M, Ribera VA, Cooper IS, Matsouk S. *Science 1965;150;*1472
23   Yap C-B. *Brain 1967;90:*887

24   Angel RW, Hoffmann WW. *Arch Neurol (Chic) 1963;8:*591
25   Dietrichson P. *Acta Neurol Scand 1971;47:*22
26   Martinelli P, Montagna P. *J Neurol Neurosurg Psychiat 1979;42:*701
27   Burke D, Andrews CJ, Lance JW. *J Neurol Neurosurg Psychiat 1972;35:*477
28   Hagbarth K-E. In Desmedt JE, ed. *New Developments in Electromyography and Clinical Neurophysiology 1973;vol 3:*428. Basle, Karger
29   Lance JW, De Gail P, Neilson PD. *J Neurol Neurosurg Psychiat 1966;29:*535
30   Marsden CD, Meadows JC, Hodgson, HJF. *Brain 1969;92:*829
31   Andrews CJ, Knowles L, Lance JW. *J Neurol Sci 1973;18:*207
32   Hagbarth K-E, Ecklund G. *J Neurol Neurosurg Psychiat 1968;31:*207
33   Bathien N, Rondot P. *J Neurol Neurosurg Psychiat 1977;40:*20
34   Andrews CJ. *Aust and New Eng J Med 1971;Suppl 1:*24
35   Hallett M, Shahani BT, Young RR. *J Neurol Neurosurg Psychiat 1977;40:*1129
36   Buchthal F, Fernandex-Ballesteros ML. *Brain 1965;88:*875

Chapter 13

AKINESIA, PHYSIOLOGICAL REST MECHANISMS, OPIATES AND THE BASAL GANGLIA

P N C Elliott, P Jenner and C D Marsden

Introduction

The function of the basal ganglia is unknown. Pathological change in this part of the brain causes either immobility, as exemplified by the akinetic-rigid syndrome of Parkinson's disease, or abnormal involuntary movements, such as the chorea that occurs in Huntington's disease. This clinico-pathological correlation has led to the belief that the basal ganglia exert influence over movement, but how they are involved in motor control is a mystery.

The finding of opiate-like encephalins in the mammalian brain has been a recent exciting discovery [1, 2]. Endogenous encephalins obviously have been considered to exert some influence on the appreciation of pain. But it has come as a surprise to discover that encephalins themselves and the opiate receptors on which they act are present in great concentrations within the basal ganglia [3, 4, 5], structures not normally considered to be concerned with pain.

In fact there is a long history of research associating opiates with motor function. The administration of morphine to rats produces a syndrome of akinesia, catalepsy and muscular rigidity [6]. These behavioural effects have been attributed to a disease in dopaminergic neurotransmission in the brain, for morphine antagonises cerebral dopamine actions such as stereotyped behaviour induced by the administration of amphetamine or apomorphine [7]. Morphine also increases firing rates of nigral dopamine neurones [8] so increasing striatal and mesolimbic dopamine turnover [9, 10], effects identical to those produced by dopamine post-synaptic antagonists such as neuroleptics [8]. However, it is unlikely that these effects of morphine, which are reversed by the specific opiate antagonist naloxone, are mediated by a direct action on dopamine post-synaptic receptors. It is more probable that the action of morphine and other narcotic analgesics on cerebral dopamine mechanisms is mediated indirectly. Opiate receptors have been shown to lie both pre-synaptically on dopaminergic neurones and post-synaptically on cell bodies in striatal and mesolimbic dopamine-containing areas of the brain [11, 12].

Recent evidence suggests that pre-synaptic actions of encephalins on dopamine neurones facilitate nigrostriatal dopaminergic neurotransmission, whereas their post-synaptic action inhibits dopaminergic activity [13].

Of the encephalin pathways within the basal ganglia identified so far, the one that is most evident is that between the striatum and the globus pallidus [14]. The function of this strio-pallidal system is not understood, but preliminary experiments indicate that manipulation of globus pallidus opiate receptors can alter motor function in rodents [15].

So opiates and encephalins exert some powerful influence on basal ganglia function and motor behaviour. Why? We propose the hypothesis that endogenous encephalins are concerned not only with the regulation of pain threshold, but also the motor responses required to protect an animal from a painful stimulus. Thus we suggest that pain evokes activation of endogenous encephalin systems so as to suppress the discomfort, and also to withdraw the injured body part from the painful stimulus. The latter involves two distinct processes. The natural and obvious response to a noxious stimulus, say the prick of a pin or the burn of a cigarette, is to withdraw as far as possible as quickly as possible. A second, more delayed and long-lasting response is to prevent use of the injured part until the wound has healed. This latter process is illustrated vividly by the injured dog who hops on three legs. Not only does he pull the hurt forepaw away from the source of damage, but thereafter he does not even attempt to use the damaged limb in walking or running, but prefers to hold it by the side out of action—a physiological rest mechanism. We suggest that encephalins in the basal ganglia initiate and maintain this physiological rest mechanism by withdrawing the injured part from use, ie. by enforcing appropriate akinesia.

To test this hypothesis we have produced tissue injury in rats, by techniques conventionally used to study pain mechanisms, and have examined the effects of the opiate antagonist naloxone on the motor behaviour of such animals.

Methods

Male Wistar rats (150–200 g) were anaesthetised using chloral hydrate (300 mg/kg ip). One forepaw was lesioned by immersion of either the foot or forearm into water at 60–65° C for periods up to 30 sec. Immediately following the lesion and at daily intervals the animals were treated with ampicillin (0.1 ml Penbritin in a suspension containing 15 mg/100 ml; Beecham Animal Health Ltd.). Prior to lesioning and following lesioning, the animals were tested for their ability to walk down a sloping runway 122 cm long by 9 cm wide, suspended 3–4 feet off the floor and terminating in the home cage. Correct use of the front paws was observed, and the number of front-leg to back-leg steps taken to traverse the runway into the home cage was counted. Four to seven days after lesioning, those animals who did not use the damaged front paw were selected for further study. Their ability to complete the walking task was assessed before and immediately following intravenous administration of either saline (0.5 ml 0.9% in HCl), or naloxone hydrochloride (20 mg/kg iv in 0.5 ml 0.9% saline; Endo Laboratories) or nalorphine hydrochloride (20 mg/kg iv in 0.5 ml 0.9% saline; Burroughs Wellcome Ltd.). In each instance the animal was placed on the walkway up to 20 times over the 30 min period following administration of either drug.

Naloxone was chosen as a specific opiate antagonist at many opiate receptor sites, with no agonist activity and few other pharmacological actions [16]. Nalorphine was chosen in comparison because at equivalent doses it produces only one-seventh the opiate antagonist activity of naloxone but has opiate agonist activity equivalent to that of morphine [16].

Results

Thermal injury to one fore-paw was produced in 50 rats, 30% of whom subsequently withdrew the damaged limb from use. Such animals characteristically began to limp on the affected fore-paw 4–7 days later, and often lifted it clear of the ground, preferring to run on three legs. Limping persisted up to 10 days, thereafter the animals gradually recovered. During this time the affected rats explored the home cage, ate, drank and slept normally.

To begin with, the effects of naloxone (20 mg/kg iv) were assessed subjectively. In all 10 animals studied, naloxone altered the rat's use of the damaged fore-paw. Within 5 min of injection of naloxone, the animals began to place the affected limb normally while running, adopting a fluent regular four-legged gait of even pace and rhythmic alternating steps. This normal gait continued for 30 min after naloxone injection, but then the animals began to limp again and to withdraw the affected fore-paw from use, reverting to a three-legged gait similar to that before naloxone.

An objective measure of this behaviour was devised by counting the number of steps taken by the affected fore-limb, compared with that taken by the ipsilateral hind-limb,as the rat ran down the 122 cm long walkway to their home cage. normal animals prior to the thermal lesion took about 7–9 steps with front and hind-limbs, and this was not altered after naloxone (20 mg/kg iv) (Table I). Seven to 9 days after lesioning, the affected rats only let the fore-paw touch the ground about 3 times, while the hind-limb still paced about 9 times. Naloxone restored normal fore-paw placing in these animals on the first trials, and greatly increased it on the second trial, but saline injection had no effect.

By comparison, nalorphine (20 mg/kg iv) administered to 5 animals had no effect on the running behaviour of such animals. Limping continued and the number of fore-paw paces remained reduced compared to those of the hind-limb.

Discussion

Effect of naloxone on running on an injured limb

These preliminary experiments suggest that naloxone can alter the use of a limb previously injured and withdrawn from the normal pattern of running. Naloxone

TABLE I Average number of paces (± 1 SE)

| Day | Treatment | LEG | |
		Rear	Front
Prior to	None	8.7 ± 0.2	8.5 ± 0.3
lesion	Naloxone	7.2 ± 0.3	7.5 ± 0.2
Day 7	None	8.6 ± 0.3	3.3 ± 0.5*
following lesion	Naloxone 20 mg/kg iv	9.9 ± 0.4	8.3 ± 0.8
Day 8	None	8.1 ± 0.2	3.6 ± 0.5*
following lesion	Saline iv	7.9 ± 0.2	3.2 ± 0.6*
Day 9	None	7.7 ± 0.1	3.2 ± 0.3*
following lesion	Naloxone 20 mg/kg iv	7.9 ± 0.2	5.7 ± 0.4*

* $p < 0.05$ compared to rear leg

Results are the mean of 10 to 20 trials for each 3 rats.

rapidly caused the animal to re-employ the affected fore-paw normally while running. The duration of this action of naloxone (about 30 min) is typical of its duration of biological action as an opiate antagonist. Thus naloxone reverses the inhibition of spontaneous locomotor activity produced by morphine for up to 10 minutes following its administration 2 min prior to morphine [17].

The dose of naloxone employed (20 mg/kg iv) is high, compared to the doses required to reverse the pharmacological action of morphine. However, we have used the drug in isolation to antagonise opiate receptors in a situation of injury where high neuronal activity is to be expected. In addition it is not certain which class of opiate receptors may be involved in this phenomenon. Thus, while naloxone is a potent antagonist at u receptors, its activity at k and σ receptors is limited [18] and high doses would be necessary to affect these systems.

Naloxone does not possess opiate agonist action, and nalorphine administered in the same dose (20 mg/kg iv) did not mimic the effect of naloxone, despite being a potent opiate agonist (this dose of nalorphine has an analgesic action equivalent to that of morphine [16]). So the ability of naloxone to restore normal running apparently is not due to any analgesic effect. Nor are there any other known biological actions of naloxone that might explain this phenomenon (although a very recent report suggests that naloxone and some other opiate antagonists and agonists may block the action of γ-aminobutyric acid in the brain [19]). We tentatively conclude that this effect is due to antagonism of opiate receptor action. Obviously, our experiments cannot specify where such an effect is occurring; we cannot even claim that it is in the central nervous system. However, this and other questions raised by the observation are open to experimental investigation.

101

The response to pain and injury

More attention has been given to the acute effects of tissue damage than to the later slower process of recovery. Pain generally is associated with acute tissue injury, but recently Wall has drawn attention to the more complex biological significance of pain and its relation to injury. Wall [20] emphasises three phases of response to injury. The first immediate response to tissue injury is characterised by the reaction to fight an aggressor or flee from the cause, and pain commonly does not occur in this phase. As the need to destroy or avoid the cause of injury subsides, the second or acute phase begins and pain commences. Wall highlights the fact that pain itself is really a poor and late indicator of tissue damage—the burnt hand is pulled from the frying-pan well in advance of the pain produced. Pain, according to Wall, may "announce the need to enter a mode of behaviour best suited to treat and cure the damage". During this acute phase of the response to injury, as pain and anxiety emerge the damaged animal or man passes from the immediate and acute attempts to cope with the cause of the injury into the third phase of recovery. The latter chronic phase of the response to injury is characterised by inactivity, sleep and re-duced bodily appetites, all of which contribute to gradual restoration of normal health.

Of course, the significance of this third chronic phase is well-known, as exemplified by that classic of medical literature, "Rest and pain" by J Hilton [21]. Hilton clearly recognised the need to rest an injured part, an infected limb, or a diseased organ if recovery was to take place. Writing in an era bereft of antibiotics and all the paraphernalia of modern medicine, Hilton harnessed the benefits of rest to aid the surgical skills of the time.

Both Wall and Hilton observed the normal animal response to pain. Wall proposed that pain provokes the third chronic phase of response to injury, in which Hilton perceived that rest was crucial to recovery. How does the injured animal rest a damaged bodily part?

A physiological rest mechanism

Whatever the mechanism, the systems responsible for resting a damaged body part are powerful. Take the example used in the experiments described above, which mimics a common everyday occurrence. The normal quadruped gait of animals is one of the most primitive, stable and enduring motor programmes known. It can persist even in the decerebrate animal, indicating that the necessary neuronal machinery exists in the lower levels of the nervous system. Yet damage a limb and that animal can override this basic mechanism for quadruped locomotion, to with-draw the injured part leaving the animal progressing on three legs for days, weeks or even months until recovery occurs. What part of our nervous system achieves this remarkable feat of enforcing physiological rest to allow recovery? We propose that it is the basal ganglia.

The basal ganglia as the source of physiological rest

The essence of an effective physiological rest mechanism is that it should stop body movement, and specifically stop movement only of the injured part. These requirements suggest that the physiological rest mechanism should:

1. Operate only after injury, and be silent during normal health.
2. Prevent movement.
3. Be highly somatopically organised.

The basal ganglia are involved with movement, but exactly how is not understood. Classical neurophysiological techniques such as discrete focal electrical stimulation or ablation, which proved so valuable in studies of cortical or cerebellar function, gave disappointing results when applied to basal ganglia (see 22 for review). But if their function operates in the chronic phase of response to injury, such acute studies in previously normal animals would not be expected to produce dramatic results. Indeed, lesions confined to the major output nuclei of the basal ganglia, the internal segment of the globus pallidus or the pars reticulata of the substantia nigra have very little long-term motor effect, while unilateral electrical stimulation in these areas or in the striatum (caudate and putamen) usually causes no more than turning of head and body, or arrest of on-going movements [22].

As far as neuronal activity is concerned, cells in the globus pallidus and pars reticulata of the substantia nigra in awake primates exhibit a high rate of tonic discharge, while those in the striatum show low discharge rates. Neuronal firing in all these areas is modulated by active movements of specific parts of the body, but there is no consistent or tight link. However, such studies have revealed somatotopic physiological organisation within the basal ganglia, and there is similar anatomical evidence for such discrete localisation of inputs from different body parts within basal ganglia structures [22].

Finally, the most obvious manifestations of basal ganglia disease concern bodily movements. Two categories are recognised, the akinetic-rigid syndrome typified by Parkinson's disease, and abnormal involuntary movements as exemplified by the chorea in Huntington's disease. Such movement disorders could be looked upon as derangements of a physiological rest mechanism, either operating too efficiently and without cause to produce akinesia, or failing to liberate dyskinesias such as chorea.

Of course, the sole function of the basal ganglia may not be to provoke rest, but a general functional capacity to suppress unwanted muscle contraction may be harnessed to this end. Indeed, perhaps the basal ganglia spend their time preventing muscular responses that might interfere with or prevent the important act of the moment, in the same way as other parts of the brain suppress the mass of sensory information from invading into the experience of the moment on which one is concentrating.

References

1   Hughes J, Smith TW, Kosterlitz HW, Fothergill LA, Morgan BA, Morris HR. *Nature* 1975;258:577
2   Simantov R, Snyder SH. *Proc Natl Acad Sci USA 1976;73:*2 515
3   Simantov R, Kuhar MJ, Pasternak GW, Snyder SH. *Brain Res 1976;106:*189

4   Yang H-Y.T, Hong JS, Fratta W, Costa E. In Costa E, Trabucchi M, eds. *Advances in Biochemical Psychopharmacology 1978;18:*149. New York, Raven Press
5   Cuello AC. *Lancet 1978;ii:*291
6   Mavrojannis M. *Comp Rend Soc Biol 1903;55:*1092
7   Puri SK, Reddy C, Lal H. *Res Comm Chem Path Pharmac 1973;5:* **389**
8   Iwatsuho K, Clouet DH. *J Pharmac Exp Ther 1977;202:*429
9   Kuschinsky K, Hornykiewicz O. *Eur J Pharmac 1972;19:*119
10   Clouet DH, Ratner M. *Science 1970;168:*854
11   Pollard H, Llorens C, Bonnet JJ, Costentin J, Schwartz JC. *Neurosci Lett 1977;7:*295
12   Pollard H, Llorens C, Schwartz JC, Gros C, Dray F. *Brain Res 1978;151:*392
13   Diamond BI, Borison RL. *Neurology 1978;28:*1085
14   Cuello AC, Paxinos G. *Nature 1978;271:*178
15   Taylor RJ, Jenner P, Marsden CD. Unpublished data
16   Jasinski DR, Martin WR, Haertzen CA. *J Pharm Exp Ther 1967;157:*420
17   Bhargava HN. *Pharmac Biochem Behav 1978;9:*167
18   Martin WR. *Brit J Clin Pharmac 1979;7:*Suppl 3 273
19   Dingledine R, Iversen LL, Brenker E. *Eur J Pharmac 1978;47:*19
20   Wall PD. In Wolstenholme G, O'Connor M, eds. *'Brain and Mind' Ciba Symposium 69 (New Series) 1979;*293. Ciba Foundation
21   Hilton J. *'On the Influence of Mechanical and Physiological Rest in the Treatment of Accidents and Surgical Distress, and the Diagnostic Value of Pain, 1863.* London, Bell and Daldy
22   Delong MR, Georgopoulos AP. In Chase TN, Wexler, NS, Barbeau A, eds. *Advances in Neurology 23 1979;*137. New York, Raven Press

Chapter 14

SPINAL REFLEXES IN PARKINSON'S DISEASE: THEIR EVOLUTION UNDER TREATMENT

P Rondot and N Bathien

Only minor importance is customarily ascribed to spinal reflex disturbances in Parkinson's disease. The tendon reflexes are present but are neither hyperkinetic nor diminished, and cutaneous reflexes are normal, at least in the earlier stages of the disease. But, electro-physiological methods allow a more accurate appraisal of the state of these reflexes, and give the opportunity of making some points of physiopathological interest.

The findings in untreated patients will be described first, then in a treated group and lastly in a group suffering from L-dopa induced involuntary movements. In each of these groups the following parameters have been studied:

- monosynaptic reflexes (RI), tested for by the H reflexes, by stimulating the tibial nerve,
- polysynaptic reflexes, the short-latency tactile reflex (R2) and the long-latency nociceptive reflex (R3) tested by stimulating the sural nerve, and
- the shortening reaction

The Untreated Parkinsonian Patient

The *H reflex* can be tested for in the presence of tremor, or in non-trembling rigid patients.

− During the tremor cycle, the H reflex decreases during the silent interval between two bursts of tremor, increasing just before the appearance of the next burst (Ekbom *et al* [1]). The decrease is not due only to a refractory phase following the motoneurone discharge, since it lasts 150–200 msec., which is too long to be accounted for by a simple state of depolarisation after motoneurone firing. The decrease in γ motoneurone excitability is brought about by the muscle contraction itself, since it can be reproduced by stimulation of the nerve or muscle where the tremor occurs, whatever the timing of the stimulation in the tremor cycle. This

105

silent interval is not caused by a spindle pause, in fact, Hagbarth *et al* [2] have shown that primary muscle spindle receptors discharge during both the contraction and relaxation phases of tremor. Thus we are dealing with some central mechanism acting on the afferent tendon or muscle impulses, as distinct from the primary spindle impulses, to dampen γ motoneurone excitability.

Angel and Hofmann [3] found the max H/M ratio in Parkinsonian rigidity to be virtually identical to that in the normal subject. However, Takamori [4], Olsen and Diamantopoulos [5] and Sax *et al* [6] showed, in studies of recovery curves of the H reflex after conditioned stimulation, that motoneurones are more excitable in the Parkinsonian patient than in the normal subject (Figure 1). This apparent con-

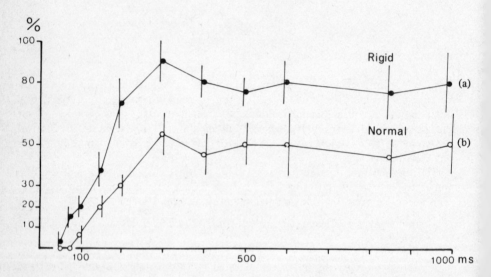

Figure 1 Parkinson's disease confined to the left side. Recovery curve of monosynaptic excitability following conditioning stimulus. a affected side, b normal side.

tradiction is probably due to a continuous decrease in γ motoneurone excitability brought about by afferent impulses from antagonist muscles. We have shown [7] in Parkinsonian patients that, after infiltration of the peroneal nerve with local anaesthetic, the amplitude of the foot extensor motoneurone H reflex is 300 per cent higher than before infiltration (Figure 2), a phenomenon not found in normal subjects.

It is supposed that this inhibition is transmitted along the disynaptic 1A pathway from the antagonist spindles, since the anaesthetic acts only after a long latent period of several minutes, whereas the small-calibre nociceptive fibres are blocked earlier.

This decrease in γ motoneurone excitability is one of the factors that tends to aggravate Parkinsonian motor disturbances.

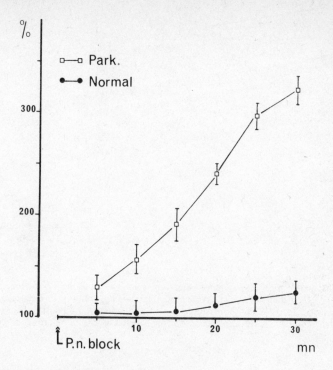

Figure 2 Comparison of peroneal nerve anaesthetic block effects on H reflex of 16 Parkinsonian patients and five healthy subjects. Mean values and two standard deviations are shown at each blocking time.

Nociceptive cutaneous reflexes

Threshold nociceptive stimulation of the external saphenous nerve triggers a long-latency response (110 ms), R3, from the biceps femoris: the nociceptive reflex is therefore normal. Sometimes a short-latency response, R2, is found with a latent period of 60-80 ms in the tibialis anterior.

The Shortening Reaction

This consists of two components: a phasic component, as in normal subject, and a tonic component which persists when shortening is sustained (Figure 3); this tonic component is an inconstant finding in the normal subject (Katz and Rondot [8]). We have shown that this reaction appears once the amplitude of the movement reaches a certain threshold and the afferent joint impulses are facilitatory. This reaction is abnormally increased in the Parkinsonian patient, probably because the central control by which it would normally be mediated has become insufficient.

107

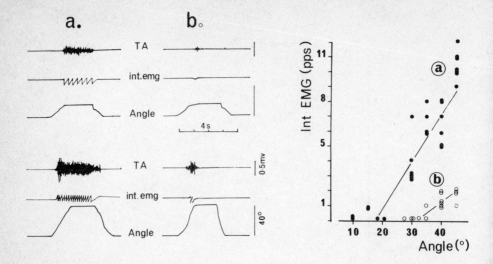

Figure 3 Parkinson's disease Shortening reaction. a before treatment, b during L-dopa treatment. EMG recordings of Tibialis Anterior, integrate emg, goniometer (angle) during passive movements of dorsiflexion (upper deflexion of goniometer) and plantar flexion of the foot at different amplitudes. In a, phasic and tonic shortening reactions are recorded; in b, only phasic.

The Treated Parkinsonian Patient

Tremor decreases, while keeping the same rhythm as before treatment, then disappears.

— Intravenous injection of the L-dopa agonist Piribedil in a Parkinsonian patient with tremor stops the tremor in 2–4 minutes (Rondot *et al* [9]), for a period lasting from half an hour to an hour.

If the tibial nerve is electrically stimulated after the tremor stops, there follows a motor response from the soleus, of an amplitude equal to that obtained before the injection; this contraction is followed by a silent phase of the same duration as before the injection, 200–250 ms. A burst of activity then follows, but is of low intensity, and the tremor tends not to reappear. This suggests that the L-dopa agonist has lowered the γ motoneurone excitability previously observed in the rhythmic burst, but that the stimulated muscle is still able to trigger a silent phase of unaltered duration. Piribedil injection allows a dissociation to be made between the facilitatory and inhibitory effects observed over the cycle of Parkinsonian tremor.

As described previously in studying the H reflex in patients with Parkinsonian rigidity, a continuous lowering of γ motoneurone excitability by afferent impulses from antagonist muscles has been found. If the H reflex is studied in the same patients before and after L-dopa treatment in the conditions which were stated earlier, ie. before and during local anaesthetic infiltration of the antagonist nerve, it is found

108

that this infiltration no longer triggers the large increase of the antagonist H reflex that caused a 3-fold increase in reflex amplitude 30 minutes after injection. L-dopa treatment abolishes the increase, and the post-infiltration amplitude curve of the H reflex returns to the same level as in the normal subject under identical conditions (Figure 4).

— *Polysynaptic reflexes* triggered by tactile stimuli, R2 and R3, are unaltered. We pointed out that they were already virtually normal in the non-treated Parkinsonian patient.

— *The Shortening Reaction* is modified by L-dopa: the phasic component of the reaction persists, as in the normal subject, but the tonic component is much more rarely found (Figure 4).

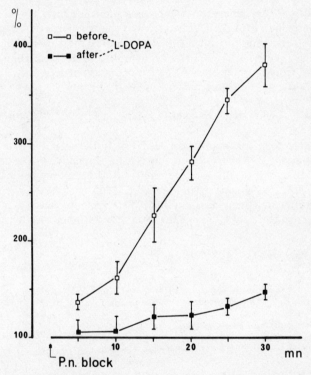

Figure 4 Effects of peroneal nerve block on the H reflex in Parkinsonian patients before and after treatment with L- Dopa over a period of one month. Mean values and two standard deviations are shown at each blocking time.

From the study of spinal reflexes during L-dopa induced *abnormal movements,* we can conclude:

— the H reflex is normal between the bursts of abnormal activity, but is enhanced during these bursts.

– Polysynaptic reflexes are unaltered as far as the short latency response is concerned,

– the long-latency Nociceptive reflex, on the other hand, is facilitated: at threshold nociceptive response, we find activity in the tibialis anterior preceding that of the biceps femoris, contrary to the findings in the normal subject. We can therefore conclude that nociceptive reflexes are being facilitated. This anomaly is to be compared with the transitory extensor response of the plantar cutaneous reflex sometimes observed during abnormal movements.

As has been shown by Jankowska *et al* [10], the facilitation of nociceptive reflex during L-dopa induced abnormal movements can be related to the dopamine facilitation of the long-acting flexor reflex. This has been demonstrated on the tibialis anterior muscle which is physiologically a flexor.

It must also be remembered that dopamine and its agonists have an antagonistic effect on morphine [11, 12]. L-dopa increases the reaction of mice to nociceptive stimuli [13]. It is therefore probable that an identical mechanism is at work during L-dopa induced abnormal movements. Nociceptive reflex facilitation could therefore be linked to a dopamine-blocking action on morphine receptors.

– The Shortening Reaction remains unmodified: only the phasic component is observed.

From this review of spinal reflexes in Parkinson's disease, 3 points deserve to be underlined:

– γ motoneurone excitability as tested for by the monosynaptic reflex is decreased periodically in tremor and continuously in rigidity. In the latter, this decrease is due to inhibitory antagonist afferents acting on γ motoneurones.

– heavy doses of L-dopa facilitate the R3 Polysynaptic Nociceptive Reflex,

– the Shortening Reaction is modified: the tonic component is recorded after the phasic component, and L-dopa tends to abolish this tonic reaction.

References

1   Ekbom, KA, Jernelius B, Kugelberg E. *Acta Med Scand 1952;141:*301
2   Hagbarth KE, Wallin G, Löfstedt L, Aquilonius SM. *J Neurol Neurosurg Psychiat 1975;38:*636
3   Angel RW, Hofmann WW. *Arch Neurol 1963;8:*591
4   Takamori M. *Neurology 1967;17:*32
5   Olsen PZ, Diamantopoulos E. *J Neurol Neurosurg Psychiat 1967;30:*325
6   Sax DS, Johnson TL, Feldman RG. *Ann Neurol 1977;2:*120
7   Bathien N, Rondot P. *J Neurol Neurosurg Psychiat 1977;40:*20
8   Katz R, Rondot P. *Electroencephalogr Clin Neurophysiol 1978;45:*90
9   Rondot P, Bathien N, Ribadeau Dumas JL. In Calne DB, Chase TN, Barbeau A, eds. *Advances in Neurology 9 1975;*373. New York, Raven Press
10   Janowska E, Jukes M, Lunds S, Lundberg A. *Acta Physiol Scand; 70:* 369
11   Major CT, Pleuvry BJ. *Brit J Pharmac 1971;42:*512
12   Pleuvry BJ, Tobias MA. *Brit J Pharmac 1971;43:*706
13   Tulunay FC, Sparber SB, Takemori AE. *Europ J Pharmac 1975;33:*65

Chapter 15

AUTONOMIC FUNCTION

G D Perkin

The description of a syndrome embracing orthostatic hypotension with Parkinsonism and other neurological features [1] has further stimulated the search for evidence of autonomic disturbances in patients with idiopathic Parkinson's disease (IPD).

Parkinson suggested [2] that patients were likely to lose control of bladder and bowel function in the later stages of the disease. In recent studies differing degrees of disturbance of autonomic function have been suggested, the variability probably a reflection of the type of patient studied, the severity of the symptoms and the method of assessment. This chapter will concentrate on blood pressure changes, including postural responses, the reaction to Valsalva's manoeuvre and the response to infusion of sympathomimetic agents. The influence of conventional and dopa therapy will be considered, and the relationship, both clinical and pathological, to idiopathic orthostatic hypotension (IOH) assessed.

The blood pressure in Parkinson's disease

Barbeau *et al* [3] concluded that patients with Parkinson's disease, particularly if akinetic, had a lower mean blood pressure than age-matched controls. The differences, particularly evident when standing, were thought to contribute to a 'chronic state of fatigue and to occasional episodes of postural dizziness'. Similarly, McDowell and Lee [4] reported a lower mean blood pressure, frequently observing a significant orthostatic fall. In a small group of patients with IPD, Aminoff *et al* [5, 6] found resting blood pressures to be lower than expected, though their cases had been chosen for study because of the presence of autonomic symptoms, particularly dizziness. Furthermore, in the first report [5], two of the eight patients were receiving dopa at the time of their assessment. Gross *et al* [7] examined 20 patients, all free of symptoms suggestive of autonomic dysfunction, and all with mild or moderate disability. The patients, many of whom were receiving anticholinergic therapy, were compared with age-matched controls, with the finding of no significant difference in supine mean blood pressures. An extensive study of casual blood

111

TABLE I Blood Pressure in Patients with Parkinson's Disease According to the Stage of the Disease: Mean Values ± SD (mm Hg)

	STAGE OF THE DISEASE				
	1 (25)	2 (152)	3 (55)	4 (25)	5 (16)
SYSTOLIC	168.0 ± 29.0	161.5 ± 27.2	158.5 ± 29.2	147.2 ± 37.4	140.3 ± 26.9
DIASTOLIC	96.0 ± 9.2	93.8 ± 12.3	90.0 ± 11.8	87.2 ± 18.3	81.6 ± 11.8

Figures in brackets are number of patients.

TABLE II Methodology of Various Studies of Blood Pressure Response to Tilt in Parkinsonian Subjects

Authors	No of patients	Tilting method	Speed of tilt	Speed of Tilt	Time when BP recording made	Current therapy C (Anti-cholinergic) A (Amantidine) D (Dopa or Combined)
Aminoff & Wilcox [5]	8	Tilt Table	15° 60°	Not given	?	6 C 1 A 2 D
Reid et al [11]	30	Tilt table	35°	Over 8 secs	1 min	28 "Routine" (probably C)
Appenzeller & Goss [12]	9	Tilt table	60°	Over 10–15 secs	Immediate	2 C
Gross et al [7]	20	Tilt table	60°	Within 5 secs	Within 10 secs	13C
Wilcox & Aminoff [14]	5	? Tilt table	?70°	?	?	5 C
Rajput & Rozdilsky [15]	6	Asked to stand	90°	?	?	?

pressure levels in Parkinsonian patients was published by Aminoff *et al* [8] in 1975. Of the 411 patients, only four had a severe form of the disease. Systolic and diastolic levels were similar in the mild and moderate groups, but significantly higher in those with tremor compared to those with bradykinesia. Controls consisted of patients previously reported who had attended various outpatient departments at another institute, having corrected for the fact that these blood pressures had been measured after five minutes rest. As a consequence, an insignificant depression of mean systolic pressures by 3 mm Hg and diastolic pressures by 1 mm Hg was found in the Parkinsonian patients, adjusted to the age of 60. A more recent report [9] is perhaps of greater value in that age and sex matched controls were studied concurrently. Blood pressures measured supine after 5 minutes rest were compared. A total of 273 patients, including seven post-encephalitic cases were analysed with the same number of controls. None of the patients were receiving L-dopa, but some three-quarters were taking anti-cholinergic drugs. Mean systolic, but not diastolic, pressures were significantly lower in Parkinsonian patients. When the stages of the disease were divided according to the method of Hoehn and Yahr [10], a decrease in both systolic and diastolic levels occurred with increasing severity (Table I) though the mean ages for the various subgroups were not given. Severity of tremor had no influence on blood pressure, but both systolic and diastolic values fell with increasing rigidity and bradykinesia. The results appear at first sight to contradict those of Aminoff *et al* [8], but in that study there were insufficient severely affected patients to allow a worthwhile comparison with the less disabled groups.

The response of blood pressure to posture

A uniform opinion regarding orthostatic blood pressure fall in Parkinsonian patients has not been expressed, perhaps partly due to the differing methods of assessment used (Table II). Aminoff and Wilcox [5] found a maximum systolic fall of 10 mm Hg and diastolic fall of 5 mm Hg on tilting to $60°$, in a group of eight patients, all complaining of dizziness, and two of blurring of vision, with posture change. Reid *et al* [11] studied 30 patients, most of whom had IPD. Twenty of the patients walked with difficulty, and a further six required support. Seven were found to have a systolic fall of 10 mm Hg or more on tilting to $35°$ (Figure 1) and all those showing a substantial fall (not defined) had impaired responses to Valsalva's manoeuvre. Appenzeller and Goss [12] reported no significant postural fall in blood pressure in nine patients tested before levodopa therapy, though the actual percentage falls in mean pressure were 16, 32, 5, 0, 0, 14, 8, 10 and 10 respectively. Bannister [13] found a greater than normal fall of mean blood pressure on passive tilting in 20 patients, and in a later communication [7] described a percentage fall of mean pressure of 16.05, compared to 12.20 in controls, a difference significant at the 0.05 level. Wilcox and Aminoff [14] reported normal cardiovascular reflex responses to standing in five patients, whereas Rajput and Rozdilsky [15] found systolic falls of 2, 24, 20, 40, 10 and 60 mm Hg respectively in six patients who were asked to stand voluntarily.

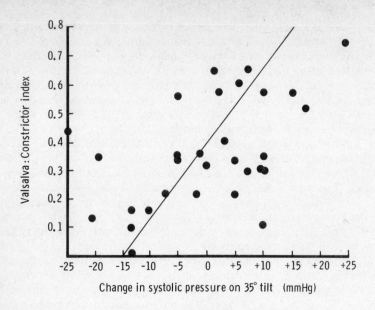

Figure 1 See text.

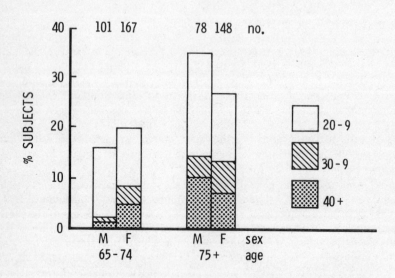

Figure 2 Prevalence of fall in systolic pressure on standing in elderly patients.

114

Quite apart from the possibility of these discrepancies being related to differing methodology, account must be taken of the occurrence of orthostatic hypotension as a normal phenomenon in the elderly. Caird *et al* [16] examined 494 patients aged 65 or over at home for evidence of postural hypotension, measuring blood pressure lying and after standing for 1 minute. Systolic pressures fell by 20 mm Hg or more in 116 (24%), by 30 mm Hg or more in 9 per cent and by 40 mm Hg or more in 5 per cent (Figure 2). The falls were more substantial in the older patients, and were common when possible aggravating factors occurred in combination. Any diastolic changes were not given, nor how often the systolic falls were symptomatic. Paradoxically, Norris *et al* [17] found greater systolic falls in elderly subjects on tilt to 45° but not on tilt to 90 °. Diastolic falls, on the other hand, were more frequent in the elderly on tilt to 90°.

TABLE III Methodology of Valsalva Manoeuvre in various studies of Parkinsonian subjects

Author(s)	Pressure	Duration of expiration	Posture
Sharpey-Schafer [18]	40 mm	About 10 secs	Supine with trunk raised to 45° to horizontal
Gross *et al* [7]	40 mm	12 secs	? Supine
Aminoff and Wilcox [5]	40 mm	Until maximum pulse pressure decrease had persisted for at least 7 secs	? Supine
Reid *et al* [11]	40 mm	10–12 secs	? Supine
Appenzeller and Goss [12]	40 mm	10 secs	Supine and 60° head up

Valsalva Manoeuvre (Table III)

In this procedure patients are asked to blow against a mercury column at 40 mm Hg for approximately 10 seconds, usually in a supine position with the trunk at 45° to the horizontal [18]. Sharpey-Schafer [18] showed a direct relationship in the normal individual between the maximum change in pulse pressure during expiration and the subsequent maximum increase in diastolic pressure during expiration and the subsequent maximum increase in diastolic pressure during the overshoot. Constrictor and accelerator indices are used to assess reactivity. The former measure rise in diastolic pressure after the release of forced expiration, reflecting γ adrenergic activity in the vascular tree, the latter increases in pulse rate during forced expiration, indicating β adrenergic activation of the sino-atrial node with inhibition of vagal tone. Both are related to the percentage falls of pulse pressure during expiration as a measure of the adequacy of the patient's effort and show a fall with increasing age in normal subjects (Figures 3 and 4). Bannister [13] reported normal responses in a group of younger Parkinsonian patients, probably the same described in greater detail one year later [7]. The age range on that occasion was given

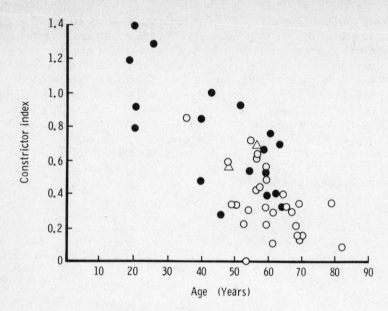

Figure 3 Black circles, controls; open circles, IPD.

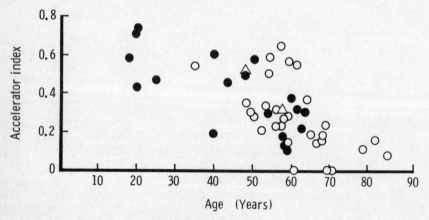

Figure 4 Triangles, post-encephalitic Parkinsonism.

as 40 to 63 years, with a mean of 54.1 years, and responses were compared with a control group of 20 patients of mean age 56.1 years. All had only a mild or moderate disability. The respective mean constrictor indices were 0.546 and 0.563, and mean accelerator indices 0.370 and 0.344; these differences were not significant. The authors noted a discrepancy between evidence of postural hypotension in some patients with normal Valsalva responses. Aminoff and co-workers [5, 6, 14] also found responses comparable to the normal range reported by Gross [19]. Reid *et al* [11] measured the same indices in 30 patients aged between 35 and 82 years. Their disability was greater, 20 walking with difficulty and six only with support. Values corresponded closely to Gross' control subjects [19], were again age related, but showed no association with severity or duration of the disease. In this study, a just significant correlation ($p < 0.05$) was found between the extent of systolic blood pressure fall 1 minute after tilting to 35° and the constrictor index (Figure 1). It was concluded that the response to Valsalva's manoeuvre was a more sensitive guide to baroceptor reflex function than postural blood pressure fall, a conclusion not shared by Gross *et al* [7].

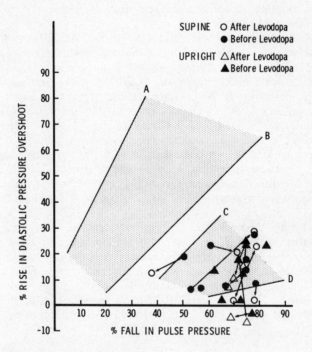

Figure 5 See text.

The findings of Appenzeller and Gross [12] appear at first sight to be discrepant. Using a standard technique (Table III), constrictor indices were measured in 10 patients. Depressed responses by some 60 to 100 per cent were found, but only when comparison was made with a control population aged between 13 and 25 years (Figure 5, A–B). If results are compared to responses in individuals over 40 years (Figure 5, C–D), no significant differences exist. It would appear, therefore, that Valsalva responses in Parkinsonian patients are similar to those in age-matched controls.

117

The response to infusion of sympathomimetic agents

An absent response to tyramine infusion, which acts indirectly by release of noradrenaline from sympathetic nerve endings, coupled with a markedly increased sensitivity to noradrenaline itself, suggests either degeneration of peripheral sympathetic nerves or a severe functional impairment of noradrenaline release at the nerve ending. It has been suggested that this combination, correlating with histochemical evidence of depletion of noradrenaline in sympathetic fibres from skeletal muscle, occurs in cases of idiopathic orthostatic hypotension unaccompanied by evidence of multiple system atrophy [20]. The findings have been contrasted with multiple system atrophy itself, where the most prominent pathological change in the autonomic system lies in the intermediolateral column of the spinal cord [21, 22], accompanied by more normal tyramine sensitivity and less marked supersensitivity to noradrenaline [23] (but see below).

There have been few studies in Parkinson's disease. Aminoff and Wilcox [5] reported responses to noradrenaline infusion in three patients all of whom were complaining of dizziness though without evidence of postural hypotension. Two of the three had constrictor indices (0.26 and 0.36) below the control value of 0.55 derived from another study [19]. Concentrations of noradrenaline needed to elevate systolic pressure by 8 mm Hg lay between 0.018 and 0.025 μg/kg/min, compared with a normal range of 0.05-0.07 μg/kg/min [24]. A year later, Aminoff *et al* [6] reported the mean concentration needed in nine patients to be 0.017 μg/kg/min compared with their own control mean of 0.113 μg/kg/min. Again, all nine patients had vegetative symptoms, most commonly postural dizziness and disturbances of bladder function. In a later study [14] of five patients without vegetative symptoms, sensitivity to noradrenaline infusion was some four times that of normal individuals.

An investigation by Reid *et al* [25] of noradrenaline and tyramine sensitivity failed to confirm these findings. In a group of 11 patients, of mean age 54 years, the mean dose of tyramine needed to elevate systolic pressure by 20 mm Hg lay in the range of 0.029-0.075 mg/kg compared with a control value, from other sources, of 0.020-0.070 mg/kg. For noradrenaline, the respective mean values to elevate systolic pressure by 25 mm Hg were 0.0135 μg/kg and 0.096 μg/kg. Bolus injections were used, though in most other studies, response to infusion of these agents has been assessed.

Other Aspects of Autonomic Function

Sweating

In four out of eight Parkinsonian patients, patchy impairment of sweating has been reported [5], and confirmed subsequently by others [6, 12, 15].

Bladder function

Disturbances of bladder function, not attributable to concurrent anti-cholinergic therapy appear to be relatively common. Frequency of micturition, sometimes with urgency and occasional incontinence, is the most frequent finding [26]. An uninhibited type of bladder response has been reported on cystometry [5, 26].

The effect of Anti-Parkinsonian Therapy

Although anti-cholinergic therapy was initially suggested as a cause of the possible relative hypotension of Parkinsonian patients [13], later studies have not shown any effect on blood pressure of these drugs [8, 9]. Amantadine is said to cause hypotension in up to 30 per cent of patients [27], but most work on the effects of treatment on aspects of autonomic function have centred on dopa or combined therapy.

McDowell and Lee [4] reported a fall of systolic blood pressure by greater than 30 mm Hg in 25 per cent of patients treated with L-dopa. Similarly Calne *et al* [28] described a significant increase in postural fall. There is universal agreement that L-dopa depresses both supine and erect blood pressures, but later work has not confirmed a significant effect on the degree of postural fall [29]. There is similar dissension over the effect of adding a peripheral dopa decarboxylase inhibitor. Watanabe *et al* [30] found a similar reduction of supine and standing mean pressures on the two regimes, though plasma levels of dopa were not compared. When such levels were comparable, Calne *et al* [31] reported supine and erect systolic pressures to be significantly higher on combined therapy, though the postural changes on the two treatments were similar. In another communication [29], the same authors concluded that supine and head up (35°) systolic and diastolic levels, and the degree of postural fall, were not significantly different when treatment with dopa plus a dopa decarboxylase inhibitor was compared with dopa alone.

Appenzeller and Goss [12] measured Valsalva responses in six patients before and after L-dopa therapy. Two showed a reduction of the constrictor index both in the supine and 60° head-up position. Reid *et al* [29] observed a fall in the mean constrictor index in 17 patients with L-dopa, the value reverting to pre-treatment levels on combined therapy. Despite the fall in mean constrictor index, some patients showed an unchanged or increased value. The mean constrictor index reverts to its pre-treatment level when a peripheral dopa decarboxylase inhibitor is added [29] suggesting that the impairment of baroreflex responses induced by dopa is mediated by a peripheral mechanism. There is, however, no correlation between the alteration of Valsalva responsiveness and dose of dopa or indeed the severity of the Parkinson's disease. Neither treatment with dopa nor with combined therapy influences response to bolus injections of tyramine or noradrenaline [32].

Few studies have been published concerning the effects of bromocriptine on autonomic function. It appears to have a similar influence to that of L-dopa on blood pressure [33].

119

TABLE IV A comparison of the Clinical, Biochemical and Pathological features of IPD, IOH with or without Parkinsonism and Multiple System Atrophy

	Presenting Symptoms	Blood Pressure And Postural Responses	Valsalva Response	Resting Noradrenaline Levels	Response of Noradrenaline Levels to Posture Change	Effect of Tyramine Infusion	Effect of Noradrenaline Infusion
IDIOPATHIC PARKINSON'S DISEASE	Rigidity, bradykinesia, tremor tec.	Possible mild orthostatic hypotension	Similar to age matched controls	?	?	? Normal	Normal or increased
IDIOPATHIC ORTHOSTATIC HYPOTENSION ± PARKINSONISM	Impotence, nocturnal diuresis, anhidrosis, postural dizziness, Parkinsonian syndrome usually late	Severe orthostatic hypotension	Depressed	Probably depressed	Depressed	No consistent findings	Increased
MULTIPLE SYSTEM ATROPHY	Autonomic symptoms usually followed by pyramidal, Parkinsonian and cerebellar features	Severe orthostatic hypotension	Depressed	Probably depressed	Depressed	No consistent findings	Increased

TABLE IV cont.

	Substantia Nigra And Locus Coeruleus	Lewy Bodies	Sympathetic Ganglia	Lewy Bodies	Intermedio-Lateral Columns	Hypothalamus
IDIOPATHIC PARKINSON'S DISEASE	Marked neuronal loss and depigmentation (predominantly middle third of substantia nigra)	Numerous	Neuronal loss uncommon	Frequent	Normal	Occasional Lewy Bodies
IDIOPATHIC ORTHOSTATIC HYPOTENSION ± PARKINSONISM	As above or Lewy bodies alone or normal	May be numerous	Various degenerative changes including neuronal loss, often normal	Frequent	Abnormal	Usually normal
MULTIPLE SYSTEM ATROPHY	Marked neuronal loss and depigmentation (predominantly lateral two thirds of substantia nigra)	Absent or occasional	Various degenerative changes including neuronal loss, often normal	Absent	Abnormal	Usually normal

The Relationship to Idiopathic Orthostatic Hypotension (IOH)

The first description of this syndrome is generally credited to Bradbury and Eggleston [34]. Their third case complained of peripheral numbness and was found to have unequal pupils, brisk knee reflexes and extensor plantar responses. The concept of a multiple system atrophy, with extensive neurological pathology outside the autonomic nervous system, has been identified with Shy and Drager following their publication of a clinicopathological study in 1960 [1], though the possibility of neurological syndromes associated with IOH had antedated their description. Ganshorn and Horton [35] reported a patient with nystagmus, dysarthria and gait ataxia, together with pyramidal signs and tremor. In a discussion of the paper, Woltman added a similar case who in addition showed widespread fasciculation.

In some early descriptions, failure to separate those cases of IOH due to specific diseases, such as tabes, led to confusion regarding the associated neurological features [36, 37]. Young [38] recorded the first case of IOH with a Parkinsonian syndrome, though in addition the patient had ataxia. Similar cases followed [39] culminating in Shy and Drager's [1] description of widespread pathological changes, including abnormalities in the inferior olivary nucleus, cerebellum, pons, substantia nigra, locus coeruleus, putamen and globus pallidus. Autonomic system changes included pallor, vacuolation and chromatolysis of the ganglia together with cell depletion of the intermediolateral columns of the spinal cord.

The time relationship of the autonomic and other neurological symptoms in such cases has been variously reported. Shy and Drager [1] considered the usual sequence of autonomic symptoms to be impotence or loss of libido, followed successively by nocturnal diuresis, then urinary retention, dizziness and blurred vision on rising. Anhidrosis was an associated feature. It was suggested that other neurological features appeared later, a view shared by Thomas and Schirger [40, 41], who found the interval to lie most commonly between two and six years. Schatz *et al* [42], however, considered neurological symptoms to antedate autonomic phenomena in the majority, sometimes by many months. Some such cases, though still apparently developing postural hypotension at a late stage, will be found to have presented with impotence or urinary frequency [43].

The description of a number of cases of IOH with close clinical relationship to IPD [38–43], but of others with a more generalised neurological disorder, has led to the concept of two separate syndromes [22, 44, 45]. The former, with autonomic failure with or without Parkinsonism, is considered to occur at a later age, and to have a better prognosis than cases of multiple system atrophy. Pathological findings have served to confirm the validity of the distinction. In the former, changes analogous to IPD are seen with Lewy bodies and characteristic degenerative changes in the substantia nigra and locus coeruleus [22, 46, 47]. In some instances, asymptomatic Lewy bodies have been reported [21, 48]. In multiple system atrophy, the process is that of striato-nigral degeneration [49, 50] with absent [22, 44, 47, 51] or only occasional Lewy bodies, as indeed may exceptionally be found in cases of striato-nigral degeneration alone [47]. The extrapyramidal changes may coexist with an olivo-ponto-cerebellar degeneration.

The pathological correlates of the autonomic symptoms of IOH have been reported more variously. In cases of multiple system atrophy, hypothalamic changes, though difficult to quantify, have either been slight [1] or absent [21, 44, 51]. Degeneration of the intermediolateral column of the spinal cord has been regarded as invariable [45], though it occasionally has been reported to be absent [50, 52] but such reports have tended not to include quantitative analysis. Reappraisal of one such case [52], led to the conclusion that significant cell depletion did in fact exist [46]. Sympathetic ganglia changes have been relatively minor [1, 44, 47, 49 50], or absent [21, 22, 51].

Pathological changes in isolated IOH or with Parkinson's alone, are somewhat similar. Hypothalamic changes appear slight and, whereas sympathetic ganglia have frequently shown Lewy bodies [21, 46, 47, 48], or atypical hyaline structures [46], cell reduction has been reported less commonly. Again, the abnormalities predominate in the intermediolateral columns [21].

Although these pathological descriptions suggested a shared basis for the autonomic changes of the two syndromes, the use of a number of biochemical characteristics has been forwarded as a method to distinguish central and peripheral types of autonomic failure. In a study of five patients with IOH alone, Kontos et al [20] found no response to tyramine infusion but enhanced vasoconstrictor responses to intra-arterial noradrenaline. Using a histochemical technique, an absence of noradrenaline was demonstrated from vasomotor nerve terminals in blood vessels of skeletal muscle. Ziegler et al [53] pursued the concept further, assessing ten patients, six of whom had multiple system atrophy. Plasma noradrenaline levels failed to rise in moving from the supine to the upright position in both groups, but were depressed in the supine posture in only those patients without evidence of neurological disease outside the autonomic system. The authors suggested patients with IOH alone had a peripheral defect and predicted they would have an absent response to tyramine with marked supersensitivity to exogenous noradrenaline. Those with multiple system atrophy were thought more likely to show a near normal tyramine response and a less marked supersensitivity to noradrenaline. This concept would be difficult to accept, knowing the shared pathological basis for autonomic failure in the two syndromes, and further experience has not supported it. Bannister et al [54], assessed ten patients, one of whom had IOH with Parkinsonism, the remainder multiple system atrophy. Plasma noradrenaline levels were markedly reduced compared to controls in the supine position and failed to rise with posture change. In a further paper [23], ten patients were studied, seven with multiple system atrophy, one with Parkinsonism and two with IOH alone. Resting supine plasma noradrenaline levels were depressed in all of them, and showed little response to tilt. Of the three patients without multiple system atrophy, noradrenaline levels were severely depressed in one, but in the other two comparable to those for cases of multiple system atrophy. Contrary to the proposition of Ziegler et al [53] there was no consistent difference in tyramine and noradrenaline sensitivity according to the presence or absence of other neurological features. Indeed, the most marked sensitivity to tyramine infusion occurred in a patient with the most marked noradrenaline reactivity, a paradox implying that tyramine-releasable stores of noradrenaline were intact, yet marked sensitivity to circulating, exogenous noradrenaline coincided. The possibility arises therefore that tyramine releasable stores of noradrenaline may not necessarily reflect the stores releasable by neurogenic activity [23]. The matter is further complicated by the contribution the deafferentation of the baroceptor reflex arc might make to the blood pressure response to noradrenaline infusion. It seems clear that a profound supersensitivity to noradrenaline with loss of tyramine response implies either degeneration of peripheral sympathetic fibres or marked impairment of noradrenaline release mechanisms. In IOH, with or without other neurological manifestations, such examples appear uncommon and the majority of these cases are indistinguishable on the basis of the biochemical characteristics considered.

In what way does IPD relate to these disorders? (Table IV). The evidence for disturbances of autonomic function in IPD is relatively minor. A significant decrease of blood pressure seems likely in those most severely disabled, but orthostatic hypotension is not prominent when compared with age matched controls, and a similar conclusion applies to Valsalva responses. Hypersensitivity to noradrenaline infusion is encountered though not to the degree found in multiple system atrophy. Furthermore, pathological changes in the autonomic nervous system have not been conspicuous. Though intermediolateral cell column degeneration is the rule in cases of IOH with Parkinsonism, such changes have not been observed in IPD [47]. Typical Lewy bodies, or atypical extracellular inclusions [15, 55, 56], are frequently found in the sympathetic ganglia of patients with IPD as indeed they are in patients with IOH and associated Parkinsonism [21, 46, 47, 48]. In the latter condition, intermediolateral cell column degeneration appears more relevant to the autonomic symptoms; furthermore, in IPD, neuronal cell loss, as opposed to inclusion body formation in the sympathetic ganglia, has been reported less commonly [15]. Rajput and Rozdilsky [15] described such changes and attempted to correlate them with the degree of postural hypotension found in life, in a clinicopathological study of six patients. Cell loss from the sympathetic ganglia occurred in three, one of whom showed some clinical features suggesting an overlap with multiple system atrophy. The changes in the other two cases were slight or moderate. Only a qualitative assessment of neuronal population was used and it remains to be established that abnormalities in sympathetic ganglia are of symptomatic relevance in patients with IPD.

Are there cases which do not fit readily into the diagnostic categories of IPD, IOH with or without Parkinsonism and multiple system atrophy? Possible examples are those described by Vanderhaeghen et al [48], the sixth case of Rajput and Rozdilsky [15] and the case of Thapedi et al [57]. The patient of Vanderhaeghen et al [48] is closest to IOH with Parkinsonism, the only unusual features being wasting of the small hand muscles (exclusion of a peripheral nerve lesion was not undertaken) and some neuronal rarefaction of the anterior horn cells. The case of Thapedi et al [57] more nearly corresponds to multiple system atrophy. The distribution of lesions in the substantia nigra was not stated, a predominant involvement of the middle third would favour IPD, but of the lateral half or two-thirds, a striato-nigral degeneration as part of multiple system atrophy. Occasionally Lewy bodies were present in the brain stem, but since these have been reported in hypoglossal and dorsal vagal nuclei and in substantia nigra and locus coeruleus in striato-nigral degeneration [58], and since there was marked astrocytic proliferation in the putamen, it seems appropriate to classify the case as an example of multiple system atrophy. The sixth case of Rajput and Rozdilsky [15] is more problematic. Though labelled as IPD by the authors, the presentation with postural dizziness, four years before a Parkinsonian syndrome developed, and the abnormalities in the intermediolateral cell columns of the spinal cord at post-mortem examination, suggest the case was most likely an example of IOH with Parkinsonism.

The concept of a division (Table IV) into three clinical and pathological entities therefore appears justified. Less certain is their relationship to circulating levels of noradrenaline and the response to infusion of sympathomimetic agents. Cases that cross the boundaries between the three syndromes are likely to be encountered occasionally, but from understanding of the typical evolution of IOH with Parkinsonism, patients presenting with a typical Parkinsonian syndrome are unlikely to subsequently manifest profound autonomic disturbances. Minor abnormalities of autonomic function undoubtedly exist in IPD but the pathological basis for such changes is yet to be established.

Acknowledgements

Table I is reproduced by permission of Dr R J Marttila and the editor, *European Neurology*. S Karger AG, Basel.

Figures 1, 3 and 4 are reproduced by permission of Dr D B Calne and the editor, *Clinical Science and Molecular Medicine*.

Figure 2 is reproduced by permission of Professor F I Caird and the editor, *British Heart Journal*.

Figure 5 is reproduced by permission of Dr O Appenzeller and the editor, *Archives of Neurology*.

References

1   Shy GM, Drager GA. *Arch Neurol 1960;2:*511
2   Parkinson J. *An essay on the shaking palsy 1817;* London, Sherwood, Neely and Jones
3   Barbeau A, Gillo-Joffroy L, Boucher R, Nowaczynski W, Genest J. *Science 1969;165:* 291
4   McDowell FH, Lee JE. *Ann Intern Med 1970;72:*751
5   Aminoff MJ, Wilcox CS. *Brit med J 1971;4:*80
6   Aminoff MJ, Wilcox CS, Slater JDH. *Acta Neurol Scand 1972;Suppl 51:*105
7   Gross M, Bannister R, Godwin-Austen R. *Lancet 1972;i:*174
8   Aminoff MJ, Gross M, Laatz B, Vakil SD, Petrie A, Calne DB. *J Neurol Neurosurg Psychiat 1975;38:*73
9   Martilla RJ, Rinne UK. *Eur Neurol 1977;16:*73
10 Hoehn MM, Yahr MD. *Neurology (Minneap) 1967;17:*427

11   Reid JL, Calne DB, George CF, Pallis C, Vakil SD. *Clin Sci Mol Med 1971;41:*63
12   Appenzeller O, Goss JE. *Arch Neurol 1971;24:*50
13   Bannister R. *Lancet 1971;ii:*175
14   Wilcox CS, Aminoff MJ. *Brit J Clin Pharmacol 1976;3:*207
15   Rajput AH, Rozdilsky B. *J Neurol Neurosurg Psychiat 1976;39:*1092
16   Caird FI, Andrews GR, Kennedy RD. *Brit Heart J 1973;35:*527
17   Norris AH, Shock NW, Yiengst MJ. *Circulation 1953;8:*521
18   Sharpey-Schafer EP. *Brit med J 1955;1:*693
19   Gross M. *Clin Sci Mol Med 1970;38:*491
20   Kontos HA, Richardson DW, Norvell JE. *Ann Intern Med 1975;82:*336
21   Johnson RH, De J Lee G, Oppenheimer DR, Spalding JMK. *Quart J Med 1966;35:*276
22   Bannister R, Oppenheimer DR. *Brain 1972;95:*457
23   Bannister R, Davies B, Holly E, Rosenthal T, Sever P. *Brain 1979;102:*163
24   Goldenberg M, Pines KL, Baldwin E de F, Greene DG, Roh CE. *Amer J Med 1948;5:*792
25   Reid JL, Calne DB, George CF, Vakil SD. *J Clin Pharmacol 1971;12:*465
26   Murnaghan GF. *Brit J Urol 1961;33:*403
27   Birdwood GFB, Gilder SSB, Wink CAS. In *Parkinson's disease. A new approach to treatment 1971;*51. London and New York, Academic Press
28   Calne DB, Brennan J, Spiers ASD, Stern GM. *Brit med J 1970;1:*474
29   Reid JL, Calne DB, George CF, Vakil SD. *Clin Sci Mol Med 1972;43:*851
30   Watanabe AM, Chase TN, Cardon PV. *Clin Pharmacol Ther 1970;11:*740
31   Calne DB, Petrie A, Rao S, Reid JL, Vakil SD. *Brit J Pharmacol 1972;44:*162
32   Reid JL, Calne DB, George CF, Vakil SD. *Clin Pharmacol Ther 1972;13:*400
33   Parkes JD, Debono AG, Marsden CD. *J Neurol Neurosurg Psychiat 1976;39:*1101
34   Bradbury S, Eggleston C. *Amer Heart J 1925;1:*73
35   Ganshorn JA, Horton BT. *Proc Staff Meet Mayo Clin 1934;9:*541
36   Chew EM, Barker NW. *NW Med, Seattle 1936;35:*297
37   Ellis LB, Haynes FW. *Arch Intern Med 1936;58:*773
38   Young RH. *Ann Intern Med 1941;15:*910
39   Nylin G, Levander M. *Ann Intern Med 1948;28:*723
40   Thomas JE, Schirger A. *Arch Neurol 1963;8:*204
41   Thomas JE, Schirger A. *Arch Neurol 1970;22:*289
42   Schatz J, Podolsky S, Frame B. *JAMA 1963;186:*537
43   Bannister R, Ardill L, Fentem P. *Brain 1967;90:*725
44   Graham JG, Oppenheimer DR. *J Neurol Neurosurg Psychiat 1969;32:*28
45   Bannister R. *Lancet 1979;ii:*404
46   Roessmann U, Van den Noort S, McFarland DE. *Arch Neurol 1971;24:*503
47   Schober R, Langston, JW, Forno LS. *Eur Neurol 1975;13:*177
48   Vanderhaeghen JJ, Perier O, Sternon JE. *Arch Neurol 1970;22:*207
49   Schwarz GA. *Arch Neurol 1967;16:*123
50   Hughes RC, Cartlidge NEF, Millac P. *J Neurol Neurosurg Psychiat 1970;33:*363
51   Spokes EGS, Bannister R, Oppenheimer DR. *J Neurol Sci 1979;43:*59
52   Martin JB, Travis RH, Van den Noort S. *Arch Neurol 1968;19:*163
53   Ziegler MG, Lake CR, Kopin IJ. *N Engl J Med 1977;296:*293
54   Bannister R, Sever P, Gross M. *Brain 1977;100:*327
55   Jage R, Waden H, Bethlem J. *J Neurol Neurosurg Psychiat 1960;23:*283
56   Forno LS. *J Neuropathol Exp Neurol 1973;22:*159
57   Thapedi IM, Ashenhurst EM, Rozdilsky B. *Neurology (Minneap) 1971;21:*26
58   Adams RD, van Bogaert L, Eecken HV. *J Neuropathol Exp Neurol 1964;23:*584

Chapter 16

VISUAL EVOKED POTENTIALS AND THE SEVERITY OF PARKINSON'S DISEASE

I Bodis-Wollner, M D Yahr and J Thornton

It is becoming clear that Parkinson's disease may involve widespread areas of the cerebral cortex in addition to the basal ganglia. Morphological studies show neuronal loss [1,2] and atrophy, while impaired cerebral function can be implied from electrophysiological and blood flow studies [3].

In 1976 we reported [4] that the visual evoked potential (VEP) latency was delayed in several patients suffering from Parkinson's disease. To summarise briefly, about two-thirds of 36 patients with Parkinson's disease had prolonged visual evoked potential latency compared to age-matched controls. There was no correlation between VEP latency and age. In five patients in whom evoked potentials were tested before initiation of therapy and then again after dopaminergic therapy was administered, it appeared that there was a change in the VEP latency at least in one eye, suggesting that catecholaminergic pathways have either indirect or direct effect on the generation of visual evoked potentials [5].

Several questions are raised by these findings. First, whether VEP latency changes in Parkinson's disease represent an epiphenomenon or an abnormality which is intrinsic to the pathophysiology of this disease. Secondly, whether or not other visual abnormalities occur in patients suffering from Parkinson's disease, and their relationship to dopaminergic neural mechanisms. In this chapter, we will address ourselves to the first question, with special reference to a relationship between visual evoked potential latency changes and the severity of Parkinson's disease.

Methods

Seventy-four hospitalised and ambulatory volunteer patients with the diagnosis of Parkinson's disease were studied. This includes retrospective data of 36 patients reported for VEP latency earlier [5]. In terms of the number of untreated patients and severity of their disease, the present group of 38 patients differs noticeably from the earlier group. Patients considered in this report predominantly belong to the less severely affected ones, as we will detail. The severity rating from I to V was in accord with that of Hoehn and Yahr [6]. A rating is routinely given to each Parkinsonian patient at the time of their visit to their attending neurologist affiliated with the authors' institution. Most patients included in this study were neurologically evaluated and rated for severity (as part of their routine clinical evaluation) by the authors and Dr R Duvoisin, so that the subjective severity rating is fairly consistent within patients. This rating was now retrospectively considered from the patient's chart. We tried to select the rating obtained closest in time to the VEP measurement. The time difference between the EP measurement and severity rating was usually less than 6 months. Often, they were obtained on the same day. Of the seventy-four patients studied with VEP, we were able to ascertain the severity rating in fifty-seven. Of the fifty-seven, thirty-seven belong to the new group, while twenty patients belong to the group whose VEP study alone was reported earlier.

Patients with ophthalmological abnormalities, opacities of the media, visual acuity of worse than 20/50, and gross eye movement abnormalities were excluded. Pupil reaction was assessed with a flashlight and in several patients, pupil reactivity was measured with pupillometric methods (Korczyn and Yahr, in preparation). Since the VEP study was conducted at a constant mean luminance after sufficient light adaptation, patients who had sluggish pupil reactions to light were not excluded from the study. The effect of pupil size *per se* on VEP latency is negligible as long as it is larger than 3 mm in diameter (S Sokol, personal communication). The mean age of the patients was 62 years. A control group consisted of 49 volunteers. Their mean age was 47 years.

Visual evoked potentials. Two sets of stimuli were used. Vertical gratings with sinusoidal luminance profile were electronically alternated at the rate of 1 Hertz on a CRT screen as described in detail elsewhere [7]. Checkerboard patterns were produced on a photographic slide which was projected on a screen with a slide projector. An oscillating mirror produced the required reversal or $180°$ phase alternation of the checkerboard pattern. The spatial frequency of both patterns was 2.3 cycles/degree, and the diameter of each circular screen subtended $3.8°$ of arc at the observer's eye. A small fixation point was provided. The mean luminance of the gratings was 10 foot lamberts, while that of the checkerboard pattern was 70 foot lamberts. The contrast, expressed as the luminance difference of bright and dark pattern elements divided by the sum of their luminances, was 0.55 for gratings and 0.9 for checks. Unfortunately we had no facility to produce checks on the CRT or sinusoidal gratings in the projection system. The difference in mean luminance and contrast between the two stimuli would tend to make a comparison between check and grating latencies rather tenuous. However, as we shall describe in detail, we compared the VEP latency of patients to controls for each stimulus separately. Following the method of Halliday *et al* [8], the latency of the evoked potential was measured as the time from the onset of pattern reversal to the peak of the major positive EP deflection recorded at the occipital electrode. The "major" positive wave was identifiable as the largest amplitude positive deflection between 98 and 220 msec following pattern reversal (Figures 1a and b).

127

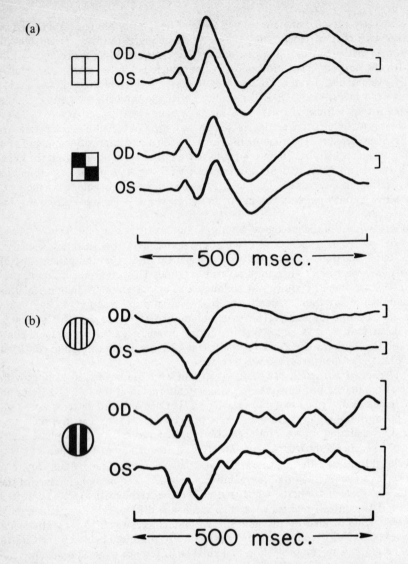

(a)

OD
OS

OD
OS

← 500 msec. →

(b)

OD
OS

OD

OS

← 500 msec. →

Figure 1a, VEPs obtained with check stimulus in a patient with Parkinson's disease at two different luminance levels. EP trace obtained for 1 Hz modulation rate. Positivity down. Latency was measured as the time taken from stimulus reversal (beginning of the trace) to the tip of the downgoing hump occurring between 96 and 200 msec. following trigger. Latencies were 114 msec. O.D. and 112 msec. O.S. (top: higher luminance) and 130 msec. O.D. and 130 msec. O.S. (bottom: standard luminance). Calibration mark corresponds to 5 microvolts. b, Grating stimulus at two luminance levels corresponding to the one used for checks (top: 128 msec. O.D. and 122 msec. O.S., and 114 msec. O.D. and 130 msec. O.S.). Calibration mark corresponds to 5 microvolts.

Statistical analysis. As detailed earlier [9], normality and abnormality of the VEP latency is reported in reference to the data of a control population studied with identical methods in our laboratory. The covariance matrix and the mean of all right eye latencies and all left eye latencies were compared between controls and patients with P.D. A multivariate analysis [10] was used to test the null hypothesis that the mean response of the control group is equal to the mean response of each of the four separate P.D. groups. Also tested was the hypothesis that the covariance matrices are equal. Discriminant analysis [11] was used to study patient data grouped under the four categories of severity of P.D. In the scattergram, representing the right and left eye latencies of the control population, an ellipse has been drawn within which 95 per cent of the normal population would be expected to fall (Figure 2). For each patient, then, a "C" score was derived based on the ob-

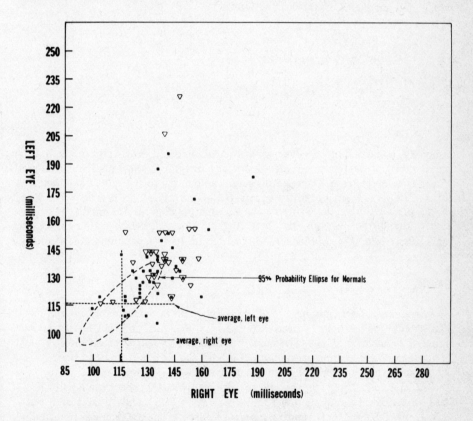

Figure 2 Scattergram of EP latencies obtained in the right (abscissa) and left eye (ordinate) of Parkinson's disease patients with grating stimuli reported in 1978 (triangles) and those studied since (squares). All data points within the ellipse represent the 95 per cent probability of belonging to the age-matched control population.

129

served right and left eye latency, representing the distance from the centre of the normal probability ellipse. The bivariate normal distribution was used to approximate the joint probability distribution of the left and right eye latencies found in a normal population. Five parameters are required to completely specify this distribution function. The parameters are 1, the expected (mean) value (b_R), and standard deviation of a normal individual's right eye latency (μ_R), 2, the expected value (b_L) and standard deviation of a normal individual's left eye latency (μ_L), and 3, the correlation (p) which exists in the normal population between the right eye latency (R) and the left eye latency (L). These parameters can be estimated from latencies measured from a random sample of the normal population.

For the bivariate normal ellipsoidal contours can be constructed which contain specified proportions of the distribution [12]. The equation of the ellipse which contains $100\alpha\%$ of the distribution is

$$\left[\frac{R - \mu_R}{b_R}\right]^2 -2p\left[\frac{R - \mu_R}{b_R}\right]\left[\frac{L - \mu_L}{b_L}\right] + \left[\frac{L - \mu_L}{b_L}\right]^2 = 2(1 - p^2)\log(1 - \alpha) = C^2$$

Using the estimates of the five parameters obtained from a study of the normal population and the measured latencies of any individual, the equation can be used to calculate a C^2 score. The resulting score can be used to assess the likelihood that this individual is a member of the normal population. The C score is directly related to the probability of belonging to the control population. The smaller the probability, the further away is the observed value from the centre of the ellipse, the higher the C score. Mean C scores for each group of P.D. patients were calculated.

Results

1 *VEP latency using grating stimuli in normals.* In 80 control subjects the mean VEP latency of the right eye was 116 ± 8.1 milliseconds, and that of the left eye was 116 ± 7.7 milliseconds. The mean interocular difference was 4.1 msec. The 95 per cent confidence limit of the normal interocular difference was 10 msec, while the upper 95 per cent limit of the normal latency was 131 msec.
2 *VEP latency using grating stimuli in patients with P.D.* The mean latency of 57 Parkinson's disease patients was 133.7 ± 14.1 msec. O.D. and 137.4 ± 23.8 msec. O.S. This is 5.3 msec (O.D.) and 5.6 msec (O.S.) shorter latency than was reported by us earlier for 36 patients of whom 20 were also included in this analysis. However, in the earlier study there were more severely affected patients. The composition of the present study is as follows. There were fifty-seven patients. In group I there were 13 patients with a mean age of 64 years. Mean duration was 2.5 years. Lat-

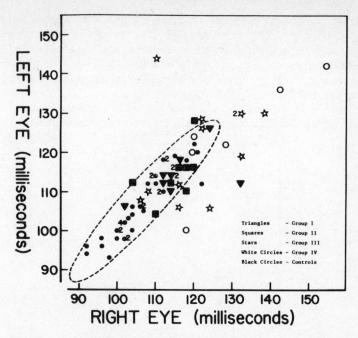

Figure 3 Scattergram of VEP latency obtained with checkerboard pattern stimulus in patients and controls. Patients' data are broken down according to the stage of their disease.

ency was 128.4 ± 8.1 msec O.D. and 127.6 ± 20.4 msec O.S. In group II there were 9 patients with a mean age of 61 years. Mean duration was 4 years. Latency was 127.6 ± 16.9 msec O.D. and 128.5 ± 10.6 msec O.S. In group III there were 23 patients with a mean age of 63 years and a mean duration of 8.2 years. The mean latency was 137.9 ± 12.3 msec O.D. and 143 ± 25.6 msec O.S. In group IV there were 12 patients with a mean age of 61 years and a mean duration of 9.7 years. The mean latency was 136.5 ± 18 msec O.D. and 145 ± 25.6 msec O.S.

3 *Checkerboard latency.* Using checkerboard stimuli in 38 control patients, the latency was 107.5 ± 7.9 msec O.D. and 107.5 ± msec O.S. In 36 P.D. patients the latency was 119.8 ± 10.9 msec O.D. and 118 ± 10.6 msec O.S. Broken down into groups of severity, the mean latency was 115.6 ± 8.4 msec O.D. and 114 ± 5.6 msec O.S. in 9 patients in Group I. In 9 patients of Group II it was 115 ± 5.2 msec O.D. and 115 ± 6.5 msec O.S. In 12 patients of Group III it was 121.5 ± 10.6 msec O.D. and 121 ± 12.4 msec O.S., while in 6 patients of Group IV it was 130.4 ± 14.6 msec O.D. and 124 ± 14.6 msec O.S.

4 *C scores.* As explained in the Methods section, the C score expresses how far away is a given observed latency of the left and right eye of a patient from the centre of the ellipse representing the 95 per cent probability of belonging to the control population. The derived mean C score representing 95 per cent probability of being normal was 2.1 for gratings and .8 for checks. The scores for each group

131

were: Group I— .7 (gratings) and 1 (checks); Group II— 3.2 (gratings) and .6 (checks); Group III— 14.4 (gratings) and 2.7 (checks); and, Group IV— 18.3 (gratings) and 2.9 (checks). The hypothesis could be clearly rejected that all patients and controls belong to the same group and thus, based on the C score, which incorporates interocular coherence or dispersion as well as absolute latency, Group II, III and IV P.D. patients can be easily distinguished from controls but group I cannot. There is an impressively clear trend toward having higher C scores and thus greater EP latency abnormality with increasing severity of the disease (Figures 3-6).

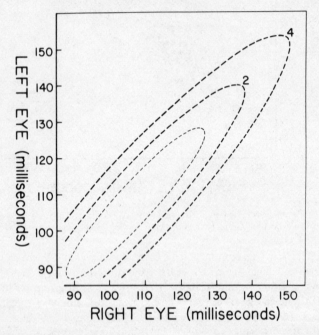

Figure 4 Illustrating the method of estimating EP latency abnormality of a population rather than of an individual patient. This figure is based on check latencies. Two ellipses labelled 2 and 4 represent "isoprobabilities" of belonging to the normal population (fine interrupted-line ellipse) based on the VEP latency of the right and left eyes of the control population. Ellipses 2 and 4 represent the "C" value which represents the degree of abnormality of a given population. For details, see Appendix and text.

5 *Unmeasurable latency*. We have encountered several patients in whom we could not with security measure the latency when the trace looked noisy, or no positive wave stood out between 98 and 200 msec. Electrode resistance and other technical factors were well under control. EP noise was not clearly related to the tremor of a patient even if he had one. Based on an evaluation of "attention", by observation it was rarely possible to predict which patients would produce noisy EPs, since some seemed to be attending to the screen with eyes open, and had no

132

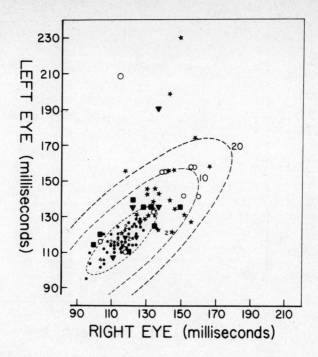

Figure 5 VEP latency obtained with grating stimulus in the control population (filled circles) and Parkinsonian patients (stage I—triangles, stage II—squares, stage III—stars, stage IV—circles). Isoprobability ellipses with C values of 10 and 20 are shown for illustration.

obvious EPs. In several patients, the record was too difficult to measure for latency before treatment, whereas following treatment it was possible to measure the latency of the major positive deflection.

6 *The effect of treatment.* Using grating patterns, in 10 patients the VEP latency could be measured before and after treatment. Untreated patients had a mean of 141.6 ± 8.6 msec O.D. and 138.6 ± 25.2 msec O.S. Following treatment the group mean was 131 ± 13 msec O.D. and O.S. The C scores were 13.1 before treatment, and became 5.2 after treatment. This is a significant change toward the "normal" score of C = 2.1, which is the C score representing 95 per cent probability of being normal. There were two patients in Group I, one in Group II, five in Group III, and two in Group IV. Apparently the large improvement in the C score represents not so much an absolute latency change but rather a normalisation of interocular dispersion. While the mean interocular difference was 21.8 msec before treatment, it was 11.6 msec following treatment. The pretreatment interocular difference is 5 S.D. away from the normal, while the post-treatment value is near the 2 S.D. limit. In three patients with large pretreatment interocular difference, the EP latency became shorter in the delayed eye but became longer in the "normal" eye following treatment, causing a disappearance of the pretreatment interocular difference. One pos-

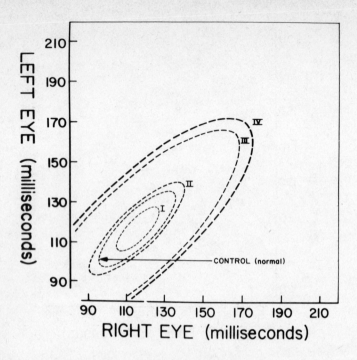

Figure 6 VEP latency abnormality using grating stimuli in different groups of P.D. patients. Ellipses were calculated based on the average C score for each group of patients. The average ellipse for patients in severity I group (mild disease) is within the normal population (control), whereas ellipses representing the II, III and IV stages of the disease are outside the normal ellipse and show greater and greater distance from it.

sible explanation of this puzzle could be that the major positive wave was mistakenly identified as such, resulting in a spurious pretreatment normal latency. However in seven of the ten patients it is clear that treatment normalised the abnormal interocular difference.

Discussion

There is a wealth of evidence which attests to the diagnostic value of VEP measurements in multiple sclerosis where both absolute delays and abnormal interocular differences occur. VEP measurements in P.D. are less important for diagnosis: rather they contribute to a new understanding of the disease. Latency was abnormal in 47 of 73 patients (64%). The present data not only reaffirm the fact that VEP latency is prolonged in Parkinson's disease, but also show in 57 patients studied that there is a correlation between VEP latency abnormalities and the severity of the disease. Since all patients were rated for severity by neurologists with experience in evaluating the clinical picture of Parkinson's disease and without knowledge of the EP latency, the concordance of objective VEP latency and subjective severity rating is encouraging. It suggests that EP changes may reflect an essential aspect of the pathophysiology of Parkinson's disease and raise the possibility that there is a slowed conduction in afferent pathways.

We do not yet know where or how EP changes and clinical manifestations of Parkinson's disease are related. Since in general the more severe the disease the more medication is used, it would be possible to argue that EP latency changes are caused by medication rather than the disease process. This is unlikely since we noticed abdominal EPs in patients who never were treated, and EP normalisation following treatment. Whether or not treatment in addition to the disease can worsen EP abnormalities in some patients rather than normalising them is left open by monocular data of three patients. On the whole, the worse the disease, the longer is the VEP latency, and treatment improves it. From these facts, it would appear that EP changes in P.D. are related to the pathophysiological changes underlying the clinical manifestations of the disease.

We have discussed several possibilities concerning the anatomy of these changes previously [5]. It is possible that the influence of subcortical circuits, involving the basal ganglia, are manifested by 100 msec component following stimulation in the "cortical" EP, and it is conceivable that subcortical pathology can change VEP latency. One must consider other explanations as well. VEP delays in this disease could occur if there was, according to earlier suggestions, a generalised dopaminergic deficiency state in the disease. Retinal [14] and visual cortical [15] dopaminergic connections have been demonstrated in animal experiments. Thus it will be fruitful to examine visual competence of patients with Parkinson's disease using psychophysical tests involving spatial and temporal contrast sensitivity measurements [16]. In addition to dopamine pathways, one should consider possible abnormalities in other catecholaminergic routes, using norepinephrine (noradrenaline) rather than dopamine as transmitter. It is known that in P.D., abnormalities may involve also norepinephrine as a transmitter [17]. A noradrenergic pathway from the locus coeruleus to the visual cortex has been established [18] and norepinephrine treatment is capable of shifting the plasticity period of binocular development of monocularly deprived kittens [19], suggesting a role of this catecholamine in the functional properties of binocular neurones of the visual cortex. In this respect, it is of especial interest that many patients tested in this study showed interocular latency differences and the most obvious VEP change following therapy was a normalisation of the pretreatment interocular difference. This was apparent as a dramatic improvement of the C score expressing interocular coherence of the treated patient group, while the mean latencies improved only modestly.

The measurement of latency has been well established as the most consistent and diagnostically useful index of the pattern VEP in man. We, too, considered latency because it has been well standardised and is subject to less variability than any other measurement. Our own "control" data reported here and elsewhere [5, 9] attest to the validity of latency measurements and the difficulty [12] of normative amplitude measurements when EP is measured at slow (1-2 Hz) pattern presentation rates. We thus adhered to this standard method of VEP evaluation. Nevertheless, as

135

we pointed out earlier, it is possible that on occasion "latency" is incorrectly measured when the EP trace and the major positive wave are not typical. In fact, when this happened we did not consider pretreatment data of patients. Significantly though, the latency could be easily measured in these patients following therapy; thus it is apparent that therapy affects the VEP, and suggests that besides latency there are other aspects of the VEP which are affected in Parkinson's disease. The problem of identifying "latency" in pathology is not unique to measuring EPs in P.D.: indeed for several differential diagnostic problems of clinical neurology and ophthalmology, it would be desirable to establish criteria for a reliable measurement of other aspects of the VEP than mere latency. For the time being, a definite measurement of latency independent of amplitude changes must await a more thorough understanding of physiologically meaningful components of the transient pattern VEP. Nevertheless it appears that abnormal VEP in Parkinson's disease is not an epiphenomenon; rather it reflects an essential aspect of its progression and clinical severity. It remains to be seen whether or not evoked potentials measure a dopaminergic deficiency in the visual pathway or other areas of the CNS of patients with P.D.

Appendix

$$Z_R^2 - 2 \times p \times Z_R \times Z_L + Z_L^2 = C^2$$

$$Z_R = \frac{R - \mu_R}{\Sigma_R}$$

$$Z_L = \frac{L - \mu_L}{\Sigma_L}$$

R = right eye latencies in msec

L = left eye latencies in msec

Constants (different values for gratings and checks depending on the stimulus)

μ_R = grating 115.8597
checks 106.9737

μ_L = grating 115.9630
checks 107.4737

Σ_R = grating 8.1950
checks 7.8894

136

Σ_L = grating 7.7141
      checks 8.4333

p = grating .8056
      checks .9308

μ = average value calculated from normal population

Σ = standard deviation for normals

p = correlation between left and right eyes for normals

Acknowledgements

We thank Mrs Sharon Simpson, whose assistance in obtaining the patients' clinical data was an invaluable contribution to this study.

Supported in part by Grant No EY 01708 of the National Eye Institute, N.I.H.; N.I.H. Grant No RR-00071 of the Division of Research Resources, General clinical Research Centre Branch; and Grant No NS 11631-5 of the Clinical Centre for Parkinson's Disease and Allied Disorders.

References

1   Hakim AN, Mathieson G. *Neurology 1979; 29:*1209
2   Alvord EC Jr, Formo LS, Kusske JA. *Adv Neurol 1974; 5:*175
3   Lavy S, Melamed E, Cooper G, Bentin S, Rinot Y. *Arch Neurol 1979; 36:*344
4   Bodis-Wollner I, Yahr MD. *Latency of the pattern evoked potential in Parkinson's disease, 11th World Congress of Neurology 1977;* 126. Amsterdam
5   Bodis-Wollner I, Yahr MD. *Brain 1978; 101:*661
6   Hoehn MM, Yahr MD. *Neurology 1967; 17:*427
7   Bodis-Wollner I, Hendley CD, Kulikowski JJ. *Perception 1972; 1:*341
8   Halliday AM, McDonald WI, Mushin J. In Desmedt JE, ed. *Visual evoked potentials in man 1977.* Oxford: Clarendon Press
9   Bodis-Wollner I, Hendley CD, Mylin L, Thornton J. *Ann Neurol 1979; 5:*40
10   Timm NH. In *Multivariate Analysis 1975;* 261. Belmont, California: Wadsworth
11   Rao CR. In *Linear statistical inference and its applications 2nd ed 1973;* 574. New York: John Wiley and Sons
12   Johnson NL, Kotz S. In *Distributions in statistics: continuous multivariate distributions 1972;* 84. New York: John Wiley and Sons
13   Bodis-Wollner I, Camisa J, Jaffe T. *Effect of stimulus orientation on latency and amplitude of the visual evoked potential 1979.* Eastern Assoc. of Electroencephalographers Annual Meeting, Mont Gabriel, Quebec
14   Ehinger B. In Costa E, Gessa GL, eds. *Advances in biochemical psychopharmacology volume 16 1977;* 299. New York: Raven Press
15   Reader TA, Ferron A, Descarries L, Jasper HH. *Brain Res 1979; 160:*217
16   Bodis-Wollner I, Bender MB. *Prog Neurol Psychiat 1973; 38:*93
17   Riederer P, Birkmayer W, Seemann D, Wuketich S. *J Neurol Trans 1977; 42:*241
18   Kasamatsu T, Pettigrew JD. *Science 1976; 194:*206
19   Kupperman B, Kasamatsu B. *Neurosci Abstracts 1979; 5:*792. Number 2666

Chapter 17

VISUAL AND AUDITORY EVOKED
RESPONSES IN PARKINSON'S DISEASE

M J Gawel, P Das and S Vincent

The development of the technique of measuring cortical evoked potentials to various stimuli [1] has led to an increased attempt to characterise the electrical properties of the human and animal brain in health and disease. Originally the techniques were used in the detection of subclinical lesions in optic nerve, spinal cord and brain stem in the diagnosis of multiple sclerosis [2]. It has become apparent recently that factors other than demyelination can affect the shape and latency of various elements of the waveforms and possibly give new insights into physiological and pathological mechanisms. Using suitable stimuli, space occupying lesions in the brain, compression of the optic nerves and vascular disease can be detected. Perhaps more interesting than identifying structural abnormalities is the possible use of these techniques to ascertain transmitter function in the nervous system.

Celesia and Daly [3] found that the latency of the first negative and the major positive wave of the VEP increased with age. This raised the possibility of studying VEPs in disorders which were perhaps characterised by accelerated senescence, such as Parkinson's disease. Of even more interest was the finding by Schafer and McKean [4] that phenylketonuric children have abnormally delayed VEP latencies which become more normal upon treatment wih a phenylalanine free diet or the addition to the diet of indole and catecholamine precursors. Furthermore, the difference in response pattern between stimulation by flash and pattern reversal, which was not present in the untreated patients, reappeared after either treatment regime. This suggested that higher level functions as well as conduction velocity were affected by pharmacological manipulations. Bodis-Wollner and Yahr [5] demonstrated an abnormally delayed latency of the major positive wave in patients with Parkinson's disease. This delay was shortened in some patients following L-dopa therapy indicating that at least some part of the abnormality causing it was amenable to pharmacological manipulation. Their original experiments were performed using a grating as the stimulus but in subsequent experiments they were able to reproduce their findings using a reversing checkerboard. They also correlated severity of disease with prolongation of latency (see previous chapter of this

138

book). Some methodological criticism must be levelled at their original paper since only 4 of the 26 controls were normal neurologically and, in our present state of knowledge of VEP changes in various conditions, this is perhaps not ideal. In their paper they examined only monocular latency of the major positive wave on stimulation of each eye.

Since binocular stimulation activates different pathways and measurement of amplitude of response has relevance in VEP studies it seemed to us that these factors needed study in patients with Parkinson's disease. Bodis-Wollner and Yahr's [5] paper also raised the intriguing possibility that there was an interocular difference in the latency of the major positive wave in Parkinsonian patients and that, in some patients, treatment altered latency in one eye only. This suggested to them that the delay was prechiasmatic and possibly retinal where there are dopaminegic cells in the interplexiform layer which appear to have D1 receptor response characteristics [6]. However this did not accord with current concepts of the sites of action of amines on evoked potentials [4, 7, 8, 9]. Further evidence for a more generalised effect would be obtained if a delay could be demonstrated upon stimulation of another modality, for instance, auditory. Accordingly we studied both visual (VEP) and auditory evoked responses (AER) in patients with Parkinson's disease comparing them with normal age matched controls.

Materials and Methods

The patients (Table I) were attending the Parkinson's Disease Clinic of the Department of Neurology of Charing Cross Hospital. Controls were either the spouses of the patients or other individuals working in the hospital of a matched age. All subjects had visual acuity equivalent to or better than J4 (corrected), normal visual fields and were free from any other ocular disorder. None had a past history of cardiovascular disease or multiple sclerosis. There were 47 patients and 26 controls in the VEP study and 21 patients and 12 controls in the AER study. 13 of the patients in the AER study also had VEPs. Ideally all patients would have both investigations and this is in progress. All but 11 of the patients who had VEPs performed were on L-dopa therapy and in these the studies were performed as near as possible to 2 hours after the previous dose. Eleven patients were newly diagnosed and had their VEPs performed before starting treatment.

TABLE I VEP in Parkinson's Disease

Patients	n = 47	30 Male
		17 Female
	age range	51–82 years
	mean age	67 years
Controls	n = 26	11 Male
		15 Female
	age range	40–90 years
	mean age	63 years

VEPs were obtained using a reversing checkerboard stimulus (Digitimer Mark II) giving a luminance of 2.0 log foot lamberts for the light squares and 0.6 log foot lamberts for the dark squares in the centre of the field. Each square was 1 cm sq. and the patient was positioned 1 metre away. Pattern reversal occurred every 500 msecs and the responses were averaged for 96 sweeps in each monocular and binocular stimulation. The recording electrode was in the midline and 5 cm above the pinion with the reference 20 cm anterior to it.

The potentials obtained were displayed on the oscilloscope screen and the P2 latency was measured automatically using a moveable cursor. Amplitudes of the P2 waves were measured from images of the potentials on light sensitive paper with reference to a calibration signal of 10 μV. The measurements taken were as follows: latency P2 was the latency (in msecs) from the onset of reversal to the major positive peak (P2); amplitude A_1, was the amplitude from the first negative wave N, to the major positive peak P2; amplitude A2 was from P2 to the following negative wave N2.

Auditory evoked responses were obtained using a click stimulus 70 db above threshold delivered at the rate of 10/sec and averaged over 2000 repetitions. Recordings were from a mastoid electrode placement and the following measures taken: latency of the fifth negative wave NV was from the onset of the stimulus to the first negative peak; amplitude of NV was from NV to the following positive peak. The latency and amplitude of the first negative peak NI were also measured.

Results were analysed using Students T test on individual measurements and a multivariate analysis (RAO) on the first amplitudes and latencies of the VEP.

Results

1 The VEP

These are summarised in Tables II, III, IV and V. As can be seen, both amplitude and latency are significantly different in patients with Parkinson's disease when taken as a group. Comparing the treated and untreated patients, no differences emerge and for the sake of this section they can be treated as one group. The same relationship of faster conduction in the binocular situation holds in both control and Parkinsonian patients. This is a feature that workers in our laboratories have found in migraine patients [10] and warrants further study in the Parkinsonian patients in all conditions; P2 latencies are longer while the amplitude of P2 is about half that of the controls.

Plotting the latencies distanced on left eye and right eye stimulation after the manner of Bodis-Wollner and Yahr [5] produces a graph almost identical to theirs (Figure 1), but attempts to correlate severity of disease with latency did not confirm their findings (see previous chapter). We were able to confirm their lack of correlation of VEP latency with age and this also applied to the amplitude; the same lack of correlation with age was found in the controls. The sex of the patients or controls did not play a significant role in VEP characteristics nor did type or duration of treatment or duration of disease.

140

TABLE II VEP in Parkinson's Disease

	Patients	Controls
P_2 Latency Binocular	109.21 ± 13.4	100.52 ± 8.7
Left	113.5 ± 16*	102.64 ± 8.6***
Right	112.17 ± 14**	102.93 ± 8.3***

* P_2B vs P_2L p = < 0.004   *** P_2B vs P_2L p = < 0.05
** P_2B vs P_2R p = < 0.02   *** P_2B vs P_2R p = < 0.05

TABLE III VEP in Parkinson's Disease

Binocular Stimulation	Patients	Controls	p
P_2 Latency (msec)	109.2 ± 13.4	100.7 ± 8.6	< 0.002
A_1 Amplitude (μV)	7.6 ± 3.2	14.3 ± 5.7	< 0.001
A_2 Amplitude (μV)	10.4 ± 5.2	17.4 ± 8.8	< 0.01

TABLE IV VEP in Parkinson's Disease

Left Eye Stimulation	Patients	Controls	p
P_2 Latency (msec)	113.5 ± 16	102.6 ± 8	< 0.001
A_1 Amplitude (μV)	7.4 ± 2.5	13.8 ± 6	< 0.002
A_2 Amplitude (μV)	9.8 ± 4.4	18.4 ± 12	< 0.05

TABLE V VEP in Parkinson's Disease

Right Eye Stimulation	Patient	Controls	p
P_2 Latency (msec)	112.17 ± 14	102.9 ± 8	< 0.001
A_1 Amplitude (μV)	6.7 ± 2.8	12.8 ± 3.8	< 0.001
A_2 Amplitude (μV)	9.3 ± 4.4	17.5 ± 10	< 0.008

TABLE VI VEP in Parkinson's Disease

Interocular Differences	Patients	Controls	p
Difference of Latencies (msec)	6.4 ± 7.4	1.8 ± 2.6	< 0.001
Difference of Amplitude A_1 (μV)	1.9 ± 2.9	3.9 ± 5.3	NS
Difference of Amplitude A_2 (μV)	2.2 ± 1.8	3.9 ± 4.1	NS

The interocular difference in the patients was 6.4 msecs ($p = < 0.001$) and 1.8 msecs in the controls, a significant difference (Table VI). There was no asymmetry of amplitude despite the interocular difference and indeed further analysis revealed that amplitude did not correlate with latency.

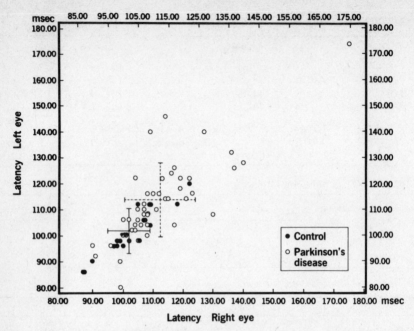

Figure 1 Graph of latency for right eye stimulation plotted against latency for left eye stimulation in patients (open circles) and controls (closed circles) with the standard deviations for each measure.

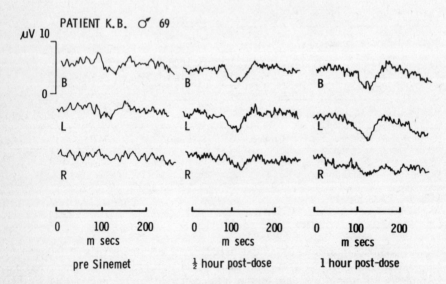

Figure 2 VEP from binocular, left eye and right eye stimulation demonstrating changes after Sinemet.

Two cases demonstrating effects of treatment on the VEP latency

Patient 1—this was a 69 year old man who had had Parkinson's disease for 4 years. The patient had very severe disability and showed changes in his condition related to dosage times. The sequence of evoked potentials obtained (Figure 2) demonstrates the effect of a single tablet of Sinemet 110. Half an hour after ingestion the evoked potential became much more clearly defined and of greater amplitude, an effect that is even more marked (except for right eye stimulation) at one hour. Two hours after the dose, the VEP had returned to a state similar to the pre-dose level. Subsequent dosage caused the same sequence of changes. His condition was improved at 1 hour post dose, but his attention, awareness and co-operation did not appear significantly altered. The latency changes were most marked on binocular stimulation.

Case 2—this patient (age 79 years) was well controlled on Sinemet 110 for 3 years and had normal VEP latencies and amplitudes in the first test (Figure 3). Six months later he had, due to social reasons, stopped taking his tablets and his condition had deteriorated. On resting, the latencies of P2 on right eye and binocular stimulation had increased, while the potential on stimulating his right eye had deteriorated to the extent of becoming immeasurable despite normal acuity and ophthalmological examination.

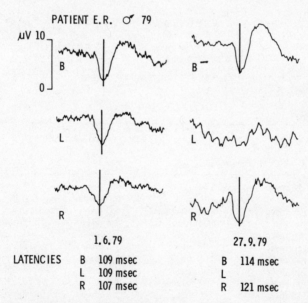

PATIENT E.R.   ♂ 79

LATENCIES	1.6.79		27.9.79	
	B	109 msec	B	114 msec
	L	109 msec	L	
	R	107 msec	R	121 msec

Figure 3 VEPs from patient ER. The first recording was taken when he was well controlled on Sinemet. Six months later he has stopped his medication and has deteriorated clinically. Note the very abnormal left eye wave form and the good but delayed waveform for the right eye.

143

THE AER (Auditory Evoked Response)

Like the VEP the waveforms obtained on auditory stimulation were odd in form, being less clearly defined than those in the controls, though measurable.

The results are summarised in Table VII and there is a significant delay in the latency of the fifth negative wave NV though not of its amplitude. There is no delay of NI indicating that delay is in the brain stem and not in the end organ. In the thirteen patients who had both AERs and VEPs performed (Table VIII), three had both delayed VEPs and AERs. Two of these (Patients 1 & 2) had had Parkinson's disease for more than 10 years and were on L-dopa treatment.

TABLE VII AER in Parkinson's Disease

	Patients (21)	Controls (12)
NV wave		
Latency	Rt 5.91 ± 0.19 msec	5.69 ± 0.18 msec p = 0.005
	Lt 5.91 ± 0.27 msec	5.73 ± 0.27 msec p = 0.05
Amplitude	Rt 0.447 ± 0.14 μV	0.522 ± 0.19 μV NS
	Lt 0.439 ± 0.18 μV	0.535 ± 0.23 μV NS
NI wave		
Latency	Rt 1.74 ± 0.12 msec	1.74 ± 0.07 msec
	Lt 1.73 ± 0.16 msec	1.74 ± 0.17 msec
Amplitude	Rt 4.19 ± 0.25 μV	3.9 ± 0.12
	Lt 4.185 ± 0.24 μV	3.98 ± 0.27

TABLE VIII

	VEP P$_2$ Latency		AER NV Latency	
	Rt	Lt	Rt	Lt
1	116 msec	124 msec	6.0 msec	6.1 msec
2	129 msec	140 msec	6.0 msec	6.0 msec
3	122 msec	113 msec	6.0 msec	6.1 msec
4	104 msec	104 msec	5.8 msec	5.8 msec
5	116 msec	116 msec	5.8 msec	5.8 msec
6	113 msec	107 msec	5.8 msec	5.7 msec
7	106 msec	102 msec	5.6 msec	5.5 msec
8	100 msec	100 msec	5.8 msec	5.7 msec
9	101 msec	108 msec	5.6 msec	5.7 msec
10	110 msec	116 msec	5.9 msec	5.8 msec
11	103 msec	104 msec	5.8 msec	—
12	108 msec	108 msec	5.9 msec	5.6 msec
13	106 msec	100 msec	5.9 msec	5.8 msec

Discussion

In this study we have confirmed the findings of Bodis-Wollner and Yahr [5] of a delay in the latency of P2 in the VEP of Parkinsonian patients and the presence of a marked interocular difference. We were unable to confirm their correlation of the VEP latency with severity of disease; although some of our patients with very severe and chronic disease did have very long latencies, the patient with the longest latencies (170 msecs) was aged 63, had had the disease for 2 years, was on Sinemet treatment and was not particularly severely affected. On the other hand, one patient with fairly severe disease had an extremely short P2 latency. It seems that there must be other factors operating which further study should elucidate.

In all stimulus conditions, we found a delay in latency on binocular stimulation and a diminished amplitude of response which was symmetrical despite the large interocular latency difference. Multivariate analysis confirmed that the Parkinsonian patients differed from controls ($p = < 0.0001$) on measures of amplitude and latency of P2.

A considerable change occurred when L-dopa was administered to the first patient we describe and we have subsequently confirmed this in two other patients. If this can be shown to correlate with clinical status, or even levels of dopamine centrally, then we may have a rapid non invasive way of assessing the amount of dopamine actually arriving at the site of action for this particular function and how long it stays there. This could be of therapeutic significance in adjusting treatment schedules to provide maximal benefit. The uniocular deterioration in the second patient, coupled with the delay on binocular and right eye stimulation, is more difficult to explain. Bodis-Wollner and Yahr [5] describe two patients in whom an interocular difference only becomes apparent on treatment. It may be that one eye was more affected by the disease than the other and that withdrawal of L-dopa had a particularly dramatic effect.

The site of the lesion is of great interest. It is suggested that dopaminergic cells in the interplexiform layer of the retina may be affected by the disease process and respond to L-dopa replacement therapy. Further evidence for the existence of these cells in vertebrates is provided by Watling *et al* [6] and they appear to be pure D_1 receptors. The involvement of such cells would explain the interocular difference but it would be difficult to explain the lack of asymmetry in the reduced VEP amplitude on this basis. Other transmitters are involved in Parkinsonism and this may be the explanation of some of the amplitude effects. The large VEP amplitude (to flash stimulation) in mongols (Down's syndrome) can be brought back to normal by administering the 5HT precursor, 5HTP, to these patients [11]. L-tryptophan, given to patients with migraine attacks, will reduce the large amplitudes of a VEP to flash, but only in those patients when migraine is ameliorated by this treatment [7]. 5HT is an inhibitory transmitter in the optic nerve and possibly in other areas, but current studies indicate that there is a deficit of 5HT in patients with Parkinson's disease [12], as well as of noradrenaline (NA), GABA and, at least in the putamen, ACh receptors. This makes studies as to the relative contributions of each of these factors difficult.

It would be interesting to attempt DI receptor inhibition with flupenthixol, chlorpromazine and haloperidol in Parkinsonian patients. There is in fact evidence that chlorpromazine does cause a delay in the VEP of normal volunteers [13].

The delay in the auditory evoked potential does suggest a more general involvement by the disease process, based on a neurotransmitter deficit or some other factor. The normal latency in the first negative wave which is thought to be derived from the acoustic nerve makes a peripheral lesion unlikely. The fifth negative wave is thought to originate in the inferior colliculus [14]. So far we have not studied the effects of dosage on the AER in our patients but are in the process of doing so. With current lack of information concerning connections between the inferior colliculus and the visual system it is unjustifiable to speculate on a direct influence, but it would seem reasonable to suggest that this effect is due to a generalised neurotransmitter abnormality.

Our studies suggest that the VEP P_2 latencies and amplitudes are abnormal in patients with Parkinson's disease and that there is a marked interocular difference in the latencies. The finding that there is also a delayed AER NV wave latency suggests that the lesion may be generalised. Rapid alterations in VEP latency and amplitude following treatment suggest that at least part of the effect observed may be due to a neurotransmitter abnormality, although there is not enough information to define this involvement. The use of EP measurement in Parkinson's disorder may be of therapeutic significance.

References

1   Arden GB, Bodis-Wollner I, Halliday AM et al. In Desmedt JE, ed. *Visual evoked potentials in man: new developments 1977;* p. 3. Oxford, Clarendon Press
2   Halliday AM, McDonald WI, Muskin J. *Brit med J 1973;4:*661
3   Celesia GA, Daly RF. *Arch Neurol 1977;34:*403
4   Schafer EWP, McKean CM. *Brain Res 1975;99:*49
5   Bodis-Wollner I, Yahr MD. *Brain 1978;101:*661
6   Watling KJ, Dowling JE, Iversen LL. *Nature 1979;281:*578
7   Kangasniemi P, Falck B, Langvik Vivi-Ann, Hyppa MT. *Headache 1978;18:*161
8   Lehtonen J, Hyppa MT, Kaikola HL, Kangasmiemi P, Lang AH. *Headache 1979;19:* 63
9   Sabelli HC, Giardinan WJ, Barbiol F. *Biological Psychiatry 1971;3:*273
10   Kennard CK, Gawel MJ, Rose F Clifford, Rudlof N de M. In Friedman AP, Granger ML, Critchley M, eds. *Research and Clinical Studies in Headache 1978;*73. Basle, Karger
11   Bigum HB, Dustman RE, Beck EC. *Electroenceph Clin Neurophysiol 1970;28:*576
12   Reisine JD, Fields JZ, Yamamura HI. *Life Sci 1977;21:*335
13   Shagass C. In Dix Efron, ed. *Pharmacology of evoked potentials in man in Psychopharmacology: A review of Progress 1957–1967 1968;*483. Washington DC, Public Health Service Publication No 1836, US Govt Printing Office
14   Stockard JJ, Rossiter VS. *Neurol (Minneap) 1977;27:*316

PART IV

NEUROCHEMISTRY

Chapter 18

NEUROCHEMICAL CORRELATES OF SYMPTOMATOLOGY AND DRUG INDUCED SIDE EFFECTS IN PARKINSON'S DISEASE

P Riederer, G P Reynolds and W Birkmayer

Parkinson's disease is characterised by degeneration of dopaminergic cell bodies in the substantia nigra and a resultant loss of dopaminergic function in the striatum. This dopaminergic subactivity can be supplemented by the administration of L-dopa (with or without inhibitors or peripheral aromatic amino acid decarboxylase). The efficiency of L-dopa therapy is dependent on the availability of L-dopa in plasma and on the utilisation of L-dopa and/or dopamine in the central dopaminergic neurones. A high L-dopa medication sometimes leads to an earlier appearance of side effects and the clinical impression that the duration of the disease is shorter than normally expected, so that the consequence of too high a dose of L-dopa seems to be the more rapid progression of the degenerative process. This may be a function of the many and varied side effects of L-dopa on neurotransmitter systems in the brain. As well as the inhibitory action of L-dopa on tyrosine hydroxylase, the rate limiting enzyme in catecholamine synthesis, it will also compete with other aromatic amino acids for uptake into the brain and into nerve endings. In addition to inducing dopamine synthesis, L-dopa increases noradrenaline turnover and can also affect serotoninergic systems by being taken up instead of tryptophan into such neurones, possibly resulting in a synthesis of dopamine as a "false transmitter" (for review see [1]).

Thus, as well as inducing dopamine synthesis in the disturbed brain areas ot parkinsonian patients, high doses of L-dopa will disturb the function of intact dopaminergic, adrenergic and serotoninergic neuronal systems, resulting in a possible exacerbation of the disease process with the appearance of side effects such as the "on-off" phenomenon and psychosis. All other drugs increasing dopamine activity, such as the dopamine agonists and monoamine oxidase inhibitors, induce these toxic reactions to a lesser or greater extent. Minimising the dose of L-dopa will correspondingly minimise these unwanted side-effects [1].

In considering the neurochemical processes of Parkinson's disease, several questions arise which are relevant to neuropharmacological approaches to treatment. Some of these are:

1 Is Parkinson's disease a facilitated "ageing" of dopaminergic neurones?

2 Are other neuronal systems involved by a functional transmitter imbalance induced by the degeneration of nigro-striatal dopaminergic fibres?

3 Is there a functional degeneration only of presynaptic nerve terminals or are the postsynaptic neurones also affected?

The Ageing Process and Parkinson's Disease

Parkinson's disease tends to occur mainly in patients over 60 years old and therefore the suggestion of a rapidly progressive ageing process might be of some relevance. In fact, there are findings in human brain studies, as well as in animal experiments, which are in line with such an assumption. It has been shown that in normal controls, dopamine decreases in the caudate nucleus with age (Figure 1) and this result is in agreement with similar studies by Bertler [2] and Carlsson et al [3]. Reduced levels of dopamine in the striatum were found by Finch [4], who noted also a reduced biosynthesis of dopamine and noradrenaline in striatum, brainstem, hypothalamus and cerebellum in senescent mice.

In this line of experiments are data showing a decrease of tyrosine hydroxylase (TH) activity in the brain of aged rats [5], as well as in specific dopaminergic regions like the caudate nucleus and olfactory tubercle [6]. A marked non-linear

Figure 1 Opposite.

H.C. (x)	:	28 healthy controls
P1 (O)	:	27 Parkinsonian patients; onset of disease aged 60 ± 1 years
P2 (●)	:	12 Parkinsonian patients; onset of disease aged 73 ± 1 years
DEP (●)	:	3 unipolar depressed patients, who died from other causes during a depressive phase
REM (O)	:	1 patient with depressive syndrome, who died from other causes during "remission"

Patients	Age Group years	Loss of Dopamine in Caudate Nucleus %
H.C.	45–55 (4)	15.3
	56–65 (7)	15.7
	66–75 (8)	9.8
	76–85 (6)	10.7
	86–95 (3)	mean = 12.87 ± 3.05 ± s.d. pro decade
P1	61–67 (14)	28.55 ± 9.0
	67–73 (13)	46.55 ± 6.85
P2	74–80 (9)	23.3 ± 4.16
	80–84 (3)	38.6 ± 5.79

for details see references [15] [17]

developing decline of TH-activity was described for the human brain by McGeer *et al* [7]. Moreover, by measuring other parameters, a similar trend towards a decreased function of catecholaminergic neurones with increasing age had been noted. Although there is no clear evidence that noradrenaline levels are substantially decreased in aged animals [8, 9], accumulation of ^{3}H-noradrenaline in the hemispheres [9], catabolism of dopamine and noradrenaline in specific brain areas [4] and uptake of ^{3}H-dopamine by striatal and hypothalamic synaptosomes [10] are reduced in aged animals and therefore support the idea of a "functionally balanced ageing of catecholaminergic neurones". In contrast to catecholaminergic neurones, cholinergic serotoninergic [12, 13] ones seem not to be so decisively dependent on an ageing process, although some reduction of 5HT in the hemispheres [9] could be observed. A hypoactivity of catecholaminergic neurones would, at

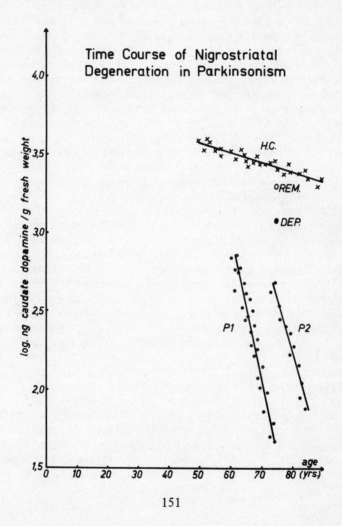

151

normal functional activity of cholinergic and serotoninergic neurones, predict an indirectly caused hyperactivity of the latter neuronal systems. Symptoms of old age, like the loss of drive and motor performance, reduced vigilance, drop of learning behaviour and memory may reflect a change in the balance of neurotransmitter systems. The progression of dopamine loss, however, is lower in older people since it appears to be logarithmic (Figure 1). This finding is in agreement with the dynamic decline of tyrosine hydroxylase [7] and its putative cofactor BH4 [4]. In a retrospective study we demonstrated that, in contrast to a control group, Parkinson's disease is characterised by an increase of dopamine loss in the second half of the disease [15].

Whether or not Parkinson's disease is a loss of some "inhibitory factor" of normal dopaminergic functional loss with age, it can perhaps be thought of as a greatly increased facilitation of this ageing process, in which high dosage L-dopa therapy (all of these patients received low doses) has, if any, only a detrimental effect, Therefore, a reduction of L-dopa dosage to as low as possible is necessary to keep the dopaminegic neurones physiologically active for as long as possible. A direct correlation between the appearance of so called "on-off" phenomena, which are symptoms of an advanced stage of the disease, and the progressive degeneration of the nigro-striatal dopaminergic neurones is assumed. This symptom is observed much more frequently in L-dopa treated patients and is further evidence that L-dopa has its limitations as a therapeutic agent in the advanced stage of Parkinson's disease [1]. This holds true especially for the "akinetic crises" at the end stage of the disease, when supplementation of dopamine in the nigro-striatal areas by L-dopa, Madopar, Sinemet, dopaminergic agonists like α-ergo-bromo-criptine, MAO-inhibitors etc., are worthless in improving motor performance but often lead to toxic psychosis [16].

Table I shows the content of dopamine in striatal areas in Parkinson's disease. Controls are compared to patients, who either died from secondary causes or who died during an akinetic crisis after a duration of the disease of 10 or more years. A greater loss of dopamine is evident in this stage of the disease.

In Figure 1 there is shown the caudate dopamine levels of three psychiatric patients exhibiting retarded depression [17]. It is tempting to speculate that some of such patients are exhibiting "pre-parkinsonian symptoms" and that their already substantially decreased dopamine levels would eventually have dropped further to the levels found in classical Parkinson's disease [1, 15]; if this were the case, L-dopa responsive retarded depression might be a marker for future parkinsonism.

Monoamine oxidase and toxic psychosis

Monoamine oxidase inhibitors improve, as do all of the dopamine-system stimulating drugs, the motor performance of parkinsonian patients but, with increasing age and process of the degeneration of dopaminergic nigro-striatal fibres, they induce pharmacotoxic psychosis. This was observed for the first time when, in the early stages of L-dopa therapy, MAO-inhibitors were included into the therapeutic

TABLE I The dopamine content of various areas of the brain in parkinsonian patients related to "akinetic crises"

Brain area	Dopamine (ng/g) Controls (9)	Parkinson's Disease died from secondary causes (6) a	died during akinetic crises (4) b
Caudate n.	3843 ± 539	401 ± 59	90 ± 25
Putamen	4183 ± 742	170 ± 44	40 ± 15
S. nigra	582 ± 103	96 ± 12	40 ± 10
Gl. pallidus	846 ± 195	83 ± 10	55 ± 13

Mean ± s.e.

Number of patients in parentheses

a Patients died in cardiac failure or bronchopneumonia; they were "responders" to L-dopa treatment and showed some surviving melanin-containing neurones in S. nigra by routine histology.

b Disability according to [1]: 80–100 (confined to bed).
   Histological examination: complete loss of melanin-containing cells in S. nigra
   No kinetic response during "akinetic" end stage when L-dopa, anticholinergics, (-)deprenyl, amantadine or dopaminergic agonists were used
   "Psychosis"during such crises were treated successfully with neuroleptics or, in mild cases, with L-tryptophan (from ref. 16).

strategy of Parkinson's disease [18]. Deprenyl, a fairly selective inhibitor of MAO-type B, is a good adjuvant in parkinsonian therapy [19–22] and it especially prevents off-phases. However, (-)deprenyl can induce psychosis, as can all other monoamine oxidase inhibitors [1, 18]. It is of special interest that selective MAO-B inhibition affects the substrates dopamine and phenylethylamine in the human brain, so that it can be hypothesised that these two amines particularly may be involved in the symptomatology of psychosis.

Parnate, the racemic form of tranylcypromine, is a MAO-inhibitor widely used as an antidepressant drug. (+)Tranylcypromine, however, acts at therapeutic concentrations (10^{-6} M) fairly selectively on MAO-B substrates [23] whereas the (-)isomer is a weak inhibitor of MAO. The (+)isomer is a potent inhibitor of platelet-MAO [23] and acts predominantly on motor behaviour in parkinsonian patients (Seemann, unpublished). In one out of 15 such patients, psychosis developed during both (±) and (+) tranylcypromine (5 mg/day) treatments. It was notable that circulating phenylethylamine in this patient reached levels substantially higher than normally found after MAO-B inhibition, while plasma dopamine was not notably increased, so that this patient was probably exhibiting a "phenylethylamine psychosis". It seems likely that further study of such toxic effects, including the more normal "L-dopa psychosis" may throw light on the aetiology of endogenous psychotic states in, for example, schizophrenia.

Dopamine receptors, drug treatment and postsynaptic changes

Up till now only a few findings indicate that the adenylate cyclase dependent dopamine receptor system (D_1-receptor) loses sensitivity with age [24, 25]. By measuring ^{3}H-haloperidol-binding, Pado *et al* [26] found a decrease in dopamine receptor binding (-35%) in 180 day old rats. Although these two-compartmental receptor systems are still far from clearly understood, a loss of response with age seems to be apparent. In Parkinson's disease, a decrease in the response of adenylate cyclase to stimulation by dopamine could be observed (Figure 2; [28, 27]. Moreover, a developing loss of sensitivity during the disease process could be assumed because patients who died from secondary causes still possessed a certain amount of dopamine-sensitive adenylate cyclase, whereas samples from patients who died during an akinetic crisis exhibited no response to dopamine stimulation (Figure 2 and table 2; [27]).

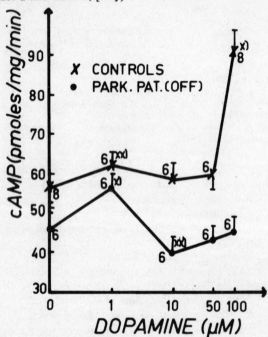

Figure 2 Stimulation of adenylate cyclase by dopamine in the caudate nucleus.

x) p < 0.01 } compared to basal level
xx) p < 0.05 }

Means in pmoles/mg protein/min ± s.e.m.
Numbers on graphs indicate number of experiments.
Brain material was taken from postmortem parkinsonian patients (group B, therapy-resistant akinetic crises; see also Table II).
Taken from [27]

154

TABLE II Stimulation of Adenylate Cyclase by Dopamine in Parkinson's Disease

	CAMP (pmoles/mg/min)	
	BASAL LEVEL	DOPAMINE STIMULATED (100 μM)
Controls [4]	542 ± 73	903 ± 165 +)
Liver Cirrhosis [5]	651 ± 138	452 ± 89
Carcinoma [4]	479 ± 129	337 ± 116
Parkinson's Disease:		
A: Kinetic p [4]	534 ± 53	736 ± 43 +) x)
(a) Nomifensine [2]	542	653
B: Therapy resistant		
akinetic crisis [8]	467 ± 119	443 ± 86 xx)
(a) Madopar [6]	799 ± 139	578 ± 109
(b) Deprenyl [6]	617 ± 149	479 ± 92
(c) 2-Bromo-ergo-cryptine [4]	766 ± 33	653 ± 106
(d) 1-Amino-adamantane [5]	785 ± 106	614 ± 92
(e) Clomiramine [4]	693 ± 83	521 ± 89
(f) Anticholinergics [3]	472 ± 64	330 ± 99

(+)   P < 0.01 when compared to basal levels
(x)   P < 0.01 when compared to controls (100 μM DA)
(xx)   P < 0.01 when compared to kinetic Park. pat. (100 μM DA)

Taken from [27]

Specific 3H-spiroperidol binding is significantly reduced in Parkinson's disease without treatment [29]. Levodopa treatment did not change the binding, while patients treated with neuroleptics had a significant increase in the number of receptors [29]. Our results confirm a decrease in 3H-spiroperone binding in parkinsonian striatum; in addition, a decrease in 3H-ADTN-binding (thought to be an agonist of the D1 receptor) was also found in samples of caudate (Table 3) (Reynolds, Riederer, Owen, Gross, unpubl.).

TABLE III 3H-spiroperidone and 3H-ADTN binding in Parkinson's disease

	3H-spiroperone (fmol/mg protein)		3H-ADTN (fmol/mg protein)	
	Control	Parkinson	Control	Parkinson
Caudate n.	1241 ± 102 [3]	505 ± 421 [4] x)	427 ± 64 [3]	307 ± 25 [4] xx)
Putamen	1386 ± 293 [4]	628 ± 61 [3]	515 ± 177 [4]	343 ± 33 [3]

(x) P < 0.05
(xx) P < 0.02

Owen F, Cross A J, Reynolds G P, Riederer P (in preparation)

In a recent review covering dopamine receptors, Kebabian and Calne [30] listed 3 receptor types in the striatum; D_1 post-synaptic receptors and both pre- and post-synaptic D_2 (adenyl cyclase independent) receptors. Thus the evidence above suggests a degeneration of post-synaptic dopamine receptors as well as a loss of pre-synaptic function. It is notable that there is little evidence to support the view that denervation supersensitivity of dopamine receptors, observed in animal models, can also occur in man.

The results of Rinne and coworkers [29] lead us to speculate that the occasional short-term application of neuroleptics with a resultant increased dopamine receptor number may be a useful therapeutic approach to optimising the residual dopaminergic function in parkinsonian patients.

Preliminary results show that this approach is of some value in depressed patients (Radmayr, unpublished).

Acknowledgement

We are grateful to Hoechst-Austria for supporting our work by a fellowship (GPR). We thank Rohm-Pharma for supplying us with Parnate ® (+) and (-)tranylcypromine and Chinoin Drug Company for (-)deprenyl.

References

1 Birkmayer W, Riederer P. *Die Parkinsonische Krankheit 1980.* Springer Verlag Wien, In press
2 Bertler A. *Acta Physiol Scand 1961;51:*97
3 Carlsson A, Winblad B. *J Neural Transm 1976;38:*271
4 Finch C. *Brain Res 1973;52:*261
5 Algeri S, Bonati M, Brunello N, Ponzio F. *Brain Res 1977;132:*569
6 Reis DJ, Ross RA, Joh TH. *Brain Res 1977;136:*465
7 McGeer E, McGeer PL. In Terry RD, Gershon S, eds. *Ageing 1976;Vol 3.* New York, Raven Press
8 Samorajski T, Rolsten C. In Ford DH, ed. *Neurobiological aspects of maturation and ageing. Progress in brain research 1973;Vol 40:*253. Amsterdam, Elsevier
9 Vernadakis A. *Fed Proc 1975;34:*89
10 Jonec V, Finch C. *Brain Res 1975;91:*197
11 Vasko MR, Dominio LE, Domino EF. *Europ J Pharmacol 1974;27:*145
12 McNamara MC, Miller AT, Benignus VA, Davis JN. *Brain Res 1977;131:*313
13 Robinson DS. *Fed Proc 1975;34:*103
14 Levine RA, Williams AC, Robinson DS, Calne DB, Lovenberg W. In Poirier LJ, Sourkes TL, Bedard PJ, eds. *Advances in Neurology 24 1979;*303. New York, Raven Press
15. Riederer, P Wuketich S. *J Neural Transm 1976; 38:*277
16 Birkmayer W, Riederer P. *J Neural Transm 1975;37:*175
17 Birkmayer W, Riederer P. *J Neural Transm 1975;37:*95
18 Birkmayer W, Hornykiewicz O. *Arch Psych 1962;203:*560
19 Birkmayer W, Riederer P, Youdim MBH, Linauer W. *J Neural Transm 1975;36:*303
20 Birkmayer W, Riederer P, Ambrozi L, Youdim MBH. *Lancet 1977;ii:*434
21 Lees AJ, Shaw KM, Kohout LH, Stern GM, Elsworth JD, Sandler M, Youdim MBH. *Lancet 1977;i:*791

22   Birkmayer W, Yahr M. *J Neural Transm 1978;43:*
23   Reynolds GP, Riederer P, Rausch WD. *J Neural Transm 1980;Suppl 16.* In press
24   Walker JB, Walker JP. *Brain Res 1973;54:* 391
25   Govoni S, Loddo P, Spano PF, Trabucchi M. *Brain Res 1977;138:* 565
26   Pardo JV, Creese I, Burt DR, Snyder S. *Brain Res 1977;125:* 376
27   Riederer P, Rausch WD, Birkmayer W, Jellinger K, Seemann D. *J Neural Transm 1978;Suppl 14:* 153
28   Shibuya M. *J Neural Transm 1979;44:* 287
29   Rinne UK, Sonninen V, Laaksonen H. In Poirier LJ, Sourkes TL, Bedard PJ, eds. *Advances in Neurology 1979;Vol 24:* 259. New York, Raven Press
30   Kebabian JW, Calne DB. *Nature 1979;277:* 93

157

Chapter 19

SUBSTANCE P IN THE CONTROL OF MUSCLE TONE

A Barbeau, D B Rondeau, and F B Jolicoeur

During the last decade, several peptides extracted from the pituitary gland and from various regions of the brain have been characterised and synthesised. New therapeutic approaches involving peptides or analogues in the management of a variety of disorders can be foreseen. Some peptides, like luteinising hormone-releasing hormone (LHRH), thyrotropin—releasing hormone (TRH) and β-endorphin, may have some clinical usefulness in the treatment of endocrine, neurological and mental disorders. Already, significant improvement of symptoms of Parkinson's disease has been observed in patients who received intravenous infusions of L-prolyl-L-leucylglycine amide (PLG or MIF-I) in combination with L-dopa or anti-cholinergic drugs (for review see 1,2). The first clinical trials of PLG, a tripeptide with unconfirmed melanocyte-stimulating hormone (MSH) inhibitory properties by Kastin and Barbeau [3] were based on experimental data which had indicated that this substance potentiated the actions of L-dopa and oxotremorine in animals [4], a finding later confirmed by numerous pharmacological studies. Recently, PLG was found also to potentiate apomorphine actions in rats treated with 6-hydroxy-dopamine in order to produce experimentally symptoms of parkinsonism [2, 5]. The study of the role of a given peptide in the central nervous system and of its possible implication in the pathophysiology of human disorders includes the examination of the behavioural effects of this peptide in animals. This chapter will review some data obtained in our laboratory concerning the behavioural effects of substance P (SP) in rats and its interaction with various treatments modifying catecholaminergic systems.

Functional roles for substance P in the central nervous system are suggested by a large number of pharmacological actions of the extracted or synthetic peptide. For instance, electrophysiological and neurochemical evidence is accumulating that SP acts as a transmitter or modulator of some, but not all, primary sensory neurones (for review see 6, 7). Intraventricular injections of SP in very low doses produced naloxone-reversible analgesia in mice while injections of high doses of SP in combination with the well known morphine antagonist produced hyperalgesia; these findings suggested a possible relationship between SP and the brain opiate peptides, endorphins and enkephalins [8]. Besides its most probable involvement in nociception, SP might play a physiological role in the control of motor function, especially via interaction with the putative neurotransmitters of the basal ganglia. High levels of SP have been detected in the substantia nigra of rats and human brain [9, 10], and the existence of a striatonigral pathway of SP containing cells originating in the anterior striatum has been demonstrated [11, 12, 13]. There is electrophysiological evidence that SP is released from the substantia nigra [14] and that it exerts excitatory actions on neurones in this area [15]. An increasing number of neurochemical studies supports the hypothesis of an excitatory input of SP on dopaminergic cells in the substantia nigra [16-19]; there is also one report suggesting that SP neurones may be under the tonic inhibitory influence of dopaminergic neurones [20]. Indirect evidence that SP may exert an excitatory action on nigrostriatal dopaminergic neurones was provided by the observation that intranigral application of SP in rats caused contralateral rotations, a behaviour primarily, but not solely, attributed to an asymmetrical activation of the dopaminergic nigrostriatal pathway [21, 22]. Administration of doses of SP higher than 10 μg/rat into the right ventricle of naive rats induced within a few minutes horizontal rotations to the left, and then rotations along the length axis of the body; the rotations were followed by a period of general excitation [16].

We undertook an experiment to establish the dose related effects of intraventricular (IVT) administration of synthetic SP (Peninsular Labs, San Carlos, Calif.) on motor activity in rats. Doses ranging from 0.07 to 80.00 μg/rat were studied. Activity scores were determined by photocell counts recorded for a 15 min test period which followed a 5 min pre-injection adaptation period. A rigid posture with extension of the limbs, interrupted by several barrel rolling rotations was a characteristic behavioural response to IVT infusion of SP in the 40-80 μg dose range. Similar abnormal postures were observed to a lesser extent with 20 μg/rat. An analysis of variance revealed significantly greater activity scores for the group of animals which received 0.30 and 1.25 μg doses of SP. A significant increase in the total number of rearings was found also in the animals injected with 0.30 μg SP. Grooming was observed, often accompanied by hypersalivation, but animals did not spend more time than control rats in such activity.

In a different experimental design allowing us to study the effects of SP on motor activity for longer periods of time, we found that the increase in activity produced by IVT 0.60 μg/rat SP did not persist for more than 15 minutes. Moreover, administration of the peptide, at this dose, did not potentiate or reduce the stereotypy and increased activity induced by 2 mg/kg d-amphetamine and 1 mg/kg apomorphine, injected simultaneously or 30 min after SP. Results of experiments in mice confirmed that SP shows little activity in the L-dopa and 5 HT potentiation tests [23] and indicated that the peptide does not antagonise or accentuate tremors induced by oxotremorine.

Photocell counts obtained when animals are placed in an activity meter are an index of gross motor activity. It is not easy from this measurement to distinguish between locomotor activity and the fine movements of grooming behaviour. Therefore, we studied the behavioural effects of SP in rats placed in a 16 squares

159

open field (88 x 88 x 60 cm) for 30 minutes. SP was administered IVT in doses of 0.60 and 2.50 μg/rat. The lower dose of the peptide significantly increased locomotion and grooming in comparison to a control group. Analyses of variance and appropriate post hoc tests revealed that locomotor activity in the 0.60 μg SP group was increased significantly for the first 10 min of the test session while grooming activity remained significantly greater almost throughout the 30 min. These results suggest that a greater frequency of grooming movements was probably an essential component of the SP induced activity initially observed when rats were tested in an activity meter.

In order to study at the behavioural level the possible interaction of SP with the catecholaminergic systems, various groups of rats were administered the following treatments at appropriate times before IVT injections of the peptide: 250 mg/kg β-methylpara-tyrosine, a tyrosine hydroxylase inhibitor, 20 mg/kg phenoxybenzamine, a predominantly post-synaptic α-adrenergic receptor antagonist, 25 mg/kg FLA-63, a relatively specific dopamine-β-oxidase inhibitor and 0.1 mg/kg haloperidol, a dopamine receptor antagonist. All four treatments produced hypokinesia in SP-vehicle treated rats, as evidenced by decreases of similar magnitude in locomotor activity measured in the open field. SP in doses of 0.60 and 2.50 μg/rat did not affect the behavioural depression produced by α-methyl-para-tyrosine, phenoxybenzamine and FLA-63. However, the peptide systematically reversed the hypokinesia of the haloperidol pretreated rats. An analysis of variance and the appropriate post hoc tests revealed that 0.60 μg SP increased locomotor activity during the whole test session while the higher dose of the peptide, 2.50 μg, produced such effect only during the first 5 min. In comparison to an appropriate control group, time spent grooming was not reduced by any of the four drug treatments. However SP did not modify significantly grooming activity in any of the group which received these pharmacological agents.

Since SP reversed the hypokinesia induced by a low dose of haloperidol, we decided to examine the actions of the peptide on some other behavioural effects of the neuroleptic. A higher dose of haloperidol, 3 mg/kg, produced catalepsy, rigidity and decreased locomotor activity in rats (unpublished data). Catalepsy was determined by placing the animal's front paws on three different objects: a horizontal wooden bar (1 cm width) suspended 10 cm above the table, a 9 cm high wooden cork (2.5 cm diameter) and a similar 3 cm high cork. The number of sec spent in each of these three positions up to a maximum of 60 sec were recorded, the sum of which constituted the result at the catalepsy test. Similarly, for the measurement of rigidity a rat was suspended by its front paws grasping a metal rod (0.5 cm diameter) which was held about 50 cm above the table and the time the animal remained in such a position was recorded; a prolonged grasping response has been correlated with direct measures of muscle rigidity [24]. Assessment of motor activity, catalepsy and rigidity in haloperidol pretreated rats was made at 30 min intervals for a period of 3 hr after SP injections. Behaviourally, the animals injected with IVT 0.60 and 2.50 μg/rat SP did not differ from controls; the peptide did not counteract the hypokinesia and catalepsy resulting from the administration of 3 mg/kg haloperidol. However, animals which received 0.60 μg/rat SP displayed

160

significantly less rigidity than controls at each test period. Changes in muscle rigidity were observed immediately after infusion of the peptide and persisted for at least 150 min. Results at the catalepsy and rigidity tests obtained 120 min after SP injections are presented in Figure 1. It appears that the occurrence of the symptoms induced by a high dose of haloperidol, catalepsy, rigidity and a considerable reduction in motor activity, cannot be attributed to a decrease of SP content in the substantia nigra.

In fact, it has been reported recently that chronic administration of haloperidol significantly reduced SP content of the substantia nigra but, also, that an acute treatment with a dose of 2 mg/kg of the neuroleptic failed to produce such neurochemical change [20]. Nevertheless, our results indicated that SP exerted differential effects on the symptoms induced by haloperidol.

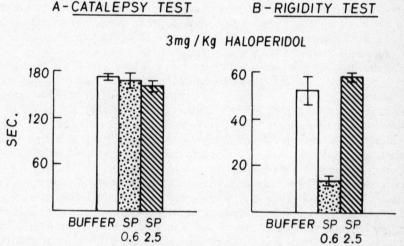

Figure 1 Results in sec ± S.E.M. at catalepsy (left) and rigidity (right) tests obtained 120 min after SP injections. All rats pretreated with 3 mg/kg haloperidol ip 2 hr prior to SP injections. Six rats per group.

Destruction of catecholamine containing neurones by microinjections of 6-hydroxydopamine (6-OHDA) into the substantia nigra and/or along the dopaminergic nigrostriatal pathway have been employed to create animal models of parkinsonism [25, 26]. Bilateral injections of 6-OHDA in the anterolateral hypothalamus produced a hypokinesia in rats which is accompanied by a generalised reduction in brain noradrenaline levels and a reduction of dopamine in the striatum and cerebral cortex [27]. The putative dopamine receptor agonist, apomorphine, and several drugs used in the treatment of Parkinson's disease were effective in reversing this 6-OHDA induced hypokinesia [27]; as mentioned earlier, apomorphine effects in this model were potentiated by the tripeptide PLG [2]. We studied the dose-related effects of IVT administration of SP, alone and in combination with apomorphine, in rats rendered hypokinetic by bilateral 6-OHDA hypothalamic lesions.

Doses ranging from 0.07 to 20.00 μg/rat were examined. An analysis of variance revealed that the dose of 0.30 μg/rat of the peptide was the only one to significantly increase motor activity as determined by photocell counts in a 5 min test session immediately after SP administration. Behavioural observations indicated that the significantly greater activity in the 0.30 μg/rat SP group as well as the higher mean activity counts in other groups which received SP were not necessarily related to the induction of locomotor activity in the hypokinetic rats. Grooming was observed in all animals injected with 0.30 μg/rat SP while only 3 out of 8 showed locomotor activity. Whenever locomotion occurred, the gait of rats consisted of extremely short steps, executed very slowly. Such abnormal walking has been reported to occur following injections of anticholinergics in akinetic 6-OHDA treated rats [28]. At all doses examined, SP did not potentiate or reduce the stereotypy and increased activity induced by 1 mg/kg apomorphine. Although the reversal of hypokinesia by SP was of much less magnitude and duration than the one produced by the administration of L-dopa or other dopaminergic agonists [27], our finding demonstrated that IVT injection of SP elicits a behavioural activation in rats with 6-OHDA hypothalamic lesions.

In summary, we observed that IVT injections of low doses of SP, between 0.30 and 1.25 μg/rat, induced behavioural activation in rats characterised by increased locomotor activity and grooming. Similar behavioural changes have been reported following administration of SP by this route in rabbits [29] and rats [30] and following intranigral injections [31]. It has been demonstrated recently that application of SP into the ventral tegmental area (VTA) elicits an increase in locomotion and exploration without affecting grooming [32]; a potentiation of the effects of d-amphetamine on activity by previous infusion of SP into the VTA was also reported [32]. The latter result is in contrast with our finding that IVT injection of SP did not potentiate the stereotypy and behavioural arousal produced by amphetamine and apomorphine. Since we administered the peptide into the ventricles, it cannot be established precisely upon which brain structures SP might have exerted its action. The use of two doses of haloperidol which produced distinct behavioural symptoms in rats allows us to study separately the effects of SP in hypokinesia and rigidity. The peptide reversed the rigidity induced by a high dose of the dopamine receptor antagonist but did not affect catalepsy and hypokinesia. SP did reverse the hypokinesia induced by a dose of 0.1 mg/kg haloperidol but did not affect the behavioural responses to α-methyl-para-tyrosine, phenoxybenzamine and FLA-63. Locomotion and grooming were briefly observed after SP injection in rats rendered hypokinetic by 6-OHDA hypothalamic lesions. It has been demonstrated that the increase in locomotor activity resulting from SP infusion into the VTA could be blocked by infusion of haloperidol into the nucleus accumbens or by 6-OHDA lesions of the ascending A10 neurones [33]. These findings suggest that SP induces its behavioural effects through activation of dopaminergic neurones; the relative contribution of the nigro-striatal, mesolimbic and mesocortical pathways to these effects, as well as the relationships of SP containing fibres with other neurotransmitter systems, for example cholinergic and GABA ergic neurones, still remain to be determined.

162

It is now widely recognised that brain peptides play physiological roles in neuronal and behavioural functions of the CNS. It has been hypothesised that an important role of the peptidergic pathway is to exert a trophic modulation on aminergic functions, and that a decrease in such trophic action of peptides could result in damage to neurones containing the putative neurotransmitters, like those associated with extrapyramidal disorders [1]. Valuable information concerning the pathophysiology and/or therapy of neurological disorders could be obtained from the study of the relationship between peptides and biogenic amines.

Summary

In recent years, many peptides have found a progressively more important role in the biochemistry and physiology of the brain in addition to their definite involvement in hormonal regulation. There is growing evidence that, among these peptides having CNS effects, the undecapeptide, substance P (SP) may functionally interact with the neurochemical mechanisms of the basal ganglia. A series of experiments were undertaken to determine the behavioural effects of SP in rats. Intraventricular injections of SP in doses ranging from .30 to 1.25 μg/rat induced motor activity in naive rats placed for 15 min in an activity meter, locomotion and grooming in a 16 squares open field were also increased temporarily. Doses over 40 μg/rat produced immobility, rigidity and barrel rolling rotations.

The interaction of SP with various treatments modifying catecholaminergic systems was investigated. Administration of SP, 0.60 μg/rat 30 min after injections of 2 mg/kg d-amphetamine and 1 mg/kg apomorphine did not potentiate or reduce the hyperactivity and the stereotyped behaviour induced by these two drugs. SP did not affect the hypokinesia produced by the tyrosine hydroxylase inhibitor, α-methyl-p-tyrosine (250 mg/kg), the α-adrenergic receptor antagonist, phenoxybenzamine (20 mg/kg) and the dopamine-β-hydroxylase inhibitor, FLA-63 (25 mg/kg). However, SP, in a dose of 0.60 μg/rat, systematically reversed the behavioural depression and the decrease in locomotor activity induced by a relatively small dose of haloperidol (1 mg/kg), a dopamine receptor antagonist. On the other hand, SP did not counteract the catalepsy resulting from the administration of a higher dose of this neuroleptic (3 mg/kg), but significantly decreased rigidity. Intraventricular injection of SP, 0.30 μg/rat, increased motor activity in rats rendered hypokinetic by bilateral microinjections of 6-hydroxydopamine into the anteriolateral hypothalamus; behavioural observations indicated that grooming and not locomotion was mainly responsible for the greater activity scores. The reversal of the hypokinesia produced by administration of apomorphine to these 6-OHDA treated animals was not potentiated by SP.

Brain peptides may modulate catecholaminergic functions and may contribute to the pathogenesis of extrapyramidal disorders such as Parkinson's disease and Huntington's chorea. The possible involvement of SP in the control of motor functions is discussed, and it is shown that substance P is probably involved in the control of muscle tone.

Acknowledgements

The authors gratefully acknowledge the contribution of F Belanger, G Fouriezos, C Robichaud-Maillet and S Gariepy. DBR and FBJ were supported by the Medical Research Council of Canada and the Conseil de la Recherche en Sante du Quebec respectively. These studies were partially supported by grants from the Medical Research Council of Canada (MA-4938) and the Seymour E Clonick Memorial Fund of the United Parkinson Foundation. Some of the data reported in this chapter was first presented at the Fulton Society Symposium in September 1979 and the original experimental results will appear in more detail [34].

References

1   Barbeau A. In Collu, Barbeau A, Ducharme JR, Rochefort JG, eds. *Central Nervous System Effects of Hypothalamic Hormones and Other Peptides 1978;*403. New York, Raven Press
2   Barbeau A, Kastin AJ. In Birkmayer W, Hornykiewicz O, eds. *Advances in Parkinsonism 1976;*483. Basle, Editiones Roche
3   Kastin AJ, Barbeau A. *Can Med Ass J 1972;107:*1079
4   Plotnikoff NP, Kastin AJ, Anderson HS, Schally AV. *Life Sci 1971;10:*1279
5   Kostrzewa RM, Kastin AJ, Sobrian SK. *Pharmac Biochem Behav 1978;9:*375
6   Mroz EA, Leeman SE. *Vitam Horm 1977;35:*209
7   Von Euler US, Pernow B. *Substance P 1977.* New York, Raven Press
8   Frederickson RCA, Burgis V, Harrell CE, Edwards JD. *Science 1978;199:*1359
9   Browstein MJ, Mroz EA, Kiser JS, Palkovits M, Leeman SE. *Brain Res 1976;116:*299
10 Kanazawa I, Bird E, O'Connell R, Powell D. *Brain Res 1977;120:*387
11 Browstein MJ, Mroz EA, Tappaz ML. *Brain Res 1977;135:*315,323
12 Hong JS, Yang H-YT, Racagni G, Costa E. *Brain Res 1977;122:*541
13 Kanazawa I, Emson PC, Cuello AC. *Brain Res 1977;119:*447
14 Jessell TM. *Brit J Pharmacol 1977;59:*486P
15 Davies J, Dray A. *Brain Res 1976;107:*623
16 Carlsson A, Magnusson T, Fisher D, Chang D, Folkers K. In Von Eulër, Pernow B, eds. *Substance P 1977;*201. New York, Raven Press
17 Cheramy A, Michelot R, Leviel V, Nieoullon A, Glowinski J, Kerdelhue B. *Brain Res 1978;155:*404
18 Cheramy A, Nieoullon A, Michelot R, Glowinski J. *Neurosci Lett 1977;4:*105
19 Waldmeier PC, Kam R, Stocklin K. *Brain Res 1978;159:*223
20 Hong JS, Yang H-YT, Costa E. *Neuropharmac 1978;17:*83
21 James TA, Starr MS. *J Pharm Pharmac 1977;29:*181
22 Olpe HR, Koella WP. *Brain Res 1977;126:*576
23 Plotnikoff NP, Kastin AJ. In Walter R, Meinhofer J, eds. *Peptides: Chemistry, Structure and Biology 1975;*645. Ann Arbor: Ann Arbor Science Publ
24 Steg G. *Acta Physiol Scand 1964;61:*Suppl 225,5
25 Smith GP, Young RC. In McDowell FH, Barbeau A, eds. *Advances in Neurology Vol 5 1974;*427. New York, Raven Press
26 Ungerstedt U, Avemo A, Avemo E, Ljungbërg, Ranje C. In Calne DB, ed. *Advances in Neurology Vol 3 1973;*257. New York, Raven Press
27 Butterworth RF, Belanger F, Barbeau A. *Pharmac Biochem Behav 1978;8:*41
28 Schallert T, Whishaw IQ, Ramirez VD, Teitelbaum P. *Science 1978;199:*1461
29 Melo JC, Graeff FG. *J Pharmac Exp Ther 1975;193:*1
30 Kubicki J. *Acta Physiol Pol 1977;28:*489
31 Kelley AE, Iversen SD. *Brain Res 1978;158:*474
32 Stinus L, Kelly AE and Iversen SD *Nature 1978; 276:* 616
33 Kelly AE, Stinus L and Iversen SD *Neurosc Lett 1979; 11:* 335
34 Jolicoeur FB, Rondeau DB, Belanger F, Fouriezos G and Barbeau A. *Peptides 1980; Vol 1,* (in press)

Chapter 20

ENKEPHALINS IN MOTOR DISORDERS

M Sheehy, M Schachter, C D Marsden and J D Parkes

Introduction

The enkephalins are pentapeptides with many of the pharmacological properties of morphine [1]. They have a high affinity for some types of opiate receptor and rapidly induce tolerance and physical dependence. Two such peptides, leu^5- and met ^{5}-enkephalin, have been identified in mammalian brain [1]. The enkephalins produce modest and very transient analgesia after intracerebral injection and, given intravenously, the analgesic potency of both peptides is extremely low. In addition to their analgesic effect, enkephalins produce immobility and catalepsy after intracerebral injection, as well as endocrine changes similar to those caused by morphine. Analgesia, immobility and endocrine effects can be reversed by the opiate antagonist, naloxone [1].

Physiological function of enkephalins

The physiological function of endogenous enkephalins remains uncertain. In addition to modulation of central responses to pain and other noxious stimuli [2], and regulation of neuroendocrine systems in the hypothalamus [3], these peptides may also act as neurotransmitters or "neuromodulators" in the extrapyramidal system. Very high concentrations of enkephalins are found in the globus pallidus and in the striatum [4]. In the striatum, but not the globus pallidus, there is also a high density of opiate receptors [4]. Destruction of the nigrostriatal tracts with 6-hydroxydopamine, which specifically destroys dopamine neurones, reduces the population of striatal dopamine receptors by about 30 per cent suggesting that these receptors are located on dopamine neurones [5]. The possible functional importance of nigrostriatal enkephalins is shown by the studies of Diamond and Borison [6]. After unilateral nigrostriatal tract lesions, met^5-enkephalin potentiates rotary behaviour due to d-amphetamine but inhibits that due to L-dopa and apomorphine. Naloxone has the opposite effect to met^5-enkephalin. Neither met^5-enkephalin nor naloxone produce rotation when given alone. On the basis

165

of these results, it has been suggested that endogenous enkephalins facilitate the action of pre-synaptic dopamine agonists and oppose that of post-synaptic agonists. However, naloxone antagonises apomorphine induced stereotyped behaviour, whereas potentiation would have been expected according to the above hypothesis [7]. Met^5-enkephalin when injected intraperitoneally in sub-analgesic doses potentiates the hypermotility that follows treatment with L-dopa and a monoamine oxidase inhibitor [8]. This contrasts with the cataleptogenic effect of enkephalin injected into the brain.

Motor effects of morphine and naloxone

The data on the effects of morphine on motor behaviour are difficult to interpret. Morphine has been reported both to potentiate and to antagonise the stereotyped behaviour caused in laboratory animals by dopamine agonists such as apomorphine and d-amphetamine [9, 10]. The precise effect is critically dependent on drug timing and dosage. Chronic morphine administration to rodents over a three-week period causes a progressive increase in stereotypes [11]. Morphine increases striatal dopamine turnover [10], an effect generally associated with dopamine antagonists such as the neuroleptic drugs, and thought to be largely due to increased pre-synaptic dopamine synthesis after post-synaptic receptor blockade. In man, morphine does not appear to cause movement disorders after either acute or chronic administration. Naloxone in low doses (0.8–2.0 mg iv) does not alter the movement disorder of parkinsonian patients [12]. The orally active opiate antagonist naltrexone, at a dose of 100 mg daily, is similarly ineffective in Parkinson's disease and in Huntington's disease [13]. In high doses, naloxone 20–28 mg iv does not cause extrapyramidal symptoms when given to schizophrenics [14].

Clinical effects of enkephalins in man

The use of natural enkephalins in clinical studies is hampered by their low potency when given po or iv, and by their very short duration of action. Many analogues of the enkephalins have now been synthesised which are much more potent than the endogenous peptides, and are highly resistant to enzymatic degradation. One of the most active of these synthetic enkephalins is DAMME (D-Aln^2, Me Phe^4, Met(0)^5-ol-enkephalin, FK 33824 Sandoz). As an analgesic it is 30,000 times more potent than met^5-enkephalin, 1000 times more potent than morphine, and over 20 times more potent than beta-endorphin [15, 16]. It is effective by the intravenous, intramuscular and oral routes. In animals, DAMME produces diminished spontaneous movement after intracerebral injection, but no motor abnormalities have been described in human subjects given DAMME 0.5 mg iv or 3 mg im [16, 17, 18]. In man, DAMME causes characteristic EEG changes differing from those caused by morphine [16]. Plasma levels of growth hormone and prolactin due to DAMME 0.5 mg im are not reversed by nalorphine 10 mg im. DAMME causes

166

a variety of side effects, including subjective heaviness of the limbs, tightness of the throat or chest, flushing of the skin, conjunctival irritation, increased bowel sounds, sweating, a metallic taste in the mouth, dryness of the mouth and nausea. These side effects are reversed by naloxone, although only in high dosage. Naloxone 4 mg iv also reverses all EEG and endocrine changes caused by DAMME. Sedation and euphoria occur in schizophrenics after DAMME 3 mg im [18], but apparently not in normal subjects given DAMME in doses of up to 1.2 mg im.

Effects of DAMME in extrapyramidal disorders

We have investigated the action of DAMME in subjects with a variety of extra-pyramidal disorders. Three subjects with idiopathic Parkinson's disease, two with Huntington's disease, one with hemichorea (probably of vascular origin), three with generalised dystonia, three with torticollis and one with tardive dyskinesia were studied. Each subject was given DAMME 0.25–0.5 mg i.v. (intravenous) as a bolus. Prior to this, all other drugs were withdrawn for at least 12 hours. In five patients, all three parkinsonian patients, the patient with tardive dyskinesia and one patient with generalised dystonia, the DAMME injection was repeated, 30 minutes after an oral dose of d-amphetamine 20 mg. Tremor, rigidity, akinesia and postural abnormality were assessed using the King's College Hospital rating scale [19], and chorea and dystonia were recorded according to the AIM scoring system [20]. Assessments were made 60 and 30 minutes before DAMME was given and at 0, 5, 15, 30, 60, 90, 120, 150 and 180 minutes thereafter.

DAMME given alone did not influence any aspect of parkinsonian disability in any of the three subjects. The severity of chorea and dystonia also remained un-altered in all cases. After d-amphetamine 20 mg, there was a 20 per cent reduction in disability score in one parkinsonian patient while the other two did not improve. The severity of dystonia was unaltered following d-amphetamine 20 mg in a single subject with generalised dystonia. The patient with tardive dyskinesia had a subjective but not objective improvement in facial movements. The subsequent injection of DAMME did not modify the effect of d-amphetamine in any of the 5 subjects.

Side effects of DAMME

Eleven of the twelve subjects reported side effects after DAMME injection. These were similar to those described in other studies and included subjective heaviness of the limbs (6 subjects), dry mouth (6 subjects) tingling in the limbs and face (4 subjects), nausea (3 subjects), facial flushing (3 subjects), metallic taste in mouth (3 subjects), sweating (2 subjects) and drowsiness (2 subjects). In one subject, there was a fall in systolic and diastolic blood pressure of 30 mm Hg associated with bradycardia. These effects began within 5–15 minutes of DAMME injection and lasted from 10 to 60 minutes.

167

Discussion

What is the role of enkephalins in human motor disorders? It is possible that enkephalins have no part in the function of the extrapyramidal system, but this is very unlikely in view of the evidence already outlined. There is no direct proof that DAMME given parenterally enters the striatum, although its endocrine effects indicate that it does penetrate the hypothalamus and its effects on the EEG also suggest a central action. The doses of DAMME used in this study (0.25–0.5 mg iv) may have been too low to produce a detectable extrapyramidal effect, since the blood-brain barrier is relatively impermeable to DAMME and repeated doses may therefore be required (Graffenried, personal communication).

Despite these negative findings, it is probable that manipulation of enkephalin systems will eventually have clinical application in movement disorders. One recent finding that supports this view is the apparent reduction in the number of opiate receptors in patients with Parkinson's disease [21]. Using naloxone-binding techniques, a reduction of nearly 50 per cent in opiate receptor populations has been demonstrated in the caudate nucleus of parkinsonian patients. It is probable that these receptors are located on dopaminergic neurones which degenerate during the course of Parkinson's disease [22], and the functional significance of this finding is uncertain. It should also be noted that there are several populations of opiate receptors in the brain, and those identified by naloxone binding are not those with high affinity for enkephalins [23].

Acknowledgements

We acknowledge gratefully the assistance of Dr B V Graffenried of Sandoz Ltd., Basle and of Dr G Kennedy of Sandoz Ltd., UK. We also thank Mrs P Asselman for help in the preparation of the manuscript.

References

1   Beaumont A, Hughes J. *Ann Rev Pharmacol Toxicol 1979; 19:*245
2   Terenius L. *Ann Rev Pharmacol Toxicol 1978; 18:*189
3   Meites J, Bruni JF, van Vugt DA, Smith AF. *Life Sci 1979; 24:*1325
4   Uhl GR, Childers SR, Snyder SH. In Ganong WF, Martini L, eds. *Frontiers in neuroendocrinology volume 5, 1978;* 289. New York: Raven Press
5   Pollard H, Llorens-Cortes C, Schwartz JC. *Nature 1977; 268:*745
6   Diamond BI, Borison RL. *Neurology (Minneap) 1978; 28:*1985
7   Margolin DJ, Moon BH. *J Neurol Sci 1979; 43:*13
8   Plotnikoff NP, Kastin AJ, Coy DH, Christensen CW, Schally AV, Coy DU. *Life Sci 1976; 19:*1283
9   McKenzie GM, Sadoff M. *J Pharmac Pharmacol 1974; 26:*280
10 Puri SK, Reddy C, Lal H. *Res Commun Chem Path Pharmacol 1973; 5:*389
11 Smee ML, Overstreet DH. *Psychopharmacology 1976; 49:*1125
12 Price P, Baxter RCH, Parkes JD, Marsden CD. *Arch Neurol 1979; 36:*661

13   Nutt JG, Rosin AJ, Eisler T, Calne DB, Chase TN. *Arch Neurol 1978; 35:*810
14   Terenius L, Wahlström A. In Hughes J, ed. *Centrally acting peptides 1978;* 161. London: Macmillan
15   Roemar D, Buescher HH, Hill RC, Pless J, Baver W, Cardinaux F, Closse A, Hauser D, Huguenin R. *Nature 1977; 268:*547
16   von Graffenfried B, Del Pozo E, Roubicek J, Krebs E, Poldinger W, Burmeister P, Kerp L. *Nature 1978; 272:*729
17   Nedopil N, Rüther E. *Pharmakopsychiat 1979; 12:*277
18   Jørgensen A, Fog R, Veilis B. *Lancet 1979; i:*935
19   Parkes JD, Zilkha KJ, Calver DM, Knill-Jones RP. *Lancet 1970; i:*259
20   Abnormal Involuntary Movement Scale, National Institute of Mental Health (Form 117)
21   Reisine TD, Rossor M, Spokes E, Iversen LL, Yamamura HI. *Brain Res 1979; 173:* 378
22   Hornykiewicz O. *Pharmacol Rev 1966; 18:*925
23   Chang K-J, Cuatredasas P. *J Biol Chem 1979; 254:*2610

Chapter 21

CSF BIOCHEMICAL STUDIES ON SOME EXTRAPYRAMIDAL DISEASES

Adrian Williams

Introduction

Biochemical studies on CSF, unlike those on brain, have contributed little to the understanding of diseases that involve the extrapyramidal nervous system. This is in spite of evidence that the CSF levels of some important neurotransmitters, or their chief metabolites, in the lumbar sac correlate moderately well with those in brain. The advantages of having access to a reflection of brain neurotransmitter levels 'in vivo' are considerable. For instance, patients can be studied before they reach 'end stage disease' by which time a number of non-specific changes may have occurred, quite apart from avoiding artefacts introduced from intercurrent illness and multiple drug therapy. Also CSF is easily sampled from a procedure with a low, and that temporary, morbidity rate and so can help elucidate diseases in which suitable brain material is difficult to obtain.

In this chapter, a number of collaborative projects, undertaken on patients attending the National Institutes of Health, will be summarised. The diseases considered are Parkinson's disease (PD), the Shy-Drager (S-D) syndrome and Progressive Supranuclear Palsy (PSP). All patients involved gave their informed consent, had typical clinical features of their respective diseases, and were not on any drug treatment. Patients with no neurological disease and with isolated torticollis, of the same average age, have been used to estimate the normal range.

Dopaminergic function

The diminished brain dopamine levels in PD have been confirmed on several occasions in CSF by the finding of a reduction of its major metabolite homovanillic acid (HVA). Representative observations are shown in Figure 1, HVA being measured by gas chromatography—mass spectrometry (GC—MS) method. It can also be seen that levels are low in the S-D syndrome and in PSP [1]. In all these diseases a tendency was present for the more disabled patients to have the lower HVA levels.

170

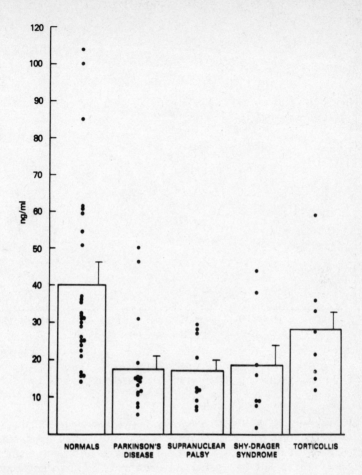

Figure 1 CSF HVA Levels.

Tetrahydrobiopterin (THB), the pterin whose availability acts as an important rate controlling factor in tyrosine and tryptophan hydroxylation, has also been used as a measure of central aminergic activity [2]. CSF levels of THB correlate with HVA (Figure 2) but not with 5-hydroxy-indole-acetic acid (5-HIAA) or nor-adrenaline (NA). CSF values are reduced in PD and also in the S—D syndrome and PSP (Figure 3). These reductions are likely to be consequent upon loss of dop-aminergic neurones, rather than due to any metabolic defect of pterin synthesis.

Noradrenergic function

NA in CSF and plasma can be measured by a radio-enzymatic method. Figure 4 illustrates that CSF levels are low in PD, as is known in brain, but are normal in

171

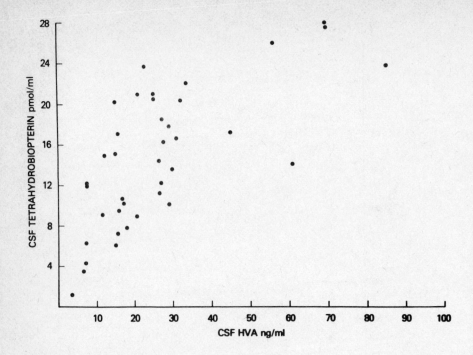

Figure 2 CSF Tetrahydrobiopterin correlated with HVA levels.

PSP despite equally severe clinical disability [1]. Levels are low in the S–D syndrome, a finding that has recently been confirmed in brain. It is not known whether this deficit is related to the extrapyramidal or to the autonomic disturbance, but the former seems the more likely. That these changes are not secondary to the known peripheral abnormalities of NA is suggested from Figure 5, where the resting plasma NA levels in the S–D syndrome are shown to be no different from normal. These data on plasma also confirm the absence of increase of NA levels on standing found in S–D patients. However, there are some curious anomalies, for instance, some patients may have a very low resting NA, similar to those seen in the syndrome, thought to be peripheral in origin, of idiopathic orthostatic hypotension, and some patients increase their levels on standing normally, despite severe postural hypotension.

Investigation of dopamine-β-hydroxylase (DBH), the enzyme responsible for converting dopamine to NA, is another potential method of investigating noradrenergic activity as it can be measured in both plasma and CSF. However, in our hands [3] little has been learnt, as shown in Figures 6 and 7. With the possible exception of some patients with S–D syndrome, CSF levels were normal and, in contrast with earlier reports on the S–D syndrome, so were those in plasma.

172

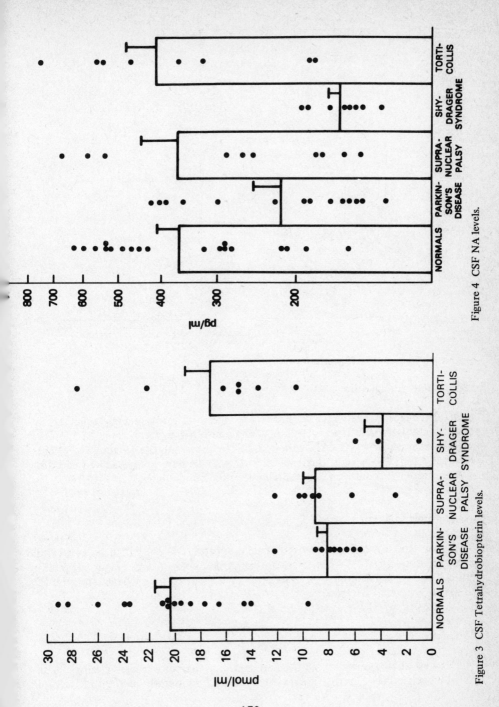

Figure 4 CSF NA levels.

Figure 3 CSF Tetrahydrobiopterin levels.

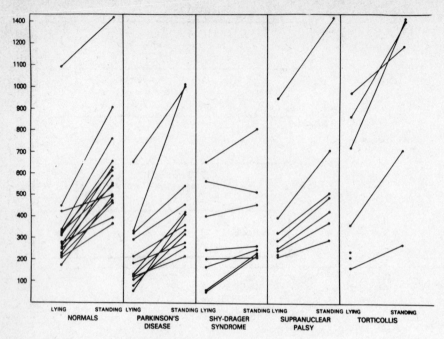

Figure 5 Plasma NA levels lying and standing.

Serotoninergic function

CSF 5-HIAA has been used as a measure of central serotoninergic function, although its usefulness is in question. Variable results have been reported and ours [1], measured by a GC—MS method, are fairly representative (Figure 8). Patients with PD and PSP have normal values. S—D patients have a tendency to have low values overall, but individuals never fell out of the normal range.

GABAergic function

The usefulness of CSF GABA levels remains uncertain. In our patients studied with the receptor assay [4], values were normal in all disease groups (Figure 9). This is in contrast to some reports on brain levels, but many of those changes may reflect a variety of agonal artefacts.

Substance P

CSF levels of this peptide have been studied in a number of diseases using a radio-immunoassay [5]. Figure 10 shows that values are modestly reduced in the S—D

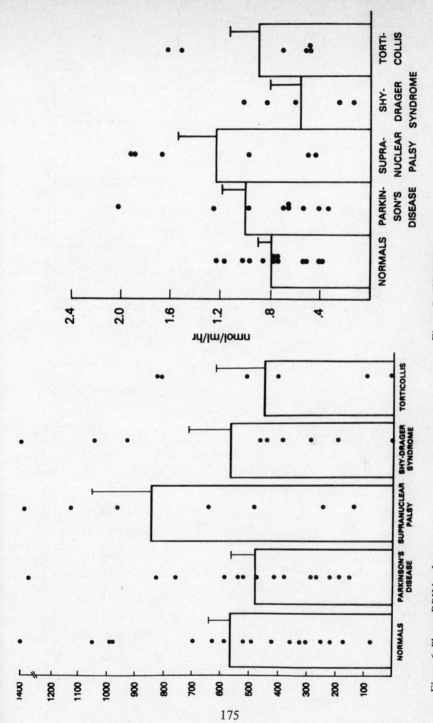

Figure 6 Plasma DBH levels.

Figure 7 CSF DBH levels.

175

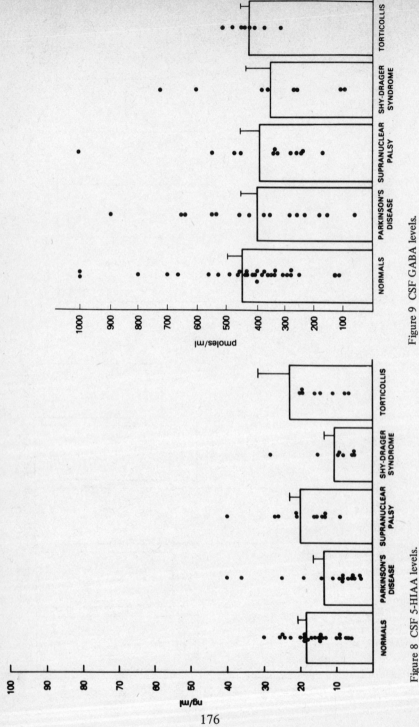

Figure 9 CSF GABA levels.

Figure 8 CSF 5-HIAA levels.

syndrome, but appear to be normal in PD and PSP. This is of some interest as substance P appears to be active in both autonomic pathways and in the basal ganglia. CSF levels are not reduced in Huntington's disease even though brain levels suggest that the relatively mild reduction of CSF levels in the S–D syndrome may represent a fairly severe central deficit.

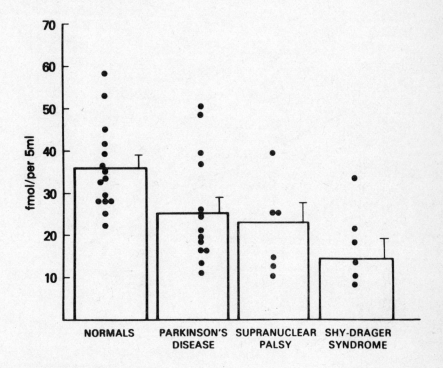

Figure 10 CSF Substance P levels.

Further Studies

Basal levels in the CSF of other substances important in the CNS could be studied with advantage in a number of neurological disorders, particularly those where suitable brain material is difficult to obtain. CSF studies may also provide useful information by following CSF chemistry after using specific agonists, or antagonists, as these changes could reflect receptor function (even though lack of normal controls would seriously hamper their interpretation). Although little need for diagnostic tests exists in this group of diseases, the examination of CSF biochemical profiles to try and identify those patients who are more likely to respond to a particular drug or who are susceptible to certain complications, eg. autonomic or psychiatric, may have practical implications.

177

Figure 11 illustrates another avenue for CSF studies [6]. Here THB, the hydroxylase cofactor, is shown to fall with age in neurologically normal subjects. This probably correlates with the known age related drop in tyrosine hydroxylase and dopamine levels in brain. Unfortunately an equivalent age range to those studied in brain was not available which would have been of interest as tyrosine hydroxylase levels fall dramatically in the first and second decade, presumably due to a

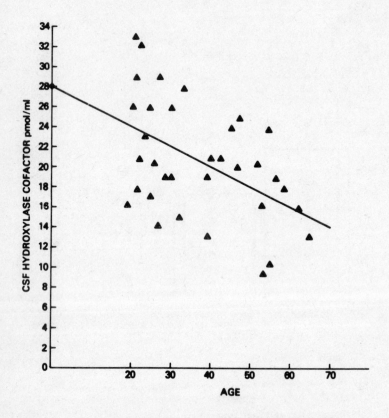

Figure 11 CSF hydroxylase cofactor levels as a function of age in normal people.

maturation rather than an ageing process, but less convincingly later in life. Figure 12 shows THB values in PD patients depending on their age (the younger patients having equally severe disease to their more elderly counterparts). Juvenile patients had relatively high values perhaps implying that the threshold loss of dopaminergic function necessary for the appearance of clinical disease in young people is less as older people have lost, in the ageing process, neuronal systems which are antidopaminergic.

178

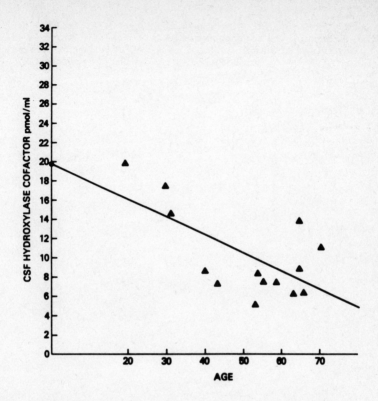

Figure 12 CSF hydroxylase cofactor as a function of age in patients with P.D.

Acknowledgement

This chapter summarises a number of studies done in the Experimental Therapeutics Branch of the NIH. These were collaborate studies and all my co-workers are acknowledged in the reference list in which this work is reported in greater detail.

References

1   Williams AC, Nutt J, Lake CR, Pfeiffer R, Teychenne PF, Ebert M, Calne DB. In Fuye K, Calne DB, eds. *Dopaminergic Ergot Derivatives and Motor Function 1979;* 271. Pergamon Press
2   Lovenberg W, Levine RA, Robinson D, Williams AC, Calne DB. *Science 1979, 204:* 624

3   Lerner P, Williams AC, Lovenberg W. In preparation
4   Enna SJ, Stern LV, Wastek GJ, Yamamura H. *Arch Neurol 1977;34:*683
5   Nutt JG, Leeman S, Williams AC, Chase TN, Engel WK. *Neurology 1980.* In press
6   Williams AC, Ballenger J, Levine RA, Lovenberg W, Calne DB. *Neurology 1980.* In press

Chapter 22

CEREBROSPINAL FLUID IMMUNOGLOBULIN PROFILES IN PARKINSON'S DISEASE

P O Behan
A M Thomas
and Wilhelmina M H Behan

Introduction

It is generally considered that there are two types of Parkinson's disease: true paralysis agitans and post-encephalitic parkinsonism. The cause of paralysis agitans is unknown: it is categorised as a degenerative process but this label merely highlights our ignorance. Clinicians are perhaps less uncertain about the aetiology of the post-encephalitic variety, classifying it as associated with viral infection but, although the original outbreak of encephalitis lethargica showed several of the features of a viral illness, no agent was ever identified or isolated from the patients.

Parkinson's disease or, not to offend the purists, a disease indistinguishable clinically from it, has been described as a complication of other virus infections, ie. coxsackie [1], herpes zoster [2], measles [3], poliomyelitis [4], Japanese B encephalititis [5], the presumed virus of Behçet's syndrome [6, 7] and influenza B [8]. Some authors, however, restrict the term post-encephalitic parkinsonism exclusively to the disorder following encephalitis lethargica.

The clinical features of this latter disorder have been well described [9, 10, 11]. The characteristic pathological findings in patients dying of the acute encephalitis, or one or two years later, are perivascular cuffs of lymphocytes and mononuclear cells in the mid-brain diencephalon. These changes are not found in the chronic cases so that it is often difficult to distinguish between post-encephalitic and true paralysis agitans material. The presence of Lewy bodies (characteristically found in idiopathic paralysis agitans but sometimes present in post-encephalitic cases or indeed in control brain material) and the finding of neurofibrillary tangles and grumous saccules (in the post-encephalitic variety) may help to differentiate the two kinds of Parkinson's disease. Some workers, however, do regard both varieties as having the same aetiology [12].

With regard to post-encephalitic parkinsonism the important question is: why does the disease process continue after the virus infection? The answer is unknown;

181

the two conditions not being mutually exclusive. Viral studies have been unrewarding in both acute and chronic cases and attempts to transmit the disorder have been unsuccessful [13].

It has recently been reported [14] that two patients with post-encephalitic Parkinson's disease had oligoclonal bands in their cerebrospinal fluid (CSF). The importance of this finding is that, if true, it would be the first indication that an immunological reaction was occurring in the brains of these patients, possibly due to a persistent virus. Because of this report, we decided to study CSF of patients with either true paralysis agitans or post-encephalitic lethargica parkinsonism. We also carried out other immunological tests, including an examination of complement metabolism and we looked for serum immune complexes.

Materials and Methods

Patients

Paralysis agitans

There were 13 patients with undisputed paralysis agitans, nine males and four females, mean age 62 years. All patients had a degree of rigidity, expressionless faces, slowness, paucity of movement and a tremor at rest. The disease had been present for from two to 28 years with a mean duration of seven years. The patients were otherwise in good health. All were being treated with Sinemet (110 mg three times a day) and in addition five took Artane.

Post-encephalitic parkinsonism

There were three patients with post-encephalitic parkinsonism, two males and one female, aged 56 to 81 years. The duration of disease was from 14 to 57 years. One of the patients had been admitted to hospital in 1923 at which time he had an expressionless face, slow mentation, unequal pupils and resting tremor. A year previously he had developed a fever and sore throat followed by delirium, drowsiness and then, some months later, diplopia. During the next year he had excessive salivation, stiffness of his muscles and oculogyric crises. The patient was affected in the Glasgow epidemic. He was one of the cases discussed in the important record made by Maine [15] of that epidemic and is still surviving. The other two patients gave a history of having developed their Parkinson syndrome within months of a pyrexial illness associated with delirium. The organism was not identified.

Cerebrospinal fluids

Controls for the cerebrospinal fluid examinations consisted of the last 850 CSFs (and paired sera) which have been examined in our laboratory. This vast number of controls includes material from normal individuals and from patients with migraine, intervertebral disc lesions, various neuropathies, multiple sclerosis, subacute sclerosing panencephalitis, bacterial and viral infections of the central nervous system, autoimmune disorders (systemic lupus erythematosus, rheumatoid arthritis and polyarteritis nodosa), myasthenia gravis, benign and malignant brain tumours and degenerative brain disorders, including Alzheimer's disease.

Immunoglobulins

IgA, IgG, IgM and IgE serum concentrations were determined by the single radial immunodiffusion technique. The following reagents were used: for IgG and IgM-Tripartigen plates (Behringwerke), for IgA—Immunoplate 3 (Hyland Laboratories), for IgE—Meloy Laboratory Kit.

Complement studies

The functional efficiency of the complement system was determined in terms of the total haemolytic complement activity (CH ^{50} units) using the method of Kent and Fife [16]. Serum anticomplementary activity was assayed by Mayer's method [17]. The following components were measured in EDTA plasma by means of the single radial immunodiffusion technique using monospecific antisera: Clq, C3, factor B and C4. Commercially available plates (Behringwerke) were used to estimate C4 concentrations. C7 concentrations were measured by the reactive lysis method [18] with activated C5, 6. C3 and factor B conversion products were sought by crossed antibody electrophoresis and immunoelectrophoresis [19]. The antisera used for the other determinations were prepared in our laboratory by standard techniques.

Electrophoresis of CSF and serum

Three millilitres of CSF (centrifuged to remove any blood cells) was concentrated 100 times in an Amicon CS. 15 concentrator. One millilitre of concentrated CSF and 1 ml of serum, taken at the same time as the CSF, were placed in sample wells of a Corning Universal electrophoresis film. Electrophoresis was carried out for 32 minutes in a Corning Electrophoresis Tank using 190 ml of barbital buffer pH 8.6. After this, the gel was stained in Amido Black for 15 minutes, rinsed in 5 per cent acetic acid, and then dried at $60°C$ for 25 minutes. This gel was then destained for five minutes with two changes of 5 per cent acetic acid and dried for a further five minutes at $60°C$. The film was then scanned on a Corning 720 Fluorometer Densitometer. The CSF/serum IgG/albumin index was then calculated from the following formula:

$$\frac{\dfrac{\% \text{ CSF immunoglobulin G}}{\% \text{ serum immunoglobulin G}}}{\dfrac{\% \text{ CSF albumin}}{\% \text{ serum albumin}}} = \text{immunoglobulin G/albumin index.}$$

Polyacrylamide electrolysis was also carried out with minor modifications to the standard technique [20].

Results

Immunoglobulins

The values for all fell within the normal range.

Complement studies

The concentrations of the complement components tested were entirely normal. Serum anticomplementary activity was negative in 15 and positive in one, of the patients with idiopathic paralysis agitans. Anticomplementary activity was positive in two controls.

CSF

The IgG/albumin index was entirely normal in all patients with paralysis agitans. No oligoclonal bands were found in any specimens using either method.

Discussion

Our study and its results have to be contrasted with that of Williams *et al* [14]. First, we examined three cases of post-encephalitic parkinsonism, at least one of which was due to encephalitis lethargica. The nature of the virus in the other two cases was unknown but the initial illness and its resultant course were exactly the same as that described in encephalitis lethargica [9]. In comparison, the two patients reported by Williams *et al* [14] certainly did not have post-encephalitis lethargica parkinsonism, according to the classical criteria. We also studied 13 cases with true paralysis agitans in comparison with the six recorded by Williams *et al* [14]. Apart from clinical criticisms, their technical work and interpretation has to be critically evaluated.

They reported that oligoclonal bands do occur in the CSF of patients with post-encephalitic parkinsonism. We examined the CSF from our patients in the light of an experience of no less than 850 previous specimens and report here that the samples could not have been more normal. The electrophoretic strips were read by three independent observers and also objectively, by a densitometer (which was not done by the other workers) [14]. We also (again unlike Williams *et al* [14]) carried out polyacrylamide gel electrophoresis on these samples, to see if the better resolution obtained would result in identification of any bands—but it did not. Calculating the cerebrospinal fluid IgG/albumin index also revealed totally negative results.

We can state with confidence, therefore, that there is no evidence of oligoclonal banding of the CSF in idiopathic Parkinson's disease or in post-encephalitic parkinsonism. The other immunological investigations that we carried out, including measurements of immunoglobulins and complement components and a search for immune complexes, were all negative.

In conclusion, therefore, we are unable to confirm the recent report by Williams and his colleagues [14] and we report also that our immunological investigations have revealed no evidence of any immune dysfunction that might point towards viral persistence in either type of Parkinson's disease.

References

1   Walters JH. *New Eng J Med 1960; 263:*744
2   Strong G. *Brit Med J 1952; 1:*533
3   Meyer B. *Brit Med J 1943; 1:*508
4   Duvoisin RC, Yahr MD. *Arch Neurol 1965; 12:*227
5   Richter RW, Shimojyo S. *Neurology 1961; 11:*553
6   Pallis CA, Fudge BJ. *Arch Neurol Psychiat 1956; 75:1*
7   Wadia N, Williams E. *Brain 1957; 80:59*
8   Gamboa ET, Wolf A, Yahr MD, Harter DH, Duffy PE, Barden H, Hsu KC. *Arch Neurol 1974; 31:*228
9   Economo C Von. *Wien Klin Wschr 1917; 30:*581
10 Buzzard EF, Greenfield JG. *Brain 1919; 42:*305
11 Bramwell E, Miller J. *Lancet 1920; i:*1152
12 Poskanzer DC, Schwab RS. *J Chronic Dis 1963; 16:*961
13 Gibbs CJ, Gasdusek DC. In Norris FH, Kurland L, eds. *Motor Neurone Diseases 1969;* 269. New York: Grune and Stratton
14 Williams A, Houff S, Lees A, Calne DB. *J Neurol Neurosurg and Psychiat 1979; 42:*790
15 Maine A. *J Hygiene 1931; 31:* 162
16 Kent JF, Fife EH. *Am J Trop Med Hyg 1963; 12:*103
17 Mayer MM. In Kabat EA, Mayer MM, eds. *Experimental Immunochemistry 2nd edition 1961;* 133. Springfield Illinois: Charles C Thomas
18 Thompson RA, Lachmann PJ. *J exp Med 1970; 131:*629
19 Laurel CB. *Analyt Biochem 1965; 10:*358
20 Davis BJ. *Ann N Y Acad Sci 1964; 121:*404

Chapter 23

[^{18}F] FLUORO DOPA FOR THE MEASUREMENT OF INTRACEREBRAL DOPAMINE METABOLISM IN MAN

E S Garnett, G Firnau and C Nahmias

It is generally agreed that Parkinsonism is associated with a deficiency of dopamine and dopamine containing cells in the nigro-striatal pathways [1, 2]. In contrast, it has been found that there is an increase in the number of post-synaptic dopamine receptors in the putamen of Parkinsonian patients, unless the patients have been recently treated with L-dopa [3]. All of this information has been derived from human autopsy material and therefore represents a static picture of the metabolic events that underlie Parkinson's disease. There are, however, suggestions based on the high ratio of striatal homovanillic acid to dopamine in Parkinson's disease, that a small pool of intracerebral dopamine may be turning over rapidly. Further, it has been noted in rats [4] that hyper- and hypo-sensitivity to catecholamines in the central nervous system is closely associated with changes in the ratio of striatal homovanillic acid to dopamine. It is clear from these considerations that a method is required whereby the turnover rates of intracerebral catecholamines can be monitored directly and atraumatically in living, and ideally conscious, animals. In our laboratory we have gone some way towards achieving this goal. Because derangements of dopamine metabolism are associated not only with Parkinson's disease but are also believed to be involved in schizophrenia, we elected to study the transport of dopa, the precursor of dopamine, across the blood brain barrier. The procedure adopted was such that the subsequent intracerebral metabolism of dopa and dopamine could also be studied. Basically, molecules of dopa, labelled with a suitable gamma emitting radionuclide, were needed. If such molecules were available then it would be possible, using the routine procedures of nuclear medicine, to monitor the intracerebral metabolism of dopa and dopamine.

The gamma emitting isotopes of the constituents of dopa have very short half lives and cannot readily be used. Instead, 3, 4 dihydroxy-5-[^{18}F] fluoro phenyl alanine, [^{18}F] fluoro dopa was synthesised [5]. ^{18}F was chosen as the label for dopa because of its high photon yield and short physical half life (110 min). In addition it was argued that the introduction of ^{18}F at the 5-position in the benzene ring of dopa would not significantly affect the biological properties of the molecule.

5-Fluoro Dopa Exhibits the Biological Behaviour of Dopa

[18F] Fluoro dopa is removed from the blood at the same rate as [14C] dopa [6]. It is decarboxylated to fluoro dopamine by aromatic acid decarboxylase derived both from hog kidney and rabbit brain and the Km for this reaction is the same as when dopa is the substrate [7]. It produces arousal in reserpinised mice [8] and turning away from the side of the lesion in rats whose nigrostriatal pathway has been unilaterally destroyed [9]. Finally it has been shown that fluoro dopamine binds to dopaminergic receptors from homogenates of rat striatum and stimulates adenylate cyclase.

The Effects of Pharmacological Manipulation of Intracerebral Dopamine Metabolism demonstrated with [18F] Fluoro Dopa

A series of experiments have been performed in which mature female baboons *(Papio papio)* were trained to sit quietly in a chair. [18F] Fluoro dopa, specific activity 2–100 uCi/mg, was then injected intravenously and the time course of 18F activity was recorded from the head with a single, well collimated, sodium iodide detector aligned along the occipito mental axis. Simultaneously, 18F activity was recorded from the peripheral blood. A second isotope, 113m In, was used to tag transferrin so that corrections could be made for 18F activity confined to the blood in the head. By subtracting this latter component the net accumulation of 18F by the brain was determined. The protocol for these experiments has already been described [9].

After [18F] fluoro dopa had been injected there was a gradual and sustained increase in the amount of 18F retained by the brain. This was taken to represent net transport of [18F] fluoro dopa across the blood brain barrier followed by retention of [18F] as fluoro dopamine. The sustained accumulation of isotope could be prevented by prior administration of α-methyl dopa, 200 mg/kg intravenously. α-Methyl-dopa, a known inhibitor of dopa decarboxylase at the concentration used [10] will also inhibit the transport of [18F] fluoro dopa across the blood brain barrier because the Km for the carrier mediated transport of neutral amino acids is 0.1 mM [11].

When reserpine, 3.5 mg/kg was given intravenously 30 min after an injection of [18F] fluoro dopa, 18F that had accumulated in the brain was discharged. Reserpin destroys the ability of neurones to store dopamine [12] and the fall in 18F activity that began soon after reserpine had been given was interpreted as being due to the release of [18F] dopamine from intraneuronal vesicles.

The retention of 18F by the brain after an intravenous injection of [18F] fluoro dopa could be augmented by the intravenous administration of the monoamine oxidase inhibitor pargyline, 90 mg/kg, or by haloperidol, 1.3 mg/kg. The latter blocks post synaptic dopaminergic receptors and as a consequence increases the rate of turnover of intracerebral dopamine and the production of phenolic acids [13]. The increased retention of 18F induced by haloperidol was particularly pleasing because it meant that [18F] fluoro dopa and an externally placed radiation detector could be used to detect changes in the rate of turnover of neurotransmitters that had been brought about by direct modification of the post synaptic receptor site.

Quantitative Measurements of Blood Brain Barrier
Transport and Cerebral Utilisation of Dopa

As before [18F] fluoro dopa was used as the tracer for dopa. It was injected intravenously into cynomolgus monkeys anaesthetised with Enflurane (Ohio Medical Products, Canada). The appearance of 18F in the head and the disappearance of 18F from the blood were each measured continuously for 10 min with simple gamma ray detectors. A 3 compartment explanatory model, Figure 1, was used to derive fractional rate consultants for the forward and backward transport of dopa across the blood brain barrier, and for the formation and degradation of neuronal dopamine [14].

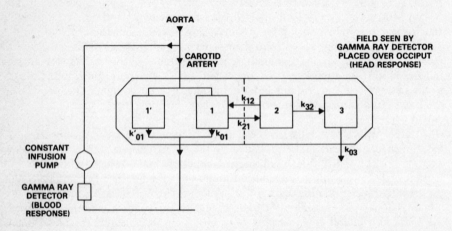

Figure 1 *Explanatory Model* Compartment 1, 1' represents vascular compartment of brain. Compartment 2 represents intracerebral capillar endothelial cells and pericytes. Compartment 3 represents brain cells. (Reproduced by permission of *Am. J. Physiol* 1979 [14]). For meaning of k numbers see text.

Anatomically the first compartment represents blood in the vessel in the brain itself. Functionally this compartment had to be subdivided because our tracer is a racemic mixture and it is known that D-dopa does not cross the blood brain barrier [15].

The second compartment represents the intracerebral endothelial cells and their neighbouring pericytes. Isolated brain capillaries from a variety of mammals have been shown to contain both aromatic decarboxylase and monoamine oxidase [16].

The intracerebral capillary can therefore be considered an anatomical and functional compartment interposed between the blood in the brain and the brain substance itself.

The third compartment is made up of the brain cells themselves together with their surrounding interstitial fluid.

The impulse response $I(t)$ of the three compartment model is represented analytically by:

$$I(t) = Ae^{-at} + Be^{-bt} + Ce^{-k_{03}t}$$

Where A, B and C and a, b and k_{03} are linear combinations of the fractional rate constants of the model, $k_{01}, k_{21}, k_{12}, k_{32}, k_{03}$

k_{01} reflects the rate at which ^{18}F in the blood in the brain turns over due to the circulation.

k_{21} reflects the fractional rate of transport of $[^{18}F]$ dopa from the blood into the endothelium; k_{12} represents the rate at which $[^{18}F]$ fluoro dopa, or its metabolite re-enters the blood from the endothalium.

k_{32} represents the fractional rate of formation of dopamine.

k_{03} reflects the rate at which $[^{18}F]$ leaves the field of view on the detector. The complete justification for the use of the model and the method of analysis is given in [14].

When the impulse response of the model was convolved with an expression that represented the time course of $[^{18}F]$ fluoro dopa in the blood supplied to the head, an expression for ^{18}F activity retained by the brain could be obtained. The

TABLE I Fractional Rate Constants for Transport and Metabolism in Whole Brain
(Reproduced by permission of *Am J Physiol* 1979)

MONKEY	Fractional Rate Constants min^{-1}					
	k_{01}	k_{21}	k_{12}	k_{32}	k_{03}	$K=\dfrac{k_{32}}{(k_{12}+k_{32})}$
1	140	2.0	0.60	0.26	0.06	0.30
2	60	1.4	0.63	0.17	0.03	0.21
3	57	1.7	0.75	0.15	0.04	0.17
4	52	1.0	0.69	0.23	0.02	0.25
5	110	1.6	0.76	0.20	0.08	0.22
MEAN	84	1.54	0.67	0.20	0.04	0.22
SD	±39	±0.37	±0.05	±0.04	±0.02	±0.04

k_{01} = fractional rate of loss of ^{18}F from capillary compartment due to blood flow
k_{21} = fractional rate of forward transport of ^{18}F from blood into the endothelial cells.
k_{12} = fractional rate of backward transport of ^{18}F from endothelial cells into the blood.
k_{32} = fractional rate of formation of ^{18}F-dopamine
k_{03} = fractional rate of loss of ^{18}F-dopamine from the neurones.
K = Fraction of dopa entering endothelial cells available to neurones.

189

fractional rate constants in this derived curve were adjusted to give the best fit to the experimental data. Table I shows the fractional rate constants that were obtained from 5 monkeys. k_{01} was higher than would be expected from knowledge of the brain blood flow and the volume of blood contained in the vascular compartment of the brain but this was not surprising since no attempt was made to fit the data during the first few seconds of an experiment. The value for k_{21} is in agreement with similar constant derived indirectly from published values for Vmax and Km for L-dopa [17]. The value for k_{03}, when applied to the concentration of dopamine in whole brain [18] gives a rate of formation of dopamine of 4nmole h^{-1}g^{-1} This compares favourably with a rate of formation of dopamine in whole brain derived from data obtained from striatum [19] and scaled for the contribution that striatal dopamine would make to the concentration of dopamine averaged for the whole brain. Of particular interest was the finding that only 20 per cent of dopa that entered the endothelial cells was available to the neurones (K in Table I).

The experiments described above have been repeated in barbital anaesthetised rats. The same pattern has emerged with rapid filling and emptying of the endothelial aromatic acid decarboxylase and monoamine oxidase. Such differences of the rats only 10 per cent of the dopa extracted by the endothelium was available to the neurones. This may reflect species differences in the amount of intra-endothelial aromatic acid decarboxylase and monoamine oxidase. Such differences have been described in rats and rabbits [16].

Summary

A gamma emitting analogue of dopa, [18F] fluoro dopa, has been synthesised and shown to have a biological behaviour very similar to that of native dopa. Using [18F] fluoro dopa and simple radiation detectors to measure the changes in 18F activity in the head and the blood after an intravenous injection of the labelled analogue, we have been able to make quantitative measurements of intracerebral dopamine metabolism in conscious live animals. We have found that the endothelial cells of the intracerebral vessels regulate the entry of dopa into the brain and normally allow less than one fifth of the dopa extracted from the blood to be retained by the neurones.

We suggest that as soon as sufficient quantities of [18F] fluoro dopa are available it will be possible to make quantitated measurements of the blood brain barrier transport and neuronal metabolism of dopa in conscious man. Further, with positron emission tomography it should be possible to measure changes in regional intracerebral dopamine metabolism in patients. We hope by these means to study the derangements of intracerebral dopamine metabolism that are associated with Parkinson's disease and to monitor in brain itself the effects of drugs that are used in the treatment of disorders both of locomotion and of mood.

Acknowledgement

We thank the Medical Research Council of Canada and the Ontario Mental Health

Foundation for financial support. We also thank L W Belbeck, R Chirakal and K Mardell for their technical help.

References

1   Hornykiewicz O. *Brit Med Bull 1973; 79:*172
2   Rinnie UK. *Acta Neurol Scand 1978; 57:*77
3   Lee T, Seeman P, Rajput A, Farley IJ, Hornykiewicz O. *Nature 1978; 273:*59
4   Schwartz JC, Costentin J, Martnes MP. *Neuropharmacol 1978; 17:*665
5   Firnau G, Nahmias C, Garnett ES. *Int J Appl Radiat Isot 1973; 24:*182
6   Garnett ES, Firnau G. In *Radiopharmaceuticals and labelled compounds, volume 1, series SM 171/77, 1973;* 405. Vienna: IAEA
7   Firnau G, Garnett ES, Sourkes TL, Missala K. *Experientia 1975; 31:*1254
8   Firnau G, Garnett ES, Chan PKH, Belbeck LW. *J Pharm Pharmacol 1976; 28:*584
9   Garnett ES, Firnau G, Chan PKH, Sood S, Belbeck LW. *Proc Natl Acad Sci (USA) 1978; 75:*464
10 Sourkes TL, Murphy GF, Chavez B, Zielinska M. *J Neurochem 1961; 8:*109
11 Pardridge WM, Oldendorf WH. *J Neurochem 1977; 28:*5
12 Carlsson A. *Pharmacol Rev 1966; 18:*541
13 Anden N-E, Roos B-E, Werdinius B. *Life Sci 1964; 3:*149
14 Garnett ES, Firnau G, Nahmias C, Sood S, Belbeck LW. *Am J Physiol 1979.* In press
15 Oldendorf WH. *Am J Physiol 1973; 224:*967
16 Hardebo JE, Edbinsson L, Emson PC, Owman Ch. In Owman Ch, Edvinsson L, eds. *Neurogenic control of the brain circulation 1977;* 105. Oxford: Pergamon
17 Pardridge WM, Oldendorf WH. *Biophys Acta 1975; 401:* 128
18 Iversen LL. In *The uptake and storage of noradrenaline in sympathetic nerves 1967.* Cambridge: Cambridge University Press
19 Costa E, Carenzi A, Cheney A, Guidotti G, Rocagin G, Zivkovic B. In Berl S, Clarke DD, Schneider D, eds. *Metabolic compartmentation and neurotransmission 1975;* 167. New York: Plenum

Chapter 24

L-DOPA EFFECT ON CEREBRAL AND EXTRACEREBRAL ENZYME SYSTEMS

A H Bone

During the course of our investigation primarily directed towards resolving the problem of the influence of prolonged elevation of tissue dopamine levels on cerebral and extracerebral protein synthesis, it was observed that, of the tissues examined, including brain, liver, kidney, skeletal muscle and testes, only the testes showed enhanced protein synthesis. In all the other tissues examined there was, under the rigorous experimental conditions used, a significant depression of protein synthesis, assessed by the ratio of the specific activity of a labelled amino acid incorporated into the proteins in a given tissue, relative to the time integrated mean specific activity of the amino acid pool of the tissue.

In outline, the experimental procedure was as follows: the experimental animals used were male albino rats of various age groups maintained on L-dopa 100 μg/g/day + monoamine oxidase inhibitor, iproniazid 10 μg/g/day. This procedure was sufficient to maintain an elevated dopamine level in the animal tissues in the region of 40 → 20 μg/g for the greater part of the twenty four hour period following the injection. Control experiments included both untreated animals and animals treated with iproniazid alone. The treatment was continued for periods up to three weeks.

Because of the problem occasionally recorded in the literature of the possible effect of L-dopa therapy on the sexual proclivity of male patients—a problem, however, often dismissed as being due only to the general improvement in the wellbeing of the patient—we examined possible mechanisms of this stimulation of protein synthesis in the testes. We were not surprised to find disharmony in the conclusions drawn by different workers on the influence of dopamine on the factors in the maintenance and development of testicular structure or function. In the words of Farnstrom and Wurtman regarding the influence of catecholamines on pituitary LH and FSH release the results of different laboratories have often been "at odds". This is no overstatement.

We were examining the effect of the L-dopa—iproniazid regime over prolonged periods and therefore had a series of animals for examining which of the factors regulating testicular function were responsible for the hypertrophy and later atrophy of the gland.

192

In immature animals, 20 days old at the commencement of the treatment, stimulation of both testosterone and dihydrotestosterone synthesis and secretion was observed. There was also very clearly defined histological evidence of mature spermatogenesis. In the later stages of the experiment there was some histological and electronmicroscopic evidence of degeneration of testicular structure. In adult animals there was a more marked amplification of testosterone production and secretion and in the later stages degeneration of testicular structure with *diminished* numbers of mature spermatozoa.

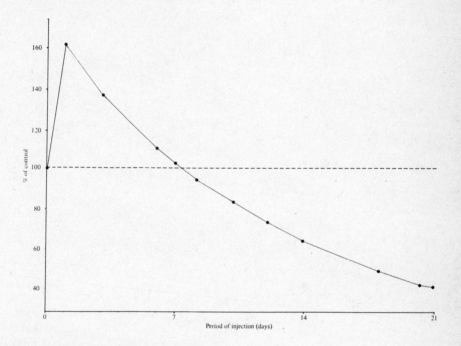

Figure 1 LH Content of whole pituitary gland.

It was, however, on the pituitary content of LH that the effect was most dramatic in both the immature and adult animals. Over the first twenty four hours following the first injection there was a sharp increase in the LH content of the pituitary (⩾ 50% increase relative to the control), but over the following six days there was a progressive decrease in this level until it became indistinguishable from that of the controls. If the treatment was continued, the LH of the pituitary continued to fall until after three weeks it was less than one half that of the controls and was still falling.

The elevated testo- and dihydrotesto-sterone are probably due to the direct stimulation of the testes by dopamine activation of testicular adenylcyclase. The initial stimulation of pituitary LH is due to the stimulation of synthesis and

193

secretion under the action of the hypothalamic LH release factor; this is followed by depression because of the negative feedback control by the elevated blood testosterone levels.

These observations on experimental animals are in keeping with the occasional early observations of the hypersexuality and infertility in dopa treated male patients. They give a possible explanation of the sometimes contradictory conclusions regarding the influence of dopamine on LH production and secretion. They are also in keeping with the known contraceptive effect of testosterone.

Chapter 25

CATECHOLAMINES AND DOPAMINE RECEPTOR BINDING IN PARKINSONISM

E G S Spokes and Sir Roger Bannister

Introduction

Parkinson's disease and striato-nigral degeneration (SND) are chronic degenerative disorders of the central nervous system. Although these conditions are separate disease entities with definite histological differences, they display certain common clinical and pathological features. Both are manifest by the clinical state of parkinsonism which is associated with loss of pigmented dopaminergic cells from the substantia nigra [1].

The evidence that the dopaminergic nigrostriatal tract has an important role in motor function by modulating the activity of striatal neurones is well established in experimental animals [2, 3]. The presence of a similar pathway in man, subserving a similar function, is suggested by the neurochemical findings in post-mortem brain tissue from parkinsonian subjects. In Parkinson's disease, dopamine, its metabolites and its synthetic enzymes are reduced in the striatum and substantia nigra [4, 5, 6, 7]. Moreover, most patients with Parkinson's disease respond well, at least temporarily, to treatment with L-dopa [8] or dopaminergic agonists [9]. However, when parkinsonism is associated with SND the response to these dopaminergic agents is disappointing [10]. This difference in therapeutic response could relate to a number of factors, such as the rate of dopaminergic cell death, loss of a neurotransmitter cell population which normally facilitates the effects of dopaminergic neurones, degeneration of striatal cells which receive a dopaminergic input or loss of, or changes in, dopamine receptors on such cells. Similar mechanisms might also operate in those patients with Parkinson's disease who gain no benefit from L-dopa or lose their therapeutic response with time.

In an attempt to shed light on the variability of response to L-dopa, we have undertaken neurochemical studies on post-mortem brain tissue from 4 cases of the Shy-Drager syndrome [11] (multiple system atrophy with autonomic failure) all of which showed parkinsonism not responding to L-dopa and the pathological changes of SND [10], and 8 cases of Parkinson's disease. We have measured dopamine and noradrenaline concentrations in a variety of brain regions and have examined the nature of dopamine receptor sites using ^{3}H spiperone, a potent butyro-phenone neuroleptic drug, as a ligand to label dopamine receptors. The values obtained have been compared with those from a control group with no antemortem evidence of neurological abnormalities.

Materials and Method

Tissue collection

Post-mortem handling of all cases was similar. Cadavers were removed to a 4°C refrigerator within 1½–4 hr of death. A total of 35 control, 8 parkinsonian and 4 Shy-Drager cases was used in the study. Ages of the groups (mean ± SEM) were as follows: controls 62.9 ± 1.6 yr; parkinsonians 75.0 ± 2.9 yr; Shy-Dragers 55.8 ± 4.8 yr. Intervals (mean ± SEM) from death to necropsy were as follows: controls 40.9 ± 3.7 hr; parkinsonians 53.3 ± 6.1 hr; Shy-Dragers 34.0 ± 4.9 hr. Subsequent handling of tissues was as previously described [10, 12].

Clinical data

Of the 9 parkinsonian patients, all of whom had received a hospital diagnosis of idiopathic Parkinson's disease, 5 had been receiving L-dopa up until death whilst 3 were receiving anticholinergic drugs. All the patients with the Shy-Drager syndrome were receiving anticholinergic drugs prior to death, one was also receiving L-dopa and another Sinemet (L-dopa plus carbidopa) and bromocriptine. A detailed description of the Shy-Drager cases has been reported elsewhere [10].

Biochemical methods

Dopamine and noradrenaline were measured by the radioenzymatic method of Cuello *et al* [13]. Tyrosine hydroxylase (TOH) activity, an enzyme marker for cells synthesising catecholamines, was measured in hypothalamic tissue from control and Shy-Drager cases by the radiochemical method of Hendry and Iversen [14]. Estimates of specific binding of ^{3}H spiperone in membrane and preparations from caudate nucleus, substantia nigra and frontal cortex were performed by Drs. M Quik and A V P Mackay as described elsewhere [15]. Protein determinations were made by the method of Lowry *et al* [16].

Tissues from control and diseased cases were always assayed in parallel, but biochemical measurements could not be performed on all areas from every case, so the total number of samples reported in the tables and figures is usually less than the total number of cases used in the study.

Results

In the Shy-Drager and parkinsonian cases dopamine and noradrenaline concentrations were reduced by a similar degree in the basal ganglia when compared with

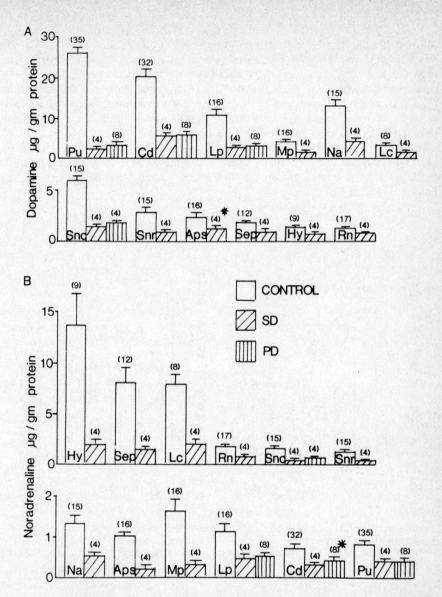

Figure 1 A, dopamine and B, noradrenaline concentrations in various brain regions from control, Shy-Drager (SD) and parkinsonian (PD) cases. Results are means ± SEM for the number of samples in brackets. Abbreviations = Pu, putamen; Cd, caudate; Lp, lateral pallidum; Mp, medial pallidum; Na, nucleus accumbens; Lc, locus coeruleus; Snc, substantia nigra (compacta); Snr, substantia nigra (reticulata); Aps, anterior perforated substance; Sep, septal nucleus; Hy, hypothalamus; Rn, red nucleus. Differences between controls and SD and PD cases are significant (P < 0.05–0.001) using Student's t-test, except where indicated: *not significant.

197

controls (Figure 1). The greatest loss of dopamine occurred in the putamen (10% mean control values), with substantial reductions in the caudate nucleus, lateral pallidum and substantia nigra (25% mean control values). In other brain regions tissue was available only from the Shy-Drager cases and showed a widespread depletion in both dopamine and noradrenaline levels, the latter being reduced particularly in those brain regions normally rich in noradrenline—the septal nuclei, hypothalamus and locus coeruleus (Figure 1).

Division of the parkinsonian cases into those who did or did not receive L-dopa prior to death revealed that striatal levels of dopamine and noradrenaline were higher in the L-dopa treated group, the differences reaching statistical significance as indicated (Figure 2).

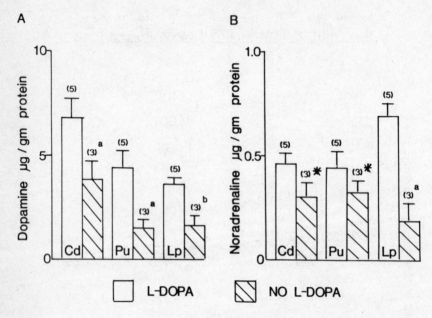

Figure 2 A, dopamine and B, noradrenaline concentrations in striatal tissue from parkinsonian patients treated with and without L-dopa. Results are means ± SEM for the number of samples in brackets. Abbreviations as for Figure 1. ^{a} $P < 0.05$; ^{b} $P < 0.01$, using Student's t-test. *not significant.

Tyrosine hydroxylase activity (results not tabulated) in hypothalamic tissues from the Shy-Drager cases was reduced to 10% of the mean control value: controls 190.9 ± 22.4 pmoles/hr/mg protein (mean ± SEM) (n=8); Shy-Dragers, 18.8 ± 4.2 pmoles/hr/mg protein (mean ± SEM) (n=4).

Scatchard analysis of dopamine-displacement ^3H spiperone binding to caudate nucleus showed that the maximum number of ^3H spiperone binding sites (B max) was similar in the control, parkinsonian and Shy-Drager groups (Table I). The

TABLE I Characteristics of Specific ^{3}H Spiperone Binding in Caudate Nucleus, Substantia Nigra and Frontal Cortex Membrane Preparations from Control, Parkinsonian (PD) and Shy-Drager (SD) Cases.

Brain Region	Group	B_{max} (fmol/mg protein)	K_d (nM)
Caudate nucleus	Control	109 ± 17 (15)	0.44 ± 0.07 (14)
	PD (-L-dopa)	106 ± 48 (3)	0.65 ± 0.25 (3)
	PD (+L-dopa)	91 ± 15 (4)	0.48 ± 0.15 (4)
	SD	81 ± 22 (4)	1.08 ± 0.14 [a,b], (4)
Substantia nigra	Control	25.0 ± 1.6 (5)	0.39 ± 0.07 (5)
	PD	12.7 (1)	0.43 (1)
	SD	10.5 ± 0.71 [a] (4)	0.72 ± 0.35(4)
Frontal cortex	Control	31.1 ± 4.6 (7)	1.07 ± 0.19 (7)
	PD	36.0 ± 7.3 (6)	1.18 ± 0.11 (6)
	SD	33.7 ± 6.2 (4)	0.62 ± 0.15 (4)

Individual results were obtained by linear regression analysis of Scatchard plots. Values in the table represent mean ± SEM of the results from control, PD and SD cases. Figures in brackets represent the number of individual samples assayed.

[a] $P < 0.001$, Student's t-test, [b] $P < 0.01$ by Wilcoxon rank test, when compared with control values.

dissociation constant (K_d) was similar in control and parkinsonian cases, 0.44 ± 0.07 nM, n=14; Shy-Dragers, 1.08 ± 0.14 nM, n=4) (Table I).

In the substantia nigra, there was a significant reduction in B max of ^{3}H spiperone binding in the Shy-Drager cases, indicating a loss of binding sites (controls, 25.0 ± 1.6 fmoles/mg protein, n=5; Shy-Dragers, 10.5 ± 0.71 fmoles/mg protein, n=4) (Table I). Due to the small amount of nigral tissue available from the parkinsonian cases it was necessary to pool tissue from 3 patients (2 treated with L-dopa, 1 with an anticholinergic drug) in order to obtain sufficient material for one Scatchard analysis. The B max was similar to that of the Shy-Drager group (12.7 fmoles/mg protein). K_d values were similar in all groups (Table I).

The characteristics of ^{3}H spiperone binding to frontal cortex were similar in all groups (Table I). However, the B max seemed suprisingly high as the frontal cortex contains little dopamine and, at most, receives a sparse dopaminergic innervation. Subsequently, near the completion of study, it became evident that ^{3}H spiperone can bind to receptor sites other than those for dopamine, particularly serotonin receptors [17]. ADTN, a rigid analogue of dopamine, emerged as a more specific ligand with which to define the dopamine receptor component of ^{3}H spiperone binding than dopamine itself [18]. In view of the difficulties this created in interpreting dopamine-displacement ^{3}H spiperone binding, it was decided to compare the effects of varying concentrations of dopamine with those of ADTN on ^{3}H spiperone binding in basal ganglia and frontal cortex. In the caudate nucleus and substantia nigra, ADTN was more potent than dopamine in displacing bound ^{3}H spiperone (IC$_{50}$ values for ADTN and dopamine were 2.0 μM and 630 μM, respectively in caudate, and 200 μM and 790 μM, respectively in the substantia nigra, at a ^{3}H spiperone concentration of 0.5 nM), but the fractions of total binding which were maximally displaced by ADTN and dopamine were similar. In contrast, ADTN caused virtually no displacement of ^{3}H spiperone from human frontal cortex whereas dopamine displaced ^{3}H spiperone with an IC$_{50}$ of 1600 μM.

The much higher IC$_{50}$ value for ADTN in the substantia nigra compared to the caudate nucleus would suggest that dopamine receptors are different in these two areas (possibly differing proportions of pre- and post-synaptic receptors) or that, at high concentrations, ADTN and dopamine are displacing ^{3}H spiperone from a mixed receptor population in the substantia nigra. ^{3}H spiperone binding in frontal cortex is likely to represent attachment to sites other than dopamine receptors, possibly serotonin receptors.

The effect of L-dopa treatment on ^{3}H spiperone binding was investigated in caudate nucleus tissue from parkinsonian subjects. Division of the parkinsonian cases into those who had received L-dopa prior to death (n=4) and those who had not (n=3) failed to show any differences in either B$_{max}$ or K$_d$ (Table I).

Discussion

The present results confirm earlier reports that Parkinson's disease is associated with a marked loss of dopamine from the basal ganglia, most pronounced in the putamen [6, 19]. The finding of similar changes in the Shy-Drager group, all of which showed striatonigral degeneration, explains the clinical state of parkinsonism in our cases and is consistent with the recent report of reduced CSF levels of homovanillic acid, the major cerebral metabolite of dopamine, in Shy-Drager patients [20]. Parkinsonian patients who were receiving L-dopa prior to death had higher striatal dopamine concentrations than those who were not on this treatment, in agreement with previous observations [6].

Apart from the nigrostriatal pathway, animal studies have indicated the presence of other central dopaminergic tracts, one of which arises from cells in the region of the interpeduncular nucleus of the midbrain and projects to limbic structures such as the nucleus accumbens, septal nuclei and anterior perforated substance [3, 21], the so-called 'mesolimbic' pathway; and another which is intrinsic to the hypothalamus [22], the tubero-infundibular system. In the Shy-Drager cases the magnitude of dopamine loss from the nucleus accumbens was similar to that seen in the caudate nucleus, an observation which has also been made in Parkinson's disease [23]. suggesting that these brain areas may receive a dopaminergic innervation from closely related cells in the midbrain. In the experimental rat, dopamine receptor stimulation in the nucleus accumbens induces locomotor activity [24, 25, 26], so it is possible that dopaminergic denervation in this area may relate to hypokinesia in parkinsonism.

The reduction in dopamine concentrations in other limbic areas and the hypothalamus in our cases of Shy-Drager syndrome may also occur in Parkinson's disease [4, 23, 24] and implies widespread involvement of dopaminergic systems in both diseases.

In mammals, central noradrenergic pathways arise from cell bodies in the hindbrain [3, 27]. There are two major ascending noradrenergic tracts: a dorsal bundle arising from the largest group of cell bodies, the locus coeruleus, and distributed mainly to the cerebellum, hippocampus, cerebral cortex and hypothalamus; and a ventral bundle, arising from diffuse cell groups, projecting to the hypothalamus, limbic structures and brain-stem nuclei. Bulbospinal noradrenergic fibres arise from cells in the caudal medulla and richly innervate pre-ganglionic sympathetic neurones and anterior horn cells.

Loss of pigmented cells from the locus coeruleus may occur in both Parkinson's disease [28] and the Shy-Drager syndrome [1]. In our Shy-Drager cases, prominent cell loss was evident in only one case, although systematic cell counting was not performed [10]. However, there was a substantial fall in noradrenaline content in all cases, which was more pronounced than that which has been reported for Parkinson's disease [29], suggesting that this biochemical change is not merely a reflection of cell degeneration. The clinical significance of this finding is not clear, but it may relate to both the parkinsonism and the autonomic disturbance observed in the Shy-Drager syndrome.

Although the role of noradrenaline in controlling normal motor activity is uncertain, noradrenaline depletion was noted in the basal ganglia of our parkinsonian subjects, confirming earlier reports [4], and in the Shy-Drager cases. It is likely that at least some L-dopa will be converted to noradrenaline within the brain and, indeed, the noradrenaline reduction noted in our parkinsonian cases was less marked in those treated with L-dopa. Animal experiments suggest that this process may contribute to L-dopa's efficacy as an anti-akinesia drug, perhaps via a facilitatory noradrenergic input from the locus coeruleus to the dopaminergic cells of the substantia nigra (see 30, for review). It is conceivable, therefore, that failure of central noradrenaline synthesis may limit the success of L-dopa therapy.

In the Shy-Drager cases there was a substantial loss of noradrenaline from the septal nuclei and hypothalamus indicating if comparisons with animal studies are valid, an abnormality in the ventral noradrenergic pathway. Moreover, the gross reduction in TOH activity in hypothalamic tissue from these cases is further evidence of impaired noradrenergic function. In contrast, near normal levels of this enzyme have been reported in the hypothalamus of two cases of Parkinson's disease [6]. Although the evidence is inconclusive, the widespread depletion in noradrenaline observed in the Shy-Drager subjects may influence autonomic function for reasons outlined below.

In progressive autonomic failure, the interruption of sympathetic and parasympathetic function has been well established [31, 32] and has been attributed to loss of pre-ganglionic autonomic cells from the intermedio-lateral columns of the spinal cord, such as was seen in our Shy-Drager cases [10]. However, it is possible that lesions in supraspinal centres, normally concerned with the control of autonomic outflow, may contribute to the overall disturbance. Animal experiments indicate that the cortex, limbic system and hypothalamus all influence cardio-vascular regulation through interactions at brain-stem level (see 33 and chapter 15 of this volume for reviews). Histochemical studies have shown that nor-adrenergic, adrenergic and serotonergic fibre systems richly innervate brain-stem nuclei involved in the central control of blood pressure and heart rate [27, 34, 35], and that bulbospinal noradrenergic and serotonergic fibres terminate in the inter-mediolateral columns where they synapse with pre-ganglionic autonomic neurones [27]. With regard to our Shy-Drager cases, it is possible that central noradrenaline depletion contributes to the autonomic failure, since there is considerable evidence that this amine has an important neurotransmitter role in central pathways sub-serving a cardiovascular function [36]. Moreover, TOH activity had been reported as greatly reduced in the locus coeruleus of patients dying with chronic autonomic failure [37].

The results of the ^{3}H spiperone binding studies are difficult to interpret. Evidence suggests that this radioligand can bind to both serotonin and dopamine receptors and that, in dopamine-poor areas such as frontal cortex, it is likely that most dopamine-displaceable ^{3}H spiperone binding occurs at serotonin receptors. With the use of the rigid dopamine analogue, ADTN, more precise identification of the dopamine receptor component of ^{3}H spiperone binding can be achieved [17, 18]. In the caudate nucleus, dopamine and ADTN appear to displace ^{3}H spiperone from the same receptor population. In the substantia nigra the situation is more complex for although dopamine and ADTN compete for the same fraction of total ^{3}H spiperone binding, the affinity of ADTN for the spiperone sites is much lower than in caudate. The reason for this discrepancy is unclear but it is possible that different types of dopamine receptor exist in the caudate and substantia nigra. In nigral tissue there may be a preponderance of pre-synaptic dopamine receptors whereas in caudate they are likely to be mainly post-synaptic. Indeed, there is in-creasing evidence, from pharmacological studies in animals, for at least 2 classes of dopamine receptor which can be distinguished by their different binding character-istics and their ability to stimulate adenylate cyclase (see 38, for review). Another possibility is that dopamine and ADTN are displacing ^{3}H spiperone from a mixed dopaminergic and serotonergic receptor population in the substantia nigra. How-ever, we feel that this is unlikely because biphasic displacement curves were not seen in nigral tissue and because in frontal cortex ADTN even at high concen-trations, caused virtually no displacement of the ^{3}H spiperone binding as reflecting dopamine receptors in the caudate and, with reservation, in the substantia nigra also, whereas in frontal cortex evidence points to an interaction with serotonin re-ceptors [17, 18].

The most striking abnormality in the Shy-Drager syndrome was a substantial reduction in the density of ^{3}H spiperone binding sites in the substantia nigra, as measured by the change in B_{max}. In this respect the Shy-Drager cases appeared to be similar to Parkinson's disease. This finding is compatible with the view that dopamine receptors are present on the cell bodies of dopaminergic neurones, so-called autoreceptors, and that receptor loss reflects death of dopaminegic neurones in both Parkinson's disease and SND. The presence of dopamine receptors on dopamine cell bodies has recently been demonstrated in rat substantia nigra [39].

In Parkinson's disease it has been postulated that dopaminergic denervation of striatal cells might induce a proliferation of post-synaptic dopamine receptors [19]; Such a compensatory increase in receptor density has been termed 'supersensitivity' [40, 41, 42] and should be reflected in increased dopamine receptor binding. Our findings do not support this hypothesis since the density of dopamine receptors in caudate was normal in both Parkinson's disease and SND. Lee et al [42] made similar observations in caudate from parkinsonian subjects, but noted a significant increase in haloperidol binding in the putamen. It is possible that dopamine receptor binding characteristics are more likely to change in the putamen since, in both Parkinson's disease and SND, dopamine loss is more severe in this region than in the caudate. Lee et al [42] also reported that L-dopa treatment of parkinsonian cases restored haloperidol binding in the putamen to normal. We found no evidence of any effect of L-dopa, but the numbers in each sub-group were too small to permit any reliable conclusion. To further complicate this issue, Reisine et al [43] reported a significant decrease in ^{3}H spiperone binding in the caudate nucleus of parkinsonian subjects, not sub-divided into those treated with or without L-dopa but normal values in the putamen. All of these studies, including our own, suffer from a paucity of available samples.

In the Shy-Drager cases, SND was associated with an approximate two-fold increase in the dissociation constant (k_d) for spiperone binding in the caudate nucleus; in other words, the affinity of the dopamine receptors for ^{3}H spiperone was reduced by about 50 per cent. Such a reduction in the affinity of receptors for dopamine might explain, in part, the poor clinical response to L-dopa and to bromocriptine [20], observed in SND.

Conclusion

In SND associated with the Shy-Drager syndrome we have found widespread reductions in brain dopamine concentrations, similar to those observed in Parkinson's disease. These cases also showed a gross depletion in noradrenaline which may be pertinent to the autonomic disturbance. Refractoriness to L-dopa replacement therapy might also arise from failure of central noradrenaline synthesis, and reduced affinity of receptors for dopamine in the caudate could be a further important factor in this regard.

Acknowledgements

We wish to thank Professor G A Gresham and his colleagues in the Department of Morbid Anatomy, Addenbrooke's Hospital, for the considerable assistance that they have offered in the study. We also thank the neurologists and pathologists who provided us with the material. Histological examination of the Shy-Drager case was performed by Dr D R Oppenheimer and binding studies were carried out by Drs M Quik and A V P Mackay. R B wishes to thank the Parkinson's Disease Society for financial support.

References

1   Bannister R, Oppenheimer DR. *Brain 1972;95:*457
2   Poirier LJ, Sourkes TL. *Brain 1965;88:*181
3   Ungerstedt U. *Acta Physiol Scand 1971;Suppl 367:*1
4   Ehringer H, Hornykiewicz O. *Klin Wschr 1960;38:*1236
5   Lloyd KG, Hornykiewicz O. *Science 1970;170:*1212
6   Lloyd KG, Davidson L, Hornykiewicz O. *J Pharmacol exp Ther 1975;195:*453
7   McGeer PL, McGeer EG. *J Neurochem 1976;26:*65
8   Cotzias GC, Papavasiliou PS, Gellene R. *New Engl J Med 1969;280:*337
9   Calne DB. In Birkmayer W, Hornykiewicz O, eds. *Advances in Parkinsonism 1976;*
       502 Basle, Editiones Roche
10   Spokes EGS, Bannister R, Oppenheimer DR. *J Neurol Sci 1979;43:*59
11   Shy GM, Drager GA. *Arch Neurol (Chic) 1960;2:*511
12   Spokes EGS. *Brain 1979;102:*333
13   Cuello AC, Hiley R, Iversen LL. *J Neurochem 1973;21:*1337
14   Hendry IA, Iversen LL. *Brain Res 1971;29:*159
15   Quik M, Spokes EGS, Mackay AVP, Bannister R. *J Neurol Sci 1979;43:*429
16   Lowry OH, Rosebrough NJ, Farr AL, Randall RJ. *J biol Chem 1951;193:*269
17   Leysen JE, Niemegeers CJE, Tollenaere JP, Laduron PM. *Nature (Lond) 1978;272:*168
18   Quik M, Iversen LL, Larder A, Mackay AVP. *Nature (Lond) 1978;274:*513
19   Bernheimer H, Birkmayer W, Hornykiewicz O, Jellinger K, Seitelberger F. *J Neurol Sci
       1973;20:*415
20   Williams AC, Nutt J, Lake CR, Pfeiffer R, Teychenne PE, Ebert M, Calne DB. In Fuxe K,
       Calne DB, eds. *Dopaminergic Ergots and Motor Control 1979.* New York, Raven Press (In press)
21   Lindvall O, Bjorklund A. *Acta Physiol Scand 1974;Suppl 412;*1
22   Bjorklund A, Falck B, Hromek F, Owman C, West KA. *Brain Res 1970;17:*1
23   Farley IJ, Price KS, Hornykiewicz O. In Costa E, Gessa GL, eds. *Advances in Biochemi-
       cal Psychopharmacology Vol 16 1977;*57. New York, Raven Press
24   Andén NE. In Birkmayer W, Hornykiewicz O, eds. *Advances in Parkinsonism 1976;*
       169 Basle. Editiones Roche
25   Pijnenburg AJJ, Honig WMM, Van der Heyden JAM, Van Rossum JM. *Eur J Pharmacol
       1976;35:*45
26   Andén NE, Johnels B. *Brain Res 1977;133:*386
27   Dahlstrom A, Fuxe K. *Acta Physiol Scand 1965;Suppl 247:*1
28   Greenfield JG, Bosanquet FD. *J Neurol Neurosurg Psychiat 1953;16:*213
29   Farley IJ, Hornykiewicz O. In Birkmayer W, Hornykiewicz O, eds. *Advances in Parkin-
       sonism 1976;* 178. Basle, Editiones Roche
30   Pycock C. In Legg NJ, ed. *Neurotransmitter Systems and their Clinical Disorders 1978;*
       99. London, New York, San Francisco, Academic Press
31   Johnson RH, Lee G De J, Oppenheimer DR, Spalding JMK. *Quart J Med 1966;35:*276
32   Bannister R, Ardill L, Fentem P. *Brain 1967;90:*725
33   Antonaccio MJ. In Antonaccio MJ, ed. *Cardiovascular Pharmacology 1977;*131. New York,
       Raven Press
34   Fuxe K. *Acta Physiol Scand 1965;64 Suppl 247:*38
35   Hökfelt, T, Fuxe K, Goldstein M. *Brain Res 1973;62:*461
36   Chalmers JP. *Circulat Res 1975;36:*469
37   Black IB, Petito CK. *Science 1976;192:*910
38   Kebabian JW, Calne DB. *Nature (Lond) 1979;277:*93
39   Quik M, Emson PC, Joyce E. *Brain Res 1979;167:*355
40   Creese I, Burt DR, Snyder SH. *Science 1977;197:*596
41   Burt DR, Creese I, Snyder SH. *Science 1977;196:*326
42   Lee T, Seeman P, Rajput A, Farley IJ, Hornykiewicz O. *Nature (Lond) 1978;273:*59
43   Reisine TD, Fields, JZ, Yamamura HI, Bird ED, Spokes E, Schreiner PS, Enna SJ. *Life
       Sci 1977;21:*335

Chapter 26

MONOAMINE OXIDASE AND PHENOSULPHOTRANSFERASE IN PARKINSON'S DISEASE

Vivette Glover, M Sandler, G Rein and G Stern

A study of dopamine metabolism may be relevant to Parkinson's disease in two ways: if we understand the enzymatic mechanisms by which dopamine (DA) is degraded, we are in a better position to design safe, selective inhibitors to increase available concentrations of this amine in the striatum; people may vary in the way they metabolise DA and such a variation may make some more liable to develop parkinsonism than others and even, conceivably, be of predictive value. In this connection, therefore, we have been studying two enzymes which metabolise DA, monoamine oxidase (MAO) and phenolsulphotransferase (PST).

Monoamine oxidase and DA oxidation

In a man, all oxidative deamination of DA can be inhibited by the MAO-inhibiting group of drugs and is, thus, presumably, mediated by MAO [1]. The development of selective MAO inhibitors has led to the classification of the enzyme into two forms, A and B [2-4]. MAO A is inhibited by a lower concentration of clorgyline than MAO B whilst deprenyl follows the opposite pattern and selectively inhibits MAO B. Both forms are widely distributed in brain and tissues but have quite distinct localisations. Although most tissues contain different proportions of each, the human platelet contains only MAO B [5] and the placenta MAO A [6]. By histochemical staining [7], we have shown that, in certain tissues, each form may be highly localised to a particular type of cell. In rat brain, for example, the high activity of MAO B in certain circumventricular structures is striking [8] (and unpublished histochemical observations). Although the physiological role of MAO appears to lie in the degradation of endogenous and dietary monoamines, it may possess other and unknown functions in particular cells. The molecular basis of the two forms is also uncertain but they appear to be physiologically independent and may, on occasion, be under independent hormonal control. For example, there is a very large specific rise in MAO A, but not B activity, in human endometrium towards the end of the menstrual cycle [9].

Monoamine oxidase A and B differ both in their substrate and inhibitor specificities. MAO is more active in oxidising low concentrations of 5-hydroxytryptamine (5-HT) and noradrenaline whilst MAO B similarly prefers phenylethylamine (PEA). However, we now realise that these properties are relative [10] and that, at high concentrations, each form of the enzyme metabolises both 5-HT and PEA. Benzylamine (Bz) is a more specific substrate for MAO B but it is also metabolised by the distinct enzyme, benzylamine oxidase [1]. Methylhistamine (the major metabolite of histamine in tissues such as brain, which lack diamine oxidase) is a specific substrate for MAO B in both rate [11] and man [12] and an important function of MAO B may be its role in histamine metabolism.

DA is predominantly metabolised by MAO B in the human striatum, [13] but it may also be degraded by MAO A; the part played by each in a particular tissue depends on the ratio of the two forms present [14]. There seems no reason to presuppose the existence of a specific MAO for DA nor that the nature of MAO A or MAO B with respect to DA oxidation varies between tissues. We have found that placenta, which contains MAO A only, and platelets, where MAO B alone is present, both metabolise DA and the activity with DA is greater than that of PEA with MAOB and less than that of 5-HT with MAO A. The Km for DA of the two forms is similar, 130 μM and 140 μM respectively for A and B. 10^{-6} M (-)-Deprenyl is the most effective concentration for distinguishing between each *in vitro;* it inhibits about 98 per cent of platelet MAO B and 23 per cent of placental MAO A. In human brain, the percentage inhibition of DA oxidation by this concentration correlates well with the MAO A/MAO B ratio ($p < 0.001$) as assessed by relative activities with 5-HT and PEA. Many peripheral tissues are also highly active in DA-oxidising ability, placenta, jejunum, liver and kidney degrading the amine even more vigorously than the brain. In the periphery also the percentage of DA oxidation by 10^{-6} M(-)-deprenyl correlates with the A/B ratio. DA oxidation in the lung, which predominantly contains MAO A, is only 22 per cent inhibited by this concentration, whereas the heart, rich in MAO B, is 85 per cent inhibited. The human striatum and accumbens contain a relatively high proportion of MAO B and here, 10^{-6} M deprenyl inhibits DA oxidation by about 80–85 per cent.

The rat is not a good model for man with respect to DA oxidation. Both brain tissues contain relatively higher MAO A activity so that a greater proportion of DA oxidation is insensitive to low concentrations of deprenyl [15]. In the rar also, but not in man, the separate enzyme, benzylamine oxidase, which is localised particularly in blood vessels, is able to oxidase DA [1].

Deprenyl

Early trials of MAO inhibitors in Parkinson's disease had to be discontinued because of dangerous and unpleasant side-effects [16]. (-)-Deprenyl differs from all other MAO inhibitors investigated both in being free from the potentially lethal "cheese effect" and in its ability to be used safely in combination with L-dopa [17]. A 10 mg dose of (-)-deprenyl, diluted in a body water mass of 40 kg would give a con-

206

centration of about 10^{-6} M [14] which, from the *in vitro* data mentioned above, would selectively inhibit MAO B and largely inhibit DA oxidation in the striatum. Platelet MAO B activity *in vivo* is completely inhibited a few hours after such a dose and urinary PEA concentrations are increased 20- to 90- fold [17]. There is, therefore, little doubt that a 10 mg dose deprenyl can inhibit MAO B throughout the body.Studies of postmortem brains from patients who had been treated with 9-0-deprenyl during life have shown an approximately 85 per cent inhibition of DA oxidation in thestriatum, [18] a finding which would also support a total inhibition of MAO B. It will be of interest to see whether clinicians with patients on (-)-deprenyl observe any effects attributable to inhibition of methylhistamine oxidation. Yahr [19] has reported one such whose quiescent peptic ulcer became active while taking (-)-deprenyl.

Deprenyl, although apparently useful in Parkinson's disease [20, 21] is not the ideal MAO inhibitor for this condition, for it does not totally inhibit DA oxidation and it is converted to (-)metamphetamine [22]. At a 10 mg dosage, few amphetamine-like effects have been observed clinically, and the drug appears to be a safe one. However, its conversion to amphetamine limits its usefulness in higher concentrations, at which it might be expected totally to inhibit MAO. This consideration raises the question of whether other MAO inhibitors, which inhibit MAO A, either in addition to, or instead of , MAO B but are without the "cheese effect", could be developed. In the pig, where tyramine oxidation is carried out predominantly by MAO B, we have recently shown [23] that deprenyl does not augment the pressor response to low doses of intravenous tyramine even though it largely inhibits tyramine oxidation. Clorgyline, on the other hand, while not inhibiting tyramine oxidation, has a substantial potentiating effect on the tyramine pressor response [22]. These results raise the possibility that the "cheese effect" in man might be independent of the inhibition of tyramine oxidation, but operate through some second mechanism. If this is so, then the development of safe and selective MAO inhibitors may become a real possibility.

Urinary MAO inhibitor

Human urine contains a reversible inhibitor or inhibitors of both MAO A and B [24]. This action can still be detected after 30-fold dilution of the urine, and cannot be accounted for by any of the major urinary constituents such as urea, uric acid, creatinine, ammonia, creatine, sulphate, glycine, hippuric acid, formic acid or inorganic ions. Nor is it caused by any of the major monoamine substrates or products of MAO found in urine. As yet we neither know whether this inhibitor has any physiological role in controlling MAO activity *in vivo,* nor its chemical nature. However, in the search for new safe enzyme inhibitors, the characterisation of an endogenous one seems a good way to begin.

207

Phenolsulphotransferase

A second major mechanism of amine metabolism in man is by conjugation. Almost all detectable dopamine in the blood is in conjugated form and the major part of urinary dopamine is also conjugated [25]. Studies which measure free DA therefore give an incomplete picture. Amines and their metabolites can be conjugated with both sulphate and glucuronide and methods for measuring conjugates usually do not distinguish between them, but there is some indirect evidence that urinary DA is predominantly conjugated with sulphate [26]. Sulphate conjugation is catalysed by the enzyme phenolsulphotransferase (PST), which uses sulphate in an activated form, PAPS, which is synthesised in the body as shown below:

$$ATP + SO_4{}^{2-} \rightarrow \text{adenosine 5'-phosphosulphate} + PPi$$
$$APS$$

$$APS + ATP \rightarrow \text{3'-phosphoadenosine-5'- phosphosulphate (PAPS)} + ADP$$

$$PAPS + DA \rightarrow DA\text{-}SO_4 + \text{3'-phosphoadenosine-5'-phosphate}$$
$$(PAP)$$

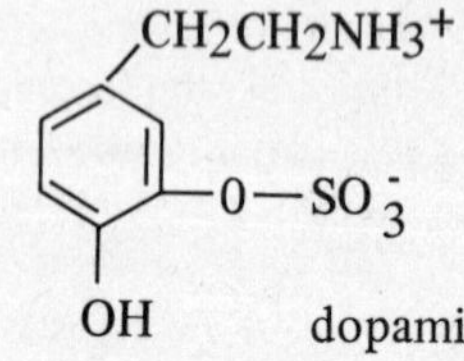

dopamine-3-0-sulphate

The sulphate seems to be added predominantly in the 3 rather than the 4 position [27]. The function of conjugation is not completely clear. One possibility is that it reduces pharmacological activity and aids excretion by the kidney [28]. There is also some evidence in the rat that conjugates may themselves act as precursors for further reactions, although not for MAO [29]. When a low dose of radioactive DA-SO$_4$ was administered to rats it was all desulphated and excreted as DA and its metabolites. This suggests that there is a sulphatase system which can metabolise DA-SO$_4$ but this enzyme or enzymes has not been studied.

PST occurs in both brain and peripheral tissues and has an uneven distribution in the rat brain, being particularly active in hypothalamus and striatum [30], suggesting a function in amine metabolism in the brain also. PST is present in human platelets [31, 32] which enables us to study it in patients. We have recently characterised the platelet enzyme and found that it is particularly active with DA. It also has a high affinity for DA with a Km of 3 μM. The relative order of activity with different substrates (all at 30 μM) with DA set at 100 was DA (100), tyramine (100), noradrenaline (71), adrenaline (66), phenol (56), 4-hydroxy-3-methoxyphenylglycol (24), 3, 4-dihydroxyphenylglycol (19), 5-HT (16), 4-hydroxy-3-methoxymandelic acid (7), 4-hydroxy-3-methoxyphenylacetic acid (4) and 3, 4-dihydroxyphenylacetic acid (4). In general then, it appears to be active with amines, less so with alcohol metabolites, and less active still with acids. The substrate specificity of PST in jejunal biopsy material, placenta and adrenal gland was similar to that in platelet, although the specific activity of jejunal tissues was much the highest. The human brain enzyme was much less active, possibly due to post-mortem changes. It has recently been characterised by Renskers et al [33] and its pattern of substrate specificity appears similar to that in the other tissues. This evidence points to a single functional form of PST and it is reasonable to use the platelet enzyme as a mirror of that in other sites. However, human PST differs markedly from that of the rat, the former being relatively more active with DA. With human PST we have found a DA/HMPG ratio of 4/1 and with rat a ratio of 1/4.

There are good reasons for considering DA conjugation in relation to Parkinson's disease. Several studies [34–37] have shown a reduction of free DA in the urine of untreated parkinsonian patients. The cause of this finding is not yet clear as only a small proportion of urinary DA probably comes from the brain, and some appears to be secreted directly by the kidney. However, conjugated DA does not appear to be reduced [35, 36] and the ratio of the output of conjugated DA to free DA is therefore increased. Crowley et al [38] have also found in a study of neuroleptic-induced parkinsonism, that the smaller the output of free DA and the higher the output of conjugated DA, the worse the parkinsonian symptoms. If this finding were to be confirmed, it would be of interest in several ways. It points to biochemical factors which contribute to vulnerability to parkinsonism, and it also suggests the possibility that an overactive DA-conjugating system may contribute to this. Bonham Carter et al [39] found that untreated parkinsonians excreted a greatly increased proportion of conjugated tyramine, again suggesting the possibility of an overactive conjugation system.

We have recently completed a pilot study, comparing platelet PST activity in parkinsonian patients with non-parkinsonian controls [40]. The mean activity of the parkinsonian group was 40 per cent greater than that of the control group (p < 0.02). Platelet MAO activity in the parkinsonian group was raised 24 per cent but the rise was not significant. This was a small study, the two groups were not age-matched, and almost all of the parkinsonians were on L-dopa plus carbidopa. The rise could, therefore, reflect an enzyme induction in response to increased peripheral dopamine concentrations. It could be a platelet phenomenon and not reflect the activity of PST elsewhere in the body. However, it is also possible that the increase indicates a biochemical vulnerability to the disease.

Thus there remain many problems concerning the significance of DA conjugation in general, and in Parkinson's disease in particular. What is the role of DA conjugation in the brain? Can DA-sulphate act as a significant source of free DA in

209

man? Does an imbalance of the DA-conjugating system or the DA-sulphate sulphatase system lead to a predisposition to Parkinson's disease?

Acknowledgments

We should like to thank John Elsworth for his contribution to the research on deprenyl and Christopher Ward for his participation in the study of platelet phenol-sulphotransferase in Parkinson's disease. We should also like to thank the Parkinson's Disease Society for its support of VG and the Cancer Research Campaign for its support of GR.

References

1   Lewinsohn R, Böhm KH, Glover V, Sandler M. *Biochem Pharmac 1978; 27:*1857
2   Johnston JP. *Biochem Pharmac 1968; 17:*1285
3   Yang HYT, Neff NH. *J Pharmac exp Ther 1973; 187:*365
4   Yang HYT, Neff NH. *J Pharmac exp Ther 1974; 189:*733
5   Murphy DL, Donnelly CH. In Usdin E ed. *Neuropsychopharmacology of monoamines and their regulatory enzymes 1974;* 71. New York: Raven Press
6   Egashira T. *Jap J Pharmac 1976; 26:*493
7   Ryder TA, MacKenzie ML, Pryse-Davies J, Glover V, Lewinsohn R, Sandler M. *Histochemistry 1979; 62:*93
8   Böhm KH, Glover V, Sandler M, Petty M, Reid JL. *J Neurochem 1979; 33:*607
9   Mazumder R, Glover V, Sandler M. In preparation
10   Lewinsohn R, Glover V, Sandler M. *Biochem Pharmac 1980.* In press
11   Waldmeier PC, Feldtrauer JJ, Maitre L. *J Neurochem 1977; 27:*785
12   Elsworth J, Glover V, Sandler M. In preparation
13   Glover V, Sandler M, Owen F, Riley GJ. *Nature 1977; 265:*80
14   Glover V, Elsworth J, Sandler M. *J Neural Transmiss 1980.* In press
15   Waldmeier PC, Delini-Stula A, Maitre L. *Naunyn-Schmied Arch Pharmac 1976; 292:*9
16   Barbeau A, Sourkes TL, Murphy GF. In Ajuriaguerra J de, ed. *Monoamines et système nerveux central 1962;* 247. Geneva: Georg
17   Elsworth JD, Glover V, Reynolds GP, Sandler M, Lees AJ, Phuapradit P, Shaw KM, Stern GM, Kumar P. *Psychopharmacology 1978; 57:*33
18   Riederer P, Youdim MBH, Rausch WD, Birkmayer W, Jellinger K, Seeman D. *J neural Transmiss 1978; 43:*217
19   Yahr MD. *J neural Transmiss 1978; 43:*227
20   Birkmayer W, Riederer P, Youdim MBH, Linauer E. *J neural Transmiss 1975; 36:*303
21   Lees AJ, Shaw KM, Kohout LJ, Stern GM, Elsworth JD, Sandler M, Youdim MBH. *Lancet 1977; ii:*791
22   Reynolds GP, Elsworth JD, Blau K, Sandler M, Lees AJ, Stern GM. *Brit J clin Pharmac 1978; 6:*542
23   Sandler M, Glover V, Ashford A. In preparation
24   Glover V, Reveley M, Sandler M. *Biochem Pharmacol 1980.* In press
25   Kuchel O, Buu NT, Unger T, Lis M, Genest J. *J Clin Endocrinol Metab 1979; 48:*425
26   Barbeau A, Murphy GF, Sourkes TL. *Science 1961; 133:*1706
27   Jenner WN, Rose FA. *Nature 1974; 252:*237
28   Williams RT. In *Detoxification mechanisms 1959.* London: Chapman and Hall

29   Merits I. *Biochem Pharmac 1976; 25:*829
30   Foldes A, Meek JL. *J Neurochem 1974; 23:*303
31   Hart RF, Renskers KJ, Nelson EB, Roth JA. *Life Sci 1979; 24:*125
32   Rein G, Glover V, Sandler M. In preparation
33   Renskers KJ, Feor KD, Roth JA. *J Neurochem 1980.* In press
34   Barbeau A, Murphy GF, Sourkes TL. *Science 1961; 133:*1706
35   Bischoff F, Torres A. *Clin Chem 1962; 8:*370
36   Weil-Malherbe H, Van Buren JM. *J Lab clin Med 1969; 74:*305
37   Hoehn MM, Crowley TJ, Rutledge CO. *J Neurol Neurosurg Psychiat 1976; 39:*941
38   Crowley TJ, Hoehn MM, Rutledge CO, Stallings MA, Heaton RK, Sundell S, Stilson D. *Arch gen Psychiat 1978; 35:*97
39   Bonham Carter SM, Youdim MBH, Sandler M, Hunter KR, Stern GM. *Clin Chim Acta 1974; 52:*327
40   Glover V, Sandler M, Ward C, Stern G. In preparation

Chapter 27

GABA FUNCTION AND PARKINSON'S DISEASE

R Kerwin and C Pycock

Introduction

The most striking neurochemical deficit in Parkinson's disease is a loss of dopamine (DA) and its synthesising enzymes, tyrosine hydroxylase and dopa-decarboxylase, in the caudate-putamen, substantia nigra and globus pallidus [1]. This dopamine deficiency is due to loss of DA containing cell bodies within the substantia nigra. The 'DA theory' of Parkinsonism is supported by the well established observations that substitute therapy with precursor L-dopa can markedly relieve the symptoms of Parkinsonism and that DA blocking drugs are capable of producing Parkinsonian like akinesia [2]. However, a wealth of other transmitters are active in maintaining functional integrity within the basal ganglia. One such important transmitter is the inhibitory amino acid, gamma-aminobutyric acid (GABA). GABA not only directly controls the activity of the DA containing cell bodies of the substantia nigra [3], but is also present as an important transmitter in other basal ganglia regions controlling extrapyramidal output [4]. Furthermore, loss of GABA and its synthesising enzymes have been observed in basal ganglia regions of patients dying with Parkinson's disease [5]. It is possible, therefore, that manipulation of GABA function within the basal ganglia may prove to be a useful therapeutic strategy in the management of Parkinsonism.

GABA in the Nigrostriatal System

GABA, its synthesising enzyme, glutamate decarboxylase, GABA receptors and GABA uptake sites are present in particularly large quantities within the substantia nigra [6, 7]. The origin of nigral GABA neurones appears to be the striatum and globus pallidus [8]. GABA terminals in the substantia nigra appear to synapse with nigral dendrites within the zona reticulata of the nigra. This striato-nigral system of GABA neurones is believed to function as an inhibitory feedback system modulating the activity of the ascending dopaminergic nigro-striatal system. GABA

212

interneurones are also present intrinsic to the striatum [9] synapsing with and modulating the activity of nigrostriatal DA terminals. Thus, both in the striatum and substantia nigra, GABAergic modulation of DA function may occur and a knowledge of these interactions is of relevance in understanding the role of GABA in Parkinson's disease.

The suggestion that GABA provides an inhibitory feedback loop to the dopaminergic nigrostriatal system is supported by many studies. Thus DA blocking agents increase the rate of firing in the nigrostriatal pathway [10], thought to be brought about by blockade of excitatory DA receptors on presumed GABAergic cell bodies within the striatum. Furthermore, stimulation of cell bodies within the caudate nucleus of cats inhibits cell firing in the substantia nigra, this effect being reversed by the GABA blocking agent, picrotoxin [11]. It is known that axotomy, or reduction in impulse flow, in the nigrostriatal system is associated with predictable changes in the levels of DA and its metabolites. Local or peripheral [12] administration of GABAmimetic agents produce essentially similar effects, thus suggesting an inhibitory function for GABA on DA cells within the substantia nigra.

Recently, it has been suggested that the role of GABA within the substantia nigra may be more than that of just simple feedback inhibition. Cheramy et al [13] have shown that nigral infusion of GABA paradoxically increases the release of DA from the ipsilateral caudate nucleus of cats. Raising GABA levels in the substantia nigra produces an enhancement of behavioural responses to dopaminomimetic drugs [14]. Furthermore, unilateral injection of GABAmimetic drugs into the substantia nigra produces contralateral turning behaviour [15] rather than the predicted ipsilateral behaviour. Several possible explanations for such effects of an inhibitory transmitter within the nigra have been proposed. Firstly, drugs may act preferentially at presynaptic GABA receptors within the substantia nigra inhibiting the tonic release of endogenous GABA onto DAergic dendrites [16]; or that GABA inhibits an inhibitory interneurone utilising a transmitter other than GABA, possibly glycine [17, 18]. These suggestions are supported by the observation that muscimol, a potent GABAmimetic agent, increases the firing rate of DA cell bodies within the zona compacta region of the substantia nigra [19]. It has also been suggested that GABA may form part of a non DAergic output relay from the substantia nigra [15].

Although the role of GABA in the substantia nigra may appear somewhat complex, the elucidation of these differing mechanisms is of crucial importance to the formulation of therapeutic strategy in Parkinson's disease employing GABAergic drugs.

GABA interneurones and axon collaterals from the descending striato-nigral pathway are present in the striatum [9, 20]. Behaviourally, GABA seems to have a facilitatory effect on DA mediated function within the striatum. Thus muscimol potentiates stereotypy induced by the DA agonist apomorphine [21]. Cools and Janssen [22] have shown that GABA is vital to the mediation of head turning behaviour produced by intracaudate injection of DA agonists in cats. Stoof and Mulder [23] have shown that release of DA from the striatum is enhanced when the catabolic breakdown of GABA is prevented. GABA itself has also been ob-

213

served to directly stimulate the release of DA from striatal tissue *in vitro* [24, 25]. GABA receptors thus appear to be present on DA terminals in the striatum. However, this may not be a useful target for GABA drugs since Parkinson's disease is characterised by loss of such terminals.

GABA in other basal ganglia regions

Globus pallidus: This nucleus is believed to regulate output of activity from the extrapyramidal system. The nucleus has a dense intrinsic GABA innervation [6, 7] and also may receive a GABA containing pathway from the striatum [26]. Manipulation of GABA systems within the globus pallidus may be particularly relevant to Parkinson's disease. Increasing GABA levels in this region, or removal of the pallidum completely, produces akinesia in rats [27]. In other words, preventing output through the pallidum either by removal or raising inhibitory tone within this region, apparently prevents the manifestation of extrapyramidal activity. Thus, enhancing transmission through this nucleus may alleviate Parkinsonism. This may be achieved by reducing inhibitory tone within the pallidum, ideally by using drugs that will inhibit the synthesis or release of GABA [28].

Mesolimbic system: This should also be considered in extra pyramidal motor disorder. Hyperkinetic responses to DA agonists in animals are believed to be mediated through nucleus accumbens dopamine receptors [29], and integrity of accumbens system is vital for the expression of normal stereotyped responses to DA agonists [30]. The anatomical proximity of the nucleus accumbens to the caudate in man should also be noted. The cell bodies of the ascending DAergic mesolimbic system are contained within the ventral tegmental region of the upper brainstem [31]. There is some controversy as to whether a long axon GABA pathway converges on this region [32, 33]. A functional interaction between GABA and DA, however, certainly seems to exist. Elevation of GABA transmission within the ventral tegmentum reduces both mesolimbic and extra pyramidal DA turnover [34]. Intrategmental injection of a GABA blocking drug, picrotoxin, increases activity in rats which is blocked by prior treatment with DA blocking agents [35]. Thus GABA seems to inhibit the dopaminergic cell bodies of the ascending mesolimbic system. In the nucleus accumbens itself GABA also seems to be functionally antidopaminergic. Elevating GABA levels, GABA uptake blockade and GABA itself abolish hyperkinesia evoked by injection of DA into this site [36]. Although the role of mesolimbic GABA systems in the aetiology of Parkinson's disease is a matter of speculation, this system should be considered in therapy using GABA-ergic drugs since it is functionally antagonistic to the effects of GABA systems in the nigro striatal system.

GABA lesions in Parkinsonism

The preceding sections have dealt with the physiological interactions of GABA in the basal ganglia and its integration with systems which may be involved in the

214

aetiology of Parkinsonism. There also appears to be a primary pathological deficit of GABA function within the basal ganglia in Parkinson's disease. The GABA synthesising enzyme, glutamate decarboxylase (GAD) resides only in GABA nerves and is a stable postmortem marker for GABA terminals. There are gross depletions of GAD within the striatum, globus pallidus and substantia nigra in patients dying with Parkinson's disease [37]. Changes in the GAD activity may represent trophic changes consequent to the dopamine lesion, since it is reversed by chronic L-dopa therapy [38]. However, this suggestion is challenged by the observation of Vincent *et al* [39] who demonstrated that the trophic change following bilateral destruction of the DA containing cells of the nigrostriatal systems was in fact an elevation of GAD activity in basal ganglia structures in the rat. These authors concluded that the loss of GAD activity in Parkinson's disease cannot be a consequence of the DA lesion but must precede it or occur independently of it. Recently, loss of binding sites for ^{3}H-GABA has been reported to occur in the substantia nigra but not in other basal ganglia regions in Parkinson's disease post mortem [40]. This simply reflects the loss of the DA containing cell bodies within the substantia nigra upon which post synaptic GABA receptors reside. If loss of GABA function is a significant pathological event in Parkinson's disease it is possible that useful GABA-mimetic drugs which can reverse this lesion may be developed and eventually be of clinical use.

Animal Models and GABA Function

A knowledge of the physiology and neurochemistry of GABA in the basal ganglia may provide insight into the mechanisms underlying GABA's role in extrapyramidal disease. On the other hand, much information about basal ganglia function can be obtained using animal models of extrapyramidal disorder produced by experimental manipulation of GABA systems within the basal ganglia. Apart from providing further understanding of the role of GABA in basal ganglia function, such models of extrapyramidal disorder, produced by experimental manipulation of GABA systems within the basal ganglia, provide a heuristic test system on which therapeutic agents can be screened. It is immediately clear from such studies that GABA has functionally opposing roles within differing regions of the basal ganglia and useful therapy using GABA drugs may await the development of specific agents manipulating GABA function only at discrete sites within the CNS. For instance, injection of GABAmimetic agents into the nucleus accumbens [36] or globus pallidus [27] of rats produces effects which include reduction in locomotor activity, akinesia, rigidity and catalepsy, a syndrome generally considered to be parkinsonian like. On the basis of these observations, it could be concluded that reduction of GABA function within these regions may be beneficial in the disease. However, such an effect at the substantia nigra would be antagonistic to this, since GABAmimetics injected into the nigra produce hyperactivity, dyskinesia and stereotypy [13, 41]. Perhaps of relevance is the more empirical observation that GABAmimetics administered peripherally potentiate the state of catalepsy produced by blockade of cerebral DA receptors [42, 43]. Thus the net effect of GABAmimetics may be to exacerbate parkinsonian symptoms. By extrapolation, drugs reducing GABA function may alleviate the symptoms.

Present status of GABA drugs in therapy: Conclusions

Several pharmacological agents which can manipulate the function of GABA systems have been tested in the clinic. In view of the theoretical importance of GABA in basal ganglia function, these drugs have been impressively unsuccessful. Drugs used include GABA itself, baclofen, imidazole acetic acid and sodium valproate [28].

GABA is of clear importance in basal ganglia function and in mechanisms underlying extra pyramidal disorder. It is nevertheless unsurprising that therapy employing GABA manipulating agents has to date been disappointing. The drugs so far tested are of dubious credibility as specific pharmacological agents. GABA itself passes the blood brain barrier only at very high doses [44]. Baclofen is a chlorophenyl derivative of GABA which passes the blood brain barrier. The drug has many potent pharmacological actions, the least impressive of which are its GABA properties! [45]. At high doses the drug may be effective in stimulating GABA release [46]. Imidazole acetic acid directly stimulates GABA receptors, but is of relatively low potency [47]. Sodium valproate can elevate GABA levels by inhibiting several of its catabolic enzymes [48]. However, at the doses of sodium valporate generally employed in anti-epileptic therapy the drug will have little effect on brain GABA levels and may not be of relevance in the drug's mechanism of action.

The successful use of GABA drugs in extrapyramidal therapy awaits the resolution of several difficulties, the most important being the acquisition of suitable and specific drugs. Many compounds are available which in experimental systems are potent and impressive agents, all of which have associated problems (for review and further reference see ref 49). Thus potent receptor agonists are available such as muscimol, but these have very low lethal ratios in laboratory animals. Potent GABA receptor blocking agents produce seizures. The newly available compounds gamma-vinyl GABA, gamma-acetylenic GABA and gabaculine have generated much interest. These agents are potent, peripherally active inhibitors of the catabolic enzyme GABA-aminotransferase, but the toxicity of these agents is unknown. Specific blockers of GABA uptake are available such as aminocyclohexanecarboxylic acid or diaminobutyric acid which will delay synaptic inactivation of GABA, but these are either inactive *in vivo*, toxic, or act as 'false transmitters'. Baclofen is a GABA release stimulating agent, but this has already been shown to be of little use in Parkinsonism [28]. It is possible to inhibit GABA release through an action at presynaptic 'autoreceptors' [50, 51]. This would be of great theoretical value [28], but compounds acting only at such receptors are unavailable. Finally, agents which inhibit the synthesis of GABA are well characterised, but like the receptor blockers these are analeptic.

216

A second problem is the fact that GABA seems to have functionally opposing roles within differing basal ganglia structures and, despite potent actions at the synapse, drugs have little or no net effect on extrapyramidal function. This may not be an insoluble problem. Supersensitivity of GABA receptors may occur at lesioned sites [52] which would be exquisitely sensitive to low doses of drug. The possibility of utilising drugs which are converted to active agents by site specific enzymes is not without precedent [53]. Furthermore, actions of a drug at the nigra which will negate the drug's action at other sites may not be of relevance since the target sites for GABA in this region will be absent in Parkinsonism [40].

Although the role of GABA in Parkinson's disease may seem to be of academic rather than of practical value, there are clear indications to suggest that continuing research in this field is fertile ground that will lead to the growth of agents acting in a new way in the treatment of the disease.

Summary

GABA is of importance in Parkinson's disease for three reasons:

1 GABA is an important transmitter within the substantia nigra controlling the activity of ascending dopaminergic neurones;
2 GABA is a major transmitter of the other basal ganglia controlling output from extrapyramidal systems;
3 Loss of GABA containing cells has been reported in Parkinson's disease post mortem.

Drugs manipulating GABA function may be of potential therapeutic use. However, behavioural and biochemical studies show that GABA has functionally opposing roles in differing regions of basal ganglia. Thus potential therapy may depend upon the development of agents acting specifically at localised sites within the brain.

References

1 Hornykiewicz O. In Lajtha A, ed. *Handbook of Neurochemistry Vol 7 1972;*465. New York, Plenum Press
2 Marsden CD. In Williams D, ed. *Modern Trends in Neurology Vol 6 1975;*141. London, Butterworths
3 Yoshida M, Precht W. *Brain Res 1971;32:*95
4 Fahn S. In Roberts E, Chase TN, Tower DB, eds. *GABA in Nervous System Function 1976;*169. New York, Raven Press
5 Hornykiewicz O, Lloyd KG, Davidson L. In Roberts E, Chase TN, Tower DB, eds. *GABA in Nervous System Function 1976;*479. New York, Raven Press
6 Kim JS, Bak IJ, Hassler R, Okada Y. *Exp Brain Res 1971;14:*95
7 Enna SJ, Kuhar J, Snyder SH. *Brain Res 1975;93:*168
8 Fonnum F, Grofova I, Rinvik E, Storm-Mathisen J, Walberg F. *Brain Res 1974;71:*77
9 McGeer PL, McGeer EG. *Brain Res 1975;91:*331
10 Aghajanian GK, Bunney BS. In Usdin E, Snyder S, eds. *Frontiers in Catecholamine Research 1974;*643. New York, Pergamon Press

217

11 Precht W, Yoshida M. *Brain Res 1975;32:*229
12 Anden NE. *N.S. Arch Pharmacol 1974;283:*419
13 Cheramy A, Nieoullon A, Glowinski J. *Eur J Pharmacol 1978;48:*281
14 Matsui Y, Kamioka T. *Eur J Pharmacol 1978;50:*243
15 Olpe HR, Schellenberg H, Koella WP. *Eur J Pharmacol 1877;45:*291
16 LeViel V, Cheramy A, Nieullon A, Glowinski J. *Brain Res 1979;175:*259
17 Cheramy A, Nieullon A, Glowinski J. *Eur J Pharmacol 1978;47:*141
18 Kerwin R, Pycock C. *Eur J Pharmacol 1979;54:*93
19 MacNeil D, Gower M, Szymanska I. *Brain Res 1978;154:*401
20 Hattori T, McGeer PL, Fibiger HC, McGeer EG. *Brain Res 1973;54:*103
21 Scheel-Kruger J, Christiansen AV, Arnt J. *Life Sci 1978;22:*75
22 Cools AR, Janssen HG. *J Pharm Pharmacol 1976;28:*70
23 Stoof JC, Mulder AH. *Eur J Pharmacol 1977;46:*177
24 Starr MS. *Eur J Pharmacol 1978;48:*325
25 Kerwin R, Pycock C. *Biochem Pharmacol 1979;28:*2193
26 Obata K, Yoshida M. *Brain Res 1973;64:*455
27 Pycock C, Horton RW, Marsden CD. *Brain Res 1976;116:*353
28 Marsden CD. In Kofod H, Krogsgaard-Larsen P, Scheel-Kruger J, eds. *GABA-Neuro-transmitters, Pharmacochemical, Biochemical and Pharmacological Aspects 1979;*295. Copenhagen, Munksgaard
29 Costall B, Naylor RJ. *J Pharm Pharmacol 1976;28:*592
30 Cools AR. In Costa E, Gessa GL, eds. *Advances in Biochemical Psychopharmacology Vol 16 1977;*215. New York, Raven Press
31 Dahlstrom A, Fuxe K. *Acta Physiol Scand 1964;62 Suppl 232:*1
32 Waddington JL, Cross AJ. *Life Sci 1978;22:*1011
33 Fonnum F, Walaas I, Iversen E. *J Neurochem 1977;29:*221
34 Fuxe K, Hokfelt R, Ljungdahl A, Agnati L, Johanssen O, Perez de la Mora M. *Med Biol 1975;53:*177
35 Stevens J, Wilson K, Foote W. *Psychopharmacology 1974;39:*105
36 Pycock CJ, Horton RW. *J Neural Trans 1979;45:*17
37 Lloyd KG, Mohler H, Bartholini G, Hornykiewicz O. In Birkmayer W, Hornykiewicz O, eds. *Advances in Parkinsonisn; 1976.* 186. Basle, Editiones Roche
38 Lloyd KG, Hornykiewicz O. *Nature (Lond) 1973;243:*521
39 Vincent SR, Nagy JI, Fibiger HC. *Brain Res 1978;143:*168
40 Lloyd KG, Dreksler S. *Brain Res 1979;163:*77
41 Scheel-Kruger J, Arnt J, Magelund G. *Neurosci Lett 1977;4:*351
42 Worms P, Willigens MT, Lloyd KG. *J Pharm Pharmacol 1978;30:*716
43 Kerwin R, Pycock C. *Neuropharmacology 1979;18:*655
44 Kuriyama K, Sze PY. *Neuropharmacology 1971;10:*103
45 Waddington JL, Cross AJ. *J Pharm Pharmacol 1979;31:*652
46 Kerwin R, Pycock C. *J Pharm Pharmacol 1978; 30:*622
47 Enna SJ, Snyder SH. *Mol Pharmacol 1977; 13:*442
48 Whittle SR, Turner AJ. *J Neurochem 1978; 31:*1453
49 Chase TN, Walters JR. In Roberts E, Chase TN, Tower DB, eds. *GABA in nervous system function 1976;* 497. New York: Raven Press
50 Mitchell PR, Martin IL. *Nature 1978; 274:*904
51 Brennan MJW, Cantrill RL. *J Neurochem 1979; 33:*721
52 Waddington JL, Cross AJ. *Nature 1978; 276:*618
53 Horton RW, Chapman AG, Meldrum BS. *J Neurochem 1978; 30:*1507

PART V

L-DOPA AND ITS PROBLEMS

Chapter 28

THE L-DOPA STORY 1958–1979

André Barbeau

Summary

The present chapter is meant to be background information for Parts V and VII on therapy. It presents, in a series of vignettes, my own view of the principal developments in the management of Parkinson's disease during the 21 years since 1958. As all such views, they are highly coloured by personal experience and should not be considered as exclusive or definitive.

The story of dopamine replacement or modulation in Parkinson's disease, to date has gone through 6 principal phases (Tables I-VI). The format utilised for this presentation will permit space economy. Details are to be found in the references given.

TABLE I PHASE 1: Levodopa–Low Dosage (1960-1967)

A   Rationale

      1 Presence of dopamine (DA) in striatum (Carlsson et al, 1958) [1]
      2 Low DA in striatum (Ehringer et al, 1960) [2]
      3 Low DA in urine (Barbeau et al, 1961) [3]

B   Results

      1 Clear modification of rigidity and akinesia with IV or oral low doses of levodopa (100 mg to 2,000 mg/day) (Barbeau, 1961 [4]; Birkmayer and Hornykiewicz, 1961 [5]).

C   Problems

      1 Short, unsustained, effect
      2 Extremely high cost of drug (up to $6,000/kg)
      3 Variable results depending on dose

TABLE II PHASE 2: Levodopa–High Dosage (1967–1975)

A   Rationale

        1   Deficit in DA (see Phase 1)
        2   Slow, gradual, titrated increase of levodopa (Cotzias et al, 1967, 1969)
            [6, 7]

B   Results

        1   Improvement exceeds 50 per cent in 70 per cent of patients (Cotzias et al,
            1969 [7] ; Barbeau 1969 [8] ; Yahr et al, 1969 [9])

C   Problems

        1   Peripheral side-effects: nausea, vomiting, hypotension, cardiac arrhythmias
        2   Central side-effects:
           a   Abnormal involuntary movements
           b   Mental side-effects (confusion, hallucinations, nightmares)
           c   Oscillations in performance

TABLE III PHASE 3: Levodopa + Dopa-Decarboxylase Inhibitors (1967–date)

A   Rationale

        1   Block of enzyme peripherally permits decrease in peripheral DA and
            increase in circulating DOPA (Bartholini et al, 1968) [10]

B   Results

        1   Same as with levodopa alone
        2   More rapid onset of response
        3   Marked reduction in peripheral side-effects
        4   Marked reduction in levodopa dosage

C   Problems

        1   Increase in central side-effects:
           a   Abnormal involuntary movements (AIMs)
           b   Oscillations in performance
           c   Mental side-effects

TABLE IV PHASE 4: Dopamine Receptor Agonists
___

A   Rationale

    1   Agonist by selecting only DA receptor would avoid complications of levodopa metabolites (Cotzias et al 1976) [11]
    2   Some agonists have longer stimulating action (Calne et al, 1974) [12]

B   Results

    1   Most imitate levodopa in action but at reduced level except with high doses.
    2   Some potentiation of levodopa
    3   Controversy as to effect upon AIM's and on/off phenomena; mainly against "wearing off"

C   Problems

    1   Extremely high cost
    2   High incidence of mental side-effects
    3   Toxicity (pre-renal azotaemia; hepatic)
    4   Short time-span of sustained effect
    5   Lack of specific agonists for D_1 and D_2 receptors
___

TABLE V PHASE 5: Dopamine Potentiations
___

A   Rationale

    1   DA concentrations could be increased by blocking metabolism
    2   MAO B more specific for DA
    3   Postulated deficit in APUD peptide producing cells (Barbeau, 1976) [13]
    4   Dopa-potentiating effect of MIF (Plotnikoff and Kastin, 1974) [14]

B   Results

    1   With Deprenyl ® (Birkmeyer et al, 1975) [15]
       a   Prolongs levodopa effect
       b   Useful against "wearing off" akinesia
    2   With PLG (MIFI) Kastin and Barbeau, 1972; 1975) [16, 17]
       a   Clear potentiation of L-dopa effect
       b   Improvement of mental constructive ability

C   Problems

    1   Deprenyl
       a   Some increase in AIM's
       b   Short lasting improvement
    2   PLG (MIF I)
       a   Only active intravenously
       b   Lack of availability of drug
       c   Short lasting effect
___

TABLE VI PHASE 6: Modulation of DA/ACH Balance

A   Rationale

    1   DA/Ach balance for symptoms (Barbeau, 1962) [18]
    2   Chronic levodopa tips balance towards low Ach
    3   Choline and Lecithin can serve as precursors to brain Ach (Cohen and Wurtman, 1975) [19]
    4   Low Ach may be involved in AIM's and dementia (Bowen et al, 1979) [20]
    5   Increased dementia after long-term levodopa

B   Results

    1   Reduction in AIM's with lecithin at expense of slightly reduced antiakinetic effect of levodopa (Barbeau, 1980) [21]
    2   Reduction in hallucinations, nightmares and confusion. Slight improvement in memory in levodopa unresponsive patients (Barbeau, 1980) [21]

C   Problems

    1   Results still preliminary
    2   Lack of control studies

The impression gained in the last few years has been one of many possible approaches, but of very few major advances over and above the use of levodopa, uniformly accepted as still the best available treatment. My own personal feeling is that the future is not in discovering a "better DOPA", but in elucidating the causal mechanism of the well-known loss of pigmented cells in the substantia nigra, the locus coeruleus and the dorsal nucleus of the vagus. No prevention of this degenerative disease will occur until this problem is solved.

References

1   Carlsson A, Lindgvist M, Magnusson T, Waldeck B. *Science 1958; 127:*471
2   Ehringer H, Hornykiewicz O. *Klin Wchs 1960; 38:*1236
3   Barbeau A, Murphy GF, Sourkes TL. *Science 1961; 133:*1706
4   Barbeau A. *Excerpta Med Int Congr Ser 1961; 38: 152*
5   Birkmayer W, Hornykiewicz O. *Wien Klin Wochs 1961; 73:*787
6   Cotzias GC, Van Woert MH, Schiffer LM. *New Engl J Med 1967; 276:*374
7   Cotzias GC, Papavasiliou PS, Gellene R. *New Engl J Med 1969; 280:*337
8   Barbeau A. *Can Med Assoc J 1969; 101:*791
9   Yahr MD, Duvoisin RC, Shear MJ. *Arch Neurol 1969; 21:*343
10   Bartholini G, Da Prada M, Pletscher A. *J Pharm Pharmacol 1968; 20:*228
11   Cotzias GC, Papavasiliou PS, Tolosa ES, Mendez JS, Bell-Midura M. *New Engl J Med 1976; 294:*567
12   Calne DB, Leigh PN, Teychenne PF, Bamji AN, Greenacre JK. *Brit Med J 1974; 4:*442
13   Barbeau A. In Yahr MD, ed. *The basal ganglia 1976;* 281. New York: Raven Press

14   Plotnikoff NP, Kastin AJ. *Arch Int Pharmacodyn Ther 1974; 211:* 211
15   Birkmayer W, Riederer P, Youdim MBH, Linauer W. *J Neural Transm 1975; 36:* 303
16   Kastin AJ, Barbeau A. *Can Med Ass J 1972; 107:* 1079
17   Barbeau A. *Lancet 1975; ii:* 683
18   Barbeau A. *Can Med Ass J 1962; 87:* 802
19   Cohen EL, Wurtman RJ. *Life Sci 1975; 16:* 1095
20   Bowen DM, Spillane JA, Curzon G, Meier-Ruge W, White P, Goodhardt MJ, Iwangoff P, Davison AN. *Lancet 1979; i:* 11
21   Barbeau A. *J Neural Transm 1980;* In press

Chapter 29

SINEMET 25/100

D W Nibbelink, R Bauer, M Hoehn,
M Muenter, S Stellar and R Berman

Introduction

The combination of carbidopa (a decarboxylase inhibitor) with levodopa has been shown to be very effective in the treatment of the signs and symptoms of Parkinson's disease. The presently available combination tablet contains a 1:10 ratio of carbidopa/levodopa. The fixed ratio combination provides assurance that patients will take the proper dosage of levodopa and carbidopa together. The usual daily dosage of carbidopa required for adequate decarboxylase inhibition is 70 to 150 mg. When patients take less than 75 mg of carbidopa per day, there may be an increase in gastrointestinal side effects (nausea and vomiting) when compared to patients receiving a higher dosage of carbidopa.

Many physicians prefer to start Sinemet treatment with Sinemet 10/100 rather than the 25/250 mg combination tablet. The usual initial dosage of Sinemet 10/100 mg is one tablet three times a day. This dosage should be increased by one tablet every day or every two days until maximum clinical response is obtained. Although the instructions specify that the dosage of Sinemet 10/100 should be adjusted rapidly, these recommendations are not always followed. The low dosage of carbidopa in the 10/100 mg preparation of Sinemet during the initial days of therapy may not be sufficient to prevent nausea and vomiting. In such instances, the patient may drop from treatment as a Sinemet failure.

Sinemet in a new fixed ratio containing 25/100 mg given as one tablet t.i.d. provides a total of 75 mg of carbidopa on the first day of treatment. This is the minimum amount of carbidopa usually required for effective inhibition of peripheral dopa decarboxylase enzyme. Such dosages should minimise nausea and vomiting during the initial days of therapy. Rather than have carbidopa used with levodopa in extemporaneous ratios with the components given separately, we considered it advisable to strive for an improved clinical response with a combination tablet of carbidopa/levodopa in the amount of 25 mg of carbidopa and 100 mg of levodopa. Patients who tolerate only low doses of levodopa (less than 750 mg of Sinemet per day) may have an increased clinical response with additional carbidopa.

For those patients, it would be convenient to supply additional carbidopa in the form of a Sinemet 25/100 mg tablet.

In investigating the efficacy of Sinemet 25/100 in Parkinson's disease, we treated the following groups of patients:

1 Patients not previously treated with levodopa.
2 Patients presently receiving daily dosages of 2000 mg or less of levodopa per day.
3 Patients who tolerate less than seven 10/100 mg tablets of Sinemet per day and who experience less than the desired therapeutic responses.

Patient Selection

This multiclinic study included 122 patients with Parkinson's disease who were being treated with a total daily dosage of 75 mg or less of carbidopa and 750 mg or less of levodopa prior to the study. Ninety-three patients were treated with Sinemet 10/100 or 25/250, 13 with L-dopa alone, and 16 had received no prior L-dopa therapy but were on anticholinergic agents.

The entry criteria in the protocol specified that each patient show at least two major, or one major and two minor, manifestations of Parkinson's disease. Patients on prior anticholinergic medication were permitted to enter the study provided the dosage was stabilised for 30 days prior to beginning treatment with Sinemet 25/100. Patients who were presently being treated with Sinemet or L-dopa alone had their drug discontinued the night before entry into the study. Following initial treatment with Sinemet 25/100 during the first two-week period, the clinical efficacy was determined and the dosage was adjusted for optimum therapeutic response. After four weeks of treatment, another evaluation was made before they entered the long-term maintenance treatment phase.

TABLE I Sinemet 25/100 for Parkinson's Disease

Investigator	No. of Patients	Duration of Disease (mo.)	Mean L-Dopa as Sinemet (mg/day)	Days in Study (Range)
RB	31	89	648	29.3 (8–43)
MH	31	118	689	30.6 (25–39)
MM	31	103	635	30.1 (19–48)
SS	29	120	411	30.2 (3–47)
Mean		108	596	30.1

TABLE II

Age (Years)	Males	Females	Total
40–49	6	2	8
50–59	15	13	28
60–69	33	26	59
70–79	13	12	25
80–89	0	2	2
TOTAL	67	55	122

Results

Four investigators in the United States carried out this open treatment study (Table I). The mean duration of treatment was 30 days (range 3–48), and the mean daily L-dopa dosage during the study was 596 mg (range 411–689 mg).

The age distribution was similar for males and females (Table II). The majority of patients (80%) were in stages 2 and 3 prior to treatment (Table III). A significant proportion of patients improved by the end of week 4 when compared to baseline (Table IV). Based on 90 patients taking Sinemet prior to the study, the mean daily dosage of carbidopa was significantly higher after two and four weeks of treatment when compared to baseline (Table V). Mean daily L-dopa levels remained nearly the same during treatment with Sinemet 25/100 when compared to baseline.

Fifty-four per cent of patients continued to use anticholinergic medication with Sinemet 25/100 therapy. The majority of these patients were on amantadine, trihexyphenidyl or benztropine (Table VI).

TABLE III Prior Therapy by Stage of Parkinson's Disease

Stage	Treatment			
	Sinemet 10/100; 25/250	Levodopa	Anticholinergic	Total
I	14	1	0	15
II	19	3	4	26
III	56	5	10	71
IV	4	4	2	10
TOTAL	93	13	16	122

228

TABLE IV Distribution of Change in Stage of Parkinson's Disease

Stage †	Baseline	Week 4*
I	14	16
II	24	38
III	57	44
IV	8	5
TOTAL	103	103

† As defined by Hoehn and Yahr

* Significantly changed from baseline P $<$0.01

TABLE V Mean Carbidopa/Levodopa dosage

	Baseline	Week 2	Week 4
Carbidopa	55.8	141.2*	140.4*
Levodopa	558.3	564.6	571.3

* Statistically Significant p $<$0.01

TABLE VI Major Concomitant Antiparkinson Medication

Drug	No.	(%)
Amantadine	32	(26.2)
Trihexyphenidyl	32	(26.2)
Benztropine	12	(9.8)

Neurological Signs and Symptoms

Nine neurological sign and symptom scores were analysed (individually and combined) at baseline and compared to the data after two and four weeks of treatment. Total neurological sign and symptom scores were significantly improved over baseline values after two and four weeks of treatment (p $<$ 0.01, Table VII). Six of the nine signs and symptoms (rigidity, tremor, gait, sialorrhoea, postural stability and bradykinesia) showed significant improvement over baseline at week 2 and week 4 (p $<$ 0.05 or $<$ 0.01). No statistically significant changes were reported for posture or seborrhoea.

229

TABLE VII Mean Scores of Neurological Signs and Symptoms

	Mean Baseline Score †	Mean Treatment Score Week 2	Mean Treatment Score Week 4
Rigidity	6.4	5.8*	5.0**
Tremor	4.1	3.7*	2.9**
Gait	1.2	1.0**	0.9**
Sialorrhoea	1.2	0.8**	0.7**
Postural Stability	1.0	0.7**	0.7**
Bradykinesia	2.1	1.9**	1.8*
Dysphagia	0.3	0.3	0.3
Seborrhoea	0.5	0.5	0.5
Posture	1.1	1.1	1.0
TOTAL	17.9	15.8**	13.8**

† 108 patients with baseline and treatment scores.
*, ** Statistically significant $p < 0.05, 0.01$, respectively.

Northwestern University Disability Scale

The total scores for the Northwestern University Disability Scale were significantly improved at the end of the four-week period when compared to baseline (9.2 at baseline to 8.2 at week 4, Table VIII). Four of the six disabilities (walking, dressing, hygiene and eating) were significantly improved over baseline ($p < 0.05, < 0.01$), whereas no significant change in scores was obtained for feeding and speech functions.

TABLE VIII Mean Scores of Northwestern University Disability Scale

Disability †	Mean Baseline Score	Mean Treatment Score Week 2	Mean Treatment Score Week 4
Walking	2.1	1.9*	1.7**
Dressing	1.7	1.7	1.6**
Hygiene	2.0	1.8	1.6**
Eating	0.5	0.5	0.4*
Feeding	1.1	1.2	1.1
Speech	1.9	1.9	1.8
TOTAL	9.3	9.0	8.2**

† 108 patients with baseline and treatment scores.
*, ** Statistically significant $p < 0.05, 0.01$, respectively.

Clinical Adverse Experiencss

Seventy-two (67.9%) of the 106 patients who received Sinemet 10/100, 25/250, or levodopa within 30 days prior to entering the study reported one or more pre-study adverse experiences. The most frequently reported pre-study adverse experiences were nausea (25 patients), involuntary movements (25), and dystonia (16).

Forty-four (36.0%) of the 122 patients reported one or more experience during Sinemet 25/100 mg therapy. A statistically significant decrease in frequency was observed after two and four weeks of therapy for nausea ($p < 0.01$), nausea/vomiting ($p < 0.05$), and hyperkinesia ($p < 0.05$, Table IX).

TABLE IX Distribution of Major Adverse Experiences

Adverse Experience	No. of Patients with Adverse Experiences	
	Prior	During
Nausea	25	5**
Involuntary Movements	25	21
Dystonia	16	15
Hypotension	8	5
Nausea/Vomiting	6	1*
Hyperkinesia	6	0*
Confusion	6	3

*, ** Statistically significant change $p < 0.05, 0.01$, respectively

Adverse Laboratory Measurements

The battery of pretreatment laboratory tests was repeated at the end of the study when clinically indicated. Most patients did not have repeat laboratory measurements. The alkaline phosphatase and SGOT tests were done most frequently and no statistically significant difference was observed between the main baseline and treatment values.

Discussion

Patients treated with Sinemet 25/100 showed statistically significant improvement in the major signs and symptoms of Parkinson's disease when compared to the baseline scores. These patients received significantly smaller amounts of carbidopa in the 10/100 and 25/250 Sinemet combination tablets. Within two weeks after beginning Sinemet 25/100 mg therapy, a significant proportion of patients improved in their rigidity, tremor, gait, bradykinesia, postural stability, and sialorrhoea. Functional disability did not improve until patients were treated for four

231

weeks. Walking, dressing, eating and personal hygiene functions improved more than feeding ability and speech functions. Another statistically significant result was the improvement in nausea, vomiting, and hyperkinetic movements during the study when compared to the incidence reported before the study.

This study was an open multiclinical investigation over a limited period of four weeks. The conclusions on efficacy of the study must be considered in that perspective. Only a double-blind study over a longer interval could provide more conclusive evidence of these preliminary results. All patients in these studies continued to be treated with Sinemet 25/100 during a long-term maintenance period of two years (mean days).

Four patients withdrew from the study during the treatment period. Two patients were unco-operative, therapy was ineffective in one, and one was hospitalised due to aspiration pneumonia. No patient discontinued treatment because of severe or increased number of adverse experiences. Mean values of weight, pulse rate and blood pressure did not change significantly from baseline.

Summary

A new combination of Sinemet (25/100 mg) was evaluated in the treatment of 122 patients with Parkinson's disease. The new combination tablet provided an increased daily amount of carbidopa (141 mg) with no increase in the L-dopa component. The patient showed a clinically and statistically improved therapeutic response with fewer adverse drug experiences as compared to the baseline response to Sinemet containing a smaller daily carbidopa dosage (55.8 mg).

No clinically significant changes in weight, pulse, or blood pressure were reported during the four week treatment period, as compared to pre-treatment values. Clinical adverse drug experiences were significantly fewer in overall incidence and in the number of patients experiencing such reactions when compared to the incidence reported during the 30 days prior to the study. Thirty six per cent of the patients reported one or more adverse experiences during Sinemet 25/100 mg therapy, whereas 78 per cent of patients reported one or more adverse experience prior to the study. The most frequently reported adverse experiences during Sinemet 25/100 mg therapy were involuntary movements (21 of 122 patients) and dystonia (15 patients). Nausea, dyskinesia and hyperkinesia were statistically significantly less frequent as compared to baseline (within 30 days prior to the study). No clinically significant abnormal laboratory values were reported.

We conclude that Sinemet 25/100 provides a significantly improved clinical response in patients who tolerate a relatively low dosage of L-dopa in the presently available Sinemet combination tablet.

Chapter 30

PHARMACOLOGICAL TREATMENT OF PARKINSON'S DISEASE IN EARLY AND LATE PHASES

Melvin D Yahr

It is now well established that the major biochemical deficit in patients with parkinsonism is a loss of striatal dopamine (DA) [1]. Concomitantly, there is a decrease in its synthesising enzymes, tyrosine hydroxylase and dopa decarboxylase. These findings are evident regardless of the nature of the causative process and are a consequence of selective degeneration of the melanin containing neurones, particularly those of the substantia nigra which gives rise to the nigro-striatal pathway. Why these melanin containing cells of the substantia nigra selectively undergo degeneration is at present unknown.

Physiologically the loss of DA causes a disturbance in the neurotransmitter relationships in the striatum—particularly that which exists with acetylcholine (ACH). These two transmitters which have opposing actions are functionally interdependent and are normally in exquisite balance. In Parkinson's disease, the DA deficiency allows for functional hyperactivity of ACH which underlies its major symptoms. The current approach to the treatment of Parkinsonism is therefore directed to re-establishing normal relationships between these two neurotransmitters which is best accomplished by using agents which decrease cholinergic or increase dopaminergic activity.

Of particular import in developing an effective therapeutic regimen is an understanding of the natural history of Parkinsonism as well as the dynamics of the evolving biochemical abnormalities. Parkinson's disease, in the main, is a slowly developing disorder where early symptoms are minimal—indeed, barely detectable in some instances. During this phase of the disease, which may persist for a number of years, the DA deficiency may be barely detectable despite damage to nigral neurones, since those which remain intact may be in a state of over-activity, synthesising and releasing more DA per unit time than normally. This phase of parkinsonism may be considered as a partially compensated phase of the disease. Treatment is best accomplished by agents capable of enhancing the remaining striatal dopaminergic activity. Those most useful are indicated in Table I.

TABLE I Treatment "Compensated" Phase Parkinsonism

---

1 Reassurance—no pharmacological agents.

2 Agents with CNS Anti-Muscarinic action.
    Trihexyphenidyl
    Benztropine
    Diphenhydramine

3 DA-Releasing or re-uptake inhibiting agents
    Amantadine HCl
    Amphetamine (Methamphetamine)
    Tricyclics (Amitriptyline, Imipramine)

4 MAO B inhibitor—Deprenyl

In those patients with little or no functional impairment, reassurance usually suffices. Indeed, it is preferable since it avoids the risk of any drug induced side effects. As symptoms become more manifest, muscarinic agents are preferred as a first drug of choice and are certainly beneficial providing they can be used in modest dosage, where few undesirable side effects are encountered. There is little to suggest that any one of the many available in this class of drugs is superior to another. They can be combined with agents that alter dopaminergic activity by promoting release or inhibiting re-uptake of DA at the presynaptic terminal. Amantadine and the tricylic compounds produce such an effect and are most frequently used. More recently, we have moved to the use of the MAO B inhibitor, Deprenyl, as the sole agent in treating early parkinsonism. This drug appears to have an action on that portion of the nigro striatal pathway which has remained intact and is still functional. In animal models it has been shown to increase the release of dopamine at nerve terminals, produce dimunition of its re-uptake and inhibit the release of acetylcholine in the striatum. These multiple pharmacological effects, all directed towards augmenting striatal dopaminergic activity, as well as its relative safety in terms of untoward action, are most desirable for a therapeutic agent to be used in the early stages of parkinsonism. Initial results are sufficiently encouraging to warrant a more extended trial which is presently in progress.

Continued degeneration of nigral cells leads to an increased degree of DA deficiency with more profound symptoms and a stage of the disease which may be termed the "decompensated" phase. Here too, certain compensatory features occur which play an important role in our present approach in treating this phase of parkinsonism. First, despite the loss of neuronal elements involved in the enzymology of DA, sufficient dopa decarboxylase remains available to convert dopa to DA and its final acid metabolite homovanillic acid (HVA), presumably the same mechanism previously noted remains operative in this phase, namely, that surviving cells are overactive and capable of carrying out an increased rate of synthesis of exogenously administered L-dopa. Additionally, the ubiquitous nature of dopa decarboxylase and monoamine oxidase allows for metabolism of this aromatic amino acid in non nigral cells. Equally important are events which occur at DA receptor sites in the striatum. As a result of degeneration of the nigrostriatal pathway, the DA receptors increase in number and show evidence of denervation "supersensitivity", which allows for increased reactivity to DA. It should be noted that changes in the DA receptors are continuous and dynamic and are further altered by the type of pharmacological agents which are administered.

The majority of patients seeking treatment fall into this decompensated phase of parkinsonism and the agents most useful for them are those capable of replenishing the functional deficit of DA in the striatum (Table II).

TABLE II Treatment "Decompensated" Phase Parkinsonism

1 Levodopa + PDI

2 Levodopa + PDI + Anti-ACH
   DA Releaser or uptake blocker

3 Levodopa + PDI + MAO BI

4 DA Receptor Agonists
   Peribedil
   Lergotril
   N-Propylaporphine
   Bromocriptine

More than 12 years ago we first began exploring the potential value of these dopaminergic agents. Levodopa alone or with carbidopa are those with which most experience is available. The advantage of this combination of agents has been well documented by a number of investigators [2]. However, long term usage shows that therapeutic effects are optimal during the first years of administration, following which a loss of efficacy occurs, which is associated with an increased number of side effects [3].

In this regard, of particular importance is the increasing incidence of abnormal involuntary movements (AIMs) and the fluctuating therapeutic response, the so-called "on-off" phenomenon. The mechanisms underlying these therapeutic limiting reactions is at best only speculative. Denervation supersensitivity of DA receptors has been invoked as the cause of AIMs. however, recent studies have shown that basal ganglia regions of those patients treated with levodopa have less DA binding sites to haloperidol than those untreated, placing this mechanism in doubt. As to the "on-off" phenomenon, depolarisation with temporary inactivation of receptors has been suggested as being operative. From a clinician's viewpoint this explanation is less than satisfactory since it does not explain the differing nature of these reactions. At least two varieties occur—one, dose related in that "on" period occurs following an ingested dose but wanes rapidly with an "off" period ensuing before

235

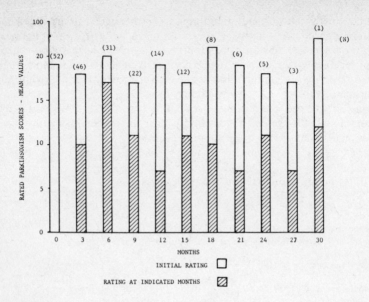

Figure 1 Parkinsonism ratings during deprenyl treatment.

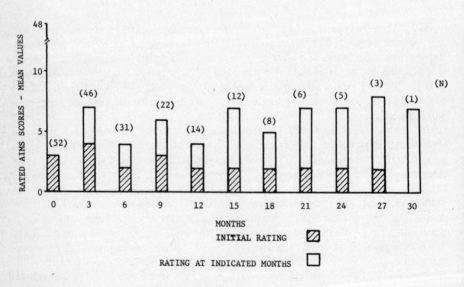

Figure 2 Incidence AIMs, during deprenyl treatment.

the next scheduled dose. The other is non-dose related and occurs randomly throughout the day. In regard to the former, which may be considered as an end dose phenomenon, we have suggested that it may relate to the lack of continuing availability of dopamine in the striatum [4]. Such may occur because its precursor levodopa is not uniformly available—its rate of conversion to dopamine impaired—or that dopamine is being degraded at an increased rate. Studies in our laboratories have shown that some patients on long term levodopa tend to clear this agent more rapidly from plasma and accumulate HVA in spinal fluid at an increased rate than those in the initial phases of treatment. For these reasons we have been particularly interested in Deprenyl since potentially it can slow the catabolism of dopamine and make it more continuously available at striatal synaptic sites.

Our studies with this agent began about two and one half years ago. Though we have carried out a variety of clinical trials I should like to present our long range findings in a group of patients whose response to levodopa has been less than optimal in that "on-off" phenomena have developed and been the major problem. The patient population treated as shown in Table III.

TABLE III Patient Population

Number	54	(M-37, F-17)
Mean Age	63 yrs	(35-80)
Duration of PD	11 yrs	(2-25)
Treatment		
L-Dopa ± PDI	7 yrs	($<$1-11)
L-Dopa + PDI + Deprenyl	9 mos	(3-30)

The overall effect of addition of Deprenyl on parkinsonism is indicated in Figure 1.

Using a rated neurological examination, a 50 per cent reduction in signs of parkinsonism is evident. No attenuation of response is noted for as long as 30 months. Associated with this improvement was an increase in abnormal involuntary movements (Figure 2).

As to the "on-off" response, which in this instance included what has been termed the end dose variety, 70 per cent of patients experienced a significant reduction in their incidence (Table IV).

Though some patients who had less than an optimal response to Dopa and Carbidopa also improved in their parkinson symptoms, the numbers are too small to make a definitive statement in this regard.

The side effects noted in this group of patients are listed in Table V. It should be noted that no real amphetamine-like reactions were seen except for isolated cases of insomnia and agitation which are not infrequent occurrences with the use of dopaminergic agents alone. We did experience two instances of induced hyper-

TABLE IV Effect of Deprenyl on "on-off" Phenomena

	No.	Improved	Unimproved
"On-off"	46	32	14
Suboptimal Response to Dopa ± PDI	8	4	4

TABLE V Untoward Effects of Deprenyl

		No.
Cardiac Arrhythmias		2
Hypertension		2
Hypotension		3
Mental		13
Confusion	7	
Depression	3	
Agitation	3	
Insomnia		5
Nausea & Anorexia		2
Peptic Ulcer (Exacerbation)		2
TOTAL		29 (54)
Increase in involuntary movement		28

tension in patients whose dietary intake did not include any excessive tyramine content. The activation of pre-existing peptic ulcer symptoms was noted on two occasions raising the possibility of excessive release of gastric histamine by Deprenyl.

The ability of Deprenyl to give sustained suppression of MAO B for extended periods of time is indicated in Table VI. MAO B was inhibited almost completely for periods up to 32 months. The concomitant decrease in plasma amine oxidase is unrelated to the use of Deprenyl but a result of Carbidopa, since its hydrazine moiety affects the pyridoxal co-factor involved with this enzyme.

Summary

Though parkinsonism remains a disorder of unknown cause, relief of its major symptoms can be achieved to a considerable degree by presently available pharmacological agents. In its early phase it is best treated by drugs which facilitate existing central nervous system dopaminergic activity. As the disease progresses it becomes necessary to resort to agents which can replenish striatal dopamine. These agents, used judiciously, can give sustained benefit for extended periods

TABLE VI Platelet MAO and Plasma Amine Oxidase Activity in Patients on Derenyl, L-dopa and Carbidopa

Sex	Age	Deprenyl (10 mg/day) MOS	Platelet MAO nmoles/10^8 platelets/hr	% of Normal Activity	Plasma Amine Oxidase nmoles/ml/hr	% of Normal Activity
M	69	32	0.015	0.14	2.21	12.06
F	63	16	0.114	0.86	3.77	19.85
M	63	26	0.019	0.17	1.38	7.53
M	79	19	0.007	0.06	0.33	1.80
M	59	8	0.006	0.05	5.11	27.89

NORMAL VALUES

	MALES	FEMALES	
Plasma Amine Oxidase	18.32 ± 0.28	18.99 ± 0.31	nmoles/ml/hr
Platelet MAO	11.04 ± 0.29	13.29 ± 0.29	nmoles/10^8 platelets/hr

of time but their usefulness is limited by a number of side effects which gradually evolve. Some, such as the "on-off" phenomena, can be diminished by the use of the MAO B inhibitor, Deprenyl. The limitation of this agent is that it tends to accentuate induced abnormal involuntary movements. It is, however, a most useful adjunctive agent in reducing the incidence of "on-off" phenomena of the end dose variety. It may have additional usefulness as a primary drug in the early phases of parkinsonism, a therapeutic response which we are presently investigating.

Acknowledgements

Supported in part by the Clinical Center for Research in Parkinson's and Allied Disease NIH Grant # NS11631–06 and NIH Grant # RR–71 Division of Research Resources, General Research Centre Branch.

References

1   Hornykiewicz O. In Costa E, Cote LJ, Yahr MD, eds. *Biochemistry and Pharmacology of the Basal Ganglia 1966;* 171. New York: Raven Press
2   Yahr MD. In *Advances in Neurology volume 2, 1973.* New York: Raven Press
3   Yahr MD. In Birkmayer W, Hornykiewicz O, eds. *Advances in Parkinsonism 1976;* 435. Basle: Editiones Roche
4   Yahr MD. In McDowell F, Barbeau A, eds. *Advances in Neurology 1974;* 397. New York: Raven Press

Chapter 31

TEN-YEAR RESULTS OF TREATMENT WITH LEVODOPA PLUS BENZERAZIDE IN PARKINSON'S DISEASE

André Barbeau and Madeleine Roy

It is now universally recognised that levodopa represents the most successful type of treatment for Parkinson's disease [1]. Its use, however, is somewhat limited by cost, the high incidence of various side-effects, and failure to respond satisfactorily in approximately 20 per cent of patients [2]. The introduction, as an adjunct to treatment, of peripheral dopa-decarboxylase inhibitors [3, 4] constituted a major advance in the management of Parkinson's disease, by permitting a reduction in the peripheral metabolism of dopa and consequently a reduction in dopa dosage and in many side-effects. The present paper aims to analyse our own experience with one of these drugs, benzerazide (Ro4-4602) in combination with levodopa over a period of 10 years.

Patients and Methods

The patients reported on in this study are the first 100 subjects studied with the combination and entered consecutively between March 1969 and March 1970. 61 were men, 39 women. The mean age of onset was 55.3 ± 0.9 years (range 38 to 69) and the average duration of illness at the time of initial treatment was 8.6 ± 0.5 years (range 1 to 18). All but four patients were classified as having idiopathic Parkinson's disease. Only eight patients had previously taken levodopa, but had had to stop because of gastric side-effects. Many, but not all, of the patients in the present series were included in the previous report, after six years, from our group [5]. After initial evaluation in the hospital, as previously described [4, 5], the patients were seen regularly at the Research Clinic of the Clinical Research Institute of Montreal at minimum bimonthly intervals, or more often if clinically indicated. For most of the first 6 years, benzerazide (Ro4-4602) and levodopa were supplied by Hoffmann-La Roche (Montreal) as separate capsules containing 50 mg of the pure Ro4-4602 and 100 mg or 250 mg of levodopa. Once the products became available on the market, the drug was given as Prolopa ® capsules containing

241

100 mg of levodopa and 25 mg of benzerazide (fixed 4:1 ratio). The initial schedule included a gradual increase of both drugs to levels sufficient for functional results but not producing abnormal involuntary movements (AIM's). Adjustments of dosage, generally downward, were often necessary. Daily dosage ranged from 100 to 900 mg levodopa in combination with 50-250 mg benzerazide. Each patient in the experimental group has received levodopa-benzerazide continuously from the start of the experiment until November 1979, date of this review. Most patients (76/100) also received either anticholinergic or antihistaminic medication, or both, for all or part of the ten years of study. 21 patients received amantadine hydrochloride in addition, after two or three years of treatment. The subjects in the present report are only the vanguard of a total of 1,052 parkinsonian patients treated by us (with levodopa alone or with potentiators) during this period [1, 5, 6]. Experience with the latter served in formulating our present evaluation of the course of treatment in this initial group.

Results

Over the 10 year period of this study, 21 patients died from a variety of causes, none directly related to levodopa treatment. All of these patients had taken levodopa-benzerazide (which we now will designate as Prolopa) until at least one month before death. Mean duration of illness in the 21 treated idiopathic patients who died was 13.8 ± 1.7 years. During the nearly 10 years of the study, 25 patients were lost to follow-up, 10 because of intolerance to the therapeutic regimen (in 4 of these cases the initial diagnosis turned out to be erroneous and should have been striato-nigral degeneration), and 15 because the patient was transferred to another centre for reasons unrelated to the treatment. In all of the latter patients the treatment results were still considered satisfactory at the time of transfer. Vomiting, dizziness, loss of appetite, and continuous nausea were the reasons given for discontinuance in 8 of the 10 drop outs. Two subjects stopped because they found our requirements for regular observations too rigorous. Thus 54 patients are still being treated and observed by us at 10 years.

For the group considered as a whole (Table I) the results of treatment based on the McDowell scale were good or very good (improvement of more than 50%) after 2 months of treatment in 82 per cent of cases, 70 per cent after 6 years and 52 per cent after 10 years in the remaining cases. In the great majority of patients (92.0%) the combination levodopa-benzerazide is satisfactorily tolerated. However, side-effects of a neurological nature increase with time, particularly somnolence, pains or cramps, abnormal involuntary movements, falls and the various types of oscillations in performance (Table II). Except for occasional but always transient elevations of blood urea nitrogen, uric acid, alkaline phosphatase and serum glutamic oxaloacetic transferase, there were no biological signs of intoxication, even after 10 years of treatment.

As for levodopa alone, a subgroup of patients (less than 10%) maintain their initial favourable result over 10 years with essentially no change in dosage, while in

TABLE I Levodopa-Benzerazide in Parkinson's Disease—Objective Results

	Start of Study	2 mos	Year 6	Year 10
Patients under treatment	100	98	68	54
Deaths (cumulative)	-	-	14	21
Drop-outs (cumulative)	-	2	18	25
Percentage of patients still taking drug improved by more than 50%	-	82	70	52
Percentage of initial group improved by more than 50%	-	80	48	28

TABLE II Levodopa-Benzerazide in Parkinson's Disease—Occurrence of side-effects (%)

		2 mos	Year 6	Year 10
1	AIM's	50	64	49
2	Nausea/vomiting	23	17	10
3	Oscillations in performance	-	60	84
4	Postural instability (falls)	33	39	50
5	Unresponsiveness	16	30	42
6	Clinically measurable dementia	21	33	65
7	Average daily dose (Levodopa)—mg	528	480	420
8	Average daily dose (Benzerazide)—mg	152	146	105
9	Average duration/dose (hrs)	4.0	3.2	2.6

most others the appearance of side-effects leads to a gradual decrease of the Prolopa dosage, with loss of many of the beneficial effects.

Of more importance to both patient and family is the improvement of the "quality of life". If a goal of treatment is independence in the activities of daily living (including, when appropriate, a return to gainful employment) the results are

243

possibly discouraging. Initially 24 per cent of our patients were functionally independent. After two months of treatment this figure climbed to 46 per cent, but gradually fell back to 30 per cent after six years and to 28 per cent after 10 years. How many of this initial group would still be independent without treatment is conjectural, especially when taking into account the age of the patients after this period and the duration of their illness.

The objective results thus seem to indicate that the disease continues its inexorable and progressive course, despite levodopa therapy. This is reflected in objective and functional tests, in a reduction of the levodopa dosage necessary, in a progressive reduction in the duration of action of a single dose, in the appearance of oscillations in performance, in the gradual impairment of mental functions and eventually in the unresponsiveness of the patients to levodopa. However, there is increasing evidence that levodopa itself could be responsible for some of these long-term phenomena.

Long-Term Side-Effects

After the initial 36 months of treatment a number of side-effects, mainly peripheral and later central, had been described [7]. It is of interest to study the picture as it evolves after 6 and 10 years (Table II). The peripheral side-effects which were so frequent and caused abandonment of levodopa alone decrease in both frequency and severity. Only a few patients still must take antiemetic medication. On the other hand, dyskinesias (abnormal involuntary movements; AIM's) of the choreic, athetotic or dystonic type become more and more frequent during the first 3 years (up to 80 per cent incidence) before they begin to taper off. At 6 years they were present in only 64 per cent of the patients. This figure further decreases to 49 per cent after the 10 years. Of course, dosage adjustments downward (see Table II) are mainly responsible for this. During the course of the last 5 years we have observed, as have others, new types of dyskinesias, the more severe of which is the so-called hemiballistic diaphasic dyskinesia (described in detail in refs 2 and 8).

The most serious problem encountered after three or more years of levodopa therapy is undoubtedly the periodic re-emergence of various forms of akinesia [2, 7, 6, 9]. Three types of oscillations can be described:
1 *End-of-dose akinesia* (wearing-off effect). This is the complete re-emergence of the symptomatic triad of Parkinson's disease some 3 to 3¼ hours after each dose of levodopa. This type of akinesia is directly related to the effective concentration of levodopa at appropriate receptor sites in the striatum. This concentration can be influenced by the plasma level of levodopa (generally low at this time), by competition in transport mechanisms from other amino acids and many other factors. With the passing years, end of dose akinesia occurs progressively earlier after each dose. As seen in Table II, this time period decreases from 4.0 to 2.6 hours in 10 years.
2 *On-off phenomenon.* This rapidly occurring biphasic phenomenon of alternating dyskinetic and akinetic phases has been described by us [2, 6, 7] so many times

that we will not repeat the details here. All that must be mentioned is the observation that as the years go by, it becomes more and more necessary for dyskinesias to be present for the patient to have an "on" period.

3 *Akinesia paradoxica*, or paroxystic hypotonic freezing, only appears after 2 years of treatment. It is different from start hesitation ("pietinement") which was present before levodopa and which reappears when the patient becomes unresponsive to levodopa [6]. This is the phenomenon which we now measure in 84 per cent of the patients still taking levodopa after 10 years. In our opinion this is due to a combined effect of levodopa chronic toxicity and the progression of the disease. Hypotonia is the major factor present.

Another frequent accompaniment of long-term levodopa therapy is the postural instability, which is manifested by more frequent falls, eventually causing fractures. After 10 years, 50 per cent of the treated patients complain frequently of such episodes.

In a certain percentage of patients there develops a total unresponsiveness to tolerable doses of levodopa. A mechanism of receptor desensitisation has been proposed, but is not yet proven [10] but it could be due to the long-term levodopa therapy itself [11], a hypothesis that has been the base for therapeutic vacations as a form of corrective measure [12].

Finally we should take special note of the increased frequency of clinically measurable dementia and progressive intellectual deterioration in these patients which we had previously noted and measured [13]. This is evidenced by increasing confusion, hallucination, nightmares, loss of recent memory, day-time somnolence and inversion of the sleep cycle [13]. Contributing to this development are undoubtedly many factors such as the progressive cortical atrophy and ventricular enlargement [14], the increased presence of neurofibrillary tangles of the Alzheimer type [15] and the decrease in choline acetyl transferase seen in ageing [16] and probably made worse by the tipping of the dopamine/acetylcholine balance consecutive to long-term levodopa therapy. This symptom is the major limiting factor of therapy at this time, but it is possibly partially reversible with the use of acetylcholine precursors such as lecithin [17, 18].

It is of interest to compare the present results obtained with the levodopa-benzerazide combination and those with levodopa alone also after 10 years [19]. For a slightly better efficacy (52% of patients still taking Prolopa and still improved by more than 50 per cent as opposed to 43 per cent with levodopa alone) the distribution of side effects is more or less the same for nausea/vomiting (10% in both groups), oscillations in performance (84% vs 87%) and dementia (65% vs 62%). However more patients have abnormal involuntary movements (49% vs 35%) and progressive unresponsiveness (42% vs 26%), while fewer have postural instability and falls (50% vs 72%).

Conclusions

When it was introduced in human physiology in 1961 and in clinical practice in

1967, levodopa caused a revolution in the approach to Parkinson's disease. With the addition of peripheral inhibitors it became the standard treatment of akinetic Parkinson's disease and, to this day, still is. There is no better therapy that can be offered to that type of Parkinsonian patient in 1979 to improve the quality of life. Unfortunately the drug has not stopped the progression of the disease, nor the process of ageing. If the patient can tolerate it, he will improve his motility for many years (5-6 at least) and this effect will be reflected in an apparent increase in survival time to an almost normal ratio. Eventually the appearance of side-effects (dyskinesias, hallucinations, etc.) will force a reduction in dosage and cause a progressive unresponsiveness of the post-synaptic receptors. There is now increasing evidence that some of the long-term problems are due to levodopa itself, probably because of chronic overdosage.

For all these reasons, we agree with Lesser and his collaborators [11] that it is preferable to delay the onset of levodopa therapy until the progressing akinesia makes it mandatory. After nearly 10 years of experience with the benzerazide-levodopa combination in the treatment of Parkinson's disease we can state that it is safe and effective. It offers a certain number of advantages over levodopa alone, such as ease of handling, a reduction in the initial side-effects of nausea and vomiting and in the total number of failures to therapy. It does not, however, overcome the neurological complications of abnormal involuntary movements, frequent falls, and oscillations in performance, particularly akinesia-paradoxica. We still have no hesitation in stating our preference for this approach over the use of levodopa alone in the symptomatic management of Parkinson's disease.

The future of levodopa therapy is excellent for new patients, but it is uncertain for the long-term patient, despite all the recent therapeutic approaches and modifications [20]. It is hoped that future research will permit, not a symptomatic replacement therapy, which this is, but a direct intervention on the cause of Parkinson's disease.

Summary

We review the results of chronic therapy with the combination benzerazide-levodopa (Prolopa®–Madopar®) in 100 akinetic parkinsonian patients treated for 10 consecutive years. At the end of this period 52 per cent of the 54 patients still taking the drug still have greater than 50 per cent improvement in performance. Long-term side-effects are numerous but while oscillations in performance, instability in posture, dementia and unresponsiveness increase, abnormal involuntary movements and peripheral side-effects decrease with time. For all these reasons, although we recognise that levodopa is still the best available therapy, we prefer to delay its onset until absolutely necessary.

Acknowledgements

The authors would like to thank their many collaborators during these studies and particularly Drs L Gillo-Joffroy; H Mars; M Gonce, Mrs Suzanne Gariepy and Miss

D Bedard. The studies from this department were supported in part by grants from the Medical Research Council of Canada (MA-4938), the W Garfield Weston Foundation and the Seymour E Clonick Memorial Fund of the United Parkinson Foundation.

References

1   Barbeau A. *Can Med Assoc J 1969; 101:*791
2   Barbeau A, Mars H, Gillo-Joffroy L. In McDowell FH, Markham CH, eds. *Recent advances in Parkinson's Disease 1971;* 203. Philadelphia: Davis & Co
3   Birkmayer W, Mentasti M. *Arch Psychiatr Nervenkr 1967; 210:*29
4   Barbeau A, Gillo-Joffroy L, Mars H. *Clin Pharmacol Ther 1971; 12:*353
5   Barbeau A, Roy M. *Neurology 1976; 26:*399
6   Barbeau A. *Arch Neurol 1976; 33:*333
7   Barbeau A. *Pharmacology and Therapeutics (Part C) 1976; 1:*475
8   Barbeau A. *Lancet 1975; i:*756
9   Barbeau A. *Neurology 1972; 22 (pt 2):*22
10 Fahn S, Calne DB. *Neurology 1978; 28:*5
11 Lesser RP, Fahn S, Snider SR, Côté LR, Isgreen WP, Barrett RE. *Neurology 1979; 29:*1258
12 Direnfeld L, Spero L, Marotta J, Seeman P. *Ann Neurol 1978; 4:*573
13 Botez MI, Barbeau A. *Lancet 1973; ii:*1028
14 Schneider E, Fischer PA, Jacobi P, Becker H, Hacker H. *J Neurol Sci 1979; 42:*187
15 Hakim AM, Matheson G. *Neurology 1979; 29:*1209
16 Samoroyski T. *J Am Geriat Soc 1977; 25:*337
17 Barbeau A. *Can J Neurol Sci 1978; 5:*157
18 Barbeau A. *J Neural Transm 1980;* In press
19 Barbeau A. In Rinne U, ed. *Northern European symposium on Parkinson's Disease 1980;* In press
20 Barbeau A, Roy M, Gonce M, Labrecque R. In Poirier LJ, Sourkes TL, Bédard PJ, eds. *Advances in neurology, volume 24, 1979;* 433. New York: Raven Press

Chapter 32

THE FREEZING PHENOMENON–PROBLEMS IN LONG-TERM L-DOPA TREATMENT FOR PARKINSONISM

H Narabayashi and R Nakamura

§1. Rigidity and tremor in Parkinsonism are now well controlled by medical and pharmacological treatment in most cases. Although there are several side-effects in the long-term use of L-dopa, such as induced dyskinesia, psychological problems and on-off phenomena in about 20 to 30 per cent of cases, these symptoms are well-manageable without much difficulty. Even in cases with severe tremor, resistant to medical therapy, this can be alleviated perfectly and permanently by stereotaxic thalamotomy using microelectrode techniques for identifying the tremorogenic neurones without producing any side-effect. About forty cubic millimetre lesion is small enough to satisfactorily control tremor, if placed exactly in the area of neurones at the base of the ventralis intermedius nucleus (Vim) of the thalamus, providing they were electrophysiologically proven as causing the tremor-synchronous burst discharges detected by the microelectrode at the tip of the needle [1].

Akinesia, lack or poverty of movement in general, is also very greatly improved by L-dopa therapy, the symptom most difficult to control before introduction of this medicine. We have therefore enough tools to treat the three main symptoms of Parkinson's disease.

However, when we observe cases treated successfully in this way for more than 10 years, it becomes gradually recognised that another difficulty tends to slowly arise, the phenomenon of so-called "freezing" in gait, speech and handwriting.

Freezing is the symptom of so-called "paradoxical akinesia" or "starting difficulty". The free commencement of gait in his own pace on the ground or floor is very difficult or impossible, so that he frequently falls down without making any step. The greatest difficulty for such patients is to pass through the door into the doctor's consultation office or through the narrow ticket entrance at the station, but he has no difficulty in walking up and down the stairs which he does steadily without hesitation, and has no difficulty stepping over an obstacle placed in front of him.

He can write well when writing in a slow rhythmic order. Repetitive movement of supination and pronation of the forearm can also be done well in a slow tempo

248

but faster repetition will easily become frozen. In speech, a similar phenomenon is observed.

Common to all these difficulties is that the patient performs slow repetitive movements almost normally but faster ones produce freezing.

§2.　In order to analyse this specific difficulty of faster repetitive movement, the following study was made by using a simple "finger-tapping test".

The sitting patient is asked to tap his fingers freely or in response to given signals. A small metal knob is attached to the tip of the middle finger which makes contact with a metal plate on the desk, thus closing an electrical circuit, which is recorded and statistically analysed automatically in several fashions.

The results of this test are as follows:

1　Maximum frequency of free tapping: Age-matched normal controls are able to perform finger tapping with maximum frequency of more than 8 Hz and younger persons can do it a little faster.

　Most parkinsonian patients can do it only 5–5.5 Hz and not faster, a frequency similar or close, but not the same, to the frequency of his tremor.
2　Response tapping: When the patient is asked to tap exactly in response to given sound signals, he can follow the signal frequency only when the latter is below 2 Hz (Figure 1). When over 2.0 Hz he is unable to follow and, within seconds, starts to tap at his own pace, ie. 5–5.5 Hz, which we call the "hastening phenomenon" or "convergence into 5–5.5 Hz". Intermediate frequency such as 3, 4 or higher is impossible and he seems to have no choice other than 5–5.5 Hz. The area of frequency, where hastening starts, is called by us the "turning frequency".

　This finding is quite in contrast to the normal individual, who can follow exactly the given frequency until 7 or 8 Hz.
3　Anticipated tapping: When the signal is interpreted in the mid course of response tapping and the patient asked to keep tapping with the same frequency, his tapping frequency quickly tends to fall and converge into repetition at 5–5.5 Hz. In this case, hastening occurs even when the signal is stopped at the frequency of one or 1.5 Hz.

All these findings suggest that the parkinsonian patient seems to have a very specific feature that he can make repetitive tapping action only at the certain frequency of 5–5.5 Hz, which is close to, but not the same as the frequency of his tremor.

§3.　In the case of long-standing parkinsonism of more than about ten years since onset where rigidity and tremor has been very well-controlled by medical therapy, with or without surgery, freezing is often the cause of difficulty in daily activities. He can feed himself, take his coat off, toilet, stand up and sit down quite smoothly, but all performances are a little slower or a little more unskilled than normal.

These cases have no rigidity nor tremor because of treatment, muscle power is almost normal and muscle tone is often hypotonic. In contrast to these relatively well preserved activities in daily living, freezing will be the only detectable motor

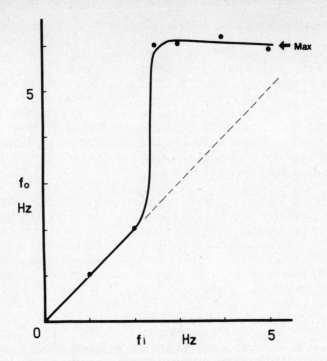

Figure 1 An example of response tapping in parkinsonism. Turning frequency is 2.5 Hz in this case and the fixed frequency of *fo* is a little higher than 5.5 Hz.
fi: frequency of given sound signals
fo: frequency of response tapping

disability, when he is asked to walk, write or to talk. In such cases, the results of the tapping test are described; L-dopa treatment does not improve the hastening phenomenon and sometimes even makes it a little worse.

In Parkinson's disease the freezing phenomenon is usually thought to be a kind of akinesia due to a starting difficulty, but such freezing or paradoxical akinesia should be clearly differentiated from the akinesia that can well be alleviated by L-dopa [2]. The latter is a lack or poverty of movement, in which the difficulty of repetitive movement does not depend on frequency and even slow repetitive movements can not be performed.

Disturbance of repetitive movement in freezing is a specific difficulty of rhythm formation except at 5–5.5 Hz, as clearly demonstrated by the finger-tapping test [3, 4]. The specific abnormalities of the finger-tapping test may suggest that, in the central nervous system of the parkinsonian patients, there is a strong and dominating pattern of repetitive neuronal activities at 5–5.5 Hz, which makes repetition at other frequencies impossible.

§4. Figure 2 illustrates some cases in which the authors could notice a gradual worsening of the freezing phenomenon in a group of patients followed for more

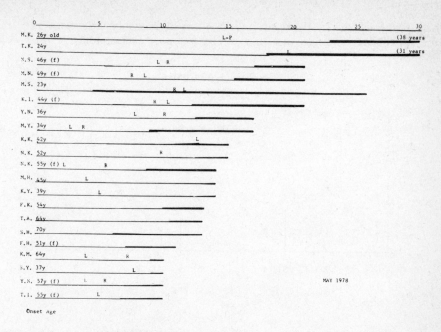

Figure 2 List of long-term observation of clinical course in 21 cases of idiopathic parkinsonism. Thick line indicates the time when the freezing phenomenon became apparent. L or R indicate thalamotomy of left-sided or right-sided brain at the time when it was done.

than ten years. Freezing is not the main symptom on the early stage of the disease, but tends to become manifest after a long-standing course of the disease-process, together with rigidity, tremor or akinesia due to striatal dopamine deficiency. The existence of the freezing phenomenon in the symptomatology of parkinsonism is well-known but the underlying dynamic mechanisms of it have not yet been interpreted with certainty.

The sign of a specific rhythm formation at 5–5.5 Hz in parkinsonism is detectable by tapping tests even in the very early stage of unilateral symptoms. In hemiparkinsonism. the affected upper extremity usually presents this feature, but even the unaffected side often shows a slight tendency to it. When the disease process is still in its early stage, the turning frequency of tapping to 5–5.5 Hz where the hastening starts is about 3 or 3.5 Hz, and not so slow as 2.0 or 2.5 Hz, which is the usual turning frequency when rigidity and tremor are manifest. In principle, hastening to 5–5.5 Hz can be found, and is the same, in all parkinsonian patients irrespective of the grade of severity. However, the turning frequency is different depending on the grade of severity or course of the disease [4].

L-dopa and thalamotomy does not essentially influence this phenomenon but surgery modifies the turning frequency from 2.0 Hz to the higher frequency of 3 or 4 Hz, which actually results in improvement of ADL since, in our daily living,

251

activities which require the repetitive movement of frequency higher than 2 Hz are few [2]. Figure 3 indicates such changes with L-dopa or thalamotomy.

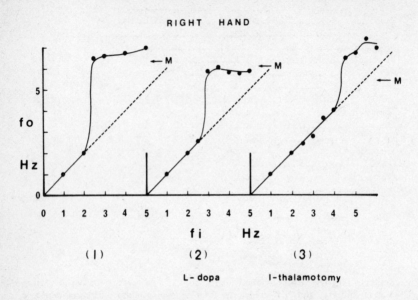

RIGHT   HAND

Figure 3   Change of turning frequency by L-dopa therapy or by thalamotomy in parkinsonism. 1 is before treatment. 2 is after enough effect by L-dopa. 3 is after abolition of rigidity and tremor by thalamotomy. Note the change of "turning frequency" from 2 Hz in 1 to 3 Hz in 2 and to 4.5 Hz in 3.

When the three cardinal motor symptoms, rigidity, tremor and akinesia, are managed well and improve with adequate treatment, the remaining freezing becomes apparent. At present, there is little knowledge about the neurophysiological mechanisms underlying this peculiar phenomenon and its morphological and metabolic basis. It is considered that dopamine deficiency would not be responsible for this phenomenon for which there is no treatment, except physiotherapy to give a sense of rhythm of movements.

§5.   The group of cases which presents only the freezing phenomenon since onset without any sign of rigidity, tremor or dopamine dependent akinesia has been reported by the authors and their colleagues and it was proposed that these were "cases of pure akinesia" and possibly a different clinical entity from parkinsonism, though no postmortem study is yet available [5].

In conclusion, the hastening phenomenon might possibly be considered as the fourth motor symptom, although it has been roughly included in the term "akinesia" and masked by the three other symptoms. When the other three motor symptoms are controlled by effective treatment, only this "hastening" tendency still remains and slowly progresses during the long-standing course of parkinsonism.

References

1   Hirai T, Shibazaki T, Nakajima H, Imai S, Ohye Ch. *Appl Neurophysiol 1980.* In press
2   Nakamura R, Nagasaki H, Narabayashi H. In Birkmayer B, Hornykiewicz O, eds.
     Advances in Parkinsonism 1976; 258. Basle: Roche
3   Nakamura R, Nagasaki H, Narabayashi H. *Percept Motor Skills 1978; 46:*63
4   Barbeau A. In Siegfried J, ed. *Parkinson's Disease 1972;* 152. Bern: Hans Huber
5   Narabayashi H, Imai M, Yokochi M, Hirayama K, Nakamura R. In Birkmayer B,
     Hornykiewica O, eds. *Advances in Parkinsonism 1976;* 335. Basle: Roche

Chapter 33

DYSKINESIAS

J D Parkes

Introduction

There have been three dyskinesia epidemics this century in Europe and America. The first followed encephalitits lethargica, the second was due to neuroleptic drugs and the third resulted from levodopa. All the dopamine-like drugs investigated in the treatment of parkinsonism will cause dyskinesias, as is also the case with tardive dyskinesia in which every commonly used neuroleptic has been implicated. Levodopa in parkinsonism, at the same time as producing improvement in akinesia, tremor and rigidity, also causes restlessness of the arms, legs or the whole body, orofacial dyskinesia, torticollis, retrocollis, limb chorea, hemiballismus and tics, blepharospasm, facial, trunk and limb myoclonus as well as disturbances of respiratory rhythm. All this bizarre range of involuntary movement appears to result from sudden changes in dopamine concentration in the brain in the presence of a damaged extrapyramidal system with denervated and supersensitive receptors [1,2].

The main clinical facts concerning levodopa dyskinesias were established early during the levodopa era [1]. Involuntary movements were seen in the first patients given large oral doses of levodopa and, with general use of the drug, it became apparent that dyskinesias occurred in between sixty and ninety per cent of all subjects, and were the main dose-limiting factor. It has never been satisfactorily explained why a small proportion of subjects with idiopathic parkinsonism, given levodopa and who respond to the drug, do not apparently develop dyskinesias. Dyskinesias are usually but not always dose-related and often increase in frequency and severity during the initial build-up of levodopa therapy.

Respiratory abnormalities, oculogyric crises, and dystonic postures acquired as a result of encephalitis lethargica may all be aggravated by levodopa therapy, and breath-holding or overbreathing can be particularly distressing to these subjects. The effect of previous bilateral thalamotomy on dyskinesias has still not definitely been decided, but the incidence of involuntary limb movements following levodopa may be reduced in this group of patients. In subjects with unilateral thalamolysis,

254

involuntary movements are most pronounced in the limbs ipsilateral to the thalamotomy in most cases.

Barbeau reported that levodopa dyskinesias were sometimes accompanied by hypotonia and reduced tendon reflexes, and certain patients could predict the appearance of involuntary movements by a feeling of warmth or tingling in that part of the body in which subsequently dyskinesias appeared.

In some patients with Parkinson's disease, involuntary movements first appear as treatment progresses and at dosages which have previously been well tolerated. In other subjects they recur at progressively lower doses. These observations suggest the need for caution in treating all subjects with parkinsonism with levodopa or dopamine-like drugs.

In most subjects, dyskinesias are of greatest severity at the time of optimum improvement from levodopa, although this is not always the case and many variants have been described including off-period dystonia with on-period chorea. The central origin of dyskinesias is shown by the finding that peripherally-acting decarboxylase inhibitors, which permit the use of large doses of levodopa without nausea. or vomiting, result in an increase in the severity and frequency of dyskinesias.

The evidence that levodopa dyskinesias result from the action of dopamine is overwhelming, Identical movements with those caused by levodopa are produced by the dopamine-like drugs, apomorphine, piribedil, bromocriptine, lergotrile and lisuride. Dopamine-depleting drugs such as reserpine and tetrabenazine, and dopamine receptor blocking drugs such as chlorpromazine, abolish levodopa dyskinesias, although at the expense of increasing parkinsonism. Unlike levodopa and ergot derivatives, amantadine and amphetamine, both of which have predominant presynaptic actions on dopamine neurones, rarely cause dyskinesias. However, the therapeutic response to these drugs is usually limited and both occasionally produce orofacial dyskinesia or limb chorea [3].

Damage to the extrapyramidal motor system is a major factor determining the appearance of levodopa dyskinesias. In our experience (see below), levodopa dyskinesias are usually of greatest severity in the limb most affected with parkinsonism in subjects with predominant unilateral disease. The long-term use of large doses of bromocriptine (20–60 mg daily) or lisuride (1–2 mg daily) in acromegaly does not cause involuntary movements. Normal subjects given large doses of levodopa for short periods of up to three months also do not develop dyskinesias.

However, there are anecdotal reports that some subjects with motor neurone disease given levodopa may develop dyskinesias [4, 5] and Lieberman and Pedersen (*Lancet* 1970, 2, 985) reported a single patient with amyotrophic lateral sclerosis who developed orofacial dyskinesia and limb chorea on levodopa 6 g but not 5.5 g daily. In other motor disorders in man, including patients with dementia but no extrapyramidal symptoms, patients with generalised torsion dystonia or torticollis, neurological symptoms induced by chronic manganese poisoning, or in schizophrenics, levodopa does not cause dyskinesias (see *Drugs* 1972, 2 369) for review). Most patients with progressive supranuclear palsy given large doses of levodopa do not develop dyskinesias. Levodopa may cause dyskinesias in normal animals although at much larger doses than used in parkinsonism, and dopamine has a much greater effect in lesioned than intact animals [6, 7]. All these findings suggest that in man levodopa dyskinesias are at least partly dependent on the destruction of dopamine neurones. Changes in the balance of the neurotransmitter systems and possibly denervation hypersensitivity are of comparatively minor importance, although they may influence the production of abnormal involuntary movements.

Effect of age, sex and race

The nature and distribution of levodopa dyskinesias in our experience is shown in Tables I and II. The prominence of facial, lip and tongue movements is obvious. With chorea due to neuroleptic drugs, the topographical distribution of involuntary movement may vary with age, and young children often show marked distal

TABLE I Influence of age, sex and other factors on levodopa dyskinesias in parkinsonism. Data from patients attending King's College Hospital Parkinson's Disease Clinic. Mean levodopa dose (g) without decarboxylase inhibitor. Disease severity as Hoehn and Yahr.

	Number of subjects :	Mean levodopa dose	Incidence of dyskinesias (percentage)
AGE			
Under 40	(5 : 3g)		80
Over 80	(6 : 3g)		50
SEX			
Male	(92 : 2.9g)		83
Female	(85 : 2.8g)		85
DISEASE AETIOLOGY			
Idiopathic	(165 : 2.9g)		85
Postencephalitic	(12 : 1.3g)		58
DISEASE SEVERITY			
I	(6 : 2g)		50
V	(8 : 4g)		85
LEVODOPA DOSE			
Under 1g daily	(10 : 0.8g)		33
Over 5g daily	(16 : 6.2g)		88
DURATION TREATMENT			
Under 1 year	(6 : 2.0g)		67
Over 8 years	(12 : 2.9g)		75
ADDITIONAL DRUGS			
On anticholinergics	(116 : 2.9g)		86
Not on anticholinergics	(16 : 2.8g)		75
SKIN COLOUR			
White	(117 : 2.8g)		85
ETHNIC ORIGIN			
Ashkenazim	(3 : 4.1g)		66
Non-Ashkenazim	(174 : 2.8g)		85
EYE COLOUR			
Blue	(24 : 3.2g)		83
Brown	(24 : 2.9g)		79

TABLE II Presentation of dyskinesias in 36 subjects given "Sinemet". Sex, age, duration and severity of disease, and Sinemet dosage comparable in these 36 subjects to 14 subjects who did not develop dyskinesias during the first 6 months of Sinemet treatment (Dr E Fagan).

Period betweencommencement of levodopa and first appearance dyskinesia (mean)		1.9 months
Initial dyskinesia:	orofacial dyskinesia	– 21 subjects
	hyperventilation	– 1 subject
	limb chorea	– 6 subjects
	dystonic posture	– 2 claw toes
		1 rotation neck
	muscle jerk or tic	– 5 subjects
Maximum severity:	lateralised	– 17 subjects
	non-lateralised	– 19 subjects
If lateralised: dyskinesias most severe:		
	on side of onset of parkinsonism	8 of 17
	on contralateral side	2 of 17
dyskinesias most severe:		
	on side with most affected limbs	12 of 17
	on side with least affected limbs	3 of 17

limb movements in contrast to adults who develop prominent orofacial dyskinesias [8], but there appears to be little difference in the distribution of levodopa dyskinesias between young and elderly subjects with parkinsonism. The frequency and security of levodopa dyskinesias are similar in men and women. In Sydenham's disease, chorea may be less common in black than in white-skinned races [9], but the presentation and severity of levodopa dyskinesias is comparable in the black, yellow and white pigmented subjects we have observed. Eastern European Ashkenazim are possibly more susceptible to drug-induced tardive dyskinesia than other ethnic groups [10], but one of three Ashkenazim with parkinsonism we have observed did not develop levodopa dyskinesias. Chronic orofacial dyskinesias due to neuroleptic drugs are sometimes more obvious in blue-eyed than dark-eyed men [11], but eye colour has little effect on levodopa dyskinesias in parkinsonism.

Effect of arousal and behaviour

Changes in the level of arousal, the stress of voluntary motor effort, and anxiety alter the presentation of levodopa dyskinesias. As with parkinsonian tremor, the severity of involuntary movements often varies greatly during a short period of observation. Parkinsonian tremor usually disappears during sleep, and the same is true with levodopa dyskinesias, although both tremor and chorea can briefly persist during stages 1 and 2 of slow wave sleep. The degree of alertness and the occurrence of sleep will likewise affect the severity of face, lip and tongue movements in subjects with spontaneous or drug-induced tardive dyskinesia [12].

257

Sedation and dopamine-stimulant drugs

Several ergot derivatives, including bromocriptine and lisuride, cause sedation. One of the first and most striking experiments to demonstrate behavioural depression caused by ergot derivatives was reported by Hess [13]. Hess administered 1 mg of ergotamine into the lateral or third ventricle of cats habituated to laboratory conditions. After 50 to 100 minutes, the cats became quiet and looked for a place to sleep. After having arrayed their bodies to a *regelrechte Schlafstellung,* the cats lowered their heads, shut their eyes and fell asleep [14]. Ergotamine induced "readiness for sleep" but not general anaesthesia. More recent studies have shown that many different ergot derivatives induce drowsiness [15], and we have observed that lisuride 0.05 mg iv not infrequently causes considerable sedation. However, behavioural excitation rather than sedation may occur with ergometrine, LSD and methysergide, levodopa and apomorphine [16], and changes in alertness with these drugs may depend largely on the environment and experimental design. As with dopamine stimulant drugs, dopamine antagonist anti-psychotic drugs frequently cause either somnolence or behavioural arousal (see Shepherd *et al*, 17, for review).

The role of dopamine and of substances acting on the dopaminergic system in sleep mechanisms has been investigated in animals and in humans (17 a, b, c, d). Bassi *et al* (17a) gave apomorphine 1.5mg sc to normal and untreated parkinsonian subjects. In both groups the drug induced sleep as well as vomiting, possibly by stimulation of hypothalamic-hypophyseal as well as medullary centres in the brain. Sedative effect with apomorphine may however only be seen with low doses and high doses of the drug reduce total sleep time in animals (17b). This apparent dual effect of apomorphine on sleep led to the concept that the drug's sedative effect resulted from a decrease and not increase in dopaminergic activity, whilst arousal with high dosages was dependent on an increase in activity. Like apomorphine in low doses most neuroleptics cause sedation but Di Chiara *et al* [17e] showed that low doses of pimozide and sulpiride, but not clozapine, inhibited the sedative effects of low doses of apomorphine. However, in man, pimozide at doses considered to block dopamine receptors has relatively little effect on sleep [17c] and dopamine mechanisms are unlikely to be of major importance in the physiology of sleep in man.

Abolition of levodopa dyskinesias

Since levodopa dyskinesias seem to be largely, if not entirely, generated by dopamine mechanisms, most attempts to prevent involuntary movements have focussed on the possibility of selective drug actions on different populations of dopamine receptors. Two different approaches have been of great interest, firstly the investigation of selective pre- rather than post-synaptic receptor stimulation to produce a reduction of dopamine turnover and release, and hence reduce dyskinesias [18], and secondly the possibility of selective blockade of a dyskinesia-generating receptor population [19].

TABLE III   Anti-dyskinetic effects of apomorphine

	Apomorphine Dose	Reported effect
Parkinson's Disease [23]	0.5-2 mg sc	Tremor improved in 8 of 13 subjects. Nausea in 4 and syncope in 2
Huntington's Chorea [33]	1-4 mg	Chorea improved in 4 of 4 subjects
Drug-induced dystonia [26]	5 mg im	Acute dystonia abolished in 7 of 13 subjects. Sedation in 3
Spontaneous orofacial dyskinesia [35]	1-1.5 mg sc	Improvement in 2, no change in 1, deterioration in 7 subjects
Torticollis [34]	1-3 mg sc	Improvement in 2 of 7 subjects. Nausea, vomiting, sedation common
Oro-Mandibular Dystonia [36]	1-2 mg sc	Improvement in 5 of 5 subjects. Sweating, yawning, sedation common.

Apomorphine and Dopamine-like drugs

Apomorphine is a directly-acting dopamine stimulant at post-synaptic receptors [20]. However, in low doses, apomorphine may specifically stimulate pre- rather than post-synaptic receptors with a consequent reduction in dopamine synthesis and release [21, 22]. Apomorphine, like levodopa, causes improvement in akinesia, rigidity and tremor in Parkinson's disease [23-25]. Despite that improvement in parkinsonism, there are many reports that apomorphine has an unexpected effect in a number of spontaneous and drug-induced movement disorders [26-36]. These include orofacial dyskinesia, oromandibular dystonia, choreoathetosis, torticollis, chorea in Huntington's disease and levodopa dyskinesias in parkinsonism (Table III). These effects with apomorphine occur with similar doses to those causing improvement in idiopathic Parkinson's disease (1-4 mg sc).

The most favoured explanation for this dual response to apomorphine is that the drug's antidyskinetic action results from pre-synaptic, and antiparkinsonian action from post-synaptic, dopamine receptor stimulation. In rodents, there is a biphasic motor response to apomorphine and other dopamine stimulants including levodopa and bromocriptine [22, 37], which all produce motor inhibition followed by stimulation. It has been suggested that the mechanism of this biphasic response results from initial pre- and subsequent post-synaptic receptor stimulation, but with bromocriptine, dopamine turnover is reduced during both phases of movement although noradrenaline turnover varies with activity [37]. Although this biphasic response is well established in laboratory animals, a biphasic response to single doses of any antiparkinsonian drug has not been described in man. However, there are anecdotal reports that during the initial weeks of levodopa, bromocriptine or lisuride therapy in parkinsonism, a transient deterioration rather than improvement may occur, and a patient has been described with classic stigma of parkinsonism treated on three separate occasions with levodopa, levodopa and carbidopa, and lergotrile, and who was made worse by each treatment. Haloperidol 1 mg twice daily also caused deterioration in this subject [38]. Despite these remarkable reports, there is insufficient evidence to justify the concept that low doses of dopamine-like drugs have opposite pharmacological effects to high doses, or that such a mechanism could explain the anti-dyskinetic action of apomorphine.

How are we to explain the apparently paradoxical effects of apomorphine on the motor system? In addition to the locomotor effect, apomorphine and other dopamine-like drugs cause nausea, hypotension and drowsiness [7, 39]. Nausea occurs in most subjects given apomorphine 2–4 mg sc and sedation is frequent. As in man, in animal models of movement disorders apomorphine produces considerable sedation [7]. It seems possible therefore that the antidyskinetic effect of apomorphine is not the result of pre-synaptic receptor stimulation and reduction in neuronal dopamine release in the extrapyramidal motor system, but is due to a less specific effect of the drug producing drowsiness. The pharmacological mechanisms involved in the production of drowsiness by apomorphine are not clear. Against this view is the finding that the specific dopamine receptor blocking drugs, sulpiride 100 mg and haloperidol 2 mg im, will prevent the antichoreic effect of apomorphine in Huntington's disease [33].

Tiapride and Dopamine Antagonists

The presentation of drug-induced dyskinesia is different in different animal species. Rodents given amphetamine sniff, lick and chew, cats show continuous head movements, dogs persistently run in circles, and monkeys make complex orofacial or trunk movements [40]. These dyskinesias have a considerable resemblance to drug-induced involuntary movements in human beings and, as in human parkinsonians, appear more readily in animals with lesions on the nervous system than without. Simultaneous with dyskinesias motor activation occurs in many animal species. There has been considerable investigation as to whether the motor and dyskinesia responses to dopamine-like drugs in animals involve the same or different mechanisms, and whether these two aspects of movement can be separated by pharmacological means. Costall and Naylor [19] showed that the intrastriatal administration of dopamine (together with a MAO inhibitor) to guinea pigs caused hyperactivity accompanied by gnawing, biting and licking, twisting of the head and neck and sometimes the whole body. Hyperactivity could be inhibited by large doses of neuroleptic drugs such as haloperidol and fluphenazine, but other forms of dys-

TABLE IV Antidyskinetic effects of neuroleptics in parkinsonism. Mean (or range) of neuroleptic and levodopa doses (po). Effect: nil, selective blockade of dyskinesias; or non-selective reduction in therapeutic and dyskinetic effect of levodopa.

| Drug | Dose | | Effect | | |
	Levodopa	Neuroleptic	Nil	Selective	Non-Select
Metoclopramide [43]	2.7g	10mg	+	+	+
[44]	0.25–2g	60mg			+
Oxiperomide [48]	3g	5–10mg		+	
Tiapride [45]	3g	200mg		+?	
[46]	0.75–1g	25–300mg		+	
Pimozide [43]	2.2g	1–4mg			+
*	2.5g	16mg			+
Promethazine [43]	2.2g	30–60mg	+		
Haloperidol [42]	2.5g	3–4mg			+

* Personal communication, Dr P Price

kinetic movement could not be prevented by these drugs, although they were inhibited by pimozide [19]. This result led to the view of two different neostriatal dopaminergic mechanisms and to the concept that levodopa dyskinesias in parkinsonism might be preventable by selective neuroleptics without interfering with the therapeutic response.

Many different neuroleptics have been investigated in parkinsonism and all will block levodopa dyskinesias to a greater or lesser extent although usually at the expense of a reduction in the therapeutic effect of levodopa (41–99, Table IV). The reduction in severity of levodopa dyskinesias as well as the degree or reduction of the therapeutic effect with different neuroleptic drugs, is usually dose related. However, with careful titration of neuroleptic dosage, it is sometimes possible to prevent dyskinesias without significant increase in parkinsonism [46, 48]. This is particularly so in the case of tiapride (see Price et al, this volume). Tiapride and oxiperomide both have a selective effect on dyskinesias whilst haloperidol and pimozide although reducing the severity of levodopa dyskinesia also impair the antiparkinsonian response. Metoclopramide 10 mg has little effect on the motor response to levodopa and will successfully prevent levodopa-induced vomiting, although metoclopramide 60 mg prevents both antiparkinsonian and dyskinetic responses to levodopa. How are we to explain the finding that some neuroleptic drugs, and in particular tiapride, block the dyskinetic but not the antiparkinsonian response to levodopa? As with apomorphine, the sedative effects of different neuroleptics [17] may be of greater relevance than specific blockade of "dyskinesia receptors". As has been discussed, levodopa dyskinesias are often markedly increased by stress and disappear during sleep although, in animals, the hypnotic drug sodium pentobarbitone does not cause selective blockade of levodopa dyskinesias to a greater extent than levodopa-induced motor hyperactivity [19], and this is also the case with promethazine in human parkinsonism [43]. However, many different factors will greatly influence drug-induced gnawing in animals whilst the locomotor response is preserved. Stereotyped behaviour, but not locomotor hyperactivity, is stimulus dependent, and altered by changes in environment or experimental design [50]. Great sophistication has not been employed in studies of levodopa dyskinesias in man (see Marsden and Parkes, this volume), although it is probable that the conditions of observation, environment, psychological factors and the level of arousal are all important determinants of the severity of involuntary movement, and have a greater effect on dyskinesias than on motor activation.

TABLE V Effects of different drugs on motor and dyskinetic response to levodopa in Parkinsonism

Neurotransmitter	Drug	Effect on	
		Levodopa Therapeutic Response	Levodopa Dyskinesia
Acetylcholine	Deanol [52–54]	Nil	Decrease in severity
	Physostigmine [55]	Increase in severity	Decrease in severity
Serotonin	Methysergide [56]	Nil	? Abolish myoclonus
Enkephalin	Damme	Nil	Nil
	Naloxone	Nil	Nil
γ-aminobutyric acid	Sodium Valproate [57]	Nil	Subjective improvement
	Halogabide	Nil	Nil
Noradrenaline	Clonidine [59]	Nil	Nil
	Nomifensine [58]	Nil	Nil

Non-dopaminergic mechanisms

Many putative neurotransmitters occur in the basal ganglia and may be of relevance to the development of dyskinesias, although the influence of non-dopaminergic systems on levodopa dyskinesias is probably of minor importance (Table V). Anticholinergic drugs by themselves occasionally produce orofacial dyskinesia [51] and may slightly increase the severity of levodopa dyskinesias. In contrast, the cholinergic drug deanol which may increase the availability of acetylcholine in the brain, and the anticholinesterase drug physostigmine, both ameliorate involuntary movements, although often at the expense of increasing parkinsonism [52–55]. Drugs which alter serotonin metabolism usually have little effect on levodopa dyskinesias, although methysergide, which may affect brain serotonin systems, has been shown to improve levodopa-induced myoclonus [56]. In our experience, drugs affecting GABA systems ([57], Sheehy, this volume), enkephalin systems (Schacter, this volume), alpha- and beta-adrenergic receptor blocking drugs, and drugs which increase the availability of noradrenaline in the brain (nomifensine) do not alter the severity of levodopa dyskinesias [58, 59].

262

Conclusion

There is little evidence that improvement in tremor, rigidity and akinesia with anti-parkinsonian drugs can be effectively separated from the involuntary movements which accompany treatment. The two properties seem to be fundamentally related [1]. The apparent selective blockade of dyskinesias by apomorphine and, alternatively, certain neuroleptic drugs may result from central behavioural changes and sedation caused by these compounds, rather than from specific drug actions on sub-populations of pre-synaptic or "dyskinesia" receptors. This indicates the need to study the patient's environment, mood, awareness and motivation in any investigation of levodopa dyskinesia.

There is increasing evidence that the long-term use of levodopa may be responsible for many of the late problems of therapy, including loss of effectiveness as well as violent fluctuations in response [60]. If this view is correct, levodopa and dopamine like drugs may be the best reserved for moderately and severely disabled patients, rather than given to all subjects with parkinsonism. The problem of levodopa dyskinesias is unlikely to be resolved until Parkinson's disease can be prevented or cured, rather than treated by brain-hormone replacement therapy.

References

1   Duvoisin RC In Birkmayer W, Hornykiewicz O, eds *Advances in Parkinsonism 1976;* 574. Basle: Roche
2   Marsden CD. In Bradford HF, Marsden CD, eds. *Biochemistry and neurology 1976;* 3. New York: Academic Press
3   Klawans HL, Weiner WJ. *J Neurol Neurosurg Psychiat 1974; 37:*427
4   Mendell JR, Chase TN, Engel WK. *Arch Neurol 1971; 25:*320
5   Lieberman et al. Cited by Marsden CD. In Bradford HF, Marsden CD, eds. *Biochemistry and neurology 1976;* 3. New York: Academic Press
6   Mones RJ. In Barbeau A, Chase TN, Paulson GW, eds. *Advances in neurology, volume 1, 1973;* 665. New York: Raven Press
7   Sanberg PR, Lehmann J, Fibiger HC. *Arch Neurol 1979; 36:*349
8   Ayd FJ Jr. *JAMA 1961; 175:*102
9   Gowers WR. In *A manual of diseases of the nervous system, 2nd edition, volume 2, 1893;* 592. London: Churchill
10   Simpson GM. *Brit J Psychiat 1973; 122:*618
11   Brandon S, McClelland HA, Protheroe C. *Brit J Psychiat 1971; 118:*171
12   Crane GE. In Boissier JR, et al, eds. *Neuropharmacology 1975;* 346. New York: Excerpta Medica
13   Hess WR. *Arch Neurol Neurochir Psychiat 1925; 16:* 36
14   Loew DM, von Deusen EB, Meier-Ruge W. In Berde B, Schild HO, eds. *Handbook of experimental pharmacology, Volume 49, 1978;* 428. Heidelberg: Springer-Verlag
15   Meldrum BS, Naquet R. *Electroenceph clin Neurophysiol 1971; 31:*563
16   Jaggi UH, Loew DM. *Experientia (Basel) 1976; 32:* 229
17   Shepherd M, Lader M, Lader S. In Meyer L, Herxheimer A, eds. *Side effects of drugs, volume 7, 1972;* 69. Amsterdam: Excerpta Medica
17a Bassi S, Albizzati MG, Frattola L, Passerini D, Trabucchi M. *J Neurol Neurosurg Psychiat 1979; 42:*458
17b Kafi S, Gaillard J-M. *Europ J Pharmacol 1976; 38:*357
17c Sagales T, Erill S. *Psychopharmacologia 1975; 41:*53

17d Corsini GU, Del Zompo M, Manconi S, Piccardi MP, Onali A, Gessa GL. *Life Sci 1977; 20:* 1613

17e Di Chiara G, Porceddu ML, Vargiu L, Argiolas A, Gessa GL. *Nature 1976; 264:* 564

18 Carlsson A, Kehr W, Lindqvist M. In Birkmayer W, Hornykiewicz, eds. *Advances in Parkinsonism 1976;* 71. Basle: Roche

19 Costall B, Naylor RJ. *Europ J Pharmac 1975; 33:* 301

20 Anden NE, Robenson A, Fuxe K, Hokfelt T. *J Pharmac Pharmacol 1967; 19:* 627

21 Walters JR, Bunney BS, Roth RH. In Calne DB, Chase TN, Barbeau A, eds. *Advances in neurology, volume 9, 1975;* 273. New York: Raven Press

22 Carlsson A. In Usdin E, Bunney W, eds. *Pre- and Postsynaptic receptors 1975;* 49. New York: Marcel Decker

23 Braham J, Sarova-Pinhas I, Goldhammer Y. *Brit med J 1970; 3:* 768

24 Düby SE, Cotzias GC, Papavasiliou PS, Lawrence WH. *Arch Neurol 1972; 27:* 474

25 Cotzias GC, Lawrence WH, Papavasiliou PS, Düby SE, Ginos JZ, Mena I. *Trans Am Neurol Ass 1972; 97:* 156

26 Gessa R, Tagliamonte A, Gessa GL. *Lancet 1972; ii:* 981

27 Cotzias GC, Mean I, Papavasiliou PS. *Adv Neurol 1974; 5:* 295

28 Tolosa ES. *JAMA 1974; 229:* 1579

29 Smith RC, Tamminga CA, Haraszti J, Pandey GN, Davis JM. *Am J Psychiat 1977; 134:* 763

30 Carrol BJ, Curtis GC, Kokmen E. *Am J Psychiat 1977; 134:* 785

31 Weiner WJ, Kramer J, Nausieda PA, Klawans HL. *Arch Neurol 1978; 35:* 453

32 Tolosa ES. *Neurology 1976; 33:* 373

33 Corsini GU, Onali P-L, Masal C, Cianchetti C, Mangoni A, Gessa GL. *Arch Neurol 1978; 35:* 27

34 Tolosa ES. *Arch Neurol 1978; 35:* 459

35 Tarsy D, Gardos G, Cole JO. *Neurology (Minneap) 1979; 29:* 606

36 Tolosa E, Lai C. *Neurology (Minneap) 1979; 29:* 1126

37 Snider SR, Hutt C, Stein B, Prasad ALN, Fahn S. *J Pharmac Pharmacol 1976; 28:* 563

38 Weiner WJ, Kramer J, Nausieda PA, Klawans HL. *Arch Neurol 1978; 35:* 453

39 Corsini GU, del Zompo M, Manconi S. In Gessa GL, Costa E, eds. *Symposium on non-striatal dopaminergic neurones 1977;* 645. New York: Raven Press

40 Randrup A, Munkvad I. *Psychopharmacologia (Berl) 1967; 11:* 300

41 Barbeau A. *Canad Med Ass J 1969; 101:* 59

42 Klawans HL, Weiner WJ. *J Neurol Neurosurg Psychiat 1974; 37:* 427

43 Tarsy D, Parkes JD, Marsden CD. *J Neurol Neurosurg Psychiat 1975; 38:* 331

44 Parkes JD, Debono AG, Marsden CD. *J Neurol Neurosurg Psychiat 1976; 39:* 1101

45 Lhermitte F, Agid Y, Signoret J-L, Studler J-M. *Rev Neurol 1977; 133:* 297

46 Price P, Parkes JD, Marsden CD. *Lancet 1978; ii:* 1106

47 Mathé JF, Cler JM, Venisse JL. *Sem Hop Paris 1978; 54:* 517

48 Bedard P, Parkes JD, Marsden CD. *Brit Med J 1978; 1:* 954

49 Caine ED. *Am J Psychiat 1979; 136:* 317

50 Ljungberg T, Ungerstedt U. *Europ J Pharmac 1977; 46:* 147

51 Fahn S, David E. *Trans Amer Neurol Ass 1972; 97:* 277

52 Miller E. *Neurology (Minneap) 1974; 24:* 116

53 Miller E. In Birkmayer W, Hornykiewicz, eds. *Advances in Parkinsonism 1976;* 582. Basel: Roche

54 Klawans H, Topel J, Bergen D. *Neurology (Minneap) 1975; 25:* 290

55 Tarsy D, Leopold N, Sax D. *Neurology (Minneap) 1974; 24:* 28

56 Klawans H, Goetz C, Bergen D. *Arch Neurol 1975; 32:* 331

57 Price PA, Parkes JD, Marsden CD. *J Neurol Neurosurg Psychiat 1978; 41:* 702

58 Bedard P, Parkes JD, Marsden CD. *Brit J Pharmac 1977; 4:* 1875

59 Tarsy D, Parkes JD, Marsden CD. *Arch Neurol 1975; 32:* 134

60 Lesser RP, Fahn S, Snider SR, Cote LJ, Isgreen WP, Barrett RE. *Neurology (Minneap) 1979; 29:* 1253

Chapter 34

"ON AND OFF"
VARIABILITY AND RESPONSE SWINGS
IN PARKINSON'S DISEASE

C D Marsden and J D Parkes

Introduction

Variations in the severity of symptoms has always been one of the most characteristic features of Parkinson's disease but, during long-term levodopa therapy, such
events have greatly increased in their complexity and frequency so that they now are
one of the major contemporary problems in management. No effective means has
been discovered to combat such response swings, which continue to interrupt the
benefits of levodopa therapy in about 50 per cent of patients treated for two years
or more. Nor have the mechanisms responsible for these curious fluctuations in
mobility and drug response been established.

Variations of disability in Parkinson's disease have made assessment of severity very difficult. When L-dopa was first introduced the therapeutic response was
more-or-less stable throughout the day. So clinical assessment could be undertaken
randomly to give a reasonable representation of disability. Indeed, clinical benefit
from anti-Parkinsonian drugs was demonstrated by single assessments after a few
weeks or months of therapy, comparing periods on placebo with those on active
drug.

The advent of increasingly severe response swings during chronic L-dopa treatment has made this simple approach to assessment impossible. Spot checks are unrepresentative in patients who may fluctuate from being normally active to being
chair-bound many times a day. In these circumstances some form of continuous
record of mobility and dyskinesias is required, but none has been developed for
routine use in Parkinson's disease. At present, clinical investigators rely on frequent
bed-side assessment many times throughout the day, coupled with self-rating
assessment by the patients themselves. Only by this means can the impact of new
therapy on response swings be established. Even so, it is critical to distinguish the
various categories of response swings that may occur in Parkinson's disease today,
because their causes and their treatment differ. The various types of fluctuation
in performance which can occur in patients with Parkinson's disease treated or untreated, were reviewed in 1976 [1] (Table I). The present paper elaborates on the
views expressed there, and introduces certain additional clinical observations.

TABLE I Types of fluctuations in performance (response swings) seen in patients with Parkinson's disease on chronic L-dopa therapy.

Probably due to underdose plus disease progression	Due to over-dose
Freezing episodes	Peak-dose dyskinesia
End-of-dose akinesia	Diphasic dyskinesia
Off-period dystonia	Peak-dose akinesia
Neurasthenia	Peak-dose delirium

Unpredictable response swings ("Yo-Yo")

Freezing episodes

Sudden episodes of immobility are a classical symptom of untreated Parkinson's disease, variously described as "akinesia paradoxica", "start-hesitation", or "freezing". The patient is abruptly riveted to the spot, and cannot get moving again. An analogy aptly chosen by George Selby is that of a car engine suddenly stalling and the starter button then failing [2]. While experienced most commonly during walking, such freezing episodes also affect speech leading to sudden silence, handwriting when the pen suddenly no longer crosses the page, and many other manual motor acts such as playing a musical instrument, knitting or peeling potatoes.

Such sudden freezing episodes are unusual in early Parkinson's disease, but appear some years after the onset when the illness is moderately advanced. In particular, they often herald the development of postural instability and more advanced disability.

Many patients may never have experienced freezing episodes before starting L-dopa treatment, so their appearance for the first time while on treatment may be taken as an adverse effect of the drug. In fact, they are an indication of progression of the underlying pathology of the illness, despite drug therapy, and are therefore an indication for an increase rather than a reduction in therapy.

An interesting finding during freezing episodes occurring in patients on long-term L-dopa therapy is that the limbs and trunk are hypotonic, despite gross akinesia [3]. This observation confirms that the mechanisms responsible for rigidity and akinesia are different, and that akinesia is not due to rigidity.

Such freezing episodes commonly appear initially as the effect of each dose of L-dopa wears off. In other words, they may be the earliest symptoms of the commonest response swing, end-of-dose akinesia or the "wearing off" effect.

End-of-dose deterioration

From the beginning of L-dopa therapy most patients are aware that benefit lasts only for a few hours after each dose. Usually improvement begins after half an hour or so, reaches its maximum within an hour, and lasts for up to about 3 or 4 hours.

Thereafter, if another dose is not taken, the patient relapses back to his untreated Parkinsonian state.

After a number of years of L-dopa treatment, the duration of action of each dose appears to shorten so that end-of-dose deterioration occurs earlier and earlier as time passes. Patients complain that they get less and less benefit from the drug, because it lasts a shorter and shorter period of time.

In our earlier publication on this topic, we interpreted end-of-dose deterioration as being due to recurrence of dopamine deficiency after the initial response to each dose—in other words, as a re-appearance of Parkinsonism modified to some extent by therapy. This conclusion was based upon our own observation that "off-periods" were associated with low or falling plasma L-dopa levels, an observation noted by others [4, 5, 6] by the demonstration that apomorphine administration during the "off" phase could restore function [7], and by the demonstration that continuous intravenous infusion of L-dopa such as to maintain a constant blood level could abolish overt end-of-dose deterioration [8]. This conclusion still seems valid, but to date no-one has demonstrated a change in the pharmacokinetic handling of L-dopa during long term therapy. Plasma L-dopa profiles appear identical at the start of treatment compared with some years later, yet the clinical response may be very different.

Nor does it seem likely that end-of-dose deterioration is the result of an increasing loss of response of dopamine receptors since apomorphine, a directly acting dopamine agonist, can restore mobility during the "off" period [7], as can other dopamine agonists such as lisuride.

Parkinsonian neurasthenia

Fatigue is probably the commonest of all symptoms in fully developed Parkinson's disease, but has received relatively little attention. The untreated patient frequently remarks on difficulty in sustaining effort, and increasing lethargy as the day progresses. Sleep may restore vigour, and many patients resort to an afternoon nap to provide strength for the end of the day.

Schwab [9] paid particular attention to this symptom, which he believed to be a manifestation of akinesia. He routinely employed a bulb ergometer to assess Parkinsonian disability and noted that the force of repetitive hand squeezes progressively declined in a manner very similar to that seen in patients with myasthenia gravis. However, unlike the myasthenic, the patient with Parkinson's disease exercised to fatigue could, if urged strongly, produce a much stronger contraction without an interval for rest. Likewise, after exercise to fatigue, an electric shock to the peripheral nerve would evoke a near normal contraction in patients with Parkinson's disease but little or no response in the patient with myasthenia. A short interval of rest would restore grip strength back to normal in both conditions.

Schwab drew attention to the similarity of this fatigue during repetitive hand squeezes to a similar apparent rapid fatigue in many other repetitive motor acts. For example, he pointed out that the initial few steps in walking might be long and strong, but that the pace became progressively shorter until quite soon the typical festinating gait was evident. Similarly, the initial few words spoken might be loud and clear, only for the voice to dwindle away as speech continued.

Another aspect of fatigue in the untreated patient with Parkinson's disease is evident in the dramatic physical deterioration that may follow severe physical effort or great mental stress [10]. It is as if such severe events exhaust the reserves of the patient, who then requires a period of rest to recover.

All these aspects of fatigue seen in the untreated patient with Parkinson's disease may be relieved initially by L-dopa therapy. Indeed, the observations that "I am no longer tired" or "I have got back my energy" are common when treatment is first started. But after years of therapy fatigue may re-appear (or in the patient started early on treatment who did not have this symptom initially, it may occur for the first time during long-term treatment). An early indication of such a sequence of events is the re-appearance of Parkinsonian disability at those times of physical or mental stress. Patients soon learn to take an extra tablet of L-dopa before unaccustomed physical effort or unusual social pressure, a phenomenon that might be termed *stress relapse.*

Another aspect of recurrence of fatigue in patients on long-term treatment is the appearance of conspicuous *diurnal fluctuations* in mobility. Many such individuals are regularly, if not always, aware that their functional capacity declines in the afternoon or evening. The response to morning doses of L-dopa or other dopamine agonist therapy may be adequate or good, but as the day wears on they get less and less benefit. As in the untreated patient this may force them to take a regular afternoon nap.

The effect of rest and sleep in such patients with marked Parkinsonian fatigue may be quite dramatic. In particular, many such patients remark on *sleep benefit,* by which is meant restoration of mobility on awakening from sleep prior to drug intake. Typically such a patient may report that "the first hour in the day is my best". They awake to find themselves capable of getting up, washing, and taking breakfast without the need for treatment, but this surge of energy soon fades after a matter of a quarter of an hour to an hour or so, and they require their first dose of L-dopa at the breakfast table.

Sleep benefit is not seen in every patient with Parkinson's disease, many of whom are at their worst and unable to move first thing in the morning before treatment works. We are in the process of analysing our data to discover whether sleep benefit is a function of duration of disease, or response to therapy. Our impression is that it is a feature of the moderately affected patient who may exhibit quite profound oscillations in response to treatment, and that it gradually disappears as the disease advances and therapy becomes less and less effective.

In summary, various manifestations of myasthenia-like fatigue may occur in the untreated patient with Parkinson's disease, and may re-appear (or appear for the first time) in the patient on long-term L-dopa replacement therapy, contributing to fluctuations in performance.

Over-dose effects

The almost inevitable consequence of the appearance of severe and progressively disabling end-of-dose deterioration is for both patient and physician to increase L-dopa dosage. This leads to a number of unwanted effects which add to the problems of fluctuating clinical response to treatment. We now recognise four unwanted over-dose effects of such treatment.

Peak dose akinesia [11] is rare, but we have now encountered twelve examples. All have manifested loss of speech at the time of greatest therapeutic benefit, some hour or so after the oral dose of L-dopa. Originally this loss of speech was attributed to depolarisation block as a result of excessive neurotransmitter action, ie, something akin to a cholinergic crisis in myasthenia gravis. However, we doubt this explanation because peak-dose dysphonia has not, in our experience, been accompanied by obvious recurrence of the full-blown picture of Parkinson's disease. Indeed, the majority of such patients have been mobile during the phase of speech difficulty and clinical examination has revealed that the latter is due to subtle dystonic spasms of mouth, jaw, and perhaps larynx. In other words, it would seem that many such cases represent examples of a peculiar form of peak-dose dyskinesia.

Peak-dose dyskinesia is very common in all patients with Parkinson's disease, but especially so in those in whom end-of-dose deterioration has developed and who, in an attempt to combat this, have increased L-dopa dosage excessively. Elsewhere [12] we have pointed out that peak-dose dyskinesia usually takes the form of chorea and oro-facial dyskinesia, but in some 10 per cent of patients may assume a frank dystonic form.

There is another type of dystonia in Parkinson's disease. Painful muscle cramps of the leg producing dystonic posturing of the foot and toes, often occurring in the morning and frequently provoked by exercise, was recognised as an intrinsic feature of Parkinson's disease [13]. A recurrence of this dystonic painful foot cramp may occur during periods of end-of-dose akinesia or first thing in the morning in patients on long-term L-dopa therapy [14]. Such "off-period" dystonia may respond to an increase in L-dopa dose [15].

An important theoretical question is whether such peak-dose dyskinesias are an inevitable consequence of successful therapeutic action of L-dopa. Recently there has been considerable interest in the possibility that two or more dopamine receptors exist in the brain [15, 16]. This suggestion is of great interest to both neurologists and psychiatrists for it means that it might be possible to dissociate abnormal movements provoked by L-dopa from its therapeutic benefit in Parkinson's disease (or anti-dyskinetic actions from unwanted Parkinsonism in movement disorders), and anti-psychotic action from extrapyramidal side effects in schizophrenia [16]. Evidence in favour of this general hypothesis has been obtained by the administration of certain drugs to patients with Parkinson's disease on optimum L-dopa therapy. Oxiperomide [17] and tiapride [18] both appear to possess the capacity to reduce or abolish L-dopa-induced dyskinesias without necessarily making Parkinsonian disability worse. Both drugs are relatively selective inhibitors

269

of that dopamine receptor not linked to adenylate cyclase (the DA2 receptor). That is to say neither oxiperomide nor tiapride inhibits dopamine stimulation of striatal adenylate cyclase. Phenothiazines, and to a lesser extent most conventional butyrophenones, do inhibit dopamine sensitive adenylate cyclase, so are DA1 receptor antagonists. But they can also act on non-cyclase linked receptors, so are relatively non-specific DA1 and DA2 dopamine receptor antagonists.

Certainly both oxiperomide and tiapride added to L-dopa can inhibit dyskinesias at a dose that does not increase Parkinsonism (although higher doses do produce increased akinesia and rigidity).

Diphasic dyskinesia [19] is quite common. The typical story is of a burst of dyskinesia occurring at the beginning of L-dopa action, often heralding improvement in mobility, followed by disappearance of this dyskinesia during the peak of benefit, followed by a return of dyskinesia as drug action wanes. However, this pattern may be modified in some patients in that only the first or only the second burst of abnormal movement occurs.

It has been suggested that while peak-dose dyskinesias are properly treated by a reduction in L-dopa dosage, diphasic dyskinesias may be managed by an increase in drug intake [20].

Paroxysmal dyskinesia is an uncommon but dramatic and distressing event. It may be an exaggeration of diphasic dyskinesia, but its explosive nature is quite exceptional. In the period during which L-dopa begins to work, such patients experience increasingly severe and dramatic dyskinesias of such severity as to completely incapacitate them. In character, such dyskinesias are often hemiballistic in nature with wild flinging movements, or alternatively are grossly dystonic, forcing the patient to bed. An episode may last a few minutes to an hour or so, and does not necessarily follow every dose. Once the dyskinesias begin to settle down the patient is mobile until the effect of the drug wears off.

Such gross paroxysmal dyskinesias occur in patients with fully developed response swings of some years duration. The impression is that it represents the severest end-stage of the problem.

Peak-dose delirium is common, particularly in the elderly. Such patients need have no persisting intellectual or cognitive defect, but at the point of maximum action of L-dopa they develop disorientation, hallucinations, and memory disturbance. Such fluctuating mental changes may occur in the setting of clear consciousness when they take the form of isolated hallucinosis (often vivid and visual), behaviour disturbance, sexual deviation, thought disorder (particularly paranoia), or simple memory lapses. We have never noticed diphasic psychiatric states, akin to the diphasic dyskinesia described above.

The stage of unpredictable response swings—"Yo-Yoing"

As time goes by, many patients begin to experience increasingly variable, unpredictable and rapid swings in functional capacity and side effects. Often patients have increased L-dopa dosage to maintain mobility as end-of-dose deterioration

270

advances, but at the expense of increasingly severe paroxysmal dyskinesia. The speed of change from mobility with dyskinesias to immbolity led to its graphic description as the "on-off" phenomenon, while the random timing and nature of the response swings led to them being likened to the ups and downs of a yo-yo. This state represents the most advanced stage of fluctuating response in long-term L-dopa treated patients. Throughout the day the unfortunate suffering patient with Parkinson's disease oscillates from active mobility to gross disabling dyskinesias to total immobility quite randomly and very rapidly. Such patients may only spend 20–30 per cent of their waking hours walking and talking, and they cannot predict when that will be.

Mechanisms of response swings

The various types of fluctuation in performance described above that may contribute to response swings can be divided into two categories—those simply due to over-dosage with L-dopa or other dopamine agonists, and the remainder. Unwanted effects due to over-dosage are managed relatively easily, simply by a reduction in dose. It is the second category that has proved so difficult to control and whose cause is so obscure. Included in this category are freezing episodes, end-of-dose deterioration, and the various aspects of Parkinsonian fatigue. There may be a number of causes responsible for these difficult problems, but we would like to conclude by putting forward a hypothesis which attributes them all to a single underlying cause, namely the progression of the underlying pathology of Parkinson's disease leading to failure to store newly synthesised neurotransmitter, especially dopamine.

Why end-of-dose deterioration should become more prominent during chronic treatment remains a mystery, perhaps to be solved by examination of how L-dopa works in the brain. It is assumed, reasonably, that its benefits are due to conversion into dopamine at striatal and mesolimbic (? mesocortical) sites deficient in the natural neurotransmitter. The question is how does this conversion come about, when there is gross destruction of the normal dopaminergic neurones innervating these regions.

A simple and obvious answer is that L-dopa entering the brain is converted into dopamine in those remaining intact neurones. In this case, a relationship between severity of disease and clinical response should be evident on the grounds that the more intact neurones there are remaining the greater capacity for synthesis of transmitter. However, soon after the introduction of L-dopa it was realised there was no clear relationship between severity or duration of illness and subsequent response to drug therapy. This had led to examination of other possibilities. For instance, it has been suggested that L-dopa is taken up into cerebral capillaries which contain the necessary decarboxylase and convert it therein into dopamine which is released onto the denervated dopamine receptors. Recent experiments [21] suggest that this is not the case, for L-dopa can exert a profound post-synaptic dopamine agonist action in rodents with near-total destruction of the nigro striatal pathway, despite effective inhibition of cerebral capillary decarboxylase activity. Another possibility canvassed has been that L-dopa is taken into 5HT-containing neurones, which also contain the relatively non-specific decarboxylase necessary for conversion of either L-dopa to dopamine or 5-hydroxytryptophan to 5HT. 5HT-containing pathways are not severely damaged in Parkinson's disease [22], so could act as the necessary reservoir of enzymic activity required. Experimental evidence on this matter has led to conflicting reports. One group [23] indicates that L-dopa no longer acts successfully in animals with destruction of one nigro-striatal pathway combined with chemical lesions of ascending 5HT neurones, but others [24] have obtained opposite results. If 5HT pathways are important for the action of L-dopa in Parkinson's disease then their progressive destruction with the passage of time could conceivably reduce the effectiveness of treatment.

The same argument can be applied to noradrenaline-containing neurones. These too are not devastated by the pathology of the illness [25], and intact noradrenaline fibres innervating mesolimbic and mesocortical dopamine-containing areas could also provide the necessary site for L-dopa decarboxylation. Elsewhere [1] we have suggested that progressive destruction of noradrenaline pathways, as evidenced by depigmentation and loss of neurones in the locus coeruleus, also might lead to a failure of cerebral decarboxylation of L-dopa.

Finally, it must be acknowledged that dopa-decarboxylase is far from being rate-limiting enzyme, so that the small amounts remaining in the few intact dopaminergic fibres may be just sufficient for adequate dopamine synthesis, but that this potential declines as more of these fibres are destroyed by the disease process.

In conclusion, we believe that end-of-dose deterioration is due not to a change in the pharmacokinetics of L-dopa, nor to some change in the responsiveness of the post-synaptic cerebral dopamine receptors, but to an alteration in the capacity of the brain to synthesise and store dopamine from its precursor amino acid. Whether this change is due to progressive loss of dopamine pathways beyond the critical level, or to progressive destruction of other neuronal systems especially those utilising noradrenaline or serotonin, is presently unknown. However, we would argue that it is *loss of neuronal storage of dopamine* that leads to progressive decline in the duration of L-dopa action with the consequent development of end-of-dose deterioration.

The phenomenon of Parkinsonian fatigue is taken as critical observation. Many of the features of the various aspects of fatigue such as sleep benefit, diurnal variation, and stress deterioration can be interpreted as the result of depletion of stores of neurotransmitter built up during periods of rest. We suggest that dopamine stores in residual intact neurones, stores synthesised from the precursor amino acid, are utilised during activity. Stores of dopamine also are important to the action of bromocriptine, for despite its post-synaptic dopamine agonist action, many of its effects are dependent upon presynaptic dopamine synthesis and storage [26]. In fact, no purely post-synaptic dopamine agonist is in routine use to treat Parkinson's disease (apomorphine proved too toxic, and lisuride and pergolide are only available for clinical trial in certain special centres). Perhaps such a drug would overcome problems of transmitter storage.

Viewed in this light, the therapeutic action of L-dopa is interpreted as due to both synthesis and storage of dopamine (and perhaps noradrenaline) from the precursor amino acid. Loss of storage capacity would lead to increasing Parkinsonian fatigue, loss of sleep benefit, and a progressive reduction in duration of therapeutic action of L-dopa. The initial response to each dose is interpreted as due to the therapeutic effect of newly synthesised dopamine, but later benefit would be due to release of stored neurotransmitter. This concept accords with the known pharmacokinetic of dopamine synthesis from L-dopa administration. Loss of storage capacity would cause reduction in duration of L-dopa action, leading to progressive end-of-dose deterioration. Such a mechanism accounts for the appearance of end-of-dose deterioration during long term therapy, without any change in L-dopa pharmacokinetics, or any alteration in post-synaptic dopamine receptor sensitivity. Freezing episodes would occur during periods of end-of-dose deterioration or stress-induced disability because of recurrence of Parkinsonian disability due to neurotransmitter lack.

The pathology of Parkinson's disease probably continues to progress despite treatment [27]. If this progressively destroys those neurones responsible for transmitter storage, the full chain of events leading to many of the features of response swings might be explained. It is trite to say that we need to know how L-dopa works in Parkinson's disease, but that is what is required to begin to understand the cause of the various "on-off" phenomena, and to produce satisfactory treatment for the many otherwise well patients with this problem of long-term therapy.

References

1   Marsden CD, Parkes JD. *Lancet 1976;i:*292
2   Selby G. In Vinken PJ, Bruyn GW, eds. *Handbook of Clinical Neurology volume 6 1968;*173. Amsterdam, North Holland Publishing
3   Barbeau A. In McDowell FH, Barbeau A, eds. *Advances in Neurology volume 5 1974;* 347. New York, Raven Press
4   Tolosa ES, Martin WE, Cohen HP, Jacobson RL. *Neurology (Minneap) 1975;25:*177
5   Fahn S. *Neurology (Minneap) 1974;24:*431
6   Sweet RD, McDowell FH. *Neurology (Minneap) 1974;24:*953
7   Duby SE, Cotzias GC, Papavasiliou PS, Lawrence WH. *Archs Neurol (Chicago) 1972; 27:*474
8   Shoulson I, Glaubiger GA, Chase TN. *Neurology (Minneap) 1975;25:*1144
9   Schwab RS, England AC, Peterson E. *Neurology (Minneap) 1959;9:*65
10   Schwab RS, Zieper I. *Psychiat Neurol (Basel) 1965;150:*345
11   Claveria LE, Calne DB, Allen JG. *Brit med J 1973;1:*641
12   Parkes JD, Bedard P, Marsden CD. *Lancet 1976;ii:*155
13   Duvoison RC, Yahr MD, Lieberman J, Antunes J, Rhee S. *Trans Amer Neurol Assoc 1973;97:*
14   Lees AJ, Shaw KM, Stern GM. *Lancet 1977;ii:*1034
15   Trabucchi M, Longoni R, Fresia P, Spano PF. *Life Sci 1975;17:*1551
16   Kebabian JW, Calne DB. *Nature 1979;277:*93
17   Bedard P, Parkes JD, Marsden CD. *Brit med J 1978;1:*954
18   Price P, Parkes JD, Marsden CD. *Lancet 1978;ii:*1106
19   Muenter MD, Sharpless NS, Tyce SM. *Mayo Clin Proc 1977;52:*163

20   Lhermitte F, Agid Y, Signoret JL. *Archs Neurol (Chicago) 1978;35:*261
21   Duvoison RC, Mytilincou C. *Brain Res 1978;152:*369
22   Bernheimer H, Birkmayer W, Hornykiewicz O. *Klin Wschr 1961;39:*1056
23   Gershanik OS, Heikkila RE, Duvoisin RC. *Neurology (Minneap) 1979;29:*553
24   Melamed E, Hefit F, Liebman J, Schlosberg AJ, Wurtman RJ. *Nature 1979;* In press
25   Rinne UK, Sonninen V. *Archs Neurol (Chicago) 1973;28:*107
26   Dolphin AC, Jenner P, Sawaya MCB, Marsden CD, Testa B. *J Pharm Pharmac 1977;29:* 727
27   Marsden CD, Parkes JD. *Lancet 1977;i:*345

Chapter 35

THE ROLE OF TRANSIENT LEVODOPA WITHDRAWAL ('DRUG HOLIDAY') IN THE MANAGEMENT OF PARKINSON'S DISEASE

W J Weiner, W C Koller, S Perlik, P A Nausieda and H L Klawans

The treatment of Parkinson's disease with levodopa or levodopa/carbidopa has been an important therapeutic and theoretical advance [1-3]. However, chronic L-dopa therapy is complicated by many problems. In this chapter we review the use of transient L-dopa withdrawal, or drug holidays, in the management of the complications of the long-term L-dopa therapy in parkinsonism.

Complications of chronic levodopa therapy

The long term use of L-dopa is complicated by various drug related side effects and possible loss of drug efficacy. Studies reporting follow-up experience of 5 and 6 years with chronic L-dopa therapy have documented a progressive diminution of therapeutic effect [3-5]. The reason for the gradual loss of efficacy during chronic treatment is unknown. Progression of the underlying degenerative disease process and unspecified pharmacological alteration of receptor sites have been suggested as possible mechanisms [5, 6]. The incidence of L-dopa induced dyskinesias increases gradually so that after 5 years of treatment 40 to 60 per cent of patients are affected [7]. Psychiatric dysfunction ranging from vivid dreams and non-threatening hallucinations to toxic confusional psychosis is directly related to duration of therapy [8, 9]. While some degree of fluctuation in motor performance in parkinsonism is well known in the older neurological literature, the unique problem of sudden dramatic changes from dyskinesia to akinesia, the on-off phenomenon is associated with long term L-dopa therapy [10, 11]. Levodopa induced myoclonus and dystonia, entities distinct from L-dopa induced dyskinesia, also become evident only after several years of therapy [12, 13]. The pathophysiological mechanisms of these complications are unknown but it has been postulated that they are related to drug induced alterations in central dopaminergic receptor sensitivity [14, 15].

275

TABLE I

RIGIDITY

0 = Absent
1 = Slight or detectable only when activated by contralateral or other movements.
2 = Mild to moderate.
3 = Marked, but full range of motion easily achieved.
4 = Severe, full range of motion achieved with difficulty.

TREMOR

0 = Absent
1 = Slight and infrequently present.
2 = Moderate in amplitude but not intermittently present.
3 = Moderate and present most of the time.
4 = Marked in amplitude and present most of the time.

BRADYKINESIA

0 = None
1 = Minimal slowness giving movement a deliberate character, could be normal for some persons.
2 = Mild degree of slowness and poverty of movement which is definitely abnormal.
3 = Moderate slowness with occasional hesitation on initiating movement and arrests on on-going movement.
4 = Marked slowness and poverty of movement with frequent freezing and long delays in initiation movement.

GAIT

0 = Freely, ambulatory, good stepping, turns readily.
1 = Walks slowly, may shuffle with short steps but no festination or propulsion.
2 = Walks with great difficulty with festination, short steps freezing and propulsion but requires little or no assistance.
3 = Severe disturbance of gait requiring frequent assistance.
4 = Cannot walk at all even with help.

POSTURE

0 = Normal erect
1 = Not quite erect, slightly stooped posture could be normal for older person.
2 = Moderate simian posture, definitely abnormal.
3 = Marked simian posture with kyphosis.
4 = Severe flexion with extreme abnormality of posture.

POSTURAL STABILITY

0 = Normal
1 = Retropulsion, but recovers unaided.
2 = Absence of postural response, would fall if not caught by examiner.
3 = Very unstable, tends to fall spontaneously with both feet together.
4 = Unable to stand without assistance.

Current Management

Since most of the side effects once present are dose related, reduction of the dosage will usually decrease these complications, but often results in an increase in the severity of parkinsonian symptoms. The addition of other dopaminergic drugs such as bromocriptine has not solved this problem [16, 17]. Bromocriptine has been found to ameliorate the on-off phenomena in some patients, but a worsening of psychiatric complications has also been documented [18]. Another approach to reduce L-dopa induced side effects has been the use of dopaminergic blocking agents. While the administration of phenothiazines or butyrophenones can decrease some of these side effects, the use of these agents blocks all dopaminergic activity, causing exacerbation of parkinsonian symptoms [4, 19].

Drug Holiday

We have studied both the acute and chronic effects of transient L-dopa withdrawal for the management of the complications of long-term levodopa therapy [20, 21]. In the initial study sixteen patients with idiopathic Parkinson's disease with an average age of 68 were investigated. The duration of parkinsonism averaged 8 years and the duration of treatment with L-dopa or L-dopa/carbidopa was 5 years. Six patients were admitted for "loss of efficacy" with increasing parkinsonian motor disability including gait disturbances and bradykinesia. The other patients were admitted because of severe dose limiting side effects including off-on phenomena and/or dyskinesia, or psychiatric complications.

Patients were initially maintained on their usual daily dose. Subsequently patients had their dosage of L-dopa reduced by one half and maintained at this level for several days. L-dopa was then discontinued for 5–7 days. Patients were administered one half of their original daily dose after the holiday. Patients then had their dosage of L-dopa titrated as thought necessary to control symptoms for 5 to 10 days while in the hospital. Patients were then followed up as out-patients every three months for a one year period. During the observation period patients were graded for parkinsonian signs on a scale of zero to four (Table I) and side effects were graded on a scale of 0 to 3 according to frequency and severity.

This study indicated that some patients with Parkinson's disease with complications of chronic L-dopa therapy benefit from a period of transient drug withdrawal. Patients given a holiday of 4 to 7 days without any L-dopa treatment had a significant increase in their parkinsonian symptoms and some became bedridden and unable to feed or dress themselves. Low dose subcutaneous heparin and other precautions were taken to avoid pulmonary emboli and infectious complications of this state. Characteristically, in any individual patient, there was a worsening of existing symptoms rather than the development of previously unrecognised symptoms, which is consistent with the observation that many patients with long-term parkinsonism never develop the complete symptom complex [2].

Following the holiday period the majority of patients responded to the first

277

dose of L-dopa given (half of the initial dose) and achieved a disability rating comparable to their admission disability (full dose). This is similar to the observation of Sweet *et al* [22] who demonstrated an enhanced motor response to low doses of L-dopa in 7 of 13 parkinsonian patients who were withdrawn from chronic L-dopa treatment, and in marked contrast to the L-dopa untreated parkinsonian patients who usually require weeks of therapy to show significant clinical improvement [23]. The basis for this increased responsiveness is unknown.

After the holiday period parkinsonian symptoms were markedly improved. Eleven of sixteen patients required only one half of their initial dose for optimal control of symptoms. Rigidity, tremor, bradykinesia, and gait disturbances all showed marked improvement. Abnormalities of posture and postural stability showed the least improvement, and were also the most drug-resistant and demonstrated the least change during the holiday period. All functional disability scores were also significantly improved after the holiday that had not been possible with drug therapy before the withdrawal period. On the other hand, five patients did not benefit since motor and functional disability scores were similar before and after the holiday, although in some of these patients the side effects were less severe after the holiday.

A 4–7 day L-dopa holiday was effective in controlling the side effects associated with chronic L-dopa therapy, psychiatric complications being the most responsive. In six patients in whom hallucinosis had become a major problem, this complication either dramatically decreased or completely disappeared after the holiday. Since severe hallucinosis often progressed to psychosis [12], controlling this symptom complex is important. Previously only reduction in L-dopa dosage decreased hallucinosis, usually at the expense of increased parkinsonism. A drug holiday, as performed here, ameliorated this side effect without loss of efficacy and usually with increased drug efficacy. On-off phenomena were also diminished following the drug holiday with 3 of 4 patients showing insignificant improvement. Several patients had L-dopa induced myoclonus and drug related nausea disappear after the holiday. One patient with dystonia of the foot related to drug usage, had no change in this symptom after the holiday. Since so few patients had these side effects the role of drug holiday in their management is unclear. Although L-dopa induced dyskinesias could always be ameliorated during the holiday, the after holiday dose adjustments often resulted in their reappearance.

The follow-up data indicate that many patients who had increased motor responsiveness after the holiday had a gradual loss of effect and increase in parkinsonian symptoms during the months after the holiday. However, significant deterioration did not occur until 6 months after the holiday and many patients retained some benefit even one year post holiday. Rigidity appeared to be the parkinsonian symptom improved for the longest period of time. Two patients appeared to regain motor responsiveness after a second drug holiday, suggesting that this manoeuvre can be successfully repeated. Drug holiday was also of long term benefit in controlling the side effects associated with chronic L-dopa therapy. During the first 6 months of follow-up there was no return of any side effect. As noted in the first phase of the study, drug holiday appeared to be the most help-

278

ful in patients with psychiatric complications [10]. At the end of one year, four of six patients remained free of this complication even though in some cases the dosage of levodopa was higher than that which was previously associated with hallucinosis. Drug holiday also had a lasting effect on several other side effects although only a few patients were studied with these complications. On-off phenomena were a problem in only one of three patients after one year. Nausea and vomiting remained absent in two patients. Thus it would appear that drug holiday has a lasting beneficial effect and is a realistic means of managing the complications of chronic L-dopa therapy although drug holiday is without any therapeutic effect in 20 to 30 per cent of those undergoing this clinical manoeuvre. In a retrospective analysis Feldman and coworkers [24] also found drug holiday to be beneficial, but more studies are needed to further define its exact range of efficacy.

Physiological mechanisms

The physiological or pharmacological basis underlying the effectiveness of a period of transient drug withdrawal is unknown. Alteration of dopaminergic receptor site sensitivity has been postulated as being responsible for drug related side effects observed during chronic levodopa administration. It has been suggested that long term dopaminergic stimulation results in postsynaptic supersensitivity [25], postsynaptic desensitisation [26], and presynaptic subsensitisation [27]. Behavioural experiments with chronic dopaminergic agonist treatment results in behavioural modifications compatible with both supersensitivity and subsensitivity, depending on which behaviour response is measured [27, 28]. Dopamine receptor binding studies yield controversial results with some investigators finding increased binding of radoligands with long term agonist treatment and others detecting no change [29, 30]. While it is not currently possible to know which theory is more valid, it is likely that changes in both postsynaptic and presynaptic receptors occur both as a result of continuation of the disease process and as a result of prolonged pharmacological therapy. Transient drug withdrawal results in changes that subsequently allow a return to a condition similar to that seen earlier in the course of treatment.

Future considerations

While drug holiday appears to have clinical efficacy in those parkinsonian patients having severe complications related to chronic L-dopa therapy the role of a drug holiday in earlier stages of treatment remains unexplored. It is possible that intermittent L-dopa therapy may help to prevent or delay some of the complications seen with chronic L-dopa therapy. If dopamine receptor sensitivity changes occur as a result of prolonged continuous treatment and this leads to complications, there may be a theoretical basis for early intermittent therapy. Clinical studies designed to evaluate this concept need to be performed.

279

Conclusions

A 5-7 day period of withdrawal of L-dopa in hospitalised parkinsonian patients whose chronic L-dopa therapy was associated with severe side effects, including dopa-induced dyskinesias, hallucinations, off-on phenomena or apparent loss of efficacy, had not only acute, but more significant long-term beneficial effects in the management of these complications. Whether drug holidays performed earlier in the course of L-dopa treatment can prevent the appearance of complications remains to be determined.

Acknowledgement

This work was supported in part by grants from the United Parkinson Foundation, Chicago, Illinois, and the Boothroyd Foundation. Chicago, Illinois.

References

1. Cotzias GC, Papavasaliou PS, Gelline R. *New Engl J Med 1969;280:*337
2. Klawans HL, Garvin JS. *Dis Nerv Syst 1969;30:*737
3. Sweet RD, McDowell FH. *Ann Intern Med 1975;83:*456
4. Barbeau A. *Can Med Ass J 1969;101:*58
5. Markham CH, Treciakas LT, Diamond S. *West J Med 1974;121:*188
6. Weiner WJ, Bergen D. In Klawans HL, ed. *Clinical Neuropharmacology volume 2 1977;* 1. New York, Raven Press
7. Fahn S, Calne DB. *Neurology (Minneap) 1978;28:*5
8. Sweet RD, McDowell FH, Ferguson JS, Loranger AW, Goodell A. *Neurology (Minneap) 1976;26:*305
9. Moskovitz C, Moses H, Klawans HL. *Amer J Psychiat 1978;135:*669
10. Markham CH. In McDowell F, Barbeau A, eds. *Advances in Neurology volume 5 1974;* 287. New York, Raven Press
11. Sweet RD, McDowell, FH. In McDowell F, Barbeau A, eds. *Advances in Neurology volume 5 1974;*331
12. Klawans HL, Goetz C, Bergen D. *Arch Neurol 1975;32:*331
13. Melamed E. *Arch Neurol 1979; 36:* 308
14. Pycock CJ, Marsden CD. *J Neurol Sci 1977; 31:* 113
15. Klawans HL, Goetz C, Nausieda PA, Weiner WJ. *Ann Neurol 1977; 2:* 125
16. Debono A, Donaldson I, Marsden CD, Parkes JD. *Lancet 1975;ii:*987
17. Lees AJ, Haddad S, Shaw KM, Kohout LJ, Stern GM. *Arch Neurol 1978;35:*503
18. Calne DB. In Klawans HL, ed. *Clinical Neuropharmacology volume 3 1978;*153
19. Klawans HL, Weiner WJ. *J Neurol Neurosurg Psychiat 1974;37:*427
20. Weiner WJ, Koller WC, Perlik S, Nausieda PA, Klawans HL. *Neurology.* In press
21. Koller WC, Weiner WJ, Perlik SJ, Nausieda PA, Klawans HL. *Neurology,* In press
22. Sweet RD, Lee JE, Spiegel HE, McDowell F. *Neurology (Minneap) 1972;22:*520
23. Yahr MR, Duvoisin RC, Shear MJ. *Arch Neurol 1969;21:*343
24. Feldman R, Direnfeld L, Alexander M, Kelly-Hayes M. *Neurology 1979;29:*553
25. Klawans HL, Margolin DI. *Arch Gen Psychiat 1975;32:*725
26. Direnfeld L, Spiro L, Marotta L, Seeman P. *Ann Neurol 1978;4:*473
27. Mullen P, Seeman P. *Eur J Pharm 1979;55:*149

28 Post RM, Kopancha RJ, Block KH. *Biol Psychiat 1976;11:*403
29 Klawans HL, Hitri A, Nausieda PA, Weiner WJ. *Effect of chronic levodopa treatment on striatal membrane dopamine binding. Sixth International Symposium on Parkinson's disease.* New York, Raven Press, In press
30 Friedhoff AJ, Bonnet K, Rosengarten H. *Res Comm Chem Pathol Pharmacol 1977; 16:*411

Chapter 36

ANIMAL MODELS IN THE EVALUATION
OF ANTI-PARKINSON AGENTS

H L Klawans, W C Koller, B I Diamond,
P A Nausieda, and W J Weiner

There are a variety of animal tests of behaviour thought to be related to stimulation of central dopamine receptors. Activation of dopaminergic mechanisms is involved in the control of locomotion, stereotypic behaviour, emesis, and thermoregulation. Animals treated with agents that deplete dopamine such as reserpine and alpha-methyl-para-tyrosine develop a characteristic motor syndrome that can be reversed with dopaminergic agents and provide another model. Methods of inducing receptor site supersensitivity such as unilateral 6-hydroxydopamine lesions of the substantia nigra and chronic agonist administration provide additional tests of dopaminergic mechanisms.

The main biochemical defect in parkinsonism is the lack of striatal dopamine [1, 2]. The major pathology in the disease is depigmentation and neuronal loss in the substantia nigra. As dopamine is the transmitter in the nigro striatal pathway it is not surprising that dopamine levels are decreased in the striatum of patients dying with parkinsonism [3]. Besides the dopaminergic system, the cholinergic representation in the striatum is also important and there is much evidence to suggest that there is antagonism of these two systems within the striatum [4]. Parkinsonism can be viewed as being due to a disequilibrium between antagonistic dopaminergic and cholinergic influences on striatal neurones [3]. Agents which decrease cholinergic or increase dopaminergic neurotransmission will improve the symptoms of parkinsonism. In this regard agents with dopaminergic activity have much greater efficacy than anticholinergic drugs. Levodopa causes marked amelioration of parkinsonian symptoms, but its chronic usage is associated with many side effects [5]. The limitations of all available therapeutic approaches make the search for newer agents most important.

In this chapter animal models of dopamine activity and their relevance to potential anti-parkinson agents will be discussed.

Locomotion and Stereotypic Activity

A common property of drugs possessing central dopaminergic activity is the production of behaviour and locomotor changes that can be observed in a variety of animal species [6-9]. The specific characteristics of these behavioural changes is species specific [6, 7]. In the rat, dopamine agonists induce a syndrome of increased locomotor activity and stereotyped behaviour characterised by repetitive movement of the head and forelegs, and by sniffing, licking, biting and gnawing [6, 10, 11]. In the guinea pig, the pattern of activity seen is less complex consisting of locomotion and gnawing behaviour [12, 13], and quantification of these changes is usually accomplished by scoring by an observer. The scale of Ernst [6] has been the most frequently used to score the intensity of the responses. This scale is illustrated below:

- − Rats showing no gnawing movements;
- + Rats walking around in the cage, sniffing over the grid, occasionally licking the wires and putting the nose into the grid;
- ++ Rats moving around, occasionally biting and gnawing at the wires;
- +++ Rats restricting their locomotion to a small area, and gnawing intensely on the bottom;
- ++++ Rats remaining on the same spot for 5-10 minutes or longer, while jerkingly gnawing and clinging their teeth around the wires convulsively for longer periods, sometimes interrupted by short intermissions.

In the guinea pig, our laboratory uses a scale 0 to 4 shown below [12, 13]:

0: Normal behaviour
1: Stereotyped sniffing, rearing, locomotion, and exploratory behaviour.
2: Intermittent chewing behaviour, occurring less than 50 per cent of the observation period of 30 seconds or more.
3: Frequent chewing behaviour, greater than 50 per cent of observation period in association with decreased level one behaviour.
4: Constant stereotypic chewing, no level one activity.

A stereotypy score is determined for each animal at 5 minute intervals following pharmacological challenge until behaviour has returned to baseline. Scores are based on observation periods of not less than 30 seconds and are performed by an observer, blinded relative to the agent and the pretreatment protocol. Animals are allowed to acclimatise one hour in the observation cages before the start of the experiments. More refined recording techniques allowing automatic quantification of the various components of behaviour have been developed [14, 15] and are becoming more widely used. Behavioural effects can be produced either by the systemic administration of drugs or by the local injection of drugs into various brain areas, in a variety of different animal species (mouse, rat, rabbits, cat, monkey). D, L-dopa or L-dopa in doses of 100 mg/kg to 1 gm/kg will produce marked stimulation of locomotor activity and various behavioural changes [16-18], such as stereotypy and increased aggressiveness, and catatonic posturing. These effects appear to reach a maximum 30 minutes after injection. The stereotypic behaviour produced by levodopa itself is of low intensity but, when a dopa-decarboxylase inhibitor is given with levodopa, a response of full intensity can be achieved. L-dopa plus RO 4 4602, a dopa decarboxylase inhibitor, will produce behavioural changes lasting almost 5 hours [19, 20].

The local cerebral injections of dopamine will also produce behavioural changes. Cools and coworkers [21, 22] have found that injections of dopamine into the rostromedial part of the head of the caudate nucleus in cats induces contralateral turning of the head and facial contractions and rapid jerking movements of the contralateral limb. Similar injections into certain sites in the caudate induces similar movements on the ipsilateral side of the body. These investigators suggest that these different effects are due to activation of different types of dopamine receptors.

Apomorphine is considered to act directly at dopamine receptor site and is a standard drug used in behavioural studies [23, 24], as it induces changes in a number of species, including mice, rats, guinea pigs, and rabbits. When the dose used is low, apomorphine appears to decrease locomotion [23] and when higher doses are used, there is an increase in locomotor activity and stereotypic behaviour [25, 26]. The latter (0.1 to 0.5 mg/kg) is dose-dependent, immediate in onset, of high intensity, and of short duration; apomorphine injected into the neostriatum of rats results in stereotypy [27, 28].

Amphetamine is considered to be the prototypic indirect-acting dopamine agonist, releasing dopamine from dopamine containing neurones, but itself having no effect on dopamine receptors [29]. Like apomorphine, d-amphetamine has been widely used as an investigative tool in neuropharmacological research, and it is well established that its administration leads to locomotor activity and stereotypic behaviour [29]. Amphetamine will induce these changes in a dose-dependent fashion (0.2 mg/kg to 10 mg/kg) with a short onset of action and a high intensity of effect. A dose of 10 mg/kg in the rat will cause behavioural activation lasting approximately 5 hours [20]. Intracaudate or intraventricular injection of amphetamine will produce similar effects as seen with systemic administration [21].

The dopaminergic systems in the striatum appear to be involved in motor regulation, since bilateral destruction of the corpus striatum prevents the production of stereotypic behaviour induced by dopamine agonists [30]. Data also exist that suggest that dopaminergic mechanisms in the nucleus accumbens may also play a role. Pijnenberg and coworkers [31–33] have found that bilateral injections of dopamine, apomorphine, or amphetamine (1–10 μg) cause an increase in locomotor behaviour after 30 minute latency; no stereotypic behaviour was reported with these injections. Destructive lesions of the nucleus accumbens will prevent agonist induced locomotion. These and other observations suggest that stereotypy is linked to mesolimbic dopaminergic systems and that the two activities are separate and do not occur in continuum [31, 34]. The ability of agents to produce these behavioural changes is a measure of their ability to act as dopamine agonists at dopamine receptors at these sites.

Emetic behaviour

Another property of drugs possessing central dopamine activity is the ability to induce vomiting in several animal species [35, 36], apomorphine being the prototypic drug for studying this action [36], and a powerful emetic in cats, dogs, and man; in pigeons, occasional emesis is produced. Of the various animal species, the dog appears to be the most sensitive animal and is used as the standard model to study emesis [36]. Besides apomorphine, a number of other dopaminergic drugs induce emesis both in dogs and man; these include levodopa and bromocriptine. Interestingly, indirect acting dopamine agonists such as amphetamine and pemoline do not seem to cause vomiting although this aspect has not been thoroughly studied. A number of drugs thought not to be concerned with dopamine neurotransmission, such as the opioids and the cardiac glycosides, often induce vomiting in the clinical setting.

As vomiting is a common clinical problem there are many studies testing the efficacy of drugs as anti-emetics [37, 38]. These drugs are usually tested as to their ability to antagonise apomorphine induced emesis in the dog [36]. The phenothiazine and the butyrophenone compounds have been found to be the most powerful anti-emetics in clinical practice [39, 40]. Experimentally, while these drugs are effective in blocking apomorphine induced emesis, they are not as effective in blocking emesis induced by morphine and are ineffective in blocking the emesis caused by the cardiac glycoside, ouabain [41]. These anti-emetic drugs are thought to act by blockage of dopamine receptors [36], but the anti-emetic efficacy does not seem to parallel their efficacy in blocking dopamine receptors in the extrapyramidal system. More detailed studies are needed to determine if there are differences between the dopamine receptors mediating emesis and those involved in motor control.

The site of action of apomorphine and other emetic and anti-emetic drugs is thought to be the chemoreceptor trigger zone located in the floor of the fourth ventricle in the medulla oblongata [42, 43]. Ablation of this area will block permanently the effects of almost all emetic agents [43], which have been shown by Borison and coworkers to accelerate unit activity in the chemoreceptor trigger zone [43, 44]. The intraventricular (fourth ventricle) injection of apomorphine induces vomiting, which is blocked by the injection of low doses of dopamine blockers into the area postrema. These experiments further suggest that the chemoreceptor trigger zone is the probable site of drug induced emesis. The ability of drugs to induce emesis in this model generally reflects their ability to activate dopamine receptors in the area postrema.

Thermoregulatory behaviour

In the last decade data have accumulated which suggest that stimulation of central dopamine receptors cause thermoregulatory changes in several species [45, 46]. The systemic administration of dopamine agonist induces hypothermia in rats and mice whilst in the rabbit, apomorphine causes a rise in core body temperature [47].

285

The hypothermic effect in rodents and the hyperthermic effect in rabbits can be blocked by dopamine receptor blocking agents but not by alpha-adrenergic blocking drugs [48]. Pimozide, a known dopamine blocker, will block apomorphine induced changes either when given systemically or injected bilaterally into the hypothalamus [48]. The location of dopamine receptors postulated to be involved in this response are those in the preoptic anterior hypothalamic region, an area considered the site for body temperature control. Apomorphine injected directly into this area induces hypothermia in a dose related manner as does the intrahypothalamic injection of dopamine [49]. Cox [47] has suggested that endogenous dopamine has a physiological role in thermoregulation and acts to lower the set-point for temperature in the hypothalamus, but thermoregulatory responses can be obtained by the direct injection of apomorphine into other brain areas, including the caudate nucleus and the nucleus accumbens [50]. Furthermore, cholinergic and serotonergic mechanisms also appear to be involved in thermoregulation [50, 51] which is complex and probably involves multiple brain pathways and mechanisms and so is of little value in screening new agents for anti-parkinsonian efficacy.

Dopamine depletion

A variety of pharmacological agents have been used to investigate dopaminergic mechanisms. Reserpine, a rauwolfia alkaloid, is such an agent and has been used as a model of parkinsonism. The administration of this drug produces effects thought to be mediated by the extrapyramidal system, both in animals and man [52], and it causes a syndrome characterised by increase in muscle tone, lack of spontaneous movements, hunchback posture, and ptosis [53]. These changes were initially designated as reserpine induced catalepsy because of its similarity to the psychiatric syndrome, or as reserpine induced parkinsonism because of the drug induced rigidity and akinesia. A dose of 5 mg/kg will produce maximal changes seen 24 hours after its administration. Similar behavioural effects can be seen with other reserpine like drugs such as tetrabenazine, a synthetic benzoquinolizine, which depletes amines more centrally than peripherally. Patients taking reserpine for psychiatric conditions and for blood pressure control often develop a form of drug induced parkinsonism which is indistinguishable from idiopathic Parkinson's disease [54].

Reserpine depletes dopamine in the striatum and also in other dopamine containing regions of the brain, because it blocks the re-uptake of amines into the storage granules in pre-synaptic neurones [55]. The findings of dopamine depletion led to the suggestion that the extrapyramidal syndrome induced by reserpine in man and other animals is secondary to a dopamine deficiency in the striatum [56], but reserpine also decreases the levels of adrenaline and serotonin in the brain. But much data exist which suggest that reserpine causes its motor symptoms through dopaminergic mechanisms in the striatum and, in most studies, there is a good temporal correlation between the motor disorders induced and the degree of deficiency of dopamine in the basal ganglia. L-dopa, but not serotonin precursors, will readily reverse the reserpine induced syndrome in both animals and man [56]. Other dopaminergic agonists, such as apomorphine and amphetamine, are also effective in reversing the reserpine syndrome.

Another drug which causes dopamine depletion is alpha-methyl-para-tyrosine, which acts by inhibiting tyrosine hydroxylase, the rate limiting enzyme in the synthesis of dopamine [57]. Like reserpine the administration of this agent in animals decreases motor activity and it causes a worsening of symptoms [58] in parkinsonian patients. In animals, a dose of 200 mg/kg given two hours before sacrifice will produce significant depletion of dopamine. Levodopa and apomorphine will reverse this syndrome but the action of amphetamine is blocked by alpha-methyl-para-tyrosine. Amphetamine releases dopamine from central, unbound, newly formed dopamine stores sensitive to alpha-methyl-para-tyrosine administration but insensitive to dopamine bound stores that are affected by reserpine administration.

Besides employing these agents to test drugs for dopamine activity, depleting agents such as reserpine and alpha-methyl-para-tyrosine, either alone or in combination, are also useful in determining whether dopaminergic drugs act through postsynaptic or presynaptic mechanisms. If a drug activates dopamine receptors when administered to animals pretreated with both reserpine and alpha-methyl-para-tyrosine, it is assumed that the agent is acting directly on postsynaptic receptors.

6-Hydroxydopamine Rotational Model

Evidence for the development of supersensitivity after degeneration of presynaptic dopamine nerve terminals was demonstrated by Ungerstedt with the 6-hydroxydopamine rotational model [59]. In this model, this agent is injected locally into the ascending bundle of dopaminergic axons in the mesencephalon. 6-hydroxydopamine is a chemical analogue of catecholaminergic transmitters and causes selective destruction of dopaminergic and noradrenergic nerve fibres [60] and will cause relative depletion of dopamine and noradrenaline [59]. 6-hydroxydopamine is dissolved in 0.9 per cent saline containing ascorbic acid as an antioxidant (1 ng/ml), the dose used being usually 5-8 μg in 2 μl of solution. Animals with unilateral injection of 6-hydroxydopamine into the substantia nigra develop a typical motor asymmetry with deviation in posture and movement towards the side of the lesion [59]. Behavioural studies of drugs in this model reveal that the systemic injection of apomorphine, a direct acting agonist, causes strong rotational behaviour toward the intact side (contralateral turning) whereas amphetamine, a dopamine releasing agent, causes rotational behaviour toward the lesioned side (ipsilateral turning). Apomorphine shows a 2 to 10 fold increase in motor response in denervated animals as compared to normal animals [61] and, at low doses, will produce locomotion and stereotypy in rats treated with 6-hydroxydopamine intraventricularly as neonates, but not in untreated animals [62]. Levodopa also induces significantly greater locomotion and stereotypy in rats treated with 6-hydroxy-dopamine [61].

These results have been interpreted to indicate that dopamine receptor super-sensitivity has developed in dopamine denervated areas as a consequence of terminal degeneration [59]. Electrophysiological studies of iontophoretically applied dopamine reveal a marked increase in the activity of denervated neurones [61]. However, biochemical studies of andenyl cyclase activity and ^{3}H haloperidol binding in the striatum after 6-hydroxydopamine lesions reveal little or no change [62]. This model is not only important in providing a sensitive behavioural test of dopaminergic activity but also provides other means of separating direct and indirect dopamine agonists based on the direction of the rotational behaviour.

Chronic Agonist Treatment

The long term administration of dopamine agonist causes an enhancement of loco-motion and stereotypy. This behavioural supersensitivity after chronic adminis-tration has been observed after various dopamine agonists including d-amphetamine, cocaine, levodopa, and bromocriptine [63]. In these experiments, the chronic administration of agonists render animals hypersensitive to subsequent challenge with apomorphine and amphetamine, an increased sensitivity which usually lasts several weeks after cessation of treatment. In this model, doses of agonists that would not induce fully developed behaviour before chronic treatment would induce the full syndrome after chronic exposure. In order to elicit this response, animals are usually challenged with doses subthreshold for stereotypy. A decrease in the latency period between the injection of the agonist and the onset of stereotypy is also seen. The chronic administration of apomorphine, the drug most frequently used as the pre-test and post-test agent itself, does not appear to produce be-havioural supersensitivity, although its inability to do so may be related to its short duration of action [64].

These experiments suggest that chronic striatal dopaminergic stimulation with dopamine agonists induces dopamine receptor site hypersensitivity. Klawans and coworkers [65] have referred to this phenomenon as "agonist induced hypersensi-tivity". The chronic administration of dopamine agonists in man results in various dyskinetic movement disorders and psychosis. Amphetamine after high dose chronic treatment is well known to produce these behavioural effects [66]. Chronic levodopa treatment in parkinsonism results in a high incidence of dyskinesias and psychiatric side effects that are directly related to the dose and duration of therapy.

It has been suggested that the mechanisms of these drug-induced involuntary movements and mental changes are related to central dopaminergic hypersensi-tivity [67]. These behavioural models have been proposed as a predictor of long-term side effects of dopamine agonists, and the validity of such a concept can be further tested in the future with the use of newer dopaminergic agents, both in animal studies and in the clinical setting.

288

Ergot derivatives

The ergot alkaloids originate in a fungus, *"claviceps purpurea"*, and can be separated into three groups; the ergotamines, ergotoxines, and ergoprovines. Chemically the structure common to all ergot drugs is lysergic acid and most of these agents are amines of this compound. Drugs belonging to this class have been used therapeutically in a variety of disorders [68]. In this section the effects of pergolide mesylate (Figure 1) and other ergolines in behavioural models will be presented, and the relevance of these results to the treatment of parkinsonism will be discussed.

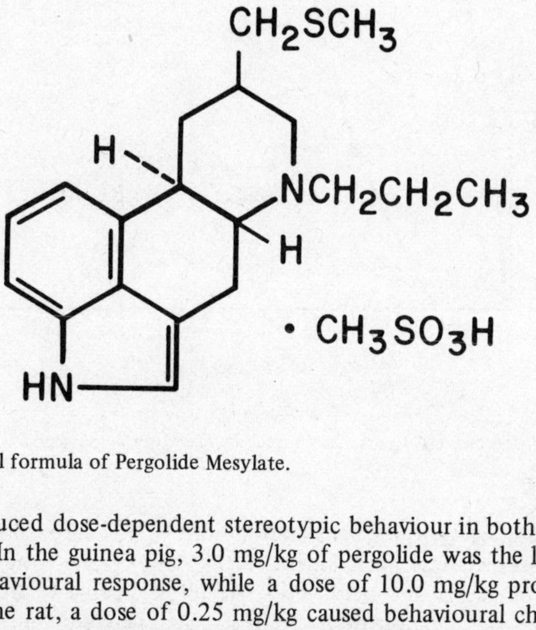

Figure 1 Structural formula of Pergolide Mesylate.

Pergolide induced dose-dependent stereotypic behaviour in both guinea pigs and rats (Figure 2). In the guinea pig, 3.0 mg/kg of pergolide was the lowest dose able to induce a behavioural response, while a dose of 10.0 mg/kg produces maximal stereotypy. In the rat, a dose of 0.25 mg/kg caused behavioural changes and a full stereotypic response could be observed with 1.5 mg/kg. The latency to the onset of stereotypic behaviour in both species was 2 to 5 minutes, and its duration is shown in Figure 3. A dose of 10.0 mg/kg in the guinea pig caused behavioural activation which lasted approximately 5 hours, whilst duration of stereotypy in the rat (1.0 mg/kg) was approximately 28 hours. These results suggest that pergolide causes a prolonged stimulation of dopamine receptors, most likely in the striatum and the nucleus accumbens. Bromocriptine and lergotrile are the best studied of the ergoline compounds evaluated for potential antiparkinson efficacy. Bromocriptine also induces stereotypy in rats, an effect that has a 1 to 2 hour latency to onset and is of low intensity, and lasts for 4 to 5 hours [69]. Lergotrile also produces low level stereotypy of short duration after a long latency. Lisuride, another ergoline, will also cause stereotypy but is not as potent as apomorphine [70].

289

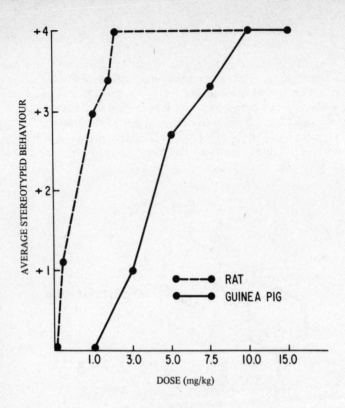

Figure 2 Dose response curve for pergolide induced stereotypic behaviour in the guinea pig and rat.

Pergolide-induced stereotypic behaviour in both guinea pigs and rats was blocked in a dose-dependent manner by haloperidol (0.05 mg/kg to 0.5 mg/kg) but was not effected by clozapine pretreatment (up to 40 mg/kg, Table I). In the rat approximately 4 hours after haloperidol pretreatment, pergolide-induced stereotypy began, presumably due to related loss of haloperidol effect.

Table II shows the effect of pretreatment with reserpine, alpha-methyl-para-tyrosine, and reserpine plus alpha-methyl-para-tyrosine on pergolide-induced stereotypy. In the guinea pig behavioural effects of low dose pergolide (2.5 mg/kg) were blocked by all of the pretreatments, but a dose of 15 mg/kg induced stereotypic gnawing without an increase in locomotion in all pretreated animals. In the rat these pretreatments, alone or in combination, were without effect on pergolide induced stereotypy and pergolide reversed the behavioural changes (catalepsy, hypo-mobility, ptosis, and hunch back) induced by these drugs.

The behavioural effects of other ergolines tested were also blocked by haloperidol pretreatment, but differential effects were seen with the pretreatment of depleting agents. Reserpine attenuates the behavioural effects of bromocriptine and

290

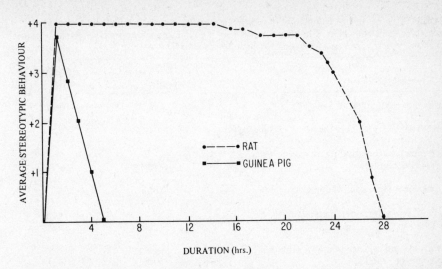

Figure 3 Duration of stereotypic behaviour by pergolide in the guinea pig (1.0 mg/kg) and in the rat (1.0 mg/kg).

TABLE I Effect of haloperidol and clozapine pretreatment on pergolide induced stereotypic behaviour in guinea pigs and rats. Pretreatment given 60 minutes before pergolide injection. Percent of animals displaying stereotypy is shown. (N = 10 for each dose)

| | PERCENT DISPLAYING STEREOTYPY | |
PRETREATMENT	Guinea Pig	Rat
Saline	100%	100%
Haloperidol (mg/kg)		
0.01	100%	100%
0.05	40%	50%
0.10	20%	20%
0.25	0%	0%
0.50	0%	0%
Clozapine (mg/kg)		
10.0	100%	100%
20.0	100%	100%
40.0	100%	100%

lergotrile but unexpectedly the actions of lisuride were potentiated [71, 72]. Alpha-methyl-para-tyrosine pretreatment significantly reduces the stereotypy induced by bromocriptine and increases the stereotypy caused by lergotrile. The inhibition of behavioural effects by depletor agents suggest that presynaptic mechanisms are in part involved in the drug's actions.

291

TABLE II Effect of pretreatment with reserpine (5 mg/kg, 24 hours prior) and α-methyl-para-tyrosine (200 mg/kg, 2 hours prior), on pergolide induced stereotypic behaviour in guinea pigs and rats. Ten animals were used for each treatment. (NT = Not Tested)

PRETREATMENT	PERCENT DISPLAYING STEREOTYPY	
	Guinea Pig	Rat
Reserpine + Pergolide (2.5 mg/kg)	0%	100%
α-methyl-para-tyrosine + Pergolide (2.5 mg/kg)	0%	100%
Reserpine and α-methyl-para-tyrosine + per-golide (2.5 mg/kg)	0%	100%
Reserpine + Pergolide (15 mg/kg)	100%	NT
α-methyl-para-tyrosine + pergolide (15 mg/kg)	100%	NT
Reserpine and α-methyl-para-tyrosine + pergolide (15 mg/kg)	100%	NT

TABLE III Effects of pergolide, amphetamine, apomorphine and levodopa, on turning behaviour in rats with 6-hydroxydopamine lesions of the substantia nigra. Ten animals were used for each treatment.

Treatment	Latency of Turning	Duration of Turning	Direction	Mean Number of Turns per Minute
Saline	0	0	None	0
Pergolide 1 mg/kg	1.0 Min	> 24 hrs.	Contralateral	17.7 ± 2.1
d-Amphetamine 4 mg/kg	3.0 Min	3,0 hrs.	Ipsilateral	8.0 ± 2.2
Apomorphine 0.5 mg/kg	1.0 Min	1.0 hrs.	Contralateral	11.1 ± 3.2
Levodopa 100 mg/kg	2.0 Min	3.1 hrs	Contralateral	6.1 ± 2.6

The effect of pergolide and known dopamine agonists on turning behaviour in substantia nigra lesioned in rats is illustrated in Table III. Pergolide (1.0 mg/kg) caused contralateral turning after 1.0 minute latency which lasted longer than 24 hours with approximately 18 turns per minute. Some animals died before 24 hours while turning, apparently from exhaustion. Neither reserpine, nor alpha-methyl-para-tyrosine, nor these drugs in combination, was able to block pergolide induced turning behaviour. Apomorphine (0.5 mg/kg) and levodopa (100 mg/kg) also induced contralateral turning after a latency of several minutes, which lasted 1.0 hours and

3.0 hours respectively. Apomorphine induced an average of 11.0 turns per minute and levodopa an average of 6.0 turns per minute. Amphetamine (4.0 mg/kg) induced ipsilateral turning after 3.0 minute latency which lasted 3.1 hours with 8.0 turns per minute. Bromocriptine mimics the action of apomorphine and causes turning behaviour towards innerved side [71].

TABLE IV Effect of pretreatment of saline and haloperidol (0.1 mg/kg) on apomorphine 6 mg and pergolide 6 mg induced emesis in dogs. Percent of animals displaying emesis is shown. Ten animals were used for each treatment.

Pretreatment	Apomorphine	Pergolide
Saline	100%	100%
Haloperidol	0%	0%

The effect of pergolide and apomorphine on the induction of emesis in dogs is shown in Table IV. Both drugs at a dose of 1.2 mg/kg induced vomiting in all dogs tested after a latency of 8 to 10 minutes, and there was no obvious difference in the behaviour caused by the two drugs. Pretreatment with haloperidol at a dose of 0.1 mg/kg blocked the emesis induced by both drugs. While lisuride causes vomiting in dogs [73], the action of other ergoline compounds on emesis has not been well studied. Clinically, vomiting due to bromocriptine is infrequent [71], while with levodopa initially in the course of treatment vomiting is often a major problem.

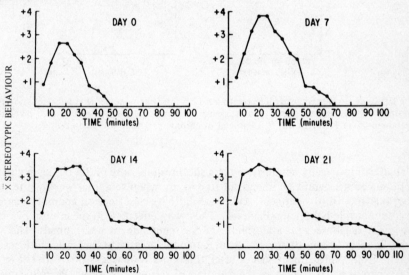

Figure 4 Effect of chronic pergolide treatment (3.5 mg/kg) on stereotypic behaviour to apomorphine (0.2 mg/kg). Stereotypic response to apomorphine is shown before pergolide treatment (Day 0) and at Day 7, 14, 21 and 28 of chronic pergolide administration.

293

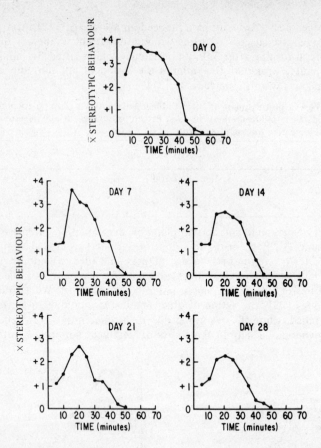

Figure 5 Effect of chronic pergolide treatment (7.5 mg/kg) on stereotypic behaviour to apomorphine (0.2 mg/kg). Stereotypic response to apomorphine is shown before pergolide treatment (Day 0) and at Day 7, 14 and 21 of chronic pergolide administration.

Pergolide chronically administered at a subthreshold dose of 3.5 mg/kg in guinea pigs produced no significant change in stereotypy when scored at weekly intervals during one month of treatment. This dose did have an effect on apomorphine induced stereotypic behaviour (Figure 4). There was a decrease in the intensity of the behavioural response to apomorphine in the pergolide treated animals. This increased in proportion to the length of pergolide treatment and was statistically different from pretreatment values after three and four weeks of treatment (p < 0.01). There was no change in the duration of response however. Pergolide given chronically at a dose of 7.5 mg/kg caused a marked enhancement of the stereotypic response to apomorphine (Figure 5). A significant increase in stereotypy was evident following one week of pergolide treatment, with both the intensity and the duration of stereotypy being enhanced (p < 0.01). The behavioural response to apomorphine was further increased when tested at two and three weeks after pergolide treatment with the duration of response being further prolonged, so that after 21 days of treatment the duration had more than doubled changing from 50 minutes to 110 minutes. Figure 6 shows the recovery of the response to apomorphine for the weeks following the discontinuation of pergolide treatment (7.5 mg/kg). The duration of response returned to baseline by one week but the intensity of response was still increased at one and two weeks. By three weeks after cessation of pergolide

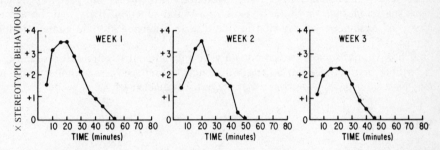

Figure 6 Time course of recovery of behavioural changes. Stereotypic response to apomorphine (0.2 mg/kg) is shown for 1, 2 and 3 weeks after cessation of chronic pergolide administration (7.5 mg/kg).

treatment the behavioural response to apomorphine had returned to normal. Bromocriptine has been the only other ergoline studied in this model and as mentioned above the chronic subthreshold treatment of bromocriptine induced behavioural supersensitivity.

The data presented here suggest that pergolide should have efficacy in the treatment of parkinsonism and also raise the possibility that it might have some advantages over the other presently available antiparkinson agents. The ability of pergolide to elicit stereotypy, reverse the behavioural effects of reserpine and α-methyl-para-tyrosine, and induce contralateral turning in unilaterally lesioned rats all suggest that pergolide acts as a direct acting dopamine agonist at striatal dopamine receptors. Since parkinsonism is due to loss of dopaminergic input into these receptors, any such agonist can be predicted to have an antiparkinson effect. These properties are shared by other direct acting dopamine agonists but not by levodopa. Studies reporting follow-up experience of 5 and 6 years with chronic levodopa therapy have documented a progressive diminution of therapeutic effect [5]. The loss of efficacy of levodopa in Parkinson's disease may depend in part upon the continued loss of neurones of the substantia nigra, raising the possibility that a direct acting dopamine agonist such as pergolide, which might not require the presence of presynaptic dopaminergic neurones for its activity, may offer a therapeutic advantage over levodopa in patients demonstrating loss of drug effect. The extremely long duration of action of pergolide noted in the current studies might also be of benefit if a similar prolonged period of action occurs in man. Patients with large fluctuations in response temporarily related to levodopa administration might be better controlled by an agent with a longer duration of effect.

Long term levodopa therapy also is associated with dose limiting side effects such as dyskinesias and psychiatric problems [5]. It has been shown that the chronic administration of known dopaminergic agents in subthreshold doses causes behaviour subsequent to supersensitivity, which is thought to be due to agonist induced receptor site hypersensitivity. Since the chronic administration of each of these agents in humans causes both involuntary movements and psychosis, it has been suggested that the induction of behavioural supersensitivity may be a predictor of dyskinetic or psychiatric side effects following chronic administration in man [65].

If behavioural supersensitisation is a valid predictor of psychomotor toxicity, it is possible that pergolide at a certain dose may not induce these complications and may have some advantages over other presently available agents.

References

1   Barbeau A. *Canad Ass J 1962;87:*802
2   Hornykiewiez O. *Pharm Rev 1966;18:*925
3   Klawans HL. *The Pharmacology of Extrapyramidal Movement Disorders 1973.* Basle, S Karger
4   Fahn S, Calne DB. *Neurology 1978;28:*5
5   Sweet RD, McDowell FH. *Ann Intern Med 1978;83:*456
6   Ernst AM. *Psychopharm 1967;10:*316
7   Amsler C. *Arch Exptl Path Pharmakol 1923;97:*1
8   Randrup A, Munkvad I. *Psychopharm 1967;11:*300
9   Fog R. *Psychopharm 1969;14:*299
10   Janssen PAJ, Niemegeers CJC, Jangeneau AHM. *Arzneim Forsch 1960;10:*1003
11   Costall B, Naylor RF. *Eur J Pharmacol 1973;24:*8
12   Klawans HL, Margolin D. *Arch Psychiat 1975;32:*725
13   Koller WC, Weiner WJ, Klawans HL, Nausieda PA. *1980,* In press
14   Morois CG, Kaufman GI. *Physiol Behav 1976;16:*493
15   Batting K. *Ann NY Acad Sci 1969;159:*880
16   Blaschko H, Chrinsiel TC. *J Physiol 1960;151:*272
17   Everett GM, Niegard RG. In *Proc first Intern Pharmacol Meeting 1960;*85. Oxford, Pergamon Press
18   Smith CB. *J Pharmacol 1963;142:*343
19   Sourkes TC. *Rev Canad Biol 1961;20:*186
20   Johnson AM, Loew DM, Vigouret S. *Brit J Pharmac 1978;56:*59
21   Cools AR, Rossum JM. *Arch Int Pharmacol Ther 1970;210:*163
22   Cools AR, Janssen HJ, Boudin HAJ, Rossum JM. In *Wenner-Gren Series volume 5 1975;*73. Oxford, Pergamon Press
23   Anden NS, Robeinstein H, Fuxe K, Hokfelt T. *J Pharm Pharmacol 1967;19:*629
24   Kebain JW, Petzold GE, Greengard P. *Proc Nat Acad Sci 1972;69:*2145
25   May JM, Gajda L. *Europ J Pharm 1971;334:*208
26   Kelly PH, Miller RJ, Nemeger J. *Europ J Pharm 1976;35:*85
27   Ernst AM, Smelik P. *Experientia 1966; 22:* 837
28   Fog RL, Randrup A, Pakkenberg H. *Psychopharm 1967;11:*179
29   Quinton R, Halliwell G. *Nature 1963;202:*178

30   Randrup CH, Munkvard I. *Neuropsychpharm 1968;1:*18
31   Pijnenberg AAJ, Honig, WMM, Van Rossum JM. *Brain Res 1973;59:*286
32   Pijnenberg AAJ, Honig WMM, Van Rossum JM. *Psychopharm 1975;41:*87
33   Pijnenberg AAJ, Honig WMM, Van Rossum JM. *Psychopharm 1975;45:*65
34   Ljungberg T, Ungerstedt U. *Europ J Pharm 1977;46:*147
35   Wang SC. In Root WS, Hofmann FG, eds. *Physiological Pharmacology volume 2 1965;* 255. Oxford, Pergamon Press
36   Borison HL, Wang SC. *Proc Soc Exp Biol 1951;76:*335
37   Rotsasen E, Wallach M, Angrist B, Gershown S. *Psychopharm 1977;26:*185
38   Janssen PAJ, Niemegeers CJC. *Drug Res 1968;18:*261
39   Cole DR, Duffy DF. *NY State J Med 1974;74:*1558
40   Lee HK, Chai CY, Chang PM, Wang SC. *Neuropharm 1978;18:*341
41   Lee HK, Chang PM, Wang SC. *Eur J Pharm 1979;49:*291
42   Share NN, Chai CY, Wang SC. *J Pharmacol Exp Ther 1965;147:*416
43   Borison HL, Wang SC. *Pharm Rev 1953;5:*193
44   Borison HL. *Life Sci 1974;14:*1807
45   Cox B. In Lomax D, Schonbaum B, eds. *Body temperature, drugs effects and thera-peutic implications 1979;* New York, Eickey, In press
46   Cox B, Lee TF. *Neuropharm 1979;18:*537
47   Hill HF, Horita A. *J Pharm Pharmac 1971;23:*715
48   Cox B, Kerwin R, Lee TF. *J Physiol 1978;282:*471
49   Kennedy MS, Burke TF. *Neuropharm 1974;13:*119
50   Glick SD, Marannico. *Brit J Pharmac 1974;51:*353
51   Grabowska M, Anden NE. *J Neural Trans 1976;38:*1
52   Bein JH. *Pharm Rev 1956;8:*435
53   Carlsson A. In Heffer A, ed. *Handbuch der experimentatlen pharmakologie 1966;* 578 Berlin, Springer Verlag
54   De N. *Trans Med College Reunion 1945;7:*27
55   Berti F, Shore PA. *Biochem Pharmacol 1967;16:*2271
56   Roos Be Steg G. *Life Sci 1964;37:*351
57   Spector S, Sjoerdema A, Udenfriend S. *J Pharm Exp Ther. 1965;147:*86
58   Birkmayer W. *J Neuro Relat 1969;9:*297
59   Ungerstedt U. *Acta Physiol Scand 1971;367:*69
60   Ungerstedt U. *Acta Physiol Scand 1971;367:*49
61   Breeze GR, Traylor TA. *J Pharm Exp Ther 1970;174:*413
62   Greese I, Iversen SD. *Brain Res 1973;55:*369
63   Klawans HL, Crossett P, Dana N. *Adv Neurol 1975;91:*105
64   Flemembaun A. *Psychopharm 1979;62:*175
65   Klawans HL, Goetz C, Nausieda PA, Weiner WJ. *Ann Neurol 1977;2:*125
66   Ellinwood FH. *J Nerv Ment Res 1967;144:*273
67   Nausieda PA, Weiner WJ, Kanapa DJ, Klawans HL. *Neurology 1978;28:*1183
68   Muller EE, Panerue FE, Cocchi D, Manbegazza P. *Life Sci 1979;21:*1545
69   Silbengild EK, Pfeiffer RF. *J Neurochem 1977;28:*1323
70   Horowski R, Wachtel H. *Eur J Pharm 1976;369:*375
71   Parkes J. *New Engl J Med 1979;301:*873
72   Podvalova I, Alabas S. *Act New Sup 1970;12:*81
73   Corrodi H, Fuxe K, Hofelt T, Lidbrink P, Ungerstedt U. *J Pharm Pharmacol 1973;25:* 409

297

PART VI
OTHER DRUGS

Chapter 37

DIPROBUTINE

Luke Harris

Diprobutine is a simple molecule—trimethylamine HC1—which has been extensively investigated in animals [1–6] as a potential antiparkinsonian agent by tests chiefly directed towards the detection of activity in the noradrenergic, dopaminergic, anticholinergic and serotoninergic systems. Early clinical studies [7] have also been carried out in France, Canada, Belgium and the Netherlands.

Effects on the Noradrenergic System

The procedures used included the effects of phenoxybenzamine, yohimbine, propranolol and alpha-methyltyrosine on diprobutine-induced stereotypy and anti-reserpinic activity and direct biochemical measurements in rat brain. Considerable activity was seen in the noradrenergic system, in particular diprobutine caused a fall in cerebral noradrenaline especially at the hypothalamic MOPEG sulphate and (at high dosage) an increased rate of utilisation of noradrenaline after blockade of synthesis with alpha-methyltyrosine.

Effects on the Dopaminergic System

The tests employed included evaluation of effects of diprobutine on neuroleptic-induced catatonia and catalepsy, apomorphine-induced and amphetamine-induced stereotypy, rotary movements after unilateral destruction of the nigrostriatal bundle, the effects of dopamine synthesis inhibition or receptor blockade on the anti-reserpine activity of diprobutine and on stereotypy induced by diprobutine. In addition, biochemical measurements have been made on rat brain including spiroperidol displacement studies and ^3H-tyrosine studies. The results of these studies indicated that diprobutine had only minor effects in the dopaminergic system, mainly by increasing the rate of dopamine turnover; in particular, it does not appear to have any effect on dopamine synthesis nor at the level of the dopaminergic receptors.

Effects on the Anticholinergic System

The models utilised included isolated rat duodenum, physostigmine mortality, tremorine test, nicotine-induced crises and the effect of atropine on diprobutine-induced stereotypy. The results suggested an absence of peripheral anticholinergic activity with conflicting evidence over the possibility of central anticholinergic activity.

Effects on Serotoninergic System

The tests included the effect of diprobutine on yohimbine toxicity and in the tremorine test and the effect of parachlorophenylalanine on diprobutine-induced trembling. The results were conflicting, but direct biochemical measurement on the rat brain demonstrated a steady fall in cerebral and hypothalamic 5 HT levels suggesting that the drug has antiserotoninergic activity.

Mechanism of Action

In many of these experiments, comparisons were made with amantadine, L-dopa and classical antidepressants and it was found that diprobutine differed from all of these in several important respects suggesting that it may have a unique mechanism of action. Studies are still in progress to try to elucidate this fully and at the present time it is only possible to speculate that its major mode of activity is probably on the noradrenergic system of the nigrostriatal tract in the presence of an intact hypothalamus. Some evidence to support this hypothesis has been obtained in man; viz. diprobutine seems to oppose probenicid induced rise in cerebrospinal fluid HVA levels, it significantly increases urinary conjugated HVA and it seems to be able to increase the urinary levels of MOPEG sulphate.

Pharmacokinetics

Radiocarbon labelled studies in the rat showed an elimination half life of 7.5 hours with 93 per cent elimination over three days and an appreciable faecal elimination indicating biliary excretion. There was a high cerebral/serum ratio and no selective sites of fixation in brain. Oral absorption indicated 100 per cent bioavailability. There was no protein binding and 90–95 per cent of serum activity was accounted for by unchanged drug, the remainder being two so far unidentified metabolites. Recent non-radioactive studies in normal human volunteers indicate a half life in man of 36–40 hours.

Animal Toxicology

Acute single dose (LD 50) studies have been conducted in rats and mice. *Repeated dose studies* of six weeks, three months and six months duration have been carried out in rats and a 12 month study has been performed in dogs. *In none of these studies was there any target organ damage or biochemical disturbance,* even in doses as high as 50 mg/kg, which is 50 times the anticipated human dose. Extensive *reproduction studies* in rats, mice and rabbits demonstrated that the drug is *not teratogenic, not embryotoxic, does not affect fertility and has no peri- or post- natal effects.*

Clinical Experience

At the time of writing data are available from approximately 300 patients treated on an open basis by 20 different neurologists for varying periods of time, at different rates of incrementation of dosage. Although preliminary, these Phase II data enable one to discern certain possible patterns. Thus, the drug appeared to be effective in about 50 per cent of cases at a dosage of 30–45 mg daily and the incidence of side effects seemed to be related to the rate of increase of dosage. The drug seemed to be even more effective against tremor (75 per cent) than against other symptoms (50 per cent) and to be a valuable addition to L-dopa in (a) control of fluctuations, (b) potentiation without developing dyskinesia and (c) increasing duration of action of doses of L-dopa.

Future development

Diprobutine now appears to merit further investigation in the form of well designed carefully controlled clinical trials to determine the optimum regimen in terms of both dose and frequency of administration and to evaluate its position in the treatment of the different problems within subdivisions of the parkinsonian population.

References

1   Broll M, Eymard P, Ferrandes B, Werbenec JP. *J Pharmacol 1977; 8:*524
2   Broll M, Eymard P, Lacolle JY, Werbenec JP. *J Pharmacol 1978; 9:*121
3   Ferrandes B, Bachy A, Lacolle JY, Simiand JM, Eymard P. In *Congrès de Pharmacologie de Paris 1978*
4   Ferrandes B, Bachy A, Lacolle JY, Simiand JM, Eymard P. In *Congrès International de Pharmacologie de Paris 1978*
5   Pigerol C, Vernieres JC, Broll M, Eymard P, Werbenec JP. *Europ J Med Chem 1977; 12:*351
6   Simiand J, Ferrandes B, Eymard P. *Etude pharmacocinetique de la Diprobutine, un antiparkinsonien potential chez l'animal et chez l'homme.* Association Francaise des pharmacologistes, UER des Sciences Pharmaceutiques Chatenay-Malabry
7   Data on file at Sanofi Pharma International, Paris

Chapter 38

BACLOFEN

A J Lees and Gerald M Stern

Introduction

Beta-parachlorophenyl gamma-aminobutyric acid (baclofen) is a lipophilic GABA (gamma-aminobutyric acid) analogue (see Figure 1) which has been widely used in the treatment of spasticity. It has been generally regarded as a GABAminergic agonist with depressant effects on the firing of neurones in many areas of the central nervous system. However, many of its pharmacological effects may be due more to its structural resemblance to the endogenous trace amine phenylethylamine. For example, it inhibits the firing of dopaminergic nigral neurones [1] and increases cerebral dopamine levels with reduction of striatal dopamine turnover [2, 3]. Furthermore it also behaves like a dopaminergic antagonist in behavioural test systems by potentiating neuroleptic-induced catalepsy [4] and restoring d-amphetamine-induced loss of discriminative behaviour in rats [5]. Baclofen also has actions on 5-hydroxytryptamine (5-HT) turnover in the central nervous system [6] and increases 5-HT levels in the corpus striatum possibly through the presence of dopamine receptors on 5-HT terminals [7]. Effects on GABA systems do occur and baclofen has been shown to be a weak GABA receptor ligand [8] and d-baclofen releases GABA from brain slices [9]. It also inhibits reflex activity [10] and possesses analgesic effects [11].

On the assumption that baclofen might act as a central GABA agonist it has been used to treat the chorea of Huntington's disease [12, 13], neuroleptic-induced tardive dyskinesia [14, 15] and schizophrenia [16, 17] with generally disappointing results and has been found to aggravate phenothiazine-induced parkinsonism [18]. Following an anecdotal observation in a patient with spastic paraparesis and levodopa treated Parkinson's disease, who developed severe visual hallucinations, confusion and choreiform movements on abrupt withdrawal of a 90 mg daily dose of baclofen [19, 20] the effects of baclofen on levodopa treated Parkinsonians were studied [21].

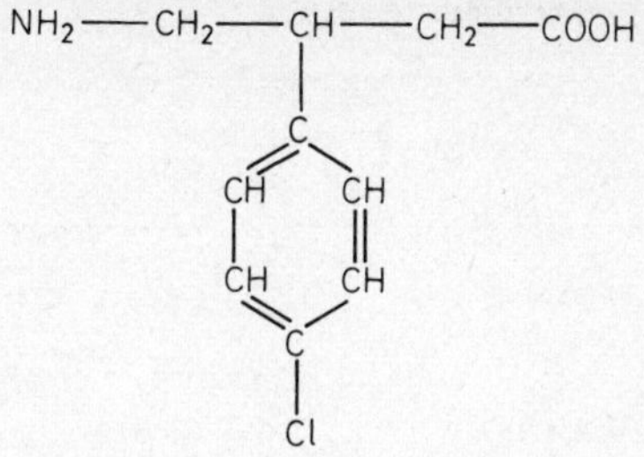

NH$_2$——CH$_2$——CH——CH$_2$——COOH

Figure 1 Structural formula of Baclofen.

Patients and methods

Twelve patients with idiopathic Parkinson's disease (7 male, 5 female, mean age 66 years, mean duration of disease 12 years and mean disease severity Grade 3 on the Hoehn and Yahr classification) agreed to take part in a controlled trial. All the patients were taking levodopa in combination with a peripheral dopa decarboxylase inhibitor (mean dose 600 mg/day) and had received levodopa for a mean period of 6 years. Oscillations in performance (10 end of dose deterioration, 2 hypotonic akinesia) and abnormal involuntary movements (12 peak-dose chorea, 4 "off-period" dystonia) were present in all patients. Patients were assessed at intervals of 14 days by the same assessor and their disabilities recorded using a modified Columbia University Disability Scale and a 4-point scale for involuntary movements. An initial daily dose of 10 mg baclofen was increased at weekly intervals by 10 mg up to an arbitrary maximum of 90 mg daily in divided doses; the L-dopa dosage remained constant. After a minimum period of two weeks on maximum tolerated doses of baclofen and at varying intervals, indistinguishable placebo was substituted unknown to the assessor or the patient and continued for at least two weeks.

Results

Baclofen significantly aggravated functional capacity although its effect on the individual components of tremor, rigidity and bradykinesia did not reach statistical significance. The results are summarised in Table I. Only two patients reached a dose of 90 mg daily and two were unable to tolerate baclofen at all and withdrew from the trial in the run-in period. No definite effects on peak-dose chorea or oscillations in performance were observed. A reduction in the pain and severity of "off-period" dystonia was observed which was maintained in two patients for six months.

305

TABLE I Effects of baclofen on patients studied

| Clinical Features | Scores ± SD | | Significance |
	Active	Placebo	
Tremor (one component)	15 (1.5 ± 0.83)	10 (1.0 ± 0.63)	NS
Bradykinesia (five components)	160 (16.0 ± 3.44)	142 (14.2 ± 3.25)	NS
Rigidity (one component)	19 (1.9 ± 0.83)	13 (1.3 ± 0.64)	$P < 0.1$
Functional Capacity (six components)	111 (11.1 ± 1.45)	92 (9.2 ± 1.47)	$P < 0.01$

Adverse Side Effects

These were more frequent than is normally seen in the treatment of spastic disorders, possibly due to the older age of Parkinsonian patients. Visual hallucinations consisting of groups of people standing in the patients' homes occurred in two patients and in a further patient during placebo phase. Toxic confusional states (three patients), drowsiness (two patients), vomiting and nausea (two patients), headaches (two patients), giddiness (two patients) and unsteadiness (one patient) also occurred.

Discussion

Baclofen aggravated Parkinsonian disability in this study. This may have been due, however, to the high incidence of toxic side-effects rather than any specific effect on dopaminergic systems. Indeed, at present, there is no evidence to suggest that baclofen alters central dopamine metabolism in man, at least as judged by the estimation of monoamine metabolites in the lumbar sac [22].

The visual pseudohallucinations, seen in some patients during chronic levodopa therapy, closely resemble the peduncular hallucinations first described by L'Hermitte [23] and it is possible that over-stimulation of the mesocortical and mesolimbic dopamine pathways is responsible. In this context it is of interest that baclofen has been reported to have more powerful effects on mesolimbic pathways in animals [24].

Segmental dystonia is well recognised as occurring occasionally in untreated patients with post-encephalitic Parkinsonism. It is also seen together with Parkinsonian features in chronic manganese poisoning and in some familial extrapyramidal syndromes [25]. Dystonic foot and hand deformities, indistinguishable from those seen in generalised torsion dystonia, have also been rarely mentioned among the clinical features of idiopathic Parkinson's disease [26, 27]. Stereotactic thalamic surgery was claimed to improve these sustained postures permitting certain patients to walk more comfortably and regain function in their hands [28]. Duvoisin *et al* [29] have considered the dystonic 'striatal' foot to be an integral part of the Parkinsonian syndrome and noted that, whereas anti-cholinergic therapy produced modest benefit, levodopa tended to aggravate it. Long-term levodopa therapy also induces a reversible peak-dose dystonia in about 5 per cent of patients. This usually develops in the first two years of treatment and in those patients who do not experience peak-dose chorea [30]. After longer periods of levodopa treatment painful morning cramps with spasm of the feet occur in many patients. In some, this occurs in the presence of otherwise excellent symptomatic control and in the absence of a pre-levodopa history of a similar disability. In these patients it constitutes the major disability, impeding mobility and causing severe pain. The foot is held in a sustained equinovarus posture with clawing of the toes except for the great toe which is dorsiflexed thus mimicking a positive Babinski sign. The posture is aggravated by standing or walking and is usually at its most severe in the early morning before the first dose of levodopa. Increasing mobility with peak-dose chorea then supervenes, only for dystonia to recur to a milder degree towards the end of each interdose period. Other varieties of focal dystonia have also been seen with the same dyskinesia sequence including spasmodic torticollis, torsion of the trunk and arms and oromandibular dystonia [20].

It is possible as Duvoisin suggests that these dystonic disturbances merely reflect progression of the basic disease process aggravated by chronic dopaminergic stimulation. The prolonged survival now being seen in many Parkinsonians might also explain adequately the increased incidence of this disability. Their occurrence, however, in relatively mildly disabled patients with no pre-treatment history of dystonia and their disappearance in some following levodopa withdrawal favours the notion that levodopa per se may induce the disturbance. The fact that baclofen can improve "off-period" dystonia and simultaneously aggravate bradykinesia suggests that different neurotransmitter abnormalities are responsible for these two symptoms.

Summary

In a controlled trial baclofen (mean dose 45 mg daily) significantly increased disability from Parkinsonism in 12 patients with the long-term levodopa syndrome. Benefit occurred, however, in 4 patients with "off-period dystonia" and the nature of this disturbance is discussed. Adverse side-effects were common and severe and included confusional states, visual hallucinations, lethargy and vomiting.

Acknowledgement

We are grateful to Miss E Edwards for typing the manuscript.

References

1   Olpe HR, Koella WP, Wolf P, Haas HL. *Brain Res 1977; 134:*577
2   Anden N-E, Wachtel H. *Acta Pharm et Toxicol 1977; 40:*310
3   Waldmeier PC, Mâitre L. *Europ J Pharmac 1978; 47:*191
4   Davies J, Williams J. *Brit J Pharmac 1978; 62:*303
5   Ahlenius S, Carlsson A, Engel J. *J Neural Trans 1975; 36:*327
6   Waldmeier PC, Fehr B. *Europ J Pharmac 1978; 49:*177
7   Waldmeier PC, Feldtrauer JJ, Kam R, Stocklin K. *Europ J Pharmac 1979; 54:*279
8   Cross AJ, Waddington JL. *Brit J Pharm 1978; 64:*380
9   Kerwin R, Pycock C. *J Pharm Pharmac 1978; 30:*622
10   Olpe HR, Deunieville H, Baltzar V, Bencze WL, Koella WP, Wolf P, Haas HL. *Europ J Pharmac 1978; 52:*133
11   Wilson PR, Yaksh TL. *Europ J Pharmac 1978; 51:*323
12   Anden N-E, Dalén P, Johansson B. *Lancet 1973; ii:*93
13   Barbeau A. *Lancet 1973; ii:*1499
14   Gerlach J, Rye T, Kristijansen P. *Psychopharmacology 1978; 56:*145
15   Nair NP, Vassa R, Ruiz-Navarro J, Schwartz G. *Am J Psych 1978; 135:*1562
16   Fredericksen PK. *Lancet 1975; i:*702
17   Bigelow LB, Nasrallah H, Carman J, Gillin JC, Wyatt RJ. *Am J Psych 1977; 134:*318
18   Gerlach J. *Am J Psych 1977; 134:*781
19   Lees AJ, Clarke CRA, Harrison MJ. *Lancet 1977; i:*858
20   Lees AJ, Shaw KM, Stern GM. *Lancet 1977; ii:*1034
21   Lees AJ, Shaw KM, Stern GM. *J Neurol Neurosurg Psych 1978; 41:*707
22   Walinder J, Wallin L, Carlsson A. *New Engl J Med 1977; 296:*452
23   L'Hermitte MJ. *Rev Neurol 1922; 29:*1359
24   Fuxe K, Hökfelt T, Ljüngdahl A, Agnati L, Johanssen O, Perez de la Mora L. *Med Biol 1975; 53:*177
25   Allen N, Knopp W. In Eldridge RF, ed. *Advances in Neurology, volume 14, 1975;* 201
26   Charcot JM. In *Lectures on diseases of the nervous system 1877;* 141. London: New Sydenham Society
27   Gowers WR. In *A manual of the diseases of the nervous system 1893;* 644
28   Gortvai P. *J Neurol Neurosurg Psych 1963; 26:*33
29   Duvoisin RC, Yahr MD, Lieberman J, Antunes J-L, Rhee S. *Trans Am Neurol Ass 1972; 97:*267
30   Parkes JD, Bédard P, Marsden CD. *Lancet 1976; i:*155

Chapter 39

GABA-MIMETICS, PARKINSON'S DISEASE AND OTHER MOVEMENT DISORDERS

M P Sheehy, M Schachter, J D Parkes and C D Marsden

The characteristic pathology of Parkinson's disease centres on death of substantia nigra cells and degeneration of the nigro-striatal dopaminergic pathway. For the last decade, replacement of lost dopamine has been the basis of standard treatment of Parkinson's disease. The response to L-dopa therapy, however, has been variable; early benefit may be lost, fluctuations in response may appear and pathology continues to progress.

In the search for a more successful therapy for Parkinson's disease, replacement of other neuro-transmitters has been considered. Gamma-aminobutyric acid (GABA), an inhibitory neurotransmitter, and its synthesising enzyme—L glutamic acid decarboxylase (GAD)—are widely distributed throughout the central nervous system, from retina and cortex to spinal cord. Both are found, however, in particularly high concentrations in the basal ganglia, particularly the striatum, globus pallidus and substantia nigra [1]. GABA's action as an inhibitory neurotransmitter is related to its capacity to increase post-synaptic membrane permeability to Cl^-, leading to hyperpolarisation [2]. GABA is inactivated by diffusion and by carrier-mediated cellular uptake into neuronal cell bodies, into nerve terminals and into glial cells [3].

GABA-ergic neurones in the basal ganglia appear to be of two types: short GABA interneurones confined to the striatum [4] and longer GABA neurones projecting from the striatum to the globus pallidus and to the substantia nigra, and possibly also from the globus pallidus to the substantia nigra [5]. Some of these descending GABA-ergic fibres terminate in the region of the zona compacta of the substantia nigra which contains the cell bodies of dopaminergic neurones [6]. There is a pharmacological interaction between the strio-nigral descending GABA pathways and the ascending dopaminergic nigro-striatal system [7]. In addition, strio-nigral and strio-pallidal GABA fibres engage the major output centres of the basal ganglia—the inner segment of the globus pallidus (in primates) and the zona reticulata of the substantia nigra [6]. So basal ganglia GABA mechanisms may be involved in the manifestations of the striatal dysfunction caused by nigro-striatal dopaminergic neuronal damage in Parkinson's disease.

GABA activity in Parkinson's disease

GABA activity is best assessed indirectly by measuring GAD levels and ^{3}H-GABA binding, rather than by assay of the unstable, quickly degraded parent compound. GAD levels are thought to reflect number and activity of GABA-ergic neurones, whilst ^{3}H-GABA binding is assumed to be an indicator of post-synaptic GABA receptor sites.

Post mortem studies of GAD levels from control and Parkinsonian patients have been reported by several groups over the last two decades (Table I). Bernheimer and Hornykiewicz [8] initially noted that GAD activity is decreased in the caudate nucleus in Parkinson's disease. McGeer et al [9] subsequently examined various regions of the brains of six Parkinsonian patients and, comparing them with three age matched patients, found a decrease in GAD activity in the substantia nigra and globus pallidus. Lloyd and Hornykiewicz [10] then examined several regions of the brains of 13 control subjects and of 11 patients with Parkinson's disease, two of whom had not received L-dopa therapy. They found a decrease in GAD activity of more than 50 per cent in the caudate, putamen and substantia nigra in the two Parkinsonian patients who had never received L-dopa. An even greater decrease of GAD activity was recorded in four Parkinsonian subjects who had received L-dopa for eight months or less in the caudate, putamen and the substantia nigra, and an approximately 50 per cent decrease was noted in the pallidum externum. Normal levels of basal ganglia GAD activity were reported in five Parkinsonian patients who had received L-dopa for 12 months or longer. These authors suggested that long term (greater than 12 months) L-dopa therapy could resore GAD levels to normal in patients with Parkinson's disease.

Rinne et al [11] reported GAD activity in several brain regions (including caudate, putamen, pallidum and substantia nigra) from four control subjects, two untreated patients with Parkinson's disease and three Parkinsonian patients treated with L-dopa. GAD levels were reduced in all areas examined in patients with Parkinson's disease, but less so in treated patients compared to untreated patients. Lloyd et al [12] examined the brains of three patients with Parkinson's disease and six controls, measuring GAD activity in the substantia nigra and other basal ganglia regions. They found less GAD activity in all areas in the Parkinsonian patients, but this loss reached statistical significance only in the substantia nigra. No mention was made of L-dopa therapy in the patients. McGeer and McGeer [13] examined many regions of the brains of several Parkinsonian patients, three of whom had received L-dopa prior to death and 22 controls, for GAD activity. GAD levels were significantly decreased in the substantia nigra and globus pallidus of Parkinsonian patients. GAD levels in the caudate and putamen were slightly less than control values. No differentiation was made between L-dopa treated Parkinsonian patients and other Parkinsonian patients in this study.

In summary, there is general agreement that GAD levels are decreased in the globus pallidus and particularly in the substantia nigra of patients with Parkinson's disease, and probably also in the striatum. But the extent of the loss is less than that seen in Huntington's chorea where GAD concentrations in striatum are re-

TABLE I GAD levels in Parkinson's disease (expressed as % of control values)
(n = number of Parkinsonian patients)

	n	Caudate nucleus	Putamen	Substantia nigra	Globus pallidus
Bernheimer & Hornykiewicz (1962) [8]	(4)	38	-	-	-
McGeer et al (1971) [9]	(6)	101	139	27	58
Lloyd & Hornykiewicz (1973) [10]	(2)a	49	47	41	70
	(4)b	26*	20*	40o	46*
Rinne et al (1974) [11]	(2)	31	50	39	53
Lloyd et al (1975) [12]	(3)	25	30	20+	28
McGeer & McGeer (1976) [13]	(10)	66	81	22*	35*

o $P < 0.001$;   * $P < 0.01$;   + $P < 0.05$

a Two patients with Parkinson's disease who had never received L-dopa
b Four patients with Parkinson's disease who had received L-dopa for eight months or less

duced to as little as 15–20 per cent of normal [14]. In addition, long term L-dopa therapy may restore basal ganglia GAD levels towards normal.

All this evidence is taken to suggest that there is a functional disorder of GABA-ergic activity in the basal ganglia in Parkinson's disease, but that this is probably due to a deprivation of dopaminergic input rather than a loss of GABA-ergic neurones. Most of the studies on which this conclusion is based, however, did not distinguish between various categories of patients with Parkinson's disease. Those who lose the benefit of treatment during long term therapy with L-dopa (L-dopa failures) may well lose striatal neurones, including those utilising GABA.

Turning to ^{3}H GABA binding in the human brain and alterations in Parkinson's disease (Table II), Lloyd et al [15] reported a reduction of ^{3}H-GABA binding to 30 per cent of control values in the substantia nigra, but not in other basal ganglia areas of six patients. Rinne et al [16] reported a loss of ^{3}H-GABA binding sites in other areas of the basal ganglia suggesting preservation of other target neurones on which GABA acts. But these studies have not examined sub-populations of Parkinsonian patients separately so it remains possible that ^{3}H-GABA binding sites are altered in L-dopa failure.

311

TABLE II ^{3}H-GABA binding in Parkinson's disease as % of control values
(n = number of Parkinsonian patients)

	n	Caudate nucleus	Putamen	Substantia nigra	Globus pallidus
Lloyd et al (1977) [15]	(8)[a]	106	135	31*	310
Rinne et al (1978) [16]	(12)	94	95	54+	79

* P<0.01;   +P<0.05

a   Nigral binding was investigated in the brains of six patients; pallidal binding in only one
    patient

GABA-mimetic drugs in Parkinson's disease

In view of the critical role of GABA systems in basal ganglia organisation, and the apparent loss of GABA in the brains of at least some patients with Parkinson's disease at autopsy, it seems rational to try to augment GABA action in this disease, when L-dopa therapy fails.

The drugs available for human use which have been claimed to exert GABA-like effects in brain are baclofen, sodium valproate, muscimol and SL76002.

Baclofen in Parkinson's disease

Baclofen was introduced for the relief of spasticity of spinal origin when it was thought to act on spinal cord interneurones. More recently, effects on the basal ganglia have been noted where it appears to possess GABA-mimetic properties. Baclofen, for instance, mimics muscimol (an established GABA agonist) in potentiating neuroleptic induced catalepsy [17] and by provoking contraversive circling in rats when injected directly into the zona reticulata of the substantia nigra [18]. Baclofen can stimulate release of ^{3}H-GABA from slices of rat globus pallidus [19]. However, the electrophysiological actions of baclofen applied iontophoretically to single spinal cord neurones are not prevented by specific GABA agonists such as bicuculline [20], suggesting that its GABA-mimetic actions may be indirect.

Lees et al [21] in a double blind trial, gave 12 Parkinsonian patients baclofen whilst routine L-dopa therapy was continued. Because of side-effects, only two patients reached the maximum projected dose of 90 mg/day; the mean daily dose was 45 mg/day. Two patients could not tolerate baclofen at all and withdrew from the trial.

Baclofen aggravated rigidity on average by 46 per cent and functional capacity by 21 per cent. Side effects were prominent and included visual hallucinations, toxic confusional states, headaches, nausea and vomiting. Other reports [22, 23] have also noted hallucinations following abrupt withdrawal of baclofen in patients with Parkinson's disease on L-dopa. L-dopa associated dyskinesias were unaltered by baclofen in Lees' study. Improvement in four of the 12 patients with morning "off-period" dystonia, did occur, however, when receiving baclofen (see also previous chapter).

In a report by Gerlach et al [24] on the effect of baclofen on tardive dyskinesia (see below) they noted a 40 per cent intensification of Parkinsonism in a group of 18 psychiatric patients receiving neuroleptics.

Sodium valproate in Parkinson's disease

Sodium valproate originally was developed as an anti-epileptic agent. It raises brain GABA levels [25] by inhibiting GABA transaminase and succinic semi-aldehyde dehydrogenase [26], the enzymes that degrade GABA.

Price et al [27] gave sodium valproate to a group of 12 patients with Parkinson's disease in a dose of 1200 mg/day. Routine L-dopa therapy was unaltered during the course of the double blind trial. They found that sodium valproate had no objective effect on Parkinsonian disability, since mean total disability scores before treatment, after placebo and after sodium valproate did not differ. Nutt et al [28] gave eight Parkinsonian patients sodium valproate in a higher dose of 2800 mg/day, routine anti-Parkinsonian therapy being maintained during the course of the double blind trial; they reported that sodium valproate had no statistically significant action on any feature of Parkinson's disease.

Both papers examined the effects of sodium valproate on L-dopa-induced dyskinesias. Price et al [27] reported subjective, but not objective, improvement of dyskinesias in 6 of 9 patients. Dyskinesias were exacerbated in 4 patients in Nutt's study, necessitating a reduction of L-dopa in 3 of the 4. This apparent enhancement of L-dopa's effects in the dyskinetic patients was not seen in patients who did not have hour-to-hour fluctuations, nor was it reported in the earlier study of Price et al where a lower dose of sodium valproate was given.

Muscimol in Parkinson's disease

Muscimol is a semi-rigid cyclic structural analogue of GABA, with potent GABA-mimetic effects, both in vivo and in vitro. It mimics the iontophoretic action of GABA and these effects are bicuculline-sensitive and strychnine-insensitive [29, 30]. Muscimol readily displaces ^{3}H-GABA from receptor binding sites [31], enhances neuroleptic induced catalepsy [32] and causes contraversive circling when injected into the substantia nigra of rats [33].

There are no reports of administration of muscimol to patients with Parkinson's disease. Taminga et al [34] found that muscimol worsened drug-induced Parkinsonism when they gave it to a group of patients with tardive dyskinesias (see below). Unfortunately in these and other studies in which muscimol was given to patients with psychiatric disorders, it was found to cause severe side effects including heightened awareness and worsening of psychosis, sedation and lowering of level of consciousness. Muscimol now is considered too toxic for human use.

SL76002 (Halogabide) in Parkinson's disease

SL76002 mimics several of the effects of known GABA agonists, including muscimol. Thus SL76002 potentiates neuroleptic-induced catalepsy and haloperidol antagonism of apomorphine-induced stereotypies [35]. SL76002 also displaces ^{3}H-GABA from binding sites, suggesting a direct agonist action [36].

We have recently given SL76002 to a group of 18 Parkinsonian patients in a double blind study, L-dopa and other routine anti-Parkinsonian therapy being unaltered during its course.

Patients commenced on 600 mg/day of SL76002 and, every two days, the drug was increased to a maximum dose of 2700 mg/day at the end of the induction phase. Patients then entered a double blind period, receiving either SL76002 or placebo. Patients were rated using the King's College Hospital Parkinsonian rating scale and the Abnormal Involuntary Movements scale at the beginning of the induction period, at the end of the induction period, and at the end of each of the two week periods of double blind observation.

SL76002 had no statistically significant effect on Parkinsonian disability nor on dyskinesias (see Table III).

TABLE III Effects of various GABA-mimetics in Parkinson's disease and drug-induced Parkinsonism

Baclofen	Sodium valproate	Muscimol
Lees et al [21] 12 patients, double blind 45 mg/day and L-dopa Parkinsonian features worsened by 21–46% "Off-period" dystonia improved	Price et al [27] 12 patients, double blind 1200 mg/day and L-dopa No effect	Taminga et al [34]* 8 patients, double blind 3–9 mg/day Parkinsonian features worsened
		SL76002
Gerlach et al [24]* 18 patients, double blind 75 mg/day, and neuroleptics Parkinsonian features worsened by 40%	Nutt et al [28] 8 patients, double blind 2800 mg/day and L-dopa Parkinsonian features no change; dyskinesias worsened	Unpublished observations 18 patients, double blind 2700 mg/day and L-dopa No effect

* Trials in patients with drug-induced Parkinsonism

GABA mimetics and other extrapyramidal disorders

Huntington's disease

Baclofen [37, 38], sodium valproate alone [39] or in combination with GABA [40], muscimol [41] and SL76002 have all been given to groups of patients with Huntington's chorea (Table IV). All investigators reported that these drugs made no difference to the chorea of Huntington's disease.

TABLE IV Effects of various GABA-mimetics in Huntington's disease

Baclofen	Sodium valproate	Muscimol
Barbeau [37] 5 patients, open study 90 mg/day No change	Pearce et al [39] 14 patients, open 0.06–2.4 g/day No change	Shoulson et al [41] 10 patients, double blind 10 mg/day No change
		SL76002
Paulson [38] 11 patients, open, film 15–60 mg/day Doubtful 25% improvement	Shoulson et al [40] 8 patients, double blind 1500 mg/day ± GABA 24.5 g/day No change	Unpublished observations 3 patients, open 2700 mg/day No change

TABLE V Effects of various GABA-mimetics in tardive dyskinesias

Baclofen		Sodium Valproate	
Gerlach et al [24] 18 patients, double blind 20–120 (75) mg/day and neuroleptics 40% improvement	Nair et al [43] 10 patients, double blind 30–90 mg/day No neuroleptics No change	Linnoila et al [45] 32 patients, double blind 900 mg/day and neuroleptics Apparent improvement	Gibson [47] 26 patients, film 900 mg/day and neuroleptics No change
			Muscimol
Korsgaard [42] 20 patients, double blind 15–60 mg/day (51) and neuroleptics 66% improvement	Simpson et al [44] 12 patients, placebo then active 20–120 mg/day No neuroleptics No change	Chien et al [46] 20 patients, double blind 1600 mg/day and neuroleptics in 15 35% improvement	Tamminga et al [34] 8 patients, double blind 3–9 mg/day 48% improvement

Tardive dyskinesias (see Table V)

Gerlach *et al* [24] and Korsgaard [42] reported improvement of tardive dyskinesias in two groups of patients given baclofen in double blind crossover trials. All patients, however, continued on regular neuroleptic therapy. Nair *et al* [43] in a double blind study, and Simpson *et al* [44] reported no improvement in two groups of patients with tardive dyskinesias who were no longer receiving neuroleptic therapy. Two double blind studies [45, 46] have been reported showing improvement of tardive dyskinesias following sodium valproate therapy. A subsequent report [47], however, employed cine films to record tardive dyskinesias before and after sodium valproate. Independent observers were unable to detect "before" and "after" films in a number of cases and it was concluded that sodium valproate had no effect on tardive dyskinesias.

Muscimol has been given to a group of 7 patients with tardive dyskinesias [34]. All were schizophrenics, free of neuroleptic therapy. Initial dose was 3 mg, increasing in 2 mg increments to 9 mg or highest tolerated dose. Involuntary movements were scored by two blind raters. Muscimol produced a diminution (of about 48 per cent) in choreiform movements at 2 and 4 hours following oral administration. Concurrent Parkinsonism was said to increase in 2 of 3 patients.

Conclusion

The GABA-mimetics at our disposal at the moment appear to be either too toxic and/or are ineffective in the treatment of extrapyramidal disorders. GABA receptors are diffusely distributed throughout the CNS, so toxic side effects may be due to widespread receptor stimulation. Conversely, lack of therapeutic effect may be due to inadequate basal ganglia GABA receptor stimulation. Clearly, before dismissing this group of drugs as possible therapeutic agents for Parkinson's disease, a more specific (ie, striatal or nigral) GABA-mimetic is needed.

In summary, GABA is the major inhibitory neurotransmitter in the CNS. Although GABA is particularly concentrated in the basal ganglia, its role in basal ganglia disease remains unclear.

Acknowledgements

We wish to thank Mrs. Pam Asselman for her invaluable assistance.

References

1   Fahn S. In Roberts E, Chase TN, Tower DB, eds. *GABA in nervous system function 1976;* 169. New York: Raven Press
2   Curtis DR, Johnston GAR. *Ergebn Physiol 1974; 69:* 97
3   Martin DL. In Roberts E, Chase TN, Tower DB, eds. *GABA in nervous system function 1976;* 347. New York: Raven Press
4   McGeer PL, McGeer EG. *Brain Res 1975; 91:* 331
5   Fonnum F, Grofova I, Rinvik E, Storm-Mathisen J, Walberg F. *Brain Res 1974; 71:* 77
6   Ribak CE, Vaughn JE, Saito K, Barber R, Roberts E. *Brain Res 1976; 116:* 287

316

7   Anden N-E, Wachtel H. In Garttini S, Pujol JF, Samanin R, eds. *Interactions between putative neurotransmitters in the brain 1978;* 161. New York: Raven Press

8   Bernheimer H, Hornykiewicz O. *Naunyn-Schmeidebergs Archiv fur Experimentelle Pathologie 1962; 243 (4):*295

9   McGeer PL, McGeer EG, Wada JA. *Neurology 1971; 21:*1000

10   Lloyd KG, Hornykiewicz O. *Nature 1973; 243:* 521

11   Rinne UK, Sonninen V, Riekkinen P, Laaksonen H. *Medical Biology 1974; 52:*208

12   Lloyd KG, Mohler H, Heitz PH, Bartholini G. *J Neurochem 1975; 25:*789

13   McGeer PL, McGeer EG. *J Neurochem 1976; 26:*65

14   Bird ED, Mackay AVP, Rayner CN, Iversen LL. *Lancet 1973; i:*1090

15   Lloyd KG, Shemen L, Hornykiewicz O. *Brain Res 1977; 127:*269

16   Rinne UK, Koskinen V, Laaksonen H, Loonberg P, Sonninen V. *Life Sci 1978; 22:*2225

17   Davies JA, Williams J. *Brit J Pharmac 1978; 62:*303

18   Waddington JL. *Brit J Pharmac 1977; 60:*263P

19   Kerwin R, Pycock C. *J Pharm Pharmacol 1978; 30:*622

20   Curtis DR, Game CJA, Johnston GAR, McCulloch RM. *Brain Res 1974; 70:*493

21   Lees AJ, Shaw KM, Stern GM. *J Neurol Neurosurg Psychiat 1978; 41:*707

22   Lees AJ, Clarke CRA, Harrison MJ. *Lancet 1977; i:* 858

23   Skausig OL, Korsgaard S. *Lancet 1977; i:*1258

24   Gerlach J, Rye T, Kristjansen P. *Psychopharm 1978; 56;* 145

25   Simler S, Ciesielski L, Maitre M, Randrianarisoa H, Mandel P. *Biochem Pharmacol 1973; 22:*1701

26   Sawaya MCB, Horton, RW, Meldrum BS. *Epilepsia 1975; 16:*649

27   Price P, Parkes JD, Marsden CD. *J Neurol Neurosurg Psychiat 1978; 41:*707

28   Nutt J, Williams A, Plotkin C, Eng N, Ziegler M, Calne DB. *Canad J Neurol Sci 1979; 6:*337

29   Johnston GAR, Curtis DR, de Groat WC, Duggan AW. *Biochem Pharmacol 1968; 17:* 2488

30   Krogsgaard-Larsen P, Johnston GAR, Curtis DR, Game CJA, McCulloch RM. *J Neurochem 1975; 25:*803

31   Beaumont K, Chilton W, Yamamura HT. *Neurosci Abst 1977; 3:*1442

32   Delini-Stula A. In Krogsgaard-Larsen P, Scheel-Kruger J, Kofod H, eds. *GABA neurotransmitters 1979;* 482. Munksgaard, Copenhagen

33   Waddington JL. *Brit J Pharm 1977; 60:*263P

34   Taminga CA, Crayton JW, Chase TN. *Arch Gen Psychiatry 1979; 36:*595

35   Lloyd KG, Worms P, Depoortere H, Bartholini G. In Krogsgaard-Larsen P, Scheel-Kruger J, Kofod H, eds. *GABA neurotransmitters 1979.* Munksgaard, Copenhagen

36   Bartholini C, Scatton B, Zivkovic B, Lloyd KG. In Krogsgaard-Larsen P, Scheel-Kruger J, Kofod H, eds. *GABA neurotransmitters 1979.* Munksgaard, Copenhagen

37   Barbeau A. *Lancet 1973; ii:*1499

38   Paulson CW. *Dis Nerv Syst 1976; 37:*465

39   Pearce I, Heathfield KWG, Pearce JMS. *Arch Neurol 1977; 34:*308

40   Shoulson I, Kartzinel, R, Chase TN. *Neurology 1976; 26:*61

41   Shoulson I, Goldblatt D, Charlton M, Joynt RJ. *Ann Neurol 1978; 4:*279

42   Korsgaard S. *Acta Psychiat Scand 1976; 54:*17

43   Nair NPV, Yassa R, Ruiz-Navarro J, Schwartz G. *Am J Psychiatry 1978; 135:*1562

44   Simpson CM, Lee, JH, Shrwastava RK, Branchey MH. *Psychopharmacol Bull 1978; 14:*16

45   Linnoila M, Vinkari M, Hietala O. *Brit J Psychiat 1976; 129:*114

46   Chien C, Jung K, Ross-Townsend A. *Psychopharmacol Bull 1978; 14 (2):*20

47   Gibson AC. *Brit J Psychiat 1978; 133:*82

Chapter 40

DA2 RECEPTOR ANTAGONISTS IN PARKINSON'S DISEASE

P Price, M Schachter, P Bedard, J D Parkes and C D Marsden

Introduction

Parkinson's disease is due to loss of dopamine-containing pathways in the brain. Treatment is aimed at replacing this dopamine deficiency either by administration of the precursor amino acid levodopa which is converted into the active amine dopamine (and noradrenaline) in the brain, or by drugs such as bromocriptine and other ergot alkaloids which act, at least in part, as direct post-synaptic dopamine agonists.

Recently there has been considerable interest in the possibility that more than one type of dopamine receptor exists in the brain. There are at least three interpretations of this statement.

1 There are dopamine receptors in different parts of the brain, ie. in the corpus striatum, in mesolimbic areas such as the nucleus accumbens and tuberculum olfactorium, in mesocortical areas in the frontal lobe, and in the hypothalamus.
2 Within a given dopamine system, dopamine receptors exist at different sites. In the nigro-striatal dopamine system there are dopamine receptors a) on the post-synaptic striatal neurones on which the nigro-striatal pathway synapses, b) on pre-synaptic nerve terminals of nigro-striatal dopaminergic fibres, c) on the cell body and dendrites of the nigro-striatal dopamine neurones, d) on pre-synaptic nerve terminals of cortico-striatal glutamate fibres, and e) on nerve terminals of strio-nigral GABA (and perhaps substance P) fibres.
3 Any of these dopamine receptors in different parts of the brain or on different sites in a given dopaminergic system may or may not be linked to a dopamine-sensitive adenylate cyclase system.

The subject that has gained widest attention in recent years is the division of dopamine receptors into those linked to adenylate cyclase (DA1 receptors), and those not linked to adenylate cyclase (DA2 receptors). Arguments have been put forward to suggest that this is a fundamental distinction between two different types of dopamine receptor [1]. Other evidence separates DA1 and DA2 receptor

318

characteristics. Thus dopamine, apomorphine, and dopaminergic ergot alkaloids are held to be agonists in nanomolar concentrations on DA2 receptors. On DA1 receptors dopamine is an agonist only in micromolar concentrations, apomorphine is only a partial agonist or antagonist, and dopaminergic ergots are believed to be potent antagonists in nanomolar concentrations and weak agonists in micromolar concentrations. Most phenothiazine anti-psychotic drugs act as antagonists both at DA1 and DA2 receptors. Butyrophenones are less effective in antagonising dopamine stimulation of adenylate cyclase than is expected from their potency in binding to receptors labelled by tritiated ligands, so would appear to be more potent DA2 than DA1 antagonists. No specific DA1 antagonist exists, but *cis*-flupenthixol shows the best correlation between receptor binding and capacity to inhibit dopamine stimulation of adenylate cyclase. A number of compounds appear to be specific to DA2 receptor antagonists, in particular the substituted benzamides [2] (which include such drugs as metoclopramide, sulpiride, sultropride and tiapride), which have no effect on dopamine stimulation of cerebral adenylate cyclase, and some butyrophenone derivatives such as oxiperomide which likewise is not active on the cyclase system in concentrations of up to 3×10^4 M.

If the therapeutic actions of L-dopa and other dopamine agonists such as bromocriptine in Parkinson's disease are due to stimulation of a population of dopamine receptors different from those responsible for unwanted adverse effects, this could lead to rational design of more selective therapy.

We have investigated a number of DA2 antagonists in patients with Parkinson's disease to assess the contribution of DA2 receptor stimulation to the therapeutic action and adverse effects of L-dopa or bromocriptine treatment. In particular we have in the past extensively studied the pharmacological and therapeutic actions of metoclopramide, studies which we will review briefly here. We will also describe the results of a comparison of sulpiride, another DA2 antagonist, with the non-specific DA1 and DA2 antagonist *cis*-flupenthixol.

Both metoclopramide and sulpiride are substituted benzamides with the typical properties of DA2 antagonists. There are, however, other DA2 antagonists which possess unusual properties. In particular, tiapride (another substituted benzamide), and oxiperomide have been shown to reduce peri-oral dyskinesias induced by intra-striatal injection of dopamine agonists in the guinea pig, without reducing locomotor effects [3]. Likewise, these drugs inhibit dyskinetic biting evoked by systemic administration of 2-(N,N-dipropyl) amino-5,6-dihydroxytetralin in the guinea pig in doses that do not inhibit locomotor hyperactivity [4]. We also describe, therefore, the effects of oxiperomide and tiapride in Parkinson's disease.

Metoclopramide and Parkinson's disease

An early study [5] showed that oral metoclopramide in a dose of 10–20 mg tds did not remove the therapeutic action of levodopa or reduce levodopa-induced dyskinesias in patients with Parkinson's disease. Subsequently others [6] have shown that metoclopramide 60 mg daily (but not 30 mg daily) reduced the

319

patient's self assessment of tremor, but had no effect on objective assessment of symptoms and signs of Parkinson's disease. However, our own further studies in which a large single dose of metoclopramide (60 mg) was given prior to a single dose of L-dopa and bromocriptine gave different results. Careful examinations of such patients showed that metoclopramide did decrease the therapeutic action of both drugs and did reduce the dyskinesia they produced (without decreasing the blood levels of either dopamine agonist) [7, 8, 9].

Thus metoclopramide can be shown to antagonise the effect of dopamine agonists in Parkinson's disease, but this pharmacological action is not of clinical importance with the usual doses employed.

Comparison of a DA2 dopamine receptor agonist (sulpiride) with a non-selective DA1 and DA2 receptor antagonist (cis-flupenthixol) in Parkinson's disease

Recently we have conducted a comparative trial of sulpiride with *cis*-flupenthixol in Parkinson's disease. Although there is no selective DA1 dopamine receptor antagonist, inhibition of dopamine stimulation of striatal adenylate cyclase activity correlates most strongly with inhibition of 3-H-*cis*-flupenthixol binding to striatal dopamine receptors [10]. This suggests that *cis*-flupenthixol, while not being a specific DA1 receptor antagonist, certainly identifies adenylate cyclase linked receptors.

Therefore we studied the effects of a single oral dose of racemic sulpiride (400 mg) or *cis*-flupenthixol (3 mg) given two hours (sulpiride) or four hours (*cis*-flupenthixol) before a single tablet of Sinemet 275 (containing 250 mg L-dopa, combined with 25 mg carbidopa) in six patients with idiopathic Parkinson's disease. All other anti-Parkinsonian disability and severity of dyskinesia were scored at 30 minute intervals (King's College Hospital rating scale) for four hours.

Sinemet alone reduced mean parkinsonian disability score by 22 ± 4%, in comparison to ratings prior to drug administration. Pretreatment with sulpiride (400 mg) reduced this benefit to 10 ± 1%, while pretreatment with *cis*-flupenthixol (3 mg) reduced benefit to 12 ± 3%. Dyskinesias were abolished by both drugs. In other words, no difference was detected between the two drugs in their ability to inhibit the anti-parkinsonian actions of Sinemet or the dyskinesias provoked by the latter drug.

Design of clinical trials of tiapride and oxiperomide

We were interested in the effect of oxiperomide and tiapride on both the therapeutic response to L-dopa, and the side effects provoked by L-dopa, in particular dyskinesias and toxic confusional states. Patients on stable L-dopa treatment were selected for study provided they had shown a useful therapeutic response and also exhibited either or both side effects. Oxiperomide or tiapride were introduced gradually in increasing dosage until either dyskinesias (or toxic confusional states)

320

were controlled, or Parkinsonian disability worsened. If the latter occurred, the dose of tiapride or oxiperomide was held constant while that of L-dopa was gradually increased to see if the lost ground could be made up.

Once optimum tiapride, oxiperomide and L-dopa dosage had been established for at least a month, matched placebo was substituted for active tiapride or oxiperomide at a time unknown to the clinical observer.

Patients were rated for Parkinsonian disability (King's College Hospital rating scale) and dyskinesias prior to introduction of tiapride or oxiperomide, an optimal dosage when arrived at and a month later, and 2–4 weeks after placebo treatment. A high score indicates severe disability and dyskinesias.

Tiapride was introduced in a dose of 12.5 mg daily and gradually was increased by increments of 12.5 or 25 mg at weekly intervals [11].

Oxiperomide was introduced in a dose of 5 mg daily and gradually was increased to 15 mg daily over two weeks [12].

Tiapride in Parkinson's disease

Ten patients with idiopathic Parkinson's disease were studied; all had dyskinesias with fluctuations in response, typical of end-of-dose deterioration.

Introduction of tiapride led to an increase in Parkinsonian disability in 7 of the 10 patients, requiring an increase in L-dopa dosage. Final optimal tiapride dosage ranged from 25 to 300 mg daily given in three doses. Initial L-dopa dosage averaged 753 (50–1875 mg) daily combined with carbidopa as Sinemet, and increased to 1009 (100–2125) mg when combined with tiapride.

L-dopa induced dyskinesias were reduced by tiapride in 9 of the 10 patients. The worsening of Parkinsonian disability in 7 of these patients was reversed by increasing the dose of L-dopa, and in 5 this increase did not result in more severe dyskinesias. Comparison of the clinical state on optimum combined tiapride and L-dopa therapy, with treatment on L-dopa alone showed an improvement in dyskinesias (score on L-dopa alone 129 ± 9 SEM, on combined therapy 88 ± 10; $P < 0.01$) without any concomitant deterioration in Parkinsonian disability (score on L-dopa alone 138 ± 21 SEM, on combined therapy 128 ± 25. NS). Placebo substitution for active tiapride caused a deterioration in the severity of dyskinesias, but no real change in Parkinsonian disability.

No untoward side effects were noted in patients taking tiapride up to 300 mg daily in this study.

In addition, tiapride was administered to 8 patients with Parkinson's disease in whom L-dopa or bromocriptine had precipitated an acute toxic confusional state. A marked improvement occurred in the mental state of 4 of these patients, without any concomitant deterioration in their Parkinson's disease, with the addition of 50–300 mg tiapride daily. No effect was seen in the remaining patients who took no more than 300 mg daily of tiapride.

In conclusion, tiapride can suppress L-dopa-induced dyskinesias, often with a concurrent increase in Parkinsonian disability. However, subsequent careful

321

titration of L-dopa dosage may restore mobility without increasing dyskinesias. Thus tiapride, carefully titrated with L-dopa, can selectively antagonise L-dopa dyskinesias without necessarily exacerbating Parkinsonism. Our study, and that of L'Hermitte and colleagues [13] show that tiapride can in critical dosage selectively antagonise L-dopa induced dyskinesias.

Oxiperomide in Parkinson's disease [12]

Oxiperomide was studied in 6 patients with idiopathic Parkinson's disease, all with dyskinesias, treated with L-dopa (4 patients) or bromocriptine (2 patients).

Oxiperomide 5–10 mg daily often decreased drug-induced dyskinesias without increasing Parkinsonian disability, but higher dosage (15 mg daily) while decreasing drug-induced dyskinesias always increased Parkinsonian disability at the same time. However, the increased akinesia and rigidity provoked by higher doses of oxiperomide was overcome by increasing the dose of dopamine agonist in 3 patients, with no increase in dyskinesias. Side effects with oxiperomide were uncommon, but one patient did complain of apathy and another of impotence.

In conclusion, oxiperomide, like tiapride, can diminish dopamine-induced dyskinesias in patients with Parkinson's disease without necessarily increasing akinesia and rigidity.

DA2 receptor antagonists in other dyskinesias

L'Hermitte and his colleagues [14] have shown that tiapride in higher doses than those used to control L-dopa-induced dyskinesias, ie. 300–1200 mg daily, can control chorea in Huntington's disease with little or no Parkinsonism, and only occasional sleepiness. Our own studies confirm this observation, and adds that tiapride has little useful effect in generalised torsion dystonia, or in adult-onset focal manifestations, such as oro-mandibular dystonia, torticollis and dystonic writer's cramp (unpublished observations).

The effects of tiapride in neuroleptic-induced chronic tardive dyskinesias has not been studied widely, but Casey et al [15] have shown that another substituted benzamide, sulpiride, is effective in controlling this movement disorder, and another selective DA2 antagonist, metoclopramide, also reduces the severity of tardive dyskinesia when given intravenously [16]. However, it should be pointed out that substituted benzamides, such as metoclopramide [17, 18], are capable of producing tardive dyskinesias, on chronic administration in high dosage.

The other DA2 receptor antagonist oxiperomide also has been found capable of reducing chorea in Huntington's disease, but to have little useful effect in the various manifestations of torsion dystonia [12], and to successfully reduce the intensity of neuroleptic-induced chronic tardive dyskinesias [19].

In summary, DA2 receptor antagonists certainly can be used to control chorea (as in Huntington's disease) and neuroleptic-induced tardive dyskinesias, but have

322

little effect on torsion dystonia. The general conclusion is that the beneficial effects of both tiapride and oxiperomide in chorea and tardive dyskinesias can be achieved in doses which do not produce evident Parkinsonism but may cause a degree of sedation. Indeed, the latter has been the most commonly reported side-effect of both drugs when used to treat such dyskinesias.

Conclusion

DA2 dopamine receptor antagonists clearly are capable of inhibiting the therapeutic action of L-dopa in Parkinson's disease, and of suppressing L-dopa-induced, neuroleptic-induced, and certain spontaneous dyskinesias. Certain DA2 antagonists such as tiapride and oxiperomide can differentially alleviate L-dopa induced dyskinesias without necessarily worsening Parkinsonism. The similarity of the effect of sulpiride to that of *cis*-flupenthixol, which also, and perhaps predominantly, antagonises DA1 receptors, may be taken to suggest that DA1 receptors are not of great importance in Parkinson's disease and dyskinesias, or that the distinction between DA1 and DA2 is artificial.

References

1   Kebabian JW, Calne DB. *Nature 1979; 277:*93
2   Jenner P, Marsden CD. *Life Sci 1979; 25:*479
3   Costall B, Naylor R. *Europ J Pharmac 1975; 33:*301
4   Costall B, Naylor R, Owen RT. *Europ J Pharmac 1977; 45:*357
5   Tarsy D, Parkes JD, Marsden CD. *J Neurol Neurosurg Psychiat 1975; 38:*331
6   Bateman DN, Kahn C, Legg NJ, Reid JL. *Clin Pharmacol Ther 1978; 24:*459
7   Parkes JD, Debono AG, Marsden CD. *J Neurol Neurosurg Psychiat 1976; 39:*1101
8   Price P, Debono A, Parkes JD, Marsden CD. *Brit J Pharmac 1978; 6:*303
9   Price P, Debono A, Jenner P, Parkes JD, Marsden CD. In Poirier LJ, Sourkes TL, Bédard PJ, eds. *Advances in Neurology, volume 24, 1979;* 423. New York: Raven Press
10   Hyttel J. *Life Sci 1978; 23:*551
11   Price P, Parkes JD, Marsden CD. *Lancet 1978; ii:*1106
12   Bédard P, Parkes JD, Marsden CD. *Brit Med J 1978; 1:*954
13   L'Hermitte F, Agid Y, Signoret J-L, Studler JM. *Revue Neurol 1977; 133:*297
14   L'Hermitte F, Signoret J-L, Agid Y. *Sem Hop Paris 1977; 53:*39B 9
15   Casey DE, Garlach J, Simmelsgaard H. *Psychopharmacol 1979; 66:* 73
16   Bateman DN, Dutta D, McClelland HA, Rawlins MD. *Brit J Pharmacol 1979; 66:*475
17   Lavy S, Melamed F, Penchas S. *Brit Med J 1978; 1:*77
18   Kataria M, Traub M, Marsden CD. *Lancet 1978; ii:*1254
19   Casey DE, Gerlach J. *J Neurol Neurosurg Psychiat 1980.* In press

Chapter 41

ACTIONS OF ERGOT DERIVATIVES IN PARKINSONISM

G Gopinathan and Donald B Calne

Introduction

The introduction of levodopa for the treatment of Parkinsonism launched an era of explosive developments in neuropharmacology. The clinical benefits it rendered to Parkinson patients held out the promise to change the face of neurological thera-peutics. The last decade has witnessed enthusiasm followed by disappointment. Im-pressive advances in the field of receptor physiology have led to the therapeutic concept of bypassing the dopamine neurone by manipulating the postsynaptic re-ceptors directly with agonists. Bromocriptine, a dopaminergic ergot derivative, has been the most promising agonist to emerge [18, 22, 30, 31]. Several groups have re-ported its clinical benefits in Parkinsonism, but again initial hopes have not been fully sustained [1, 2, 4, 13, 14, 35, 38]. While the quest for safer and more effic-acious therapeutic agents continues, bromocriptine does have an important role in treatment which can now be defined with some precision. We report here our ex-perience with this drug for over 5 years.

Materials and Methods

Most of our 118 Parkinsonian patients were already receiving L-dopa by the time they were referred to us. All the patients were screened for the presence of dis-orders other than Parkinson's disease (PD). Patients with significant cardiovascular, renal or hepatic disease were excluded from the study, as were patients with signifi-cant psychiatric disorders. Patients with prior cardiovascular illness, but currently stable, were accepted; they were all admitted to hospital for observation at the start of the treatment. Except for two who had post-encephalitic parkinsonism, and one patient with basal-ganglia calcification, all the other patients had idiopathic parkin-sonism.

The indications for starting bromocriptine were as follows:- diminishing response to L-dopa, 52; marked dyskinesia and/or on-off phenomena, 40; other adverse re-actions to L-dopa, 12; no specific indications (patients who wanted to try new treatment), 13.

An initial 1 mg of bromocriptine was given, this low dose being employed to avoid nausea and the occasional severe hypotension encountered with higher starting intake. Increments were undertaken stepwise, over a period of 4 weeks—until a beneficial clinical response was elicited or signs of intolerance emerged. Patients who were receiving amantadine and/or anticholinergics continued to take these drugs without any changes in dosages. Adjustments of L-dopa intake were made (reductions or discontinuation) when required, during the period of building up bromocriptine doses. Patients received a mean bromocriptine maintenance dose of 72 mg daily (range 24 to 150).

Patients were reviewed in the clinic every month, when their response was assessed, blood pressure checked lying down and standing up, and mental status was evaluated. Laboratory tests at each visit consisted of a complete blood count, with red cell indices, estimation of haemoglobin, uric acid, blood urea, creatinine, serum glutamic oxaloacetic and pyruvic transaminases, serum protein, alkaline/phosphatase, bilirubin and electrolytes.

Patients who developed abnormalities during bromocriptine therapy were admitted to hospital for further evaluation and management. They continued taking bromocriptine as long as they benefited from it, and did not encounter intolerable side effects.

In the computations of the L-dopa dosage reported here, allowance is made for concomitant administration of carbidopa by multiplying the L-dopa dose by four.

Results

Table I summarises the number of patients, mean duration of therapy and mean dose of bromocriptine. Forty-eight patients (41%) continued on the study (Group A). 70 patients (59%) stopped taking the drug (Group B). The proportion of patients still receiving bromocriptine is 11 per cent less than we reported in our last communication, in 1978 [6]. The Group B patients were taking 20% more bromocriptine (and 11% more L-dopa) than those in Group A, implying that the former had more refractory disease.

Table II depicts experience with the patients who took L-dopa in addition to bromocriptine. 75 per cent of the total group of 118 were receiving L-dopa when they entered the study. The 30 patients (25%) not taking L-dopa were either newly diagnosed, never having received any dopaminergic agents, or subjects who were at one time treated with L-dopa but later discontinued because of intolerance.

Forty-eight patients (41% of the total group of 118) underwent a reduction of L-dopa intake (mean 57%) when they reached peak bromocriptine dosages (mean 68 mg/day, range 35 to 150). The reduction was usually required because of appearance or exacerbation of side effects (mainly dyskinesia, on-off phenomena or hallucinations). The proportionately greater reduction of L-dopa (28% more) in Group B patients derived from: (1) their receiving higher doses of bromocriptine and L-dopa initially (20% and 11% respectively); (2) adverse reactions developed earlier

325

TABLE I Patients treated with Bromocriptine

Patient Category	Number of Patients	Mean Age	Mean Duration of Disease (Years)	Mean Dose (mg)	Mean Duration of Therapy (Months)
Patients continuing treatment	48	59	10	64	33
Patients Who Discontinued Treatment	70	59	9	79	15
Total	118	59	9	72	21

TABLE II Patients receiving L-dopa in addition to Bromocriptine

Patient Category	Number of Patients	Mean Dose of L-dopa (mg)	Number of Patients who had reduction of L-dopa	Mean % reduction
Patients still on Bromocriptine	34	2685	10	45
Patients who Discontinued Bromocriptine	54	3010	38	63
Total	88	2885	48	57

and more severely in this group, as shown by the much shorter duration of therapy (mean 14.5 months).

The clinical responses of 118 patients to bromocriptine therapy are summarised in Figure 1. The patients were separated into two groups: those who improved and those who did not. A total of 88 patients (75%) benefited from the bromocriptine therapy: 25 per cent had a good clinical response, 28 per cent obtained moderate benefit and a further 21 per cent experienced slight amelioration of deficits.

In the non-responding group, 13 per cent did not show any improvement at all; 4 per cent were lost to follow-up and a further 4 per cent died during the course of the study. The causes of death are as follows: two patients who had advanced parkinsonism and severe dysphagia were found dead in bed (they probably died of

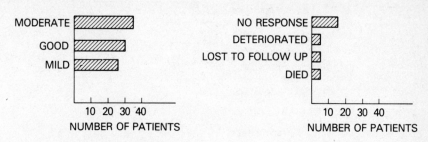

Figure 1 Responses to bromocriptine.

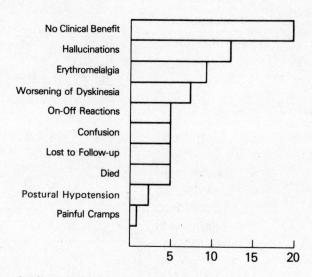

Figure 2 Reasons for discontinuing bromocriptine.

aspiration); one patient died after emergency open heart surgery for coronary artery disease; one died following massive mesenteric thrombosis, and the last died after acute myocardial infarction which occurred while the patient was being treated in hospital for intestinal obstruction secondary to faecal impaction.

A variety of side effects were encountered with long term use of bromocriptine. These are grouped as major and minor reaction and are summarised in Figure 3 and Figure 4. The commonest problem encountered was dyskinesia, which occurred in 42 per cent of our patients. Four patients, who were on bromocriptine without L-dopa, did not develop dyskinesia and are still taking this drug. The other major clinical reactions encountered were "on-off" phenomena (19%), nausea (16%),

327

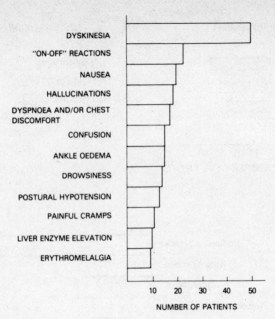

Figure 3 Major side effects.

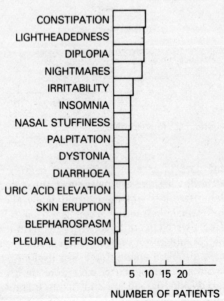

Figure 4 Minor side effects.

328

hallucinations (15%), paroxysmal dysponea and/or chest discomfort (14%), confusion (12%), pedal oedema without erythema or tenderness (12%), drowsiness (11%), postural hypotension (10%), painful cramps (9%) and erythromelalgia (6%).

The erythromelalgia syndrome comprised erythema, oedema and tenderness seen most frequently on the feet and anterior aspect of the legs and below the knees. This reaction was considered an indication to reduce or stop bromocriptine. As a result, eight patients were discontinued from bromocriptine and one patient, who is still on bromocriptine, is receiving only 20 per cent of the dose he was taking at the time when he developed this complication. The patients who developed erythromelalgia were receiving a mean daily dose of 101 mg (range 24–150) bromocriptine for a duration of more than 10 months (range 2 weeks to 5 years). The skin lesions disappeared within 10 days (range 3–16) after discontinuation of bromocriptine.

Pleural effusion was encountered in one patient. He developed bilateral pulmonary infiltrates when he was receiving 100 mg of bromocriptine daily. Bilateral pleural effusions appeared 2 weeks later, and persisted for several weeks. The pleural aspirate revealed 3.3 gm/dl protein and 200 white cells—54 per cent lymphocytes, 28 per cent polymorphs and 18 per cent histocytes. Investigations for tuberculosis, malignancy and collagen diseases were negative. A needle biopsy of lung did not reveal any abnormalities. Bromocriptine was discontinued and the effusion and pulmonary infiltrates improved to a considerable extent, but did not resolve completely. Eventually the patient responded well to a short course of prednisone and is now doing well. The nature of this respiratory illness is unclear; while it may have been related to administration of bromocriptine, there is no firm evidence to support this conclusion.

One patient had urinary incontinence, which resolved 3 days after bromocriptine was stopped. One patient with a history of old duodenal ulceration developed backache while receiving bromocriptine. He was given aspirin without our knowledge, and presented with haematemesis. He made an uneventful recovery when both aspirin and bromocriptine were withdrawn.

The only abnormal laboratory finding was asymptomatic transient elevation of SGOT and SGPT. This was encountered in 10 of the patients (8%); such findings were always viewed seriously and were considered an indication for reducing or stopping bromocriptine. With a decrease in intake of bromocriptine, the enzyme levels usually returned to normal and subsequent increments in dosages did not cause recurrence of elevations in liver enzymes.

Discussion

Our experience with 118 patients treated over a period of 5 years with bromocriptine has shown that 75 per cent of the patients studied so far have benefited from the drug to some degree; this is 23 per cent more than our previous results. Factors contributing to this change include: (1) The mean dosage of bromocriptine has increased by 23 per cent since our last, report. (2) The 26 new patients who entered the study since our last report have done well; this may reflect improved selection of suitable patients.

Among the side effects of bromocriptine, dyskinesia was prominent, and this deserves an explanation. Most of the patients were receiving L-dopa in addition to bromocriptine and of these, many had some degree of dyskinesia before they entered the study. Even though a temporary amelioration of that symptom was noted when giving bromocriptine in addition to L-dopa, dyskinesia reappeared or gradually increased in these patients during prolonged use of bromocriptine. The failure of dyskinesia to develop in patients receiving bromocriptine without L-dopa is in accord with other reports [12, 26, 27, 33] and supports our general conclusion that bromocriptine itself causes less dyskinesia than L-dopa.

Most of the patients with "on-off" reactions showed some initial improvement following introduction of bromocriptine. However, within a period of months "on-off" phenomena returned or increased, requiring either reduction of drug intake or discontinuation of bromocriptine. As in the case of dyskinesia, we conclude that while bromocriptine induces "on-off" reactions in patients who have developed this problem during L-dopa therapy, they are less frequent and less severe with the ergot derivative. We are not aware of any reports of bromocriptine causing "on-off" phenomena in patients who have never received L-dopa.

The most important adverse effects of bromocriptine are psychiatric reactions, and we regard a history of psychosis or dementia as a contraindication to this drug. Erythromelalgia induced by bromocriptine seems to arise from a localised vasculopathy; we have reported our analysis of this reaction in more detail elsewhere [42].

Elevation of liver enzymes was transient and not associated with a clinical picture of hepatitis [27]. In most patients, the enzymes returned to normal levels without any adjustments in dose of bromocriptine, but one had to be temporarily withdrawn from ergot therapy because of more prolonged abnormalities; in this case the values returned to normal levels without any adjustments in dose of bromocriptine, but one had to be temporarily withdrawn from ergot therapy because of more prolonged abnormalities; in this case the values returned to normal levels within a few weeks. These findings, and the more prominent hepatic complications reported [43] with lergotrile (another ergot derivative), imply that it might be an appropriate precaution to monitor transaminase values in all patients receiving long term bromocriptine therapy.

Although we accepted compensated cardiac patients for this study, we consider bromocriptine to be contraindicated in patients with severe angina pectoris, recent myocardial infarction, or an unstable cardiac rhythm. We also avoid giving bromocriptine to patients with active peptic ulcers, and we do not administer aspirin to patients receiving ergot derivatives.

In a small minority of patients, we have observed increasing Parkinsonian deficits when administering bromocriptine, and improvement when this drug was stopped. This paradoxical response may derive from selective stimulation of presynaptic dopamine receptors, or partial agonism at postsynaptic receptors.

While we have discussed the adverse effects of bromocriptine at some length, we should emphasise that we consider this drug to be a worthwhile addition to the therapeutic compendium for Parkinson's disease. It is particularly useful in certain patients who, in the course of conventional treatment with L-dopa, encounter severe dyskinesia, or "on-off" reactions.

The most significant fact emerging from experience with bromocriptine is that artificial agonists which act directly on dopaminergic receptors are capable of inducing a potent therapeutic response in some parkinsonian patients. This finding has led to the investigation of congeners of bromocriptine as potential treatment in Parkinsonism. We wish to conclude on a cautiously optimistic note by reporting a preliminary finding with another dopaminergic ergot, lisuride. From a double blind study which has, up to now, involved fourteen patients, we have evidence that this drug is efficacious. Over a period of 14 weeks of treatment we have found a therapeutic response is usually attained on a dose range of 2.5–5.0 mg lisuride daily. We are extending this investigation to determine whether lisuride is capable of eliciting safe and sustained benefit.

Summary

One hundred and eighteen patients with Parkinson's disease were treated for a period of over 5 years (mean 33 months) with bromocriptine (mean dose 72 mg). 70 patients (59%) dropped out of the study. 48 patients (41%) continued on the drug. In 88 patients (75%), who were receiving L-dopa concomitantly with bromocriptine, 48 (41%) underwent a mean reduction of 57 per cent of L-dopa requirement at a peak mean bromocriptine dose 68 mg/day. 75 per cent of the patients benefited to some degree from bromocriptine therapy. The reasons for withdrawal of the drug are discussed. In addition, we report our preliminary findings with a new dopaminergic ergot derivative, lisuride.

Acknowledgement

We wish to thank Mrs Helen Krebs and Ms Marjorie Gillespie for assisting with patient evaluations, and Ms Pamela Barnicoat for typing the manuscript.

Bibliography

1   Bateman DE, Tunbridge WMG. *Drugs 1979;17:*359
2   Besser GM. *Triangle 1978;17:*33
3   Besser GM, Thorner MO, Wass JAH et al. *Brit med J 1977;2:*868
4   Besser GM, Wass JAH, Thorner MO. *Acta Endocrinol (Suppl) (Copenh) 1978;216:*187
5   Boyd AE, Reichlin S. *New Engl J Med 1975;293:*451
6   Calne DB, Plotkin C, Williams AC et al. *Lancet 1978;i:*735
7   Calne DB, Teychenne PF, Claveria LE et al. *Brit med J 1974;4:*442
8   Caraceni TA, Celano I, Parati E. *J Neurol Neurosurg Psychiatr 1977;40:*2243

9   Clark BJ, Fluckiger E, Loew DM. *Triangle 1978;17:*21
10   Clark BJ, Scholtysik G, Fluckiger E. *Acta Endocrinol (Suppl) (Copenh) 1978;216:*75
11   Fahn S, Calne DB. *Neurology 1978;28:*5
12   Fahn S, Cote LJ, Snider SR. *Neurology 1978;28:*343
13   Fluckiger E. *Acta Endocrinol (Suppl) (Copenh) 1978;216:*111
14   Frank S. *Drugs 1979;17:*337
15   Godwin-Austen RB, Smith NJ. *J Neurol Neurosurg Psychiatr 1977;40:*479
16   Greenacre JK, Teychenne PF, Petrie A et al. *Br J Clin Pharmacol 1976;3:*571
17   Hutt CS, Snider SR, Fahn S. *Neurology (Minneap) 1977;27:*505
18   Johnson AM, Loew DM, Vigouret JM. *Brit J Pharmacol 1976;56:*59
19   Kartzinel R, Calne DB. *Neurology (Minneap) 1976;26:*508
20   Kartzinel R, Shoulson I, Calne DB. *Neurology (Minneap) 1976;26:*511
21   Kebabian JW, Calne DB. *Nature 1979;277:*93
22   Keller HH, Da Prada M. *Life Sci 1979;24:*1211
23   Kirstensen O, Hansen E. *Acta Neurol Scand 1977;56:*274
24   Lees AJ, Shaw KM, Stern GM. *Lancet 1975;ii:*709
25   Lieberman A, Kupersmith M, Estey E et al. *New Engl J Med 1976;245:*1400
26   Lieberman AN, Kupersmith M, Gopinathan G. *Modification of the 'on-off' effect with bromocriptine and lergotrile.* Presented at the International Symposium on Dopaminergic Ergot Derivatives and Motor Function 1978. Wenner-Gren Center. Stockholm
27   Lieberman AN, Kupersmith M, Gopinathan G et al. *Neurology 1979;29:*363
28   Marsden CD, Jenner P, Parkes JD et al. In Fuxe K, Calne DB, eds. *Dopaminergic Ergot Derivatives and Motor Function 1979;*313. New York, Pergamon Press
29   Mashiter K, Adams E, Beard M et al. *Lancet 1977;ii:*197
30   Mehta AE, Tolis G. *Drugs 1979;17:*313
31   Miyamoto T, Battista A, Goldstein M et al. *J Pharm Pharmacol 1974;26:*452
32   Parkes JD. In Harper N, Simmonds A, eds. *Recent Advances in Drug Research 1977;* 247. New York, Academic Press
33   Parkes JD, De Bono AG, Marsden CD. *J Neurol Neurosurg Psychiat 1976;39:*1101
34   Price P, Debono A, Parkes JD et al. *Brit J Clin Pharmacol 1978;6:*303
35   Rolland R, Schellekens LA. *Acta Endocrinol (Suppl) (Copenh) 1978;216:*119
36   Silbergeld E, Pfeiffer RF. *J Neurochem 1977;28:*1323
37   Teychenne PF, Calne DB, Leigh PN et al. *Lancet 1975;ii:*473
38   Vaisrub S. *JAMA 1976;235:*2854
39   Wass JAH, Moult PJA, Thorner MO et al. *Lancet 1979;ii:*66
40   Wass JAH, Thorner MO, Morris DV et al. *Brit med J 1977;1:*875
41   Parkes JD, Marsden CD, Donaldson I et al. *J Neurol Neurosurg Psychiat 1976;39:*184
42   Eisler T, Hall RP, Kalavar KAR et al. *Erythromelalgia-like eruption on parkinsonian patients treated with bromocriptine.* In preparation
43   Teychenne PF, Jones AE, Ishak KG et al. *Gastroenterology 1979;76:*575
44   Wass JAH, Thorner MO, Besser GM. *Lancet 1976;i:*1135
45   Griffith RW, Turkaji I, Braun P. *Brit J Clin Pharmacol 1978;5:*227

Chapter 42

DOPAMINE-LIKE ACTIONS OF ERGOT DERIVATIVES IN PARKINSONISM AND ENDOCRINE DISORDERS

M Schachter, C D Marsden, R George, J Dick, J D Parkes, B Smith, A Wilson, R Horowski and R Dorow

Introduction

A great number and variety of chemical substances have been isolated from the parasitic fungus, *Claviceps purpurea*, that grows on rye and grain and an immense amount of pharmacological work has been devoted to these compounds [1].

Dale's work on adrenaline remains the cornerstone of the pharmacology of ergot (Dale, 1906) [2]; he showed that many ergot alkaloids selectively block alpha-adrenoceptors whilst beta-adrenoceptors are relatively unaffected. However, in addition to these actions on the adrenergic nervous system, research in the last decade has been directed to the powerful effects of ergot alkaloids on the dopamine nervous system.

In medieval times it was recognised that milk cows eating contaminated grain failed to lactate and this also occurred in suckling women with St. Anthony's Fire. But only in the last 25 years has the mechanism of this emerged with the recognition that dopamine is the major inhibitory factor influencing production of the milk-controlling hormone, prolactin, by the pituitary, and the ergot derivatives have a similar action to dopamine. Fluckinger's work (1968) [3] on prolactin inhibition by ergot derivatives led to the production of the first of a new and exciting class of compounds, bromocriptine. Subsequently Corrodi *et al* (1974) [4] showed that bromocriptine had the same effect as L-dopa on motor behaviour in animals and because of this similarity bromocriptine was introduced as an antiparkinsonian drug. In addition to these actions on prolactin and the extrapyramidal system, bromocriptine is also effective in acromegaly in which there appears to be a defect in the normal dopaminergic control of growth hormone secretion.

This Chapter will briefly analyse the major therapeutic advances due to this class of compounds, many of which have now been investigated in the treatment of hormonal and motor disorders (Fuxe and Calne, 1979) [5]. Bromocriptine is the only member of this class that at present (1979) is readily available, although lisuride has been extensively used in the treatment of hormonal disorders [6, 7].

Structure

Ergolines are easier to prepare and less toxic than many other ergot derivatives. Examination of the basic ergoline molecule shows several similarities with the biogenic amines, with the structure of tryptamine and methyl tryptamine contained in the molecule. There is also some resemblance to phenylethylamine molecules and dopamine. This similarity of structure is probably the basis for the similar actions of certain ergolines and the biogenic amines at both pituitary and CNS level [8]. The 9, 10-dihydrogenated ergot compounds, including bromocriptine and lergotrile, dihydroergocornine and dihydroergokryptine do not have the toxic vasoconstrictive properties of other ergot derivatives that lack this group, but the dopamine-like actions remain intact. The stereo-chemical configuration of the molecule at the 8-position is important for this action, and D6-methyl-8 β-ergolineacetonitrile (lergotrile) and N-(D-6-methyl-8-isoergolenyl)-N', N'-diethyl-urea hydrogen maleate (lysenyl, lisuride) are amongst the most potent inhibitors of prolactin secretion known.

In 1960, Zikan and Semonsky [9] synthesised lisuride hydrogen maleate, 1, 1-diaethyl-3-(6aR, 9S-7 methyl-4, 6, 6a, 7, 8, 9-hexahydroindolo (4, 3-f, g) chinolin-9-y) urea, hydrogen maleate, an isoergolenyl derivative stereochemically related to d-isolysergic acid. Lisuride possesses many of the classic properties of other ergot derivatives and is an extremely potent dopamine-like drug. Horowski *et al* (1977) [10] showed that in normal women oral administration of lisuride 100–200 μg lowers prolactin levels, and reduces TRH and sulpiride-induced hyperprolactinaemia. Lisuride, like bromocriptine, causes stereotyped behaviour in normal and reserpine-treated mice and antagonises the motor depression caused by reserpine (Horowski and Wachtel, 1976) [11]. These effects of lisuride are similar to those of apomorphine and are not affected by pre-treatment with alpha-methyl-p-tyrosine, an inhibitor of tyrosine-beta-hydroxylase; but are antagonised by haloperidol, a drug which blocks dopamine receptors. In addition to this action on dopamine systems, lisuride, like LSD, inhibits the electrical activity of 5-hydroxytryptamine containing neurones [12, 13].

There is some evidence that ergoline derivatives, including lisuride, may have a selective action on dopamine systems in the limbic regions of the brain and also may be especially active in supersensitive systems [14, 15] in which case lisuride should stimulate the supersensitive nigro-neostriatal pathways in Parkinson's disease at doses lower than those causing stimulation in areas where denervation has not occurred.

The motor effects of lisuride, unlike bromocriptine, are independent of intact dopamine stores. If this pharmacological finding is relevant to man, lisuride may possibly prove a slightly more effective antiparkinsonian drug than bromocriptine in parkinsonian patients with severe neuronal loss but intact dopamine receptors. In many other respects lisuride resembles bromocriptine and both drugs inhibit ^{3}H spiroperidol binding from striatal membranes, but do not activate striatal adenylate cyclase linked dopamine systems [16]. There is some evidence that the motor actions of bromocriptine are prevented by interference with drug metabolising hep-

334

atic microsomal enzyme systems but this does not seem to be the case with lisuride [17].

Lisuride is approximately 10 to 15 times more potent than bromocriptine in causing prolactin suppression; and in rodents with 6-OH-dopamine lesions lisuride is amongst the most potent stimulants of turning behaviour investigated.

Actions of Ergot Derivatives on Prolactin

The role of ergot alkaloids in affecting reproduction and lactation has been studied extensively for many years. Animals fed ergot or its derivatives fail to lactate or reproduce normally [18-20]. This effect can be attributed to the inhibitory action of these compounds on prolactin release. Prolactin secretion is essential to normal lactation.

Dopamine is released from the hypothalamus and inhibits prolactin release from pituitary cells [21]. It is not clear how dopaminergic stimulation causes prolactin suppression but, in animals, bromocriptine reduces pituitary cell division and there is now definite evidence that treatment with bromocriptine will reduce the size of prolactin and growth hormone-producing tumours in man. Both *in vivo* and *in vitro* bromocriptine has a more prolonged action on prolactin suppression than dopamine and effects can be prevented by specific dopamine antagonists [22, 23]. These findings give definite evidence for a direct action of bromocriptine upon dopamine receptors situated on pituitary cells.

Bromocriptine, lergotrile and lisuride have all been used to treat lactation disorders and to suppress normal lactation [24-26]. Bromocriptine 7.5 mg daily, lergotrile 6 mg daily and lisuride 0.6 mg daily all reduce elevated prolactin levels to normal values with an immediate and sustained response that has now been maintained in the case of bromocriptine for over 8 years without the development of tolerance. Prolactin suppression with a single oral dose of all 3 drugs lasts for 4-12 hours. When hyperprolactinaemia is the result of intense dopamine receptor blockade due to neuroleptic drugs, or occasionally initial prolactin levels are extremely high, bromocriptine dosages of up to 50 mg daily are sometimes necessary to reverse hyperprolactinaemia and the clinical consequences of this. The most important of these is infertility occurring in both sexes and bromocriptine has been outstandingly successful in the treatment of infertility as a result of hyperprolactinaemia.

Bromocriptine 7.5–50 mg daily and lisuride 0.6 mg daily when used in a young and mainly female patient group with hyperprolactinaemia causes few side effects. However, a very few subjects may complain of sickness with faintness and sometimes collapse, occasionally accompanied by yawning and hiccup. Nausea and vomiting appear to be slightly less common with bromocriptine than lisuride in equipotent doses for endocrine and motor effect. Neither drug causes abnormal involuntary movements in endocrine disorders, although both drugs occasionally produce neuropsychiatric changes, altered awareness, and hallucinosis.

335

Growth Hormone

Dopamine-like drugs including ergoline derivatives cause a rise in plasma growth hormone levels lasting 60-120 minutes in most normal and also parkinsonian subjects but a sustained fall in plasma level lasting 6 to 8 hours in patients with acromegaly. The effect of bromocriptine and other ergot derivatives has been extensively investigated and it seems probable that the action in normal subjects results from hypothalamic dopamine receptor stimulation, whereas inhibition of growth hormone in acromegalics results from a direct inhibitory effect of the drug on pituitary dopamine receptors [27]. As with the nomal prolactin-producing cell, the neoplastic growth hormone producing cell may possess cell surface dopamine receptors.

Bromocriptine and dopamine have no effect on growth hormone production by normal cultured pituitary cells, but both inhibit growth hormone release from pituitary tumour cells *in vitro* [28]. The effects of L-dopa and dopamine infusion in acromegalic subjects are inconsistent but usually dopamine, which does not readily cross the blood-brain barrier, causes a fall in plasma growth hormone levels in acromegalics indicating a pituitary, or possibly hypothalamic, effect, whereas dopamine may cause a slight elevation of plasma growth hormone levels in normal subjects [29].

Bromocriptine and lisuride cause a fall in plasma growth hormone level in acromegalics although, unlike prolactin, growth hormone levels may not return to normal values and some subjects do not respond. However, bromocriptine 5-20 mg three times daily causes a sustained and dose related decrease in plasma growth hormone levels in about 80 per cent of all acromegalics [30-32]. The fall in plasma growth hormone level is usually obvious in the first week of treatment and metabolic changes occur in the first 2 weeks with clinical improvement commencing in the first 4-8 weeks. Complete clinical remission with bromocriptine in acromegaly is rare but most subjects respond to some degree. Hormonal and clinical response has now been maintained for over 5 years although occasionally tolerance develops, possibly owing to a change in pituitary tumour receptor characteristics. If treatment is stopped, plasma growth hormone levels return to previous values and disability returns. Lisuride has not been extensively investigated in acromegaly as yet but appears to have similar actions to those of bromocriptine [26]. Slightly higher doses of bromocriptine and lisuride used in acromegaly as compared with hyperprolactinaemia result in a slightly higher incidence of unwanted effects including nausea, hypotension, and altered awareness.

Effects of bromocriptine, lergotrile and lisuride on parkinsonism

Bromocriptine, lergotrile and lisuride all cause contraversive turning in animals with 6-hydroxydopamine induced degeneration of one nigro-striatal dopamine system, stereotyped sniffing and gnawing behaviour and relief of tremor in monkeys with surgical ventromedial segmental lesions [35-37]. The biochemical consequences of post-synaptic dopamine receptor stimulation result in a decrease of striatal dopamine turnover with these compounds [36] and all these drugs cause displacement of radioligands from striatal membranes which presumably label the post-synaptic dopamine receptor.

The effects of bromocriptine, lergotrile and lisuride in hyperprolactinaemia and acromegaly are likely to be due to direct stimulation of pituitary dopamine receptors and the pituitary appears to lack pre-synaptic receptor components. The motor effects of ergoline derivatives in Parkinson's disease are likely to result from both pre- and post-synaptic actions and, in the case of bromocriptine, drug metabolites may be involved [38, 39]. The motor effects of bromocriptine, but not those of lisuride, are prevented when dopamine synthesis or storage is inhibited, and interference with drug-metabolising hepatic microsomal enzyme systems will alter the motor response to bromocriptine but not to lisuride [17, 39].

The effect of bromocriptine, lergotrile and lisuride in Parkinson's disease may depend on the high dosages used (in comparison with hormonal disorders), and on the presence of a damaged nervous system and receptor sensitivity. All three drugs have broadly similar effects, although lergotrile is unsuitable for prolonged clinical use on account of hepatoxicity, and lisuride has not yet been fully evaluated. Single dose equivalents in the treatment of parkinsonism are very approximately L-dopa 100 mg (combined with a decarboxylase inhibitor), bromocriptine 10 mg, lergotrile 10 mg and lisuride 1 mg.

Although bromocriptine and more recently lisuride have been very successful in the treatment of hormonal disorders, their effect in parkinsonism may be more limited. In parkinsonism the effect of bromocriptine rarely quite equals that from optimum doses of L-dopa [40], and most clinical trials describe the additive effects of the two drugs. Bromocriptine may require adequate dopamine stores to exert its full therapeutic effect. However, the action of bromocriptine and L-dopa on tremor, rigidity, and akinesia is qualitatively similar and both drugs cause similar dyskinesias. There has been some debate about the value of bromocriptine in so-called "dopa failures" [41] and usually bromocriptine is not of great value in subjects who do not respond at all to L-dopa, although a few dopa-resistant subjects do respond [42]. Bromocriptine is of definite value to partially or completely replace L-dopa in parkinsonian subjects with dose-related response swings on L-dopa that cannot be avoided despite frequent administration of this drug.

The long-term benefits and side effects of bromocriptine have been summarised by Calne et al [43] (and see previous chapter). Bromocriptine appears to cause hallucinosis more often and nausea and vomiting less often than L-dopa. With bromocriptine, hallucinations may persist for several weeks following drug withdrawal. Many subjects on bromocriptine complain of drowsiness.

The antiparkinsonian actions of lergotrile and its side effects including dyskinesias, orthostatic hypotension, behavioural alterations and nausea and vomiting have been documented by Lieberman et al (1975) [44]. These appear to be qualitatively and quantitatively similar to those of bromocriptine, although with lergotrile there may be an early and marked amelioration in tremor. Lergotrile, like bromocriptine, causes mental changes more often than L-dopa and lergotrile will produce personality disorders, paranoid ideation and delusions [45], although these are all reversible on drug withdrawal. The mechanism of neuropsychiatric changes

337

with ergot derivatives used in the treatment of parkinsonism is still uncertain and other antiparkinsonian drugs including anticholinergics that lack both the dopamine stimulant action and LSD chemical grouping of ergoline derivatives, commonly produce hallucinations.

Lisuride 1–4 mg daily has about the same antiparkinsonian action as bromocriptine 10–50 mg daily, although the long-term potential and possible hazards of lisuride have not yet been evaluated. Lisuride is highly soluble and given iv caused an immediate improvement in tremor, rigidity and akinesia lasting for 2–4 hours, whilst dyskinesias occur in some subjects immediately after injection. With oral treatment, the antiparkinsonian action of lisuride is not quite so prolonged as with bromocriptine and lisuride is unlikely to be of greater value than bromocriptine in the control of L-dopa dose-related response swings. It is not yet known whether lisuride will be a more effective drug than bromocriptine in subjects with severe dopamine depletion.

There is limited evidence that bromocriptine is an incomplete dopamine agonist in man and in the treatment of parkinsonism high doses are sometimes less effective than low doses (Price *et al,* 1978) [48]. A transient deterioration, rather than improvement, has been observed at the commencement of both bromocriptine and lisuride therapy in parkinsonism; this has not been described in hormonal disorders, and is unlikely to be either clinically important, or related to a possible dopamine antagonist rather than agonist actions of these drugs in low dosages, but is likely to be due to natural variation in disease severity. With some dopamine-like drugs, including norpropylaporphine, tachyphylaxis develops during initial treatment but this does not appear to be the case with bromocriptine, lergotrile of lisuride.

TABLE I Clinical effects of different dopamine stimulants

	Bromocriptine	Other ergot derivatives	Levodopa	Amphetamine Amantadine
Average daily dose i) hyperprolactin- aemia ii) Parkinsonism	i) 5 mg ii) 100 mg	Lergotrile: i) 2 mg ii) 12 mg	i) Not used ii) 2–3 g	i) Not used ii) d-amphetamine 20–60 mg
iii) acromegaly	iii) 40 mg	Lisuride i) 0.4 mg	iii) Not used	iii) amantadine 200–300 mg
Duration of action	6–8 hours	Varies	2–3 hours	about 6 hours
Prolactin	Very potent, prolonged suppression	Bromocriptine more potent than other ergot derivatives, less potent than lisuride	Brief suppression only	Potentiate action of levodopa

	Bromocriptine	Other ergot derivatives	Levodopa	Amphetamine Amantadine
Growth hormone (normal)	Brief increase plasma levels	Methysergide: slight fall in plasma levels	As bromocriptine	Increase levels or potentiate action of levodopa
Growth hormone (acromegalics)	Sustained reduction in plasma GH with clinical improvement	Methysergide: little or no effect Lisuride: lowers GH level	Inconstant brief reduction in plasma GH levels	No effect
Parkinsonism	Almost as potent as levodopa. May have minor antagonistic effect	Lergotrile as potent as bromocriptine but tolerance may develop	Very potent	Minor improvement. No dyskinesias
Vascular toxicity	Uncommon but may cause Raynaud's phenomena and erythromelalgia	Some compounds (eg. ergotoxine) may cause gangrene in toxic doses	Slight or nil. Increases renal blood flow	Livedo reticularis
Emesis	10% all subjects	Varies widely	30–80% of all subjects	Rare
Neuropsychiatric	Rare (5–10%) in hormonal disorders. Common (30%) in parkinsonism and may be prolonged	LSD potent hallucinogen	15% of all parkinsonians	Hallucinations, CNS stimulation
Major advantages in hyperprolactinaemia or parkinsonism	High prolactin specificity. Prolonged and potent response. No tolerance. Safe	None established at present	High antiparkinsonian specificity. No tolerance. Safe	Occasionally useful adjunct in parkinsonism. Not useful in hormonal disorders
Major disadvantages	Few. High cost. Occasional syncope	Lergotrile is hepatotoxic and causes marked fall in BP. Not useful clinically	Development of response swings after 2–3 years use in parkinsonism	Not very effective. Amphetamine abuse

References

1   Berde B, Sturmer E. In Berde B, Schild HO, eds. *Ergot Alkaloids and Related Compounds, volume 49, 1978;* 1. Berlin: Springer-Verlag
2   Dale HH. *J Physiol 1906; 34:* 163

3   Flückiger E, Wagner HR. *Experientia 1968; 24:* 1130
4   Corrodi H, Fuxe K, Hökfelt T, Lidbrink P, Ungerstedt U. *J Pharmac Pharmacol 1973; 25:* 409
5   Fuxe K, Calne DB. In *Dopaminergic Ergot Derivatives and Motor Function 1979.* New York: Pergamon Press
6   De Cecco L, Foglia G, Ragni N, Rossato P, Venturini PL. *Clin Endocrinol 1978; 9:* 491
7   Liuzzi A, Chiodini P, Verde GG. *1979.* In press
8   Clemens JA, Shaar CJ, Smalstig EB, Bach NJ, Kornfeld EC. *Endocrinology 1974; 94:* 1171
9   Zikan V, Semonsky M. *Collect Czech Chem Comm 1960; 25:* 1922
10 Horowski R, Wendt H, Graf KJ. *Acta Endocrinol (Kbh) 1977; 85:suppl 212:* 53
11 Horowski R, Wachtel H. *Europ J Pharmacol 1976; 36:* 373
12 Aghajanian GK, Foote WE, Sheard MH. *Science 1968; 161:* 706
13 Carlsson A, Lindqvist M. *J Neural Trans 1972; 33:* 23
14 Fuxe K, Agnati LF, Corrodi H, Everitt BT, Hökfelt T, Löfström A, Ungerstedt U. In Calne D, Chase TN, Barbeau A, eds. *Advances in Neurology, volume 9, 1975;* 223. New York: Raven Press
15 Horowski R. *Europ J Pharmacol 1978; 51:* 157
16 Fujita N, Saito K, Yonehara N, Yoshida H. *Neuropharmacology 1978; 17:* 1089
17 Keller HH, da Prada M. *Life Sci 1979; 24:* 1211
18 Nordskog AW, Clark RT. *Am J Vet Res 1945; 6:* 107
19 Nordskog AW. *Am J Vet Res 1946; 7:* 490
20 Tindal JS. *J Endocrinol 1956; 14:* 268
21 MacLeod RM, Lehmeyer JE. *Endocrinology 1974; 94:* 1077
22 Pasteels JL, Danguy A, Frerotte M. *Ann Endocrinol (Paris) 1971; 32:* 188
23 Besser GM. *Triangle 1978; 17:* 33
24 Horrobin DF. *Drugs 1979; 17:* 409
25 Cleary RE, Crabtree R, Lemberger L. *J Clin Endocr Metab 1975; 40:* 830
26 Verde G, Luizzi A, Chiodini PG. *Acta endocr (Kbh) 1979; 91: suppl 225:* 395
27 Liuzzi A, Verde G, Chiodini PG. *Triangle 1978; 17:* 41
28 Mashiter K, Adams E, Beard M, Holley A. *Lancet 1977; ii:* 197
29 Verde G, Oppizzi G, Colussi G, Cremascoli G, Botalla L, Müller EE, Silvestrini F, Chiodini PG, Liuzzi A. *Clin Endocrinol 1976; 5:* 419
30 Liuzzi A, Chiodini PG, Botalla L, Müller EE, Cremascoli G, Silvestrini F. *J Clin Endocr Metab 1974; 38:* 910
31 Wass JAM, Thorner MO, Morris DV, Rees LH, Mason AS, Jones AE, Besser GM. *Brit Med J 1977; 1:* 875
32 Besser GM, Wass JAM, Thorner MO. *Acta Endocrinol (Copenh) suppl 1978; 216:* 187
33 Corrodi H, Fuxe K, Hökfelt T, Lidbrink P, Ungerstedt U. *J Pharmac Pharmacol 1973; 25:* 409
34 Johnson AM, Loew DM, Vigouret SM. *Brit J Pharmacol 1976; 56:* 59
35 Miyamoto T, Battista A, Goldstein M, Fuxe K. *J Pharmac Pharmacol 1974; 26:* 452
36 Fuxe K, Corrodi H, Hökfelt T, Lidbrink P, Ungerstedt U. *Med Biol 1974; 52:* 121
37 Lew JY, Hata F, Ohashi T, Goldstein M. *J Neural Trans 1977; 41:* 109
38 Clark BJ, Flückiger E, Loew DM. *Triangle 1978; 17:* 21
39 Marsden CD, Jenner P, Parkes JD. In Fuxe K, Calne DB, eds. *Dopaminergic Ergot Derivatives and Motor Function 1979;* 313. New York: Pergamon Press
40 Parkes JD. *New Engl. J Med 1979; 301:* 873
41 Lieberman AN. *New Engl J Med 1977; 297:* 508
42 Fahn S, Cote LJ, Snider SR, Barrett RE, Isgreen WP. *Neurology (Minneap) 1979; 29:* 1077
43 Calne DB, Plotkin C, Williams AC, Neophytides A, Nutt JG, Teychenne PF. *Lancet 1978; i:* 735
44 Lieberman A, Miyamoto T, Battista AF, Goldstein M. *Neurology (Minneap) 1975; 25:* 459

45   Lieberman AN, Kupersmith M, Estey E, Goldstein M. *Lancet 1976; ii:* 515
46   Price P, Debono A, Parkes JD, Marsden CD, Rosenthaler J. *Brit J Clin Pharmacol 1978; 6:* 303

Chapter 43

DEPRENYL

G M Stern, Cecilie M Lander, A J Lees and C Ward

During the past decade the potential and also the limitations of L-dopa administered alone or in combination with a peripheral decarboxylase inhibitor in Parkinsonism has become well known. Many agents which might on theoretical grounds
improve the quality and duration of L-dopa therapy have been studied and amine-
oxidase inhibitors were among the first to be tried. Blashko (1952) [1], in his
authoritative review of the history of amine-oxidase and amine metabolism, points
out that as early as 1877 Schmiedeberge had shown that, in the dog, benzylamine
was excreted as hippuric acid, and correctly speculated that probably all monoamine bases are broken down in a similar manner. In 1928, Mary Hare discovered
an enzyme which catalysed the oxidative deamination of tyramine and, during the
1930s from studies of the metabolism of adrenaline *in vitro,* the concept of amine-
oxidase, an enzyme system which catalyses the oxidation of a large number of amines, was firmly established. It was soon recognised that MAO systems were widely
distributed in the animal kingdom and were present in many different tissues including neurones, glia, liver, kidney, heart, lung and various kinds of smooth muscle
bound to outer mitochondrial membranes. Subsequent studies illustrated considerable substrate specificity and indicated how MAO participates physiologically in
regulating intracellular concentrations of certain monoamines, including dopamine.
It is now well established that in the brain the major enzymatic pathway of catecholamine degradation is oxidative deamination by MAO which functions intra-
neuronally and O-methyl-action by catechol-O-methyl transferase (COMT) which
functions extraneuronally.

Following the seminal finding that in patients with Parkinsonism the substantia
nigra and corpus striatum were deficient in dopamine, attempts were speedily made
to inhibit the degradation of this neurotransmitter. In 1962 Birkmayer and
Hornykiewicz [2] gave a number of the then available monoamine oxidase inhibitors
alone and in combination with L-dopa. Although clinical improvement was recorded, distressing side-effects such as toxic delirium, increased involuntary movements and potentially catastrophic hypertension led to the temporary abandonment of this form of adjuvant therapy.

Recent advances in knowledge concerning monoamine oxidase systems and inhibitors have shown that MAO exists in several forms with different substrate specificities and these can be classified according to response to potent and selective irreversible inhibitors. Johnston [3] proposed two main types, A and B. Type A-MAO deaminates 5-hydroxy-tryptamine and noradrenaline and is selectively inhibited by clorgyline; type B deaminates phenylethylamine and benzylamine and is effectively inhibited by deprenyl. The latter, (-)(N-methyl-N-propynyl)(2-phenyl-1-methyl-ethyl)ammonium chloride, was synthesised and introduced by Knoll who demonstrated in tissue preparations that this inhibition is free from the 'cheese effect' [4]. We were able to confirm that deprenyl is an extremely potent drug causing complete inhibition of the human platelet enzyme within an hour or two by doses as low as 2–5 mg, whilst relatively complete inhibition of MAO-B throughout the body follows the administration of a 10 mg dose. We were also able to confirm Knoll's claim of safety by giving volunteers up to 200 mg of tyramine during deprenyl administration [5]. A balanced crossover study in six healthy young male adults showed that deprenyl acted like other MAO inhibitors and was associated with an increase in frequency of periods of wakefulness and stage 2 sleep and decreasing REM sleep and sleep stages 3 and 4.

Apart from inhibiting the degradation of dopamine, deprenyl may have other significant actions. The drug is metabolised almost quantitatively to a mixture of approximately 80 per cent methamphetamine and 20 per cent amphetamine, and Reynolds et al [6] have shown in post-mortem human brains that in addition to increasing the concentration of dopamine, there is a tenfold or more increase in the concentration of 2-phenylethylamine and also of amphetamine. Phenylethylamine has an indirect effect on dopamine activity and also a direct effect on dopaminergic receptors; amphetamine has a direct central stimulant effect on dopamine releasing mechanism. Whatever the precise mode of action of oral deprenyl on dopaminergic and other neurotransmitter systems in the brain, there have now been several studies to confirm its safety and to show that it has a useful but limited role in alleviating the symptoms and some of the complications of patients treated with L-dopa.

In 1975 Birkmayer et al [7] showed that when deprenyl was given orally, intravenously or intramuscularly, the anti-akinetic effect of L-dopa was potentiated and that deprenyl could reduce functional disability within sixty minutes of a single oral dose, a benefit might persist for up to three days. In an open trial of constant medication, he and his colleagues [8] found sustained benefit after two years and reported that side-effects which occurred during combined treatment were of the same order and magnitude as occurring with L-dopa therapy alone.

We found in a double-blind, crossover trial [9] in 41 patients receiving maximum tolerated doses of L-dopa alone or in combination with carbidopa, that 10 mg of deprenyl daily prolonged the benefits of L-dopa and was helpful in about half the patients who had end-of-dose akinesia or wearing-off effect of the previous oral dose, also helping those with nocturnal and early morning akinesia. We found no definite improvement in those with severe, unpredictable on-off disabilities, rapid oscillations of motor performance and akinetic freezing. In previously untreated

343

patients, deprenyl alone in doses of up to 40 mg produced only slight relief in disability, but when 10 mg daily was given in combination with L-dopa or carbidopa, a mean dosage reduction of 200 mg of L-dopa was possible. Drug-induced dyskinesia was unacceptably aggravated in 14 patients and no specific antidepressant effect was noted.

Rinne and his colleagues [10] reported their experiences in 47 Parkinsonians on long term L-dopa therapy with and without on-off changes and found a significant reduction in on-off disabilities in 68 per cent, but considered that this degree of improvement was mostly in the moderate or minimal range and no patient showed a dramatic response. They also found that peak dose dyskinesia was aggravated in about half the patients. Csanda *et al* [11] reported improvement in two-thirds of their 152 patients and considered that all Parkinsonians merited a trial of deprenyl.

Recently, 18 of our original patients who had shown initial and unequivocal benefit from combined therapy with deprenyl during double-blind studies were followed for up to thirty months and then participated in a further double-blind assessment when deprenyl was replaced with placebo. Two thirds of the patients showed deterioration on placebo, but only four of the original eighteen were gaining substantial, sustained benefit from deprenyl. These impressions have been confirmed in uncontrolled observations when patients were questioned after supplies of deprenyl had been unexpectedly curtailed. Thus although there seems to be evidence that deprenyl is an effective adjuvant to conventional L-dopa therapy and is safe and devoid of a cheese reaction, it remains to be determined whether the beneficial effects are sustained and whether patients who are treated in this manner throughout the course of their illness will run a more benign course with fewer late complications.

References

1   Blashko H. *Pharm Rev 1952;4:*415
2   Birkmayer W, Hornykiewcz O. *Wr Klin Wachr 1962;74:*555
3   Johnston JP. *Biochem Pharmacol 1968;17:*1285
4   Knoll J, Vizi ES, Somogyi G. *Arzneim Forsch 1968;18:*109
5   Stern GM, Lees AJ, Sandler M. *J Neurol Transm 1978;43:*245
6   Reynolds GP, Riederer P, Sandler M, Jellinger K, Seeman D. *J Neurol Transm 1978; 43:*271
7   Birkmayer W, Riederer P, Youdim MBH, Lihauer W. *J Neurol Transm 1975;36:*303
8   Birkmayer W, Riederer P, Ambrosi L, Youdim MBH. *Lancet 1977;i:*439
9   Lees AJ, Kohout LJ, Shaw KM, Stern GM, Elsworth JD, Sandler M, Youdim MBH. *Lancet 1977;ii:*791
10 Rinne UK, Siirtola T, Sonninen V. *J Neurol Transm 1978;43:*253
11 Csanda E, Antal J, Antony M, Csanaky A. *J Neurol Transm 1978;43:*263

Chapter 44

NOMIFENSINE

G W Hanks and D M Park

Nomifensine ("Merital") is a new antidepressant which has been available in the UK for the last two years or so. It is a tetrahydroisoquinoline and thus differs structurally from the standard tricyclic antidepressants (Figure 1) but has a similar phar-

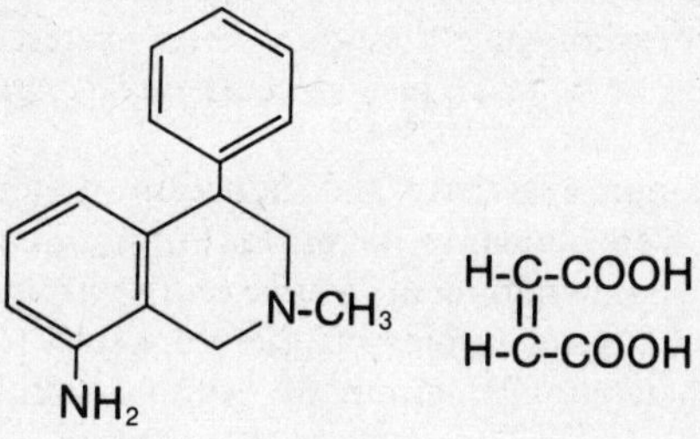

Figure 1 Nomifensine (Hoe 36 984). 8-Amino-1,2,3,4-tetrahydro-2-methyl-4-phenyliso-quinoline.

macological profile and shares with them the property of being a mono-amine uptake inhibitor [1-4]. *In vitro* and *in vivo* studies using various animal models demonstrated that nomifensine differs from the tricyclics in that it possesses potent dopaminergic activity and this prompted investigation of its possible therapeutic use in Parkinson's disease. This chapter reviews the relevant pharmacological and clinical data relating to the use of this drug in parkinsonism.

Pharmacology

Nomifensine was selected for development as an antidepressant after initial pharmacological screening indicated that it had a favourable therapeutic index in the

345

standard animal models for antidepressant activity (reserpine and tetrabenazine-induced syndromes in rodents) [1]. Early studies also demonstrated that nomifensine increases spontaneous motor activity in rats and is a potent inducer of stereotypy [5-7] behaviour which is believed to reflect dopaminergic activity [8]. Nomifensine produced similar effects to reference dopaminergic drugs such as amphetamine and apomorphine, but these effects could be differentiated from both those of amphetamine and of apomorphine *in vivo* on the basis of pre-treatment with α-methylparatyrosine (α MPT) and reserpine.

Sayers and Handley [9] divided CNS stimulants into three groups on the basis of their ability to induce stereotypy or produce an increase in locomotor activity in rats pre-treated with a α MPT or reserpine, or both. The first group is represented by amphetamine, whose effects in these animal models are abolished by pre-treatment with a α MPT but are resistant to pre-treatment with reserpine. Amphetamine is believed to act indirectly by releasing recently synthesised catecholamines from the non-granular (reserpine resistant) pool; α MPT inhibits dopamine synthesis.

The second group, represented by methylphenidate, is not affected by pre-treatment with α MPT plus reserpine. It is postulated that the action of this group of drugs depends on both the granular and non-granular amine stores. Drugs in the third group, represented by apomorphine, produce their effects by a direct action on the post-synaptic receptor, and these are therefore resistant to combined pre-treatment with α MPT and reserpine, since these agents can only affect pre-synaptic function.

The increase in locomotor activity and induction of stereotyped behaviour induced by nomifensine were shown to be resistant to pre-treatment with α MPT but were abolished by the combination of α MPT and reserpine, or by pre-treatment with haloperidol [5, 6]. Nomifensine was therefore seen to have some characteristics of the methylphanidate-like group of drugs, according to the Sayers and Handley criteria.

Subsequent work further alluded to the similar pharmacological profiles of nomifensine and methylphenidate [7, 10]. Nomifensine was shown to produce a marked increase in brain levels of homovanillic acid (HVA) and 3, 4-dihydroxyphenyl acetic acid (DOPAC—a dopamine (DA) metabolite). Methylphenidate also induced an increase in DOPAC whereas amphetamine, apomorphine and benztropine, a powerful amine-uptake inhibitor, did not induce any change in DOPAC. This suggested that nomifensine is not merely an amine-uptake inhibitor, but that it causes *release* of catecholamines in a similar way to methylphenidate.

The possibility that nomifensine may cause release of catecholamines had been examined earlier. Gerhards and his colleagues [5] showed, however, that nomifensine fails to increase DA turnover in the striatum in doses which elicit hypermotility in rats, unlike amphetamine, and they concluded that nomifensine does not induce release of catecholamines.

The weight of evidence from other biochemical studies supports this latter conclusion. Using a crude rat brain synaptosome preparation, Schacht and Heptner [3] demonstrated that nomifensine is a potent inhibitor of noradrenaline (NA) uptake and has a relatively weaker effect on serotonin (5HT) uptake. They were unable

346

to demonstrate any releasing effects on the efflux of noradrenaline. In a similar model, nomifensine was shown to be a very powerful inhibitor of dopamine uptake, being more active in this respect than both amphetamine and benztropine, and thus one of the most active inhibitors of dopamine uptake known [4]. Again, no releasing effects on dopamine could be demonstrated with nomifensine. Further studies using electrically stimulated brain slices did not show any releasing effects of nomifensine on catecholamines [11]. These results conflict with the conclusion of Braestrup and Scheel-Kruger, but their data could also be explained on the basis of DA-uptake inhibition rather than release. Costall and her colleagues [6, 12] further suggested that nomifensine may have some direct receptor activating properties. This was on the basis of its resistance to α MPT pre-treatment and its relative resistance to dopamine blockade by haloperidol, together with observations of its effects in circling models in which the response elicited by nomifensine more closely resembled those produced by apomorphine than by amphetamine. This assumption has been disputed by other workers, on the basis both of the abolition of stereotyped behaviour of combined α MPT and reserpine pre-treatment—which indicates a pre-synaptic mode of action; and by the observation that nomifensine causes ipsilateral circling in animals with a unilateral 6-hydroxydopamine induced lesion of the nigrostriatal dopaminergic pathway, whereas direct agonists such as apomorphine and bromocriptine induce contralateral circling [13].

Costall and Naylor [12] discuss this particular point and suggest that the direction of circling induced by dopaminergic agents is not a reliable basis for differentiating between pre- and post-synaptic activity.

Further doubt on a post-synaptic action of nomifensine is, however, raised by the different effects produced by nomifensine and apomorphine in animals with bilateral 6-hydroxydopamine lesions of the substantia nigra [14]. Poat *et al* [15] using a dopamine-sensitive adenylate cyclase receptor model, were also unable to demonstrate any direct agonist effect of nomifensine or of its 4'-hydroxy metabolite.

It appears, therefore, that the predominant effect of nomifensine in relation to amine neurotransmission is to inhibit re-uptake of the catecholamines, dopamine and noradrenaline, with a much weaker inhibitory effect on serotonin reuptake. The evidence that the drug either causes release of catecholamines or that it possesses direct DA-receptor activating effects is unconvincing.

The precise site and mode of action of nomifensine in relation to NA and DA are important in the context of its therapeutic potential in Parkinson's disease, a disease characterised by neuronal degeneration in the substantia nigra and loss of nigrostriatal dopaminergic pathways. Drugs which have a purely pre-synaptic mode of action are unlikely therefore to produce profound therapeutic benefits or to help at all in patients with advanced chronic disease where there is extensive pre-synaptic dysfunction. This is true of amphetamine, which causes release of dopamine from the pre-synaptic neurone and has only mild therapeutic activity in parkinsonism [16], and of amantadine [17].

There is some evidence that the ideal anti-parkinson drug should possess noradrenergic as well as dopaminergic activity [18]. Tricyclic anti-depressants have been used in Parkinson's disease but with little success. The various tricyclic anti-depressants block the reuptake of NA and 5HT to varying degree but none have any significant effect on DA uptake [19, 20]. Nomifensine is therefore unusual in its combination of dopaminergic and noradrenergic effects, and certainly differs in this respect from the tricyclics. This, with the potent dopaminergic activity of nomifensine in animal behavioural models, was the stimulus for clinical investigation of the drug in patients with parkinsonsim.

Clinical studies

Clinical investigation of the antidepressant activity of nomifensine began some ten years ago and the drug is now widely available around the world as an anti-depressant.

In some early trials of nomifensine as an antidepressant it was observed that schizophrenic patients on long-term neuroleptic treatment experienced an amelioration of the extra-pyramidal side-effects of these drugs when nomifensine was added to their regimen. This was followed by specific studies in patients with Parkinson's disease.

In the first reported trial, 28 patients with idipoathic parkinsonism and one patient with post-encephalitic parkinsonism were studied [21]. Of the twenty patients who completed the trial, sixteen were receiving maximum tolerated doses of L-dopa, two were receiving anticholinergics and two were not taking any drugs. The mean maximum tolerated dose of nomifensine was 150 mg/day added to existing therapy and the results suggested that nomifensine does have a moderate therapeutic effect in parkinsonism; all aspects of functional disability improved with the addition of nomifensine, with tremor and facial expression improving most. The major adverse effect was dyskinesia and, although this was most marked in patients already receiving L-dopa, three patients who were not receiving L-dopa also developed dyskinesias with nomifensine.

In a small single blind study [22] eight patients with idiopathic Parkinson's disease presented much more difficult clinical problems. Four had developed the "on-off" phenomenon and four had failed to respond or had lost all response to L-dopa. Nomifensine in doses of 50–150 mg/day failed to produce any benefit in these patients.

Barbeau *et al* (1979) [32] looked at two groups of patients: the first (n = 17) had not previously received L-dopa; in the second (n = 10) all patients were receiving L-dopa either alone or with a peripheral decarboxylase inhibitor. Patients were treated with 75–150 mg nomifensine daily for a maximum of four months. Though there was a trend in favour of nomifensine, overall the drug produced no significant benefit in either group of patients.

In a recently completed trial [23], nomifensine was studied in eighteen patients with idiopathic parkinsonism who had not previously received L-dopa or bromocriptine. Six patients were receiving no other medication, nine were receiving anticholinergics alone, one amantidine alone and two patients were receiving a com-

348

bination. They were entered into a double-blind crossover study in which they were treated with nomifensine or placebo for six weeks and then crossed over. Clinical evaluation was carried out every two weeks using a standard scoring system [24].

The result of the aggregated ratings showed a difference in favour of nomifensine but this failed to reach the 5 per cent significance level. Some individual items of the clinical rating did improve significantly: tremor and rigidity were reduced ($p < 0.02$; $p < 0.01$) and speech disorder and arising from a chair improved ($p < 0.02$; $p < 0.01$). No involuntary movements were provoked nor were there other notable adverse effects attributable to nomifensine.

Conclusions

The moderate therapeutic effects in Parkinson's disease demonstrated for nomifensine in the clinical studies are consistent with the biochemical data on this drug. Its effects on dopaminergic transmission are largely or wholly confined to presynaptic inhibition of dopamine reuptake and, predictably, it does not produce marked beneficial effects in parkinsonism. Nomifensine may, however, have a specific place in the treatment of certain patients with Parkinson's disease. As suggested by Findley and his colleagues, its good tolerability and lesser tendency to provoke involuntary movements may make it preferable to L-dopa for the patient in the early states of the disease. Depression in a patient with Parkinson's disease may also be a specific indication for the use of nomifensine rather than an alternative antidepressant. Nomifensine is now established as an effective antidepressant [25] and has particular advantages in the treatment of an elderly population, namely a relative lack of anticholinergic effects [26, 27] and absence of serious cardiovascular effects, either in therapeutic dose or overdose [28–30].

Depression is common in Parkinson's disease [31] and can frequently be a difficult problem; this would appear to be a particularly appropriate situation for the use of nomifensine.

References

1   Hoffmann I. *Arzneim-Forsch (Drug Res) 1973; 23:* 45
2   Hoffmann I. *Brit J clin Pharmac 1977; 4:*69S
3   Schacht U, Heptner W. *Biochem Pharmac 1974; 23:*3413
4   Hunt P, Kannengiesser MH, Raynaud JP. *J Pharm Pharmac 1974; 26:*370
5   Gerhards HJ, Carenzi A, Costa E. *Naunyn-Schmideberg's Arch Pharmacol 1974; 286:*49
6   Costall B, Kelly DM, Naylor RJ. *Psychopharmacologia (Berl) 1975; 41:*153
7   Braestrup C, Scheel-Kruger J. *Europ J Pharmacol 1976; 38:*305
8   Fog R. *Acta neurol scand suppl 1972; 48:*50
9   Sayers AC, Handley SL. *Europ J Pharmacol 1973; 23:* 47
10   Braestrup C. *J Pharm Pharmac 1977; 29:*463
11   Schacht U, Leven M, Backer G. *Brit J Clin Pharmac 1977; 4:*77S
12   Costall B, Naylor RJ. *Psychopharmacologia (Berl) 1975; 41:*57

13   Pycock C, Milson JA, Tarsy D, Marsden CD. *J Pharm Pharmac 1976; 28:*530
14   Price MTC, Fibiger HC. *Pharmac Biochem Behav 1976; 5:*107
15   Poat JA, Woodruff GN, Watling KJ. *J Pharm Pharmac 1978; 30:*495
16   Parkes JD, Tarsy D, Marsden CD, Bovill KT, Phipps JA, Rose P, Asselman P. *J Neurol Neurosurg Psychiat 1975; 38:*232
17   Hunter KR. In Turner P, ed. *Topics in Therapeutics 2 1976;* 121. Tunbridge Wells: Pitman Medical Ltd
18   Hornykiewicz O. In Yahr MD, ed. *Advances in Neurology 1973;* 1. New York: Raven Press
19   Horn AS, Coyle JT, Snyder SH. *Mol Pharmac 1971; 7:*66
20   Fuxe K, Ungerstedt U. *Europ J Pharmacol 1968; 4:*135
21   Teychenne PF, Park DM, Findley LJ, Clifford Rose F, Calne DB. *J Neurol Neurosurg Psychiat 1976; 39:*1219
22   Bédard P, Parkes JD, Marsden CD. *Brit J Clin Pharmac 1977; 4:*187S
23   Findley LJ, Hanks G, Park DM, Sandler M. Submitted for publication
24   Calne DB, Teychenne PF, Claveria LE, Eastman R, Greenacre JK, Petrie A. *Brit Med J 1974; 4:*442
25   Stonier PD, Jenner FA. *Nomifensine Roy Soc Med Int Cong Symp Series 1980.* No 25. Academic Press London
26   Malsch V. In *Alival Symposium über Ergebruisse der experimentellen und Klinischen Prüfung 1977;* 141. Stuttgart: Schattauer
27   Chan M-Y, Ehsanullah R, Wadsworth J, McEwen J. *Brit J Clin Pharmac 1979.* In press
28   Burrows GD, Vohra J, Cunmorie P, Scoggins BA, Davies B. *Med J Aust 1978; 1:*341
29   *Drug and Therapeutics Bulletin 1979; 17:*13
30   Dawling S, Braithwaite R, Crome P. *Lancet 1979; i:*56
31   Mindham RHS. *J Neurol Neurosurg Psychiat 1979; 33:*188
32   Barbeau A, Roy M, Gonce M, Labereque R. In Poirier LJ, Sourkes TL, Bedard PJ, eds. *Advances in Neurology, volume 24, 1979;* 433. New York: Raven Press

Chapter 45

OXPENTIFYLLINE

R B Godwin-Austen

In the treatment of Parkinson's disease the main emphasis since the introduction of L-dopa has been on improvement in the effectiveness of that drug and the development of dopamine agonists. However, with both L-dopa and synthetic dopamine agonists, problems of receptor hypersensitivity reactions lead to a substantial rate of failure of treatment. Thus between one third and a half of patients on L-dopa for more than 3 years have lost most or all of their benefit because of the development of abnormal movements or 'on-off' attacks. While these toxic manifestations of L-dopa treatment in the Parkinsonian undoubtedly relate partly to varying brain concentrations of dopamine, variations in receptor sensitivity play a part. Compounds, therefore, which affect receptor sensitivity are of great interest especially in the patient suffering from a late failure of L-dopa treatment. Of the two dopamine receptors in the striatum, one is dependent on cyclic AMP. Inhibition of cyclic AMP phosphodiesterase raises the intracellular levels of cyclic AMP and should therefore enhance dopaminergic activity.

Oxpentifylline is a methylxanthine derivative related to theophylline which inhibits phosphodiesterase in a wide variety of tissues including brain [1]. There is some evidence from animal work that it may potentiate dopaminergic agonists. We wished to study whether a similar potentiating effect could be demonstrated in man. Since oxpentifylline has a mild central stimulating effect, an attempt was made to monitor such effect in our patients and distinguish it from any specific effect on Parkinsonian symptoms and signs.

13 patients with Parkinsonism were studied, all of whom were suffering 'on-off' attacks, dyskinesias or deterioration while on L-dopa. The trial was designed as a double blind, within patient, comparison of oxpentifylline and placebo added to existing therapy, the dose of levodopa and anticholinergic drugs being continued unchanged. The patients were assessed as to their Parkinsonian symptoms and signs fortnightly, had their critical flicker fusion threshold measured as a measure of central arousal [2] and carried out a daily self assessment of severity of dyskinesia 'on-off' attacks.

Two patients were withdrawn during the initial period of the trial, when oxipentifylline was being introduced in increasing dose to establish tolerance; one

TABLE I Clinical details and response to oxpentifylline

Patient	Sex	Age (Yrs)	Length of History (Yrs)	Drugs on Admission to Trial
1	M	66	13	Sinemet (275) ½ t.d.s. Benzhexol 2 mg b.d.
2	M	66	14	Sinemet (275) ½ 5 daily Orphenadrine 50 mg t.d.s. Amantadine 100 mg t.d.s.
3	F	68	7	Sinemet (275) ½ 7 daily Benzhexol 2 mg t.d.s.
4	F	66	6	Sinemet (110) 1 t.d.s. Benzhexol 2 mg t.d.s.
5	F	52	10	Sinemet (110) ½ t.d.s.
6	F	67	12	Levodopa 500 mg 8 daily
7	F	57	6	Sinemet (110) t.d.s. Orphenadrine 50 mg t.d.s.
8	M	51	7	Sinemet (110) ½ b.d. Benzhexol 2 mg q.d.s.
9	F	42	10	Sinemet (275) 1 q.d.s. Benzhexol 2 mg q.d.s.
10	F	48	14	Sinemet (110) ½ 7 daily Benzhexol 2 mg t.d.s. Bromocriptine 2.5 mg 6 daily
11	M	75	6	Sinemet (110) 3½ daily Benzhexol 5 mg b.d.

Significance

+   Improved
-   Worsened
0   No change
N.S. Not significant

Oxpentifylline (mg/day)	Functional Capacity	Rigidity	Hypokinesia	Abnormal Movements
1200	0	+	0	-
1200	+	+	0	0
1200	0	0	+	-
1200	0	0	+	-
1200	0	-	-	-
1200	+	+	+	-
1200	+	0	+	-
1200	-	0	-	-
1200	0	+	+	-
1200	-	-	+	+
900	0	0	0	0
	N.S.	N.S.	N.S.	P < 0.01

patient developed severe nausea, whilst the other suffered marked exacerbation of involuntary movements and asked to be excluded.

The remaining 11 patients ranged in age from 42 to 75 years; the mean duration of Parkinsonism was 9 years and there were 7 females and 4 males. All were taking L-dopa and 9 out of 11 patients were taking anticholinergic drugs as well.

On a dose of oxpentifylline 1200 mg/day in addition to L-dopa, no therapeutic effect could be demonstrated. Table I illustrates the most important parameters of assessment and it is clear without any statistical analysis that no benefit occurred. It is noteworthy that one patient (No. 10), who was the only patient on bromocriptine, deteriorated subjectively and objectively with regard to rigidity while on oxpentifylline.

In the majority of cases the abnormal involuntary movements were exacerbated. The only exception—again—was the patient on bromocriptine whose abnormal movements were less.

Critical flicker fusion threshold showed no significant change with oxypenti-fylline and our patients did not report any symptoms that might be interpreted as indicative of an alerting or stimulating effect such as insomnia, tremor or agitation. We believe therefore that the deleterious effects of oxpentifylline are not due to any non-specific central stimulating effect.

Animal work and previous studies with oxpentifylline in human subjects have not caused abnormal involuntary movements. What then is the mechanism of the exacerbation of abnormal movements in L-dopa treated Parkinsonians by oxpenti-fylline?

If the abnormal movements observed in our study derived from a noradrenergic mechanism they must only develop in patients with the specific neurochemical defect of Parkinson's disease. There is no published evidence to suggest that dopa dyskinesia is mediated via a noradrenergic mechanism.

At least three types of dopamine receptor are present in the striatum—pre and post synaptic DA2 receptors and post synaptic DA1 receptors [3]. The DA2 receptor is unassociated with adenyl cyclase whereas DA1 is dependent on adenyl cyclase mechanisms. Oxpentifylline is only to be expected to have any action on DA1.

The increase of abnormal involuntary movement induced by oxpentifylline suggests that this side effect of levodopa may be partly or wholly dependent on this DA1 receptor site in the striatum.

Our evidence is therefore in direct conflict with that presented by Price and his colleagues (in Chapter 40 of this volume) who, from their work on DA2 antagonists have suggested that the DA2 receptor is responsible for dopamine-induced dyskinesia. Our results are, however, compatible with the conclusion that the therapeutic effect of dopamine agonists is predominantly on the DA2 receptor.

Only one patient was taking bromocriptine during this trial but her response was different from all the other patients. Her Parkinsonian symptoms and signs deteriorated without any increase in abnormal involuntary movements. This response was similar to that reported in 1976 by Kartzinel et al [4]. We would like to suggest that our patient may not have developed hypersensitivity at the DA1 receptor—the potentiation of which by oxpentifylline would have resulted in abnormal movements. There has been evidence presented by Goldstein in New York and Stern's group at University College Hospital to suggest that such hypersensitivity phenomena are less commonly induced in patients treated with bromocriptine.

Finally these results raise the possibility of utilising the differential action of the two dopamine receptor types to avoid some of the late hypersensitivity phenomena of dopa treatment.

References

1   Stefanovich V, Macukat M, Hurn G. *RCS Med Sci 1976; 4:*506
2   Smith JM, Misiak H. *Psychopharmacology 1976; 47:*175
3   Kebabian JW, Kebabian PR, Munemura M, Calne DB. In Fuxe K, Calne DB, eds. *Dopaminergic Ergot Derivatives and Motor Function 1979.* New York: Pergamon Press
4   Kartzinel R, Shoulson I, Calne DB. *Neurology 1976; 26:*741

CHAPTER 46

PARKINSONISM: CURRENT PROBLEMS AND FUTURE RESEARCH

Heikki Teravainen, Christopher Ward and Donald B Calne

Introduction

We shall review current research on Parkinsonism in the following stages: (i) diagnostic considerations, (ii) aetiology and classification, (iii) pathology and physiology, (iv) pharmacology. This discussion ranges freely over some growth areas in current research and attempts to stress some gaps in our knowledge, with suggestions as to how they might be filled. The future is promising, but history teaches us to expect the unpredictable. There is a natural tendency to exaggerate the extent to which current knowledge has accrued from the orderly progression of hypothesis and experiment. Progress in Parkinsonism has often been dependent on fortuitous clinical observation (Table I).

TABLE I Accidental Observations in the History of Parkinson's Disease

1874	Empirical use of belladonna
1954	Reserpine induces parkinsonism
1954	Ligation of anterior choroidal artery alleviates parkinsonism
1969	Amantadine alleviates parkinsonism

Diagnostic Considerations

Definition: A central issue is the definition of Parkinsonism as a separate clinical entity among disorders of motor function. There have been remarkable advances in our understanding of the morbid anatomy, biochemistry, pathophysiology and rational treatment of Parkinsonism. Nevertheless, the process of diagnosis and the definition of this disorder has remained strictly traditional, depending upon the identification of tremor, rigidity and poverty of movement as the central triad of clinical features.

356

Diagnosis: Methods are available to quantify various aspects of poverty of movement, including delay in initiation ("akinesia"), reduced speed ("bradykinesia") and decreased amplitude ("hypokinesia") [1]. Commercially available devices which measure motor performance are likely to become available in the near future. Such approaches can be expected to improve the specificity of clinical observations. The evaluation of rigidity (resistance to passive movement) is technically more difficult, while methods to quantify parkinsonian tremor are cumbersome and convey somewhat different information from that attainable by visual inspection [1]; the clinical phenomenon has greater diagnostic specificity than does any objective measurement, a fact which again emphasises the continuing pre-eminence of a clinical approach.

Investigations: It has been found that striatal dopamine is depleted by about 50 per cent before the clinical features of Parkinson's disease are manifest [2]. Clinical diagnosis thus lacks sensitivity. Since clinical ascertainment occurs late in life, genetic studies tend to underestimate the true prevalence of a parkinsonian trait among relatives of a parkinsonian proband [3]. Delay in clinical expression has been attributed to compensatory effects, possibly involving neurotransmitters other than dopamine, and on this premise a provocative test manipulating noradrenaline has been suggested [4]. Cerebral dopaminergic metabolism may be reflected by urinary dopamine excretion and by cerebrospinal fluid (CSF) concentration of dopamine catabolites. Both measurements have been reported to indicate pre-disposition to drug-induced Parkinsonism [5, 6]. Correlations between CSF dopamine catabolites and both pre- and post-treatment parkinsonian disability have been reported but are not reliable [7]. The measurement of these substances in jugular venous blood might provide a more sensitive, although more invasive, test. Intracerebral aromatic aminoacid decarboxylase (AAD) is depleted in parkinsonian brains [2] and the activity of this enzyme may reflect the size of a nigrostriatal lesion. The use of labelled dopa in positron emission tomography would enable the regional activity of cerebral AAD to be estimated *in vivo* [8]. Other enzymes and substrates could probably be evaluated in a similar way; this method has potential as the first direct technique for measuring the extent of nigrostriatal biochemical dysfunction *in vivo*. It remains to be seen whether nuclear magnetic resonance imaging will prove to be a technique with similar capability [9].

Unfortunately, none of these investigations are currently of value in the routine diagnosis of Parkinsonism.

Aetiology and Classification

The clinical syndrome of Parkinsonism may develop as an idiopathic disorder, in which primary neuronal degeneration occurs for unknown reasons, or secondary to a variety of diseases affecting the central nervous system. Table II shows the classification of Parkinsonism employed by Fahn [10], with minor modifications to include recent reports of Parkinsonism following traumatic childbirth [11], chronic inhalation of carbon tetrachloride [12] and chronic organophosphate intoxication

[13]. Treatment with lithium may also cause Parkinsonism [14], even if it more commonly leads to hyperkinetic extrapyramidal syndromes [15, 16]. Fahn states that "the classification of Parkinsonism into the major categories of primary, secondary and heterogeneous system degenerations is arbitrary not ideal". Nevertheless, we agree with him that this approach is the best available at the present time.

Table II illustrates the multiplicity of aetiologies which may cause Parkinsonism and it is outside the scope of the present paper to go into all of these in any greater depth. Attention is primarily focused on idiopathic Parkinsonism (Parkinson's disease, paralysis agitans), including aspects of secondary Parkinsonism only if these are of aetiological interest. It should be emphasised that there may exist multiple aetiologies, as yet unidentified, for the large group of patients with idiopathic Parkinsonism. The situation might be analogous to the numerous different neuropathological mechanisms involved in the various clinically diagnosed myopathies.

TABLE II Classification of Parkinsonism

I   Primary

          Idiopathic parkinsonism (Parkinson's disease, paralysis agitans)

II   Secondary

       A   Infections

                 1   Postencephalitic (encephalitis lethargica)
                 2   Other encephalitides
                 3   Jakob-Creutzfeldt
                 4   Luetic

       B   Toxins, Mn, Li, CO, CS_2, CCl_4, CN, organophosphates, methanol

       C   Drugs

                 1   Phenothiazines
                 2   Butyrophenones
                 3   Reserpine
                 4   Tetrabenzine

       D   Brain tumours

       E   Trauma—physical, electric shock

       F   Vascular

       G   Metabolic

                 1   Hypoparathyroidism and basal ganglia calcification
                 2   Chronic hepatocerebral degeneration

III   Heterogeneous system degenerations

A   Striatonigral degeneration

B   Olivopontocerebellar atrophy

C   Ophthalmoplegia—Steele Richardson Olszewski syndrome

D   Orthostatic hypotension—Shy Drager syndrome

E   Dementia

         1   Parkinsonism—dementia of Guam
         2   Normal pressure hydrocephalus

F   Hereditary disorders

         1   Wilson's disease
         2   Hallervorden-Spatz disease
         3   Pallidal atrophy
         4   Joseph's disease

(Modified from: Fahn, S (1977) In *Scientific Approaches to Clinical Neurology*. (Eds) E S Goldenshon and S H Appel. Lea and Febiger, Philadelphia. Page 1160).

Viral hypothesis: The possibility of a viral aetiology for Parkinson's disease has been suspected since the pandemic of lethargic encephalitis between 1915 and 1926 which established beyond doubt that a virus could induce akinesia, rigidity and tremor (postencephalitic Parkinsonism). Interest in the possibility of virus infection has been reactivated following i) the disovery of infections of the CNS in man caused by atypical exogenous agents (such as Jakob-Creutzfeldt's disease), ii) the demonstration of viral antigens in the brains of patients with postencephalitic Parkinsonism [17] and iii) the existence of both chronic virus infections [18] and acute encephalitides [19, 20] with parkinsonian signs.

The fact that viral infection can induce Parkinsonism does not necessarily implicate this mechanism in the pathogenesis of the idiopathic syndrome. In a large group of such patients, complement fixing antibody to Herpes simplex virus was increased, but no differences were observed in antibodies to a number of other viruses [21, 22]. Brains from patients with idiopathic Parkinsonism have shown no immunological evidence of the presence of a virus [17]. Attempts to transmit Parkinsonism to primates by the injection of brain tissue of patients with idiopathic Parkinsonism have been unsuccessful [23].

Both the possibility of viral infections and an abnormal immune response in Parkinsonism remain important areas for research. Too little information is available on the extent of immunological isolation of the CNS from the rest of the body, and on the immune responses of the normal CNS [24]. Incorporation of viral genetic material into the host genome can occur and herpetic material has been reported in nucleic acid hybridisation experiments on human brain [25]. Among the potential results of such a mechanism could be the modification of the function

359

of the host cell. In this connection, it is interesting to note again that amantadine, a pre-synaptically acting agent with dopamine releasing properties, also inhibits the entry of infuenza A virus into cells [26]. Are these two properties coincidental, or do we have here a clue to how a virus may cause acute or post-infective extra-pyramidal disease?

Hypothesis of premature ageing. Idiopathic Parkinsonism is one of the classical degenerative CNS diseases in which nerve cells progressively die. The prevalence of Parkinson's disease increases with advancing age [27, 28] and some support for the concept that the causal mechanism is premature ageing [29, 30] derives from observations of loss of substantia nigra neurones [31, 32, 33] and the fall of brain tyrosine hydroxylase activity [32] with advancing age. Additional features of Parkinson's disease encountered in elderly subjects include death of neurones in regions other than the nigra [33, 34], brain atrophy [35], and impairment of various neuroendocrine and neurochemical functions [36–39].

Ageing animals display a progressive decrease in the number of neurones in certain regions of the CNS [40, 41, 42], degeneration of axons [43], and changes in dendrites [44]. There is, in particular, degeneration of catecholamine neurones [45], a decrease in synaptic receptor sensitivity [46] and diminished synaptic potentiation [47]. L-dopa can improve movement (swimming) of aged rats [48] and extend the life span of mice [49]. At present, the ageing hypothesis remains unproven and is, at best, only vaguely formulated. Testing of the hypothesis is hampered by lack of knowledge of what is cause and what is result. More work is needed to study changes in the various components of the CNS concomitantly, not only neurones, but also glia, and the vascular system including the blood-brain barrier. Furthermore, ageing does not explain why there may be a decreased risk of Parkinsonism among cigarette smokers [27] and why marked racial and geographical differences exist. Parkinsonism is relatively uncommon among the black compared to the white population in Africa and the USA [27, 50]. Geographical distribution indicates some threefold differences in the death rates between Scandinavian countries and Australia, Israel and Belgium [51]. It is difficult to explain these findings in terms of varying quality of reporting in countries with comparable standards of medical care.

Ambani [52] has suggested that impaired catalase or peroxidase activity could permit hydrogen peroxide, a product of catecholamine oxidation, to cause enzyme denaturation, depigmentation, and finally cell death. An acute example of this process is produced by direct application of 6-OH-DA, which induces degeneration of the dopaminergic nigrostriatal pathway [52]. Reduced catalase and peroxidase have been reported in parkinsonian brains [52], but no further support for this hypothesis has been forthcoming. This theoretical construct does, however, illustrate how a simple defect may lead to a complex sequence of events. Such models would appear more useful for future research than non-specific statements about processes such as ageing.

The cause of the development of CNS changes leading to Parkinsonism may be multifactorial [3]. Normal ageing processes may be accelerated by, for example, changes in the blood-brain barrier in the region of the basal ganglia, leading to preferential damage by toxic substances in the circulation. One of the possible agents, not mentioned in Table II, is iron, which has been reported to be present in considerably higher concentrations than normal in the basal ganglia of parkinsonian brains [53, 54, 55]. The presence of iron in the form of vascular siderosis is a feature of Parkinsonism, but has not been considered an essential part of the lesion [56]. Vascular siderosis was recently reported to contain lead, aluminium, sulphur, manganese and barium in parkinsonian, but not in non-parkinsonian patients [57]. Of these elements, the association of lead with Parkinsonism was statistically significant.

The contribution of genetic factors to a multifactorial process is controversial. An autosomal dominant form of the disease exists, but for the great majority of patients a multi-gene model is more appropriate [3]. The finding that monozygotic twins are usually discordant for idiopathic Parkinsonism [58] favours the importance of environmental factors over heredity in the genesis of the disorder, placing particular emphasis on exposure to an exogenous agent after childhood, when twins are usually living separately.

Pathology and Physiology

Pathology: The pathology of Parkinsonism is confusing [59–64]; there have been variable and contradictory observations of either intact or altered substantia nigra, pallidum, putamen, cerebral cortex, brain stem and spinal cord. The present state of knowledge indicates that the severity of Parkinson's disease correlates best with the degree of neuronal loss in the substantia nigra [63]; and that there is more diffuse brain atrophy than in age matched non-parkinsonian patients [63, 64, 65]. Other pigmented and some non-pigmented neurones degenerate, their distribution corresponding to monoaminergic cell bodies [66, 67], and certain hypothalamic nuclei [68]. There is purported to be some overlap between the pathology of Parkinsonism and presenile dementia [63, 69, 70].

The fundamental neurochemical defect seems to be the loss of dopamine in the striatum [71, 72]. This apparently results from degeneration of dopaminergic nerve endings, due to the disappearance of the neurones in the pars compacta of the substantia nigra, from which the dopaminergic nigrostriatal pathway originates. This may be an oversimplified view, since lesions in the substantia nigra without Parkinsonism have been reported [61].

The problem of inconsistent pathological observations has been attributed to variations in the handling of the postmortem material, as well as disparities of interpretation [60]. Furthermore, patients with different disease may not have been clearly identified, and there may have been coexisting disease. Thus, Schober *et al* [73] described two cases of idiopathic orthostatic hypotension, one associated with striatonigral degeneration and the other with Lewy-body Parkinsonism. This clearly illustrates the difficulty of interpreting the earlier pathological literature, since neither idiopathic orthostatic hypotension nor striatonigral degeneration were distinguished as separate disease entitites prior to 1980.

It is evident that more work is needed to elucidate many aspects of the pathology in Parkinsonism. One would expect that much clearer concepts could be formed by an interdisciplinary effort including careful clinical evaluation and classification, utilising as an essential part of the study the patient's clinical and neurochemical response to drugs, combined with physiological and pathological analysis. This approach would not only enhance diagnostic precision, but would also lead to better understanding of both the pathophysiological phenomena and sites of drug action. A start in this direction has been made by Bernheimer *et al* [71].

Physiology: The basic abnormal clinical findings of rigidity, tremor, and poverty of movement are combined with abnormalities in both simple and complex motor functions, such as delay in starting movement, decreased speed of movement, enhanced fatiguability, impaired ability to perform complex repetitive movements, defective correction of erroneous movement, difficulty in performing simultaneously separate motor acts and reduced postural reflexes [74-81]. These deficits reflect the problem experienced by the patient in daily functions, such as difficulties in writing, dressing and walking [82, 83]. This listing gives only an incomplete illustration of this extensive field of study and further references can be obtained from several monographs and reviews [1, 59, 64, 81, 84, 85, 86].

Current evidence indicates that the physiological disturbances in Parkinsonism predominantly involve abnormal supraspinal modulation of normal spinal mechanisms [87-91]. Recent studies on voluntary eye movements, with and without visual feedback [92] suggest that the motor programming and internal monitoring of the programme are intact in Parkinsonism; the execution is defective. Whether this can be generalised to the motor control of the axial and limb muscles remains to be determined.

Another important area for investigation is the physiology of postural mechanisms in Parkinsonism. In normal subjects, postural control and voluntary movements are precisely integrated. Experimental evidence is needed to support or refute Martin's [93] proposal that some of the motor deficits of Parkinsonism result from postural reflexes interfering with voluntary movements. A start in this direction has recently been made [92] by measuring the delay in initiation of voluntary eye movements with and without postural disturbance (rotation of the head). This study failed to reveal an abnormal impact of vestibular mechanisms on voluntary movement; again it remains to be seen whether the ocular findings can be extrapolated more generally. Since knowledge of the disturbed physiology in Parkinsonism is so limited, we cannot even come close to defining the relationship between biochemical abnormalities at synaptic level and functional disorders at the level of organised electrophysiological interactions between networks of neurones.

Pharmacology

Animal models. A wide range of animal models are available for the study of Parkinson's disease and its treatment. The earliest paradigm was the akinetic syndrome induced by giving reserpine to rats. This was followed by studies on rats with unilateral lesions of the nigrostriatal pathway, produced by injection of 6-hydroxydopamine into the substantia nigra. Once the therapeutic potential of L-dopa was established, a number of pharmacological indices of dopaminergic activity became recognised. *In vitro* measurements included changes in tissue concentrations of homovanillic acid, in binding of labelled ligands to dopamine receptors, in release of dopamine from synaptosomes, and in the activity of dopamine sensitive adenylate cyclase. *In vivo* indices of dopaminergic activity include the induction of loco-motor activity and stereotyped behaviour rotation in rats with unilateral nigral lesions, alterations in the firing rate of neurones in the pars compacta of the sub-stantia nigra, suppression of plasma prolactin, and production of hypothermia in rodents exposed to a cold environment.

While these animal models have yielded successful predictions of the antiparkin-son efficacy of several new drugs [94], precise analogies have not yet been est-ablished. We do not know which, if any, of the models gives the best correlation with relief of akinesia, tremor or rigidity. Of much greater importance is the failure to identify correlates with adverse reactions. We cannot predict answers to such critically significant questions as whether a drug will cause prominent hallucin-ations, dyskinesia, or fluctuations in response. A major task for the future is the quest to sharpen the discrimination in the areas attainable with animal models of Parkinson's disease and pharmacological tests for dopaminergic activity.

Dopaminergic agonists. One advance to have emerged from the development of animal models relating to the antiparkinson therapy is the identification of a range of new compounds that stimulate dopamine receptors directly—dopamine agonists [95]. The first group to be studied were apomorphine and N-propylnoraporphine, which were demonstrated to have both dopaminergic properties in animal models, and antiparkinson actions in man. Unfortunately, these compounds proved nephrotoxic, so they were abandoned.

The second group of dopamine agonists to undergo development comprised the dopaminergic ergot derivatives. Those containing a peptide moiety are classified as ergopeptines, while those without a peptide component are termed ergolines. Bromocriptine is an ergopeptine with considerable dopaminergic potency. It has antiparkinson properties which are sufficiently useful to justify its administration to certain categories of patients [96, 97, 98]. The main advantage of bromocrip-tine is its low propensity to induce dyskinesia; its major drawback is a relatively high incidence of psychiatric reactions. Lergotrile is an ergoline which is active against Parkinsonism, but a high incidence of hepato-toxicity has been encountered with this drug so it is no longer used [99]. Newer ergolines which are currently undergoing evaluation include lisuride and pergolide.

The search for new agonists of dopamine is likely to continue, in an attempt to achieve more efficacy with less toxicity. One recent finding, of considerable inter-est, has led to a reappraisal of the significance of the ergot structure. Hitherto, the active component of the ergot molecule was thought to be the benzene ring with nitrogen on its side chain. New observations [100] indicate that the benzene ring may not be critical in conferring dopaminergic properties. This discovery is likely to lead to the synthesis of a series of new tricyclic compounds for evaluation as potential antiparkinson drugs.

Receptors for dopamine. Accumulating evidence indicates the existence of at least two types of synaptic receptor for dopamine [101]. The category associated with an adenylate cyclase has been designated D-1 type, while that independent of the cyclase has been termed D-2. Selective D-2 receptor antagonists, such as molindone and sulpiride, are capable of inducing or exacerbating Parkinsonism, while D-2 agonists, such as the dopaminergic ergots, alleviate Parkinson's disease. It may be inferred, therefore, that the predominant deficit in dopaminergic transmission that leads to the clinical features of Parkinsonism involve defective transmission at D-2 receptors. Future studies are likely to allow further characterisation of the D-1 and D-2 forms of receptor, and perhaps lead to a subclassification. The development of an array of compounds with more selective agonism and antagonism for the various categories of receptor should allow an improvement in the therapeutic ratio for drug regimens. Clarification of the role of D-1 receptors in the nervous system is desirable; the quest for selective D-1 agonists and antagonists is an obvious approach to this problem.

Another aspect of receptor pharmacology that is relevant to the treatment of Parkinsonism is dopaminoceptive sensitivity. The neuropathology of Parkinson's disease leads to denervation supersensitivity, which may be of importance in enabling dopaminergic agents to elicit a therapeutic response without causing too many adverse effects by excessive stimulation of normal dopamine synapses. It is also possible that transient changes in receptor sensitivity may contribute to some of the "on-off" reactions that are seen so commonly after several years of L-dopa therapy. However, no precise hypothesis has been formulated, and it is also evident that pharmacokinetic factors determine fluctuations of response in some patients.

Neurotransmitter interactions. The most clearly defined neurotransmitter interaction that is of importance in Parkinsonism is the antagonism between dopamine and acetylcholine. This is illustrated by the established therapeutic action of drugs which either increase dopaminergic function or decrease cholinergic transmission. The details of dopamine–acetylcholine relationships in the striatum have not been worked out. A similar level of ignorance obscures the interaction between noradrenaline and dopamine; on the one hand, noradrenaline concentrations in the brain are known to be decreased in Parkinsonism, but on the other, drugs which modify noradrenergic function do not alter the clinical deficits. A step has recently been made towards elucidating the role of GABA in nigrostriatal function. It has been thought for some time that an inhibitory pathway runs from the striatum to the dopamine neurones in the pars compacta of the substantia nigra. A recent analysis of the electrical activity of single cells in the brainstem has revealed a neuronal organisation in which GABA fibres project to the pars reticulata of the substantia nigra. Systemic administration of GABA agonists leads to inhibition of reticulata neurones, which appears to result in excitation of the compacta dopamine cells [102].

One problem in attempting to define the role of neurotransmitters in the basal ganglia and substantia nigra is the profusion of so many active substances found in such high concentration in these regions. In addition to the high levels of dopamine, acetylcholine, noradrenaline and GABA, there are also notable concentrations of neuropeptides such as the enkephalins and substance P. Future research on the pharmacology of Parkinsonism can be expected to begin to unravel some of the functions of the large assortment of transmitters and modulators with which the extrapyramidal system is so richly endowed.

Summary

While there has been an explosive increase in our understanding of Parkinsonism over the last 20 years, some of the recent observations have led to the recognition of new problems and still many of the old questions remain unanswered.

Acknowledgement

We wish to thank Mrs A Miller for typing this manuscript and Mrs P Barnicoat for collating the references.

References

1   Teräväinen H, Calne D. In *Parkinson's disease. Current Progress, Problems and Management 1980.* Holland, Elsevier, In press
2   Hornykiewicz O. *Brit Med Bull 1973;29:*172
3   Kondo K, Kurland LT, Schull WJ. *Mayo Clinic Proc 1973;48:*465
4   Antelman SM, Caggiula AR. *Science 1977;195:*646
5   Crowley TJ, Hoehn MM, Rutledge CO, Stallings MA, Heaton RK, Sundell S, Stilson C. *Arch Gen Psychiat 1978;35:*97
6   Chase TN, Schnur JA, Gordon EK. *Neuropharmacology 1970;9:*265
7   Bianchine JR, Shaw GM. *Clin Pharmacokinet 1976;1:*313
8   Korf J, Reiffers S, Beerling van der Molen HD, Lakke JPWF, Paans AMJ, Vaalburg W, Woldring MG. *Brain Res 1978;145:*59
9   Hinshaw WS, Andrew ER, Bottomley PA, Holland GN, Moore WE, Worthington BS. *Brit J Radiol 1978;51:*273
10   Fahn S. In Goldensohn ES, Appel SH, eds. *Scientific Approaches to Clinical Neurology 1977;*1159. Philadelphia, Lea and Febiger
11   Murphy RP. *J Neurol Neurosurg Psychiat 1979;42:*384
12   Melamed E, Lavy S. *Lancet 1977;i:*1015
13   Davis KL, Yesavage JA, Berger PA. *J Nerv Ment Dis 1978;166:*222
14   Lutz EG. *J Med Soc NJ 1978;75:*165
15   Hartizsch BV, Hoenich NA, Leight RJ. *Brit med J 1972;4:*757
16   Kane J, Rifkin A, Quitkin F, Klein DF. *Amer J Psychiatry 1978; 135:* 851
17   Gamboa ET, Wolf A, Yahr MD, Harter DH, Duffy PE, Barden H, Hsu KC. *Arch Neurol 1974;31:*228
18   Miyasaki K, Takayoshi F. *J Neuropathol Exp Neurol 1977;36:*1
19   Bojinov S. *J Neural sci 1971;12:*383
20   Schultz DR, Barthal JS, Garrett G. *Neurology (Minneap) 1977;27:*1095
21   Marttila RJ, Arstila P, Nikoskelainen J, Halonen PE, Rinne UK. *Eur Neurol 1977;15:* 25
22   Rinne UK. *Acta Neurol Scand (Suppl 67) 1978;57:*77

23 Gibbs CJ Jr, Gajdusek DC. *J Clin Pathol 1971;25 (Suppl 6):*132
24 Johnson RT, ter Meulen V. *Adv intern Med 1978;23:*353
25 Sequiera LW, Jennings LC, Carrasco LH, Lord MA, Curry A, Sutton RNP. *Lancet 1979;ii:*609
26 Parkes JD. *Adv Drug Res 1974; 8:* 11
27 Kessler II. *Amer J Epid 1972;96:*242
28 Marttila RJ, Rinne UK. *Acta Neurol Scand 1976;53:*81
29 DeJong JD, Burns BD. *Can Med Assoc 1967;97:*1
30 Barbeau A. In Yahr MD, ed. *The Basal Ganglia 1976;*281. New York, Raven Press
31 Pakkenberg H, Brody H. *Acta Neuropathol 1965;5:*320
32 McGeer PL, McGeer EG, Suzuki JS. *Arch Neurol 1977;34:*33
33 Mann DMA, Yates PO. *Acta Neuropathol (Berl) 1979;47:*93
34 Bugiani O, Salvarani S, Perdelli F, Mancardi GL, Leonardi A. *Eur Neurol 1978;17:*286
35 Earnest MP, Heaton RK, Wilkinson WE, Manke WF. *Neurology (Minneap) 1979;29:* 1138
36 Robinson DS. *Fed Proc 1975;34:*103
37 Finch CE. *Quart Rev Biol 1976;51:*49
38 Shelanski ML. In Terry RD, Gershon S, eds. *Neurobiology of Ageing 1976;*339. New York, Raven Press
39 Iwangoff P, Reichlmeier K, Enz A, Meier-Ruge W. *Interdiscipl Topics Gerontol 1979; 15:*13
40 Diamond MC, Johnson RE, Gold MW. *Behav Biol 1977;20:*409
41 Hsu HK, Peng MT. *Gerontology 1978;24:*434
42 Peng MT, Lee LR. *Gerontology 1979;25:*205
43 Naranjo N, Green E. *Brain Res Bull 1977;2:*71
44 Machado-Salas JP, Scheibel AB. *Exp Neurol 1979;63:*347
45 Masuoka DJ, Johnsson G, Finch CE. *Brain Res 1979;169:*335
46 Govoni S, Loddo, Spano PF, Trabucchi M. *Brain Res 1977.138:*565
47 Lanfield PW, McGaugh JL, Lynch G. *Brain Res 1978;150:*85
48 Marshall JF, Berrios N. *Science 1979;206:*477
49 Cotzias GC, Miller ST, Nicholson AR Jr, Waston WH, Tang LC. *Proc Natl Acad Sci 1974;71:*2466
50 Lombard A, Gelfand M. *Cent Afr J Med 1978;24:*5
51 Kurland LT, Kurtzke JR, Goldberg ID. In *Epidemiology of Neurologic and Sense Organ Disorders 1973.* Cambridge, Harvard University Press
52 Ambani LM. *Indian J Med Sci 1977;31:*21
53 Hallgren B, Sourander P. *J Neurochem 1958;3:*41
54 Earle KM. *J Neuropath Exp Neurol 1968;27:*1
55 Still CN. *Adv Exp Med Biol 1977;90:*291
56 Denny-Brown D. *Int J Neurol 1961;2:*25
57 Duckett S, Galle P, Kradin R. *Ann Neurol 1977;2:*225
58 Duvoisin RC, Eldridge, Williams A. *Neurology 1979; 29:* 578
59 Denny-Brown D. *The Basal Ganglia and Their Relation to Disorders of Movement 1962.* London, University Press
60 Scott TR, Netsky MG. *Int J Neurol 1961;2:*51
61 Stern G. *Brain 1966;89:*449
62 Lewis PD. *Brit med J 1971;3:*690
63 Alvord EC, Forno LS, Kusske JA. *Adv Neurol 1974;5:*175
64 Fahn S, Duffy P. In Goldenshon ES, Appel SH, eds. *Scientific Approaches to Clinical Neurology volume 2 1977;*1119. Philadelphia, Lea and Febiger
65 Schneider E, Fischer P-A, Jacobi P. *J Neurol Sci 1979;42:*187
66 Ohama E, Ikuta F. *Acta Neuropathol (Berl) 1976;34:*311
67 Rajput AH, Rozdilsky B. *J Neurol Neurosurg Psychiat 1976;39:*1092
68 Langston JW, Forno LS. *Ann Neurol 1978;3:*129

69   Hakim AM, Mathieson G. *Lancet 1978;ii:*729
70   Kosaka K, Mehraein P. *Arch Psychiatr Nervenkr 1979;226:*241
71   Bernheimer H, Birkmayer W, Hornykiewicz O, Jellinger K, Seitelberger F. *J Neurol Sci 1973;20:*415
72   Hornykiewicz O. *Brit med Bull 1973;29:*172
73   Schober R, Langston JW, Forno LS. *Eur Neurol 1975;13:*177
74   Schwab RS, Chafetz ME, Walker S. *Arch Neurol Psychiat 1954;72:*591
75   Draper IT, Johns RJ. *Bull Johns Hopk Hosp 1964;115:*465
76   Perret E, Eggenberger E, Siegfried J. *J Neurol Neurosurg Psychiat 1970;33:*16
77   Angel RW, Alston W, Garland H. *Neurology (Minneap) 1971;21:*1255
78   Knutsson E, Mårtenson A. *Scand J Rehab Med 1971;3:*121
79   Cassell K, Shaw K, Stern G. *Brain 1973;96:*815
80   Velasco R, Velasco M. *Neuropharmacol 1973;12:*89
81   Evarts EV, Teräväinen H, Beuchert D, Calne DB. In Fuxe F, Calne D. *Dopaminergic Ergot Derivatives and Motor Functions 1979;*45. Oxford, Pergamon Press
82   Anden N-E, Carlsson A, Kerstell J, Magnusson T, Olsson R, Roos, B-E, Steen B, Steg G, Svanborg A, Thieme G, Werdinius B. *Acta Medica Scand 1970;187:*247
83   Murray MP, Sepic SB, Gardner GM, Downs WJ. *Amer J Phys Med 1978;57:*278
84   Calne DB. *Parkinsonism: Physiology, Pharmacology and Treatment 1970.* London, Edward Arnold Ltd
85   Denny-Brown D, Yanagisawa N. In Yahr MD, ed. *The Basal Ganglia 1976;*115. New York, Raven Press
86   Teräväinen H, Calne DB. *Acta Neurol Scand 1979;60:*1
87   Wallin BG, Hongell A, Hagbarth K-E. In Desmedt JE, ed. *New Developments in Electromyography and Clinical Neurophysiology volume 3 1973;*263. Basle, Karger
88   Hagbarth K-E, Wallin G, Löfstedt L, Aquilonius S-M. *J Neurol Neurosurg Psychiat 1975; 38:*636
89   Burke D, Hagbarth K-E, Wallin BG. *Scand J Rehab Med 1977;9:*15
90   Mortimer JA, Webster DD. In Desmedt JE, ed. *Cerebral Motor Control in Man: Long Loop Mechanisms. Progr Clin Neurophysiol volume 4 1978;*343. Basle, Karger
91   Teravainen H, Evarts EV, Calne D. In Poirier LJ, Sourkes TL, Bedard PJ, eds. *Advances in Neurology volume 24 1979;*161. New York, Raven Press
92   Teräväinen H, Calne D. *1979,* unpublished
93   Martin JP. *The Basal Ganglia and Posture 1967.* Philadelphia, JB Lippincott Co
94   Klawans HL Jr. *Models of Human Neurological Diseases 1974.* Amsterdam, Excerpta Medica
95   Calne DB. In Klawans HL, ed. *Clinical Neuropharmacology volume 3 1978;*153. New York, Raven Press
96   Calne DB, Williams AC, Neophytides A, Plotkin C, Nutt JG, Teychenne PF. *Lancet 1978;i:*735
97   Lieberman A, Kupersmith M, Estey E, Goldstein M. *New Engl J Med 1976;295:*1400
98   Debono AG, Marsden CD, Asselman P, Parkes JD. *B J Clin Pharmacol 1976; 3:* 977
99   Teychenne PF, Jones EA, Ishak KG, Calne DB. *Gastroenterology 1979;76:*575
100 Bach NJ, Kornfeld EC, Jones ND, Chaney MO, Dorman DE, Paschal JW, Clemens JA, Smalstig EB. *J Med Chem 1980;* In press
101 Kebabian JW, Calne DB. *Nature 1979;277:*93
102 Waszczak BL, Eng N, Walters JR. *Brain Res 1980;* In press

367

PART VII

ASSESSMENT AND NON-DRUG THERAPY

Chapter 47

PSYCHOLOGICAL ASSESSMENT IN PARKINSON'S DISEASE

John McFie*

In spite of James Parkinson's [1] original assertion that in the disorder he described "the senses and the intellect [were] unimpaired", there is general agreement
that the majority of patients suffer some degree of intellectual impairment—beyond
that normally expected at their ages. This is consistent with the fact that, at ventriculography prior to stereotaxic operation, many Parkinsonian patients showed
some degree of ventricular dilatation [2].

Psychometric assessments, although all based upon use of the Wechsler intelligence scales, have not all yielded the same conclusions. The first significant study
of 71 patients [3], reported only the IQs: with a mean Verbal IQ of 110.6 and Performance IQ of 102.5, there appeared to be no *prima facie* evidence for a significant degree of deterioration. Similar results are shown in the study by Asso *et al*
[4] whose 31 operated patients of 30 control patients showed comparable Verbal–
Performance IQ differences of 10 to 12 points. (It may also be observed that the
results presented by Pearce *et al* in chapter 7 of the present volume also show no
significant IQ differences). On the other hand, the series of 63 patients tested by
Loranger *et al* [5] showed a mean Verbal IQ of 115.6, compared with a Performance IQ of 95.3: looked at as frequencies, 57 per cent of their patients showed
a Verbal–Performance difference of more than 20 points (ie. of significant degree).
Impairment, they suggest, is the rule rather than the exception, and does not
emerge as a result from the many studies either because of inadequate tests used or
because of inadequate norms.

Comparison of Verbal and Performance IQs is not, however, a valid method for
ascertaining deterioration of cerebral function. Although in cases of generalised
atrophy there is commonly a difference in the expected direction (ie. Performance
less than Verbal), this is often due to non-specific motor retardation rather than to
intellectual impairment, and is frequently so in cases of Parkinson's disease. When
the atrophy is non-symmetrical, with emphasis on the left hemisphere, or if there is
a lesion in the left hemisphere, then the likelihood is that the Verbal IQ will be less
than the Performance. According to the "Verbal minus Performance" formula, this
would represent negative deterioration, which is plainly invalid.

* Dr John McFie died in the summer of 1980.

The correct method of assessing deterioration is that proposed by Wechsler [6], based on comparison of the age-scaled scores on those subtests which are most sensitive to cerebral lesions with scores on subtests which are not. For the non-sensitive ("Hold") group, Wechsler proposed four subtests, but experience shows that two are sufficient, Vocabulary and Picture Completion [7, 8]. The mean of the two "Hold" subtest scores may be compared with the mean score of all the remaining subtests given (excepting Information and Comprehension) either as a ratio or as a percentage of the "Hold" mean: in the latter case, the result is the Deterioration Loss per cent.

Using this formula on the series of cases for which adequate data are presented, it will be noted that in the study by McFie [2], the 40 patients who subsequently underwent stereotaxic operations on the left had a mean Deterioration Loss of 13.8:, ie. more than the 10 per cent suggested by Wechsler as the upper limit of normal: for the 29 patients subsequently operated on the right, the mean DL of 9.5 per cent was the upper limit of normal. Loranger et al [5] presented the subtest scores of their 63 patients as IQ equivalents; but the DL may be calculated similarly, with a resulting value of 11.4 per cent. This confirms the conclusion reached by these authors based on comparing Verbal and Performance IQs, but on a more valid basis, since "asymmetrical" impairment is given equal weight (whether primarily Verbal or Performance) and natural decline in ability associated with age is also taken into account. This method of assessing deterioration is that used by Fisher and Findley in chapter 8 of the present volume.

References

1   Parkinson J. *An Essay on the Shaking Palsy 1817*. London: Sherwood, Neely and Jones
2   McFie J. *J Ment Sci 1960; 106:*1512
3   Riklan M, Diller L, Weiner H, Cooper IS. *Arch gen Psychiat 1960; 2:*22
4   Asso D, Crown S, Russell JA, Logue V. *Brit J Psychiat 1969; 115:*541
5   Loranger AW, Goodell H, McDowell FH, Lee JE, Sweet RD. *Brain 1972; 95:* 405
6   Wechsler D. *The Measurement of Adult Intelligence 1944*. Baltimore: Williams and Wilkins
7   McFie J. *Assessment of Organic Intellectual Impairment 1975*. London: Academic Press
8   Uzzell BP, Zimmerman RA, Dolinskas CA, Obrist WD. *Cortex 1979; 15:*391

Chapter 48

SPEECH ASSESSMENT OF PATIENTS WITH PARKINSON'S DISEASE

Alison R Perry and P K Das

Until recently, speech pathologists and therapists have not been closely involved in attempting to assess patients with Parkinson's disease, perhaps because it is a progressive disease and it was thought that speech therapy cannot help. This view is changing and various attempts have been made to scientifically assess the motor speech disorder in these patients, the rationale being fourfold:

1 To assess the type of disorder
2 To assess the degree of disorder (ie. severity)
3 To assess type of intervention needed (ie. appropriate therapy)
4 To assess degree of intervention (amount of therapy)—which is linked to the expectations of improvement

How much success has there been in the area of assessing motor speech disorders or "dysarthria"?

There are various parameters involved in speech, and one can try to assess any or all in isolation and/or give a qualitative rating of overall speech adequacy. The main parameters involved are: respiration, phonation, rate, pitch, intonation, nasality, loudness and diadochokinesis (rate of articulation). These may be observed informally and a purely descriptive assessment given, or one can try to evaluate each parameter scientifically and give measures relating to the 'normal population'. The problems which influence the type of assessment are:

— The bias of the tester (in the choice of test administered)
— The bias of the tester (in interpreting the test)
— The bias of the test originator (in weighting that test)
— The tester's selection of items (eg. if patient is fatigued)

It is therefore preferable to use objective measurements, rather than a subjective evaluation wherever possible, or both, in order to give a clear picture of overall speech performance. Unfortunately, all too often, there is little quantitative data to support clinical (qualitative) judgements.

In Parkinson's disease, the outstanding characteristic is a marked limitation in the range of movement. Individual movements are often slow and restricted and repetitive movements are either slow and moderately restricted, or fast with limited range and arrested movement.

Consequently, one finds hypokinetic dysarthria with a loss of inflection, weak phonation, poor voice quality, blurred articulation and sometimes palilalia [1].

Various attempts have been made to assess the speech characteristics of patients with Parkinson's disease. Canter [2, 3, 4] in his experiments, compared 17 Parkinsonian patients with 17 controls, matched for age, and came to the following conclusions:-

— There was no significant difference in voice intensity in the two groups.
— The Parkinsonian patients had a more limited pitch range, and the pitch was raised.
— Patients with Parkinsonism were unable to sustain phonation for as long as the control group.
— Patients with Parkinsonism had reduced ability to phonate at a loud level.

He also investigated diadochokinesis (articulation rate) and concluded that this had a high relationship with speech adequacy. Canter hypothesised that there was a physiological support for speech being reduced in Parkinsonian patients due to a neuromotor impairment of the phonatory/respiratory mechanisms.

These results contrast with a study by Kreul [5] who compared a group of Parkinsonian patients with geriatric patients and concluded that a reduced ability to prolong vowels and to read rapidly was associated both with advanced age and Parkinson's disease. He also noted that the more open a vowel, the more difficult to prolong it for a patient with Parkinson's disease.

Canter concluded his study by suggesting that speech therapy should be aimed at *increasing* the capacity of Parkinsonian patients and not simply using residual functions to the optimum. This compares with Sarno [6] who investigated 300 Parkinsonian patients and found that speech only improved with therapy during treatment but, once treatment was discontinued, the patients regressed.

In an investigation of the presence of difficulties in speech by Logemann *et al* [7] on 200 patients, the most frequently found problem was voice disorder > articulatory disorders > speech rate > nasality. It was hypothesised that clusters of symptoms may represent a progression in dysfunction, beginning with laryngeal changes and progressing to problems with lips and tongue. Treatment for parkinsonian patients with speech problems have included drug therapy, and various evaluative studies have been done. Wolfe *et al* [8] looked at voice quality, pitch and articulation rate before, and after, administration of L-dopa on 17 patients. Patients were evaluated on a 0–4 point scale and the conclusion was that speech was 'not such a valuable measure of effectiveness of L-dopa therapy as physical measures'. A possible progression in impairment of voice quality → pitch → articulation → rate was suggested.

Rigrodsky and Morrison [9] rated patients on a 1-7 point scale, considering various speech parameters: overall adequacy, clarity of articulation, nasal resonance and time factor in speaking. They concluded that a trend was observed in the direction of improved scores during L-dopa therapy, but the improvement in speech symptoms only became evident after maximum L-dopa dosage had been continued for a considerable period.

Mawdsley and Gamsu [10] investigated periodicity of speech in Parkinsonian patients and stated that in 20 patients there was a difference in phonation time for single digits after drug treatment. However, no attempt seems to have been made to evaluate *exactly* what aspects of voice or speech L-dopa improves, if indeed, it improves any.

Some attempts have been made to amplify the speech of Parkinsonian patients, [11] but it was concluded that there was little point in amplifying poor speech quality, and consequently perhaps one should re-consider Canter's conclusion that "therapy should be aimed at increasing the capacity of these patients" [2-4].

Before such an attempt at therapy can be made, it is valuable to improve assessment techniques to try and evaluate which parameters of speech are affected and to what extent.

A pilot study was conducted at Charing Cross Hospital to investigate the speech involvement in Parkinsonian patients with special reference to measurement of peak flow, length of phonation of speech and optimum loudness of speech.

The aim of the study was to detect:

1 The speech characteristics of Parkinsonian patients.
2 The degree of speech involvement and its correlation with other parameters of the disease.
3 The short and long term effect of speech therapy on modification of Parkinsonian speech involvement.
4 Drug effect on different parameters of speech.

Material

Three groups of six people were taken:

PP + SI Parkinsonian patients with clinical speech involvement
PP – SI Parkinsonian patients without clinical speech involvement
CONTROLS Normal control group to distinguish speech changes related to the normal ageing process.

All the above groups were age and sex matched, and were screened for any other neurological disorders or any primary cardiac, respiratory or laryngeal disease. All patients were considered by themselves and by their families to have had no impairment of speech prior to the onset of Parkinson's disease.

All patients were screened for dementia using Raven's Progressive Matrices.

Methods

All patients who were selected had been stabilised for at least 3 months on L-dopa treatment. Patients were graded as follows during selection:-

a *Tremor:-*

    0 — None
    1 — Amplitude < 1″ in a limb/head (rest or walking)
    2 — Amplitude < 4″ in a limb/head (rest or walking)—not constant
    3 — Amplitude < 4″ in a limb/head (rest or walking)—constant

b *Rigidity*

    0 = None
    1 = Detectable in neck/shoulder/or limbs, reversible by medication.
    2 = Detectable in neck/shoulder/and limbs, reversible by medication.
    3 = Detectable in neck/shoulder/and limbs irreversible by medication.

c *Bradykinesia*

    0 = None
    1 = Slowing of arm swing, expressive gestures of hand; doing up buttons; using utensils; mild facial immobility.
    2 = 1 + mild difficulty in walking (slow steps and turns); moderate facial immobility, stares; looks depressed.
    3 = Difficulty in getting out of chair; shuffling gait, forceful heel strikes, turns very slow, shortened steps, masked facies, open mouth; requires help for day to day activities.

Speech Assessment

a *Subjective*

The patients were asked to answer the questionnaire for Subjective rating of their speech difficulties (Table I).

b *Objective*

All tests were conducted in a quiet room with closed door, with the subject seated comfortably. The speech of each patient was recorded and analysed independently by two speech therapists and a four point rating given:

0	1	2	3
No problem	mild	moderate	severe

376

This was later compared with the cardinal clinical features of the disease and was correlated with the duration of disease and length of drug treatment.

Peak flow in each patient was measured using a peak flow meter: duration and quality of phonation using a laryngograph and a stop watch while the patient sustained a vowel sound for as long as possible. Each subject attempted to say the vowel "A" as loud as possible on a single breach; the loudness being recorded with a sound level meter. All of these tests were done three times in succession, and a mean value calculated. This was done to rule out any possible progressive decrease in performances as a result of prolonged effort.

TABLE I

Date . . . . Name . . . .

Because of the nature of Parkinson's Disease, we are interested in finding out how it affects your life. Put a cross in the appropriate box to show how much difficulty you have with the following situations.

SITUATIONS	0 No Difficulty	1 A little Difficulty	2 Some Difficulty	3 Severe Difficulty
1 Making telephone calls				
2 Answering the telephone				
3 Talking in pubs				
4 Asking for goods in shops				
5 Asking for fares				
6 Talking in other people's homes				
7 Talking to strangers				
8 Talking to friends				
9 Talking to family				
10 Attending social events				
11 Speaking in a group of people				

To investigate the effect of L-dopa on the above three parameters, assessments on the study groups were conducted at hourly intervals. All patients had their usual first dose of L-dopa medication at 8 a.m. prior to the first assessment and subsequently had taken a single dose of Sinemet (275) at 12 o'clock.

Effect of Speech Therapy

As a second part to this project, the group of PP + SI were offered one month's intensive speech therapy (ie. four times per week, hourly sessions) and re-assessed a) immediately afterwards to evaluate therapeutic effect and b) six weeks after termination of therapy (to establish long term effects of therapy).

Results

Effect of L-dopa

In neither patient group (PP + SI, PP – SI) was there any significant effect, after taking drugs at 12 o'clock, on any of the three speech parameters: peak flow, loudness, or length of phonation. A graph was plotted for each patient on each measure throughout the day with no significant change following drug intake. It was, therefore, assumed that each patient was stabilised on his/her drug therapy.

Speech characteristics

The mean values of the three parameters were compared amongst the groups. It can be seen from the results (Table II) that in both the study groups the mean value for peak flow is lower than in the Control group.

TABLE II Results

PEAK FLOW (in 1/min)	Mean	Range
PP + SI	264	82–463
PP – SI	275	160–437
Controls	312	180–417
LENGTH OF PHONATION (in seconds)	Mean	Range
PP + SI	6.5	0.6–13.7
PP – SI	5.2	1.8– 8.3
Controls	14.3	7.2–34.7
LOUDNESS (Decibels)	Mean	Range
PP + SI	76.3	67.7–87.7
PP – SI	82.0	74.0–96.2
Controls	81.7	73.3–96.3

However, this difference could not be confirmed statistically in view of the small number of cases involved. Again the study groups had apparently a reduced length of phonation compared with the control group; a comparison of the values in PP - SI patients with those in the controls revealed a significant difference at the 5 per cent level (Mann-Whitney test).

On the loudness scale there was a noticeable difference amongst the study groups themselves. The value in PP - SI was nearer in score to the group of control subjects. It is difficult to draw significant conclusions in view of the small numbers involved, but *possibly* the marked reduction in loudness is a significant assessment result, distinguishing the PP + SI and PP - SI groups. The peak flow and duration of sustained phonation was definitely less in all Parkinsonian patients. A much larger sample would clearly need to be taken to investigate this further.

A comparison was made of the severity of speech rating; the clinical rating of tremor, rigidity and bradykinesia; and the duration of the disease, and length of treatment when the results were as in Table III.

Clearly all of the PP + SI group had some bradykinesia clinically. In the PP - SI group, three out of six patients had bradykinesia. It is interesting to note that, although the PP - SI group were "without reported speech involvement" on their neurological rating; three did in fact, indicate on their subjective ratings (Table I) that they had speech difficulties in certain situations. These three patients are asterisked in Table III, and two of these three have bradykinesia. Thus there may possibly be a trend towards speech problems being more evident in patients with bradykinesia, but a much larger study would need to be done to confirm this result.

There was no apparent relationship between the duration of the disease and the degree of speech involvement; many patients without speech problems had had the disease far longer than those with speech involvement. Obviously, many Parkinsonian patients do *not* have speech problems, despite having had the disease for many years. Similarly some acquire speech difficulty relatively soon after the onset. Again there appears to be no connection between the length of treatment of the disease and the speech difficulty experienced.

Effect of Speech Therapy

Three patients in PP + SI eventually completed the full course of treatment, thus the results can not be taken as conclusive but the records were as in Table IV.

Each patient improved in length of phonation and in loudness during therapy and this improvement was maintained in two patients for six weeks after cessation of treatment. No patient was assessed by the same therapist who had given the course of treatment. In addition, patients and spouses (where appropriate) were asked to fill in an "evaluation of therapy" form (Tables V and VI) to see whether they felt therapy had been beneficial. Questions 3 and 6 were included as a "lie detector"! All three patients genuinely felt their speech had improved but, in fact, when voice tape recordings were re-assessed by two therapists individually, two patients' ratings did not vary from the initial ones but one patient had an improved rating from mod. (2) to mild (1).

379

TABLE III

Patient Number	Age	Duration of disease (months)	Duration of treatment (months)	Speech Rating	Tremor	Rigidity	Bradykinesia
PP + SI							
1	72	26	8	Mild 1	0	2	2
2	70	22	22	Mild 1	0	0	1
3	59	98	98	Mod. 2	0	0	1
4	66	78	78	Mod. 2	0	1	1
5	66	48	48	Severe 3	0	1	1
6	70	240	186	Severe 3	0	1	1
PP – SI							
7	70	58	47	0	0	1	1*
8	71	70	55	0	1	1	0*
9	74	40	1	0	2	1	0*
10	65	36	26	0	0	0	0
11	74	8	2	0	0	1	1
12	79	36	3	0	1	1	1*

* = Patients whose self-assessment indicated speech difficulty in certain situations, despite clinical rating of no speech involvement.

TABLE IV Length of Phonation (seconds)

Patient No.	Pre-treatment	Post-treatment	6 weeks post
1	3.6	5.1	7.1
2	11.7	16.3	15.8
3	2.1	4.5	3.2

TABLE V Questionnaire for Patients on Speech Therapy Project

Do you feel that the following have improved after therapy?
Please put a circle round your answer.

1	Your speech	YES/NO
2	Your breathing	YES/NO
3	Your ability to hear the radio/television	YES/NO
4	Loudness of your voice	YES/NO
5	Clarity of your speech	YES/NO
6	Your walking ability	YES/NO
7	Your ability to talk for a longer time	YES/NO
8	Your confidence in mixing with people	YES/NO

NAME . . . .

DATE . . . .

TABLE VI Questionnaire for Relatives of Patients on Speech Therapy Project

After your relative has had speech therapy do you feel that the following have improved?
Please put a circle round your answer.

1	Your relative's speech	YES/NO
2	Your relative's breathing	YES/NO
3	Your relative's ability to hear the radio/television	YES/NO
4	Your relative's loudness of voice	YES/NO
5	Your relative's clarity of speech	YES/NO
6	Your relative's walking ability	YES/NO
7	Your relative's ability to talk for a longer time	YES/NO
8	Your relative's confidence in mixing with people	YES/NO

NAME OF RELATIVE. . . . .

DATE . . . .

TABLE VII Loudness (decibels)

Patient No.	Pre-treatment	Post-treatment	6 weeks post
1	80.3	84.0	86
2	82.3	84.0	86
3	75.1	78.0	73

This pilot study would seem to indicate that useful areas for further research in assessment of speech involvement in Parkinsonian patients would be:-

a Scientific methods of evaluating the various parameters of motor speech.
b A correlation of these individual aspects of speech production with the overall speech adequacy, and an attempt to find those paramters most closely connected with speech effectiveness.
c An attempt to correlate the cardinal clinical features, especially bradykinesia, with the degree of speech involvement and to find out whether bradykinesia at the onset of disease predicts future speech problems.
d Role of effective speech therapy in improving overall speech adequacy.

Summary and Conclusions

In a pilot study, 3 groups of patients (PP + SI, PP − SI and Normal controls) were screened for other primary cardiac, respiratory and laryngeal disease and dementia. The parkinsonian patients had been stabilised on L-dopa for at least 3 months. The speech and other cardinal clinical features were scored.

Overall speech adequacy and peak flow, length of phonation and loudness of speech were recorded in all the subjects. Any possible effect of L-dopa was investigated. The parameters of speech were compared with the clinical score of tremor, rigidity and bradykinesia in Parkinsonian patients.

The group of PP + SI were offered one month's intensive speech therapy and reassessed immediately afterwards, and six weeks after termination of therapy, to investigate the immediate and long term effect.

No significant effect of L-dopa was found on the parameters of speech investigated. There was a trend of reduction in loudness in PP + SI group, compared with PP − SI and Controls.

The peak flow and duration of sustained phonation was less in all Parkinsonian patients.

All of the PP + SI had bradykinesia. The degree of speech involvement had no correlation either with the duration of the disease or with the length of treatment.

All patients improved in length of phonation and in loudness of speech during treatment, but the overall speech improvements were not significant.

Acknowledgements

We are grateful to the Parkinson's Disease Society of the United Kingdom for financial support (to PKD).

Many thanks to the following people:-
1 Mrs C Flood and Mrs E West, fellow speech therapists involved in assessments.
2 Mr A G R McClelland for analysis of results.

3 Mrs R Ward, Secretary, for typing and clerical help.
4 Mrs J Frederick, Secretary, for typing.

References

1   Darley FL, Aronson AE, Brown JR. *Motor Speech Disorders Chapter 8, 1975* Eastbourne: WB Saunders
2   Canter GJ. *J Sp Hear Disord 1963; 28:*221
3   Canter GJ. *J Sp Hear Disord 1965; 30:*44
4   Canter GJ. *J Sp Hear Disord 1965; 30:*217
5   Kreul EJ. *J Sp Hear Res 1972; 15:*72
6   Sarno MT. *Archives of Phys and Mental Rehab 1968; 49:*269
7   Logermann JA, Fisher HB, Bosches B, Blonske ER. *J Sp and Hear Dis 1978; 43:*47
8   Wolfe VI, Garvin JS, Bacon M, Waldrop W. *J of Comm Disord 1975; 8:*271
9   Rigrodsky S, Morrison EB. *J Amer Geriatrics Soc 1970; 18:*142
10 Mawdsley C, Gamsu CV. *Nature 1971; 231:*315
11 Green MCL, Watson BW. *Folia phoniatrica 1968; 20:*250

Chapter 49

THE ASSESSMENT OF GAIT

F J Imms

If we observe a person walking, we can all quickly pass a judgement on whether the person is progressing with a normal gait or whether the gait is abnormal. If the gait is abnormal, then we often find it difficult to describe the abnormalities. We need to be able to 'freeze' the action so that we can examine its components either visually or by calculation of mathematical indices. A normal gait requires adequate ranges of movement in the joints of the lower limb, normal muscle power, the absence of pain and deformity in the legs and high levels of integrated function of the sensory and motor components of the central nervous system. In patients with Parkinson's disease impairment of the control of motor function often affects the gait. Studies of gait may therefore be a convenient method for monitoring the course of the disease and in evaluating therapy. A wide range of methods are available and it is important to choose a method appropriate to a particular clinical or experimental situation.

Biomechanical analysis

A precise description of the movements of the limbs during walking may be obtained from frame by frame analysis of cinefilm. This technique may be quantified by measuring for each frame the angles subtended by the thigh on the trunk, or the angles of flexion at the knee and ankle joints, and plotting these against time. Alternatively, we may plot these angles against each other [1]. For example, plotting the angles subtended at the hip and knee joints when a normal person is walking gives loop diagrams of the form illustrated in Figure 1. Any abnormality of the gait will alter the shape of this loop. To take an extreme example, if the patient were walking without bending the knee then the loop would become a horizontal line. This type of analysis is obviously very time-consuming, but fortunately similar results can be obtained using a polarised light goniometer [2].

Biomechanical analysis may also include the measurement of forces acting across joints and especially those exerted by the foot on the floor. These may be measured using suitably instrumented shoes [3] or a force plate [4]. The contributions of

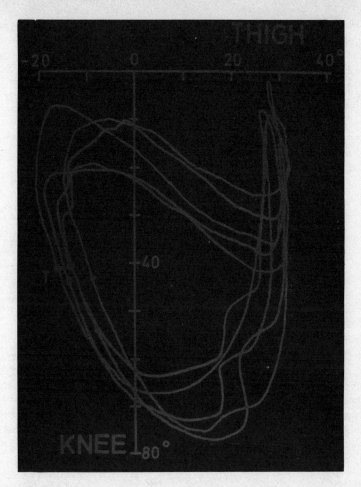

Figure 1 'Thigh-knee' angle charts for a normal adult male walking at moderate speed. Heel strike at top right-hand corner. Closed circles and 'T' refer to toe off (from Grieve [1]).

individual muscles during walking, in particular the phases of the cycle for which they are active, may be defined by electromyography.

Time and distance factors

When studying locomotion in patients with a disease which may cause gross abnormalities of gait, much useful information can be obtained using less sophisticated techniques. Simple data such as the velocity of walking, the length of stride, or the time taken to turn around may be better indicators of the patient's clinical condition than a detailed biomechanical analysis. To obtain such information we have used a technique originally described by Grieve [1, 5]. The apparatus consists of a metal walkway (Figure 2) on which the patient walks in shoes which have metal foil

Figure 2 Apparatus for recording gait patterns (From Imms and MacDonald, [5]).

contacts on the soles and heels. Two light beams cross the walkway towards either end and activate photocells. The breaking of these beams by the patient permits calculation of stride length and step frequency, of the duration of contact and swing phases of the walking cycle, and of the symmetry of the gait.

We have examined the gait of 50 patients with established diagnoses of Parkinson's disease, who were receiving a variety of drug therapies, and of 50 elderly control subjects (Table I) who have been subdivided into three groups according to their locomotor abilities [6].

TABLE I Subjects used in the studies of temporal and distance factors

		Number	Age
Parkinson's disease		50	66 ± 11
Controls	— housebound	8	80 ± 7
	— limited outdoor activity	16	78 ± 8
	— unlimited outdoor activity	26	77 ± 6

There were marked differences in the performances of the control subjects; the housebound patients walked more slowly than the fitter groups; they took shorter strides, and they turned around more slowly (Figure 3). The data for the Parkinsonian patients show a wide variation, spanning almost the complete range of the control subjects. It has been suggested by Knutsson [7] that the periods of double support during the walking cycle are specifically increased in Parkinson's disease. This hypothesis is not supported by our observations. Although the double support time of many Parkinsonian patients was longer than that for controls with unimpaired locomotor activity, many control patients with locomotor difficulties were double supporting for longer than the Parkinsonian subjects (Figure 3). We conclude that although the walking performance of many Parkinsonian patients was worse than that of the fittest group of controls, there were no indices which were altered specifically by the condition. This does not preclude the use of the test to study patients with Parkinson's disease, for it is to be expected that a change in clinical condition will result in appropriate changes in the test results.

The use of film and videotapes

Many of the locomotor problems of the Parkinsonian patient are not so much concerned with the form of the gait as with associated acts such as rising from a chair or bed, and the initiation and stopping of walking. Such factors may conveniently be assessed by asking the patient to carry out a standardised test routine (Table II)

TABLE II Tasks suitable for recording on film videotape

Rise from chair, walk across room, turn and return to chair

Rise from chair, walk until commanded to stop

Rise from chair, pick object from floor

Transfer from lying to sitting position on bed, sit on edge of bed, rise to stand clear of bed.

and recording the performance on cinefilm or videotape [6]. The test may be scored by measuring the times taken for various stages of the tasks, and for abnormalities of gait and mobility, eg. undue use of the arms in rising from a chair, carrying of a walking aid and episodes of 'freezing'.

Ambulatory monitoring

The methods described above are all hospital or laboratory based. One important aim of therapy in patients with Parkinson's disease is to improve their mobility, and

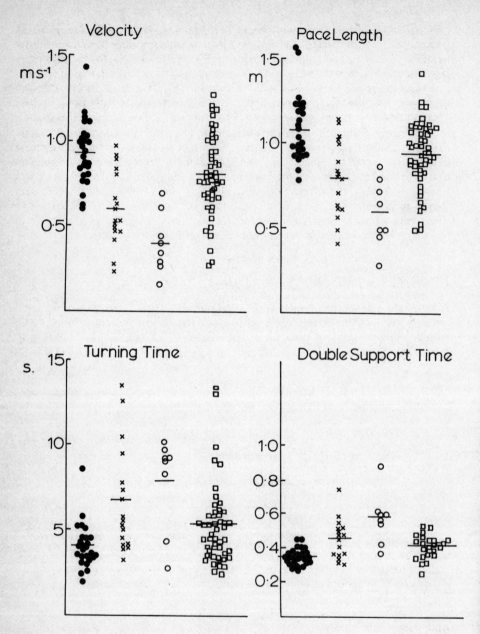

Figure 3 Time and distance factors in walking of control subjects (Table 1) claiming unlimited outdoor activity (●), limited activity (x) and to be housebound (○), and of patients with Parkinson's disease (□).

hence their independence, in their homes and at work. Assessment of the patient's habitual activity may be made by using small body-borne tape-recorders to record physiological variables [8] over periods up to 24 hours. Periods of walking may be identified from records of a small pressure transducer placed in a shoe, and an estimate of the energy costs of the task made from the heart rates calculated from recordings of the ECG. Furthermore, it is possible, using suitable transducers, to record whether the patient is lying, sitting or upright. The recordings may be analysed by computer to determine the duration during the day of different levels of physiological activity and to give a profile of the patient's habitual locomotor activity [9].

References

1   Grieve DW. *Physiotherapy 1969; 56:*452
2   Capildeo R, et al. Chapter 51 in this volume
3   Spolek GA, Day EE, Lippert EG, Kirkpatrick GS. *Experimental Mechanics 1975; 15:*271
4   Paul JP. *Proc. Instn Mech Engrs 1967; 181:*8
5   Imms FJ, MacDonald IC. *Scand J Rehabil Med 1978; 10:*193
6   Imms FJ, Edholm OG. *Age and Ageing 1979, suppl; 8:*261
7   Knutsson E. *Brain 1972; 95:*475
8   Bassey EJ, Fentem PH, MacDonald IC, Scriven PM. *Clin Sci Mol Med 1976; 51:*609
9   Karagozoglu. *PhD Thesis 1977.* University of Strathclyde

Chapter 50

THE MEASUREMENT OF PARKINSONIAN GAIT
USING POLARISED LIGHT GONIOMETRY

Rudy Capildeo, Beryl Flewitt and F Clifford Rose

Introduction

The Parkinsonian gait is so characteristic that the diagnosis is usually made by the neurologist as soon as the newly-referred patient enters the clinic room in the out-patient department. On hearing his name being called, the patient has initial difficulty in getting out of the chair in the waiting room, particularly if the chair has no arm rests. He stands stooped, appearing uncertain as how best to initiate walking, his feet appearing to 'stick' to the floor. Tremor may be noted in one or both legs before the first step is taken. When walking begins, the steps are small (marche à petits pas) and shuffling. Once walking is under way, the typical 'festinant' gait is seen. The patient may almost break into a run as he tries to catch up with himself since his forward stoop pushes his centre of gravity further and further in front of him. On reaching the entrance to the consulting room he pauses, seemingly disturbed by his conception of the narrowness of the doorway, and may stop altogether and hold on to the door lintel. Having stopped, he tries to initiate movement again and the whole cycle is repeated. The longer the period of observation whilst the patient negotiates the problems imposed by his disability, the easier the 'spot diagnosis' is made.

Having confirmed the diagnosis of "Parkinson's Disease" or "Parkinsonism" by history-taking and examination, the neurologist decides upon the initiation of treatment with a choice of medication. In clinical practice, improvement is measured subjectively rather than objectively, Procedures for objective assessment, necessary for the evaluation of new drugs in the treatment of the disease, are seldom continued over into routine clinical practice, chiefly because of the time factor; out-patient clinics are busy and assessments are time-consuming. The type of gait disturbance that has been described is seen in those patients with rigidity and marked bradykinesia. Difficulty with walking can be the most incapacitating aspect of the disease whilst tremor may socially be the most embarrassing. Loss of confidence, depression, other causes for disability and increasing age may compound the walking problem. Medication may "speed the patient up" but this does not necessarily mean that the patient can now walk more safely. Since no two patients are ever identical, it is necessary to assess each patient separately, and to define their individual disabilities rather than employing an empirical approach to management.

In this chapter, we shall discuss how to assess the different walking patterns of Parkinsonian patients with particular reference to a new objective method using a polarised light goniometer. New physiotherapy techniques have been devised based on the results obtained from a large number of patients. The principles behind these new treatment techniques and the physiotherapy regimes involved are further discussed in the other chapters of Part VII.

Assessment of Gait

The type of assessment performed depends upon the training and skill of the personnel involved. The problems of assessing neurological disability and some of the ways to overcome them have been recently described [1]. The physiotherapist traditionally measures power in limbs, using either the MRC (Medical Research Council) 0–5 scale or a modified form, whilst commenting on the tone of the limbs, whether spastic or flaccid. When observing walking, if possible, the 'good' leg is compared with the 'bad' leg. The occupational therapist is more concerned with assessing the activities of daily living—can the patient walk aided or unaided; can he manage stairs; can he manage stairs at home, etc. Although both types of assessments are quantifiable, the results are liable to interobserver and intraobserver bias particularly when the number of points on the assessment scale is over 3. 'Can perform the activity normally', 'some improvement' and 'cannot perform the activity' is hardly a sensitive measure, although in purely functional terms it indicates the patient's abilities and needs sufficiently. A simple way to quantify walking ability is to measure the time taken for the patient to walk say, 10 metres, 5 metres forward and 5 metres back. The main disadvantage is that this will not highlight two common problems that the Parkinsonian patient may have; i) initiating walking and ii) turning. When assessing walking, it has to be remembered that all the body participates in this activity in a co-ordinated fashion. The Parkinsonian patient may lose the ability to swing either arm when walking. His posture changes as there is a considerable reduction in the mobility of the spine and trunk due to muscular rigidity. It is also dangerous to consider 'good' and 'bad' legs since any abnormality in one leg will affect the range of movements in the other leg. This has been clearly demonstrated in hemiplegic patients following a stroke using polarised light goniometry to measure gait patterns [2]. In these patients, the range of movements in the 'unaffected' leg may initially be very restricted, but when good recovery has occurred, the range of movements may become exaggerated. it can be questioned whether the walking pattern ever returns to the pre-ictal 'norm' despite the patient's opinion that this may have occurred.

When assessing Parkinsonism, the variation in physical performance and tolerance of each patient during the day and the timing of medication in relation to these events must be taken into consideration. It is also important to know whether the particular gait problems observed are constant for each patient despite the apparent daily variation in physical performance.

Photographic techniques have been used extensively in gait research. The obvious advantage over other techniques is that a complete picture of the subject is obtained without the need for transducing devices and other equipment which may affect movement. The disadvantages outweigh the advantages for every-day clinical use [3]. The cost has been prohibitive but video-cassette recorders now provide a much cheaper alternative to cine-film, and also have the further advantage that replay is instantaneous and shots can be frozen. In a previous study [4] cine-film was used to analyse Parkinsonian gait. Two major differences compared with normal were observed:

i   altered patterns of movement occurred at the knee during the support phase and
ii there was an altered pattern of 'foot-to-floor' contact.

Our initial experience with polarised light goniometry was in stroke patients where the gait characteristics were obtained in the form of angle to angle charts comparing thigh and calf. In the Parkinsonian patients, the crucial measurement was found to be the recording of the ankle/knee movement. It is also important to measure the length and speed of stride since the normal gait pattern varies as these parameters change.

Crane-Mitchelson Polgon Goniometer

The characteristics of this equipment have been previously described [1, 3]. In summary, a beam of polarised light is directed from the polgon at right angles to the direction of gait. Photoelectric sensors, covered with polarised material, are attached to the thigh, calf and foot of the leg nearest the light source. Recordings of angular movement of the ankle and knee are plotted against each other on a two channel 'XY' pen recorder at a rate of 50 angles per second. The subject is also asked to walk on a foil covered walkway. Stride is measured from the foot imprints on the foil using a metre ruler and is expressed as a fraction of stature (relative stride). The time taken to complete the walking cycle can be measured through the polgon goniometer linked to the 'XY' recorder. If stride is measured at the same time then it is possible to calculate speed from the measurement of relative stride divided by the time taken for the walking cycle (relative speed).

Normal Gait

In the normal ankle/knee charts, three loops can be seen which indicate the changes in direction at these joints as the leg moves backward in the support-phase and forward in the swing-phase. All the angular changes are shown that occur during the course of a walking cycle (heel-strike to next heel-strike). The ankle angles are read against the horizontal; extension (or plantar flexion) to the left and flexion (or dorsiflexion) to the right. The knee angles are read against the vertical; extension is upward and flexion is downward. The alternating support and swing phases of the two legs induce the forward horizontal progression of the centre of gravity in walking.

Loop 1. The walking cycle begins as the foot strikes the ground heel first ('heel-strike'). Plantar flexion occurs at the ankle and flexion at the knee follows as the forefoot is lowered flat to the ground. Dorsiflexion of the ankle follows as the body-weight is carried forward over the foot which is now the single support as the opposite leg is in the swing phase.

Loop 2. The foot 'rolls over' from dorsiflexion to plantar flexion and at the same time the knee flexes and the heel is raised. The body-weight is now transferred to the opposite leg as the foot continues to plantar flex against the floor. The knee continues to flex until 'toe-off' occurs and the leg moves forward into the swing-phase.

Loop 3. The ankle dorsiflexes so that the foot is clear of the ground. With continued knee flexion the leg 'folds under' the trunk. At the end of the swing-phase, the knee has extended forward ready for the heel to strike the ground for the beginning of the next cycle. The 3 loops are referred to as 1. 'foot flat', 2. 'foot roll-over' and 3. 'fold under of the leg'.

Parkinsonian Gait

Comparing this chart with the normal subject, *Loop 1* is not present. The foot contact with the ground is 'toe-down' and the knee is more flexed than normal. Knee extension commences after 'toe-down' and the heel is then lowered. This is a reverse of the normal pattern seen on slow-speed charts, when heel-strike occurs first after which the forefoot is lowered. Knee extension immediately after ground contact with the foot is another abnormal feature.

At 2. there is a gradual change to knee flexion with the foot plantar flexing. Instead of the normal loop, a wide arc is seen on the chart at 'foot roll-over'. During weight transference, the range of plantar flexion is also reduced.

At 3. a normal 'fold under' of the leg occurs in swing but this is followed by a reduced range of knee extension and the ankle plantar-flexes to contact with the ground when it should be dorsiflexed ready for the next heel-strike.

These gait abnormalities have been confirmed in a large number of assessments and in those patients stabilised on medication they appear to be remarkably constant throughout the day. In normal subjects, electromyography techniques have demonstrated that there is a change from eccentric to concentric action of the gastrocnemius muscle during 'foot roll-over' [5]. During this phase of weight transference, premature concentric contraction of the gastrocnemius muscle may account for the characteristic patterns seen in the Parkinsonian patients.

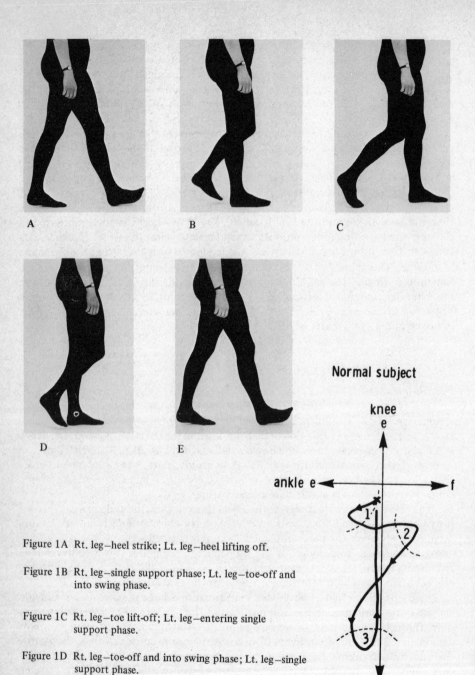

Normal subject

Figure 1A Rt. leg—heel strike; Lt. leg—heel lifting off.

Figure 1B Rt. leg—single support phase; Lt. leg—toe-off and into swing phase.

Figure 1C Rt. leg—toe lift-off; Lt. leg—entering single support phase.

Figure 1D Rt. leg—toe-off and into swing phase; Lt. leg—single support phase.

Figure 1E Rt. leg—heel strike and into next gait cycle.

A B C

D E

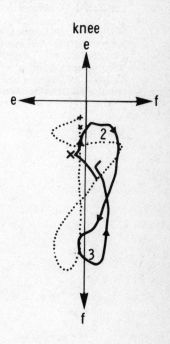

Parkinsonian patient

Figure 2A   Rt. leg – floor contact is plantigrade and knee is more flexed than normal; Lt. leg – support phase.

Figure 2B   Rt. leg – single support phase; Lt. leg – toe lift-off.

Figure 2C   Rt. leg – moving to heel-raise. Lt. leg – floor contact is plantigrade, flexed knee. Both legs supporting.

Figure 2D   Rt. leg – swing phase; Lt. leg – single support phase.

Figure 2E   Rt. leg – about to make floor contact with foot plantigrade, no heel strike, and into next gait cycle.

395

Summary

In order to objectively assess gait, a technique is required which is 1. quantifiable, 2. visually displayed, 3. quick to perform, 4. readily reproducible, 5. sensitive to small changes, 6. capable of being carried out by medical or paramedical personnel after minimum training and 7. cheap to run and maintain. After the initial capital outlay, we have found the running cost and servicing of the polarised light goniometer to be negligible. The technique is very sensitive and provides a quick record which can be analysed and used as the basis of physical treatment (Chapter 53). The graph can be measured in mathematical terms using planimetry techniques and it is possible to store the information on computer to provide a range of normals and also to measure 'abnormality' in terms of variation from normal.

It should be possible to assess all newly diagnosed Parkinsonian patients before treatment is initiated. When repeated at intervals over a long-term period, gait records provide important information on the course of the patient's disease.

References

1   Capildeo R, Clifford Rose, F. In Greenhalgh RM, Clifford Rose F, eds. *Progress in Stroke Research 1 1979.* Tunbridge Wells: Pitman Medical Ltd

2   Capildeo R, Mitchelson D, Clifford Rose F. *Chest, Heart and Stroke Journal 1979; 3:*13

3   Mitchelson D. In Grieve DW, Miller DI, Mitchelson D, Paul JP, Smith AJ. *Techniques for the Analysis of Human Movement 1975.*London: Lepus Books

4   Flewitt B. *Study of gait in Parkinsonism. FCSP Thesis 1975.* Chartered Society of Physiotherapy, London

5   Cavanagh PR. *Patterns of muscular action and movement associated with the range of speeds used in normal human locomotion. PhD Thesis 1973.* University of London

Chapter 51

PHYSIOTHERAPY IN PARKINSON'S DISEASE

S Franklyn, L J Kohout, G M Stern and M Dunning

Since the advent of L-dopa, less attention has been paid to physiotherapy as a possible treatment for Parkinson's disease but, as limitations of this and similar drugs have become apparent, interest has recently been revived. Much of the published work in this field was written before or during the inception of L-dopa, and few, if any, controlled studies have appeared.

The aims of this study are to evaluate the efficacy of current physiotherapeutic techniques, to develop an effective treatment programme, and to record as accurately as possible any change in the patient's condition before and after treatment and ten weeks after the end of treatment. All those treated were out-patients.

When planning such a study the problem of a control group must be considered but, after careful consideration, we decided that each patient should be his own control. Although not ideal, ethical considerations finally made us settle for this arrangement.

Assessment is also of vital importance. Two major problems associated with this group of patients must be taken into account: their extraordinary variability of performance, which largely depends on the drug cycle, and frequently, impairment of concentration for long periods of time. We have tried to overcome variability of performance by assessing the patient at the same time of day on two occasions, thus having two base-lines from which to work. While it would seem necessary to have more assessments, we had to compromise with clinical realities, and so used an assessment programme that is reasonably short and simple.

The assessment consists of 4 sections:

1 *Subjective Assessment* This consists of numerous daily living activities, ie. turning in bed, walking indoors and out, and is scored on a 6 point scale.

2 *Objective Assessments* which include: *Timed assessment* where the physiotherapist times the patient while he performs tasks such as turning in bed or doing up buttons.

3 *Video-recording* where the patient is asked to perform such tasks as standing up from a chair.

4 *Independent assessment* by a doctor, who grades each patient on the Northwestern University Disability Scales (NUDS).

Psychometric tests

We felt it was necessary to include psychometry to attempt to gauge the degree of anxiety and depression, since these two emotions are common to Parkinsonian patients and doubtless have an effect on their response to treatment. We employ the Multiple Affect Adjective Check List (Zuckerman and Lubin, 1965). (We had used a Personal Questionnaire (D Mullhall) to score depression and motivation but we found this too long and repetitive and patients often fell asleep while completing it).

Difficulties

Each patient was asked to list his particular difficulties in daily tasks.

Turning and manoeuvring in bed
Standing up from sitting
Walking indoors, caused by freezing, particularly through doorways
Loss of confidence walking outdoors, sometimes caused by a fall
Bad balance

While treating these patients, it became obvious that there were certain symptoms commonly shared by many patients which had to be taken into account by the physiotherapist, when planning a logical treatment programme. These are:

Disturbance of movement patterns
Poverty of movement
Bad memory for recent events
Tires easily
Disturbed balance

While watching a patient perform certain activities we noticed that one of the major factors preventing them from performing the required task was a disturbance of the pattern of movement. We tended to concentrate on this, breaking up the total pattern so that patients could practise certain elements of the movement they find difficult and then integrate them to form the complete movement.

Bad memory for recent events means that the tasks described had to be repeated many times on subsequent visits so that the patient would be able to remember and utilise the information.

If a patient tires easily he needs to employ his energy towards performing a task successfully, which he can do better if he knows the sequence of movements required to complete the total pattern.

This technique appears to work when performing activities that are encountered a few times a day but for walking and trick movements, for example, the constant thought needed to perform them appears to require too much concentration by the patient, and he reverts to his Parkinsonian gait.

Disturbed balance is another symptom often complained of in varying degrees. Patients who fall without warning or have attacks of loss of consciousness do not usually respond to physiotherapy.

Each patient in the study is given a list of simple mobility exercises to practise at home. Included in this list and emphasised are breathing exercises to maintain chest expansion and ankle movements to maintain the flexibility of the calf muscles.

A number of problems became apparent from the onset of the study. Without doubt, transport was a major problem for patients who were dependent on the ambulance service, and previous adverse experience made many patients unwilling to come for treatment on a twice weekly basis. Some became rigid in anticipation and were unable to leave their homes without maximum assistance. We have partly been able to overcome this difficulty with the help of the Parkinson's Disease Society who have been able to provide a volunteer car service to ferry patients to the hospital. Even so, two patients found the journey too exhausting, one falling asleep on arrival. A few patients were too disabled to travel comfortably in a car.

The study, so far, is divided into two parts:

1 *Group treatment* which was given on a twice weekly basis for 10 weeks.
2 *Individual treatment* given on a twice weekly basis for 8 weeks.

This section was further subdivided into physiotherapy given either in home or hospital.

We ran 3 groups with between 5 and 8 patients in each group (21 total). The first comprised patients at stage II, III, and IV on the Yahr scale but it was found that the more severely disabled patients were unable to take part fully in the activities. Subsequent groups had patients at stage II and III on the Yahr scale. The basic treatment scheme described above was used, taking into account the group's difficulties, and was augmented by various group activities including gait analysis.

Results

Of those treated, 10 showed a modest improvement on varying parameters at the end of treatment, and 7 retained that improvement 5 weeks after treatment ended. What was most disappointing was that the subjective rating often did not correlate with the patient's improved ability in hospital, for example, some patients complain of festinating at home yet walk normally in hospital.

Many patients reported the continued practice of the home exercises and most said they enjoyed the classes.

Patients often mentioned benefits from treatment that were not apparent in the assessment results, and this brings into question the limitations of conventional scoring systems.

The transport difficulties and the discrepancy between home and hospital performance led us to consider domiciliary physiotherapy.

In the individual treatments, by which is meant that each patient is treated on a one to one basis, his specific disabilities dictate the treatment programme, and patients at Stage III and IV on the Yahr scale are included. Both domiciliary and hospital patients were treated in a similar way with the methods discussed above. This part of the study has still to be completed. Those patients treated in the home environment seem to be able to utilise the new information more successfully and more quickly than those treated in hospital. The physiotherapists working on the project found it easier to treat a patient at home, which is where most of the difficulties occur.

In conclusion, we appreciate that it is impossible to judge how much of the improvement is physical, how much is psychological, or both. Nor can we say how enduring the improvement may be, but this applies to any medicinal treatment in this field. Even so about half of the patients treated reported improvement, but in some this was not sustained.

Chapter 52

A CONTROLLED TRIAL OF PHYSIOTHERAPY
FOR PARKINSON'S DISEASE

F B Gibberd, N G R Page, K M Spencer, E Kinnear and J B Williams

Introduction

Physiotherapy is used routinely in many hospitals in the treatment of Parkinson's disease. However, controlled trials of its efficacy do not exist. In carrying out such a trial there are many problems. The patients, almost without exception, come from an ageing and frail population so that difficulties in maintaining regular out-patient attendances occur. During a prolonged trial, as this must be, there are frequent intervening illnesses and even deaths. Some patients comply poorly with drug treatment so that variables may be introduced unwittingly. We have met all of these problems and overcome some of them.

Methods

Only patients who have been stabilised on drug therapy were admitted to the trial. Furthermore, if a home visit and domestic aids were considered necessary these were carried out before patients entered the trial.

All patients entering the trial were assessed initially by a doctor. Subjective assessments of speech, gait, posture, tremor in the worse arm and rigidity in the worse arm were carried out and graded as absent (0) to severe (4). Objective timings were made of the patient carrying out several activities. These included the time taken to rise from a seat, walk six metres, turn round and walk back to the chair, the time taken to insert a set of six pegs into a peg board, the time taken to insert a sheet of cardboard into an envelope and the time taken to write a standard phrase. The number of times the patient could open and close his fist in 10 seconds was recorded.

The diagram shows the layout of the trial. After an initial assessment the patients were randomly divided into those to receive active therapy and those to receive inactive therapy. Immediately after the courses the patients were reassessed by the doctor, who was unaware of which treatment individual patients had received. The

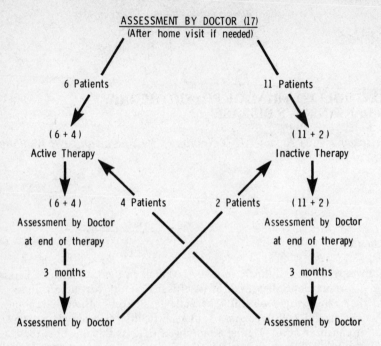

ASSESSMENT BY DOCTOR (17)
(After home visit if needed)

6 Patients   11 Patients

(6 + 4)   (11 + 2)
Active Therapy   Inactive Therapy

(6 + 4)   4 Patients   2 Patients   (11 + 2)
Assessment by Doctor   Assessment by Doctor
at end of therapy   at end of therapy

3 months   3 months

Assessment by Doctor   Assessment by Doctor

Figure 1 Physiotherapy in Parkinsonism (see text). This shows the flow diagram for the trial. The numbers in brackets refer to the number of patients.

patients were reassessed after a three-month gap in therapy, and some then proceeded to cross over and receive the opposite type of therapy.

During either type of therapy the patients attended hospital eight times in four weeks.

Active therapy started with a joint physiotherapy and occupational therapy assessment, after which the treatment programme was planned according to the individual patient's problems. When necessary the speech therapist and the dietician were requested to join in the treatment programme. Active physiotherapy was geared to positive treatment using Proprioceptive Neuromuscular Facilitation, Bobath and Peto methods. These were used for improving rotation, balance, walking, reducing festination and increasing range of movement where rigidity was a problem. Active occupational therapy was aimed at improving personal independence. Functional activities such as transferring to and from a toilet or chair, feeding, dressing, writing and cooking were practised where appropriate and in order to facilitate mobility, coordination and speed of action. Various activities to improve trunk rotation, standing balance and upper limb coordination were also used, e.g. woodwork, printing and table tennis.

During active therapy relatives were invited to observe treatment and to encourage the patient's activities at home.

402

Inactive physiotherapy consisted of infra-red radiation to the thoracic region for 20 minutes at a session. Inactive occupational therapy consisted of diversional activities such as table games and crafts, with minimal supervision.

Results

So far 23 patients have entered the trial. Six have dropped out because of illness other than Parkinson's disease, death or a change of drug therapy; 17 patients have completed a course of therapy (diagram); 6 patients have completed an initial course of active therapy and 4 patients have completed a second course of active therapy. Eleven patients have completed an initial course of inactive therapy and 2 patients have completed a second course of inactive therapy making 13 patients in all who have had inactive therapy.

Results obtained for each test in the assessment made by the doctor before therapy were compared with those obtained immediately after therapy using the Wilcoxon Rank Paired test. This was carried out for results of both active and inactive therapy. Out of 9 tests for each type of therapy in only one case was a trend for changing condition demonstrated. This occurred after inactive therapy and p was only 0.05.

Conclusions

According to our results remedial therapy in a hospital outpatient department is not useful in treating Parkinson's disease despite its widespread usage.

So far only 17 patients' results are available and one wonders if the results could be explained by small numbers. However, if remedial therapy was useful, one would have expected to see a trend of improvement after active therapy even if that trend was not yet significant. There is no trend and statistically it is unlikely that even with large numbers we would be able to show a significant improvement after therapy.

If some patients were too well on entry to the trial to show significant benefit from treatment, this might have reduced the overall significance of the results. But, again, if this were the case, one would have expected a trend, even if insignificant, to emerge.

It is possible that progression of the disease might veil any benefits of therapy, but then we should have seen a deteriorating trend in patients receiving inactive therapy, and this did not occur.

It may be that if we had chosen other forms of therapy or other tests of assessment we might have demonstrated an improvement. Nevertheless our tests of walking and manual dexterity are testing everyday functions so that our results are valid and significant.

Further research in physiotherapy and occupational therapy may show other ways in which it could be helpfully used. Perhaps, instead of concentrating resources on outpatient hospital remedial therapy, we should also be turning our attention to ways of helping parkinsonian outpatients within their own homes. Future research should be directed towards the community and the home, rather than towards outpatient treatment within a hospital environment.

Chapter 53

PHYSIOTHERAPY AND ASSESSMENT IN PARKINSON'S DISEASE USING THE POLARISED LIGHT GONIOMETER

Beryl Flewitt, Rudy Capildeo and F Clifford Rose

Introduction

Patients with Parkinson's disease present with a variety of gait problems which do not appear to be related to a single mechanical cause. If a common aetiological basis could be established, it would then be possible to devise specific physio-therapy treatment programmes which could be subsequently evaluated. At present, the physiotherapist has little to offer the patient with Parkinson's disease. Further-more, the inability to distinguish the reason for improvement, transient or per-manent, or no improvement discourages both the patient and the therapist.

In a previous study [1], gait patterns were observed in a group of 39 patients with post-encephalitic Parkinsonism. Cine film was used to record and analyse the various components of the walking cycle in six of these patients. A number of different gait styles were noted in those patients who had suffered from Parkin-sonism for a long time. In addition to the typical 'festinant' gait, three other patterns were commonly observed, 'loping', 'scooting' and 'martial stepping'. (Figures 1a, 1b and 1c). Common features to all types were that:

(1) the foot was held plantigrade or plantarflexed at the point of floor contact, i.e. the normal 'heel-strike' was absent,
(2) the knee was extending at the point of 'foot-roll over' (see Chapter 50), which is normally seen in a fast gait pattern, and
(3) the ankle was plantar-flexing during the 'swing' phase.

Calf muscle shortening or even contractures were noted in the majority of cases. These results suggested that the different gait patterns represented each patient's individual adaptation to an underlying mechanical disturbance [2].

We have carried out a number of different studies to investigate the mechanics of gait disturbance in patients with Parkinsonism at various stages in the disease process, comparing those with early signs of the disease with those considered 'intermediate' or 'late'. In addition, patients have been reassessed after the initiation of medication, or when it has been changed, during the course of a 24-hour period,

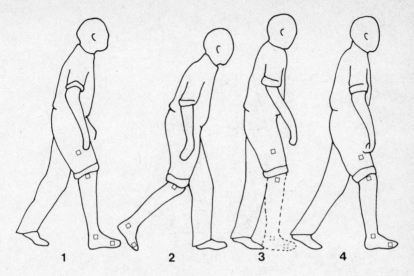

Figure 1(a)

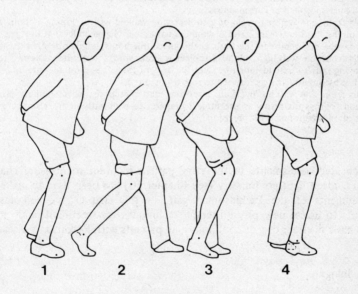

Figure 1(b)

405

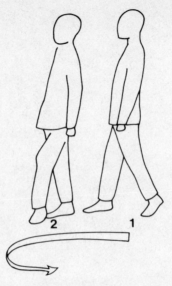

Figure 1(c)

Figure 1 Outlines from images of projected film, illustrate different patterns of gait in subjects with post-encephalitic Parkinsonism.
(a) Stills from one walking cycle of a subject who walked with a 'loping' action. The vertical lift of the head between 2 and 3 would equal a 9cm change in level at life-size. The dotted line represents tremor in the limb as the knee straightens, which obscured the true outline.
(b) Stills from one walking cycle of a subject walking with a 'scooting' action. The right limb in swing fails to extend much beyond the level of the left at ground contact (2–4). The left limb subsequently swings forward to repeat posture 2.
(c) Stills from one walking cycle of a subject 'martial stepping' with soldierly precision. The action follows the arrow as the subject prepares to turn with an erect stance and the foot placed on the ground with precision.

and repeated assessments in the same patient in order to measure changes over time. Polarised light goniometry (see Chapter 50) has been used to make objective measurements of the Parkinsonian gait. In this chapter, we will describe our attempts to assess new physiotherapy techniques for treatment, and our concept of the basic disorder of gait common to all patients with Parkinson's disease.

Methodology

Forty patients with Parkinson's disease were initially assessed. Twelve patients were excluded from the study because of co-existing orthopaedic or other causes of disability which affected their gait.

Group 1

Fourteen patients were selected for this study who had been stabilised on medication for at least the preceding four months. All patients were fully assessed and gait measurements recorded. Seven patients were then treated for between three and six weeks, the other seven patients acting as controls. At the end of the course of treatment, all patients were reassessed and further assessments were carried out at monthly intervals for a further three months. Assessments were made on the same day of each month and at the same time of day for each patient.

Group 2

Seven patients were selected, including three patients from the control group, and their gaits assessed and measured. Physiotherapy treatment was given twice a week for three weeks. Patients were shown exercises to continue at home and each received an instruction pamphlet with diagrams of the exercises. At the end of three weeks, reassessments were carried out and repeated one month later. Shoe modifications or metatarsal pads were introduced as necessary. Patients were also supervised walking out of doors if this was a major problem.

Gait assessment

Polarised light goniometry has been described in Chapter 50. The polarised light source was set at a distance of 2 metres from a walkway and at right angles to it. The walkway consisted of strips of honeycomb rubber flooring, 6 metres long, the central 3 metre section being covered by 50m aluminium foil (Alcan), held in place by a wood and metal frame. Transducers were attached to the leg facing the light source at the thigh, and calf and foot. The leads from the transducers were connected to a junction box carried on a belt worn by the patient. A trailing cable ran from the junction box to the goniometer linked to an XY recorder. After attachment of the transducers and belt pack, each patient initially obtained practice by walking along the floor before measurements were made on the walkway. The length of stride was measured from the imprints on the walkway. Four charts were recorded of the ankle/knee patterns from four traverses—two for each limb, one with the patient walking with shoes followed by the patient walking without shoes.

A record was kept of (i) the case summary, (ii) the medication and any subsequent changes, (iii) the ankle/knee charts, (iv) the range of active and passive movements at the joints of both legs, (v) the standing posture and (vi) the patient's description of his gait problems.

Concepts of physiotherapy treatment

One of the principal aims of treatment was re-education, to teach the patient how to control his balance when his equilibrium was threatened and to concentrate on 'foot-to-floor' activity throughout the entire walking-cycle. The patients found the concept of the forefoot acting as the 'drive' and the heel striking the ground as the 'brake' to be particularly useful in understanding their own gait problems. The calf muscles are plantar-flexors, acting as propulsors in walking or running and to restore the balance of the trunk to the upright position in standing. When acting concentrically, the calf muscles can tilt the body weight in all directions and, conversely, movement of the trunk from the midline will cause stretch in the calf muscles.

Control of plantar-flexor 'drive' in walking relies on the patient striking the ground heel first at the beginning of each step; this will 'brake' the forward momentum of the leg at the end of the 'swing-phase'. After the 'heel-strike', the centre of gravity will move forward as the weight is transferred on to the forefoot at the beginning of the next walking cycle. This type of control is lacking in patients with Parkinson's disease who are unable to perform a normal 'heel-strike', who have calf muscle shortening or contractures or scoliosis of the spine. Physiotherapy treatment was designed to reduce the effect of stretch on the sole of the foot, the tendo achillis and back of the knee by ensuring that full ranges of movement were maintained at the knee and ankle joints during active (or assisted-active) movements. The patients performed exercises lying, and also standing holding on to a support. In some patients, metatarsal padding (molefoam) was used to hold the toes in a plantar-flexed posture in order to reduce the range of stretch on the calf muscles during 'foot roll-over' ('heel-strike' to 'toe-off'). In other patients, shoe heels were raised in order to improve 'heel-strike'. Any possible undesirable effects of the raised heel were counteracted by instructing patients to walk indoors in low-heels or stockinged feet. The use of sticks or walking aids were discouraged since they cause the trunk to lean forward. Daily exercises were written down for the patient to practise at home, and instructions to walk out of doors each day for at least 20 minutes, in quiet streets, practising walking with good 'heel-strikes', the body relaxed and upright. The importance of walking at a moderate pace, with moderate stride lengths, was stressed to the patients as this will help to reduce any extremes of stretch on the tendo achillis prior to 'foot-roll-over'.

Results

Group I. Five of the seven patients in the treatment group completed their course of physiotherapy. One patient withdrew because of intercurrent illness, the other was reluctant to continue attending because of domestic problems. In three patients, subjective and objective assessments indicated a return to normal walking. In the other two patients, one had improved ranges of joint movement but still some gait disturbance was present as indicated by the ankle/knee charts, although less pronounced than before treatment, and the other patient felt he was back to normal, although his right ankle still inverted during the swing phase and his left knee tended to flex during the phase of single support, confirmed by the ankle/knee charts. The seven control patients did not change during the trial periods, either by subjective or objective assessment.

Group II. In five out of seven patients, walking returned to normal, the ankle/knee charts showing return to normal gait patterns. The patients were free from sudden episodes of gait disturbance. One patient was satisfied with his walking and was unaware that he walked with an 'up and down' motion of the trunk with exaggerated knee extension patterns during the phase of single support as demonstrated by the ankle/knee charts. This pattern of gait can be compared to that following treatment. She veered as she walked which made chart recordings difficult to obtain. She was extremely slow in all her actions and generally debilitated.

Parkinsonian patients who had other causes of disability present which influence their gait patterns were not included in Groups I or II. Individual treatment of these patients was, however, of particular interest. In one patient, shortening of the leg after a hip operation made the exercises difficult to perform. Raising the heel of the shoe made the shoe too heavy and the patient did not respond to treatment. In another case, raising the heel of the shoe improved the patient's walking with improved ranges of joint movement and exercise ability. In the case of a patient with an old fracture of the shaft of the femur accompanied by shortening, the ankle/knee charts showed considerable improvement, and the subject can now walk without a stick. A full return to normal was not possible, particularly as the patient had difficulties with the adjustment of medication. This was clearly indicated by the ankle/knee charts which varied from session to session. Three patients with severe scoliosis failed to respond to physiotherapy because of the forward lean of the trunk. This could not be corrected by using walking sticks or Zimmer walking aids. 'Rollator' walking aids keep the trunk more upright and have been tried with some success. Two illustrative cases are described from Group II. For normal gait patterns see Chapter 50.

Case 1

A female patient, aged 63 years, with a two-year history of Parkinson's disease. Her main problems were tremor and an unstable gait, with occasional 'sticking' and festination. The patient always wore shoes with a 1½-inch heel. She did not go out alone. Medication: Sinemet 110, 2 tablets b.d. There had been no change in medication during the previous four months.

Ankle/knee Charts

The gait charts before treatment (Figures 2a and 2b) show no heel-strike (loop 1) in the right leg (Figure 2a) and the ankle is plantar-flexing on floor contact. In the left leg (Figure 2b) all loops are present but the ranges of knee flexion and extension are reduced.

After the first physiotherapy session, the patient was asked to wear low heels at home for part of the day or stockings only, walking carefully, putting the heel down first at each step. By the fourth treatment the patient had recovered the ability to fully dorsiflex both ankles. By the fifth treatment, the patient had gained enough confidence to walk out-of-doors alone. Her husband also commented that she no longer walked with a limp.

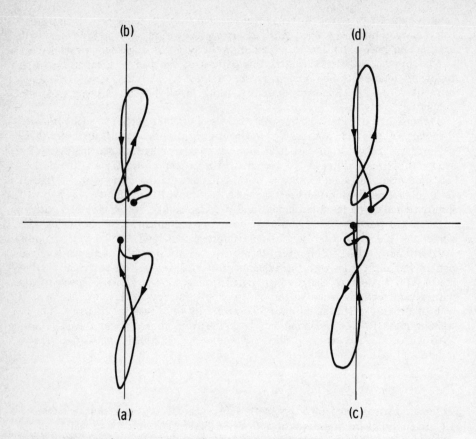

Figure 2 The ankle/knee charts are for the right (a), and left (b) legs of Case 1 before treatment. For convenience of recording the charts for the left leg are presented inverted and reversed. 'Heel-strike' is marked by a closed circle. Arrows indicate the pathways of the movement from heel-strike—ankle dorsi-flexion to the right, plantar-flexion to the left; knee extension upward and knee flexion forward. The charts (c) and (d) are for the right (c) and left (d) legs after treatment. (See text).

The ankle/knee charts after treatment (Figures 2c and 2d) show an improvement towards normal. Three loops are present in both legs and the ranges of knee flexion and extension are equal. Monitoring the gait charts over the next two months showed that improvement was maintained. The patient continued to go out alone, for example, to do her shopping.

Case 2

A female patient, aged 75 years, with a four-year history of Parkinson's disease, had as her main problem loss of balance. Two years previously, she had suffered from an episode of myocardial infarction and her exercise tolerance was now limited.

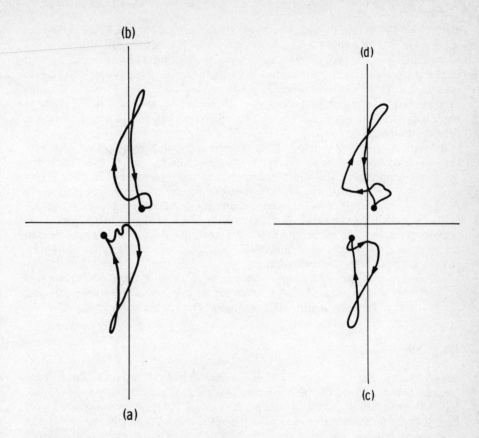

(b)

(d)

(a)

(c)

Figure 3 The ankle/knee charts are for the right (a) and left (b) legs of Case 2 before treatment. Charts (c) and (d) are for right and left legs respectively, of the subject after treatment. Signs are the same as for Figure 2 (see text).

Medication was Madopar 125mg t.d.s. and Artane 2mg t.d.s., there having been no change in medication during the previous four months.

Assessment of both legs, with the patient lying down, showed that there was resistance to passive dorsiflexion of the ankle. These findings were more marked in the right leg than the left. Hip movements were in the normal range. The patient always wore shoes without heels and did not go out often, except with her husband. She walked with short steps and, when standing, rocked forward and backward with the right foot in front of the left, a habit of which she was unaware.

Ankle/knee Charts

The gait charts before treatment (Figures 3a and 3b) showed no heel-strike (loop 1) in the right leg (Figure 3a). Instead, the foot is plantigrade to the floor and is followed by alternating flexion and extension at the knee as the leg straightens

411

almost to $180°$ before flexing. The charts of the left leg (Figure 3b) and right leg show no loop 3 since both ankles do not dorsiflex after 'toe lift-off' into the swing-phase. The charts suggest a 'scooting' action, the right leg being carried in advance of the left leg with neither leg folding through during the swing-phase. This type of action is outlined in Figure 1b and suggests an adaptation of gait which avoids the need to carry the centre of gravity over the base when the leg is in the phase of single support. This gait pattern was made less obvious in this patient because she took short strides.

By the second physiotherapy treatment, the right ankle could actively dorsiflex in the normal range. At the third treatment, shoes with higher heels were worn and the stride length increased and the steps were more symmetrical. However, there were some problems with the shoes because of ankle swelling. After six treatments, the gait was reassessed. The ankle/knee charts showed the normal features of three loops for both the right leg (Figure 3c) and the left leg (Figure 3d). The range of ankle dorsiflexion is much greater in the left leg during the support stage. A normal follow through for both legs during the 'swing-phase' was apparent, and joint movements were in the normal range.

Monitoring the gait charts over the following three months confirmed that improvement was maintained. Later, when her general health deteriorated, the gait charts remained unchanged although the range of the gait cycle was reduced.

Discussion

Physiotherapy trials in Parkinson's disease are extremely difficult. Direct comparisons between 'treated' and 'untreated' patients are subject to many biases, not least the difficulty of matching patients. Individual variation on a daily or hourly basis and the individual's tolerance to therapy further confound the problem of trial design. It is not possible to exactly define a 'unit of physiotherapy' in order to quantify total treatment given when comparing outcomes of different amounts or types of physiotherapy treatment.

For these reasons, we decided to adopt a different approach. If we could find an easy, readily reproducible method for objective gait measurement, then each patient could act as his or her own control for the evaluation of different types of physiotherapy treatment. Polarised light goniometry has proved to be a highly successful method for the objective measurement and analysis of different gait patterns in a variety of neurological and orthopaedic conditions (see Chapter 50). Using this approach it was possible to test new concepts of physiotherapy treatment outlined in this chapter. In the physiotherapy treatment programme, it was found to be essential to choose exercises which will reduce passive stretch to the calf muscles. In some cases it was found that even touching the patient to give assistance during episodes of 'sticking' might result in the patient leaning in that direction. Similarly holding on to the wall or a helper's arm might make the problem of balance worse. Gait interruptions of this type could simply be resolved by instructing the patient to take a step backwards on to the heel or forwards on to the heel. When patients festinated, the physiotherapist would calmly stand in front of the patient taking the patient's hands lightly and guiding the elbows backwards, held in flexion. This manoeuvre would halt the interruption in gait.

This investigation into parkinsonian gait suggests that the mechanical cause for the disturbance of gait is primarily due to a minor fault in leverage at the floor level during walking. Since this mechanical fault disturbs the person's balance, serious deterioration in the person's gait ability will result. The fault happens unexpectedly and, because righting the balance relies on the same principle of leverage, the usual method of correction is no longer reliable in Parkinsonism. 'Exaggeration', 'misphasing' or 'misturning' of plantar-flexion is the result of the individual's adaptation to this basic problem. 'Sticking', festinating or falling suddenly without cause is a complete mystery to the patient and increases the degree of disability. When this happens once or twice, apprehension naturally occurs and rigidity and tremor are made worse.

Patients with early changes of gait disturbance soon learn the value of walking with a good 'heel-strike' at every step and a relaxed upright stance. If daily exercises are carried out which will bend and stretch the ankle, correction at this stage will become automatic. Re-education in Parkinsonism should always be considered as soon as the problem arises. Ankle/knee charts will show a fault developing in one joint of one leg often before an enquiry elicits an account from the patient of 'one or two' falls. Physiotherapy methods, which increase the patient's control of sudden interruptions in their walking, will help the parkinsonian patient to see their walking problems in a proper perspective; this will have the effect of reducing anxiety and improving confidence in the everyday activities of daily living.

References

1   Flewitt B. *FCSP Thesis, registered with the Chartered Society of Physiotherapy 1975*
2   Grieve DW. In Grieve DW, Miller DI, Mitchelson D, Paul JP, Smith AJ, (eds). *Techniques for the Analysis of Human Movement 1975;* 109. London: Lepus Books

Index

415

418

Hallucinations, *continued*
from bromocriptine, 329
lergotrile causing, 337
Halogabide, in Parkinson's disease, 314
Haloperidol, 146, 160, 260
binding, 203
reducing substance P content of
substantia nigra, 161
Handwriting, freezing in, 248, 266
Hastening phenomenon, 250, 252
Hemiballistic diphasic dyskinesia, 245
Hemichorea, DAMME in, 167
Hemi-parkinsonism, tremor in, 78
Heparin, 277
Hippocampus, noradrenaline in, 201
Home care, 403
Homovanillic acid, 234
action of nomifensine on, 346
in CSF, 170, 200
striatal, 186
H response, 91, 92, 105
amplitude, 106
effect of baclofen on, 95
in treated patient, 108
in tremor, 105
in untreated patient, 105
Huckman index, 44
Huntington's disease, 98, 102, 166
apomorphine in, 259
baclofen in, 304, 315
DA 2 receptor antagonists in, 322
DAMME in, 167
muscimol in, 315
sodium valproate in, 315
substance P in CSF in, 177
Hydrocephalus ex vacuo, 48, 50
6-Hydroxydopamine, 161, 182
inducing parkinsonism, 362
6-Hydroxydopamine rotation model, 287
5-Hydroxy-indole-acetic acid, 171
5-Hydroxytryptamine, 4, 5, 145, 272
action of baclofen on, 304
action of diprobutine on, 302
age affecting levels of, 151
deficiency in Parkinson's disease, 145
MAO and, 206
receptors, 199
Hyperalgesia, substance P causing, 158
Hyperkinesia
reversed by substance P, 160
Sinemet causing, 232
Hypersecretion *See Drooling*
Hypertension, MAO inhibitors causing, 342
Hypochondriasis, 38
Hypokinesia, 357
substance P and, 161, 163

Hypotension
in juvenile parkinsonism, 38
orthostatic *See Orthostatic
hypotension*
postural, 114, 115, 116 *See also
Orthostatic hypotension*
Sinemet causing, 231
Hypothalamus, noradrenaline in, 201
Hypothermia, dopamine-induced, 285
•
Idiopathic dystonia, in juvenile
parkinsonism, 38, 39
Idiopathic orthostatic hypotension, *See also
Orthostatic hypotension*
relationship to parkinsonism, 121
Idiopathic parkinsonism
CT scans, 43, 45
nomifensine in, 348
tremor in, 75
Imidazole acetic acid, use of, 216
Immune response in parkinsonism, 359
Immunoglobulins, determination of, 183
Impotence, 121
Incidence
familial, 35
of cerebral atrophy, 50
of juvenile parkinsonism, 35, 38
of post-encephalitis parkinsonism, 40
Incontinence, 111
Inflammation, aetiology and, 40
Influenza A virus, 5
Injury, response to, 102
Insomnia, 38
Intellectual changes, treatment and, 53–60
Intellectual deterioration, in treatment with
L-dopa and benzerazide, 245
Investigations, 357
Involuntary movements
drug-induced, 288
oxpentifylline affecting, 354
IQ, 53, 371
during treatment, 55, 58
Iron, in parkinsonian brains, 361

Jakob–Creutzfeldt's disease, 359
Jakob's disease, 41
Jendrassik's manoeuvre, 90
Joseph's disease, 30
Juvenile parkinsonism
age of onset, 35, 38
autonomic signs in, 38
clinical features of, 35–39
dopamine in, 38
dyskinesia in, 35, 37
familial incidence, 35, 38
incidence of, 35, 38

Locomotion, animal models, 283
Locus coeruleus
    cell loss from, 25
    changes in, 120, 121
Long-latency nociceptive reflex, 105, 110
Long-latency response, in untreated
        patient, 107
Lower oesophageal sphincter pressure,
        dopamine depletion and, 61
L-prolyl-L-leucylglycine amide, 158
Lung cancer, Parkinson's disease and, 14, 67
Luteinizing hormone, 192, 193
Lysergic acid, 289
    sedative effects, 258

Madopar, 152
Manganese, 40
Manganese poisoning, 256
Marche à petits pas, 391
Maximal twitch response, 91
Melanocyte-stimulating hormone, 158
Mental symptoms, 43
Merital *See Nomifensine*
Mesencephalitis syphilitica, 40
Mesolimbic system, GABA in, 214
β-Methyl-para-tyrosine, 160
Methylphenidate, 346
Metoclopramide, 261, 319, 322
Micturition, frequency of, 119
Migraine, 145
Mobility
    diurnal fluctuations in, 268
    exercises, 398
Mongolism, 145
Monoamine oxidase, dopamine oxidation
        and, 205
    forms, 343
    in Parkinson's disease, 205–211
    in platelets, 209
    physiological role of, 205
    systems, 342
    toxic psychosis and, 152
Monoamine oxidase A, 343
Monoamine oxidase B, 343
    suppression by deprenyl, 238
Monoamine oxidase inhibitors, 205
    side effects of, 206
    urinary, 207
Monoamine oxidase inhibitors A, 205
Monoamine oxidase inhibitors B, 205
    effect on dopamine, 153
    effect on phenylethylamine, 153
    use in treatment, 234
Morbid anatomy, 25–31
Morphine
    action of, 98

Morphine, *continued*
    effect of dopamine on, 110
    motor effect, 166
Mortality rates
    age-specific, 10
    cohort analysis, 11, 12
    encephalitis lethargica, 11
    trends in, 9
Motor functions
    abnormalities of, 362
    opiates and, 98
Motor neurone disease, 22
Motor neurone excitability, decrease in, 106
Movement transducers, 76
Multiple system atrophy
    features of, 120, 123
    noradrenaline levels in, 122
Muscimol
    in Huntington's disease, 315
    in Parkinson's disease, 313, 314
Muscle
    cogwheel effect *See Cogwheel effect*
    contraction 'at rest', 90
    dynamic shortening reaction, 89
    H response, 91, 92
        effect of baclofen on, 95
    relaxation, 90
    shortening reactions, 89
    slow (tonic) stretch response, 89
    static shortening reaction, 89
    vibration of, 93
    voluntary contraction, 91
        rigidity and, 93
Muscle cramps, 269
Muscle tone control, substance P in,
        158–164
Mutism, 38
Myasthenia gravis, 267
Myoclonus, levodopa induced, 275

Nalorphine, 101
Naloxone
    action of, 99
    action on side effects of DAMME, 167
    effect on running on injured limb in
        rats, 100
    motor effects, 166
Nausea and vomiting
    animal models, 285
    from baclofen, 306
    from bromocriptine, 327, 335
    from Prolopa, 242, 243
    in levodopa therapy, 279
    Sinemet causing, 231
Nervousness, 38
    Neurasthenia, parkinsonian, 267

Pergolide mesylate, 289
Peristalsis, 64
Peroxidase, impaired activity, 363
Pharmacology, 362
Phenocybenzamine, 160
Phenothiazines, 270, 277, 285
   as dopamine receptor antagonists, 319
Phenylethylamine, effect of MAO B on, 153
Phenylketonuria, visual evoked response in, 138
Phenylsulphotransferase
   dopamine conjugation with, 208
   in Parkinson's disease, 205–211
   in platelets, 209
Physiology in Parkinson's disease, 362, 397–400, 401–403, 404–413
Physiotherapy
   assessment, 397
   benefits of, 401
   concepts of, 407
   methods, 401
   problems, 401
   psychometric tests in, 398
   results of, 402, 408
   treatment pattern, 398
   using polarised light goniometer, 404
Physostygmine, 262
Picrotoxin, 213, 214
Pimozide, 258, 286
Piribedil, effect on tremor, 108
Platelets
   MAO activity in, 209
   phenylsulphotransferase in, 209
Pleural effusion from bromocriptine, 329
Polarised light goniometer, 404–413
Polysynaptic reflexes, 109, 110
Post-encephalitis parkinsonism, 5
   aetiology of, 181
   association of rigidity with putamen damage, 88
   course of, 181
   distinction from idiopathic disease, 9
   gait problems in, 404
   immunoglobulins in CSF, 182, 184
   incidence of, 40
   nomifensine in, 348
   schizophrenia and, 67, 68
Postural disability, 278
Postural hypotension, 114, 115 See also Orthostatic hypotension
   Valsalva's manoeuvre and, 116, 117
Posture, 401
   changes in, 391
   effect of Prolopa, 243
   effect of Sinemet on, 229, 231

Posture, *continued*
   instability in L-dopa with benzerazide treatment, 245
   physiology of, 362
Procaine, shortening response affected by, 90
Progressive lacunar degeneration, 41
Progressive supranuclear palsy
   CSF noradrenaline levels in, 172
   homovanillic acid in CSF in, 170
   serotoninergic function and, 174
   substance P in CSF in, 177
   tangles in, 26
Prolactin
   action of bromocriptine on, 333
   action of ergot derivatives on, 335, 337
   action of lisuride on, 334
Prolopa *See under L-dopa with benzerazide*
Proprioceptive neuromuscular facilitation, 402
Proteins in Lewy bodies, 25
Psychiatric disorders, 59
   bromocriptine causing, 330
   from levodopa therapy, 275, 279
Psychological assessment, 371–373
Psychological traits in juvenile parkinsonism, 38
Psychometric measurements, 45, 48
   correlated with clinical features, 45–51
   tests, 398
Psychosis
   correlation with ventricular size, 50
   from levodopa therapy, 278
   monoamine oxidase and, 152
Pterin synthesis, 171
Pulmonary emboli, 277
Punch-drunk boxers, 41
Putamen, 4
   dopamine in, 198
   glutamic acid decarboxylase in, 310
   noradrenaline in, 198

Quadriceps muscle, slow stretch response in, 89
Quality of life, 243

Research, 359
Reserpine, 4, 362
   dopamine depletion and, 286
Reserpine induced parkinsonism, 286
Respiratory abnormalities, in encephalitis lethargica, 254
Response swings, 265
   mechanism of, 271
   unpredictable, 270

Rest
  parkinsonian fatigue and, 268
  physiological mechanism, 102
Rest and pain, 102
Retina, dopaminergic cells in, 145
Rigidity, 21, 88–97, 248, 251, 363, 376,
      379
  association with damage to putamen, 88
  blood pressure and, 113
  co-existing with resting tremor, 90
  effect of apomorphine, 259
  effect of baclofen, 305
  effect of Sinemet, 229, 231
  effects of treatment on, 95
  freezing and, 251, 252
  from oxiperomide, 322
  GABA reducing, 215
  H response in, 105
  in juvenile parkinsonism, 35
  L-dopa affecting, 95
  mechanism, 266
  physiological basis of, 86
  reduced by substance P, 160, 162
  shortening reactions, 89
  slow (tonic) stretch response, 89
  tendon jerks in, 91
  tonic vibration response and, 93
  treatment, 278
  voluntary contraction and, 93
  Westphal phenomenon, 89
RO 4 4602, 284

Schizophrenia, 255
  dopamine metabolism in, 67, 186
  drug induced, 67
  nomifensine in, 348
  Parkinson's disease and, 67–71
Schottky detector, 76, 81
Sedation, in levodopa dyskinesia, 258
Segmental dystonia, 306
Senile dementia, 25
Serotonin See under 5-Hydroxytryptamine
Serotoninergic function, CSF and, 174
Sex, effect on levodopa dyskinesia, 256
Shortening reaction, 105, 110
  in treated patient, 109
  in untreated patient, 107
Short-latency response, in untreated patient,
      107
Short-latency tactile reflex, 105
Shy-Drager syndrome, 30
  CSF noradrenaline levels in, 172
  dopamine deficiency in, 200
  dopamine levels in, 196
  dopamine receptors in, 195
  homovanillic acid in CSF in, 170

Shy-Drager syndrome, *continued*
  noradrenaline levels in, 196
  pigmented cells in locus coeruleus in,
      201
  reduction of spiperone binding sites in,
      202
  serotoninergic function in, 174
  substance P in CSF in, 177
  tyrosine hydroxylase in, 198
SL 76992 (Halogabide) in Parkinson's
      disease, 314
Sialorrhoea, effect of Sinemet on, 229, 231
Sinemet *See Carbidopa*
Sleep
  absence of tremor in, 257
  apomorphine affecting, 258
  dopamine in, 258
  dyskinesia in, 261
  in parkinsonian fatigue, 268
Sleep benefit, 268, 272, 273
Slow viruses, 6, 16, 21
Smoking, Parkinson's disease and, 14, 15,
      360
Social aspects, 23
Sodium valproate, 216
  in Huntington's disease, 315
  in Parkinson's disease, 313, 314
Spearman rank correlations, 47
Spectral analysis, 75, 76, 84
Speech
  articulation rate, 374
  assessment, 373, 376, 401
  characteristics, 374, 378
  effect of levodopa on, 378
  freezing in, 248, 266
  periodicity of, 375
Speech therapy, 374, 402
  effect of, 378, 379
Spinal cord
  cell loss from, 30
  degeneration of, 122
Spinal reflexes, 105–110
  during L-dopa treatment, 109
  monosynaptic, 105
  polysynaptic, 105, 109, 110
Spiperone, measuring dopamine receptor
      sites with, 196
3H-spirioperidol binding in Parkinson's
      disease, 155
Starting difficulty *See Freezing*
Stereotypic activity, animal models, 283
Stereotypy, nomifensine inducing, 346
Striato-nigral degeneration, 30
Stress, 268
  levodopa dyskinesia and, 261
  tardive dyskinesia and, 70